LEMKOVYNA

A History of the Lemko Region of the Carpathian Mountains in Central Europe

by
Fr. Ioann Polianskii
(writing as I. F. Lemkyn)

Translated and edited by

Paul Best
Michael Decerbo
Walter Maksimovich

Carpathian Institute
The Lemko Association
Higganum, Connecticut
2012

Lemkovyna: A History of the Lemko Region of the Carpathian Mountains in Central Europe
General editors: Paul Best, Michael Decerbo, and Walter Maksimovich
Translation: Dimitri Gallik and Walter Maksimovich with Paul Best, Michael Decerbo,
    Stanisław Stępień, Katarina Mihaly, Anna Antoniewska-Dubiel, and Ludmila Kozlowska
Cover: Andrew Best
Layout: Dawid Kwoka

Original Lemko language edition published 1969 as
Istoriia Lemkovyny by I. F. Lemkyn (pseudonym of Father Ioann Polianskii)
Original edition published by Lemko Association of USA and Canada,
Copyright © 1969 by Lemko Association of USA and Canada.
Editorial board (1969) was Stephen Kychura, Nikolai Tsisliak, Michael Savchak, and Teodor Dokla.
Production committee (1969): cover by Michael Savchak, layout by Teodor Dokla, printing coordinated by Andrei Tsisliak.

English language edition published 2012 by
Carpathian Institute
The Lemko Association
184 Old County Road
Higganum, CT 06441-4446
USA
Tel. 1-860-345-7997
Fax 1-860-345-3548
www.lemkoassociation.org

Library of Congress Control Number: 2012934017

Publisher's Cataloging-In-Publication Data
(Prepared by The Donohue Group, Inc.)

Polianskii, Ioann.
    [Istoriia Lemkovyny.]
    Lemkovyna : a history of the Lemko region of the Carpathian Mountains in Central Europe / by Ioann Polianskii (writing as I. F. Lemkyn) ; translated and edited by Paul Best, Michael Decerbo [and] Walter Maksimovich.

    p. : ill. ; cm.

    Translated into English from the original Lemko language.
    Original Lemko edition published: Istoriia Lemkovyny / I. F. Lemkyn. S.l. : The Lemko Association of USA and Canada, 1969. This translation contains additional new material, mostly contained in appendices.
    Includes bibliographical references and index.
    ISBN: 978-1-938292-00-2 (hardcover)
    ISBN: 978-1-938292-01-9 (paperback)

    1. Lemky--History. 2. Lemkivshchyna (Poland and Slovakia)--History. 3. Carpathian Mountains--History. I. Best, Paul J. (Paul Joseph), 1939- II. Decerbo, Michael. III. Maksimovich, Walter. IV. Title. V. Title: Istoriia Lemkovyny.

DJK28.L4 .P6513 2012
909.04917   2012934017

This book is dedicated to our Carpathian ancestors
and to their descendants, wherever found.

The editors especially wish to recognize:

Metropolitan Nicholas (1936-2011)

Metropolitan Nicholas (born Richard Smisko) was the titular bishop of Amissos under the Ecumenical Patriarchate of Constantinople and the presiding bishop of the American Carpatho-Russian Orthodox Diocese (the "Johnstown Diocese"). He was noted for his ecumenical spirit, especially in relation to the Byzantine (formerly "Greek") Catholic Church to which many Carpatho-Rusyns belong, which he recognized as a brother church. He was devoted to Carpathian plain chant church music in the original language, and in his last public appearance insisted that singing go on: *"Zaspivaime!"* he kept saying. He actively encouraged research and writing about Rusyns whether in the homeland or the diaspora, and followed the work of at least two editors of this book. The last Carpatho-Rusyn bishop of his era, he is truly missed. *Vichnaia pamiat!*

Alexander Herenchak (1926-2010)

Alexander was a civil engineer by training and co-founded the firm Barnett and Herenchak, Inc. Active in both domestic and foreign projects, he was a noted bridge and road builder. He served in Europe during WW II where he witnessed the results of Nazi war crimes. He was a lifelong Carpatho-Russian patriot based on the grounding he got from his father Stefan of Newark, New Jersey. At various times, usually with the assistance of Victoria Windish, he was President of the Lemko Resort, Inc., of Monroe, New York, the Carpatho-Russian American Center, Inc. – Lemko Hall, of Yonkers, New York, and the Lemko Association of the United States and Canada. He also edited and published the Karpatska Rus' newspaper for two decades. With the help of his wife Lyudmyla and his nephews Mark and Walter Andrew, the inheritance of the aforementioned organizations was passed on to today's Lemko Association, the publisher of this history. Hail and Farewell.

Victoria Windish (1928-2008)

Vicki was born into the Merena family and was a Lemko-Russian activist all her life. Along with Alexander Herenchak, she was involved in the Lemko Resort, the Carpatho-Russian American Center, the Karpatska Rus' newspaper, and the Lemko Association of the United States and Canada. She kept voluminous records of these organizations, acting as Secretary and/or Treasurer, and managed their finances. She was able to pass all this material, via her son Michael, to a new generation of the Lemko Association in the twenty-first century. Thank you!

CONTENTS

Wooden Lemko church in Ropki, twenty years after the ethnic cleansing of 1945–1947. Ropki, 1968.

FOREWORD

Ioann Polianskii and His *Magnum Opus*

Ioann Polianskii (1888-1978) was a Greek Catholic priest who witnessed and to a certain extent took part in many events of the twentieth century important for Lemkos. He was born early enough to be submerged in the Russophile ideology which dominated the Lemko Region before the outbreak of World War I. As were hundreds of others, he was arrested during the early stages of the war, imprisoned and eventually sent to an internment camp in Talerhof. This suffering and the martyrdom of his fellow Rusyns contributed to the strengthening of his ethnic and political beliefs.

Relatively long service at a village parish in Smolnik (1918-1935) brought
Father Polianskii back to the type of environment he knew from his childhood years in the Lemko village of Banica, in Nowy Sącz county. But now
he was the most important person in the village, where life was simple, hard
and not always fulfilling. In his autobiography *"Droga Ciernista kapłana ka-
tolickiego"*[1] [A Priest's Thorny Path]— which is published in this book in an
English translation but remains unpublished in its Polish language original—
he claimed that those years were actually personally very fulfilling. His flock
appreciated his work, which was not limited to ecclesiastical matters, but also
included efforts to raise the cultural and economic level of his parishioners.

Father Polianskii eventually moved to a bigger stage, the Lemko Apostolic
Administration, where he served as a chancellor and later as an interim administrator, while also serving as a pastor in Wróblik Królewski.[2] The Lemko
Apostolic Administration was established in 1934 by the Vatican with the
goal of removing Lemko parishes from the jurisdiction and Ukrainian propaganda of the Greek Catholic Bishop of Przemyśl. This ecclesiastical separation was very much to the liking of Father Polianskii who also got involved
in the activity of the Lemko Association, the organization which promoted
the view of Lemko distinctiveness from their eastern neighbors.

The official Polish policy favorable for Rusynophile Lemkos ended quickly.
Polianskii witnessed this change firsthand when he went to Warsaw as a member of a Lemko delegation ignored by the prime minister. Even more changes
occurred under Nazi rule, during which Father Polianskii encountered persecution, several arrests and imprisonment. Although the "liberation" was a wel-
come development for Father Polianskii as it removed Ukrainian rule from
the Lemko Region, the resettlement to the East and the subsequent Operation "Vistula" shattered the Lemko world in the Carpathians.

Under Communist rule,[3] Father Polianskii had to do what other Greek
Catholic priests did in this new environment. He had to find a place for himself within the structures of the Roman Catholic Church as the Greek Catholic

---

1   I received a typewritten copy of this work from Jerzy Starzyński of Legnica, Poland.
2   Dmytro Blažejovskyj, *Historical Šematism of the Eparchy of Peremyśl Including the Apo-
     stolic Administration of Lemkivščyna (1828-1939)* (Lviv, 1995): 808.
3   In addition to his memoir, his activities in Communist Poland and some of his let-
     ters are presented by Jarosław Zwoliński in his *Rapsodia dla Łemków* (Koszalin, 1994).
     http://lemko.org/pdf/rapsodia.pdf See also: Aniziia Put'ko-Stekh, *Ukraïns'ki svia-
     shchenyky Zakerzonnia. Khronika represïï* (Ukrainian priests of Zakerzonnya) (Lviv,
     2007): 306–307.

Deportations conducted by soldiers of the "Poznań" battalion, 2nd brigade of Ministerstwo Spraw Wewnętrznych troops. Ustrzyki Górne, 1947.

Church ceased to exist. He is, however, credited with celebrating the first Eastern Rite liturgy in Poland after 1947. Apparently for this act he was transferred to Opole Diocese where he briefly served in a few parishes before settling in Rogi (1953), a village located some thirty kilometers west of Opole where he spent the rest of his working years. He became ill in the late 1960s and was paralyzed and bedridden after September 1970, but he continued to write.

Father Polianskii was indeed a "priest unlike any other" as Petro Trokhanovskii described him.[4] Throughout his life he was always very resourceful and very much capable of finding sometimes surprising— or even eyebrow-raising— connections that allowed him to move on with his life and work. Under Communist rule it meant some level of compliance with the government's policies. In return, he was able to use his contacts and favorable opinion in governmental circles to lobby for Lemkos, or at least to find out what sort of Lemko activities would be permitted by the Communist regime independent of Ukrainian influence. He tried to keep in touch with and influence Lemko activists in various parts of Poland and in the United States. After the political thaw of 1956 he was instrumental in spreading information about Lemko activities and linking Lemko leaders with each other. He also lobbied the highest Roman Catholic circles on behalf of Lemkos.

---

4   Petro Trokhanovskii, *"Sviashchennyk inchyi od inchýkh,"* in *Lemkivskii kalendar 1998* (Krynica-Legnica, 1998): 84-87.

It was in Rogi that he wrote his History of the Lemko Region. The text was written at the request of Lemko activists who lived in western Poland and were engaged in the post-Stalin era's Lemko renaissance. The first part of the text, called "Geography," was sent to Nikolai Tsisliak (1910-1988), the editor of the American Lemko newspaper *Karpatska Rus'*, by March of 1959. The second part, called "History," was at that time almost ready. In 1959, Father Polianskii planned one more part which was to deal with current developments. It is not known how much time it took him to finish the text but it did spend considerable amount of time in a drawer perhaps due to internal power struggles within the Lemko Association. The book was finally published by the Lemko Association of the United States and Canada in 1969 thanks to the efforts of Teodor Dokla (1931-1982), a high ranking member of the Association.[5] The final, printed work consisted of five parts, with history and contemporary developments stretched over four parts and the fifth part carrying biographies of accomplished Lemkos.

While it is the work of a person not trained to be a researcher or a historian, it is nevertheless based on a sizable number of works in a number of languages. It is clear that Father Polianskii had a long-lasting interest in history which allowed him to write a monographic overview of Lemko history, a task which could not be achieved without considerable work and knowledge. He also had to assemble a sizable library. After all, materials that he used while working on his History were not readily available anywhere close to the village of Rogi. One may speculate that libraries of Wrocław, where he traveled to meet with Lemko activists, could have been utilized by him.

Father Polianskii also used scholarly apparatus in the form of footnotes, which in the original version were sometimes erroneously printed in the middle of a page. In his undated "Observations on the History of the Lemko Region"[6] he voiced his displeasure at this and other shortcomings. He pointed out that some pages were left blank and his collection of some one hundred photographs was not used in the book. Instead other illustrations were used as well as additional text that was not written by him (it was added at the end of the book and marked as such).[7] Most importantly, Father Polianskii complained

---

5 For more on him see: Petro Trokhanovskii, "Teodor Doklia," in *Lemkivskii richnyk 2002* (Krynica-Legnica, 2002): 108-113.

6 I received a copy of this text from John Madzik of Ansonia, Conn. It is also reprinted in this volume.

7 This part consists of articles from a book edited by Ivan S. Shelepetskii, *Priashevshchina: istoriko-literaturnyi sbornik* (Prague, 1948).

that some parts of his text were excluded from the book, but we do not know which. Therefore he was eager to prepare a second revised edition but it is impossible to say with any certainty whether he ever set out to do that.

Technical problems that occurred in the first edition are not repeated in this English translation, but other shortcomings could not be removed. Despite a substantial bibliography some may question the sources of information for some of Father Polianskii's statements. In some parts of the work a reader will ask: "what is this statement based on?" Back in 1959 Father Polianskii announced to his Lemko friends that he wrote a brand-new, scholarly treatment but the emotionally-charged-language of some of its passages does not belong to a scholarly work. It may, however, be somewhat acceptable in a memoir. Father Polianskii's book could actually be considered to consist of two parts. One of them deals with the distant past up until the time when he entered adult life. The other one, which covers the first part of the twentieth century, could be treated more like a memoir as he either witnessed or was a contemporary to the events that he wrote about.

Father Polianskii's ethnic, religious and political viewpoints had significant impact on his work but that can be said about many— if not all— other works written by amateur scholars who were deeply involved in their ethnic group's life. Actually, the value of this work is precisely in the reflection of how a person of certain ethnic, religious and political convictions viewed the historical evolution of his own people. His occasional harsh words towards Ukrainians or Poles have their roots in what Father Polianskii would describe as the long-lasting suffering of the Lemko nation. Although a staunch Catholic until his last breath he was not shy to criticize some Catholic priests, whether Polish or Ukrainian, for their actions that in his opinion hurt Lemkos.

What a reader will find puzzling in a book published in America are the author's praises for the Communist system. Father Polianskii writes about Lemkos' involvement in the fight against fascist Germany and about some support for and high hopes for a better life under "the people's rule." He is quick to point out major disappointments: (1) the resettlements, (2) the liquidation of the Greek Catholic Church, and (3) the official treatment of Lemkos as Ukrainians and associating them with what he calls "Ukrainian nationalism." Writing the book during the post-Stalin era he blames those undesirable developments on decisions of flawed leaders of the previous period.

It is obvious now and was without doubt obvious to Father Polianskii that an official distribution of his book among Lemkos in Poland could be achieved only if the book presented a favorable picture of Communist Poland. While this may have been the reason for his rosy picture of Communism, it is also possible that a person who originated in an underdeveloped, impoverished, and struggling environment (his parents were illiterate) could have been somewhat receptive to Communist propaganda.[8]

While we do not know how many copies of the book were printed it is quite possible that the still formidable Lemko Association (with its own printing shop) produced a sizable number of copies.[9] They were made available to American Lemkos and some did make it to Poland where they were cherished by many and known as *Istoriia Lemkyna* (A history by Lemkyn), as Father Polianskii published it under the pseudonym of Y. F. Lemkyn. Hardbound, with the title and author's name in golden letters, and produced in America it was at the least intriguing if not impressive. Even today people continue to ask for it, as it is still the largest history of Lemkos written— as many would describe it— *po nashomu* [in our own language].[10]

Lemkovyna: A History... is the love-child of a person who was not a trained historian but most of all a Lemko patriot. A person who during his short reign as interim Administrator of the Lemko Apostolic Administration made sure to communicate to all Lemkos, whether Greek Catholic or Orthodox, that unity is what they need the most. For him, Lemkos came first, before anything else.

Bogdan Horbal
New York Public Library

---

8   In his memoir, which was finished in 1972, he concentrates on his pastoral service and dealings with Roman Catholic priests and hierarchy without addressing the issue of the current political system in Poland. Thus we do not know what his real attitude towards it was.

9   Before the sale of Lemko Hall in Yonkers in the late 1990s, boxes with dozens of uncirculated copies of the book were removed, eventually to end up in storage in Higganum, Connecticut, twenty-first century headquarters of the Lemko Association.

10   The somewhat complex issue of the language of the original edition book is addressed separately in this volume. For a listing of monographic works on Lemkos see Bogdan Horbal, *Lemko Studies: A Handbook* (New York, 2010): 317-323.

PREFACE

Although they are a small stateless people, the Lemkos of the Carpathian Mountains of Central Europe have the right to a history too. Despite not ever having a united political entity of their own, although several parts tried to wrench free from the grasp of neighboring states right after the First World War, and despite the magnetic pull of the East Slavic Russians and Ukrainians plus the assimilationist pressures of living within a space claimed by Poland, nonetheless there is a provable historic continuity of the Lemko people going back at least a thousand years.

As European populations approached modern times, the concept of nationhood/nationality became popular, especially with governments, which attempted to draw to themselves the greatest number of people possible. The Lemkos, in their mountains, were not immune to this and in the early

The Maslei family. Berest, 1938. (Photo © M. Maslej).

nineteenth century these Carpathian mountaineers felt the first stirrings of nationalism. Near the middle of the century Aleksander Dukhnovych became active in Prešov and in 1849 the imperial Russian army went through the Carpathian passes to crush the Hungarian nobility's rebellion against the Habsburgs. The Russians and Lemkos recognized in each other fellow East Slavs of similar culture and religious persuasion.

Eventually, while most Lemkos probably ignored the situation, several political/social/religious orientations developed: Staro-Rus' (Old Ruthenian)/ Russophile, Ukrainophile, and Carpatho-Rusyn. The Staro-Rus' idea included the notion of a commonality of all East Slavs, a single social and religious Rus' entity. Russophiles carried that idea further into the *Rus'ka Idea* that not only was there a common East Slavic identity, but that there ought to be a single united, undivided state "from the Carpathians to Kamchatka" or "from the Poprad [river] to Vladivostok," ruled over by "our Tsar" in Moscow— a concept which, for some, after 1917 transmogrified into rule by Soviet Moscow. Ukrainophiles, on the other hand, rejected a common East Slavic identity, whether Staro-Rus' or Russophile (much less a common state) and claimed all "Ukrainian lands"; this included the Carpathian region and the Lemko area, as "Western Ukraine." The Carpatho-Rusyn idea is that *Karpatska Rus'* is simply *Karpatska Rus',* an ethnic territory not dependent on any other entity for its right to exist.

The author of *Lemkovyna: A History*, Father Ioann Polianskii, clearly was of the Staro-Rus' persuasion with leanings towards Carpatho-Rusynism. He thought that Ukrainophilism was a negative force, inimical to a common East Slavic identity. Yet while he was sympathetic towards Russians he never indicated that he wanted to be ruled by them. In fact, when forced to choose between East and West he went west, never joining the Orthodox Church even though he had been constantly oppressed and persecuted by the Latin Rite Catholic Church. It is interesting to speculate, as Petro Trokhanovskii does in his article "A priest of a different sort" (see bibliography), why, since he was sympathetic to Orthodoxy, Polianskii didn't transfer to that church, as others had done in similar circumstances. Perhaps the answer lies in his writings on the powers of the successors of St. Peter (see bibliography) which, unfortunately, are not available to us.

The current volume is an attempt to present to readers of English an overview of the Lemko Region of Central Europe written by a man who experienced much of its recent history firsthand. We have also included new

Lemko school children from Chyrowa on a field trip to a shrine in Dukla.
Between the two adults stands Pavlo Hranychnii.

material by Mykhailo Almashii, Paul Best, Bogdan Horbal, and Walter Maksimovich which analyzes Polianskii's book in its historical and linguistic context. Finally, a brief biography of the author, as well as his own autobiography, also appear here for the first time in English.

Although most copies of the 1969 Lemko language edition of Polianskii's *Lemkovyna: A History* sat gathering dust in storage for forty years for reasons discussed in "The Lemko Association and *Lemkovyna: A History*," the idea to translate Polianskii into a world language is nonetheless decades old. It only came to fruition with the revival of the Lemko Association in 2010 as a non-profit, tax-exempt, non-partisan, non-political organization for furthering knowledge about Lemkos, the Lemko homeland, and the Lemko diaspora. We hope that the readers of this volume will profit by gaining a greater knowledge of the unique Lemko people.

The Editors

Last remains of human habitation, Lemkovyna, 2001.

ACKNOWLEDGEMENTS

The editors gratefully acknowledge the assistance of the following institutions and individuals.

Book cover
 Andrew Best

Layout
 Dawid Kwoka

Contributed translation
 Dimitri Gallik

Additional translators
 Katarina Mihaly, Anna Antoniewska-Dubiel, Ludmila Kozlowska, Stanisław Stępień

Institutions
 ELPIS Center for Orthodox Culture — Gorlice, Poland
 The Lemko Studies Workshop of the "Kyczera" Lemko Dance and Song
   Ensemble — Legnica, Poland
 Muzeum Kultury Łemkowskiej — Zyndranowa, Poland
 Muzeum Okręgowe — Nowy Sącz, Poland
 Narodowe Archiwum Cyfrowe— Warsaw, Poland
 Ruska Bursa — Gorlice, Poland
 Sanok Historical Museum — Sanok, Poland
 Southeast Research Institute — Przemyśl, Poland

Individuals
 Mykhailo Almashii — Uzhhorod, Ukraine
 Wiesław Banach — Sanok, Poland
 Roman Dubec — Gorlice, Poland
 Bogdan Gambal — Gorlice, Poland
 Bogdan Horbal — New York, New York, USA
 Bogumiła Gruszczyńska Kozan — Ostrów Wielkopolski, Poland
 John Madzik — Ansonia, Connecticut, USA
 Maksymilian Maslej — Toronto, Canada
 Jerzy Starzyński — Legnica, Poland

Financial and release-time support for basic research necessary to prepare this volume is gratefully acknowledged from the Faculty Development Fund of the Office of Academic Affairs of Southern Connecticut State University. Additionally, we wish to recognize financial support for overseas research from the Faculty Research Abroad Program of the United States Department of Education; the International Research and Exchanges Board (IREX), Washington, DC, USA; and the Kosciuszko Foundation, New York, NY, USA.

NOTES ON TERMINOLOGY AND TRANSLITERATION

There are multiple uses of the word *Rus'* in the original Lemko language text of 1969. The editors have endeavored to translate this term into English according to its contextual situation, whether as "Russia" (the political entity), "Rus'," (the common East Slavic territory), "Rusnak" or "Rusyn" (referring to East Slavs within that territory, particularly in the Carpathians), or "Rus'" as an alternative ethnonym to the word "Lemko."

Also, Fr. Polianskii frequently conflates, under the term "German," the German-speaking Austrians of the Vienna-based Austro-Hungarian Empire and the Germans of the Berlin-based German Empire. The editors have tried to make clear which is which.

There are a number of schemes for transliterating the Cyrillic alphabet used in the 1969 text into English. Since this is not a text for linguistic specialists, we have applied the principle of Occam's Razor: to paraphrase, "Don't make things too complicated." Some inconsistency in transliteration of personal names is unavoidable because some people spelled their names differently at different times. However, in keeping with standard scholarly practice, place names appear according to the current spelling in the country where they are now located, e.g. Lviv (Ukrainian) rather than Lwow (Polish), Lvov (Russian), or Lemberg (German).

Fr. Polianskii's notes appeared in a non-standard format in the 1969 edition; he complains about this in his letter to Dokla, reproduced in "The Lemko Association and *Lemkovyna: A History*." While the editors have corrected their placement, we have not attempted to standardize their content or check them for accuracy, since many of the referenced materials are not available in North America. Some materials that would otherwise be difficult or impossible for the North American reader to obtain have been made available by Walter Maksimovich on the lemko.org Web site; we have augmented Fr. Polianskii's notes with references to these copies, where available.

Material, including notes, appearing in square brackets [ ] was added in this edition to further elucidate the text. Additionally, while the popular Wikipedia Web site is not generally considered a reliable source, for some subjects or persons about which little other material is available in English we provide links to Wikipedia as a convenience, to serve as a jumping-off point for further research.

As a matter of record, the term "Lemko Association," the publisher of both the original and this English version of Polianskii's text, is often used generically. In reality, there were six Lemko entities in North America with interlocking directorates: The Lemko Association of the United States and Canada; The Carpatho-Russian American Center, Inc. – Lemko Hall; the Carpatho-Russian American Congress; The Lemko Resort, Inc.; the Thalerhof Chapel Fund; and the Lemko Relief Committee of the United States and Canada, Inc. Lemko organizations in both Poland and North America have often been referred to generically as *Lemko Soyuz*; in this usage, *soyuz* or *soiuz* is not a Soviet or communist term, but rather a common Slavic word with no particular significance, having the meanings of alliance, association, or union, e.g. Polish *sojusz*.

LEMKOVYNA

Tombstone detail from a cemetery in Krywa, 2000.

INTRODUCTION

Лемковино моя люба,
Мой ты земский раю.
За тобою сердце тужит,
О тобі мечтаю.

Ты для мене найдор ожча,
Бо ты моя мати,
Ах, як рвеся моє сердце
О тобі писати.

Добре давно нам там было,
Як ты нас корми
Як нас разом обнимала –
До сердця тулила.

Як счастливо мы ся чули,
Як мы с тобом жили.
Ты нас сердцем голубыла –
Мы ти вірни были.

Але пришол лютый ворог,
Хотіл нас згубити,
Нашы села, нашы хыжы –
До тла вынищити.

И сталося страшнее діло:
Нас з гор вышмарили,
С тобом, наша люба мати,
На все розлучили.

My beloved Lemkovyna,
You are my earthly paradise.
My heart is yearning for you,
I dream of you.

You are most dear to me
Because you are my mother,
Oh, how it tears at my heart
To write about you.

Long ago it was so good for us there,
How you fed us
How you once embraced us–
Nestled next to your heart.

How lucky we felt,
How we lived with you.
You loved us with all your heart–
We were true to you.

But a cruel time came,
They wanted to break us,
Our villages, our homes–
To raze to the ground.

Terrible things happened,
We were chased from our
     mountains,
From you, our loving mother,
Separated from us forever.

О як тяжко мі на сердци,
Што мы розлучены,
И по цілой чужой землі
Мы роспорошены.

Але приде ище время,
Што нас доля злучит,
Товды жадна вража сила
Нас уж не разлучит.

Не тіш-же ся лютый враже
З нашой горькой долі,
Приде на тя кара Божа –
Будеме на волі.

Нашы горы розвеселят,
Солнце засияє,
Лісы громко зашуміют,
Што ворог конає.

За терпіния, нашы мукы
Бог вынагородит,
Наше горьке, тяжке житье
Нам знов осолодит.

Приймий, люба, тото письмо
Кровью написане
З горя, туги, болю сердця –
Слезами обляне.

Oh, how heavy is my heart
That we are separated,
And throughout this strange land
We are scattered.

But there will come a time
That our fate will bring us together,
At that time no hostile force
Will separate us.

Do not rejoice, cruel enemy
About our bitter plight,
God's wrath will come upon you–
We will be free.

Our mountains will rejoice,
The sun will shine,
The wind will blow through the
     forest,
That evil doing is ending.

For our struggles and our tortures
God will reward us,
Our bitter difficult life
Will become sweeter for us.

Receive with love this letter,
Written in blood,
From our aching hearts
Watered with tears.

Destroyed stone cross behind the village church. Before... Chyrowa, 2002.

...and after restoration. Chyrowa, 2004.

PART I:
GEOGRAPHY OF LEMKOVYNA

Local Eastern Rite wooden church after restoration work. Kotań, 2007.

Prologue to Part I

Лемковино, родный краю,
Моя прелесть, земский раю,
Мой ты світе найсолодшый,
Мой ты скарбе найдоросшый.

Иду спати, рано встаю,
Лем о Тобі я думаю,
Ци роблю я, спочываю,
Лем о Тобі все мечтаю.

А як в сердци тугу маю,
Або горе отчуваю,
То до Тебе ся звертаю,
Своє сердце открываю,
Перед Тобом ся выжалю,
А уж в сердци спокой маю.

Лемковино, люба Мати,
Я не в силі описати
Свойой тугы, свого горя,
Слез выляных цілы моря.
За Тобою, мой Ты скарбе,
Всьо без Тебе нич не варте,
За тобою плачу, гыну,
Так у ночы, як и в днину.

О Тобі я все мечтаю,
Тобою ся возхищаю,

Lemkovyna, land of my birth,
My beautiful earthly paradise,
You are my sweetest thing,
You are my treasure.

I go to sleep and arise in the morning,
Only thinking of you,
When I work or rest,
I always dream of you.

Or when I don't feel well,
I return to you,
With an open heart,
I pour out my heart to you,
And I am quieted.

Oh Lemkovyna, loving mother,
I hardly have the strength to write
About your grief and your woe,
Enough tears are shed to fill an ocean.
For you are my treasure,
Without you nothing matters,
I cry out for you and perish
At night, and during the day as well.

I always dream of you,
I find delight in you,

В Тобі всю надію маю,
До Тебе я все вздыхаю.
Як счастливы мы ся чули,
Коли разом з собом жыли.
Ты нас сердцем голубила
И в обнятих нас пестила,
Хлібом, сольом нас кормила,
Хоц сама голодна была.

Ворогы нас розлучыли,
На погыбель засудили,
По світі розпорошылы,
Штобы марно мы згынули.

Днес от себе отдалены,
Дольом нашом засмучены,
Бо з любых гор выселены
И по світі розшмарены.

Буд проклята тота хвиля,
Коли з пекла вража сила
Брутально нас выселила,
Наше счастье закончыла.

Тяжко было ся розстати,
З собом ся попращати,
За Тобом люба Мати
З болю, жалю зарыдати.
В світі долі сой шукати,
Нераз горко поплакати.

Вельку рану в сердцу ношу
И штодня Бога прошу,
Штобы горе пережыти,
Счастливо вік докончыти.

I put all my hope in you,
I always sigh to you.
How lucky we felt
When we lived together.
You loved us with all your heart,
And in your embrace you spoiled us,
You fed us with bread and salt,
Even though you yourself were hungry.

The cruel enemy separated us,
Condemning us to perish,
And scattered us throughout the
    world,
So that we would disappear.

Today we are apart from you,
Our plight is sorrowful,
For we are transferred from our lov-
    ing mountains
And scattered around the world.

Cursed be the moment
When the strong enemy came from hell
And brutally deported us,
Our happiness came to an end.

It was difficult to depart,
To bid farewell to you,
For you are our loving mother.
Pain, sorrow, crying out.
To seek our fate out in the world,
Crying out bitterly often.

We carry a great wound in our heart,
Daily we ask God to help us
Survive our bitter life,
So all will end well.

В сердцю туга, вельке горе,
Вылятых слез ціле море
З жалю, тугы за горами,
За лугами и лісами,

There is great bitterness in my heart,
I shed tears enough to fill an ocean,
Out of sorrow, yearning for the
          mountains
For the pastures and the forests

За хыжыном з краю села,
За стежечком, што нас вела
До церковці на горбочку,
Серед дерев, як в віночку.

For our homes in our country villages,
For the path which guides us
To our church on the hill,
In between the trees like in the mid-
dle of a wreath.

О, як тяжко мі на сердцю,
Што мы розлучены
И по цілом земском гльобі
Мы розпорошены.

Oh, how heavy is my heart
That we are separated,
And all over the round earth
We are scattered.

Не тішыся сило вража
З нашой горькой долі,
Сплыне на нас ласка Божа,
Будем знов на волію

Do not rejoice, O powerful enemy
In our bitter plight,
God's love will come upon us,
We will be free again.

За терпіния и страдания
Бог вынагородит,
Нашы мукы и рыдания
Он нам осолодит.

For our patience and suffering
God will reward us,
Our torment and our wailing
He will make sweet.

Нашы горы розрадуют,
Солнце засияє,
Лісы громко зашуміют:
—Лемко повертає!

Our mountains will rejoice
And the sun will shine
The forests will sing out–
Lemko return!

Цілы вікы переминут,
Мы ся розроснеме,
Нашы врагы всі погыбнут,
Мы тут зостанеме.

A whole century will pass,
We will grow,
Our enemies will perish,
We will remain here.

Бо то наша русска земля,
То наша отчына.
Ту наша спадчына.
Ту колыбель Святой Руси,

Рукы проч, сволоч германска,
И ты клятый Прус,
Ту єст земля праславянска,
Ту родился Лех, Чех, Рус.

Because this is our Rusyn land,
It is our fatherland,
It is our inheritance,
It is the cradle of Holy Rus'.

Take your hands off it, you German
    scum,
The same to you, cursed Prussians,
This is our ancient Slavic land,
For here Lech, Czech and Rus were
    born.

....

Лемковино, чар природы,
Ліси, лугы, загороды,
Боры, рікы и потокы
Очаруют, якбы врокы.

Над ріками гарды села,
Околиця барз весела.
Серед села річка плыне,
На закруті деси гыне.

Хыжы з ялиц будуваны
И на ясно малюваны.
Кажда хыжа з загородом,
Як не з садом то з городом.

Люде, што в них замешкуют,
Хоц сут бідны, не бідуют,

Бо землиця их не зводит,
Лем все красні им зародит.

Lemkovyna, miracle of nature,
Leaves, brooks and gardens,
Pine forests, streams and rivers
Hover magically.

Over the rivers of beautiful villages,
The whole area is happy.
Through the village the stream flows
And disappears around the bend.

The houses are built of wood
And are painted brightly.
Every house has a garden
And where the garden stops the
    town begins.

People who live in them,
Even though they are poor,
    do not suffer,
The land does not deceive them
But produces very well.

Хоц не родится пшениця,
Ани гречка, кукуриця,
Але грулі, овес, ярец
И капусты хоц окраєц.
Жыют собі люде в згоді
И єст спокой в каждом роді,
Хоц роскошы не зазнают,
Ани балів не справляют,

Чуются ту счтастливыми
И зо собом згодливыми.
Вшыткы добры сердця мают
И сой в біді помагают.

В каждом селі церков стоит,
Бо лемко ся Бога боит.
В ней то часто ся зберают,
В піснях Бога величают.

Свои сердця к Богу взносят
И у Него ласкі просят,
Штобы в счастю вік прожыти,
А по смерти в небі быти.

Чудны пісні в церкви поют
И ними то жалость коют,
Взносят сердця ген до Бога,
Бо там их ціль, там дорога.

Ах, то прелест Лемковина,
Найдоросша нам краина.
Хоц быс світ ногами сходил,
По пояс по счастю бродил,
Не знайдеш такого краю,
Лемковина пресмак раю.

Even though wheat will not grow,
Nor buckwheat nor corn,
Potatoes, oats, barley
And cabbages thrive.
People live in harmony
And there is peace in every home,
Even though they don't know luxury,
They don't live badly either

Here they feel lucky
And of the same mind,
Everyone has a good heart
And in their poverty they help each
other.

In every village a church stands,
Because a Lemko fears God.
Often they gather there,
And sing praises to God.

They carry God in their hearts
And they ask God for mercy,
So that they would live a happy life
And after death go to heaven

They sing wonderful songs in church
And in them express their sorrows,
They carry God in their hearts,
That is their strength, that is their way.

Oh, you are a beauty, Lemkovyna,
Our country, you are priceless to us.
Even if one were to go over the
whole world
From pole to pole,
One would never find such a place,
Lemkovyna is a foretaste of paradise.

Смуклы верхы, стромы горы
Стырчат в гору без подпоры,
Вытягнены барз высоко,
Ледво их увидит око.

Над Избами єст Лацкова,
Под ньом лісы дооокола,
Єй всі «тетом» называют,
За астронома уважают.

Як Лацкова рано плаче,
Термометр з горы скаче.
Як Лацкова усміхнена,
То погода запевнена.

Але як єст засмучена,
А до того захмарена,
Будут громы, блискавиці
И то в цілой околиці.

И тым важна єст Лацкова,
Же, хоц стара, завсе нова.
Сідит собі на скалиці
И пильнує нам границі,
От Чех, Мадяр и Словаков,
Не допущат к нам бортаков.

А Магура Маластовска,
Якбы сестра єй лемковска,
Смотрит на ню кривым оком,
Обернена задным боком.

Над Крыницьом Яворина,
Барз вызока, як драбина.

Cloud-draped peaks, steep
    mountains
Projecting upward, unsupported,
Stretching skyward up so high,
Your eye can barely see them.

Above Izba is Lackowa,
Below her forest all around,
Everybody calls her "Auntie,"
And consider her like an astronomi-
    cal observatory.

When Latskova cries in the morning
The thermometer jumps upwards,
When Latskova smiles
Then the weather is better.

But when she is sad,
Then added to those clouds
There will be lightning and thunder
In the whole area.

And this is why Latskowa is important
Despite her being old, there's always
    something new.
Sitting as a barrier
And protecting our borders
From the Czechs, Magyars, and Slovaks,
    Not letting those fools get to us.

The mountain Magura Malastovska
Is like a Lemko sister
Looking at us with a screwed up eye.
Turned to one side.

Above Krynica is Iavoryna,
Very high up like a ladder

Жебы на ню мог вылізти,
Мусиш горнец чыру зісти.

If you are to be able to climb her,
You would need to eat a bowl of
        oatmeal first.

И мериндю з собом взяти,
Жебыс по ней мог скакати.
Яворина красна гора,
Але не все на ню пора.

And bring your lunch with you
So that you could get up on her.
Iavoryna is a beautiful mountain,
But not in every season.

В зимі она засніжена,
А на яри захмарена,
В осени знов наіжена,
Зато в літі усміхнена.

In winter she is covered in snow,
In spring with clouds,
In fall, again,
Thus summer is the best.

Над Фльоринком, Холм высокий
Пильнує нас от голоты,
Што крыівку в Ропі мала
И нас з села выганяла.

Over Florynka, high Kholm
Protecting us from hunger,
Like a wing over the Mała Ropa
From where they drove us away.

А так само от Концльовы,
Бо там люде иншой мовы.
Маме ищы иншы горы,
Малы, велькы и просторы.

And the same is Kąclowa
where people speak differently.
We have other mountains,
Large, small and simple.

Равка, Бердо и Магура
И Хрещата велька дзюра.
Они вшыткы нам дорогы,
Для нас щыры, не ворогы.

Rawka, Berdo and Magura
And Chreszczatyk the great pass.
All of them are dear to us,
For us they are friends, not enemies.

Горы нашы, горы красны,
И счастливы и несчастны.
Вы кормите нас грибами
И ріжными овочами.

Our mountains, our beautiful
        mountains
Both lucky and unlucky.
You feed us with mushrooms
And various fruits.

Вы нас в зимі огрівате,
В літі тіни достарчате,
От бурі нас хороните,
Ціле жытя нам служыте.
Нехай же вам буде слава,
Честь, подяка и похвала.

Як сой лемко гукне з горы,
То зашумят лісы, боры.
Ехо взнесе ся высоко,
Де юж не взритлюдске око.

Як сой лемко ногом тупне,
То найліпший слух оглухне,
Як сой лемко пястук стисне,
А потом языком свистне.

То озвутся цілы горы,
Лісы, лугы, вшыткы творы,
Медведі зачнут рычати,
А вовкы, як псы гавкати

И по дзюрах ся ховати,
Псы по земли ся качати
Діти будут верещати,
И до буды утікати.
Птахы заворот доставити
И на землю упадати.

А як хлопці заспівают,
Як з гор домів повертают,
А голосы красны мают
И співанок дуже знают,

А дівчата завторуют,
Як лем пісню гев почув,

You warm us in winter,
And in summer you provide shade.
And you protect us from storms,
All of our lives you cater to us.
May you have glory,
Honor, gratitude and praise.

When this Lemko shouts from the
 mountains,
Then forests and thickets
Will echo on high
As never before seen.

When this Lemko pounds his foot
The best of hearing will go deaf.
When this Lemko will make a fist
And then whistle,

All the mountains will answer,
Forests, meadows and all creatures,
Bears will begin to growl,
And wolves will bark like dogs

And will hide in holes,
Dogs will roll around on the ground,
Children will scream
And run into the sheds.
Birds will get dizzy
And fall to the ground.

When boys will sing as they return
Home from the mountains,
They have beautiful voices
And they have plenty of songs,

And the girls will join them
When they hear the song

То забудем вшельке горе,
Хоц быс то мал ціле море.

Пісня сердце розрадує,
Веселость в нім запанує.
Ах, то концерт, як бы з неба,
Больше сердцю нич не треба.

Душа так розрадована,
Як бы уж єй была дана
З небес вічна нагорода,
Ожыдана от род рода.

Піснь лемковска мельодийна,
Чаруюча, гармонійна.
Хоц быс перешол цілий світ,
Такой пісні нигде ніт.

Красні собі лемкы жыли,
На отпустах ся сходили,
Рано в церкви ся молили,
По полудни ся гостили.

Палюночку попивали,
Келишками ся здравкали,
Ідла у них дост вшыткого,
И ліпшого и планьшого.

На столі єст ружна страва:
Хліб, кобаса, біла кава,
Грулі варены, печены,
Обераны и смажены.

Then you will forget all sorrows
Even though you might have an
    ocean full.

Songs will make hearts happy,
Happiness will remain.
Oh! That concert is as though from
    heaven
The heart does not need anything else.

The soul would be so joyous
As though it were given
An eternal reward from heaven,
Given from generation to
    generation.

Lemko songs have great melodies,
Enchanting and harmonious.
Even if you traveled all over the
    world
Such songs do not exist elsewhere.

Lemkos lived beautifully.
They got together at a pilgrimage,
In the morning they prayed in church,
In the afternoon they celebrated.

They drank *palunka*,
Toasting with glasses,
For them there is enough of everything
Some good and some bad

On the table is various food:
Bread, *kobasa*, coffee with milk,
Potatoes, cooked and baked,
Peeled and fried.

Кеселиця, варянка,
И мастило, и стеранка.
Яшниця на солонині,
Вытягненой впрост зо скрині.

Росол, мясо и капуста,
Ни не худа, ни не тлуста,
На остатку сут періжкы,
З самой брындзі, просто з діжкы.

Кто хтіл собі попоісти,
Мусіл за стол собі сісти.
Одталь выліз з повным бріхом,
Вертал домів з вельком втіхом.

Кто лакомый на палюнку,
Для такого ніт ратунку,
Без палюнкы можна жыти
И терезвым завше быти.

Лемкы любят палюночку,
Выпили бы цілу бочку.
Кєбы она туньша была,
Або в поли ся родила.

Же палюнка єст дорога,
Мало містця ма небога,
В хыжах нашой Лемковины,
Богом даной нам краины.

Keselitsa,[1] *varianka*[2],
And *mastilo*[3], and *steranka*[4]
Scrambled eggs with bacon
Pulled out straight from the pantry.

Soup, meat and *kapusta*
Neither lean nor fat
At the end there is
Bryndza [cheese] straight from the cloth

Whoever wanted to eat
Just had to sit at the table.
You left with a full belly,
Returned home very happy.

Whoever yearned for liquor,
For that kind there is no help.
You can live without alcohol
And always be sober.

Lemkos love home-brew [alcohol],
They would drink whole barrels full,
If only it were less expensive,
Or if it would grow in the field .

That liquor is expensive,
That there is very little room for it
In our homes in Lemkovyna,
Is a gift God has given our country.

---

1) A dish made of fermented oatmeal.
2) Soup made of sauerkraut juice, potatoes, and bits of sauerkraut.
3) A dish made of boiling milk, flour, butter and chives.
4) A dish made of dough bits dropped into boiling milk.

Лемкы, як пют Бога хвалят,
По земли ся никто не валят.
Пред келишком здравя жычат,
Бо такый єст а них обычай.

На ярмаках ся зберали,
Бо статочку досыть мали.
Єдны статок продавали,
А што треба купували.

Газды волами торгували,
Бабы яйця продавали,
Одомашом честували,
Фаталашкы купували.

И холошні и запаскы,
Веретена мотовила,
Скірні, керпці, ріжны фрашкы,
Граблі косы и повила.

А циганкы ворожыли,
Штобы люде довго жыли.
Бабы карты вытігали,
А циганкы им шептали.

Добры часы товды были,
Як на ярмак ся сходили
Лемкы з цілой околиці,
Дакотры аж з заграниці.

В єдной группі шли дівчата,
В другой бабы и пацята,
В третой хлопи з коровами
И газдове зо сейками.

Lemkos praise the Lord when they
    drink,
Nobody falls to the ground.
With their glasses they wish every-
    one good health,
Because that is their custom.

They went to market-fairs,
Because they had enough animals.
Some they sold,
And when they needed stock they
    bought some.

Farmers traded oxen,
Women sold eggs,
Treated people to bread samples,
Purchased odds and ends.

And men's pants and aprons,
Hand spindles and winders,
Boots, moccasins, various things,
Rakes, scythes, and pitchforks.

And Gypsies told fortunes
That people might live longer.
Ladies selected cards
And Gypsies whispered to them.

Those were good times
When they gathered at the fair.
Lemkos came from all over,
Some from beyond the border.

There were girls in one group,
The second was women and pigs,
The third was men and cows,
And farmers with their wagons.

А на конци паробчакы,
А за ними уж хоц-якы
Діти, жены их камраты.
Волоцюгы и жебракы.

Ясным солнцем освіченых,
На тлі лісов, гор зеленых,
Як шли люде цілом массом,
Отбивался фольклор красом.

Зеленіли ся запаскы
И горсеты ріжной краскы,
Оплічата, як сніг білы
И вышывкы на них цілы.

А у хлопов гуні, чугы,
От их френзлів довгы смугы
И холошні, и керпчата,
А в них білы онучата.

Калап з пером и крисами,
Обведеный встожечками.
Ах, прекрасный строй
    лемковский,
Бо той строй наш власный,
    свойский.

Сусіде нам завидуют
И барз часто ся дивуют,
Одкаль у нас така краса,
Хоц мы з ними єдна раса.

And at the end young men,
And after them all kinds of folks,
Children, wives, and their friends,
Vagabonds and beggars.

Bright sun shines on them
In the forest, and green mountains,
When masses of people traveled,
It was beautiful folklore.

They wore green aprons
And various beautiful vests,
Blouses white as snow,
With embroidery all over.

And the men's jackets and coats,
And their long lines of fringes,
And the pants and moccasins,
On them are white pieces of cloth.

A hat with feathers and a brim,
Outlined with ribbon.
Oh, Lemko garb is beautiful
Because this clothing belongs to us,
    ours alone.

Neighbors are jealous of us
And often they wonder
From where we have such beauty
Even though we are the same people.

(Из Пісні о Лемковині)   (From *A Song About Lemkovyna*)

Apple trees in blossom in Lemkovyna, late May 2007.

Enjoying the serenity of Chyrowa, 2007.

1. A Geographic Outline of Lemkovyna

(Geographic Location, Expanse, and Boundaries)

In the southern part of Poland and the northern part of Czechoslovakia, on both sides of the Carpathian Mountains, on a background of beautiful nature, between the rivers San and Uzh on the east and the Poprad on the west, within a time frame of over a thousand years, lives an interesting people now known as Lemkos, while the land they live on is called Lemkovyna, or Lemkivshchina. This is a long and narrow strip of the Carpathian mountain range, divided politically into two parts. The northern part belongs to Poland, and the southern to Czechoslovakia. Between the two parts, the boundary is an irregular line that follows the crest of the mountains. The total expanse of Lemkovyna is about 10,000 square kilometers, and its people number about 500,000. There are about fifty people per square kilometer.

The northern part of Lemkovyna, which is located on Polish territory, takes up parts of seven counties, which are: Nowy Sącz, Gorlice, Jasło, Krosno, Sanok, Lesko, and a small portion of Nowy Targ. The ethnographic boundary

View of Lemkovyna. Mochnaczka Wyżna, 2005.

between the Polish and Lemko peoples starts at Leluchów on the Poprad River and goes through the area of Mnišek, then through Hanušov, Barnowiec, and Czaczów in the direction of Kamionka, then turns east through Ptaszkowa, Kąclowa, Chełm, Ropa, Szymbark, Cieklin, Żmigród, Dukla, Bałucianka, Wróblik, Besko, Grabownica, and Witryłów, to the San River, following that to its source and down the Uzh River all the way to Uzhhorod.

Beyond this boundary line, and still in Poland, are two "islands" of Lemko villages. One of these is in Nowy Targ County and consists of four villages: Szlachtowa, Jaworki, Biała Woda, and Czarna Woda. The other island is in Krosno County with the villages of Czarnorzeki, Pietrusza Wola, Bratkówka, Łączki, Oparówka, Golcówka, Brzeżanka, Wysoka, Krasna, Lutcza, Iwanówka, Bonarówka, Blizianka, Gwoździanka, Baryczka, Żarnowa, and Niebylec.

Creating boards from logs the old-fashioned way. Zyndranowa, 2002.

According to some historians and experts, such as the professor Dr. Mykhailo Ladyzhinskii in his work *Sanok i ioho okresnosti* (Sanok and its surroundings) and the professor Fr. Dr. Tyt Myshkovskii in his *Severno-zapadnaia hranitsia Halitskoi Rusi* (The northwestern border of Galician Rus'), the ethnographic boundary of Lemkovyna once went much farther west and north. In his work *Istoricheske izvistie o vedenii khristianstva v prikarpatskykh stranakh* (Historical evidence on the introduction of Christianity into the Carpathian countries), the very learned historian Fr. Antonii Petrushevych notes the existence of Eastern Rite churches in the towns of Rzeszów and Hoczew in Brzozów County, and of sections of land found in Szczawnica that are still called "priest's field" and "cantor's field," which is evidence of Rus' parishes in these localities. The names of some cities, such as Grybów (not Grzybów) and Gorlice (not Gardlice) also show that the founders and early residents of these places were Rusyn Lemkos.

2. Nature

Lemkovyna lies in the Carpathian Mountains, which trend in an East-West direction and are intersected by the valleys of rivers that flow to the north. For this reason there are no east-west roads. The roads all go north-south. Communication there is difficult. The rivers Poprad, Kamienica, Biała, Ropa, Wisłoka, Jasionka, Osława, and San all come out of the mountains and flow north. Roads have been built from the north up these rivers, cutting through the crest of the mountains in places like Tylicz, Izby, Konieczna, Grab, Bar-

View from land belonging to Petro Maslei towards land belonging to Evylia Maslei. Berest, 1919. (Photo ©M. Maslej).

winek, Czeremcha, and Łupków, and leading to Czechoslovakia. As far back as the sixteenth century, there were roads from Poland to Hungary through Dukla, Jaśliska, Tylicz and Muszyna, which were used for bringing wine to Poland. These roads were very bad, muddy in the spring and impassable in the fall. The first paved roads were built during Austrian times.

The mountains of Lemkovyna attain altitudes of over a thousand meters above sea level. Among the highest peaks are Jaworzyna, Lackowa, Magura, Chełm, Cergowa, Bukowica, Kamień, Pasieczna, Chryszczata, and others. The

Roadside shrine/cross in Czyrna, near Krynica, pre-1939.

hills and mountains are covered with forests, with open glens near the peaks, and along the brooks are wonderful valleys that create romantic views. Up to a certain height in the valleys, there are tilled fields, with pastures above that. With this background, villages have been established along the streams. Among the oldest villages are Ropica, founded in 1279, and Macyna in 1342. In his *Sandetska Rus'* (Sącz Rus'), Ioann Petrovych maintains that the oldest villages in Lemkovyna are Wawrzka and Andrzejówka. The fields higher on the hills are rocky and infertile, lower down they are more productive, and those in the San valley are the best.

The climate of Lemkovyna is rugged, continental, of average temperature, dry. Winds are predominantly from the south. Precipitation is average. The rough mountain situation forced Lemko farmers to adapt to the special conditions of the environment. Difficult access reduced the influence of other cultures, which made for a retention of the Lemko's old spiritual and material values and created durability in his way of life.

3. Mineral Resources

Although the Lemko highlands are poor in regard to soil fertility, they are rich in forest and pasture land, petroleum, and mineral waters. However, these resources do not belong to Lemkos but to the State. Lemkos merely provide the labor. Petroleum and oil seeping out of rocky areas are found in the foothills of Lemkovyna, in the counties of Jasło, Krosno, and Lesko. In the mountains themselves there is an entire series of health resorts with beneficial mineral waters.

The following resorts are widely known: Krynica, Żegiestów, Słotwiny, Muszyna, Wysowa, Wapienne, Rymanów, Iwonicz-Zdrój, and others. The most important one is that in Krynica, which was built in fields and pastures that had previously belonged to the Greek Catholic parish of Krynica. In 1772, Franc Stix von Saubergen, commissioner of Sanok County, bought an area of springs from the Krynica parish, for 203 Polish zlotys. Most active in the development of the Krynica resort were a Dr. Starby and Dr. Dietl.

4. Forest Resources

Lemkovyna is a lovely remote corner of Europe, densely covered with fragrant trees, primarily conifers. The most prevalent are pines, firs, and spruces, with only a few stands of beech. In earlier times, the owners of the forests were manorial estates and the state, but now it is only the state. In the woods there are many wild animals that do damage to homesteads. People often have to drive wild animals away from their crops with clubs. Wolves often appear in the pastures and do away with sheep and young heifers. Sometimes it is hard to keep a wild animal away.

View of Lemkovyna in the summer. Mochnaczka Niżna, 2005.

The woods are rich in wild berries, mainly strawberries, raspberries, black-berries, and blueberries. There is also a great abundance of mushrooms of many varieties. To go into the forest to pick its bounty it was necessary to go to the [government] Administration of Forests and buy a special pass. The fee for such a pass was very high, and not everyone was in a position to purchase one. Anyone caught in the forest without such a pass was a great criminal. He would be beaten, have his clothes torn off and his implements confiscated, and would have to pay a heavy fine. In addition, he would have to work several days without pay for the Administration of Forests.

The mushrooms that were gathered would be dried in the sun or in a stove, strung on a string and sold. Wagonloads of mushrooms were shipped everywhere, including America. Picking of mushrooms provided Lemkos with a nice income and tasty food for the winter. The local health resorts were well supplied with wild berries and mushrooms picked by Lemko women.

5. Population

The population of Lemkovyna on both sides of the mountains is approximately six hundred thousand. Most of them are light-haired and blue-eyed, but there also are some short, sturdily built, dark-complexioned people. Gypsies are found in almost every village, but they are only a small proportion of the population. Their settlements are usually outside of village boundaries or otherwise isolated. Since Gypsies have been living alongside Lemkos, it is not inconceivable that they have left traces of swarthy skin and black hair, of the southern type. Villages almost entirely populated by Gypsies are Rokytov, near Zborov, and Hamry near Ustrzyki. From a cultural viewpoint, the residents of the four villages in Nowy Targ County noted above, and those of Leluchów and Dubne differ from the rest of Lemkovyna. The first have been influenced by Polish Górals, and the other two by Transcarpathia.

Located as they are along mountain streams and amid meadows and forests, Lemko villages present a scenic view. For the most part, the villages are shaped in the so-called "chain" form, that is, houses are built along a single road with orchards and fields behind them. Also occurring, although rarely, is the so-called "oval" form, where the houses are situated around a market oval. The village is usually irregular in shape, depending on the valley in which it is located. Houses are most often set with the longer side facing the road, less frequently with an end to the road.

The homestead is usually of the one-building type, which means that both the living quarters and the farm components are housed under one roof. However, in the Ropa River valley and in Nowy Sącz County there are homesteads with several buildings for farm operations and a separate one for living quarters enclosed with a stone wall or wooden fence. In earlier times, houses were roofed with thatches of straw, later with wood shingles, and most recently even with tin or tile. The style of houses has also been changing. The older four-slope roof style is changing to one with two slopes and wide eaves. The space between the edge of the roof and the frame of the building is partitioned off. This space is called the *zahata* and provides insulation against the cold and a place for storing household goods. Lemko houses are never painted in one color but in parallel stripes from roof to ground. In Jasło County, the stripes are black, in Sanok County red, and in other counties white.

The interior of Lemko houses is modest, rather primitive: a wide bed on tall legs, a shelf for kitchen utensils, a rod for hanging clothes, a table. and fixed benches along the walls. A large fireplace with a hearth, painted with whitewash, stands in a corner. Until recently, Lemko houses were quite smoky.

Residents with their Orthodox priest, Fr. A. Ivanovych. Królowa Górna, 1925.

An exterior view of a Lemko dwelling in Radoszyce near Komańcza, pre-1939.

A serious misfortune for Lemkos has been the fact that Lemkovyna is not a single political entity but was divided into two parts, one belonging to Poland, the other to Hungary, and after the First World War, to Czechoslovakia. Both parts have been split into national minority areas within Polish and Slovak administrative districts. Not having their own political center, they have never been able to elect their own representatives to county councils, or legislatures and parliaments. Nor could they have their own administrative authority, not even a partial one. About 250,000 Lemkos were encompassed within seven Polish counties, of which only Sanok County had a majority of Lemkos. The situation on the other side of the Carpathians was similar. There are over seven hundred communities of various size in Lemkovyna, including two large towns, Sanok and Krynica, and about ten smaller towns: Tylicz, Łabowa, Uście Ruskie [now Uście Gorlickie], Dukla, Rymanów, Bukowsko, Baligród, Łupków, Cisna, and Lesko.

6. Farming

Lemkovyna should not be regarded as a strictly crop farming region, with the exception of the Sanok and Sącz valleys, where wheat, rye, and other such crops are often grown. The Lemko highlands are more suitable for animal husbandry, but the Lemko also sows some grain, to stave off hunger.

Arable fields have been established mainly in areas cleared of forest, so most Lemkos have had little land, and that was poor soil, not very fertile. The most important products of this land were potatoes, cabbage, turnips, and oats. Usually, the homesteader was not able to buy and keep a horse, so he used cows as harnessed power to till his fields. And as a result he would get less milk and its products from his stock. Farmers who were better off worked their fields with oxen. As time went by, wild and greedy forestry practices led to elimination of oxen from Lemko fields and replacement by horses, because it was easier to earn money using horses to haul logs from the woods to a sawmill or railroad station.

The subdivisions of land were called whole section, half section, quarter section, half quarter, stripe, turnaround, lump, and slip. A whole section was a wide and long band that stretched from the home buildings in both directions to the borders of the neighboring villages. It amounted to more than thirty acres, and included arable land, hayfields, pastures, wasteland, and often a piece of woods. But such holdings became increasingly fewer, because

Petro Maslei behind the plow. Berest, 1923. (Photo © M. Maslej).

Oxen-pulled cart. Berest, 1923. (Photo ©M. Maslej).

a dying father would divide his land among his heirs. Years ago, sheep and cattle could be pastured in forest glens, but this aspect of farming died out after the First World War, when Polish landlords revoked the peasants' ancient right to free pasture in forest glens and meadows.

Agriculture in Lemkovyna was a primitive operation. Wooden wagons, wooden plows, wooden harrows were used until just recently. Straw was chopped with a cutter that the farmer had constructed himself. Grain was winnowed by fanning and threshed with a flail. Threshing took up all winter, and in that time half the grain was destroyed by mice. In most recent times farmers have acquired factory-made equipment, making the work easier and the gain greater.

7. Animal Husbandry

Before the First World War, a farmer in Lemkovyna could get a good income from raising oxen. A richer man would buy two or three pairs of oxen in the spring, pasture them through the summer in forest glens and meadows, and sell them in the fall for a large profit. A poorer man might do the same with one pair. Some would keep a good pair and train them to work in a yoke. Before the war there were well known markets for oxen and barren cows in such places as Grybów, Tylicz, Gorlice, Baligród, Żmigród, Dukla, Rymanów and Krosno. From these market places wagon loads of cattle raised by Lemkos would be carted out to places like Vienna and Berlin. After the war, raising oxen was no longer lucrative and was discontinued.

Sheep were also raised in Lemkovyna. Usually, a couple of farmers would buy fifty or a hundred sheep at a market in Rychwałd, Żdynia, Uście, Łabowa, Żmigród, Rymanów, or Bukowsko. Some even went as far as Semigorod [in Transylvania] and drove from there huge flocks of up to three thousand sheep, which they then sold at local markets. Sheep were grazed, shorn, milked, and sold in the fall. This made for a good income. At night and through the noon hour, the sheep would be held in movable pens made of willow branches and called *koshary*. There they would be shorn and milked. In the morning and afternoon they would be let out to graze. Beside the *koshary* there would be a hut for the shepherd. The *koshary* would be moved to a different place every day. In this way the farmer enriched his fields with manure for growing rye or barley. The milk from the sheep would be heated in a brass kettle over an open fire and made into a cheese called *bryndza*. This would be put into wooden kegs covered with stones. To make this cheese tastier and more elastic, some curdled milk might be added to the warm milk.

In earlier times, the *sołtys* or village chief and bailiffs had the most sheep-grazing rights. Bailiffs had the obligation to pay the landowner a pasture fee, which amounted to five rams and one large cheese per year for pasturing three hundred sheep. Village chiefs were exempt from this fee.

The residents of Uście Ruskie had a special privilege giving them the right to raise pigs in manorial forests that had many beech trees. For this they had to pay the forest owner a fee of pigs, chickens, butter, cheese, and eggs.

Residents of the village of Rychwałd [now called Owczary] had an extraordinary privilege to slaughter rams and sell them in the market in Gorlice, during the period between the holidays of St. Nicholas and St. Catherine. Without any fee or license, they could sell either live or butchered rams. This privilege was granted to the Rychwałdians by some king for saving the king's army from starvation. Use of this privilege led to a court case in 1923. The Rychwałdians won the case on testimony that they had had this right from time immemorial. In existence is an 1845 document attesting that Rychwald had been admitted to the butcher's guild in Gorlice.

8. Industry

Nature has endowed the Lemko people with the great gift of an ability to adapt to all the hard conditions of life in the highlands. This ability made for the development of cottage industries in Lemkovyna. These satisfied their most urgent needs and also brought in some income. The most notable of these are woodworking, stone working, weaving, and traveling craftsmanship.

The making of wooden shingles for roofing has been widespread in Lemkovyna since ancient times. These products were in great demand and were even exported. Shingles were used not only for roofing houses but also churches and chapels, and not only for roofs but also for siding. Almost all the churches in Lemkovyna were roofed with wooden shingles, even those built of stone.

A center of the manufacture of small wooden items was the village of Nowica in Gorlice County, which was situated among forests. There, with the aid of simple hand operated lathes and curved knives, men made wooden spoons, ladles, spindles, boxes, churns, whistles, and all kinds of toys for children. Production of spoons spread out from Nowica to surrounding villages, especially to Leszczyny and Banica. In the first few years after the First World War, these items were shipped out to America and other countries. The greatest profit was made by middlemen, usually Jews, but even the Lemkos got paid for their labor. In time this export business closed down completely, and the Lemko had no other recourse but to hoist his wares on his shoulders, carry them around to other villages, and sell them for mere pennies.

Another element of wood working is sculpture, that is, the carving and etching of wood. Several villages neighboring Rymanów-Zdrój– Bałucianka, Wólka, Wołtuszowa, and a few others– have formed a center of this craft. The beginning of wood sculpture in Lemkovyna is dated to the latter half of the last century. The Countess Potocka, owner of Rymanów and grandmother of the present Ignacy Potocki, was a very pious and noble lady. When she saw the poverty in the surrounding villages, on the one hand, and the available skills of carpentry and wood carving on the other, she established a three-year school for Lemko boys in Rymanów-Zdrój, at her own expense. Many young Lemkos went through this school, where they learned how to carve wood into beautiful objects, which knowledge was then passed on from generation to generation. All the carved wood articles, such as small cases, chests, trays, canisters, plates, canes, etc., that are sold at the health resorts in Krynica, Żegiestów,

Wood-carving, widespread around Rymanów Zdrój before WWII, continued among Lemkos in emigration. Ivan Maksymovych from Wołtuszowa and wife Maria Hranyczna plied their skills in western Poland in the 1960s and later in the US. New York City, 1978.

Muszyna, Wysowa, Rymanów-Zdrój, Iwonicz-Zdrój, and elsewhere, are produced by Lemko hands in the villages around Rymanów. At the resort itself, only the name of the place is etched into the wood. The sale of these articles was handled by Jews, who bought them wholesale from the villagers at low prices and then distributed them among the resorts, and made good money.

There is also another kind of wood sculpture in Lemkovyna, and that is the making of all kinds of objects and adornments for churches. The center of this craft is the village of Bielanka. Almost all the figurines of saints, all the altars, holy portals, and other such church objects are the work of Lemko hands. These articles are very artistic and are highly valued by connoisseurs.

Beautiful wooden chests and boxes are made in Szlachtowa. In Świątkowa they weave wicker baskets out of juniper roots, and in Wróblik they make large willow baskets for wagons and for export. Birch twig brooms are produced in Pielgrzymka and sold at local markets.

In every Lemko village there are craftsmen who use wood to make various things needed for the household, such as cupboards, shelving, picture frames, candle holders, washboards, flax strippers, shoe lasts, yarn reels, kneading troughs, kegs, and other household utensils.

Over a hundred years ago, the most important center of stonework was Krempna in Gorlice County. Its products were highly valued throughout the entire Austro-Hungarian Empire. Now, stone work is most highly developed in Bartne, where millstones and handmills are produced, and in Florynka, where they make various kinds of whetstones for sharpening knives, scythes and axes. Figurines of saints for roadside chapels are produced in Krempna and Przegonina.

The most important occupations for traveling craftsmen are glassworking, wiremending, and the peddling of lubricants.

The first wood-carving marketing cooperative organized for deported Lemkos by Stefan Kyshchak. (left) Andrei Sukhorskii (Wólka), Ivan Kyshchak (Bałucianka), Vasyl Kyshchak (Bałucianka) and Petro Orysik (Wólka). Lviv, 1949.

Glassworkers carry their wares on their backs from village to village, and fit glass into windows and set it with caulking. In western Lemkovyna, glassmen are called *bvanari*.

From the villages around Szczawnica, such as Biała Woda, Czarna Woda, and Szlachtowa, come *drotary*, tinkers who travel all over Lemkovyna and repair dented kettles, pots, and bowls. They also carry with them artistic things made of wire, such as traps for mice and rats and toys for children. Well known in western Lemkovyna was the figure of Pavlik the tinker, who has even entered into Lemko literature.

Another kind of traveling occupation, but on a broader scale, was the peddling of various oils and lubricants for wagons. Black grease for wagon wheels was made from melted down pine tar or from crude oil with the addition of mineral wax. Greasemen would fill large barrels with this grease and with

Typical grease wagon from the village of Łosie. Interwar period.

a team of horses hitched to a large wagon would haul it all over Europe. They would usually start out in May and return home in late fall. The people of Łosie in Gorlice County have been engaged in this grease business for a long time. Those in Bielanka, Leszczyny, and Ropki have done it on a smaller scale. Years ago greasemen used to keep stocks of grease in Warsaw, Lublin, and Lviv. Still living are many old greasemen who in their youth drove grease wagons through Russia all the way to the Ural Mountains, and all over Austria, Germany, Hungary, and many other parts of Europe.

The grease business meant a lot to a village, mainly because it was a profitable undertaking. The residents of Łosie alone had more money in banks and safes than did all the rest of Lemkovyna, considering that a prosperous greaseman probably had about a hundred thousand florins in the bank, which at today's rate of exchange would amount to over a hundred thousand American dollars. From the standpoint of wealth and culture, Łosie surpassed all other Lemko villages. Many intellectuals have come from Łosie. The greasemen learned a lot in their roving over foreign countries, and when they returned home they used what they had learned to their own advantage. So the grease business also had an educational aspect. Łosians were regarded as the most cultured people in Lemkovyna. Their grease peddling educated and distinguished them. The greaseman was respected in other countries and had free entry into the homes of aristocrats. Foreigners learned to honor the Lemko spirit more than our own folks did.

The weaver's craft was widely practiced in Lemkovyna. Excellent linen cloth was produced on homemade looms, and wool was felted in fulling mills. Years ago Lemkos did not buy cloth or any other material for home use but made everything at home. They dressed entirely in materials they made themselves, and for a long time they kept their own styles. In recent times, however, tawdriness has begun replacing the attractive Lemko fashions.

Another home craft was production of oil by pressing flaxseed in a so-called "masher." This oil was used to replace animal fat during periods of fasting. The residue of the pressing process is called *makukha* and was used as cattle feed.

At the Pavlo Sefanivskii Lemko Museum. Bielanka, 2000.

Beekeeping was not well developed in Lemkovyna. Beehives were cut out of logs and later made of boards. There were many wild bees in the forests of Lemkovyna, black in color and fierce stingers, but productive. These bees lived in the hollows of old trees and usually accumulated a lot of honey, which was hard to get at. Some people managed to transfer some into regular hives, but they often wouldn't stay. Beeswax was used to make large candles called *triytsi*, which were carried to church on major holidays.

9. Tourism and Interest in Lemkovyna

For many long years, nobody paid any attention to Lemkovyna. It was as though it were walled off from the world and of no general interest. However, when through their efforts and knowledge, through their accomplishments, the Lemkos converted this wild little corner into a functional society, when they developed their own cottage industries, when Lemko goods and products began showing up in foreign countries, Lemkovyna attracted more attention and interest in it grew. The Lemko highlands attracted tourists and sportsmen who visited there more and more frequently, individually and in groups. Tourists have traversed the length and breadth of Lemkovyna.

Along with the tourists have come scientists, anthropologists, ethnographers, ethnologists, geologists. They have been researching the history and characteristics of the people, the natural resources of the land, and the beauty of its scenery. Their studies of Lemkovyna have been issued in print, and there is a growing body of scientific literature on this land and its residents.

The works written in Polish are tendentiously one-sided. They don't give a truly authentic picture of the situation. There are many health resorts in Lemkovyna, and they are frequented by foreign guests. These foreigners often visit Lemko villages and display an interest in the people. "Sanation" Poland [a reference to the 1930s government] bared its teeth at Lemkovyna and exerted its brain power to find ways of destroying the Lemko people forever. Its aristocratic ambition could not allow a people of different faith and different nationality to live in this prettiest piece of Polish territory. Polish tourism rendered no benefit to the Lemkos, but rather brought harm to them. There will be more on this in Part III, Section 12.

10. Food

The everyday food of the Lemko is potatoes, cabbage, turnips, oat bread or oat pancakes (called *adzymka* and *podpalok*), oatmeal, and *kiselitsia*, a sour soup made of oats or barley. One who was better off might allow himself some

Children and teenagers participating in May 3rd celebrations. Gorlice, May 3rd, 1933.

better food, such as eggs, butter, lard, barley gruel, cheese, or barley bread. For a major holiday there might be *pirohi* with cheese, well basted with fatback or butter, or dumplings and salt pork. Meat is rarely eaten, and when it is, it is usually rabbit or chicken. A typical meal in Lemkovyna is oatmeal, *kiselitsia*, and lard.

Although simple, the Lemko cuisine is very tasty. Nowhere in the world can you find bread as flavorful as Lemko *paskha* (Easter bread), or sausage as savory as Lemko *kolbasa*, or pasta as tasty as Lemko *pirohi*. Similarly, you won't find any tastier drinking water than that in the Lemko highlands. Lemkos drink alcoholic beverages only in moderation, usually at events like weddings, christenings, or when a dear friend comes to visit. After the First World War, some drank *kropka* [diethyl ether] instead of vodka, but now they are giving up this harmful drink and turning to *oranżada* (orangeade) instead. Drunkards were rare in Lemkovyna.

Despite their simple diet, Lemkos are healthy, strong, enduring, and long lived. In some villages, though, such as Nowa Wieś and Roztoka [Mała?], people have become afflicted with tumors due to a lack of iodine in their water.

II. Clothing

As often in a theater one gazes in wonder at the costumes of the actors, so also worthy of admiration is the native apparel of Lemkovyna. In its beauty and diversity, it surpasses the attire of the Polish Górals or the residents of Cracow. A detailed description of Lemko attire would require a long treatise. Here we shall give only a short sketch of the clothing used most commonly among Lemkos.

On their feet they wear *kerptsi*, homemade of pigskin or cowhide, or of wool felt. These *kerptsi* are tied up with black wool strings called *navoloky* or *nastrochanky*, which go up around the leg to keep leggings up. Some wear high boots called *skirni* or *chereviky (tsizhmy)* instead of *kerptsi*.

A man would put on a linen *koshelia* (shirt) and linen *gachy* (underpants), and over that *nohavky* or *kholoshni* (trousers). *Nohavky* are made of linen and *kholoshni* of wool. Over the shirt he would have a *drushliak* or *laibyk* (vest), embroidered in front. A *laibyk* is made of wool and has metal buttons. Over the laibyk he might put on a *hunia* or *hunka* (light coat) made of wool and over that a *chuha* (greatcoat) of the same kind of wool. The *chuha* is used in cold or rainy weather. A *chuha* is the kind of cloak that has wide sleeves narrowed tight at the ends and fringed with long thongs. The sleeves of a chuha are used for carrying *merindia* (lunch). Sewn on the shoulders of the chuha are squares of fringed felt for decoration.

On his head he might have a black *kapeliukh* or *kalapik* (hat) with a high brim, and in winter a lambskin or wool cap with flaps that could be lowered to cover the ears and neck. In very cold weather he would wear a sheepskin coat instead of the *chuha*, and sheepskin mittens. Around the house, he might have on a sheepskin *serdak* (jacket) instead of the *laibyk* under the *hunia*.

Sketch from the mid-nineteenth century, "Lemkos" by G. Hoffman.

Lemko men wearing festive hunias. Olchowiec, 2001.

Men's attire is not very fanciful, but the women like to dress up and display Lemko styles on every occasion.

Women would put on a linen *podolok* (petticoat) and *oplicha* (chemise). The oplicha is decorated with Lemko embroidery on the sleeves and chest and around the neck. Over the *podolok* they would wear a *kabat* or *spodnitsia* (skirt) of various colors, and over the *kabat* an apron or overskirt. Over the *oplicha* she might have a vest or jerkin. The jerkin would be decorated with embroidery and shiny buttons. Her neck might be adorned with a necklace of glass or coral beads. Girls would tie their hair up in back with *basamunky* (ribbons) of various colors. In summer the girls would go bareheaded, and would wear their hair in long braids. Married women wound their hair into a *preshpilianka* (pinup), put a cap or hairnet over it, and a *fatselik* (kerchief) over that. In winter they would wear a wool vest, jacket, or coat, and a large woolen shawl over their head or shoulders. On their feet they would have *kerptsi* or *chereviky*. In severe winter weather, older women would wear a heavy sheepskin coat.

12. Nationality

In terms of nationality, Lemkos belong to the large [East] Slavic Rus' family. The name Rus' [pronounced *Roosh*] has always been sacred to them, and Slavic ideals have always been close to their hearts. They have always felt a kinship with all other Slavic peoples, and have always thought of the German as their enemy. They call themselves Rusyns, Ruthenians, Rusnaks, or Lemkos. The term "Lemko" stems from the word *lem*, meaning "only," which they use with great frequency. Although in recent years there has been a drive to call them "Ukrainians" in defining their nationality and also to change their political orientation, so far Lemkos have not accepted this label, nor have they changed their political views. This drive had its roots in Berlin and Vienna and has been propagandized by Ukrainian nationalists and Polish fascists in the service of Bismarck's policies with his slogan of *divide et impera* (divide and rule), and the policy of world domination followed by that evil malefactor Hitler.

The people living in the Carpathian Mountains are divided into three groups called Lemko, Boiko, and Hutsul. This division is based on differences

Girls in local folk costumes. Berest, 1923. (Photo © M. Maslej).

The church committee in charge of planning construction of a new St. John Chrysostom church, after fire destroyed the wooden church. Standing from left: Petro Prokopyk, Petro Bugel, Ivan Bogush, Teodor Myshkovskii, Nykolai Fedak, Ivan Shpak, Ivan Hardysh. Sitting: Sava Dzhugan, Havrilo Dytko, Fr. Nykolai Felenchak, deacon Sydor Iatsenyk, Iakym Vyshnovskii, Danylo Dytko. Polany, 1912-1914.

in their speech. Historically, however, taken together all three of these groups have been called Carpatho-Rusyns or Carpatho-Rusnaks, and the territory in which they live as *Karpatska Rus'* (Carpathian Rus'.) Lemkos, therefore, are a part of Carpathian Rus'. But over the centuries, each of these groups has developed a separate language, a separate dialect. The reasons for these linguistic differences are the geographic location and the history of the three groups.

As noted above, the Carpathian Mountains are arranged in a chain fashion, so that the Carpathian roads run mostly North-South. For a Lemko to reach Boikivshchyna (the Boiko region) or Hutsulshchyna (the Hutsul region), he would have to climb a high mountain or else go down one valley to the lowlands, then go eastward to another valley and back up again. For this reason there was no steady contact between the Lemkos and Boikos or Hutsuls, and the people of these three groups could not merge into a single entity. Instead, it was easier for them to mingle with the Carpatho-Rusyns to the south of them; because that's the way the roads ran. This also explains why there is no significant difference between the Lemkos on either side of the Carpathians, despite the fact that these two parts belong to different countries, the northern to Poland and the southern to Slovakia. But differences did develop between Lemkos and the Boikos and Hutsuls, even though they are all on the same side of the mountain range and belong to the same country. [Poland, at that time.] Another reason is that both the Boiko and Hutsul lands are located among Rusyn peoples, while Lemkovyna lies between Poland and Slovakia. Both the Boikos and the Hutsuls have been subjected to influences flowing from Galician and Transcarpathian Rus', while the Lemkos were affected by Poles and Slovaks.

13. The Lemko Language

In both structure and pronunciation, the Lemko language is the most singular of all Rusyn local dialects. Since Lemkos have been neighbors of Poles, Slovaks and Hungarians, their speech has incorporated many Polonisms, Slovakisms, and Magyarisms. Nevertheless, Lemko speech is based principally on Old Slavonic and has become so well developed and independent that it is used not only by the common people but also by Lemko intellectuals. For more than half a century, books and periodicals have been written and printed in the Lemko language. It differs from both Ukrainian and Russian primarily in accent, which, as in the Polish language, always falls on the next to last syllable. A principal virtue of this language is that it can be understood by every Slav, and vice versa, the Lemko can understand every other Slav.

In recent years, bilingual dictionaries have been published even for Slavic languages, as for example, Russian-Polish, Ukrainian-Polish, Czech-Polish, and so on. But there is no need for such dictionaries with the Lemko language. Lemko can be understood by both the Great Russian and the Little Russian, and by the Pole and the Czech and every other Slav. None of the other Slavic languages has been able to preserve so well the character of the Old Slavonic language, the forefather of all Slavic languages, as the Lemko language has. If sometime in the future a great Slavic nation should arise, which some Slavophiles dream about, a pan-Slavic literary language would best be based on Lemko. It is no surprise that the monthly *Slavianski Viek* (Slavic Century), published in Vienna, has for over fifty years carried articles written in Lemko. The Lemko language has already made substantial gains. Although it finds itself in very unfavorable circumstances, Lemko literature is growing daily. Finally, it should be noted that the Lemko language in Lemkovyna is not stagnant. There are many localisms, many names for the same object, and this is evidence that the language is developing. As a characteristic example, there are about a dozen words for potatoes in Lemkovyna [*bandurky, gruli, kartofli, kompery, krompli,* etc.]

14. Religion

Lemkos profess both the Orthodox and the Catholic faith, but of the Byzantine rite. Among themselves, they call their faith either Orthodox [*pravoslavna*] or Rus' Faith [*Ruska Vira*], without regard as to whether it is Catholic or Orthodox. They acquired Christianity from Moravia through the sainted missionaries Cyril and Methodius in the latter half of the ninth century, a hundred years before it was brought to Kyivan Rus' by St. Volodymyr the Great. For the span

Polany near Dukla, before 1914 when the church burned down. Parishioners with their priest, Fr. Nykolai Felenchak, in their Easter Sunday best.

of an entire millennium there was religious unity in Lemkovyna, and no heresy or foreign religion could gain entrance to the Lemko highlands. The pure doctrine of Christ in its glorious Eastern rite has held there to this day, always faithfully guarded by the Lemkos. They did not scrutinize the truth of the pronounced dogmas of their faith, but believed strongly in God's truths as they were propounded by their priests and were handed down from generation to generation. As regards faith, the practice of religion, and morality, the Lemko people have always stood very high.

After the First World War, a battle over religion broke out between Orthodox and Catholics. This was brought about by the chauvinistic policies of Ukrainian nationalists with the Bishop of Przemyśl at their head, and it was a demonstration by both warring sides of their willingness to defend their most cherished values of faith, nationality, and ritual. There will be more on this in the historical part of this elaboration.

The Lemko people have distinguished themselves for their piety and adherence to their church and their rite. Everyone would go to church service on holy days, leaving only infirm old-timers and small children at home. A significant factor in maintaining faith, nationality, and rite was the fact that Lemko priests were married and had large families. Lemko intellectuals came principally from priestly families. The people lived in close association with their priest and his family. A parish was like a spiritual family, in which the priest was father, teacher, and counselor, while his wife was like a mother and taught the housewives how to manage their households. Sons of priests acted as organizers of choirs, drama groups, and reading sessions, at which they gave readings, produced plays and concerts, and brought enlightenment and culture to Lemko villages.

Clerical matrimony brought great benefits to the Lemko people. In conversation with a Lemko priest, an old Latin priest expressed it thus: "Your people have a great moral strength, because your priests are married and have their own families. As soon as celibacy becomes established among you, however, you and we will be on the same footing and your morality will weaken." That priest's words were truly well-spoken. When unmarried priests started arriving in Lemkovyna then people lost faith in them and drifted farther and farther from them, because they could not feel that warm kinship with them that they had been accustomed to in priests' homes before. Among Lemkos, such unmarried priests were called "bachelors," because it often happened that such a priest was lower in morality than

Fr. Alexander Ivanovych with wife Julia, son Viacheslav, and five parishioners. Królowa Górna, 1939.

a confirmed Lemko bachelor. Gone was the kindly familiarity that had formerly warmed all who came to the parish house. Instead, an evil began creeping into Lemkovyna, an evil that the celibate priests could not counteract, and after that faith began weakening also.

15. The Lemko Character

The marvelous natural setting of the Carpathian Mountains has left its mark of beauty on the Lemko soul. No other peoples are characterized by such great spiritual gifts, such virtue, and such high integrity as the Lemko people.

Lemkos are exceptionally hard-working, considerate, thrifty, conscientious, scrupulous, honest, reliable, peaceful, tolerant, and very versatile. Also among the characteristic features of these people are a well tempered and enduring disposition; a strong attachment to their own history, tradition, nationality, and faith; love for their cherished hills and dales; conservatism in habits and

Brother and sister Mykhal and Paraska Vovk pose as "newlyweds" during annual "Mountain Holiday" celebrations. Sanok, 1937.

customs; strong resolution in defense of their own; distrust of foreigners; desire for proper socio-religious education; and a highly developed sense of honor and justice. In respect to desirable features of character, the Lemko is a kind of Slavic role model.

The Lemko is so upright and so much a man of his word that he will never take advantage of anyone. When he borrows something he always tries to get it back on time, at least before Saturday night, because he considers it sinful to keep a borrowed object over Sunday. He considers money loaned to a neighbor as being safer than in a bank. It is always paid back on time. Among themselves, a man's word is good in all things. Each believes the other and will never cheat. It is not necessary to sign any notarized or court documents. A Lemko's word is more reliable than any written contract.

The Lemko is an ethical person. He has a deep seated respect for another's property. There was no thievery in Lemkovyna. Anything could be left anywhere– in the yard, out in the field, or beside a road– without the slightest fear that it would disappear. Locks were unknown in Lemkovyna until recently. In summer, the house was always left unlatched, or at worst it would be wedged with a wooden shim to keep dogs out. All the members of a family could go far out to some field for all day, and no one would have a qualm that someone might steal something, for such a thing never happened.

16. Superstitions and Customs

When a Lemko begins the task of building a new house, he must first verify that the site he has chosen for the house is the right one for that purpose, whether it would be good or harmful. To determine this, he makes some tests. In the

Lemkos celebrating the Jordan holiday in western Poland after Operation "Vistula." Zimna Woda, Wrocław district, 1957.

evening he will lay a piece of bread at each of the four corners of the proposed house. If next morning the bread is gone, the spot is not suitable and he must find another. If on the other hand the bread is still there, the site is a good one and he can proceed with building his house.

He first plows a furrow all around the proposed house, to keep evil spirits out. While this is going on there must be no shouting or cursing, else there will be no peace in the new house, the wife will not respect her husband, and the children will not obey their parents. Then he prepares the footing. He places large rocks at the four corners of the outlined rectangle and connects them with fir beams. When the footings are all laid, he asks a priest to bless the new site and foundation. He sets a cross at each corner and drills a deep hole in each one. In these holes he puts a silver quarter coin (so that there would always be plenty in that house), some periwinkle leaves (so that the girls of the house would be quickly married off), blossoms of aspen or willow trees (so no sins would be committed in that house), poplar leaves (so the children would be happy and would grow strong), a piece of *prosfora*, unconsecrated bread cut from a communion loaf, wrapped in a handkerchief (so that the Lord would always provide food and some gain for the master of the house), and a piece of glass (so that no evil spirit could get into the house and so that all the members of the household would always be healthy).

The Lemko would never dare to cut down an old fruit tree. That could bring some great misfortune down on him or his family. He might die within the year, or his children might become ill, his animals could die, a hailstorm might destroy his grain crop, etc. He would hire a gypsy or some other tramp for this job.

When it is time for the farmer to go out to the field to sow oats at the start of the season and he has everything ready to go, his wagon loaded with oats ready for sowing, and his team hitched to the wagon, his wife puts on a sheepskin coat, hair side out, thrusts a piece of bread in her bodice, and takes a sprinkler of holy water in her hands. She then walks three times (clockwise) around the rig, sprinkling the wagon, the grain, the horses or oxen, and her man, and reciting portions of the Psalms as she goes around. She places bread in front of the team. The farmer makes the sign of the cross three times over the bread and drives his horses or oxen over it. He then takes that bread with him to the field, plus another piece of bread in a sack with some cheese and an egg. When he turns the first furrow, he puts the egg in it. He takes some dirt from that furrow and smears his horses (oxen) with it, so that they would be strong and healthy.

If the first bird to set down on the plowed area is a crow, then the harvest will be good, but if it is a wagtail then there will be windstorms and lightning. It is a good sign if the first person he sees when plowing is a man. If it is a woman, there may be trouble.

Before he starts out to sow his grain, he first fastens a piece of *prosfora* and seeds inside the sack or pouch that he will use to sow his grain from, to ensure a good harvest. Rye, wheat, peas, and beans must not be sowed or planted during the new moon; else the food prepared from them will be harmful to the health. Also, clover should not be sowed on freshly plowed sod, because the cows and heifers could bloat from it. To protect the sprouting grain from rainbows, a piece of shiny metal should be placed in that field to cast back the bad rays of the rainbow.

During the grain harvest, one must not drink *palunka* ["fire water," i.e., home-brewed alcohol] so that no scabs form on one's face or hands. In loading the sheaves on a wagon, not a single word should be spoken until the wagon is full, else there would be a great misfortune. When the load of sheaves gets to the barn, the farmer or his son must take a knucklebone in his teeth and walk around the wagon with it, and then scatter some fine sand where the grain is to be placed, so that mice can't get into the barn. Some of the straw should be left in the field, as a bribe to the mice to keep them away from the barn.

One should not laugh when pounding out barley or groats, because in cooking the grain it will boil out of the pot and will turn sour if left until evening. Young girls should not do the pounding in a mortar, because their breasts will not develop.

When baking bread, one should say "God have mercy on me" twelve times. In baking *paskha*, along with that one should repeat ten times the "Our Father" and the "O Virgin Mother of God." If the dough rises properly, the children will grow nicely and will soon be able to help. Duck and goose eggs must not be eaten, because ducks and geese eat frogs, lizards, beetles and other nasty things. The herder who dares to disturb a bird's nest will have to run around for his cattle all day long, because they won't want to graze. He who beats and kicks livestock will suffer beatings and kicks from his own children in his old age. Livestock that is well fed and often cleaned will never be troubled by any witch or demon.

The various superstitions and customs given above really do have some deep meaning and are evidence of the high degree of morality existing in Lemkovyna.

17. Customs in Family Events

In Lemkovyna, christening (baptism) was conducted solemnly after a Divine Service held specifically for the child and its parents. Many *kums* (godfathers) and *kumas* (godmothers) were usually invited to the christening. For a Lemko it is a great honor to be a godparent, and so everyone tries to perform this obligation properly. Godparents bring all kinds of gifts for the babe, such as a *kryzhmo* (white christening linen), kerchiefs, butter, milk, white rolls, wheat bread, rice cooked in milk, honey, and money. The food at a christening would be pirohi with cheese, cabbage with meat, oil, pot cheese, and honey. Alcohol is rarely served, for that would not be fitting. No music is played, but there is a lot of singing. The lyrics of the songs are permeated with best wishes for the child and the parents. Godfathers also present gifts to godmothers, chiefly money which they hold in their hands and press into the godmother's hand in a handshake. During the feasting, money is again put into a plate as a gift for the mother and child. Noisiness is not allowed at a christening when the babe is sleeping, because that might cause the child to hiccup or it might bring epilepsy. The child must not be spanked while feeding, because later it might lose its mind. Small children have their eyes and ears washed: girl's eyes with sweet cream and ears with olive oil; boy's with whey of sheep's milk. The mother breastfeeds her baby. Breast milk is a good cure for rheumy eyes. A sick child is treated with chamomile or linden tea, or with raspberry or strawberry juice. To induce a child to begin talking sooner, herbs that have been blessed are placed under its

A village funeral. Bartne, 2002.

pillow, and nuts are rattled loudly. A badly frightened child is wreathed in herb smoke or curses are cast into the fire.

Weddings in Lemkovyna involve many ceremonies. The most suitable time for weddings is autumn, because that is when food is most plentiful. A Lemko wedding comprises three feasts: at the homes of the groom, the bride, and the father-in-law or mother-in-law. Several days are required for this; earlier it used to take a whole week. Foods at a wedding are pirohi, noodles, rice, groats, butter, cheese, and meat. *Palunka* and beer are imbibed. Everyone has a merry time, dancing and singing. A wedding requires special costumes. The bride wears a beribboned periwinkle or myrtle garland on her head. The groom wears a hat striped with periwinkle and ribbons, and carries a hatchet bound in ribbons. The wedding bread, called *korovai,* is beautifully decorated with periwinkle, flowers, fruits, and ribbons. Everyone in the locality is invited to the wedding. All the neighbors bring gifts for the bride and groom: grain, butter, cheese, poultry, and money. Gift money must not be picked up in a bare hand, only through a kerchief or piece of cloth. The bride and groom also exchange gifts. The groom gives his bride a *kolach* (loaf of twisted white bread) and a kerchief for her head. She gives him a kolach and a white shirt. During the walk to the altar, the mothers-in-law give their children ribbons and honey cakes. When leaving the church, the bride puts an egg in her bosom so that it falls to the ground, ensuring that childbirth will be easy. As the newlyweds arrive at their home, grain is tossed at them. When the bride is handed to the groom they both go to the brook to wash. When they come back, the bride pours water on all the guests and then sprinkles the entire homestead. The best man splashes water on the bride with his wedding cane, so that she could still become pregnant if somebody should put a curse on her. The most artistically decorated *korovai* is given to the priest as a gift from the newlyweds.

The entire parish takes part in a funeral. Beginning with a person's death and right up until the burial is over, the church bell is rung three times every day. The deceased is laid out on straw and a holy candle is placed in his hands. He is then dressed in his best clothes, laid on a bench, and the body is covered with a white shroud. All mirrors in the house are either covered or turned to the wall. If there is a clock in the house, it is stopped. Lanterns with candles are placed near the body, and a wooden cross wound with hemp yarn is set up in the midst of them. Candles are kept burning all the time. Years ago they would put whiskey in the coffin of a drunkard and a pipe with tobacco in that of a smoker. A young girl is dressed as if for a wedding. Small children are given a candle in the hands, a wax finger ring, and toys. In some areas, they put money in the coffin, so the soul would have something to redeem itself

Wedding of Rosalia Wyslotskii and Andrei Yavorskii. Berest, 1923. (© M. Maslej).

with. As a sign of grief, girls unbind their tresses and dress in black. A *prosator* (invitor) invites everyone in the parish to come for the burial. The body is either carried on men's' shoulders to the cemetery, or is drawn by wagon in the summer or by sleigh in the winter. Long ago, the oxen used to haul the deceased to the cemetery were given as a gift to the priest. After the burial, everyone returns to the home of the deceased for a grieving feast called the *horiachka*, where there is bread, cheese, cabbage, dumplings, and barley pancakes. Meat is not eaten during a funeral. A week after the funeral a Divine Service with a *panakhida* (requiem) is held for the deceased. All invited guests take part in this. After the service is over everyone sits down to a meal with the priest. Meat is now permitted, but only veal or mutton; poultry is not allowed. After the meal, a requiem is held for the deceased. At the end of this the priest draws a cross on the table with candle wax, and everybody sings "Eternal Memory." Then the priest reads from the Gospel at each corner of the house and sprinkles holy water over the house. A Divine Service is held again on the first anniversary of the death, with a feast for the participants.

The subject of Lemko customs at christenings, weddings, and funerals is very broad, and deserves extensive treatment. We have discussed it here only briefly, because our primary concern is a general description of Lemkovyna.

18. Lemkovyna Today

Because of thuggish activities in the Carpathian Mountains at the end of the Second World War, and other incidents generated by Ukrainian and Polish nationalists, in May of 1947 the [remnants of the] Lemkos were forcibly evicted from their mountains and exiled to western Poland. Through this, people lost their fatherland, their homes, all the rest of their property, and the land that they had worked for generations. They were replaced by colonists recruited from among landless Poles who had not the vaguest notion of how to operate a hill farm, and also were not accustomed to hard work. These were mostly outcasts who lived at the expense and effort of others, without the slightest qualms of honesty or morality.

Harvest season in the village. Berest, 1923. (Photo ©M. Maslej)

When the Lemkos departed from their mountains they left their lands well tilled and planted. These new colonists came to established farms and appropriated the results of Lemko labor. In the fall [of 1947], they gathered up all the harvest of the fields. Through the winter, they ate, drank and played. When spring arrived, there was nothing left for planting and no one to do it. The empty fields began to go fallow and wild. Instead of growing grain and potatoes, they grew weeds and shrubs. There was famine among the colonists,

Home of Petro Hodio, fifteen years after forced deportations. Wołowiec, 1962.

and they deluded the local and county authorities. They cried, "Give us help. We need food, we are dying of starvation. Lemko land is poor. It will not grow anything," and so on. The government responded to these cries with large sums of money intended for welfare and for improving the land. It established state farms and cooperative farms, and made every effort to invigorate the local economy. None of this did any good, however, because there were not enough people around who could make proper use of mountain land, as the Lemkos had done. The colonists were interchanged as though in a kaleidoscope, with many leaving and others coming in to take their places. Nevertheless, the situation did not improve despite the millions allocated by the government for this purpose. The land of the Lemkos stubbornly rejected its new masters and would not produce.

The colonists carried out a plundering operation. They sold the assets left by the Lemkos, the tools and equipment. When that was gone, they dismantled the buildings and sold or burned the lumber. They cut down the fruit trees, ruined the gardens, and so on. In the course of a single decade, they converted Lemkovyna into an African wasteland, where at least half of the homes and other buildings have disappeared from the face of the earth. There now are many villages with only a few houses still standing, and even those badly damaged.

Lemkovyna now is a sorry spectacle. It is now an empty land, depopulated, and covered with the cinders of burned out villages, where weeds flourish and

Nature has taken over what used to be a Lemko cemetery. Bartne, 1985.

feral cats breed. Arable fields are overgrown with trees, shrubs, and thistles. Roads are eroded, overgrown with brush, and totally useless. Anyone wanting to travel in Lemkovyna would have to cut his way with an axe, like in an African jungle, because truly the once lively Lemko villages have been transformed into jungles. In the past, the harmonious sound of Lemko singing and the music of Lemko fifes trilled through field and forest, but now there is no life there. Even the song of some poor little bird or the croaking of a frog is missing. Only the wind blows from time to time with a mournful wail, as if trying to express sorrow for what is no longer there. Even the sun no longer shines as brightly as it once did, and Lackowa, Magura, Kyczera, and other mountain tops are hidden in fog, as if trying to hide the crime committed against this land.

Government officials are now seriously concerned with the question of how to restore Lemkovyna economically. Various commissions and various specialists, such as agronomists, geologists, engineers, and scientists, have recently been going to the area to study and test the process of mountain farming. And they almost unanimously have come to the conclusion that Lemkovyna can be made productive only by Lemkos, who lived in harmony with this land for centuries, who know its requirements, and who have learned by prolonged practice how best to make use of it. The Polish Academy of Sciences has arrived at this conviction, as have the Committee on Water Management and the Committee on Developing Mountain Lands.

A conference of members of the Polish Academy of Sciences, attended by such specialists and scientists as Director Bodnar, Professor Krzysik, Dr. Kubica, Dr. Nowak, the engineer Dąbek, Dr. Szmagała, and others, unequivocally expressed the opinion that only Lemkos or some other mountain people would know how to manage such areas properly. In accordance with a plan developed there, they proposed a project to establish by 1960 at least four thousand farmsteads to go with the five hundred already in place, and to increase the number of such farmsteads every year. Interested officials have been inviting and urging Polish people through newspapers to take up farming in Lemko lands (specifically, the Bieszczady Mountains part), promising very good conditions and monetary aid. There has not been any eager response by volunteers. On the other hand, activities to allow Lemkos to return to their former homesteads are being paralyzed by chauvinistic Polish groups.

Posted in the executive committee chambers of the county councils in Rzeszów Province are announcements in the Polish language such as the following: "The Council needs men for work. The State Land Fund has eighteen thousand hectares of arable land for sale. The price is four thousand zlotys per hectare. The purchase can be made on a twenty-year payment plan, with only ten percent down. For those wanting to settle there, the state will grant credit of up to fifty thousand zlotys for building a house and other buildings. Land can also be bought in neighboring counties under similar conditions. The land is waiting for people. Act today! Act now!"

In contrast, however, in a speech to Lemkos on June 16, 1956, Minister [Witold] Jarosiński, speaking as representative of the Government and the Party, made the following statement:

Our Government and Party appeal to the Ukrainian (Lemko) people to not return to their former area, because in general living conditions there are not good. The fact of the matter is that on the basis of our laws, settlers in the east, as well as those in the recovered territories, have full rights of ownership in good farmsteads. It is the duty of local authorities to explain this matter thoroughly to interested persons. They should also be warned that local authorities can not and will not give any material assistance to those who risk returning to their former place. They should have the good sense to remain in their designated place.

At another point in that same speech, the same Minister had this to say:

No explanations can in the slightest degree justify the method and forms by which the resettlement was accomplished. In no way can the wrongs suffered by innocent people as a result of this action be justified. It has left profound sorrow among those resettled and a sense that unwarranted injustice has not yet ended to this very day. It has created conditions for the growth of nationalistic attitudes not just among those resettled but also among the Polish people surrounding them. An important failing of that time was a lack of concern for the resettlers. Individual elements of local authority in many cases did not react to the material needs of the resettlers and, what is even worse, tolerated and in some cases even practiced discrimination. The cultural and educational requirements of the Ukrainian people were ignored. Such a situation was not conducive to consolidating Polish and Ukrainian sensibilities in a spirit of international friendliness and goodwill. There were cases of Ukrainian people being assigned to unproductive farmsteads– in huts, and sheds, and stables, and their language, traditions, and culture being ridiculed. Ukrainian residents in cities were passed over in factory and community promotions, were discharged from work without reason, and were denied representation in local government.

Any comments on this speech by Minister Jarosiński would be superfluous.

19. Reflections

By evicting the Lemkos, the Polish government showed itself to be one of the worst persecutors of a people in the history of the world. These peaceful, submissive, hardworking, loyal, and congenial people were brutally treated and expelled from their own land, from their own homes, deprived of all their properties on which entire generations had labored, deprived even of the opportunity to pray in their native language, and dispersed throughout all of Poland's western lands, abandoned to the whims of fate. This terrible tragedy

Zabavskii family a year before being resettled deep into the eastern Ukrainian
Soviet Socialist Republic, to Nykolaiv district. (1) Maria Gluz, (2) Ioanna
Zabavska, (3) Lukach Zabavskii, (4) Bohdan Stanchak, (5) Antonina Zabavska,
(6) Milko Zabavskii, (7) Iosafat Stanchak, (8) Pavlo Zabavskii. Skwirtne, 1944.

is a crime that cries to Heaven for redress! This is how the Polish government repaid the Lemko people for sending thousands of their best sons to the front to fight for a free Poland, for the hundreds of Lemko soldiers who gave their lives in battle for the Polish nation!

And although now many Poles beat their breasts, admit their guilt in the crimes that have been committed against the Lemkos, and sympathize with the lot of these people, and even though they see the tremendous losses suffered by the Lemkos when the Polish regime evicted them from their beloved mountains, still they will not agree to letting the dispossessed return to their previous holdings. This is clear evidence of ill will, the reason used to justify the eviction of the Lemkos. Today, most painful of all is the fact that the Poles have eliminated the historical name Rus' for the Lemko people and are using the spurious title "Ukrainian," which the Lemkos fought against for decades when enemies tried to foist it on them.

The Poles should not forget Lenin's doctrine, which states that a people who oppress other peoples cannot endure, but must perish.

Wooden Lemko church in Przysłup near Gorlice, twenty years after the ethnic cleansing of 1945-1947. Przysłup, 1968.

PART II:
EARLY TIMES TO WWI

Local church brotherhood, Kalnica, 1935.

Prologue to Part II

Горы нашы, горы святы	Our mountains, holy mountains
Бескиды, Карпаты,	The Beskids and Carpathians,
Ту мешкали нашы предкы,	This is where our ancestors lived,
Білый Хорваты.	The White Croats.
Стада овец в лісах пасли	Herds of sheep grazed in the woods
И землю орали,	And the land was plowed,
Штобы больше земли мали,	So that they would have more land,
Лісы корчували.	The forest became smaller.
На Карпатах и Бескидах	In the Carpathians and Beskids
Русь ся формувала,	Rus' was formed,
По Європі в ріжных місцях	To various places in Europe
Ся розпространяла.	It spread.
Тож мы Лемкы автохтоны	Thus we Lemkos are autochthonous
Тут на власной земли,	Here in our own land,
А не якысь пройдысвіты,	And not some kind of nomads,
Ци приблуды вредны.	Or pernicious strays.
Нашы предкы праславяне	Our ancestors were proto-Slavs
В Карпатах мешкали,	Who lived in the Carpathians,
Як потреба заходила	And when the need arose
З врагом воювали.	They fought with the enemy.
Надармо пан Мацієвскі	It is useless that Mr. Maciejowski
В истории голосил,	Proclaimed in his history

Што Лемков на польску землю	That the Lemkos were invited
Круль Казимір спросил,	To Poland by King Casimir,
Што не было ани сліду	That there was no trace
О нас у Карпатах,	Of us in the Carpathians,
Аж прийшла на свою біду	Before we arrived, to our misfortune,
По Білых Хорватах.	After the White Croats.
Простый парох из Тылича	A simple priest from Tylicz
Вченому доказал,	He showed the scholar ,
Што он вченый без облича	That he, the priest, is educated
Дурным ся показал.	And only appeared to be unlearned.
Тяжко было ученому	It was difficult for that scholar
Свой блуд поправляти,	To fix his error,
Бо было му барз прикро	Because it was very unpleasant
Блудов ся встыдати.	For him to acknowledge his mistakes.
Ей панове историкы	Oh, gentlemen, historians
Пиште вшытко правду.	Write everything truthfully.
Як сте добры политыкы,	If you are good politicians
То не кричте гвалту	Do not create turmoil.
.	
Не фальшуйте истории	Do not falsify history
О то вас благаме	We ask that of you
И не робте комедии	And do not make a comedy
З фактов, котры знаме.	Out of facts that we know.
Мацієвскы у нас были	Maciejowski's type were around
Вчера и сут нынi,	Yesterday and are here now,
Историю, яку пишут,	The kind of history they write,
Най чытают свинi.	Let the pigs read it.
Мацієвскы, як писали,	When Maciejowski-types wrote,
Много фактов опущали.	They left out many facts.

Де не треба, додавали
И так правду закрывали.

Where they didn't need to, they
    added material
That is how they buried the truth.

Цілу нашу историю
Так поциганили,
Што барз вельку меж народом
Незгоду зродили.

Our whole history
They lied about,
So that they created
A lot of discord among people.

Они внесли в нас руину,
Народ поріжнили,
Відумали Украину,
Штобы Русь нищыли.

They brought ruination upon us
The people were forced out,
They invented Ukraine
To destroy Rus'.

Украину Берлин сплодил,
А відень уродил,
Польскы паны выховали,
Для германской хвалы.

Berlin sired Ukraine,
Vienna gave birth to her,
And Polish gentlemen raised her,
For German glory.

Украину Русскым дали,
Польских панов дябли взяли,
А хоц Гитлер уж не краче,
То Бонн за ньом горко плаче.

Ukraine was given to Russia,
The devil took the Polish gentlemen,
And though Hitler is no longer
    squawking
Bonn bitterly cries over her.

Маме своих историков
И ученых политиков:
Ключевского, Третякова.
О них ище буде мова.

We have our own historians
And educated politicians:
Kluchevskii, Tretiakov.
That will be discussed later.

Маме ищы Рыбакова.
Горьечку, Шахматова,
Соловия, Пришнякова,
Историков-то голова.

We have others: Rybakov,
Horechka, Shakhmatov,
Solovii, Prishniakov,
We have plenty of historians.

Маме ище много других,
Умных и ученых,

We also have many other
Smart and educated people,

Не треба нам вченых чужых,
Маме досвідченых.

We don't need educated strangers
We have our own experienced people.

Всі солідны политикы
Так нам повідают,
Як историкы робят крикы,
Рации не мают.

All honest politicians,
They tell us that
When historians make a lot of noise,
They have no rationale.

На Бескидах и Карпатах
Русь ся народила,
Пред Києвом, на Моравах
Водом ся крестила.

In the Beskids and the Carpathians
Rus' was born,
Even before Kyiv, in Moravia
Rus' was baptized with water.

Русску віру мы приняли
Из уст Методия.
Всім Славянам показали,
Де свята Мисия.

We received the Rus' faith
From Methodius's mouth.
His holy mission
Applied to all Slavs.

Зостали зме окрещены
Во престольном граді,
Через учнів Методия
В церкви Велеграді.

We were baptized
In the capital city
By the disciples of Methodius
In a Velehrad church.

До Києва свята віра
Прийшла з Подкарпатья.
Обі Руси полюбились,
Бо то родны братя.

The holy faith came to Kyiv
From Subcarpathian Rus'.
Both Rus's loved it
Because they were twins by birth.

Русскый Києвобрадовал
А народ наш заваровал
«Русьом» Подкарпатье,
Слово тото святе.

Kyivan Rus' gave us a gift
And safeguarded our people
The word Rus' is sacred
To Subcarpathian Rus'.

Од товды то Прикарпатье
З Києвом ся зляло,
Од той хвилі слово «Русин»
Для нас святым стало.

Since then Transcarpathia
Was merged with Kyiv,
From that time the word "Rusyn"
Became sacred to us.

Два тысячы літ минає
Од предков начала,
Богу нехай честь быває,
Святой Руси хвала.

Лемковино, люба Мати
Притуль мя до себе.
Ци єст лекше де спочати,
Як ту близко Тебе?

Two thousand years have passed
From our ancestors' beginning.
May God be praised
And Holy Rus' honored.

Lemkovyna, beloved mother
Hold me close to you.
Is there a better place to rest
Than being near to you?

(Из *Пісні о Лемковині*)   (From *A Song About Lemkovyna*)

Lemko Region delegation marching in annual parade, Sanok, 1938.

1. Tribal Origins and Ethnic Affiliation of the Lemkos

As a group, Lemkos belong to the great Slavic family. The Slavs appeared on the world scene long before the time of Christ. They are mentioned by Greek, Roman, and Syrian historians, such as Herodotus, Ptolemy, Pliny, Tacitus, Procopius of Caesarea, John of Ephesus, and others. From these sources we learn that even in those times the Slavs were already divided into two branches, Western and Eastern, and occupied areas around the rivers Dnieper, Dniester, Bug, Vistula, Oder, and Elbe. In time a third group of Slavs, the southern, came into being.

By the first century of our era, the Slavs were a powerful people. They began raiding neighboring peoples and then pushing out in various directions, primarily to the south. They migrated through the Moravian Gate and the Carpathian mountain passes into the regions of the present day Czechs, Moravians, and Slovaks. The fourth century assault by the Huns on the Roman Empire, which began its decline, opened the way for the Slavs farther south. In the fifth century, they intruded into the lands of the Polabians and Moravians, the Czech basin, and Pannonia. Some of them went as far as the Dalmatian coast, areas around the Danube River, and the Balkans.

The result of these migrations and political upheavals was a regrouping of all Slavdom. Three principal groups were formed, and these became the basis of further development. With some admixture of a foreign element, the southern group, which stemmed from the eastern group, created the Bulgarian nationality. And with admixtures of western elements it gave rise to the Serb, Croat, and Slovene subgroups.

The western group of Slavs developed into two groups– southwestern and northwestern. The southwestern group occupied the region south of the Sudeten and Carpathian mountains, along the Morava and Dina rivers. In the seventh century, Samo's kingdom arose in this region. In the ninth century it became the Moravian state, which grew into Greater Moravia, a state that developed a high level of culture and extended beyond the Carpathian

Mountains. The Moravian state fell before the advance of the Magyars, a no-madic people of Ugro-Finnish origin who had moved from the Ural portion of Bashkiria to the Black Sea steppes in the sixth century, and in the early tenth century barbarously occupied the lowlands of the Danube and Tisa riv-ers. Another group of southwestern Slavs settled in the valleys of the Elbe and Vltava rivers. The Czech state was formed in this region in the ninth century.

The northwestern group was composed of Polabian Slavs, who were di-vided into three smaller groups– Serbs [or Sorbs] (between the Saale and Silesia), Obodrites (between the Elbe and the Baltic Sea), and Veletians (be-tween the Oder and the Varnava).

The Slavs of the eastern group comprised ten different territorial tribes. Some of these were large individual tribes, while others were political alliances of small tribes. In the Bug River valley lived the Buzhany (Volhynians) and the Duliby, on the Pripet were the Derevliany, on the Bog and Dniester were the Ulichy and Tyvertsy, around Kyiv were the Poliany, on the Desna were the Siverzhany, in Polesie were the Dregovichy, on the Sozha the Radimichy, on the Oka the Viiatichy, on the Dvina, Dnieper, and Volga the Kryvichy, on Ilmen Lake the Novgorodtsy, on the Polota the Polochany, on the upper Dniester and the Vistula the White Croats. At the core of their political or-ganization was the concept of *Ruska zemliia* ("Rus' land"), with Kyiv as the initial city along with other cities such as Chernihiv and Pereyaslav. In the tenth century the Kyivan Rus' state was the largest and strongest political or-ganization in Eastern Europe.

This raises a question. Where should we look to find the forebears of our unfortunate Lemkovyna in this great sea of Slavic tribes and their groupings? With a paucity of sources on the history of Lemkovyna, we cannot draw con-clusions with hundred percent certainty. In view of the widespread movement of Slavic tribes, it can be deduced that the Lemko people were formed from a number of tribal groups.

As northern Slavs moved southward through the Carpathian passes, it is quite probable that some of the migrants stopped off in the mountains and began their organized life there. Some scholars and historians, such as Šafarik, Barsov, Wojciechowicz, and others, argue that the Slavic tribe of *Bilo-Hor-vaty* (White Croats), lived long ago on both sides of the Carpathian Moun-tains around the headwaters of the rivers Dniester, San, Biała, Vistula, and tributaries of the Tisa. The Kyivan Rus' chronicler Nestor also says the White Croats were a Slavic tribe.

In 981, the Kyivan prince Volodymyr the Great invaded Poland, took over the Cherven cities, *Chervona Rus'* (Red Rus'), and annexed them to Kyivan Rus'. The land of the White Croats lay open before him. In 993, he advanced against them and added the White Croats to his state, according to Nestor's Chronicle. On this basis some scholars claim that Lemkos are descended from the ancient Slavic tribe of White Croats, who at some time in the past inhabited the inaccessible region of present day Lemkovyna.

In time, some of those White Croats emigrated out of the Carpathians, crossed the Danube, and settled in present day Croatia, keeping the old name that they brought out of the mountains. Those that stayed in the mountains lost their tribal name through the influence of Rus' culture and adopted the name common to all the tribes that were part of Kyivan Rus'.

It has now been proven and verified by scholars that Lemkos inhabited the most inaccessible portion of the region that was known in the tenth century as White Croatia, and because they were secluded by the difficult terrain they retained their linguistic and cultural singularity. The forebears of today's Lemkos belonged to those Slavic tribes that, under the influence of the state organization prevailing in princely times, adopted and retained Rus' culture and the name Rus', Rusyn, Rusnak, which is what Lemkos call themselves today. It is affirmed that the Lemko forebears have been, throughout their history, a strong part of the great Rus' people [that is, the East Slavs], spiritually and ethnically. The descendants of those old Lemkos have retained such a strong life force that they have been able to assimilate a number of German, Wallachian, and Cossack colonists who found refuge in their mountains.

2. State Subordination of Lemkovyna

During the time of principalities, [some of] Lemkovyna belonged to Rusyn princes from 993 to 1340, when the Polish king Casimir the Great annexed it as the first of the Ruthenian lands that were incorporated into Poland. It stayed as part of Poland until 1772, that is, until the first partition of Poland. In 1772 it was taken over by the Austrian monarchy. After the First World War, it was divided into two parts. One part fell to the Republic of Poland, the other to Czechoslovakia. After the Second World War, the Lemkovyna within the borders of Poland ceased to exist. Its residents were transferred in part to the Soviet Union and in part to the "Recovered Territories" in the west of the new Peoples' Poland.

Noteworthy is the historical fact that after the First World War three Lemko republics arose in Lemkovyna. One of them began in [Florynka, in] Gorlice County. It was initiated by Dr. Iaroslav Kachmarchyk of Binczarowa. The second Lemko Republic was organized in Wisłok Dolny by the priest Panteleimon Shpilka, vicar of the local parish. The third arose in Prešov under the leadership of Dr. Antonii Beskyd, former delegate to the Hungarian Parliament. None of these republics lasted more than a few months. The organizers and council members were arrested, and the republics were quashed.

3. Introduction of Christianity Into the Lands of the Carpathian Region and Lemkovyna

According to studies by noted Russian historians and Slavophiles, such as Antonii Petrushevych,[1] Iuliian Pelesh,[2] and other scholars, the beginnings of Christianity in Lemkovyna are to be found in the missionary work of those Slavic Apostles, Sts. Cyril and Methodius, who were sent from Byzantium to Moravia in 864 to expound Christ's teachings there in the Slavonic tongue. Sts. Cyril and Methodius were brothers of Greek origin, born in Salonika (Thessaloniki). Cyril's baptismal name was Constantine. He took the name Cyril shortly before his death when he entered a monastery, where he died. Because of his extensive education he is often referred to as "the philosopher." Both brothers were well versed in the Slavonic languages from their youth.

Methodius was at one time an administrator of some Slavic region. As a man of great learning, Constantine was librarian at the patriarchal library, but a career as a librarian was not to his liking. He dreamed of a life of solitude. For a time he was a professor of philosophy. He then went, with his brother

---

1　Antonii Petrushevych, *Geschichte der Union* (History of the Union).
2　Afanasii M. Selishchev, *Staroslavianskiy iazyk* (The Old Slavonic language), pt. 1-2, Moscow, 1951-1952.

Sts. Cyril and Methodius.

Methodius, to live in the Slimpis-ki Monastery where he learned the Coptic and Old Hebrew scripts. Before going to Moravia, he had been sent on missionary trips to the Saracens in Asia Minor. Then he and Methodius went on a mission to the Khazars, where Constantine's great gifts made an especially great impression. In Kherson, on the way to the Khazars, he found a Gospel and a psalter written in a "rushky" script[3] and a man who knew that language. Through this man he learned to read both books. There he also learned the Samarian script and language. With his tremendous knowledge of various languages, Constantine devised an alphabet [Glagolitic] for the Slavic language and translated the gospel from the Greek into Slavic.

In 862, the Moravian Prince Rostislav wanted to paralyze the harmful activity of the German Latin clergy in Moravia and dispatched an emissary to Byzantium to obtain for the Moravians preachers who knew the Slavic language. The Greek Emperor Michael III, sensing some political value in this, sent missionaries to Moravia in 864. This group included both the brothers Constantine and Methodius, with a few other persons who knew the Slavic tongue.

In the early years of the saintly brothers' stay in Moravia they occupied themselves with training a cadre of literate people and in preparing more Slavic translations from the Greek. From the very beginning, use of the Slavic language in church writings was met with hostility by the Latin clergy of Moravia, who insisted on Latin in everything. The Latin clergy were no less hostile to the persons of Constantine and Methodius, because it saw in them dangerous opponents of German lordship over the Slavs. German bishops flooded Rome with false accusations, denunciations, and libels against Constantine and Methodius. They were slandered as using a barbaric language to spread unrest among the people.

---

3   [It is a very contentious question as to just what this script was.]

After three years of intense labor, Constantine and Methodius took a group of their students and left for Rome to give the Pope an account of their activity, to ask for ordination of the students with them, and to protest against the improper actions of the Latin clergy. Along the way they stopped for a while in Pannonia, where they arrived in 867. There they were welcomed very hospitably by Prince Kotsel, who gave them fifty students to teach from their Slavic books in preparation for becoming priests.

From there they traveled to Venice where they had a heated argument with the "tri-lingualists," those who insisted that writing was lawful only in Hebrew, Greek, and Latin [the three languages the sign Pilate had placed on the top of Christ's Cross.] This was a viewpoint that was broadcast throughout the West by the Latin clergy in their animosity toward the Slavic language. The "tri-lingualists" were discomfited by Constantine's conclusions which were based on Holy Scripture.

In the summer of 868, the Apostles arrived in Rome. Pope Adrian II received them warmly and ceremoniously. When their textbooks and sacramental books in the Slavic language were examined, the Pope confirmed the Slavic language as a liturgical one and blessed the sacramental books in the Church of the Most Holy Virgin. It was in this Church that Sts. Cyril and

Roadside monument commemorating 950th anniversary of Christianity in Rus'. Skwirtne, 2003.

Methodius chanted the first Divine Service in the Slavic language. The Pope ordained the accompanying students to the priesthood.

Constantine never returned from Rome. He became seriously ill and died there in 869. Before he died he entered a monastery and adopted the name of Cyril. It is by this name that he is known as the Apostle of the Slavs. Pope Adrian II appointed Methodius an Archbishop with extensive powers for spreading Christianity among the Slavs. He restored an old Roman metropolitanate and appointed Methodius its head. This metropolitanate encompassed Pannonia and Moravia. In addition he gave Methodius permission to conduct Divine Service in the Slavic language throughout his metropolitanate.

Methodius went back to Moravia. The enemies of the Slavic language now began persecuting him. Three German bishops, namely Adalvin, Hermarik, and Ano, brought charges against Methodius in court. When Methodius did not appear, they seized him and imprisoned him in a monastery at Freising [near Munich] in Bavaria. For about two months, Methodius suffered much there from those German bishops, who treated him brutally. He sent many messages to Rome in complaint, but the messages were intercepted by those bishops and destroyed. The Pope learned of the treatment of Methodius from Lazarev, one of his students. He sent Bishop Paul to Germany as his emissary to have Methodius released. He was freed in 873. The Pope suspended all three of those bishops who had treated him so unjustly. And soon after, all three of them died, suddenly and unexpectedly.

Despite the great harm the German clergy had done him, Methodius now carried on extensive apostolic work in his large metropolitanate. The fruits of his pastoral efforts could be seen on all sides. Genuinely Christian life flourished everywhere. Pagan customs declined, and the number of devout priests rose. Methodius's students went in all directions preaching the faith of Christ. Czechs, Poles, Croats, and our forefathers who lived on both sides of the Carpathian mountains listened to the lessons those students taught, and they heard them in their own tongue. Along with the religion of Christ, Slavonic script also spread widely.[4]

German bishops again brought complaints against Methodius, alleging that he was not a true believer and was spreading heresy. They were joined by Prince Sviatopolk with his own accusations. Pope John VIII summoned

---

4   [The Slavonic script which eventually was used in the church was not, however, Glagolitic, but an amalgam of Greek, Latin, and special letters, given the name of the "Cyrillic" alphabet after St. Cyril.]

Methodius to Rome. After examining the case, the Pope responded with praise for Methodius's zeal and orthodoxy, reinforced Old Slavonic as a liturgical language, and confirmed Methodius's authority in the metropolitanate of Moravia. He made a big mistake, however, when he appointed a German named Wiching as Bishop of Nitra. This man was one of the worst plotters and enemies of Methodius, one who belittled and falsified papal letters, and opposed Methodius everywhere. Wiching was not a bishop of Christ but a servant of the devil.

Toward the end of his working life, Methodius had many problems. He had to concern himself with training young priests and with translating the Holy Scripture and other theological books. His pupils came from the common people, so he had much to do to teach them the necessary knowledge and instill goodness in them. For twenty-five years he had carried the missionary's heavy cross, which had taken a toll on his physical vitality. He had passed his seventieth year, and his time was nearing the end. In the midst of his disciples, with the words "Father, I give my soul into Your hands" he gave up his saintly soul to Almighty God so that he could receive the wreath of heavenly glory for his lifetime of work for the glory of God. Methodius died on April 6, 885. His body is buried in the Cathedral of Belgrade. The Holy Church has added Cyril and Methodius to the array of saints and has awarded them the title of Apostles to the Slavs.

The enemies of the Slavic language got Pope Stephen V to prohibit use of the Slavic tongue in church services in Moravia.[5] Gorazd was named as successor to Methodius, but he was not elevated to the rank of bishop and was even arrested. In 970, Pope John XIII prohibited use of the Slavonic rite in the Prague Eparchy. In the Czech lands and in the land of the Vistulans, who were subject to the Czechs, the Slavonic rite held on until 1253 and, according to the historian Czermak[6], until the conquest of Little Poland by Bolesław Chrobry.

After the death of Methodius, all of his disciples, about two hundred of them, were driven out of Moravia. They scattered throughout other Slavic lands to continue the work of the saintly Apostles. Some went to the Croats, others to the Serbs and Bulgars, and everywhere they spread Slavic books and readings from Cyril and Methodius. They were especially successful among

---

5   Afanasii M. Selishchev, *Staroslavianskiy iazyk* (The Old Slavonic language), pt. 1-2, Moscow, 1951-1952.

6   Wiktor Czermak, *Illustrowane Dzieje Polski do X Wieku* (Illustrated history of Poland to the Tenth Century), Nakład Fr. Brod., Warsaw, 1935.

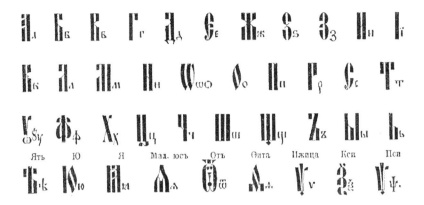

Old Church Slavonic alphabet.

the Croats. They introduced Slavonic (Glagolitic) even into the Latin Mass, and it has lasted to the present time in three eparchies of Croatia (Senj, Krk, and Sibenik.) The Slavonic script (as Cyrillic) expanded most rapidly in Bulgaria, and spread from there to Rus' in subsequent centuries.

St. Methodius's missionaries traversed our Carpathians several times in their apostolic work, reaching as far as Cracow and the Vistula area, and spreading Christ's gospel in the Slavonic rite. Our forefathers, the inhabitants of those mountains, received this gospel directly from those missionaries, the students of Sts. Cyril and Methodius, about a hundred years before the official Christianization of Rus' by St. Volodymyr the Great in Kyiv in 988.[7]

In 874, the Czech Prince Boryvoy and his wife Ludmila adopted Christianity in the Slavonic rite. They were baptized at the court of Sviatopolk, the king of Great Moravia.

In a biography of St. Methodius we read that in the Vistula region reigned a very strong prince who tyrannized Christians. Methodius advised him to adopt Christianity willingly; if not, he would be baptized forcibly in a foreign land. That is what happened. The prince of the Vistulans was forcibly baptized in Moravia in the Slavonic rite. The Moravian Prince Sviatoslav annexed the Vistulan state to his own in that same year.[8]

---

7   Pelesh, *ibid.*; Petrushevich, *ibid.*
8   T. Manteuffl (ed.), *Historia Polski* (History of Poland), Vol. 1, Part 1, Warsaw, 1958, p. 156.

In his treatise *Opis starożytnej Polski* (Description of Ancient Poland), Tomasz Święcicki, one of the most eminent historians of Poland, notes[9] that Poland received Christianity in the Slavonic language from the enlighteners of
the Slavs, Sts. Cyril and Methodius and their disciples, through Moravia near
the end of the ninth century.

*Unidentified Lemko ensemble (left) with women in folk costumes from Uście/
Hanczowa at the Royal Castle "Wawel" in Cracow, late 1930s.*

The prince of Mazovia, Miechyslav I (Mieszko), a pagan, adopted Christianity only after he married Doubravka, daughter of the Czech Prince Boleslav
I, in 965.[10] Doubravka enthusiastically supported Mieszko in total eradication of paganism and in construction of churches.[11] Doubravka died in 977,
and two years later Mieszko was married again, this time to Oda, daughter of Margrave Dietrich. Under the influence of his wife and father-in-law,
he began changing the language of divine service from Slavonic to Latin.[12]
He brought German Latinist clergy into his country. By 986, Mieszko I was
already warring against the Czech king Boleslav II, in alliance with Saxon

9   T. Święcicki, *Opis starożytnej Polski* (Description of Ancient Poland), Vol. 1, Warsaw, 1816, p. 9.
10 The historian Fruze states definitely that Mieszko adopted the Eastern/Greek rite of
    Christianity.
11 *Wielka Powszechna Encyklopedja* (The great universal encyclopedia), illustrated, Vol.
    47, p. 33. It is stated there that Christianity was adopted in 960.
12 *ibid.*,Vol. 47, p. 33; Vol. 9, p. 33.

troops. He then stationed Polish garrisons in the Cherven cities, which in 981 had belonged to the Kyivan state.

The first bishops in Cracow were of the Slavonic rite.[13] The first bishop of Cracow was named Prokhor and was of the Eastern rite. We have historical data that at one time there were churches and monasteries of the Slavonic rite in Cracow, that services were conducted in that rite, and that there still remain traces of the Byzantine style (for example, in Wawel Castle.)[14] Coins issued by Bolesław Chrobry carried impressions of church cupolas and inscriptions in Cyrillic.[15]

The scholar and historian, A. Shishko-Bohush, states that the church at Wawel was Slavonic and was built in the ninth century. One of the latest indications that the religious faith of Cracow in the early days of Christianity was of the Slavonic rite was found in excavations made this year in Wiślica near Cracow. This revealed the church of Sts. Cyril and Methodius, dating to the ninth century, that is, before the official Christening of Poland in 966 by Mieszko I. Only one church of the Greek rite survived in Cracow to our times, and after World War II it was immediately converted to a Latin church. In that church (St. Norbert's[16]), there was a beautiful and valuable iconostasis, painted by the renowned Polish artist Matejko. This iconostasis was recently removed by some invisible hand.[17]

In Moravia, as in Poland, the Slavonic rite did not survive pressure and opposition from the Latin rite that was spread by German and French missionaries, even though there were many defenders of the Slavonic rite among the Poles. In Lemkovyna, however, the Slavonic rite has survived to this very day, and this must be attributed to the fact that as far back as the tenth century our forefathers came under the influence of princely Rus', which then had a rich culture. Still, our Byzantine rite has always been salt in the eyes of

---

13   *Shematysm Apostolskoi Administratsii Lemkovshchiny* (Manual of the Apostolic Administration of Lemkovyna), p. xii.

14   *Nasza Kultura* (Our culture), No. 6, 1958, p. 16.

15   Chr. T. Fruze, *Historia kościoła polskiego* (History of the Polish Church).

16   [See http://pl.wikipedia.org/wiki/Cerkiew_św._Norberta_w_Krakowie .]

17   [At the end of the nineteenth century, a stone iconostasis designed by Thaddeus Stryjeński was erected in the church. The icons for the iconostasis were designed by Jan Matejko, but painted by his student Władysław Rossowski. In 1947 the communist authorities closed down the parish and the iconostasis was dismantled and transferred to the archives of the Museum of Jan Matejko. In 1998 the parish was legally granted ownership of the church building, which they took over at the end of 2001. After a contentious process, the original iconostasis was re-erected and dedicated in 2004 by the Greek Catholic metropolitan, Archbishop Ivan Martyniak.]

Unidentified Lemko folk ensemble in front of the Battle of Tannenberg/ Grunwald (1410) statue, destroyed by the Germans in 1940. Cracow, 1938. The statue was rebuilt after WW II. See http://pl.wikipedia.org/wiki/ Pomnik_Grunwaldzki_w_Krakowie

the Latin clergy, which has pressed our people *per fas et nefas* (through right and wrong) to convert to the Latin rite, despite precise decrees against this from the highest church authorities.

Christianity came to the regions of the Bug and Dnieper rivers not from Kyiv but from the Slavic Great Moravian state, which in its struggle for independence from Germans and Roman bishops had asked Byzantium for help. And from those regions Christianity spread to Kyiv, where Rus' was officially baptized in 988.

4. Administrative Subordination of the Church in Lemkovyna

Velehrad [now Stare Mesto] in Moravia was St. Methodius's capital city. Velehrad was where the missionaries who spread the faith of Christ in our mountains came from, and the first priests were appointed from Velehrad.

Therefore, it must be assumed that in respect to church administration, Lemkovyna at first belonged to Velehrad. When the first bishopric in Cracow was established, Lemkovyna came under the administrative authority of Cracow bishops of the Slavonic rite. This situation lasted until the establishment of a Slavonic Rite bishop in Przemyśl, which came about in the latter half of the eleventh century.

Because of a lack of sources, it is hard to determine the exact date of establishment of the Przemyśl bishopric. Though it is certain that Lemkovyna was assigned to it in the latter half of the eleventh century, it is not possible to fix the date of this action exactly. In 1492, the Sambor bishop was added to the Przemyśl eparchy (diocese). Since that time, every Przemyśl bishop has called himself the Bishop of Przemyśl and Sambor.

Although Lemkovyna belonged to the Przemyśl eparchy and shared its history for centuries, still it always held on to its own individuality and its detachment. The greatest difference between Lemkovyna and the Przemyśl bishopric developed at the time when it was a question of accepting the decision of the Brest Synod, that is, bringing the church Unia (Union) into the Przemyśl eparchy (1595). Mykhailo Kopystynskii, Bishop of Przemyśl and Sambor at the time (1591-1610) refused to join those prelates who accepted the Brest Unia. Another bishop, one who would agree to Unia, was appointed to his position.

For a hundred years, two bishops functioned in the Przemyśl Eparchy at the same time– one Orthodox, the other Uniate. An intense struggle went on between them. The Uniate bishops had allies among the Latin clergy and among government officials. In the course of this struggle, Lemkovyna lost its connection with the Przemyśl episcopate and became an individual unit under the jurisdiction of a vicar general, who performed the functions of a bishop for the region.

Sts. Peter & Paul's Greek Catholic Church, made Roman Catholic after 1947. A long struggle over ownership followed before its return to Greek Catholics in 1996. Krynica, 1945.

A new masonry Orthodox church was built in Krynica and was consecrated in 1996.

The last Orthodox bishop of Przemyśl and Sambor was Antoni Winnicki (1650-1679). In 1675, he transferred his residence to Sanok, and began calling himself Bishop of Przemyśl-Sambor-Sanok. This title for the Przemyśl bishops continued from then on. Antoni Winnicki's successor, Innocent Winnicki (1679-1700), accepted the Unia for the entire Przemyśl eparchy. After that, Lemkovyna remained part of the Przemyśl Greek Catholic Eparchy.

However, not all Lemkos were happy belonging to the Przemyśl Eparchy. They often had the dream and idea of having their own eparchy with the bishop's seat in Krynica, a very presentable locality. Monsignor Viktor Zhehestovskii, a brilliant and zealous priest, was named vicar at Krynica in 1848. He started out to make this idea a reality. To this end, in 1865 he built a beautiful brick church in Krynica, under the patronage of the Apostles, Sts. Peter and Paul. This church was intended to be a cathedral in the future. Beside the church he erected a single story building as the residence for a bishop. At the Krynica health resort he built two large villas, the income from which was to go toward the subsistence of a bishop. He also tried to get the support of the Pope of Rome. He never achieved success. In 1945, the Polish government converted the vicar's residence into a so-called machinery center. Inside the church the iconostasis was torn down, other Byzantine icons were painted

Consecration of an Orthodox church, Piorunka, 1936.

over, and the church became a [Latin Rite] Catholic temple.[18] All Lemko churches have become victims in the same manner.

Fr. Viktor Zhehestovskii's plans had been realized after the First World War. Because a third of the Lemkos converted to Orthodoxy, because of incessant fighting between Orthodox and Uniate Lemkos, and because of the danger that all of Lemkovyna would convert to Orthodoxy, the Holy See, acting in agreement with the Polish government, established, through a decree of the Congregation of the Eastern Church *"Quo aptius consularet,"* a separate eparchy for the Lemkos entitled the Apostolic Administration for Lemkovyna *ad nutum S. Sedis* (directly dependent on the Holy See.) The first Apostolic Administrator was a Lemko, Fr. Dr. Bazyli Mastsiukh. This Administration lasted only until 1945, at which time the authorities of People's Poland eliminated it, and resettled [the remnants of] the Lemkos in the western lands.

---

18   [The Greek Catholic church under the patronage of Sts. Peter and Paul in Krynica became very important to the local community after its return to Greek Catholic control on December 20, 1996. This church became very important to the local Lemko community, emboldening the community and stimulating further activities. In 1997 a new iconostasis was erected. Between 2000 and 2003 the building underwent thorough repairs. In recent years, the parish also recovered other possessions that belonged to it before the Second World War. A new masonry Orthodox church was built in Krynica from 1983-1996.]

5. Linguistic and Archaeological Research on the First Inhabitants of the Carpathian Mountains

In the very earliest of times, the Carpathian regions were settled by various foreign tribes, such as the Germanic, Celtic, Pannonian, Illyrian, and Vlach [today called Romanian]. During the time of tribal migration [*Volkswanderung*], these people moved around and yielded to the Slavs, who began steadily moving into these areas in the fifth through seventh centuries. Historical sources for those times are very meager. However, some information can be gleaned from the place names that were set by those other tribes and that the Slavs encountered here. These names pertain primarily to mountains, streams, and occupations.

Scholars derive the name "Carpathian" (*Karpathes óros*) from the Albanian [or Thracian] word *karpe*, which means mountain. Albanian was one of the Illyrian dialects. The name "Carpathian" appeared as far back as the second century A.D. The name "Beskid" comes from the old German word *beschet*, or *besheid*, which means the top of the lowest mountain, or a pass. The name "Tatra" (*Turtur, Tisrtra, Tatry*) is from an Illyrian [or Thracian] word *Triti*, which means rocky mountains. The name *Dunai* (Danube), and its diminutive Dunayets, is of Celtic origin; it was adopted by the Germans and then by the Slavs. "Orava" is of German origin from words meaning "river" or "brook." On the other hand, the names *Mahura (Magura), Kychera (Kyczera), Sihly (Sigly), Gruny* are of Romanian (Vlach) origin. Also Romanian in origin and still in use in the Carpathians are such words as *bacha, bryndza, bundz, kliah, helstka, gruli,* and many other words like that. This is evidence that the Romanian (Vlach) tribes who lived in the Carpathian region were pastoral. The words *chuha, gazda, yuhas* are Hungarian in origin.

Archeological research on the residents of the Carpathians in prehistoric times has begun only recently. Roman coins have been found in Sanok and Grybów counties, attesting to the fact that people lived there in the Roman era and had contact with the Roman empire.

6. Settlement and Colonization

Slavs came to the Carpathian Mountains in about the fifth or sixth century, settling in the river valleys. During the period of population movement, they pushed southward through the mountains and reached as far as the Adriatic Sea, forming a large mass there. Invasions by the Avars, and later the Magyars[19], divided them into southern and northern groups. It was then that our forefathers settled in the Carpathians and in Transcarpathia. At the dawn of history the western part of Carpathia belonged to White Croatia, which in the ninth century became part of the Great Moravian Empire until Volodymyr the Great annexed it to Kyivan Rus'. The White Croats are the forefathers of the Lemkos of today. Casimir the Great took over [the eastern part of] Lemkovyna for Poland in 1340. Lemkos are the indigenous peoples in their land.

At first, the Lemkos lived a free pastoral life in their Carpathians. The forests and meadows were not registered to anybody but belonged by natural right to the residents of the area.

This state of affairs still held true under the early Polish and Hungarian kings. Change began when those states turned to feudalism. Then those Hungarian and Polish kings declared themselves owners of all the land that had not yet been claimed by any other sovereign.

Since these wilderness lands did not yield them any gain, the kings began bringing in settlers who would be exempt from taxes and other duties for a specified period of time, usually twenty years, so that they could get well established. These would be given rights according to Polish, Magdeburg, or Wallachian (Vlach) models of law. However, this kind of settlement did not go well for the kings, so they began giving grants to their nobles. When someone distinguished himself in war or did some service for the king, he would be granted large tracts of forest land for his own, on condition that he establish settlements there. By virtue of such grants, the king's domain was reduced so that in the course of three hundred years kings lost almost all of their estates, while the grantee lords became powerful magnates. Beginning in the twelfth century, knights and nobles acquired large estates, brought in colonists, and established villages and towns. The period of most intensive colonization lasted from the thirteenth to the sixteenth centuries. It was during this period that the settlements in the Carpathians today, that is, the towns and villages with present-day names, came into being.

---

19   [It may have been the reverse, Magyars first and then the Avars.]

7. The Rise of Large Estates

In 1359, Casimir the Great, in the presence of his royal council, granted Jan Gładysz a large tract of forest on the Ropa River. Already existing on this tract re the villages of Łosie, Regietów, and Smerekowiec. Jan Gładysz and his descendants chartered all the villages now in existence in this district: Wysowa, Blechnarka, Żdynia, Konieczna, Ług, Ropki, Hańczowa, Kwiatoń, Gładyszów, Uście Ruskie, Klimkówka, Nowica, Bielanka, Ropa, Ropica, Szymbark, and the no longer existing Gryfów and Unewiczy. This was called the "Szymbark Estate," because the Gładyszes resided in Szymbark. It was also known as the "Gładysz Estate" or *Dominium Ropae* (Domain on the Ropa River). Still extant in Szymbark today, although badly damaged, is a castle built by the Gładyszes; judging from its style of construction, it must be from the original settlement. Szymbark was burned down by Rákóczi's army. The Gładyszes went off to their Sandomierz and Lublin properties, and smaller estates grew up on the ruins they left.

Along the Wisłok River and its tributaries was the great estate of the Stadnicki family. Nineteen Lemko villages belonged to them— Desznica, Długie, Grab, Jaworze, Wola Cieklińska, Krempna, Myscowa, Nieznajowa, Ożenna, Olchowiec, Polany, Ciechania, Huta Polańska, Chyrowa, Rozstajne, Ropianka, Skalnik, Świątkowa Mała, Żydowskie. This was called the "Żmigród Estate," because the Stadnickis lived in Żmigród. Between the sixteenth and eighteenth centuries, the Stadnickis acquired another parcel of land in Lemkovyna, known as the "Nawojowa Estate."

Petro Bogori, governor of Cracow, defeated Prince Daniel of Galicia at Koprowince. As a result, the prince ceded to him a large estate, and his descendants attained great wealth. They owned Lubna, Dukla, Chyrowa, Zagórzany, Mszana, Tylawa, Zyndranowa, Trzciana, Stróże, and many Polish villages.

Zyndram of Maszkowice, a knight at the battle of Grunwald, acquired from the king the large "Jaśliska Estate" and the title *haeres de Jasiel* (lord of Jasło). He founded Królik Wołoski, Królik Polski, Jasionka, and Lubatowa. The Jaśliska Estate later became the property of the Latin bishops of Przemyśl, and was known as "The Bishops' Second Estate."

The reign of Casimir the Great was a period of rapid colonization in all of the Carpathian region. Many cities and villages were set up on the model of German [Magdeburg] Law. The estates of magnates became rich.

In Eastern Lemkovyna, the Sanok area was a "golden apple" for the Polish nobility. Colonization pushed deep into the valley of the San River. It gave the aristocratic families an opportunity to play a more than minor role in the area. This colonization also extended far into the Carpathian wilderness. Colonization on the German Law model was supplemented by colonization on the Wallachian Law model, which was adapted to the needs of Vlach pastoral life. From the fourteenth to the sixteenth centuries Wallachian sheep herders spread all through the Carpathian Mountains from east to west.

An outstanding role in the colonization of the San, Hoczewka, and Solinka river valleys was played by the Baly family, which had its origins in [Sáros County in] Hungary. They founded many villages in those valleys, such as Baligród, Hoczew, Nowotaniec, Średnia Wieś, and Żubracze. For faithful service, Casimir the Great granted them Boiska, Radoszyce and Wisłok.

In addition to the Balys, there were many other Hungarian families who began some settlements, as for example, the Uherce, who left the name of a village as evidence. Also of Hungarian extraction were the Humnicki (Humecki) and Dydinski families, both of whom had property in the Sanok region. The towns of Humniska and Dydiowa were begun by them.

Considerable credit for the region's colonization is due the Kmit family, especially Piotr Kmit who founded the villages of Dwernik, Dołżyca, Tarnawa, Skorodne, Rosochate, Lutowiska, Tworylne, Krywka, Hulskie, Zatwarnica,

Lemko church, abandoned in 1945 by forcefully deported villagers of Królik Wołoski, as it appeared in 2002. Unlike most Lemko churches, this one was not made of wood and it therefore survived.

Jaworzec, Smerek, Wetlina, Berehy Górne, Chmiel, Procisne, Stuposiany, Radoszyce, Ustrzyki Górne, Łupków, Mików, Wola Michowa, Maniów, Szczerbanówka, Solinka, Turzańsk, Komańcza, Smolnik, and others. Most of these villages no longer exist. They have fallen victim to raids by all kinds of bandits. Their people have scattered all over the world.

8. The Episcopal Estate

A great estate, known as the *Klucz Muszyński* or Muszyna Estate, was established in the fourteenth century. It encompassed all the settlements on the Poprad, Kamienica, and Biała rivers, from Piwniczna to Czertyżne. At first it belonged to the king, but in 1391 King Władysław Jagiełło granted it to the bishops of Cracow under the title of *Państwo Biskupie* (Episcopal Estate). Other villages besides Muszyna had been established in that region even before 1391. These included Andrzejówka, Brunary, Kunczowa (now Kąclowa, a Polish town), Porui (no longer in existence), Szczawnik, Łomnica, Florinkowa (now Florynka), Jaszkowa, and Milik. Maciejowa, owned by the Tyniec Convent, was founded even earlier, before 1229.

Among the oldest of the king's villages are Łosie, Binczarowa, Tylicz, and Ropica Ruska [now (2011) Ropica Górna].

By the end of the sixteenth century, the Episcopal Estate incorporated twenty-three Rus' villages, with localization (foundational) charters issued in the years indicated: Czyrna (1574), Czarna (1575), Banica (1574), Berest (sixteenth century), Biliczna (1595), Czertyżne (1589), Florynka (1574, chartered a second time), Izby (1547), Jastrzębik (1577), Kamianna (1577), Krynica (1547), Powroźnik (1565), Sołotwiny (1595), Śnietnica (1596), Stawisza (1574), Szczawnik (1578, chartered a second time), Wawrzka (1574), Wierchomla Wielka (1595), Złockie (1580), Zubrzyk (1545), Żegiestów (1575).

Most of these villages were chartered by the Cracow bishops Franciszek Krasiński, Piotr Myszkowski, and Jerzy Radziwiłł in the period 1570-1595. Written in bloody letters in the history of Lemkovyna are the names of later Cracow bishops, such as Jakub Zadzik, Marcin Szyszkowski, Jan Małachowski, and others, who tried everything possible to Latinize and Polonize the Rus' Lemkos. They confiscated Rus' church properties and turned them over to Polish priests. They forced Lemkos to attend Latin church services, restricted the rights of Rus' priests, forbade expansion of Greek Catholic parishes, and wiped out the "disunited" (Orthodox) population. There will be more on this at other points in this exposition.

The center of this Episcopal Estate was Muszyna, where every one of the heads of the estate lived. Known as the "Muszyna Governor," he had great power and many privileges. He was not only the administrator but also chief justice and commander of the armed forces. The villages located within the area of this estate had to carry out special obligations as well as performing the duties associated with their situation. Among other things, they were responsible for maintenance of manorial buildings, inns, and breweries; for repair of bridges, ditches, roads, and cemeteries; for providing police service; for hauling wine from Hungary and salt from Stara Solia for the manor houses. There were four categories of special obligations, benefiting the bailiff, the bishop, the Latin clergy, and the manor.

In addition there were other levies, such as labor, cloth, eggs, cheese, and kitchen labor. A tithe called *desiatyna* (a tenth) had to be paid for the Latin clergy. There was also a military obligation. Every draftee had to provide a uniform and weapon at his own expense and

Typical roadside religious statue that has survived to this day. Bartne, 2004.

be ready for military service. The most important service was that with the "Bishop's Dragoons." This was a kind of militia that did not take part in war. It was composed mainly of bailiffs. Another unit of a military character was the *harniki*, called in documents *pedites Ruthenici* (Ruthenian infantry). Of interest to us is the fact that the Lemko *hunka*, which was worn until very recently in Nowy Sącz County, is a copy of the Bishop's Dragoons' uniform.

At the beginning of the seventeenth century, some new villages were chartered: Dubne (1603), Mochnaczka Niżna (1648), and Wierchomla Mała (1603). The Polish-Hungarian border went through frequent changes. It was finally set in 1772, after the first partition of Poland. Even before 1770, 16 towns and 273 villages had been taken from Poland and allotted to Hungary, including Nowy Sącz, Stary Sącz, Nowy Targ, Krościenko, Muszyna, and Tylicz. This region was ruled by Hungary until 1772, when the Austro-Hungarian border was redrawn. This boundary divided Lemkovyna into northern and southern sections. The northern part went to Galicia and the southern to Hungary.

The Muszyna assets remained unchanged until 1782, when Austria took over and granted them to Count Skrzyżyński. This status lasted until 1802.

Lemkos, nineteenth century lithograph by C. Hofmann.

In 1809, they were purchased by the firm of Arnstein, Eskeles, Heimiller, and Stainer for ten thousand florins. They eventually came into the hands of the [Government] *Religionsfonds* (Foundation for the Support of Religion). From various sources and notes we learn that our forefathers did not lead very happy lives under the rule of the Cracow bishops. They were severely oppressed both materially and morally. They had to work hard physically, and the fruits of their manual labor went into the hands of their oppressors, who tried to wrest from them their most valuable possessions– their faith and their nationality.

9. The Jaśliska Estate

Different in character was another section of land owned by the Przemyśl bishops that was known as the *Klucz Jaśliski* or Jaśliska Estate. This other episcopal estate spread from the San to the Wisłok rivers. Its center was the little town of Jaśliska. In 1366, Casimir the Great established a town called Wysokie Miasto (Hohenstadt) and gave one Ioan Hansel, a Hungarian, charter privileges under Magdeburg Law. The name of the town was soon changed to Jaśliska.

In 1434, King Władysław Jagiełło granted Jaśliska and the villages of Królik, Daliowa, and Jasionka to Janusz, the Latin bishop of Przemyśl. Soon other villages were established, such as Wola Jasielska, Trzciana, and Zawadka. As the number of villages grew, they were classified as *potoky* (hollows).[20] There were five such hollows: (1) Wola Niżna and Rudawka, (2) Lipowiec and Czeremcha, (3) Daliowa and Szklary, (4) Królik Wołoski and Królik Polski, (5) Zawadka and Abramów. Kamionka and Posada constituted half a hollow.

The obligations here were those of serfdom. In addition, each hollow was obligated to haul to Czeremcha a every year sixty-four barrels of salt from Stara Solia and an equal number of barrels of wine from Hungary. Also, fifty-seven wagons were to be provided to Jaśliska for various purposes each year,

---

20   [The word *potoky* means literally "streams" but here it has the meaning "hollows" as in the Appalachian mountain "hollows" of the USA, i.e., a deeply indented, depressed basin with a stream running through it.]

Former residents of Zawadka Rymanowska, now residents of Poltava district in eastern Ukraine. 1964.

and all the roads in the area had to be kept in repair.

The village of Deszno was chartered in 1389, and by 1885 it belonged to the Rymanów Estate of the Potocki counts.

Among the older villages in the Jaśliska Estate was Jasionka, chartered in 1386. Along with Posada Jaśliska it was not included in any hollow. Szklary was chartered in 1527 by Bishop Andrzej Krzycki, and Kamionka in 1541 by Bishop Tarło. In the domain of the Przemyśl bishops there was no form of militia comparable to the Bishop's Dragoons of the Muszyna estate.

10. The Nawojowa Estate

The *Klucz Nawojowski* or Nawojowa Estate arose from the ruins of the great Episcopal or Muszyna Estate when that estate became the property of the Stadnicki counts in 1828 and the Stadnickis moved into the region of Nowy Sącz and Muszyna. From Elena Apolonia Massalski, who had acquired Muszyna assets through the Austrian Senate, Count Franciszek Stadnicki purchased the following villages: Czaczów, Łabowiec, Uhryń Wyżny and Uhryń Niżny, Roztoka Mała and Roztoka Wielka, Łosie, Składziste, Maciejowa, Nowa Wieś, Jaworki, Szlachtowa, Biała Woda, Czarna Woda, and Łabowa as a town. The farthest west of these are Szlachtowa, Jaworki, Biała Woda, and Czarna Woda. The residents of these four villages differ from other Lemkos in both dialect and apparel; their culture is closer to that of the Slovaks. In 1794, Prince Paweł Sanguszko, a previous owner of Szczawnica, endowed the Greek Catholic parish of Szczawnica with some revenues.

According to the Russian historian Fr. Iuliian Nikorovych, all the villages listed above were founded during the era of princes of Rus'. As such, they came under the dominion of Poland, along with other princely assets, in 1340 by way of the Polish King Casimir the Great. Tradition and fact tell us that since then the little stream flowing through Szlachtowa has been known as *Ruski Potok*. This prudent route was used at one time by the Phoenicians, Romans, and later by the warriors of Kyivan Rus'.

Not far from Szlachtowa are two Polish towns: Szczawnica and Krościenko. The residents of these towns had been Rusyns, and they had their Rusyn

Lemko residents of Jaworki in their Sunday best. From left: Seman "Galaidiv", Sylwester "Sandriv", Ivan Surmiak, Ivan Breida, Tymko Ikoniak, Ivan "Sych" Krupiak, Ivan Shest. Jaworki, 1933.

churches and Rusyn parishes. Evidence of this is the fact that a hayfield belonging to the parish in Szczawnica is still called *łuka Popova*,[21] and in Krościenko
they still point out a place where a Rusyn church stood centuries ago.

In the church in Szlachtowa there was until recently a Bible that had been
given to that church as a gift in 1542 by the then owner Andrzej Jordan of
Zakliczyn. A dedication is inscribed on the last page. Similarly, mementoes
like that have recently been found in other churches of the old Episcopal Estate. For example, in the church at Milik there was a bell from 1484 with an
odd apparatus for ringing the bell with a hammer; the church at Mochnaczka
had a bell dated 1626; the Powroźnik church had a picture of the Last Judgment from 1627 and another of the Suffering Mother from 1644; in Piorunka
there was a Liturgicon from the era of principalities. After the Second World
War some invisible hand made all of these relics disappear.

Some time ago, large Greek Catholic parishes were established in this region. Parish warrants and other documents, such as village charters, are evidence that Andrzejówka, Bogusza, Żubryk, Muszynka, and Piorunka were
independent parishes. However, the guardian hand of the Cracow bishops
deprived them of this privilege, and they became something like daughter
parishes of neighboring villages.

On the Polish-Czech border, near Wojkowa, is the "spring of three kings," Kela-
likut. According to tradition, three kings are supposed to have met here. Scholars consider this to have been the event mentioned in the Volhynian-Galician
Chronicle as having occurred in the year 6776 from the creation of the world. In
that we read: "Herewith was a council of the Rusyn princes with the Polish prince
Bolesław and held in Tarnów. Prince Danylo with both his sons Lev and Shvarny
and Prince Vasylko with his son Volodymyr, and they agreed among them on
a line between Rusyn land and Polish land, swearing to this by the Holy Cross."

11. Defensive Castles

To defend boundaries and protect roads, building of castles began as far back
as the twelfth century. In addition, for defense against enemy raids there were

21   [In Polish, *pop* is a reference to an Eastern/Byzantine Rite Catholic or Orthodox priest.]

ramparts, forts, ditches, and forest roads obstructed with logs, stumps and brush. There were also *kotchy zamky* (from Hungarian *kotse*, wagon, and the Slavic *zamky*, castles), lines of dozens of wagons arranged side by side for defense against an enemy.

Castles were built in towns through which the principal roadways ran. The oldest towns in Lemkovyna are Biecz, Jasło, Krosno, Sanok, Żmigród, Brzozów, Zagórz, Dukla, and Muszyna. There were several roadways through the Carpathians. These were trade routes for moving goods from Poland to Hungary and from Hungary to Poland. The most important product for Poland was wine, which was brought in large quantities from Tokai. Our lords in their great mansions liked this wine very much. This wine was still young, for the Hungarian vintners were not in a position to provide enough aged wine for our nobles. The barrels and casks were all inscribed in Latin: "Wine made in Hungary and aged in Poland."

The main Poland-to-Hungary route led from Tarnów through Pilzno and Jasło to Żmigród, and from there through the Polany Pass to Zborov, Bardejov, Košice, and finally Tokai. To the east a road led through the Dukla Pass, Svidnik and Ungvar [Uzhhorod] to Munkacs [Mukachevo]. A third route connected Poland with Hungary through Sanok and the Osława valley. The valleys of the Vistula and the San gave access to Subcarpathia from the north and east. Roads intersected with each other, and traffic never stopped. From Poland salt was transported to Hungary. On the roads, highwaymen often raided the wagons. And marauders often attacked the mansions of the gentry. Some defense against all this was necessary. From this need rose castles, called *hrody*; the places where castles were built were termed *hrodowy mista* (castle towns). From this we have the Rusyn word for city– *horod*.

One of the oldest castles was the one in Muszyna on the Poprad River. It was built in the twelfth century, originally out of wood. Casimir the Great enlarged it and encompassed it with a stone wall, which can still be seen today. Many castles were erected in the Carpathian foothills, especially in Nowy Sącz, Rytro, Szymbark, Biecz, Dukla, Jaśliska, Sanok, Odrzykoń, and Lesko. Traces of these castles can still be found in some of these towns, and some have been restored.

Right at the border, not far from Tylicz, is an old *okop* or earthwork abutted by a dense forest on one side and a rocky cliff on the other. This is where men from Muszyna and Tylicz fought against the Hungarians.

12. The History of Lemko Towns

Muszyna

Muszyna is one of the oldest settlements in Lemkovyna. It was established in 1209. It was just a village at first, and was originally called Plokhe, which testifies to the Rusyn nature of its inhabitants. It was chartered by Casimir the Great in 1356, and by 1364 had grown considerably and was called Nowe Misto (in Latin, *Nova Civitas* or New Town). In time it came to be called Muszyna. Above the Poprad River is a castle that guards the Poprad valley and the highway to Bardejov. In 1391, Muszyna became the center, or capital, of the growing Episcopal Estate. The highest court, which sentenced highwaymen to torture or death, was located there. In 1656 it acquired the privilege of regulating trade and the right to distill alcohol. In 1647 it had gained the right to hold four *iarmarky* (market-fairs) each year.

Muszyna was a Rusyn settlement from the very beginning. It was Polonized and Latinized during the period when the Cracow bishops reigned there. This is shown by the Rusyn surnames of Polonized residents. The first Latin church in Muszyna was built in 1686 with construction materials gotten by Poles through demolition of an Eastern Rite church in Tylicz.

Tylicz

Tylicz is one of the oldest settlements in Lemkovyna. It is mentioned in the Galician-Volhynian Chronicle. During the reign of the Rus' princes, Tylicz was called Ornawa, or Orawa. This is a German name, and thus it can be assumed that the first residents of Tylicz were Germans. During the period of Tatar invasions, Tylicz declined both materially and in numbers. It didn't recover until about 1363. In time it obtained some privileges, including the right to trade, from the Polish kings, and became a town with its name changing to Miastko. Its residents by then were Rusyns, who built a church around 1400 on the site where the church now stands.

In 1391, Miastko, along with the entire Muszyna estate, came under the control of the Cracow bishops. In 1612, Bishop Piotr Lubicz Tylicki enclosed the settlement with a wall, restored its municipal rights, and changed its name to Tylicz, after his own surname. He gave the local Rus' church two *łany*[22] of land, on condition that the people help build a Latin church in the event one became necessary. However, no such church was built for a long time because there was nobody to use it. There was not a single Latin worshipper in Tylicz at that time. A Latin church was built in Tylicz about a hundred years later, with the help of the Rusyn residents of the town. After a while, a Latin priest arrived in Tylicz. When he saw that the church was empty during services, he tried to force the Rusyn residents to go to his church instead of their own. The Rusyns refused, however, and so in 1636 the Cracow Bishop Jakub Zadzik locked the Rus' church and transformed it into a chapel where a Rus' priest could hold service only once a year. The Rus' priest at that time was Fr. Ioann Fedorovych.

The people of Tylicz didn't want to desert their faith and nationality, so they went to church in Muszyna all year round. It was not until after Bishop Andrzej Trzebicki died that the Cracow administrator, Bishop Zebrzydowski, permitted the church to be opened at the request of the people of Tylicz in 1680. The joy of the Tyliczans did not last long, however, because their church was again closed, two years later, in 1682, on the order of Jan Małachowski, the next bishop of Cracow. At that time, the Latin priest was Fr. Martin Timkowski, and the Rus' vicar of Tylicz was Fr. Tymofei Krynytskii.

That event is described in stirring words by Fr. Petro Kaminskii, chief deputy at that time for the Przemyśl Uniate bishop, in his report on the barbaric demolition of the Tylicz church:

It is impossible to describe what a lamentation there was among the Rusyn people when they saw their church being removed, what a wailing and weeping. Women and children at home and in the streets threw themselves on the ground and raised their voices even unto High Heaven. Not a single soul present that was not awash with tears. At the time there also were some Hungarians in Tylicz, trading at the distillery.... and they too wept to see such devout people in such agony. And everyone was amazed that the Uniates were being deprived of their church.

Not only did the weeping and the bitter pain of the victimized Uniates at this separation do no good, neither did the attempts of the Uniate bishop to restore the church nor the intervention of the king himself lead to any success.

22 [A *łan* is an ancient and indeterminate Polish measure of land. A medium-size farm measures roughly one *łan*.]

On the contrary, despite the entreaties and legal actions of the Tylicz people, their church was demolished in 1686, and the materials taken to Muszyna and used there to erect the first Latin church in that area.

Because of this, the people of Tylicz were without an Eastern Rite church for a long time– from 1686 to 1743. After much strain and trouble, Fr. Stefan Mokhnatskii finally managed to get a new church built in Tylicz in 1763 and the Greek Catholic parish revived. He also tried to get some of the property in Tylicz returned to the parish, but without success. His son Ioann Mokhnatskii did eventually accomplish that. At that time, Tylicz had 784 Greek Catholics and 130 Roman Catholics.

A Polish historian described that event as follows:

The Bishop [of Cracow], Piotr Tylicki, permitted construction of a church for the Uniate [Greek Catholic] parish, but he stipulated that the people live in obedience to the Catholic Church. Moreover, additional settlement there for people of the Eastern Rite was prohibited, on pain of loss of property. This gave rise to controversy. A commission appointed by Bishop Jakub Zadzik found that the blame was on the Rus' side, expelled the Rusyns from the town, did away with their church and converted it to [Roman] Catholic. Transfer of the Orthodox/Eastern Rite priest's land to ownership by the Catholic priest remained in force.

Members of the church choir and of the Kachkovskii Society. Andrzejówka, 1937.

Bishop Jakub Zadzik issued the following administrative order, presented here verbatim:

So that everyone [meaning the Uniates] would go to church, and those who do not be punished by monetary fine, or who miss the blessing several times, and because there is no one to carry the banner around the church when the procession starts...

Our place was settled by authority of the Roman Catholic Church and serves Catholics, not the Rus', and these people stay away from the Holy Church and eat meat on Saturday, which is forbidden by the Church.

These then are to be punished by a fine of twenty [unit unspecified], and if one of them should be troublesome and is notified three times of failure to pay, he is to be deprived of all his property and goods, which shall be turned over half to the parish priest and half to the Tylicz Church...

Since funds are for the benefit of [Roman] Catholics, and even more Rusyns have been arriving, and when Catholics wish to purchase real estate, they are confronted with unfair pricing, so edicts of the Bishops have been issued, to force Rusyns to sell all their properties... we empower the local governor and the priest to chase out of town those individuals who demand payment in three equal payments, so that the buyer is to make one payment every year. With the priest's permission, the fourth payment shall be considered to be tax; otherwise Rusyns will continue with their intolerable contention, thus oppressing Catholics.

"Here rests a victim of Talerhof, 1914-1917," Archpriest Emilyian Ioanasevych Venhrynovych. Tylicz, 2007.

This edict sheds some light on the attitude of the Poles toward Rusyns, particularly the attitude of the Cracow bishops.

On the basis of reliable historical documents, Fr. Mykhailo Krynytskii, parish priest at Tylicz (1843-1863), proved to the Polish historian Wacław Aleksander Maciejowski, a professor at Warsaw University, that the Rusyn Lemkos are not colonists or late-arriving settlers but are the autochthons of their own land. He published his conclusions in a book entitled *Istoricheskoe sostoianie namistnichestwa Mushinskogo* (The Historical status of the Muszynka Vice-regency), published in Vienna in 1853.

The last Rus' parish priest in Tylicz was Fr. Volodymyr Mokhnatskii. He was born in Łabowa and had been dean at Muszyna and Councilor to the Apostolic Administration of Lemkovyna. He performed some great services for the people of Tylicz. He built a beautiful parish house, completely rebuilt the local church, and elevated the moral and religious level of the parishioners. During the First World War, he was arrested by Austrian police, and together with Fr. Petro Sandovych was tried in a military court, found guilty of treason to the Austrian state, and sent to Talerhof, where he stayed to the end of the war. During the Second World War, he was again arrested, this time in 1941 by Hitler's Gestapo, imprisoned in Nowy Sącz, and then transferred to Kielce for confinement. After this war he was driven out of Tylicz to the west and never saw his beloved Lemkovyna again. He died in Cracow, at the home of his son Dr. Rodion, a professor at the university.

Krynica

Krynica is an old Rusyn settlement. We have no historical information on the first few centuries of its existence. Fr. Nikolai Nikorovych speaks of semi-barbarian tribes attacking Krynica and savagely destroying the settlement, and of an epidemic of disease that wiped out the population to such an extent that the region was devoid of human beings for a long time.

The earliest historical information we have for Krynica comes from the sixteenth century. Samuel Maciejowski, Bishop of Cracow, through a deed dated January 8, 1547, granted one Danko of Miastko (Tylicz) two *łany* of land for a village office, a mill, and an inn, to accommodate craftsmen and seven prosperous farmers. This same document also exempted the village chief from payment of two hundred sheep. From this it would seem that an extensive pastoral economy was flourishing in the area even then.

It can be assumed that a Greek Catholic parish was established that same year (1547), because in 1581 the Governor of Muszyna permitted the priest, Fr. Mykhailo, to buy a plot of land from Tymko Luchkovych that was to remain the property of the Krynica parish forever.

In a document dated May 10, 1664, the Bishop of Cracow, Andrzej Trzebicki, permitted Fr. Stefan Krynytskii to build a mill with two wheels, one of which was designed for milling grain, the other for fulling (cleansing and thickening) cloth. The leaseholders in 1664 were Iuri Tsikhanskii and Hryhory Krynytskii. In 1780, the parish holdings were increased by large tracts of field and forest in the direction of Tylicz and Mochnaczka. Those fields are now occupied by the Krynica resort.

The church and parish house were burned down in the mid-seventeenth century, with all their records. A new church, rather small, was built in 1651. The present church and one-story house were erected in 1865 through the efforts of Fr. Viktor Zhehestovskii, the pastor at that time, who dreamed of detaching Lemkovyna from the Przemyśl Eparchy and establishing a separate eparchy with the bishop's residence to be in Krynica. The church built by Fr. Zhehestovskii was blessed in 1861 by the Przemyśl Bishop Iosyf Sembratovych, a native of Krynica and later Metropolitan of Galicia. Sembratovych was appointed Metropolitan of Galicia on May 18, 1870. In 1882, after the trial of Ivan Naumovych, he was forced, by order of Emperor Franz Joseph, to resign from the metropolitan throne, in favor of his nephew Sylvester Sembratovych, an alumnus of Rome and later Cardinal. Iosyf Sembratovych was compelled to retire to Rome, where he died in sorrow for his native land in 1896, a victim of the Vatican-Vienna policy of that time.

Fr. Havryil Hnatyshak, born in Wierchomla Wielka, was pastor in Krynica for a long time. He performed great services for Krynica and for Lemkovyna. In his time he was a serious candidate for the Vienna parliament. During the First World War he was arrested by Austrian police and sent to the concentration camp at Talerhof, from which he never returned to his native land. There his bones were laid "under the pines," together with his sons Teodor and Iosyf.

The last Greek Catholic priest in Krynica was Fr. Evhen Khyliak. He beautifully renovated the parish house and church, brought order to the parish and raised its morale, but in his late years he had to leave it. During the German occupation, he was arrested by the Gestapo, sent to prison in Nowy Sącz, and then transferred to Kielce for internment. He was imprisoned there until the end of the war, after which he was driven out of Krynica with his entire family and all his parishioners.

Eugeniusz Dziadosz standing by the Talerhof Memorial in the village. Pielgrzymka, 2001.

His Greek Catholic parish was taken over by the Roman Catholic priest Duchiewicz, who transformed the *tserkva* [Eastern Rite church] into a Roman Catholic church. He had the beautiful icons and a Byzantine style painting of Sts. Volodymyr and Olga at the entrance plastered over with whitewash, and he threw out the stylish iconostasis. The parish house renovated by Fr. Khyliak became the property of a "Machinery Center."

One of the greatest Lemko patriots was the Krynica resident Nikolai Hromosiak, who became a victim of Austro-Ukrainian hatred. Along with many other Lemkos, he was incarcerated at a military prison in Vienna, where he, along with others, was sentenced to death.

From the very beginning of its existence, Krynica has been a strictly Rusyn settlement. Foreigners first began coming there when mineral springs were discovered and baths were established. As time went on, the resort was taken over completely by Poles, but the village of Krynica stayed entirely Rusyn until recently.

Krynica has always been the center of western Lemkovyna from the viewpoint of religion, as well as culture and politics. People from all over would gather there for Krynica festivals, of which the most ceremonious was Sts. Peter & Paul Day. It was here that the political and cultural organization, *Lemko Soyuz* (Lemko Association), was developed. It was here that the newspaper *Lemko* was published. It was here that school textbooks in the Lemko language were produced. It was here that the educated life of western Lemkovyna was concentrated.

Today there still are a few score Lemko families living in Krynica. However, these are not the former full-of-life Lemkos, but rather walking corpses—fearful, disheartened, and hopeless.

Church choir with Fr. Evhen Khyliak. Krynica, early 1940s.

Łabowa

Łabowa is an old Rus' settlement. In a document from 1585, Jan Branicki, owner of Zabelecz and Łabowa, sold to Doroshov, a man of Rusyn nationality, for eighty florins, a large tract of land along with the Uhryń brook for the purpose of establishing a village. In this document, Branicki stipulated that the settlers would have to pay a tax and would be subject to Rus' law [*ruske pravo*]. Six years later, in a document dated 1591, Lord Branicki assigned four tracts of farmland to the brothers Nazar and Petro of Uhryń to establish a village in Łabowa, stipulating that the rules for pastorage and farming] be based on the Rus' system of law. In all likelihood, the first document pertains to Uhryń, the second to Łabowa.

According to a document dated October 8, 1627, Stanisław, count of Lubomir, sold to the Łabowa presbyter Fr. Vasyl Vyslotskii for one hundred zlotys a tract of land called Demisiszakowska for the establishment of a parish house in Łabowa. From another document we learn that a church was already in existence in Łabowa in 1581. In a document dated May 29, 1695, Stanisław's son Aleksander Michał, count of Wiśnicz, along with Jaroslaw Lubomirski confirmed the previous grant, and later, in a document dated March 26, 1697, added to it another field known as Drahomanowka.

The abovementioned first church was erected in 1581 and was given the name of Protection [*Pokrov*] of the Virgin Mary. It was located on a site between Łabowa and Maciejowa and served both localities.

In a warrant dated November 18, 1810, Łabowa was declared a major town (Latin *oppidum*) for an entirely Rusyn population.

Łabowa was transversed by the main highway from Nowy Sącz to Tylicz and Bardejov. Merchants traveled through it carrying goods from Poland to Hungary and from Hungary to Poland. They would stop in Łabowa for rest and refreshment. There arose a need for large inns and taverns. Such shelters for merchants and travelers were soon erected, and they brought great profits to their owners, who were Jews. Well known to Lemkos until recently was the Frayir family, who operated a tavern and inn in Łabowa for a long time.

The last two parish priests in Łabowa, each serving their people well for many years, were Fr. Iosyf Mokhnatskii and Fr. Ioann Khryzostom Durkot. The latter died in Talerhof. Born in Łabowa was Dymytrii Vyslotskii, well known to Lemkos by the pseudonym Vanio Hunianka, a talented Lemko writer, poet, journalist, and social activist both in the old country and abroad.

Ensemble "Lemkovyna" from Lviv at the Lemko "Vatra". Andryi Baisa, Atanas Petronchak, unknown and Lev Reha. Zdynia, Poland, 2002.

During the German occupation, many Łabowians fell victim to the Hitlerite and Ukrainian terror. On the basis of accusations by the Ukrainian lackey of the Gestapo Pidsadniuk, many Łabowians were arrested and then executed. Pidsadniuk became so conscience-stricken for all his innocent victims that to obtain God's absolution for his great sins he got himself ordained as a priest and served in the Czyrna parish, from which he went to Russia [Soviet Ukraine].

In 1947, all [remaining] Łabowians were exiled to Poland's western lands, and Łabowa became a Polish town with a Latin parish. Those who tried to return to their ancestral lands fell to armed Polish chauvinist paramilitary units.

Nowy Sącz

In a lovely valley in the Carpathian foothills, on the rivers Dunajec and Kamienica, with large castles built for the defense of the town and its surroundings, lies the town of Nowy Sącz. In ancient documents, it has been called "Cymer" (also Zandecz, Nova civitas, Sandecz), which would indicate that its first inhabitants were Rusyns.

Nowy Sącz was established by a grant from Vaclav, King of the Czechs as well as Prince of Cracow and Sandomierz, on November 8, 1292. There had been a village called Kamienica on the site where the town was located. Vaclav

*Stefan Shkimba (1) at the Rusyn Boarding School/Ruska Bursa in Gorlice, Poland,
May 10, 1938. Sitting next to him is Iaroslav Siokalo (2), a cultural and political
activist among Lemkos before 1939, and (5) Fr. Soboloveskii from Uście Gorlickie.
Among other identified persons there are students Stefan Zabawskii (3) from Skwirtne,
Lubomyr Bubniak (4) from Wapienne, and (6) Petro Fetsitsa. Gorlice, 1938.*

granted seventy-two plots of land to two brothers, Bertold and Arnold.

The history of Nowy Sącz would require a special treatise, but we shall restrict ourselves here to the facts that interest us.

We will present here the history of the Ruska Bursa [Rus' boarding house/
hostel for students], which illustrates best the attitude of the Polish authorities of that time toward the Lemko people.

In 1898, an association named "The Ruska Bursa in Nowy Sącz" was legally established in that town. The founders were Fr. Teofil Kachmarchyk,
rector in Binczarowa; Fr. Havryil Hnatyshak, rector in Krynica; Fr. Iosyf
Mokhnatskii, rector in Łabowa; Fr. Ioann Durkot, rector in Szlachtowa; Fr.
Miron Cherlunchakevych, rector in Banica; Fr. Emilyian Venhrynovych, rector in Maciejowa; Vasyl Iavorskii, owner of oil wells and delegate to the Vienna parliament; Petro Lipinskii, chief judge in Nowy Sącz; Ioann Cherkavskii,
gymnazium professor in Nowy Sącz; Ioann Ivanishov, government official;
and Vasyli Tvardievych, government official in Nowy Sącz.

In the first year of its existence, that is, the school year of 1898-1899, the
Bursa could accommodate twenty pupils in its one-story four-room boarding house. Its first pupils were Ioann Bohuskii from Wierchomla, Viktor Khoroshchak from Bohusha, Aleksander Chychylo from Mochnaczka

"Lemko" weekly, the first Lemko weekly written in the language of the Lemkos. Lviv-Nowy Sącz - Gorlice, 1911-1914.

Wyżna, Ioann Russyniak from Maciejowa, Vasyli Dziuba from Wierchomla, Dymytrii Kobanyi from Bogusza, Symeon Khoma from Stawisza, Iulian Tyminskii from Grybów, Tyt Bohachyk from Bartne, Vasyli Mylianych from Szczawnik, Volodymir Hreniak from Brunary, Ihnaty Polianskii from Łabowa, Stefan Tyminskii from Grybów, Ioann Polianskii from Banica, Iulian Ostrovskii from Żegiestów, Pymen Kostelnyk from Binczarowa, Sofron Lukachyn from Smerekowiec, Hryhory Piroh from Hańczowa, Iaroslav Perfetskii from Jaroslaw, and Stefan Lavronskii from Przemyśl. Except for the author of this history, none of them are alive today.

The Bursa grew rapidly. The number of pupils increased every year. As early as 1898, a Greek Catholic gymnazium-level cathechistic program was established in Nowy Sącz. The first cathechist was Fr. Iuri Hensiorskii, who was also director of the Bursa. By virtue of many contributions from both the old country and America, and especially through a princely donation of six thousand Austrian florins by Benedykt Miiskii, a senior engineer with the Lviv Vice-regency who was born in Wierchomla, a large lot with two buildings on Jagiellonian St. was purchased in 1900, and Bursa attendees were housed there. By that time the number of pupils had risen to sixty. In that same year, the name of the association was changed to "The Benedykt Miiskii Ruska Bursa in Nowy Sącz." Three years later, another plot of land was purchased and a brick building was erected there for the use of the Bursa.

A division arose among the founding members of the association at their

general meeting in July of 1901. This led to the formation of another school in
Nowy Sącz called "The Ukrainian Bursa." At the suggestion of Fr. Kachmarchyk, who had a personal quarrel with Petro Lipinskii, the members present
at this meeting expelled founding member Lipinskii from the association. In
protest against this expulsion, Vasyl Iavorskii announced that he was resign-
ing from this association. At the start of the following school year, these men
established a Ukrainian Bursa that provided lodging for students and was
maintained entirely by funds donated by Iavorskii.

This thoughtless move by Fr. Kachmarchyk and the members present at the
meeting led to deplorable consequences. The Bursa suffered a great loss in the
departure of two important members, especially that of Vasyl Iavorskii, a powerful financier and a man of good will who gave the Bursa large sums out of his
own pocket and who as a member of parliament was highly respected by the
local school authorities. A much worse result, not only for the Bursa but for
all of Lemkovyna, was the fact that this Ukrainian Bursa nurtured renegades
and confidants for the Austrian government. It became a nest of Ukrainianization and aggravation for Lemkos. The fruits of this Ukrainianization came

*Paying homage to those who perished by the Talerhof Memorial at the Lychakiv
Cemetery. Members of the Kusyk and Wenhrynovych families from Krynica. Lviv, 1937.*

to light at the start of the First World War.

While our two bursas in Nowy Sącz were accommodating 110 students, the Polish Bursa had only thirty. And so there began harassment of our students, especially those staying at the Miiskii Bursa. The principal role in this harassment was played by the gymnazium director Stanisław Rzepiński and a professor named Błażej Gawor-Sławomirski. The name of the latter is written in black letters on the soul of every Nowy Sącz Bursa student of that time. Fleeing from harassment by these pedagogues, students either dropped out of school, transferred to gymnazium-level schools in other places (mostly in Sanok and Jasło), or went out of the country (to America or Russia). That is why the number of Rusyn students at the Nowy Sącz gymnazium declined each year.

Fr. Iuri Hensiorskii was dismissed from the faculty at Nowy Sącz, on the charge of Russophilism. He was replaced by Fr. Zachary Lekhitskii, who was a Ukrainian but nevertheless a tactful clergyman. In addition to teaching, he took over management of the Ukrainian Bursa. The directors of the Ruska Bursa were, in sequence, Mykhailo Sekunda, Dr. Ioann Cherlunchakevych, Teofil Kostetskii, and Ioann Hassai.

The Ruska Bursa in Nowy Sącz lasted until August of 1914. With the outbreak of the world war, Austrian authorities showered harsh acts of repression on the entire Lemko populace, and especially on the Lemko intelligentsia and nationally conscious villagers, accusing them of sympathy toward Russia. In line with this, the Lviv Vice-regency [the Galician government] of that time issued an order dated August 4, 1914, dissolving the Benedict Miiskii Ruska Bursa Association and arresting its members, who were sent to Talerhof and Vienna.

After the war, in Decision No. T. I, 1148, dated April 26, 1919, the county court of Nowy Sącz, Section I, affirmed the local government's appointment of the attorney Dr. Mawrik Kerbela as administrator of the Association's property. This man inflated and inflated his authority to the point where he petitioned the court for permission to sell all the real property of that Association, without consulting any of the Association members still alive. He received this permission in court order No. 1138/19, dated September 14, 1921.

Ownership of all the Bursa property, including buildings, was transferred to the town government of Nowy Sącz through a sales contract dated September 30, 1921 and confirmed by the court on October 10, 1921. The selling price was 935,634 Polish marks. At that time, [because of hyperinflation] this sum was worth about one box of matches.

The Association brought suit to revoke this contract, but the case has still not been resolved and probably never will be. The suit was filed in the name of the Association by the chairman, Fr. Roman Pryslopskii, parish priest in Żegiestów. The case was lost at the first hearing, won at the second, and undecided at the third. And that is how the fine Lemko property in Nowy Sącz was lost to the insatiable members of the City Council.

The Rusyn residents of Nowy Sącz obtained permission to use a side altar in a Latin church, where services were held every day. After some time, they felt a need for their own church. Construction of a new church was begun in 1902 on the above-mentioned plot of land on Jagiellonian St. The foundation was completed and walls two meters high were constructed. Further work was delayed by various impediments set up by administrative authorities. Finally, construction was stopped entirely on the pretext that the foundation was not sound. With funds donated by Vasyl Iavorskii, a chapel was built on Kunegunda St. to serve the religious needs of the Nowy Sącz Greek Catholics. In 1924, Iavorskii received the Papal award "Pro Ecclesia et Pontifice"(For Church and Pontiff) for his service to the church.

Biecz

The little town of Biecz, at one time the foremost Lemko town after Cracow, got its name from German colonists and in German was called Beutsch or Beitsch. Some Polish historians, trying to give the town a Polish character from the beginning, claim that Biecz was founded by some Hungarian marauder named Bech and the town was named after him. Other historians think that notion is improbable. A document from 1446 attributes the founding of this town to a fellow called Karwacjan. This document was issued by one Jan, *didych* (lord) of Gorlice, through his brother and sons, and confirms the right of this settlement to become a town.

Biecz was chartered by Casimir the Great on February 23, 1363. As a self-governing town, it had jurisdiction over 243 villages, only twenty-one of which actually belonged to the Biecz governor, while the rest were leased. Biecz was a center of trade, especially in wine and salt. Weaving developed there on a large scale in the sixteenth century, and Biecz competed with Bardejov in the production of cloth. There was a court and a school for executioners in Biecz. In 1614, 120 criminals were sentenced there to torture and death.

Queen Jadwiga constructed a castle in Biecz and funded a hospital for poor people. In 1710, Wilhelm Siemieński was the ruler of Biecz and all the villages belonging to it. Biecz was the best defended of all the towns in the Carpathian region, but it was almost completely destroyed during the Swedish wars. Very few of its many historical monuments have been preserved to this day. During the period 1386-1389, its rulers were Germans and Rusyns, but not a single one of them was Polish, which attests to the Rusyn character of the town during this period of history.

Jaśliska

Jaśliska originated in the time of Casimir the Great. By a decree dated January 28, 1366, Casimir gave what is now Jaśliska as a gift to Zyndram of Maszkowice, a hero of the battle of Grunwald. In a document dated October 4, 1389, Zyndram then gave one Ioan Hansel (Latin *Ion de Hanselino*) a forest between Jaśliska and Deszno to establish a settlement. This town was established on the basis of Magdeburg Law and was named in German as *Hochstadt*, High City.

In a decree dated May 8, 1434, King Władysław Jagiełło gave Jaśliska and the villages of Daliowa, Królik, and Jasionka as a gift in perpetuity to the bishop of Przemyśl Januszow and his successors. It was then that the name of the town was changed to Jaśliska.

The oldest historical sources indicate that Jaśliska was already in existence in the time of the princes of Kyivan Rus'.[23] Of particular interest is a royal act of May 8, 1434. The following is its text:

In the year of 1434, the generous king Władysław Jagiełło granted to the Rusyn people the property of the town of Jaśliska and the villages of Królik, Biskupice, Daliowa, and Nowa Jasienka in Rus' land *(terra Russiae)* in the district of Sanok which belongs to Janusz, Latin Rite Bishop of Przemyśl.[24]

From the words "Rusyn people... the property... in Rus' land" *(ruskie narodowe dobra ... in terra Russiae)* it follows that Jaśliska was a purely Rusyn settlement. According to one Russian historian[25], a Greek Catholic parish was established in Jaśliska and a church was built, for which two lots of meadow

---

23   Dr. Mykhailo Ladyzhinskii, *Sanok i ioho okrestnosti* (Sanok and its environs).

24   Denis Zubritskii, *Granice miedzy polskim i ruskim narodem w Galicji* (The boundary between the Polish and Rus' people in Galicia.)

25   Dr. Izidor Sharanievich, *Rzut oka na benficje kosciola ruskiego za czasów Rzeczypospolitej polskiej* (A glance at the benefices of the Rus' Church in the time of the Polish Republic).

and pasture were allocated from the property of the bishop as an endowment for the Rus' priest. It is not known how long this parish lasted. There is not a single trace of it left today. The Poles managed to Polonize the settlement quickly and to erase all traces of its Rus' origin. Antonii Ossendowskii[26] makes the following comment: "In the year 1611, the Jaśliska Council hurriedly enacted into law that Rusyns, a people of the Greek faith, were not permitted to settle in this place."

Like Biecz, Jaśliska was a center of wine trade. The Hungarian merchant Iuri Ozheshko stored stocks of wine there and constructed stone cellars, which are still in existence today. Jaśliska also had defensive walls, which withstood a siege by Rákóczi in 1657.

Jaśliska was a woeful nest of criminal behavior that Polish aristocrats, not excepting women, indulged in. The town archives are full of offenses committed by Polish nobles, not only against our people but also among themselves, predominantly involving eroticism. Here are a few examples: Lady Beata Zawisza Solikowski attacked her husband Yakov Solikowski with an ax, and then smothered him to death with a pillow. Her Highness Sofia of the Podolia Herbuts choked her husband Kasper Herbut to death with the help of her mother-in-law Lady Ewa Wielżyńska. Two minor nobles named Czernecki and Polanski murdered Aleksander Klofas, another petty noble, at the instigation of his wife "the beautiful Lady Helen" and his mother Lady Regina Brzesdyński.

Bukowsko

Southwest of Sanok, in the valley of the Sanoczek River, lies the little town of Bukowsko, once a purely Rusyn settlement that had its own Rusyn parish and Rusyn church. In the middle of the seventeenth century, the residents of this locality were colonized and Latinized by the Polish clergy and the Polish nobility because they would not accept the Union of Brest but instead held on to Orthodoxy. To this day, the older residents of Bukowsko can point out where the Rusyn church had stood. The registers of this ancient Rusyn parish are still held by the Latin Rite rector of Bukowsko.

Years ago, there was located here the private residence of some Polish bishop who claimed to be a great scholar and supposedly took part in learned symposiums in Cracow. Later it turned out that he was neither learned nor even ordained but just an ordinary scoundrel and impostor. This man did our

---

26   Antonii Ossendowskii, *Karpaty i Podkarpacie* (The Carpathians and Subcarpathia).

people a lot of harm. He destroyed our church and built a Latin one which, however, soon burned down. Another Latin church was erected and this also was soon burned, together with all of Bukowsko. The present church is the third in that series.

This brief observation on Bukowsko is characteristic of the Latinization and Polonization of the Rusyn people in Lemkovyna. For a better appreciation of this process let us take a look at a few other nearby Rusyn villages that were transformed into Polish ones in a relatively short time. The village of Dołhe, near Zarszyn, was an ancient Rusyn settlement with a large Rusyn church, but all traces of its Rusyn past are gone now except for a field still known as *pole cerkiewne* ([Eastern Rite] church meadow). The villages of Dudyńce, Pobiedno, Markowce, Pisarowce, and Jędruszkowce were strictly Rusyn settlements, each with its own church, and a few even with their own rectorates. In a relatively short time they were all completely Latinized and Polonized. The church in Pobiedno was burned down in 1830, and the people were compelled to convert to the Latin rite. Pisarowce soon followed Pobiedno. In Jędruszkowce in 1921, the owners of plots of land needed for a churchyard would agree to sell only on condition that the parish change from Byzantine to Latin rite; it did. Various impediments were set up to prevent the building of new churches. For example, when the building of a masonry church was begun in Nowosielce, the governor himself, Kazimierz Badeni, a fanatic Rusyn-hater, came to the village to stop work on the church. But the staunch will of the Nowosielce residents was stronger. A beautiful Church of the Protection *(Pokrov)* of the Virgin Mary was completed in 1895.

Sanok

Oldest of all the towns on the northern side of the Carpathians is Sanok. It has been in existence for more than a thousand years. It was mentioned as far back as the second century A. D. by the Greek scholar Ptolemy in his geographical treatise on the various tribes inhabiting the areas of the Baltic Sea, the Vistula River, Germany, the Tatra Mountains, the Black Sea, and the Don River. He called this region "European Sarmatia" and its inhabitants Sarmatians. Among these Sarmatian tribes he mentions the Saboki (*Sabokoi* in Greek). In the opinion of the Czech scholar Pavel Šafarik, these Sabokis were the progenitors of the people living in the Sanok region, and he includes them among the Slavs. The word "Sabokoi" is made up of two parts. The first part is "Sa" (a shortened "San"). The second, "bokoi," indicates a river bank. So "Sabokoi" means simply those living on the banks of the San River. To Ptolemy this was a purely geographical term, but it also pertains to the actual situation. In East Slavic philology, the name "Sanok" is composed of two parts -- the word "San" and the suffix "ok". Sanok's very name is indicative of its ancient Rusyn origin.

We know from a number of sources that from 568 to 797 the San River region formed part of the Avar state, while from 830 to 905 it was incorporated in the Great Moravian Empire. Under Sviatopolk, Moravian power extended even to the Transcarpathian White Croats. These White Croats were an East Slavic people occupying the San and Dniester river regions. In 907, a corps of them formed part of the army of Prince Oleh and took part in his assault on Tsarhorod [Tsar City, Constantinople]. In the middle of the tenth century the White Croats were added to the Czech state and remained part of it until 981 when Volodymyr the Great conquered the White Croat and Buzhan cities and incorporated them into the Kyivan state. By 993 all the Eastern Slavic tribes were united and the borders of the Kyivan state were secured.

After the tragic death of Sviatopolk in 972, the rulers of the Kyivan state became acutely aware of the catastrophic danger presented by the Pechenegs to their main trade route, the Dnieper River. The Dnieper was used to import salt from the Black Sea area. So they turned their attention to the Carpathian salt mines such as Tyrawa Solna near Sanok, Dobromil, Drohobych, and Kalush. They also learned of peaceful trade routes going through the White Croat and Buzhan lands, routes that gave them secure access to the Danube River, to the Black Sea, and even to Constantinople. These reasons were why Volodymir the Great began his invasion of those lands as soon as he gained the throne.

It was then that Sanok appeared on the historical scene, as an important town and also as a strongpoint on an important trade route. The massive stone foundations of the original fortress can still be seen underground of the present-day castle, now a museum. It is notable that the exceptional breadth of the old foundation walls is not matched at all by that of the castle walls, even though the latter are up to two meters thick. So that old fort must have been a massive structure. The first floor of the castle was built in the time of Casimir the Great, while the next story was erected in the sixteenth century. The original fortress disappeared some time during the Kyivan era.

The original Sanok was not located in the same place it is today but rather where Dubrówka now stands. It was situated in fields now adjoining the villages of Stróże Wielkie , Stróże Małe , Płowce, and the no longer in existence Sanocka Posada. The castle, however, was located where it is now. The area from Polish Dąbrówka, formerly known as German Dubrowka, right up to where the hospital now stands used to be swampland, spotted with ponds. On the other side of this were the two villages of Stróże Wielkie and Stróże Małe (The Greater and Lesser Watch-Bastions). Beyond that, nearly a score of kilometers to the southwest lay a belt of primeval, impassable forest on both banks of the Wisłok River. The only passage through this was by way of man made *presiky* (cuts), from which came the name of Prusiek ("Prosek" in ancient documents), a village southwest of Sanok. Wooden barricades served as defensive positions, which were guarded by the local populace. Hence the names of the villages Stróże Wielkie and Stróże Małe.

As far back as the time of the White Croats, the entire valley of the San River, from its very source all the way to Przemyśl, was dotted with strongpoints that guarded and controlled the trade route from Pannonia and Hungary through Sanok to Przemyśl. That period marked the disappearance of the White Croats, who were probably assimilated into the various Tyvertsy tribes that had been forced out of the area between the Bug and Dniester Rivers and migrated to the Carpathian region, becoming the forebears of the present-day Lemkos. Associated with this movement is the very old village of Ulucz on the San River, not far from Sanok.

During the second half of the eleventh century, exiled princes promoted a new concept of inheritance. They based it on the proposition that a father's estate is exclusively the property of his children. In the end, this led not just to the political independence of a given estate, but to the breakup of the Rus' state then in existence. The first exiles who managed to acquire territory by this means were the Rostislavovyches. When the first Rostislav died he left three sons: Rurik, Volodar, and Vasylko. These three compelled Grand Prince Vsevolod to set up a new province for them in 1087. This comprised the areas of the Wisłok and San Rivers and the Dniester and Prut Rivers, as well as lands around Zvenyhorodka and Terebovla. Rurik was the first of the brothers to make a claim when he settled in Przemyśl about 1078. This was the beginning of a new province named Galicia, which eventually crystallized into a western Rus' nation.

Sanok and the area around it became part of this new province. From the administrative viewpoint it was under Przemyśl and thus subject to the Prince of Przemyśl. After that its fate was uninterruptedly linked with the fate of this new province, even though the latter underwent profound reorganization. This was accomplished by Prince Volodymyrko of Zvenyhorodka (died 1152), the son of the Przemyśl Prince Volodar (d. 1125). He united the provinces of Przemyśl, Zvenyhorodka, and Terebovla into a single governmental entity that stretched southeastward as far as the Danube River, with its capital at Halych. And it is precisely for this period that we have the oldest written report on the town of Sanok, in the Galician-Volhynian Chronicle for 1150. In a struggle for Kyiv between Iziaslav II, the Prince of Vladimir (d. 1154), and Iuri of Suzdal (d. 1157), the Galician Prince Volodymyrko sided with Iuri.[27] Opposing him was the Hungarian King Geza II (1141-1161), brother-in-law of Iziaslav.

While Volodymyrko held his army at the city of Belz, King Geza marched his Hungarian army through the Carpathian Mountains at Uzhok. He then took the towns of Myczkowce, Hoczew, Wola Postołowa, Lukawica, and Zagórz, and approached Sanok. He conquered that town and imprisoned its mayor. From there he went on to Przemyśl and took many villages in that region.

Later reports on Sanok are very scanty and deal mainly with Hungarian affairs. The most interesting of these is again one in the Galician-Volhynian Chronicle, this one for 1205. This tells that in the year 1205 the Hungarian King Andre II (1205-1253) met in Sanok Castle with the widow of Roman, Prince of Galicia-Vladimir. She had fled there from the Galician boyars along with her children, four-year-old Danylo and two-year-old Vasylko. The widow made a pact with King Andre wherein he, as friend of the deceased Roman, became the guardian of the two boys and pledged to defend their rights to the principality of Galicia-Vladimir. Taking advantage of this pact and of his rank, Andre II proclaimed himself sovereign of Galicia-Vladimir and made Danylo and Vasylko his vassals.

In a decree dated January 20, 1339, Sanok's sovereign Iuri II (1324-1340) initiated Magdeburg Law in the town. Someone named Bartko of Sudomir obtained a localization charter, by virtue of which he became mayor of the town and also established mills in Trepcza and Ostrowiec on the San River. This grant revoked the powers of the prince's municipal administrators and judiciary and delegated them to the mayor, and it freed the people from various tolls exacted by the prince. It also foresaw the need for bringing foreigners, principally Germans and Poles, into Sanok to stimulate industry and trade.

---

27   Juri's coalition included the Prince of Chernihov; Byzantium; the Polovtsy, and Hohenstaufen. Allied with Iziaslav were Bolesław IV Kedzierzawy, King of Poland; the Welfs; the Czech King; Roger the King of Sicily; and Rostislav the Prince of Riazan.

This is the last available source of information on the period of the Galician-Volhynian Principality, which at that time encompassed three quarters of the lands settled by the Rus' people.[28]

In 1340, Casimir the Great, King of Poland, brought Sanok under Polish rule, along with other towns of *Chervona Rus'* (Red Rus'). In 1366, he established Magdeburg Law there. In 1377, Sanok was taken over by the Hungarian King Ludwig (1370-1382).

In the era of princes, Sanok was entirely Rusyn. And even during the Polish period it retained its Rusyn character, Rusyn culture, and Rusyn faith for a long time. Individuals of other nationalities also migrated to Sanok, chiefly from the adjoining countries of Poland and Hungary. During the time of the Rusyn princes of Galicia, Sanok had its own chief magistrate. From time to time it was ruled by titled governors sent by princes who recognized it as one of the important towns of Galician Rus'. Its jurisprudence was based on the laws of *Ruska Pravda* (Rus' Truth). All important civil matters were adjudicated by a judiciary panel, which consisted of the *voievoda* (governor), judges, a steward, a scribe, and assessors. Monetary claims were settled with silver coins known as *kunitsias*, which is attested to by both Rusyn and Polish documents.

Churches are also a part of Sanok's Rusyn history. At one time after its transfer Sanok had five churches. In view of the importance of ancient Sanok, this figure should not be considered an exaggeration. It is a historical fact that as far back as 1250, in the time of princes, a wooden church was built in the courtyard of the castle. It was named the Church of St. Dymytrii the Great Martyr, and it housed a miracle-working icon of Christ on the Cross. This church witnessed the fall of the Rusyn princes' Galician state and lasted until 1550. It was then dismantled in preparation for the anticipated residence in Sanok of Isabella, sister of King Zygmunt August. In a part of the town known as "the ramparts," a piece of land was granted to the Rusyn residents by Piotr Zborowski, the governor of Sanok, for a church to be named after St. Nicholas. This grant was confirmed by King Zygmunt August in 1551 and by King Władysław IV in 1632:

> We were shown a letter that confirms the letter of the one time mighty Piotr Zborowski, which on the one hand granted the residents of the town of Sanok an empty plot with the Lechow garden inside the town walls, and on the other hand gave them permission to build a church of

---

28   Dr. Iaroslav Konstantynovych, *Z Minuvshiny Sanoka* (From the past of Sanok).

the Greek faith there...

However, we do not know whether this church was actually built or just remained a project, because in 1667 we find on that particular plot a wooden church dedicated not to St. Nicholas but to the Holy Spirit. It would be odd for the Rusyn people of Sanok to build a church to the Holy Spirit in the place intended for a church to St. Nicholas. This uncertainty may be explained in part by a note found in the church annals:

> The residents of Sanok were ordered by the local Council to erect a building on the designated lot in three days, at the expiration of which time they would not be allowed to build a church. They hurriedly bought an abandoned wooden church in the hamlet of Jasielnica near Krosno, and with the lumber from this they erected in Sanok a church in the style of the church in Jabłonica. And this church lasted until 1789.

It is also possible that the St. Nicholas church was actually built but for some unknown reason it lasted only a short time and was replaced by a Holy Spirit church. This possibility is suggested by the fact that a St. Nicholas altar was still in existence in the early nineteenth century in a later masonry Church of the Holy Spirit in Sanok. In all cases the sentiment noted above is evidence of the harsh religious intolerance of Orthodoxy that prevailed in old Poland under King Zygmunt August in the latter half of the sixteenth century. And the Rusyn residents of Sanok were all Orthodox at that time.

A new masonry church, also named for the Holy Spirit, was built in Sanok on the site of the old wooden church in 1784-1789 during the pastorate of Fr. Ioann Kunevych, by collecting voluntary good-will offerings. It is still standing today. In addition to the icon of Christ Crucified from the castle church and another of the Holy Mother of God from a suburban church, housed in this new church are pieces of the true Cross of the Lord. A masonry bell chapel was erected beside it in 1827, and in 1876 major repairs were performed by Fr. Vasyli Chemarnyk. It was again repaired and repainted in 1907 and 1933 by Fr. Emilyian Konstantynovych. In 1909, Fr. Konstantynovych erected a beautiful one-story parish house with funds provided by the parishioners.

On the fringes of Sanok, from time immemorial there stood another wooden church, named for the Birth of the Virgin Mother of God. This was removed in 1790 on Order No. 27453 of the Lviv Provincial Council. The Council issued this order on the basis of false testimony given by some Poles that the church had burned down. In memory of the old church, a side altar with an image of the Virgin Mother of God from that church now stands in the present Sanok church. The last pastor of this Sanok "suburb" was the presbyter Fr. Ioann Vaitsovych, who was there as far back as 1772.

We read in the parish chronicle that above this old church was a hill "formerly called Wladycz after the Bishop of Sanok whose palace stood at the foot of this mound; it was the size of an entire town and was slowly taken over by the local townspeople." Later, that hill was called "Aptykark," and it is now known as "Mickiewicz's Park." Less than a tenth of the land occupied in the past by the many Sanok Eastern Rite churches is still held by the Rusyn parish of the town. Taking advantage of rights granted them by the town, townspeople have taken over these lands.

In addition to all those churches, there also were supposed to be in Sanok a Holy Trinity Church and a St. Onufrii Monastery, but all traces of them were erased by some invisible hand. Their existence is revealed by the fact that lists of miracle-working Sanok icons mention icons of the Holy Trinity and St. Onufrii. Near the end of the seventeenth century, some Lady Herbury established there a monastery for Uniate monks, as attested to by letters of Fr. Petro Kaminskii dated in 1685.

In the sixteenth and seventeenth centuries Sanok was lively, the religious and cultural center of all Lemkovyna. As far back as 1551 there was a school there that produced manuscripts and church books, for example an Epistle Book from 1551. There were two well organized youth groups, one of which was in the Holy Spirit Church and the other in the Birth of the Mother of God Church on the outskirts of Sanok. The latter group lasted until somewhere around the mid-eighteenth century. One of its graduates was the son of Archpriest Mykhailo Vasylevych who, at the prompting of the Princess Holszanska, translated the Gospel from Bulgarian into Rusyn in 1556. [A copy of] this translation was later discovered in the monastery at Peresopnitsa in Volhynia, the so-called "Peresopnytska Gospel."

During the time when the Union of Brest (1596) was being promoted, that is, throughout the seventeenth century, the people of Sanok and its environs were strongly attached to the Orthodox faith and resisted adoption of the Union. That is why when the Orthodox bishop of Przemyśl, Antoni Winnicki (d. 1679), lost his seat there, he sought protection and support in Sanok, where he lived from 1668 to 1675. By settling in Sanok and taking over existing institutions, he intended to establish a new Orthodox eparchy

*"An evening of Lemko national dress." From left: Petro Khraptsio, (unk), Anna
Koval, Kateryna Krasovska, Yulia Beblo, all from Deszno near Rymanów.
Sanok, February 16, 1941.*

with the help of the Sanok residents and the surrounding aristocracy, in the
hope that Orthodoxy would overcome the Union. When he died in 1679,
the Sanok Orthodox eparchy collapsed under pressure from those in power.
However, its memory lives on in that the Greek Catholic bishops of Przemyśl
have also titled themselves "Bishop of Sanok" ever since.

During the period of the Boleslavs many aristocratic families settled in
Sanok and its environs. After the partition of Poland they were attracted by
foreign capital and most of them moved to the regions of Przemyśl, Sambor,
and Cracow. Władysław Jagiełło lived in the Sanok castle, and while there he
married Elizabeta Pielecka in the Franciscan Church. After his death, his widow Sofia ruled Sanok and instituted many improvements. Various merchants
settled in the town, trading mainly in salt from the Tyrawa Solna salt mine.
Two fires, one in 1470 and the other in 1680, inflicted complete destruction
on the town, which in those days was considered very rich.

King Zygmunt August assigned Sanok to Isabela, who was the widow of
King John Zapoli and had been exiled from Hungary. However, it soon became
the property of the Italian-born Bona, mother of the last of the Jagiellonians.
Bona reconstructed the Sanok castle, and on the opposite bank of the San River

she built the *Mysliwski Zamok* (Hunter's Castle) and *Królewski Atelier* (Royal Studio). In time, a factory producing railroad cars and rubber products was established in Sanok. After the war, it became an automobile factory.

Sanok was also well known for the atrocities committed there by Polish gentry in the seventeenth century. A petty noble named Piotr Ramult of Hołuczków rampaged through Sanok and its vicinity and sheltered highwaymen in his own home, for which Pienionżek, the deputy mayor of Sanok, had him put in irons and locked up in the tower dungeon. The petty nobles Grochowski, Dwernicki, and Buczacki murdered anyone who reported on them. Minor noble Jacek Dydyński was cut to ribbons with a sword by his enemy Mikołaj Tarnowski. The petty noble Lady Suzanna Krohulecki attacked her relatives like an ordinary bandit. The renowned adventurer Stanisław Stadnicki, known among the Polish nobility as "the devil of Łańcut," stained his hands with blood and betrayal. Our people, always oppressed, suffered so much torture and persecution from those and many other desperados that it could fill volumes. The invisible hand in feudal Poland always took care to cover up all traces of the maltreatment and coercion of the Rusyn people. That is why so much is concealed from the historian and known only to God.

Sanok has also played an important role in recent times in the national

Administrators of Kachkovskii Reading Room. Fr. Polianskii is second from right. Wróblik Królewski, late 1930s. Photo © Kyczera.

religious and cultural life of all of Lemkovyna. For a long time before the
World War, and for a short period after it, Lemko youth were raised and edu-
cated in two boarding schools there, one Rusyn and one Ukrainian. Branches
of both national trends began and operated there. Worthy of note among the
Rusyn organizations and institutions are the Beskid National Home, a Com-
mercial Hall, a Mykhailo Kachkovskii Reading Room,[29] the Student Circle of
Friends, and the Dniester Society for Mutual Protection, the National Home
Boarding School, a Drama Group, a Rusyn Ladies' Boarding School, a Rusyn
Choir, and many others. Ukrainian institutions were younger. Noteworthy
among them were *Prosvita* (Enlightenment Society),[30] National Trade, The
Rural Agriculturalist, and others. On the whole, relations between the Rusyn
and Ukrainian organizations were proper. Both one and the other often arranged imposing processions, held national ceremonies, and organized national performances. All of Lemko Rus' took part in the general conference of

*Founders of the "Lemkivshchyna" Society Museum (1930-1940). Sitting left to right:
1. B. Shulakevych, 2. Lev Getz, director (1896-1971), 3. Dr. Franz Kokovskii, 4. Fr.
E. Konstantynovych. Standing left to right: 1. Fr. S. Venhrynovych, 2. B. Chaikovskii,
3. V. Blavatskii, 4. (unknown). Not shown: I. Dobrianska, I. Fiunt. Sanok, 1935.
(Photo © Sanok Museum.)*

---

29   [A Russophile institution which even had branches in the USA.]
30   [The Ukrainian equivalent of the Kachkovskii Reading Room.]

the branches of the Mykhailo Kachkovskii Society, held in Sanok every year. After listening to the patriotic thunder of Lemko orators, people returned home inspired with hope for a better future. Today, all of this is just a dream.

A succession of Lemko intellectuals came from the state gymnazium in Sanok. It may be that no other gymnazium in Galician Rus' graduated intellectuals of such character, patriotic and devoted to the Rusyn spirit, as did the Sanok gymnazium. This is due primarily to the Rusyn professors and educators of that school. One unforgettable name is that of Volodymyr Bankovskii, son of a Rus' priest and director of the gymnazium, who nurtured many generations of students and was a true father to them. All the Rus' students who had been persecuted by Polish professors throughout all of our towns and were forced to look for aid elsewhere found refuge under the protective wings of Director Bankovskii, who treated them all with tenderness.

We also cannot forget the catechist of the Sanok gymnazium, Fr. Iosyf Moskalyk, a man of good heart, a patriot, renowned educator and organizer, and a friend of young people, who provided great service to the gymnazium, the Sanok intellectuals, and the Sanok people. Dr. Mykhailo Ladyzhinskii, long-time professor and teacher at the gymnazium, author of *Sanok i ioho okrestnosti* (Sanok and its environs), a man of profound education, took care to instill that spirit deeply in his students. His pupils are now in their elderly years but they can still recite a few Greek or Latin verses from Homer or Virgil. Professor Roman Kovalyk has left a good memory in the hearts of his students. Despite the fact that he was of a Ukrainian bent, he treated all his students sincerely and kindly, made no distinctions among them, and acted toward them like a father. The higher educational authorities, knowing that Rus' was flourishing in Sanok, took great care to make sure that no Rusyn or Ukrainian professor should make it into Sanok. For this reason, with the exception of the two above, the Sanok gymnazium had only Polish professors.

The Sanok parochial archives, which were kept by the last parish priest, date back to 1573, with copies from 1550. There are registration statistics for the years 1686, 1731, and 1750. After World War I, a Lemko Museum was established; it already had many valuable artifacts. After World War II, those items were moved to a Polish museum located in the Sanok castle. This museum contains two copies of the Acts of the Apostles dated from 1502 and 1551, which were donated by the Sanok church.

In Dąbrówka Ruska near Sanok is a masonry church founded by a native son, Fr. Valerian Slavikovskii, Archimandrite of the monastery in

Nikolayevsk-on-Amur.

Following World War II, in 1947 the Rusyn population of Sanok was [mainly deported to Soviet Ukraine while the rest were] exiled to the west (with very little property), and the Greek Catholic parish church became Roman Catholic.

After much work and many difficulties on the part of Dr. Iosyf Perelom, a lawyer in Sanok, and Iuri Chertezhynskii, an engineer from Bóbrka, the provincial authorities at Rzeszów granted ownership of the Sanok church to the Orthodox residents in early January of 1959.

On January 19, 1959, after a twelve-year gap, a solemn Divine Service was held at the church, and after the service a solemn procession went to the San River. Over two thousand people participated in a Jordan-type blessing of the waters. Over twenty-four years earlier there was a similar ceremony in Sanok when Fr. Dr. Bazyli Mastsiukh, the first Apostolic Administrator of Lemkovyna, marked the beginning of his office with an Epiphany Liturgy and blessing of the San River. The history of the town of Sanok provides much material for us to meditate on our sad misery.

Uście Ruskie

Uście Ruskie[31], located on the main road from Gorlice-to-Wysowa, is one of the oldest settlements in Lemkovyna. The term *Uście / Ustie* refers to the confluence of the Ropka and Żdynka rivers. The town was in existence as far back as 1359 when the Gładyszes were granted huge estates. In 1528 it belonged to the lords of Szymbark. The so-called "location privilege" document is dated 1504. It was in that year that brothers Iakow and Stanisław, sons of Stanisław de Górka Gładysz, granted a localization charter to one Juszkowicz as a reward for some service to the brothers. The pertinent document does not give the extent of this grant. It just mentions fields which define the village chief's holding. It specifies in detail the obligations of the peasants to the lord and the village chief, from which we can surmise about the economy of a village of that day. In addition to tilling the soil, the inhabitants engaged in hunting large animals (wild boars and bears), raising livestock (sheep and pigs), and beekeeping. The document requires a peasant to render to the lord five sheep out of every hundred owned, a tenth of the pigs raised, a quarter of the honey from every hive, and every fourth boar, bear, or other wild animal killed. Bees

---

31 [Uście Ruskie was renamed to Uście Gorlickie in 1949.]

were kept in the woods or near the home.

From this same document we learn that a Rusyn priest was already living in Uście at that time. He was given a field to use, for which he had to pay the lord a quarter of a *hriwen* [a monetary unit] and six grosz annually. He was allowed to graze ten pigs in the estate forests, but he had to give the lord a saddle and a horse blanket. We learn from a deed dated March 3, 1539 that the land belonging to the priest was purchased that year by the chief's office. Nearly a hundred years later, in a deed dated October 9, 1601, Jan Tarło of Tenczyn, Governor of Sandomierz and Lord of Uście Ruskie, certified all the existing properties of the church and the incomes from them, and freed the church of all estate taxes. In addition, he allowed, free of charge, the Uście priest to graze a hundred sheep in the estate forests, operate a water powered mill and stamper, distill alcohol, brew beer, and bring in four outsiders.

This document also lists the parishioners' obligations to the priest, for which the latter had to perform divine services and keep a cantor. In those days, the villages of Przysłup, Kwiatoń, and Smerekowiec belonged to Uście. This situation was confirmed by a later owner of Uście, Anna Rybinska of Grochowce, in a deed dated July 28, 1695, and again by Jan Wiktor of Wola Sękowa in a deed dated January 9, 1805. The parish lands in Uście Ruskie were held by parish priests from 1601, when Fr. Ioann Krynytskii was the priest until recent times, that is, until the last of the parish priests, Fr. Mykhailo Sobolevskii.

After the Tarłos, Uście Ruskie became the property of Martina De Rybno Rybiński, and then in 1720 it went to Kasyr of Roplin and Marianna Potoka Bojańska. On December 25, 1782, an agreement was made between Jan Wiktor of Natrowice and Vasyl Vyslotskii, a Kwiatoń official, by which Wiktor relieved Vyslotskii of all manorial duties.

In the times of serfdom, the inhabitants of Uście Ruskie and its neighboring villages were oppressed and exploited by the stewards and officials of the nobility. For this reason they often brought charges in the district court. Considerable light is cast on relations in those days by a "register of grievances and losses" enacted on April 27, 1811 in the form of forty-three points proposed by councils from Uście Ruskie, Kwiatoń, Przysłup, and Smerekowiec and addressed to the Central Committee of the District Legislature in Tarnów. The villagers note that they delivered the required products to the manor, and that cart trips to Bardejov, Biecz, Bochnia, Jasło, and Polanka were not reimbursed. This register gives some interesting details about economic relations, such as prices for labor, transport, etc. It also tells about wrongs that were common in Lemkovyna. For example, "When Iatsko Kovalchyk, mayor of Uście Ruskie, did not comply immediately with some order of the steward because he was christening a child that day, he was punished by five blows with a club." A complaint about a brewery in Smerekowiec that threatened fire to the village was signed by Ioann Lukachyn, plenipotentiary from Kwiatoń; Hryhory Stefanovskii, Ioann Kordash, Stefan Vyslotskii, and Mykhailo Khovanets of Uście Ruskie; Aleksei Andreychyn, Fedor Voitovych, Ilko Voykovskii, and Iatsko Kostelnii of Przysłup; Mykhailo Mainych and Ioann Hraban of Uście; Iatsko Kovalchyk, mayor of Uście; and Seman Fetsiukh, mayor of Smerekowiec. Such cases happened often.

In 1836 the owners of Uście Ruskie were Tit and Franciszek Przedeski. In 1871, Magdalena Milkowski was the owner. Later on it was Sofia Stawiarski Milkowski, the last patron of the Uście parish.

As far back as 1581, Uście Ruskie consisted of five homesteads, steward's land, and a parish house. In 1683, a noble took over the steward's office and required ten *korets* [a hundred kilograms dry weight] of wheat, ten *korets* of barley, and six *korets* of oats; he paid four zlotys for them. There were eleven peasants in Uście at that time and their taxes were as follows: rent was due half on St. Martin's Day and half on St. Ioann's: ninety zlotys, plus two zlotys, plus ten grosz. In addition, each peasant had to pay a "salt tax" of one zloty, twenty grosz and a "harvest tax" of two zlotys, four chickens, two geese, six

Weekly farmers' market. Grybów, 1923. (Photo © M. Maslej.)

eggs, half a quart of butter, ten sheep out of every hundred, and one ram. Besides that, each had to furnish a wagon to go to Hungary for the lord's wine, and footmen as needed.

On September 18, 1840, Uście villagers sent a complaint to the district authorities complaining about high work levies and the non-issuance of permits to cut trees, or their issuance only for places that could not be reached. They also complained that the forester punished the felling of a tree by jailing the accused, fining him, or giving him fifteen blows with a club. This letter was sent to the Jasło district Central Committee and demanded free access to forests, mills, and liquor licenses. It asked for a scribe who could write contracts and notices for the villagers, because they could not write. This petition was signed by Leshko Andreychyn, Iosyf Vakhnovskii, Stefan Kovalchyk, Pavlo Stefanovskii, Fedor Merena, Ioann Kapelnyk, Petro Okal, and Pupchyk.

Starting about fifty years ago, Uście Ruskie began to present a nicer picture. In 1876, an [Austrian military] Royal Road was built from Ropa to Wysowa [and on into Hungary] going through Uście, and traffic increased significantly. Prior to the First World War, sheep-raising thrived in Uście. A farmer would have had from ten to one hundred head. But after the war, the number fell to zero, with heavy loss to the farmers.

In 1931 Uście Ruskie had 127 houses and 120 families. From about 1876 to World War I, there was heavy emigration to America. The first Lemko priest in America was Onufrii Obushkevych, former pastor at Uście Ruskie. There are many Uścians now living in America. Many of them engage in cultural-educational work and materially help their countrymen left in the old country.

There is a wooden Greek Catholic church in Uście Ruskie, built in 1765 and dedicated to the Holy Mother Paraskevia. Before the Second World War, it was restored by Fr. Mykhailo Sobolevskii. After the Rusyn residents of Uście were deported [to Soviet Ukraine in 1945-1946 and] to western Poland in 1947, it was converted to a Roman Catholic church and Latin Rite services have been held there since.

Before the Second World War large *iarmarky* (market fairs) were held in Uście, for cattle, horses, pigs, sheep, and rams. They were attended by numerous villagers from neighboring counties. Handicrafts from the surrounding villages were brought for sale. Live demonstrations of beautiful Lemko crafts took place there, with the Carpathian Mountains in the background.

Land consolidation known as *komasatsia* [gathering strips of land into a single piece] to improve soil tillage was implemented in Uście after World

War I. Prior to the war there was a Mykhailo Kachkovskii reading room and a Rus' cooperative called *Syla naroda* (People's Power) and later *Iednost* (Unity). The last parish priest of Uście, Fr. Mykhailo Sobolevskii, and the mayor Teodor Voitovych made considerable contributions to cultural and educational activities.

In 1947, the Rus' people of Uście Ruskie were deported to the western lands of Poland, and to erase all traces of Rus'ianness the name of the village was changed first to Uście Górne and then in 1949 to Uście Gorlickie.

13. Outlaws in Lemkovyna

The proprietors of large estates could not manage their properties by themselves so they turned to vassals, stewards, overseers, and lackeys. In the view of their subordinates these officials were merciless in performing their duties. Occasionally they would resort to repression and terror, and they often persecuted the poor villagers in dreadful ways. Complaints to district officials or kings were never successful because the persecutors simply ignored royal rules that might help the accused. Those who dared claim such a royal defense would be "knouted" (clubbed on the bare back twenty or more times) and then had heavier workloads imposed on them.

Driven to extremes by such actions of the nobility, some villagers began organizing in self defense, uniting into groups and taking revenge against their oppressors. Archives give the names of the most prominent of those oppressors– Samuel Jabłonowski, Hrabinski, Szaniawski, Pawłowskii, Rykowski, Trojecki, the Jew Shaya, the Jew Berko, Opalinski, Mniszech, Iuri Krasytskii, Stadnicki, and many, many others. These self-defense groups would find cover in woods, caverns, and taverns, and then raid lordly homes, taking severe revenge. Their numbers increased almost day-by-day. Many of them would also attack wealthy merchants that were carting goods from Hungary or Poland through the mountain passes of the Carpathians. These people's avengers have come down in history by the term *zboiniky* (brigands) or *Beskidniks*. Headed by a *harnash*, they consisted of anywhere from a few brigands to a few dozen. In the archives they are identified as *latrones Beskidens in montio Carpathicis*

Sypko from Męcina Wielka near Gorlice, painting by Viacheslav S. Urusov.

("Beskid thieves in the Carpathian mountains").

Strictly speaking, these men were originally defenders and avengers of the people. As time went on, however, various undesirable elements began infiltrating their bands and they became highwaymen. Most of them were Hungarians, Slovaks, and Poles, but Lemkos were not lacking among them. Most famous among the latter were Savka, Cherep, Bachinskii, Lazarchuk, Prochpak, Kvochka, Fedor from Nowa Wieś, Kapka, Shuhai, Makovitskii, Pushkarik, Rostotskii, Hrits Iakhno, and many others. These men had their special places where they could hide and felt safe. Such hideouts were the caves near Maciejowa, Krainia Hala near Krynica and Wierchomla, two taverns near Krzyżowa Huta, the Rosticki home in Roztoka [Wielka?], the Danchaks' home in Łosie, the Robbers' Hole in Izby, Huta near Uście, the robber's hollows in the woods of Czarna, Huta near Polany, and others. From Krainia Hala thieves used eight pairs of horses to cart away a block of gold. Outlaws found good protection with some Hungarian noble families, such as the Drugeths from Humenné, the Asperments, the Nagytuches, the Peteys, the Rákóczis, the Veselenys, the Tekelys, and the Bizas, who not only protected them and hid them in their dungeons at Humenné, Trenčín, and Uzhhorod, but also used them for their own purposes and got good gains from them. When the Swedes were threatening Poland, the Polish kings recruited these outlaws for their armies. Jewish merchants made good returns from brigands, for whom they acted as gatherers of intelligence. They supplied them with weapons, ammunition, horses, and hideouts. Jews that had contacts with them ended up with huge estates.

The most frightful of these brigands were Savka and Chepets. In 1649, they attacked Jamgród (near Dukla) and manors in Ropa and Rogi. Each in his own time was in the ranks of Polish national hero Kostka-Napierski [alias of Stanisław Bzowski]. In 1653, Savka befriended Hrits Iakhno of Cegelka and they raided together.

Savka participated in the Swedish War, and when that ended he returned to brigandry. He often spent nights with his friend Rostotskii (from Roztoka [Wielka?]) or with Danchak (from Łosie.) When Rostotskii was imprisoned in Muszyna, Savka threatened the court that if they didn't free Rostotskii he would burn the village down. The judge feared that Savka would do just that so he let Rostotskii go.

Savka often used the nickname Hanchovskii. He was really a goodhearted man. When one time near Krasny Brod his comrade got shot, Savka gave him a horse, guided him to a safe place, bought two zlotys worth of ointment in Bardejov, and nursed him back to health. He preyed only on evildoers, and he shared his loot with the victimized.

Savka was caught by Muszyna police, trying to fight them off with a knife. On December 22, 1654, a criminal court in Muszyna sentenced him to death by impalement, which at that time was the most severe punishment. The sentence was carried out that same day. Savka has left his name in Lemko memory, no less a popular hero than Oleksa Dovbush for Hutsuls or Janosik and Ondraszek for the Poles.

Governors and magistrates would issue decrees ordering superintendents and judges to punish outlaws severely. They organized various raids on outlaws and set bounties to get rid of them. Outlaws were judged at criminal courts in Muszyna, Levoča, Biecz, Sącz, Krosno, and Sanok, and the penalty was death for all of them. There were various forms of death penalty– breaking on the wheel, quartering, decapitating, impaling, and more. The easiest was hanging. Various tortures were used during the proceedings, for example exposure to fire. In 1614, 120 outlaws were executed in Biecz in one day. In 1735, Iosyf Bachinskii was executed in Cracow, while in 1736 it was Lazaruk with his comrades in Levoča.

In 1654, great fear was created in the mountains by Fedor of Nowa Wieś. He used the aliases Semchak, Potopok, and Nohavitskii. He mostly attacked merchants. In Łosie he killed the guardsman Petro Krainyk of Jastrzębik. In

Czarna he attacked some merchants, and in Puste Pole he attacked the count of Lubovňa. His unit consisted of eleven men. Savka also ganged up with him for a while.

In 1649, Matyi and Andrei Kvochka had eight men in their group. They raided mainly on the Hungarian side. He [*sic*] was caught and brought to court in Levoča, and that judge sent him to Muszyna where he was executed.

The region also suffered from fear in the eighteenth century, caused by Prochpak, from Hungary. In the end, he too could not avoid torture and a death sentence.

Stefan Baius, opryshok *par excellence, as painted by Teodor Kuziak (1926-2010). Bartne, 1969.*

In 1656, brigands attacked and killed the Polish priest in Wrocłaniec near Krosno. In 1768, a gang attacked the Ruthenian priest of Izby, Fr. Ioann Ropskii. They killed him and destroyed all the parochial documents.

There were no regrets or complaints against all those brigands on the part of the village people; the brigands spared the lowly peasants and focused their revenge entirely on the aristocracy that oppressed the people. Brigandry was generated and nurtured by the nobility through their inhuman attitude toward the village population. Thus, acts of vengeance are recorded on the pages of history of the seventeenth and eighteenth centuries. The father and patron of brigandry was George Rákóczi. It is not so long ago that old Lemkos would tell stories about how the brigands lived and protected our poor people.

14. Rebellion in Lemkovyna

In the period from 1619 to 1622, Lemkovyna was an area of activities for *Lisow-czycy* or *Lisovshchiki* (Forest Raiders)[32] who passed through it twice, first on their way into Hungary and then on their way out of Hungary. These *Lisovsh-chiki* were a volunteer army composed of petty nobility, townsmen, and villag-ers, formed to quell the revolt of Gabriel Bethlen. They were guided through the Carpathian Mountains by Adam Lipskii, brother to the Bishop of Cracow. During their passage they indulged in raids on noble estates and caused consid-erable damage and deprivation. Lemkos suffered greatly from them.

At this same time, Khmelnytskii's emissaries were urging the people to rise against the Polish nobility. A spirit of rebellion enveloped the Lemkos en masse in hopes of throwing off the yoke of the Polish nobility. Meanwhile, in 1631 the Polish national hero Aleksander Kostka-Napierski, an officer in the Royal Army, was preparing an uprising in the Carpathian foothills, and Lemkos began filling his ranks. In the lead we see two already known to us, Savka from Orawa and Chepets from Stropkov. They are followed by others such as Sipko from Męcina Wielka, Vanio Malyk from Roztoka [Wielka?], Iurko Tsiupa, Sidoryk from Blechnarka, Iatsko Vatral from Regietów, Marko and Pańko Shcherba from Smerekowiec, Dańko from Hańczowa, Senko from Makowica, and many, many others. Kostka gave command of the Lemko con-tingent to Stefan Baius from Małastów. The rebels traversed all of the Car-pathians and unmercifully battered the gentry and the nobility in revenge for old wrongdoings. In their raiding they reached the castle at Czorsztyn, surrounded and captured it.

The rebels paid dearly for it, however. The Bishop of Cracow, Piotr Gem-bicki, sent out from Muszyna a well armed detachment of the bishop's army, which routed Kostka-Napierski's force. The rebels were subjected to terrible tortures. The Criminal Court in Muszyna sentenced some of them to death by hanging, others by impalement. Executed along with Poles were a few score of Lemkos. Kostka-Napierski and his two comrades and chief aides, Stanisław Lentowski and Martin Radotski, were taken to Cracow and executed there. Napierski was just as famous as Khmelnytskii or George Rákóczi.

---

32 [See http://en.wikipedia.org/wiki/Lisowczycy.]

15. The Confederates in Lemkovyna

In 1768, a Polish military organization called the Confederation of Bar was formed, supposedly to defend the borders of Poland but actually aimed against Russia. After its bloody birth at Uman, the Confederation left Russia and crossed over into Poland. There, except for a few skirmishes with Russian troops, they concluded their "heroic" exploits with raids against the defenseless Lemkos. In Lemkovyna, their activity took place in the period 1769-1771. Their original commanders were adventurous Polish petty noblemen who hated Russians with a passion, such as Casimir Pulaski,[33] Michał Krasiński, Józef and Joachim Potocki. Their general staff was located at Prešov in Hungarian Rus'. In addition to Polish aristocrats their ranks comprised castle guardsmen, police, bishop militia, and many Hungarians enticed by the slogan *"Polak, Madziar, dwa bratanki i do dziewki i do szklanki"* (Pole, Magyar, two fast friends, girls and drinking are their ends) and other such trash. This diversity was the cause of endless intrigues, quarrels, and fights among the Confederates and their leaders, who could not control the situation.

Pulaski's march from the southern side of the Carpathians crossed through Kąty and Kłosów into Galicia. He passed through Turka and Czeremcha, and on April 7, 1769 arrived at Barwinek

Memorial to victims of Confederate occupation, Stefan Hladyk during dedication at Shybenychnii Verkh (Hangman's Hill), 2011. (Photo © Watra 2012, № 76.)

---

33   [This is the Casimir Pulaski of U.S. Revolutionary fame who died leading a cavalry charge against British positions in Savannah, Georgia.]

where he met fresh units organized by Martin Lubomirski. A furious dispute arose between Pulaski and Lubomirski. Each of them had pretensions to being the principal leader. Pulaski issued a general proclamation to all the manor estates to furnish mercenaries for the Confederates, but the response was scant. A similar argument arose between Joachim Potocki and Michał Krasiński. Taking advantage of the situation, Biedrzycki, who had been chosen by the Muszyna Confederates to lead their regiment, marched out of Muszyna in the direction of Gorlice and Jasło in order to split Pulaski and Lubomirski and take over command.

Russia soon appraised the situation and sent its troops into the Carpathians. The Rusyn clergy warned the people that the Confederates were enemies, and in view of that the Lemkos did not give them any help. A powerful Russian force commanded by General Drevych routed the Confederates. Pulaski fled to Zborów, and Zawadski hid in the Carpathian Mountains. Some Confederates remained in Grab, and Pulaski brought some fresh units there. On January 13, 1770, Russian troops commanded by Elchanikov completely demolished the Confederates, while at the same time the Russians defeated Mączyński at Żmigród and strengthened their positions in the area. Pulaski fled to Izby and then to Konieczna [directly on the border with Austria.]

On July 21, 1770, Russian troops defeated the Confederates at Świątkowa. Pulaski retreated from Konieczna to Wysowa, and Mączyński came to Konieczna with the main force of Confederates. The Russian armies finally crushed the Confederates completely. The Lemko populace had stood solidly with the Russians, and the defeated Confederates, furious, exacted bloody revenge for this stand. They erected a gallows near Izby, where they tortured and hung several hundred Lemkos. This place is still known as *Shybenychnii Verkh* (Gallows Hill or Hangman's Hill). Referring to this place, the Lemko writer Ieronim Anonim (Fr. Volodymyr Khyliak) gave the same name to his novel about Confederate times in Lemkovyna [*Shybenychnii Verkh*, Lviv, 1882].

There are many reminders of the Confederates left in Lemkovyna, especially in Izby where they had stayed the longest and had the largest group. Their Izby camp numbered over two thousand men. The village of Izby ranks among the most historic places in Lemkovyna.

Izby was chartered in 1574 on the basis of a patent granted to Hryćko by the Cracow Bishop Samuel Maciejowski. It belonged to the Muszyna estate of the Cracow bishops. In 1782 it was leased to Count Skrzyński, while under Austria it was attached to the *Religionsfonds*. By a document dated November

20, 1862, the Cracow bishop granted the village priest Danyło a watermill in Izby with all its appurtenances, but with the stipulation that if Fr. Danyło's son was unworthy of being a priest then the value of the buildings must be paid to a worthy successor appointed to that position by the bishop. Later on, a special contract was agreed upon between one Ioann Medved and Fr. Danyło Izbianski that ensured a flow of water across Medved's field to the parish mill. For that, Fr. Danyło gave Medved a swatch of white woolen cloth worth six zlotys and sixty sheaves of oats worth twelve zlotys.

Earlier, on April 26, 1758, soon after one of the priests serving in Izby, Ioann Ropskii, was killed in a brigand attack on the parish house and the parish archives stolen, a verification of all the church's rights in Izby had been undertaken. This was done by order of the Cracow bishop, Kaietan Sołtyk, at the request of Fr. Ioann Shchavynskii, the parish priest in Izby and dean of Muszyna and Spiš. During this verification, Fr. Shchavynskii discovered a document dated November 12, 1732 showing that the local priest had the rights to all the parish lands in Izby, including Medved's field. A decree by Bishop Andrzej Zaluski of Cracow released all of these properties from manorial obligations.

A document dated April 6, 1759 shows that the village community also laid claim to Medved's field. The document says that the villagers also had claims to Medved's field, by being willing to legally have the title to it transferred to Fr. Shchavynskii and his descendants, since he cleared all liens on this land [it was used as collateral for loans] and he did not ask for any contributions during the blessing of a new church in Izby. At the same time they made a pronouncement that Fr. Shchavynskii should discontinue a twenty-five-year tradition of collecting "smaller" and "annual" loaves of bread.

There are many mementos of Confederate times in Izby: a Confederate trench near the forest above Izby, opposite Mt. Lackowa and about 30 meters from the border; Gallows Hill; a well below Izby near the road to the border, beside which an Austrian customs shed stood over a hundred years ago; and a rock in the Izby trenches with the inscription "N. XXV. Izb. 1787." The most prominent Confederate memento is the roughly eight thousand square meters of trenches near Muszyna.

A historic Eastern Rite church of the Apostle Luke is located in Izby. Built in 1888 out of stone, its design is interesting. It has a beautiful baroque iconostasis and an image of an armed knight in a red cloak and a lady with a crown and a courtly dress. On a side altar is a miracle-working image of the Mother of God of Izby, while beside it there was formerly supposed to have been

Parishioners, descendants of Lemkos, in front of their church, which was erected in
1992. Lviv, 1995.

a painting showing Casimir Pulaski, on the background of a Confederate
camp, praying to that same Mother of God. The painting of the picture was
supposed to have been commissioned by Pulaski himself in gratitude for the
kindness of the Mother of God of Izby. In the parochial archives of Izby there
was a document written in Latin in 1799 by the parish priest, extolling Pulaski's miraculous escapes from certain death in Confederate battles, once at
Plzeň and again at Świątkowa. This document says:

> *Huius Beatac Mariac expertus est gratiam Illustrissimus Dominus Casimi-*
> *rus Pulaski marsalcus confoederationis Lomzinensis anno Domini 1771,*
> *dum de villa Izby egresus easet contra Moschcos prope oppidium Pilzno,*
> *ibi undequaque circum datus existens a Moschis, cum nullum svandendi*
> *modum haberet, ad B. Virginem Mariam in ecclesia Izbiensi existentem*
> *suspirium fecit...*

(The illustrious Lord Casimir Pulaski, Marshal of the Łomża Confederation, experienced the kindness of the Virgin Mary in 1771 A.D.

After he had set out from the village of Izby against Russians, he was surrounded on every side by the enemy near the town of Plzeň. Seeing no way out, he addressed the Virgin Mary of Izby...)

Pulaski then broke away from the hands of the enemy almost without a scratch, going on to report that shortly afterwards:

dum in silvis Swiątkoviensibus contra Moschos et Kozakos vigilas ageret ad ortum solis correptus somno vix paullulum odormire ocepit, miles Moschovitieus reperter eum invasit et disperse eius militia, vivum capere contabatur et fere in manibus habebant...

(...while keeping watch against Russians and Cossacks in the forests of Świątkowa, at sunrise he started somewhat dropping off as overcome with sleep. Suddenly, he and his dispersed troops were attacked by Russian soldiers who were trying to capture him alive. And they nearly succeeded...)

However, Pulaski made a bow to the Mother of God and started to flee on a fast horse. The horse stumbled on a stump and threw him, but he still managed to escape unhurt by the fall and from the hands of the enemy. For this he funded the painting of the image of the Mother of God.

The last parish priest in Izby was Fr. Dymytrii Khyliak, who had been persecuted by Bishop Kotsylovskii after World War I. He returned to Orthodoxy with his parishioners and established an Orthodox parish in Izby.

After the Second World War, a large portion of Izbians were moved to Soviet Ukraine, and in 1947 the remnants were deported to western Poland. Their places in Izby were taken over by Polish squatters. In 1958, with permission from the Polish government, the Oleshnevych and Kokovskii families returned to their farms in Izby. They were constantly terrorized by the Polish settlers. On January 6, 1958, both families were sitting in Kokovskii's house observing Christmas Eve. Suddenly the house, set on fire by those settlers, collapsed on them. The fire swept through the room that the families were sitting in. With the room ablaze, they couldn't get out through the door and had to escape through a window to save their lives. The house was burnt to the ground. All that Kokovskii had worked for went up in flames, and he was left without a roof over his head, without food, without the basic necessities of life. That's how the Polish squatters treated the Lemkos who returned to their homeland.

16. Freedom Movements in Lemkovyna

Although Lemkos are a peaceful people, gentle and modest, in them lives a spirit of freedom, striving for liberty. For millennia, Lemkos have always struggled for freedom and have fought for the freedom of their people. They fought independently against the Polish nobility, which was oppressing them with its feudalism, and they organized groups against it. They fought together with the Polish rebels led by Kostka-Napierski. And they fought in the volunteer ranks of Ataman Khmelnytskii for a better lot for their people. In recent times they have fought in Russian armies against the German occupiers. The Lemkos gave great help to the allied forces, raising an army of twenty-five thousand young men. Many of them sacrificed their lives in the very flower of their youth, hoping to improve the lot of their people. In return, Poland [in 1947] expelled the [last group of] Lemkos from the Carpathian Mountains, scattered them all over Western territories, and left them to their fate. The deportation of all the Lemkos from their homeland remains the darkest episode in their history.

The Lemko spirit of freedom was strengthened by four of Pugachev's insurgents. Four rebel brothers distinguished themselves with bravery while fighting in the famous Cossack rebellion started by Emilyian Pugachev, a folk hero in Russia. After the execution of their beloved leader, they fled from Russia and hid in the Carpathian Mountains, in Lemkovyna, to save their lives from the tsar's *Okhrana* (security service). The Russian government promised a huge reward for the capture of the fugitive brothers' heads, and a massive search was launched. To throw off the bounty hunters, the four rebels changed their names and went separate ways. One brother who had assumed the surname Moskva settled in the village of Śnietnica; another reached the village of Czyrna, adapting the surname Kopystianskii; the third got to the village of Mochnaczka where he took the name Garbera, while the fourth, having crossed the Carpathian Mountains, settled in Transcarpathian Rus' under the name Dukhnovych.[34] The celebrated families that produced many Lemko luminaries were started by these very brothers. Some of Garbera's descendants changed their name into Mokhnatskii; Kopystianskii and Mokhnatskii are the patriarchs of the priest families in Lemkovyna. As for the Dukhnovych family, their role in the awakening of Transcarpathian Rus' is well known.

---

34 Dr. Andrian Kopystianskii, *Semeinaia istoria* (Family history), unpublished manuscript.

17. The Origin of Names in Lemkovyna

The oldest names of Lemko inhabitants derive from the name of a village or town, e.g. Banytskii (dweller of the village of Banica); Baranskii (dweller of Baranie); Bilanskii (Bielanka); Bohuskii (Bogusza); Bortnianskii (Bartne); Brunarskii (Brunary); Vesolovskii (Wesoła); Vyslotskii (Wisłok); Volanskii (Wola); Hamerskii (Hamry); Hladyshovskii (Gładyszów); Hrabskii (Grab); Hrushevskii (Hruszówka); Dolynskii (Doliny); Dubynskii (Dubne); Zhehestovskii (Żegiestów); Zavadskii (Zawadka); Zavoiskii (Zawoje); Kaminskii (Kamianna); Kotovskii (Kotów); Krynytskii (Krynica); Labovskii (Łabowa); Lipynskii (Lipna); Lishchynskii (Leszczyny); Malynovskii (Malinówka); Matsiiovskii (Maciejowa); Mokrytskii (Mokre); Mushynskii (Muszyna); Mokhnatskii (Mochnaczka); Nahorianskii (Nagórzany); Novitskii (Nowica); Oparovskii (Oparówka); Polianskii (Polany); Pototskii (Potok); Pryslupskii (Przysłup); Ropskii (Ropki); Ropytskii (Ropica); Rostotskii (Roztoka); Rudavskii (Rudawka); Shvatkovskii (Świątkowa); Seniavskii (Sieniawa); Stavynskii (Stawisza); Tarnavskii (Tarnawa); Tsekhanskii (Ciechania); Florynskii (Florynka); Chertezhynskii (Czerteż); Chyrnianskii (Czyrna);

The cemetery in Królik Wołoski has been taken over by nature, 2002.

Shklarskii (Szklary); Shchavynskii (Szczawnik); Iablonskii (Jabłonica); Ia-vorskii (Jaworze); etc.

All the names mentioned above are of Lemko origin, deriving from the name of a village. The name of a village, in turn, may refer to the following:

1) the name of its founder, e.g. Gładyszów (the village founded by a Gładysz), Andrzejówka (Andryi), Jaszkowa (Iashko), Bogusza (Bohusz), Zyndranowa (Zyndram of Maszkowice), Jurowce (the Rus' prince Iuri II), etc.

2) the name of a forest or a tree growing nearby, e.g. Dubne – from *dub* (oak tree); Smerekowiec and Smereczne – from *smerek* (spruce); Jaworki and Jaworze – from *jawor* (sycamore); Hraby and Hrabówka – from *hrab* (hornbeam); Lipowa and Lipna – from *lypa* (linden tree); Olchowiec as well as Olchowce – from *olcha* (alder); Czeremcha – from *czeremcha* (bird-cherry tree); Ożynna – from *ożyna* (blackberry); Leszczyny and Lesko – from *liszczyna* (hazel-nut tree); Berest – from *berest, bereza* (birch tree);

3) the name of a river, e.g. Sanok (derived from the river of San); Ropki (from the Ropa river); Wisłok and Wisłoczek (Wisłok); Jasionka (Jasionka); Uście (a tributary area of the Ropa river); Międzybrodzie (the village situated between the two tributaries of the San river);

4) land types, e.g. Wapienne (calcium/limestone rich soil); Kamienne (stony terrain); Skalnik (rocky land); Surowica (raw land); Zabłotce (muddy soil);

5) the occupation of its inhabitants, e.g. Powroźnik – derived from *poworoz* (rope) as its inhabitants were occupied with rope-making; Bednarka – from *bodnar* (cooper), someone who made barrels; Bartne – from *bartnik* (beekeeper); Folusz – from *folusznyk* (fuller), someone whose job involved cleansing of cloth in order to make it thicker; Szklary – from *szklar* (glassmaker); etc.;

6) landform features, e.g. Długie (long); Krywa (curved); Krzyżówka (intersection); Głębokie (deep); Rozstajne (crossroads);

7) villages of royal founding (korol), e.g. Królowa, Królik, Wróblik Królewski;

8) land owned by the nobility (Pol. "szlachta"), e.g. Szlachtowa, Dobra Szlachecka, Wróblik Szlachecki;

9) historic events, e.g. Binczarowa – from "Biltsareva" (this village is said to have given shelter to some princess); Banica (from *banicja*, exile; the village where criminals were exiled to); Izby (where the first living quarters, *izba*, was built), Piorunka (from *perun*, lightning; the village in which the god of lightning was worshipped), and many others.

18. The Union of Brest in Lemkovyna

Not only were the Lemkos persecuted and exploited by Polish magnates and nobles, they were also forced to defend their religion.

Since the Great Schism, the Lemkos adhered to Orthodoxy which proved to be of great significance in sustaining their national identity and culture. The Eastern Orthodox Church was subordinated to the Patriarch of Constantinople. Senior Orthodox posts were usually held by the nobility, to whom matters of the common people were foreign. Hence the Orthodox hierarchy did not enjoy the trust of the people. An important position was held, however, by brotherhoods, societies of a religious and culture-oriented character including townsmen, craftsmen, merchants, and petty nobles within their ranks. The Lviv Stauropegial Brotherhood was one such association.

Scarcely had the Polish-Lithuanian union been created when the Latin hierarchy along with state officials began making efforts to subordinate the Orthodox Church to their jurisdiction. On several occasions, they tried to place Orthodoxy under the authority of the Pope of Rome.[35] With this end in view, Jesuits made great efforts to persuade both hierarchs of the Orthodox Church and magnates of Orthodox faith to sign onto union. Piotr Skarga was the most vigorous advocate of this cause. The union first became concrete at a synod at Brest-Litovsk in 1595, at which an agreement on the conclusion of a union with the Roman See was reached between the Roman Catholic Church hierarchy and a majority of Eastern Orthodox bishops. In 1596, an agreement was concluded between the Pope and the Orthodox bishops Mi-

---

35 In 1352, Pope Clement VI via letter encouraged King Louis the Great of Hungary to go on a crusade against the "schismatics," promising to donate to him all villages and towns he would capture from the Orthodox and infidels with God's help. In 1471, Pope Sixtus IV told his cardinal to order King of Hungary Matthias Corvinus "to wipe out and destroy each and every Ruthenian heretic in Hungary regardless of their origin." The papal legate Antonio Possevino, a Jesuit, was sent to Moscow in order to persuade the tsar to enter into union with Rome. His eloquence nonwithstanding, the legate did not achieve the desired results; the tsar flatly refused to submit to the Pope. After his return from Moscow, Possevino arrived at Vilnius where he said to the Jesuits, "There is no chance that the union will be formed in Eastern Europe, or in the Grand Duchy of Moscow. There the tsar and his nation are of the same faith. The western part of Rus' which is under the rule of the King of Poland seems more likely to accede to the union as its king belongs to the Roman Catholic Church. Consequently, with a view to creating the union, it is worth influencing the King, as well as Ruthenian princes and clergymen, to accept the Union."

chael Rahoza, Cyril Terletskii, and Adam Potiej by which the Eastern Orthodox Church moved to the rule of the Pope with respect to administrative and
dogmatic matters, imposing, however, the condition that all its laws, privileges, and Byzantine rite should be preserved.

This Union of Brest was created to the advantage of the Polish nobility and
aimed to alienate the Rusyn people that lived within the Polish borders from
the influence of Russia. However, the Orthodox bishops cannot be suspected of
ill will. They entered into the union for the sake of the church and the nation;
they believed that the Church would enhance its prestige through the union,
and that it would be strengthened under the Pope. Yet Poland did not maintain
the rights and privileges described at Brest. Ruthenian [Rusyn] bishops were
refused participation in the sessions of the Sejm, and in general did not enjoy
the same privileges as Latin bishops.

The prince Konstantin Ostrogski, one of the most prominent magnates of
Rus', protested against the
union, becoming its bitter
opponent. The Rus' nobility, however, quickly became
Polonized and Latinized.
The clergymen and people
did not accept the union
happily, with many fighting
against it. But adherents of
the union, with the full support of the government and
Polish magnates, intimidat-
ed and sometimes terror-
ized people into accepting
it. The Dioceses of Lviv and
Przemyśl entered into the
union very late, namely at
the end of the seventeenth
century. Lemkovyna, in
turn, embraced it even later.
Up until 1675, the town of
Sanok was presided over by
the Orthodox bishop Antoni

Icon of the Virgin Mary and Jesus in an
abandoned church. Kuńkowa, 1968.

Winnicki who had considerable influence over Lemkos. If we assume that the Diocese of Przemyśl entered into the union in 1692 while headed by the bishop Innocent Winnicki, then Lemkovyna must have joined it at the beginning of the eighteenth century.

A wide range of methods was used to get Lemkos to adhere to the union. Eastern Orthodox churches would be closed and turned into Catholic ones; they would be pulled down, providing materials for Catholic temples to be built somewhere else; people were terrorized, expelled from their villages, burdened with various duties, and so forth. In those times, many Orthodox churches and Rusyn parishes were simply wiped off the face of the earth. These are some of them: Bukowsko, Długie, Pobiedno, Dudyńce, Markowce, Pisarowce, Nagórzany, Haczów, Jaśliska, Muszyna, Bachórz, Dynów, Ulanica, Wara, Izdebki, Witryłów, Krywe, Temeszów, Dubno, Pawłokoma, Dąbrowa, Krzemienna, and many others. Within less than a hundred years, purely Rusyn villages were Polonized and Latinized.

19. The Union in Transcarpathia

Subcarpathian Rus' / Transcarpathian Rus' under the House of Habsburg proved to be more resistant to the union than did Lemkovyna under the Polish Crown. At the beginning of the sixteenth century, the Reformation arose in Europe. Numerous Catholics broke with the Roman Catholic Church and flocked to Protestantism and Arianism. A substantial number of Hungarian nobles joined the Reformation. Action against the movement was taken by the heirs of the Habsburg dynasty, Charles V and Ferdinand I. Their troops were followed by carts loaded with torture devices and tar barrels for the burning of heretics. In 1526, the Archduke Ferdinand I from the House of Habsburg was crowned as King of Hungary, but he failed in his attempts to establish control over the whole country. The Kingdom of Hungary split into two halves with its northwestern part under the rule of the Habsburgs and the southeastern one (known as Transylvania) ruled by a king supported by the Turkish sultans.

The Habsburgs inaugurated their reign with severe persecution of infidels, especially the Orthodox. In 1561, the Jesuits were invited to Royal Hungary to wipe out all the heretics. Their arrival inspired an uprising against the German and Jesuit persecutors. In 1606, the rebels forced concessions from the Habsburgs. The principality of Transylvania strengthened its autonomy.

The cardinal Piotr Pazman, a fighter against the Reformation, turned his eyes towards the wealthy Count Gyorgy Drugeth who exercised full feudal rights in Humenné. They reached an agreement with each other. The Count accepted Catholicism and poisoned the Count Bálint Drugeth, his relative and the Uzh-horod estate owner as well as killing his son, Stephen. In this way, Gyorgy became the feudal lord of Uzhhorod. From then on, he carried out all of Pazman's wish-es. Not only did he establish a Jesuit college in Humenné, he also asked Atanazy Krupetskii, the Greek Catholic bishop of Przemyśl, to introduce the union in the Transcarpathian region. But the bishop and his helpers achieved nothing. Con-versely, they had to run away from the rage of the people. Drugeth's supporters barely managed to deliver Krupetskii from the angry mob.

The Count John Drugeth followed in his father's (Gyorgy's) footsteps and followed the lead of the Jesuits in everything. In 1640, the Jesuit College moved from Humenné to Uzhhorod. This school would cause much bitter-ness for the Transcarpathian people.

As the first attempt to introduce the union in Subcarpathian Rus' had proved unsuccessful, the Habsburgs and the Jesuits came up with another idea. This time, their plan involved Vasyli Tarasovych, the bishop of Mu-kachevo, who came from Galicia. The bishop had been promised that if he succeeded in planting the Uniate Church in the region, he would be granted privileges and his career would be boosted. Accompanied by some like-mind-ed supporters, Tarasovych unleashed a campaign to popularize the union. Then he was arrested by the Transylvanian authorities, which prevented him from carrying out his plans. Thanks to the intervention of Ferdinand I, Tara-sovych was released from prison, but he no longer had the desire to continue his campaign, and even returned to Orthodoxy in his old age.

The Latin Rite clergymen possessed large estates and led lives of luxury. An estimated thirty thousand to fifty thousand hectares of land belonged to each diocese. A Catholic priest was financially secure and surrounded by honor and privilege. The more dedicatedly he served the Emperor, helping keep the Ortho-dox people under control, the higher he could climb in the ladder of hierarchy.

The Jesuits invited two Basilian monks named Petrovych and Kosovych from Galicia to Uzhhorod and with them began using a carrot-and-stick ap-proach to propagate the union across the Uzhhorod district. But they failed to obtain what they aimed for. The people had a negative attitude towards the union as the arguments of its proponents did not appeal to the peoples' hearts.

In the end, only sixty-three persons were won over to the union, a majority of them recruited from Ann Drugeth's servants. On April 24, 1646, the union was officially proclaimed in the Uzhhorod Castle.

Having submitted to Rome, the organizers of Union in Transcarpathia set out to erect a Uniate eparchy. The Basilian monk of Halych, Parfentii Rostopchynskii, was elected its first Greek Catholic bishop. However, he did not have the courage to openly admit to his people that he had become a Uniate church hierarch. So he kept pretending to be a zealous adherent of the Eastern Orthodox Church. In 1652, he arrived at Alba Iulia, Transylvania, where he was consecrated bishop by the Orthodox bishop of Alba Iulia. Within three years, he managed to gain the confidence of the nation who believed that he was an Orthodox clergyman. No sooner had these three years elapsed than he declared himself a Uniate bishop, regretting publicly that he had ever been a member of the "false faith." That allowed him to be confirmed by the Pope himself.

Such intrigues resulted in a split within the Eastern Orthodox Church in Transcarpathia. The eastern region (Transylvania) came under the jurisdiction of an Orthodox bishop with residence in Mukachevo, while the western part, under the rule of the Habsburgs, had a Uniate bishop with his seat at Uzhhorod. In order to get Mukachevo to prostrate itself to the union, the Jesuits urged the prince of Transylvania, George Rákóczi II, to marry Sophia Bathory, a Catholic. After his premature death, she asked the Jesuits to persuade his minor son and heir to the throne to adopt Catholicism. As he was too young to govern the Principality of Transylvania, Sophia served as queen regent until he became capable of ruling by himself.

On the order of the Jesuits, Princess Sophia Bathory expelled the Orthodox bishop Zoikin from Mukachevo, appointing the Uniate bishop Rostopchynskii his seat. The people seethed with anger and rebelled against the German Catholic oppressors. The Mukachevo monastery returned to Orthodoxy. The Catholic landlords and Greek Catholics took refuge under the Habsburg roof.

In 1685, the Turkish army under Kara Mustafa Pasha besieged Vienna. Realizing the gravity of the situation, the Pope appealed to all Catholic countries to help the Germans defeat the Ottoman forces. The Polish king John III Sobieski set out for Vienna to relieve the city and support the Habsburgs. Eventually, the combined Polish-German army won a remarkable victory over the Turks at Vienna. The German troops entered Hungary and taught all non-Catholics a lesson. By the order of Emperor Leopold I, almost all the inhabitants of Prešov were butchered and the Protestant nobility arrested. The Magyar hopes of gaining independence from the Holy Roman Empire were drowned in blood.

Now Transcarpathia, when its turn came to fight for liberty, for three years mounted a heroic defense of Mukachevo against a German siege, and for three years the Germans broke their teeth against its walls. Neither the eventual fall of the castle, nor severe punishments broke the people's spirit. When fifteen years had passed, they took up arms again to fight for their freedom. This time they were headed by the last Prince of Transylvania, Francis II Rákóczi. In 1703 near Mukachevo, he started an uprising against the oppressors which spread across all Hungary. Under Rákóczi's leadership, peasants, craftsmen, and petty nobles fought in the rebellion while magnates and Catholic clergymen supported the Habsburgs.

For five whole years, the Austrian Emperor would call for reinforcements from all directions, yet could not suppress the revolt. Then the Habsburgs, following the example of the Jesuits, mounted a deception. Count Sigbert Heister treacherously attacked Rákóczi's *kuruc* forces at Trenčín, which gave the Habsburgs a decisive victory over the rebels. Subcarpathia's dreams of liberation from German and Catholic oppression unfortunately did not come true.

After the liquidation of the Principality of Transylvania, Transcarpathia found itself encircled by a ring of hostile countries, in imminent danger of being attacked by any of its neighbors. Its western, southern, and eastern frontiers were threatened by the German and Magyar lords, deadly enemies, and its northern one by the arch-Catholic magnates of Poland.

In addition, Uniate priests within Transcarpathia became internal enemies to a greater and greater degree. In 1692, Emperor Leopold I had issued a decree releasing Uniate priests from serfdom and granting them the same rights as Latin Catholic clergymen. Whatever the cost, the Unite priests became determined to prove their loyalty towards the Habsburg executioner of the nations. During Rákóczi's reign, while all Subcarpathian Rus' waged holy war against its old enemy, the Uniate priests clung to the Habsburg throne "on bended knee" and followed imperial orders, as if spies or saboteurs. Although the Jesuits were to do away with the Orthodox remnants in Transcarpathia, it was the Uniate intelligence service that did the job for them. At the request of the Uniate bishop Ioann Hrodemarskii, Austrian troops rounded up sixty Orthodox clergymen to the town of Sighetu Marmaţiei and forced them to accept the Union.

The population of Máramaros elected the Archimandrite Dosyfei as their new bishop. The Uniate clergymen cast aspersions on him and denounced him to Vienna, following which imperial forces imprisoned him in the Khust castle. After five years of physical and moral torment, Dosyfei died in prison. With his death, the Transcarpathian Orthodox Diocese vanished. The Uniate [Greek Catholic] rite became the official religion of Transcarpathia.

20. How the Orthodox Church Reacted to the Accession of Transcarpathia to the Union

The unlucky people of Transcarpathia, poor, persecuted and ruined, loathed the Union and Uniates, just as they hated their German and Magyar Catholic landlords and the Holy Roman Emperor. The popular hatred reached the consciences and hearts even of some Uniate clergymen. The best known of these was Father Mykhailo Andrella. He had been educated abroad, in Vienna and Bratislava, and did not see up close the circumstances in which the Union had been introduced. He accepted the Union with the best of intentions. But when he returned to his homeland and saw the machinations of the Jesuits and how state officials treated the common people like dirt, his eyes were opened and the ghastly truth dawned on him that the union was an evil. Realizing what harm the union caused to people and whose interests it served, Andrella and two other brethren abandoned Catholicism. For this they were to pay dearly. They were chained and imprisoned. The Latin and Uniate clergymen subjected Andrella to interrogation. They promised him the moon if he agreed to rejoin the union, a death sentence if he didn't. Setting these conditions stripped Andrella of his dignity. Yet he was neither scared by the thought of being killed nor interested in what they were trying to bribe him with. Owing to the determination of the people, who had demonstrated their sympathies with the brethren since the beginning of their imprisonment, the Uniate prelates were frightened into setting the priests free. On his release from prison, Mykhailo Andrella decided to dedicate the rest of his life to the people. He devoted all his knowledge and talent to fighting against the German and Magyar tyrants, regarding them as the greatest enemies of the Slavs. During his long painful life, Father Andrella wrote a lot of works in which he harshly attacked the enemies of the people with his razor-sharp tongue and wise words. Since many of his books have survived, we are provided with a reliable source revealing a real and convincing view of the political and religious struggles in Transcarpathia during the seventeenth and eighteenth centuries.

The fate of the Uniate clergymen was not to their satisfaction. They were dependent on Latin Rite priests, any of whose orders they had to follow immediately. Similarly, the Uniate bishop was subordinated to a Latin Rite bishop; he was completely dependent on him and obliged to obey his orders and instructions. In a word, Unite bishops were literally just administrators of affairs settled by Magyar or German Latin Rite hierarchs.

In 1760, another uprising, led by the hieromonk Safronii, was sparked off against the odious union in Transcarpathia. Uniate clergymen fled the uprising, and within a short period of time, 416 out of 749 parishes which had been forced to unite with Rome returned to the Orthodox Church. But the rebellious forces again turned out to be too weak. Peasant pitchforks and spades yielded to the imperial musket and cannon fire. The rebellion was suppressed; Habsburg bayonets secured the victory of the Union.

21. The Consequences of the Union's Enforcement in Transcarpathia

The enforcement of the Union in Transcarpathia quickly proved harmful. The Rusyn language, which had so far been the only means of communication in Transcarpathia, began to be spoken exclusively by peasants. With further development of the native tongue prevented, the nation found itself in imminent danger of being Magyarized and Germanized.

To safeguard the interests of Uniate clergymen, the hated government imposed duties known as *kobłyna* and *rokowyna*, which obliged peasants to give a share of their crop to Uniate priests. Along with this, on specified days of the year each peasant was bound to work for free on Uniate church lands. The Uniate clergymen made full use of this right given them by the Germans.

No less a transgression was the role of the Greek Catholic clergy in Transcarpathia's cultural life. Regardless of the borders, Transcarpathia had been cultivating cultural and political relations with the north since the earliest times. A variety of manuscripts from Kyivan Rus' and Galician Rus' had been transported there. After the Tatar raids, Moscow became the cultural center for Transcarpathia. The grateful nation kept alive the memory of how Tsar Peter the Great had supported Rákóczi's uprising, and when the rebellion headed by Bohdan Khmelnytskii began, the Transcarpathian people waited impatiently for a signal to begin fighting. The Habsburgs knew perfectly well that Transcarpathians' sympathies were with their brothers in the north. The Empress Maria Theresa of Austria forbade the import of books from Russia to Transcarpathia. At the same time, she tried to change Greek Catholic priests into loyal gendarmes who would kill the Rusyn people's desire for unity with their brothers, turning the nation into a shapeless mass detached from their roots and national heritage. With this aim in mind, the Empress founded a Greek Catholic seminary at Saint Barbara's church in Vienna, which came to be known as "Barbareum."[36] She also granted a few buildings to the Greek Catholic Eparchy of Uzhhorod, including the Uzhhorod Castle, the Jesuit College and their monastery, in order to make Uniate clergymen dependent upon the Habsburg dynasty. Maria Teresa was not mistaken. Within a short period of time, the Uniate priests forgot even their native language. Some few decades later, almost any Unite priest would have claimed Hungarian as their native language. As they became Magyarized and Germanized, Greek Catholic clergymen also became a powerful tool of assimilation in the hands of Magyar and German landlords.

In nineteenth-century Transcarpathia, however, one could have also encountered a group of Greek Catholic clergymen who did not betray their beliefs, but rather remained faithful to the nation. With oral and written words, they tried to either awaken or inject the Rusyn spirit into the people. This group included, among others, the following priests: Dukhnovych, Pavlovskii, Stavrovskii (known as Popradov), Dulyshynovych, Sylvai-Meteor, and others. But no matter how hard they tried, they were not able to cut themselves off completely from the environment in which they had grown and had been raised. They exhorted the nation to what Fr. Ivan Naumovych called for in Galicia: "Pray, learn, sober up, and work." Yet they did not encourage the nation to fight, because they knew that any popular

---

36   Many highly educated Rusyn priests graduated from Barbareum, among them the bishop Iuliian Pelesh, Ph.D., Tyt Myshkovskii, Ph.D., Panteleimon Skomorovych, and many others.

uprising would be against those to whom they had many connections. They loved the nation, but loved it in the fashion of liberal aristocrats, trying to reconcile water with fire at the lowest cost. Their works were written in two languages. When writing for the common people, they used the vernacular (the people's language); in other cases, they made use of an obscure mixture of Rusyn, Church Slavonic, Polish, and Magyar words, which was incomprehensible to the people. They often sharply criticized the Budapest government, considering it less effective than the one run in Vienna. Consequently, they preferred the Austrian Emperor to the Hungarian king, although both functions were performed by one person. As these priests were entirely devoted to Austro-Hungarian counts and barons, they were incapable of securing a better future for their nation. A typical example was the bishop Stefan Pankovych, who uttered these clergymen's credo when talking to Ivan Sylvai: "Under Magyar rule, we have to be Magyars; if we are ruled by Germans, we will become Germans." Father Dukhnovych characterized these clergymen's policy with these words: "For their own advantage, our priests will bring a poor people to the edge of a precipice."

The people's situation was getting worse year by year. At the beginning of the eighteenth century, the Magyar authorities remarked that the Subcarpathian peasants lived on a mixture of mustard flour as well as on tree buds, bran, acorns, and orach plants. But worse was yet to come. That protector of the Union, the count Shenborn, possessed 139,000 hectares of the best land along with two hundred villages inhabited by 70,000 people, while the peasants had merely twenty percent of the land— and stony, generally uncultivable land at that. While villagers had little to eat, well-fed Greek Catholic clergymen, speaking Hungarian, wished longevity and good fortune to various landlords of the Shenborn type as well as bowing before images of the Holy Roman Emperor Franz Joseph I.

22. The National Movement and the First Maramaros Trial

The Transcarpathian nation exerted itself to find a way out of its situation. Surrounded by enemies on all sides, people turned their thoughts toward their formidable Russian brother beyond the Carpathian Mountains. Out there, on the wide steppes of Russia and Ukraine, they sought support to set them free from their unbearable suffering. However, the political circumstances of that time were unfavorable for fulfilling these hopes and dreams. The Romanov whip was upon the people of the Russian Empire. The tsarist powers were interested in Transcarpathia, but their interest was that of empire-builders eager to swallow another morsel. The wealthy Russian landowner [Count Aleksei] Bobrinskii and the Transcarpathian people couldn't have had any common interests.

Nevertheless, the people's hope of liberation coming from the East did not die out. The Transcarpathian poor truly believed that one day all the peoples of the Romanov Empire would cast off their yoke, set the people in power, and under the leadership of their powerful Russian brother bring freedom to all the enslaved nations of the world. But, sitting on one's hands and waiting for this to happen meant certain death. Therefore, the nation rose in struggle against its oppressors. This struggle took the form of Rusyn peasants' return en masse to the fold of the Orthodox Church. In this way, they demonstrated their opposition to the religion imposed on them and to the enemy regime itself. What's more, the return to Orthodoxy was at the same time a manifestation of national unity with their brothers living along the Dnieper and Volga, revealing the people's desire for political unification of the three Rus' nations.

This movement started simultaneously in Transcarpathia and across the ocean, in places with the largest concentrations of peasant Rusyn immigrants. The movement's center was the village of Iza, in which within the shortest period of time ninety percent of the inhabitants broke with Rome. The movement made the Magyar authorities frightened and the Greek Catholic clergymen anxious. The latter began uttering threats from the pulpit, but all in vain. Gradually, the movement spread across all Carpathian Rus'.

The Greek Catholic consistory found itself in danger. Supported by Magyar gendarmes, the Magyarophile Uniate clergymen counter-attacked. A Greek Catholic priest, Andrei Arada, arrived at the village of Iza to hold an inquiry into the case; he acted as a gendarme investigator. Going from cottage to cottage, he interrogated all the villagers, searched everywhere, looked into wardrobes and drawers, and eventually found an American pamphlet entitled *Hde iskat pravdu* (Where to find the truth). He immediately sent a denunciation, and shortly a whole detachment of the gendarmerie arrived in Iza, where they made mass arrests. Dozens of peasants were chained and taken to Sighet prison.

Soon, the first Máramaros trial was staged in Sighet. The accused were charged with struggling to separate Subcarpathian Rus' from the Hungarian Kingdom so as to unite it with the Russian Empire. The judges were deaf to the arguments of the defense. The peasants from the village of Iza were given a year or more in prison. However, it was already too late for the repression to be of any use. The suffering people of Transcarpathia had awakened.

23. The Second Maramaros Trial

The first Máramaros trial failed to produce the results desired in Budapest. Conversely, the Rusyn masses became so furious that even the strictest measures taken by the authorities would not have stopped the nation from fighting for their rights. In Transcarpathia was heard the cry, "We don't want any more of the damned Union. We're fed up with the Magyar leeches and their supporters!" Yet the leeches continued doing as they had been doing. Wild boar and deer belonging to the Count Shenborn devastated peasant fields, yet the Count's forest rangers were ready to shoot Rusyn people who dared enter his forest. With the help of bayonet-wielding gendarmes, Uniate clergymen forcibly herded people into Greek Catholic churches where the Gospel was read in Hungarian, even ordering them to greet each other with "Praised be Jesus Christ" in Hungarian, instead of the Rusyn *Slava Isusu Christu*. Yet even this was still not enough to satisfy the Uniate clergy. In conjunction with the Budapest government, they set up a sophisticated entrapment. Arnold Dulishkovych, the son of a Greek Catholic priest, was given the main role. His assignment was to persuade residents of Transcarpathia to make contacts within the Russian Empire, so he could then supply the police with grounds to arrest and charge the suspects.

The provocateur Dulishkovych traveled to Russia and soon returned with ready evidence. Royal gendarmes searched the peasants and found "evidence" of treason against the state—religious books published in Russia.

Hundreds of peasants were arrested, beaten, tortured, and taken half-dead to Máramaros prison for two years of excruciating torture, after which the second Máramaros trial began. Ninety-four Rusyn peasants stood in the dock, accused of committing treason against the state, against the Magyar nation, and against the Greek Catholic Church.

The chief defendant was Aleksei Kabaliuk; as soon as he found out about the mass arrests of his countrymen, he voluntarily returned home from abroad to join them on the defendant's bench.

Testimony at the trial revealed how horribly the accused had been tortured in prison. They were beaten and tortured to the point that many of them went mad, for example, Babynets, Borkaniuk, and Bakariv.

The trial itself was a complete farce. Neither the judges, nor the prosecutor, nor the defense knew the Rusyn language; the accused, in turn, were not familiar with Magyar. The court interpreter insolently twisted the statements taken from the defendants, translating them as whatever the prosecutor wanted to hear. The main lawyer for the defense, Batory, happened to be the Greek Catholic Consistory's legal adviser as well a Magyarophile, thus advocating a guilty verdict for the defendants. More than two hundred witnesses gave evidence at the trial. Each witness's testimony had been rehearsed in advance before a panel of carefully selected specialists. Gendarmes controlled all the Rusyn villages; they beat the people, tortured them, and forced the peasants to lie under oath in the court of law. If they hadn't followed orders, they would have been severely punished for disobedience. However, even the head of the Khust town, Bela Ryshko, who appeared as a witness in the court of law, was incapable of keeping to himself that the Greek Catholic clergy cooperated with the gendarmes. At the trial, he said, "We made inquiries into those who were known to feel like converting to Orthodoxy, and if they happened to have broken even the health code, or something like that, we punished them severely for everything..."

During the Máramaros trial, the prominent Slovak politician Milan Hodža (who was later elected Prime Minister of Czechoslovakia) described the Greek Catholic Church negatively, as follows: "There, in Transcarpathia, the Greek Catholic Church is completely subordinated to the government; nearly all Greek Catholic priests have been Magyarized and cooperate with the government officials. For long years, the people have patiently tolerated it all (the *koblyna* and *rokowyna* levies)..."[37]

Three years later, Hodža wrote these words: "The Rusyns are a starving nation. They suffer hunger as they have nothing to eat; they starve mentally, and suffer as no other nation in Europe. As soon as they are born, they are sucked dry by the Magyar priest and by the *likhvar* [money-lender], both of

37   "Slovackij tyžnevik" newspaper, October 3, 1913.

whom are supported by the government. They have the worst land to cultivate... Out of a hundred people, five or maybe ten can read..."

Finally, few months before World War I broke out, the Máramaros farce
ended. The verdict: thirty-two people were found guilty of treason against
the state and sent to prison.

24. Lemkovyna under Austria

Two years before Poland was divided, upon the order of Maria Theresa on July
19, 1770, the Austrian government took Spiš from Poland and, in expanding its border northward, parts of the districts of Nowy Targ, Czorsztyn and
Nowy Sącz. With the first of the three divisions of Poland, which occurred in
1772, all of Galicia was made part of Austria, and divided into twelve, then
in 1782 into nineteen districts, and finally in 1868 into seventy-nine counties. Lemkovyna now consisted of Nowy Sącz, Grybów, Gorlice, Dukla (for
a short time), Jasło (separated from Krosno County in 1878), Krosno, Sanok
and Lesko Counties. All legal, land and administrative questions had to go to
state representatives for resolution, and with the introduction of the German
language, people had difficulty in communicating. In addition to the German,
the Rusyn and Polish languages were used for state business.

The Austrian government immediately began certain reforms. The taxes that
had gone previously to the religious owners of the Muszyna Estate were diverted
to a so called *Religionsfonds* or Religious Fund. Under Joseph II serfdom was
abolished [this was later rescinded] and taxation was revised by introducing
new forms of taxation such as those levied on peasants and alcoholic beverages
as well as salt and tobacco monopolies. The number of Greek Catholic parishes
was decreased while the number of Latin Rite parishes was raised to 995 within
Galicia. The Latin clergy were granted pensions from the Religious Fund upon
retirement and the government favored them. Complaints by the Greek Catholic clergy were usually resolved in favor of the Latin clergy.

The policy of the Austrian government was based on the phrase *divide
et impera* (divide and rule). They divided the Poles into two hostile camps
[landowners and peasants] and, likewise, they divided Lemkos, instigating

one group against another, while at the same time exploiting this fratricide. Joseph II implemented what Maria Theresa had thought about: active German colonization. All the more important and better jobs were assigned to Germans. On the one hand, the government aimed to weaken the Polish *szlachta* (landed gentry) as the strongest element of opposition, but on the other hand, they also handed important duties over to them. Villagers suffocated under the burden of high taxes. They also became obligated to serve in the army which they had not been used to before. Previously in "noble" Poland only the village chief or *soltys* and selected individuals had to serve. In order to avoid taxes and the draft, villagers would go on the move from village to village, or would move to undeveloped areas, abandoning their households to fate.

Demeaning serfdom, discrimination, oppression and compulsory army service contributed to the rebellion of 1846 during which, in an organized manner, the Polish villagers threw themselves on the landed gentry and took revenge for their misfortune. Polish peasants from Krosno beat up the lord Tytus Trzecieski and the poet Vincenty Pol. Badly beaten, they were taken to Jasło. Hearing about the rebellion, the owners of Grybów, Ferdinand and Jules Hoshy, and the owners of Biała and Polany, Kiryl and Amela Zielińska fled for their lives. The most aggressive leader during the rebellion was the chieftain Szelya and his gang. In Lemkovyna everything was relatively quiet as Lemkos did not participate in this unrest.

In 1848, serfdom was [definitively] abolished by the [Austrian] Constitution, and ownership of peasants was abolished in 1849 and 1851.

To more fully understand the economic, political and cultural life of Lemkos under the Habsburg dynasty we must examine the prevailing conditions of the entire Rusyn population in Galicia and Hungary.

25. Galicia, including Lemkovyna, under Habsburg Tyranny and Oppression

Austria-Hungary was one of the most backward European countries, and Galicia was one of its poorest provinces, with agriculture its principal industry.

The autonomous government of Galicia had a provincial Sejm (legislature) but it merely carried out the central government's instructions. The little latitude of county and local governments was restricted to school and hospital business and road maintenance. All important decisions were made by the central government, which was represented by a Namiestnictwo (administration) in Lviv and a delegate of the Namiestnictwo in Cracow, supplemented by bailiffs. Bailiffs were powerful people in each village. They had control of all administrative power and the police force. They decreed fines and issued arrest warrants, and represented the villages in meetings of county authorities. Under the Habsburgs, as previously, only Poles could be administrators and bailiffs. They were men trusted by the Polish magnates. Galicia, a colony of the Habsburg empire, was governed by the Vienna bureaucracy with the help of the Polish magnates, proud of their titles as special Advisers to his Majesty and as Polish Senators of the House of Gentry in the Vienna Parliament.[38]

In 1905, the Galician Sejm had 761 representatives; including ninety-two landowners, six knights, eighteen lords and a baron. In addition there were eighteen attorneys, an interpreter, a merchant, an owner of oil wells, a bank director, two directors of credit firms, etc. but only ten villagers, and no workers, craftsmen or teachers. Count Andrzej Potocki was the *namiestnik* (administrator/governor/viceroy). Count Leon Piniski, Count Kazimierz Badeni and Count Ewstachy Sanguszko were the administrators preceding Potocki. Count Stanisław Badeni was a Marshal and his substitute was Archbishop (and Count) Andrei Sheptytskii. Ninety percent of the county marshals were Poles. The secretarial work of the villages was performed by landowners, attorneys, judges and notaries public. The village police force consisted of bankrupt landowners, former military men and retired gendarmes.

---

38 Take for example, Dawid Abrahamowicz, who was Jewish and had the following titles: *Dawid Ritter won Abrahamowicz seiner Kaiserf, und Konigl. Apostolischen Majestak wirklichen geheimen Rot, Ritter des Osterr, Kaiserl. Ordens der Eiserneh Kroe 1. klasse, Komandeur des Osterr, Kaizerl. Leopold- Ordens, K.K. Minister a D., Lebenslanghichens Mittklied des Herrenhanses des Österreichischen Reichsrates, Landesabgeordneter Ehrenmitglied des K.K. Galiz. Landwirtschaftlichen Geselischaft, Grossgrundbesitzer, Vertrauensmann der Hypothekar Kreditbabteilung der Österreichisch-Ungarischen Bank, etc.* [David, Knight von Abrahamowicz, Privy Councilor to his Royal and Imperial Apostolic Majesty, Knight of the Imperial Austrian Order of the Iron Cross, 1st Class, Commander of the Imperial Austrian Order of Leopold, Royal and Imperial Minister (retired), Lifelong Member of the House of Lords of the Imperial Austrian Council, District Delegate, Honorary Member of the Royal and Imperial Galician Agricultural Society, Landed Proprietor, Trustee of the Mortgage Credit Department of the Austro-Hungarian Bank, etc.]

Galicia was completely run by magnates such as Potockis, Badenis, Lubomirskis, Czartoryskis and others who owned vast tracts of real estate in the region.

Galicia was an exceptionally good agricultural province, yet harvest yield from cultivated lands was lower than harvests in hilly regions in the Alps. Communications, trade and business were not faring better, either. The existing oil wells and forests were owned and controlled by foreign elements or absentee landlords. Lack of any industry made it difficult to find employment. The only livelihood that the poor people and villagers could seek was the use of their manual labor. Wages in Galicia were the lowest in the entire Austro-Hungarian Empire. Unemployment was chronic. Millions of people had no work and little bread. At the beginning of the twentieth century there were approximately 1,200,000 unemployed. They were ready to do any work for meager wages to survive. However, the central government was generous with Galicia's bureaucracy, politicians, policemen and others in authority. Due to poor living conditions and bad hygiene, epidemics such as plague, polio, small pox and cholera took the lives of many people. In one year, 1902, forty-seven thousand people died from these diseases. Tuberculosis was another real disaster for the people. The hygiene in hospitals was primitive. Doctors and medicines were not within the reach of ordinary people.

A unique hierarchy of oppression existed in Galicia: Austrians oppressed the Poles and the Poles in turn oppressed the Rusyns, in spite of the fact that the Austrian Constitution of December 21, 1867 recognized the equality of nationalities. The provincial and central governments treated Galicia as a Polish province with a Rusyn [East Slavic] national minority. In reality, Poles were not in the majority. Austrian statistics were in terms of language rather than nationality. According to the census of December 31, 1900, there were 3,932,033 Polish speaking people and 3,080,443 Rusyn speaking people. Out of 7,315,930 people 54.4% were Poles and 42.1% were Rusyns. If we account for the fact that the Polish language was spoken not only by Poles, but also by Jews, some Rusyns, and some Germans, the percentage of the Polish speaking population decreases to 45% and the percentage of Rusyns climbs to 43%. These numbers are still not accurate and need to be corrected in favor of the Rusyns because they were at a disadvantage thanks to the landowners. They would call the language of their peasants Polish, even though it was Rusyn. The same situation would happened with Polish landlords and their tenants. Also, the census forms passed through the bailiff's hands, where they were often altered in favor of the Polish language. Taking all this into consideration, we can see that the Poles in Galicia did not outnumber the Rusyns. Therefore, the Poles had no right to treat Galicia as Polish territory.[39]

The nationality statistics show vividly the debasement of the Rusyn population in the governmental and socio-political spheres. Poles occupied the top spots in industry, administration and the free professions, while Rusyns were in agriculture. Also debased was the Rusyn worker, who worked as an unskilled laborer, usually at a day rate, while skilled workers were recruited exclusively from among the Poles. The Rusyn peasant went head-to-head with his landlord, who was a Pole, and because of this the nationality question was inseparably linked with the agrarian question.

At the beginning of the twentieth century, Polish colonization was extensively developed. Colonists were transferred from western Galicia onto eastern lands that were purely Rusyn. In 1902 alone, several hundred Polish peasants were moved from the Myślenice district to the Stryj district. The primary objective of the Polish landlords in this colonization was to set the Polish peasant against the Rusyn peasant, to foster hostility between them and to strengthen their own mastery of the villages.

The Rusyn populace was no less debased in political and cultural affairs. Of 145 delegates to the Lviv Sejm scarcely sixteen were Rusyns, and for 72 seats in the Vienna Parliament there were 10 Rusyn candidates while all the rest were Poles. In the entire region the official language, alongside German, was Polish. Only at the district and village levels might a little Rusyn be heard. In 1900, there were 5,449 Polish teachers in the schools, and only 2,284 Rusyns. There was not a single institution for training Rusyn teachers in the entire region. The school authorities assigned Rusyn teachers mainly to Polish villages, and instead placed Polish teachers, who did not know the language, in Rusyn villages. In 1904, there were fifty-two Polish high schools and only five Rusyn. Of eleven professional schools, not a single one was Rusyn. There were 20,664 Polish high school students and only 4,557 Rusyns. Establishment of a Rusyn high school required authorization from the provincial Sejm, while an ordinary warrant from the local school authorities was enough to establish a Polish school. Rusyns had no university of their own, and only at the University of Lviv were there seven Rusyn [Ukrainian] chairs, which were shortly reduced to two.

---

39   *Wiadomości statystyczne o stosunkach krajowych* (Statistical information about the provincial situation), Lviv, 1909; Stefan Dnistrianski, *Natsionalnaia statistika* (National Statistics), Lviv, 1909.; V. Okhrymovych, *S polia natsionalnoi polityky Halychyny* (National policy of Galicia), Lviv, 1909.

The dominant religion was the Roman Catholic faith, although Roman Catholics, at 45.7%, did not constitute a majority. Polish nationalists fanned the flames of ethnic hatred between the Polish and the Rusyn peasantry. In a speech in 1904, Professor Stanisław Głombiński, a candidate for delegate to the Sejm, proclaimed a program of conflict between Poles and Rusyns under the slogan "No yielding to Rusyns in politics, economics, or culture," while Władysław Studnicki expounded a zoological chauvinism in respect to Rusyns that earned him the epithet of "the Polish hatchet man."[40]

Toward the end of the nineteenth century, under conditions of a growing terror initiated by Badeni regarding spurious elections in 1897, relations between the two peoples in Galicia became very tense. Ivan Franko exhibited great love also toward the Polish people, as he expressed in his brochure in Polish,[41] but he had some bitter experiences with Poles and Polish elections. Three times (in 1895, 1897, and 1898) he was a candidate for Parliament, but each time the Polish reactionaries rejected his candidacy. Disappointed and discouraged, he parted from his Polish friends and never again cooperated with the publisher of any Polish newspaper. Polish nationalism was the poisoned arrow of the reactionaries.

Marx's statement to the effect that a people who suppresses other peoples cannot itself be free acquired particular meaning as applied to Polish social conditions in Galicia.

26. The Agrarian Question in Galicia

In Galicia, 83% of the population earned their living from agriculture, forestry, or fishing, while 39.2% of the land belonged to nobles who often owned dozens of estates covering several thousand hectares. For example, here are a few of them:[42]

---

40   Wł. Studnicki, *Wyodrębienie Galicji* (Separation of Galicia), Lviv, 1901.
41   Ivan Franko, *Nieco o stosunkach polsko-ruskich* (Some comments about Polish-Rus' relations), Lviv, 1895.
42   J. Buzek, *Własność tabularna w Galici według stanu z końcem r. 1902* (Property ownership in Galicia as of late 1902).

Baron Jan Libig owned 66,756 hectares in 62 estates
Count Roman Potocki owned 49,874 hectares in 104 estates
Archduke Karol Stefan owned 44,079 hectares in 53 estates
Wilhelm Adam Schmidt owned 35,516 hectares in 20 estates
Baron Bertold Popper owned 33,421 hectares in 28 estates
Count Yakov and Maria Potocki owned 25,586 hectares in 34 estates
Count Stanisław Badeni owned 22,761 hectares in 16 estates
Count Karol Lanckoronski owned 20,077 hectares in 38 estates
Wilhelm Friedrich Schmidt owned 19,722 hectares in 13 estates
Count Andrzej Potocki owned 18,996 hectares in 39 estates
Maria and Count Olivir Ressegnir owned 15,452 hectares in 10 estates
Count Stanisław Siemieński-Lewicki owned 14,303 hectares in 23 estates
Prince Jewstachy Sanguszko owned 13,490 hectares in 42 estates
Prince Hieronim Lubomirski owned 13,179 hectares in 24 estates
Prince Kalikst Poninski owned 12,582 hectares in 16 estates

The masters of these great manors included not only Galician magnates but also a list of foreign aristocrats headed by Archduke Karol Stefan. Among them were Poles, Germans, and Jews. Estates in Galicia were accumulated not only by Austro-German aristocrats but also by various merchants and speculators. Ownership of landed property made it easier to play a more important role in politics.

Also among the large landholders was the Catholic Church. Ecclesiastical holdings reached the sum of 129,028 hectares. The Latin archbishop in Lviv had 14,787 hectares, and the Greek Catholic archbishop had 30,991. The Latin Rite bishop in Przemyśl had 7,808 hectares, the Greek Rite bishop 1,000. A Latin Rite order in Lviv owned 6,318 hectares. Some Latin parishes also owned large holdings. For example, the Tomb of the Lord parish in Cracow owned 708 hectares, the parish in Olesko had 693, that in Trembowla 578, and that in Dolina 1,592.

As the landed gentry became richer, the peasantry grew poorer. In 1898, there was an average of four morgs[43] of land per peasant family. Because industry was poorly developed, work opportunities for the villagers were limited, and the land had to be divided into parcels (separated strips.) For 1,009,000 households there were 19,340,321 parcels listed. That means there were nineteen scattered parcels for every average four morg holding. Besides establish-

---

43 [A *morg* was a unit of land measure equivalent to about 1.4 acres.]

ments of three or four morgs, there were many dwarf holdings of only one or two morgs. There also were many peasants who did not have even a piece of land. These were the *chalupniki* (cottagers), and *komorniki* (roomers). A cottager had his own hut set on somebody else's land, for which he owed the owner a rent payable in labor for the rest of his life. A roomer did not even have a hut of his own and had to work for a miserly wage on the fields of the lord or a wealthy peasant. Professor Napoleon Cybulski of the University of Lviv described these poor wretches of his time as being in a state of "near starvation":

They make their bread by mixing flour with potatoes, cabbage, beans, peas, ground corn cobs, apples, etc. Instead of bread they often bake ash cakes and eat them half raw and covered with ashes, hot out of the stove, because the cakes would be inedible when dried out. To sustain life they resort to rotten potatoes, oil cake, bran, pigweed and other weeds, beet and cabbage greens. Often, ten percent of the people do not have bread all year round. The poorest eat no bread for most of the year.[44]

Attesting to the wretched state of the Galician peasantry was the fact that they were often unable to pay their taxes and had to pay a high rate of interest for late payment. In 1904, Galician peasants paid the state treasury 1,230,000 zlotys[45] in interest for late payment of taxes. In 1900, there were 4,028 auction sales of peasant properties for nonpayment of taxes. In all these cases, the amount of the tax plus interest did not come to one hundred zlotys. In one such case, a peasant's property valued at 1,400 zlotys was auctioned off for eight zlotys of unpaid tax, which sum had risen to eighty zlotys when court costs were added. Another peasant had his eleven morg homestead auctioned off to Count Lubomirski for 250 zlotys, while in the Allotment Bank's report its value was listed at no less than 8,000 zlotys.

Poor people were not allowed to serve on local councils. And when sometimes one did manage to get on, neither the executives nor the other members of the council paid much attention to him. They would often not notify him of meetings, would make it hard for him to get a look at the village books, and so on. The executives would deny poor people their workbooks, which were necessary to get work abroad, while the prefect would deny them passports, needed to enter another country. A poor man would be denied the certificate of poverty

---

44   N. Cybulski. *Proba badan nad zywieniem sie ludu wiejskiego w Galicyi* (Attempted research on the diet of peasants in Galicia), Cracow 1894.

45   [Polianskii does not indicate what the monetary unit is here; we assume it to be the zloty.]

he would need to be exempted from hospital costs, but a wealthy person could easily get such an exemption. To pasture a cow on public lands, a cottager or roomer had to pay a much higher fee than a rich landholder. In Czerniec, Nowy Sącz County, landholders paid nothing for public pasture, but the landless had to pay up to ten kronen per cow. With such treatment of poverty, conflict often arose, and in such cases both the prefect and the policeman sided against the injured party. Peasants were deprived of field and pasture. Cattle were the salvation of poor peasants, but there wasn't enough forage. The owners of land took advantage of this and forced people to pay dearly in both money and labor for pasturing on their lands. Those who lacked pasture had to put their cattle on stubble or fallow, or graze them along roads, hedges, or yards. This practice often caused damage to the fields and brought heavy penalties.

The peasantry in general suffered from lack of firewood. To gather brush in the lords' forests, a person had to pay dearly or work off several, sometimes several score, days in the lord's fields. The manorial forest was a wellspring of constant conflict. The lord's servants dealt harshly with women and children caught gathering brush or picking mushrooms, with herders who moved their animals through roadside hedges, with those who dared to take a shortcut through the woods, with the farmer whose dog wandered in the woods. Every year, peasants fell wounded and slain in the forests of the lords. In Żelechów, a seventy-year-old man was beaten nearly into unconsciousness, and his coat was taken, all because he was grazing his cow in a grove that marked the border between the lord's fields and the commons. On the property of Archduke Stefan, a forester who shot a peasant was sentenced to seven days or seven kronen.[46] Another forester who had raped a girl and then shot her with birdshot served only eight months.[47]

A source of incessant conflict between the village and the manor were the hunting regulations. Only holders of no less than 115 hectares of combined lands could have a chance of getting hunting charters. Peasants could form hunting associations. In the management of such an association, each owner of four morgs had one vote, an owner of eight morgs had two votes, etc. Those who had the most votes came out the best in this arrangement.

Hunting charters were granted for a period of six years. The holder of such a charter also had to have a hunting license, which for ordinary country folk was impossible to get. In practice, the authorities would not allow peasants

---

46   *Prawo Ludu*, No. 28, April 19, 1906.
47   *Wieniec-Pszczółska*, No. 15, April 15, 1900.

to keep firearms. The local council granted hunting charters in accordance with instructions from the prefecture. If it should happen that, despite pressure from the prefect and the manor, the council did issue a hunting license to someone else, then both the prefect and the lord would spare no effort to harass him and force him into submission. Such a person could not find work for hire, could not buy firewood or lumber, and would be fined stiff penalties for gathering brush in the forest. That's how Count Roman Potocki took vengeance on peasants in his neighborhood.

The fees paid for hunting on peasant lands were very low, while the peasants' losses from damage caused by wild life were very high. Peasants complained constantly: "Bears, deer, wild geese destroy our potatoes, oats, beans, and forage; wolves raise havoc in our sheep pens; foxes carry off our geese and our chickens." People would keep bonfires going all night, but that didn't help much. The animals would become accustomed to yells and fires and come right up to dwellings. In practice, damages were never paid for. In the first place, it was very hard to prove a hunter's guilt under the hunting laws. And even if guilt were proven, the hunter would have hundreds of ways to get out of it, supported by the prefect, who would even assess court costs against the poor plaintiff. For this reason, the peasants seldom brought charges. Experience had taught them that it made no sense to take legal action against the gentry.

Equally harmful to the peasants was the fishing law of April 26, 1885. The rivers were divided into fishing reserves, each of 150 or more hectares of surface. Reserves were leased out to large manors or businesses for very low prices. A reserve would be leased out by the prefect without any consideration for the needs of the local communities involved and without even taking into account the size of the lease. On the San River near Sanok, fishing licenses on the territory of eight communities were leased for forty kronen, which averaged out to five kronen yearly for each community. Another reserve on the San together with the tributaries and estuary of the Osława River was chartered from ten communities for seventy-five kronen, which came to seven kronen yearly for each community. The community of Mrzygłód tried to get its quit rent reduced by thirteen kronen fifty heller for a fishing reserve, but this amount was disputed.

In short, landholders paid pennies for hunting and fishing reserves chartered from peasant communities, but paid nothing for the damages incurred and also charged the peasants high quit rents for the land allotted to them.

The manor brought the peasants to ruin by means of taverns. To be sure,

the ancient right of propination [the landowners' monopoly over alcohol sales
to peasants] had been purchased [by the state] from the magnates in 1889 for
a price of 134 million kronen, but the great overlords of the settlements did
not give up these revenue sources that had proven themselves over centuries.
They leased propination districts from the regional authorities and then li-
censed individual inns to their henchmen for returns up to fifty percent higher than they had projected for themselves. Among the delegates to the Lviv
Sejm there were eighty-four propination lease holders. Their incomes from
this must have been great, since they paid up to a hundred thousand kronen
yearly into the treasury under the rubric of quit rent. According to Michał
Bobrzyński's account, there were sixteen thousand inns in Galicia. The innkeepers, who were principally Jews, knew how to get people drunk and were
also good facilitators who could drum up cheap labor for the landholders.

The manor rapaciously defended its rights, which were almost feudal in nature. Open use of force on the part of the lord was hard to withstand. On his
side he had the prefect, the gendarme, and the judge. When the plaintiff was
a peasant and the defendant a lord, the case was quashed. No lawyer dared to
come out in defense of the community of Zubazucha near Zakopane against
Count Zamojski. The presiding judge in the Jasło district court, Maldzinski,
told a plaintiff: "It doesn't pay to bring a complaint against the Lord Count,
best you withdraw." A peasant woman who wanted to enter a charge against
Count Tyszkewicz for destruction of her property was laughed out of the Kol-
buszowa court. When Count Stanisław Badeni's former steward wanted to
bring a case against the count and asked the magistrate for a poverty permit
so he could be exempted from paying stamp taxes, the attending gendarme
tore up the permit with the cry: "You scum, how do you get to sue the Lord
Count?"[48] A woman in Wola Sękowa, who had been beaten into unconsciousness, was ridiculed when she wanted to enter a complaint against the overseer
of the estate.[49] Going to the authorities could even be dangerous. When a forester tore the clothes off a woman he met in the lord's forest and then chased
her naked on a public road, the prefecture sentenced not the forester, but the
woman, to two days in jail.[50] Having clothes torn off and being chased naked
to the village by the lord's lackeys was a matter of daily routine. When a forester in Bochnia beat up a woman from Domuszczyce, a widow and mother

48   *Służba Dworska*, No. 2, July, 1905.
49   *Prawo Ludu*, No. 38, September 21, 1901.
50   *Służba Dworska*, No. 4, September, 1905.

of five children, the woman was jailed while the attacker got off scot free.[51] When a peasant in Kaclubiska tried to defend his meadow, which was being illegally ditched by the lord's servants, he was shot by a forester. It was not the forester who was arrested, but the injured villager and his brother.[52] When a twelve-year-old boy led out of the manor his father's horses, which had been taken for damages, the father was sentenced to eight days in jail and the son to a cudgeling, during which the father was forced to hold his boy's feet.

Entire volumes could be written about the harsh attitudes of the Austrian administrative authorities, the nobility, and their servants toward ordinary peasants, and about the atrocities that called to heaven for vengeance. But even from what has been written here we have a picture of the terrible oppression suffered by the peasantry.

Manorial service in the fields and in the household was exempted from the basic statute of the Austrian state, which preached about the personal freedom of citizens. The worker was at the mercy of the landholder and the gendarme.

The rules that governed the relationships between servant and master were established by an imperial edict of July 1857, which in Galicia was implemented by a decree of March 20, 1872. This law introduced into hired labor relations an order that placed the entire administrative and police apparatus at the disposal of the landholder. The police and the local authorities were required to provide servants for the manor. In practice, this meant a police escort into servitude. The servant had no rights and no defense. Here are a few examples from the instructions to a deputy governor:

A servant who is not employed must be put to work in community or public service. Furthermore, if he makes excuses that he is obligated to work for relatives, he is to be grabbed on sight. Housemaids who are not working and do not take advantage of offers to work are to be driven out of the community.

A servant hired for a specific term could be fired without notice before the term was up. It was enough for a servant to get sick and he could be cast out without treatment or provisions. As manager of a manorial estate, Prince Lubomirski wrote to a prefect: "I respectfully request the honorable Royal and Imperial Prefect to bring Maria Lianoska, as soon as possible, back to my

---

51   *Wieniec-Pszczótska*, No. 12, March 25, 1900.
52   *Przyjaciel ludu*, No. 1, January 27, 1906; *Prawo ludu*, No. 20, October 14, 1900.

service, which she has secretly run away from without any cause on my part." From the further content of this letter, it turns out that the girl was afraid of being raped by the petitioner; he tries to vindicate himself by saying that when he called her to his room he "did not molest her."

A worker could not readily leave his job because of the insecurity that would face him; he was supposed to give advance notice to the local authorities or the management of the manor. This meant that a young woman, beaten and molested by a lord and threatened with rape, would have to accuse him face to face and furnish proof by herself, something rarely possible for a frightened girl. Even if she could prove maltreatment and rape, the lord would not be punished with arrest but would only pay a small fine at most. When a maidservant would not give in to him, petty lord Michał Łukaszewicz ordered his grooms to unhinge the door to the room where the distraught girl had fled, disrobe her naked and lash her mercilessly. This incident was published in the newspapers. Since his guilt was proven, the court perforce fined the accused two hundred kronen for "disturbing the domestic peace."

The club, the cane, and the flail were common means of punishment, authorized by regulation. Quitting service without permission was forbidden, even after marriage.

Well known for torturing their servants were the Austrian chamberlain Gniewosz, Xavier Potocki's constables, the squire Uznański, Przylucki, and many others.[53] Slapping with a hand loaded with rings was not considered abuse. There were many cases of severe injury, disablement, and mental derangement brought about by beatings.[54] Rarely did such incidents come to court, and when that could absolutely not be avoided, punishment was very light. All disputes between worker and employer were decided by political authorities, primarily by the prefect. A worker could not turn to the courts until at least thirty days had passed.

Another means of terrorizing workers and forcing them to accept service were the workbooks given to manorial servants. Retention of the workbook by the lord made it impossible to seek work elsewhere. Galician manors made very little use of permanent servants; they preferred to take advantage of day workers, to whom they had absolutely no obligation whatsoever. The wages of a day worker in Galicia were the lowest in the entire Austrian empire.[55]

---

53 Służba Dworska, No. 2, July 1905 and No. 3, August 1905.
54 Prawo Ludu, No. 1, 1905 and No. 37, June 1906.
55 The relative percentages of daily wages were: in Lower Austria 87.7%, in the Czech

A correspondent wrote in 1896: "Last year the prefect issued an order requiring peasants to dig potatoes at the manor for nothing. This was enforced by the magistrates."[56] Even ten years later there were instances of forced labor. Władysław Wiktor, manager of an estate in Sękowa Wola, beat a peasant woman into unconsciousness because she would not go to work on the manor, saying that she had her own place to take care of.[57]

Manorial managers ensured a supply of cheap labor by means of loans for fertilizer. The cost of this labor was reckoned to be considerably less than average. Workers were compelled to do something for nothing in exchange for work on the manorial lands. For example, in order to get a job planting potatoes they would first have to work for free spreading manure; to be able to work at gleaning, they had to tie up to thirty sheaves of grain for the field master or the head stockman.[58]

The wife and children of a stable hand were a reserve of labor that did not have to be paid until they were needed. A family man working on a manor received produce, that is, payment in kind, which was enough for subsistence but not for a normal life. An unmarried lad or girl got leavings instead of produce. His or her value, either in money or in kind, was very low.[59] As an example, in Baron Romaszkan's household the servants did not get any breakfast at all; for dinner they were given potatoes or hulled barley gruel, for supper ground barley or corn meal. Tardiness to work brought a fine of four kronen, which amounted to several days' wages. A bricklayer who worked for this lord discovered on payday that after his fines were deducted he not only had nothing left but even owed the baron thirty kronen. For servants, getting into an argument could lead to a beating or even torture.

Deductions from wages could be made for illness or even militia duty. Rozwadowski penalized a man two kronen for a half day's illness and thirty kronen for a week of military training, this while his pay for the whole year was only sixty kronen.[60]

The average daily wage in manor households was fifty-five heller for men and forty heller for women, which was barely enough to buy two kilograms

---

lands 57.0%, in Silesia 47.9%, in Galicia 29.0%.

56 Letter from Mykhailo Herman of Nadlesie, September 6, 1896.

57 Prawo Ludu, No. 38, September 21, 1906.

58 Swoboda, May 25, 1902.

59 The wage per day was, in heller: in Lower Austria 88.75, in the Czech lands 61.25, in Silesia 43.75, and Galicia 22.50.

60 [Reported by author and member of the Austrian Parliament Ernst] Breiter, October 1902.

of bread.[61] Living conditions were simply catastrophic. Servants with families lived in communal dormitories, and often there were several families in each room. Adults slept on benches made of poles and planks and lightly covered with straw, while children slept on the ground with rags for cover. Unmarried men slept in barns, and unmarried women in cowsheds. A field worker's day lasted fourteen to eighteen hours. A stable hand had to be

Ivan Tymura (left) from Krynica, an Austrian soldier. 1903.

on his feet at three o'clock in the morning and could not lie down to sleep earlier than ten o'clock.

Hatred of the manor and its masters grew stronger from day to day. The most bitterly detested aspect of the system was the tax in blood that was the military draft. Draftees were taken for three years, and the Austrian army was foreign to both Rusyn and Pole. Between the ordinary solider and the officer, who was usually a German, there was an impassable stone wall, not that anybody ever tried to get over it. Reporting "here" with the Rusyn word *yesm*, the Polish *jestem*, or the Czech *zde* instead of the German *hier* meant two to five months in prison.[62] The military courts did not recognize any due process. Justice was administered without witnesses, with no defense, and even without the presence of the defendant. Plaintiff, investigative judge, and auditor were all combined in one person, who was also the reviewer in the event of appeal.

---

61 According to Ivan Franko, one day's salary in Galicia varied from sixteen to forty hellers.
62 "Secret military tribunals," speech by representative Daszynski at the Rada Panstwa (National Council) meeting, Nov. 8, 1902. [The language of command in the Austro-Hungarian army was German.]

Sadism was rife among the officers. The common soldier was mercilessly beaten where he stood with whatever happened to be handy– beaten about the face, on the head, and over the entire body; beaten with fists, with sword, with rifle butt. Facial beatings were often so fierce that eardrums and noses were crushed. In 1903, an order was issued to discontinue shackling men to stakes or racks for many hours. Utter contempt for the man and his dignity was the rule.[63] It is not surprising that military service was regarded by the peasants as penal servitude [*katorga*] to be avoided at any cost, even the cost of mutilation, imprisonment, or death. In the Tenth Army Corps, stationed at Przemyśl, the following incidents were reported in 1901 alone: eight suicides by soldiers, ten suicides by officers, seventy cases of severe self-mutilation by soldiers, four hundred desertions, thirteen fatal beatings, forty cases of madness with loss of speech and hearing, seven hundred twenty-five sentences to hard labor, four cases of madness among officers, and three cases of officer degradation.[64] Such was the frightening nightmare prevalent in the Austrian military.

To get away from starvation-level wages and unemployment, from the misery of life in village and manor, from the arbitrariness of the masters, and often from military service and the hated Austrian army, Galician peasants and workers fled to foreign lands.

The oppression, exploitation and atrocities suffered by peasants, workers and manorial servants at the hands of the Polish magnates gave rise to agrarian strikes in Galicia that reverberated throughout Europe. Such strikes went on continuously from 1898 to 1904. They started in western Galicia and spread eastward to encompass principally the estates of Prince Adam Sapieha, Count Roman Potocki, Count Lanckoroński, Count Siemieński, Count Dzieduszyński, Count Baworowski, Count Kazimierz Badeni, and others. Although these strikes resulted in many being sacrificed, nevertheless these disciplined peasant masses showed great strength and solidarity, and they put pressure on the manorial system. Ivan Franko estimates that the participants in these strikes were eighty percent Rusyn and twenty percent Polish.[65]

---

63   *Prawo Ludu*, No. 5, Nov. 2, 1906; Prawo Ludu, No. 52, Dec 28, 1906.
64   Daszynski, "Secret military tribunals."
65   Ivan Franko, *Bauerustrikes in Ost Galizien* (Peasant strikes in East Galicia).

27. Emigration

Lemkovyna was the poorest region of Galicia. Lemkos had little land, because their plots were scattered and divided among individual family members. The plots up in the hills were stony and infertile, which made them hard to till and not very productive. Even with the very primitive Lemko life style, the produce of the land could not meet their most basic requirements. There was almost no way to earn anything extra. Even to gather a small cartload of brushwood for fuel required spending several days working for the owner of the forest.

But Lemkos are an enterprising people. He who had a horse would extricate himself from his misery by getting together with his neighbor, and with their carts they both earned a living. They would go to Cracow to purchase trade goods. This made for risky and strenuous earnings, but the tough Lemko character could overcome anything. Others would haul logs from the magnates' forests to the sawmill and then haul the lumber to the city or the railroad. People from Łosie and Kuńkowa traded in grease and oils for lubricating wagons and machinery. They shipped their goods all over Europe and made good money at it. He who didn't have a horse because he couldn't afford one would try something else. This is how the production of various kinds of wooden items came about in Lemkovyna. Still others went to Hungary or Germany for seasonal work.

Everyone did what he could to somehow provide for his family and not let the specter of death come near it. And then one day he would hear that somewhere far beyond the ocean there is a rich country called America that needs working hands and where good money can be made. So began the emigration to America, which increased from year to year. The beginning of Lemko emigration to America dates from around 1865.

The flow of emigrants to America and other overseas countries sprang up all over Galicia. The peak of this flow came between the end of the nineteenth and the beginning of the twentieth century. Here are some statistics: in 1903-1904 9,415 Rusyns and 20,243 Poles emigrated to America; in 1904-1905 14,250 Rusyns and 50,785 Poles. In total, from 1901-1905 46,516 Rusyns and 173,997 Poles emigrated to America, and in 1907-1908 12,298 Rusyns and 26,423 Poles did so.[66] The statistics do not show how many of these were Lemkos, yet it can be taken for a fact that the highest percentage came from Lemkovyna, and that in Lemkovyna emigration assumed mass proportions. However, no one went to

---

66 *Podręcznik statystyki Galicji* (Handbook of Galician statistics), Vol. 9, No. 1, Lviv 1913.

America with the idea of staying there forever, but merely to earn some money and return to his native land to improve his material situation there. On the average, half of the emigrants returned after three to four years.[67]

Prior to World War I Lemko emigration to America, from both sides of the Carpathian Mountains, had grown to such proportions that out of seven hundred Lemko villages there was not a single Lemko family that had not sent abroad at least one of its members. There were cottages from which all the residents had gone to America. They locked up the house, boarded up the windows, and gave their plots of land to relatives or neighbors. Thanks to this emigration, the economic situation of the Lemkos improved. The emigrants sent dollars back to the old country, with which more land was purchased, cattle were added, and the whole situation was improved.

Returning emigrants brought not only money but also new ideas about living. They knocked down their old smoke-blackened houses and built new ones that were nicer and more convenient. They also bought mineral fertilizers, and their land began to produce better. On the fertilized soil they sowed new species of grass, and so their oxen grew fatter, their cows gave more milk, and their material situation and living conditions improved. Lemkos were so closely linked with America that some of them went there several times, always for just a short while, returning to their families and their mountains, which they loved above all.

Some Lemkos also went to Prussia and Hungary. This, however, was only a seasonal emigration for periods of intense agricultural labor such as grain harvesting.

Michał Bobrzyński, governor of Galicia, stated that the export of human labor was the most important item in Galicia's balance of trade.[68] In Lemkovyna, this export of working hands was so significant that in some counties the population increased very little, or even decreased.[69]

Emigration had a significant effect on the labor market. It brought about improvement in working conditions and wages. The peasant's character changed, his independence and self-confidence grew, and the scope of his thinking expanded. The money brought back and sent back by emigrants not only improved the working and living conditions of the people but also played a significant role in the region's balance of payments. It is impossible to

---

67   *Ibid.*; W. Grabski, *Materjały w sprawie włościańskiej* (Materials about the peasantry), Vol. III, Warsaw-Lviv, 1919.

68   M. Bobrzyński, *Z moich pamiętników* (From my memoirs), 1908-1913.

69   For example, in Gorlice, Krosno, and Nowy Targ Counties.

determine the total amount of money sent back to the old country by Lemko emigrants, because Lemkos rarely took advantage of the services of banks or post offices in sending money back. They often sent back cash in registered letters, but this money usually disappeared in the Galician post offices.[70] Large amounts were carried by the emigrants themselves or were sent through friends or relatives. The total annual revenue from emigration to America has been estimated at twenty million kronen. Postal money orders sent from the United States to Galicia in 1904 amounted to 5,922,663 kronen.[71]

The émigrés were inhumanly exploited. The attitude toward them was one of extreme contempt. It was expressed in an unceasing debasement of their personal worth and complete disregard of their most basic needs. Travel to Germany for seasonal work was a horrible journey in jam-packed, unheated railroad freight cars, standing or sitting on your own bundle all the way. From February to June, when seasonal workers were going out, and from November to January, when they were returning home, the travelers filled to overflowing the courtyards and compounds at Oświęcim, Mysłowice, and Racibórz. It was even mentioned in the Sejm that these migrants were treated worse than cattle in cattle cars. Government officials introduced "fourth class" railcars for the migrants, to legalize the transfer of people as transfer of cattle or hogs.[72] At the Oświęcim compound, a special police unit was organized, consisting of four or five police officials, seven or eight ordinary patrolmen, and five gendarmes.[73] At every step the migrant was controlled, or rather he was exploited by a mob of all kinds of middlemen. These were special agents surrounded by a network of assistants. This role was often played by Jewish innkeepers in the villages. Some "benevolent societies" that appeared to be acting as protectors of the migrants, such as the societies of St. Rafael, Providence, Patrice, Columbus, and others, were actually hidden agents of emigration and transportation firms. This was just ordinary human trafficking.[74]

---

70 [One translator of this book has personally read letters from the old country, dating to about this period, in which the writer complained that money sent to her was stolen at the post office.]

71 Z. Gardas, *W sprawie ruchu pieniężnego między Ameryką a Galicją* (Concerning the question of the movement of money between America and Galicia), Cracow, 1907.

72 Prawo Ludu, No. 52, December 28, 1906.

73 Stenographic records of the eighth provincial Sejm, second session. Vol. II, Lviv, 1905.

74 M. Bobrzyński, *"Emigracya pośrednictwo pracy* (Emigration middlemen)", in Prawo Ludu, No. 5, March 4, 1900. [See also (in German) Martin Pollack, *Kaiser von Amerika: Die Grosse Flucht aus Galizien* (The emperor of America: the great flight out of Galicia) (Vienna: Paul Zsolnay Verlag, 2010), or (in Polish) *Cesarz Ameryki: Wielka*

No better and no less unscrupulous was the situation with the emigrant going abroad. If he had bought a ticket for a Dutch ship, the German border guards would not let him cross. They recognized only tickets for German firms. When in 1904 the government established its own shipping line, Austro-Americana, the village prefects began to compel emigrants to ship out through Trieste.[75] Emigrant diaries describe a terrible picture of the suffering of Rusyn peasants and workers thrust into the virgin forests of Brazil, without a roof over their heads, starved and deceived at every step. "We are beginning to forget that we are people," wrote one of them.[76]

Both the landholders and the authorities were displeased with the growing emigration. They were afraid that the wages of workers would go up, that there would be a shortage of cheap labor for the manors. Passport requirements were made more stringent, issuance of documents was dragged out, and those leaving were terrorized. In a secret letter, Governor Andrzej Potocki issued an order to restrain the emigration of Rusyn peasants.[77]

Intense propaganda against emigration was carried on through newspapers and brochures, playing on religious and patriotic sentiments. Some bishops put out pastoral letters in which they cautioned against emigrating. All of the landowners' organizations tried to influence government officials against emigration through resolutions and petitions.[78]

Although the landholders made emigration more difficult, they nevertheless managed to profit from it. Whatever savings our peasant managed to accumulate through hard labor in a foreign country he usually invested in land, which he bought from the large estates. The owners of the land quadrupled its price. According to a report of the Parcelization Bank in Lviv, the average price of a hectare of land rose from 700 to 1150 kronen in 1901, and then jumped higher every year.[79] It reached four to five thousand kronen. The most costly land was in western Galicia. Lemkos didn't profit too much by buying land from the manors.

Difficult and tragic was the lot of our emigrants who sought work abroad, especially in the early days. The first of our emigrants to America found themselves

---

Ucieczka z Galicji (Wołowiec: Wydawnictwo Czarne, 2011.)]

75 Speech by Daszynski, in Stapiński's memoirs.

76 *Pamiętniki emigrantów, Ameryka Południowa* (Emigrant memoirs, South America), Instytut Gospodarstwa Społecznego, Warsaw, 1939; Ivan Franko, *Do Brazyli* (To Brazil), 1898.

77 Głos Robotniczy, No. 18, April 30, 1904 and No. 20, May 15, 1904.

78 Prawo Ludu, No. 9, March 2, 1906.

79 Fr. Bujak, *Galicja* (Galicia), Vol 1, Lviv, 1909; Z. Ludkiewicz, *Kwestja Rolna w Galicji* (The agriculture question in Galicia).

in an impossible situation. They had to work fifteen to sixteen hours a day in the mines, and for this hard labor they received scarcely three to five dollars a week. Their earnings were not even enough for a meager living, to say nothing of buying other necessities or sending money back to the old country. They lived in primitive barracks, existing mainly on dry bread and sugared water. Striking Irishmen, who had been working in the mines, regarded our Lemkos as strikebreakers and killed them at every opportunity. They even organized outlaw gangs, attacked the Lemko workers, and battered them en masse. Our people did not dare go out alone into God's world, because they were threatened from all sides with danger to their lives. For this reason, Lemkos went to and from work in large groups. Many Lemkos died at the hands of the striking Irishmen. Hundreds of graves of our Lemkos, killed by the Irish, can be found in the spacious cemeteries of Shenandoah, Pennsylvania and other mining towns. Many years and several generations went by before our emigrants were treated on the same level as other people.

No better fate awaited seasonal workers in Germany, who usually went there to work on a fixed contract. In a foreign land, deprived of the means of making a living, our peasant agreed to the working conditions that were dictated to him. Once the contract was accepted, he was left to the favor or disfavor of the lord and the gendarmes. He was threatened with dismissal for the slightest misstep. A worker's monthly wage in Prussia came to thirty-four kronen for men and nineteen for women when exchanged from German to Austrian currency.[80] The work day was sixteen hours or more. The laws allowed monetary fines to be levied against a worker. He could be fired for any reason. His contracted wages and reimbursement for travel costs would be gone. These conditions opened the door for abuse by the employers, and they gladly took advantage of them.[81] Every large land owner had the police on his side, and he could order a worker to leave the vicinity immediately and get out of Germany in three days. If the owner did not have this power himself, the district council would come to his aid. The worker dismissed from his job was escorted to the border by gendarmes.

The Galician authorities also did not look with favor on internal migration. On the pain of being charged with vagrancy, the police forced people who were looking for work to stay put at their place of residence. This was the renowned "Galician detention," used against the unemployed or politically suspect. In the course of twenty years (1880-1900), 150,000 people were detained by this method. For every social problem, the Galician authorities'

---

80   Bobrzyński, "Emigracya pośrednictwo pracy."
81   Prawo Ludu No. 5, March 4, 1900.

remedy was police and gendarmes.[82]

Hard and unenviable was the lot of people looking for work in either their own or a foreign country. But finally there came a time that brought an end to their tyrannization.

28. The Political Atmosphere in the Austrian State Before the First World War

From the Rusyn point of view, the political atmosphere in the Austrian state before World War I was oppressive and insufferable. The Austrian government was morbidly jealous of Russia and its people and regarded with mistrust all Slavic peoples living within its borders. Surrounding itself with all kinds of agents, spies, detectives, and provocateurs, the government terrorized the Lemkos. The most innocent manifestation of cultural, educational, or economic life was considered an act against the Austrian state and was often brutally crushed. Rusyn institutions like reading rooms, cooperatives, student hostels, and boarding schools were salt in the eyes of Austrian officials, who saw treason everywhere. Austrian gendarmes, loyal servants of the government, ran around like hound dogs through towns and villages sniffing out "Moscophiles" and stirring up provocations everywhere; they would then carry tales to the administrative authorities against completely innocent people. Under the cover of tradesmen selling holy icons, Ukrainian provocateurs would scamper through Lemko villages, go into people's homes and talk about political subjects, presenting themselves as friends of the Rusyns and enemies of Austria. They would draw out a person's political inclinations, taking careful notes on everything, which they would then send, flagrantly edited, to the political authorities. In this way they compiled a list of "Moscophiles, who in the event of war will be ready to betray His Imperial Highness [Emperor Franz Josef]." On the basis of this list, all of the Lemko intelligentsia and hundreds of thinking peasants were arrested at the start of the war.

In such a political atmosphere, there were a number of arrests even before the

---

82   Gorzycki, *Szupaśnictwo w Galicji na podstawie materyałów urzędowych* (Police control in Galicia based on government materials).

war: the Orthodox priest Father Maksym Sandovych, born in Żdynia, Gorlice
County, just called to the parish in Grab, Jasło county; Vasyl Koldra, law student,
born in Świątkowa, organizer of reading rooms in Lemkovyna; Father Mykhailo Iurchakevych, rector in Czarna; and many others. Their only crime was that
they loved their people and worked for them. Father Maksym Sandovych and
Vasyl Koldra were sent to prison in Lviv, and in 1914 they were brought before
the district court, together with Fathers Gudima and Bendasiuk, and were accused of treason against the Austrian state. This trial was well known throughout Lemkovyna, as hundreds of Lemkos testified as witnesses, and Ukrainian
nationalists tried by all possible means to prove that the accused were guilty of
treason. The trial lasted continuously for three months. Over a thousand witnesses were heard. The accused were defended by Dr. Volodymyr Dudikevych
of Kolomyia, Dr. Maryian Hlushkevych of Lviv, Dr. Kyryll Cherlunchakevych
of Przemyśl, and Dr. Alekseevych of Stanisławów. All of the defendants were
found innocent in the Lviv District Court and were freed.

Relations in the religious sphere were also not promising. At the request of
the Austrian authorities, the bishops would not accept seminary candidates
of a Rusyn orientation. At a selection held in Przemyśl in 1911, only one of
forty Lemko seminary candidates was accepted, and in the subsequent years
prior to the war not a single one was. In that same year, among three hundred students at the general seminary of two eparchies there were only eleven
Rusyns, of whom two were Lemkos, even though at that time both the Rusyn
clergy and the Rusyn peasantry outnumbered the Ukrainians.

Rusyn students at the seminary in Lviv had a hard time and had to be of
a strong spirit to undergo all the humiliation brought on them by their Ukrainian comrades. These future altar servers organized hunger strikes and demonstrations and used whatever means came to hand to terrorize their Rusyn comrades. In 1912, such a dangerous situation arose that the Rusyn students twice
had to flee from the seminary in the dark of night to save their lives from their
crazed Ukrainian comrades. The late Father Botsyan, rector of the seminary at
that time, upon seeing this dangerous situation told the Rusyn students: "Run
away, for I cannot vouch for your lives." The Gehenna that our students had to
undergo at the theological seminary in Lviv at that time cannot be described
by inert letters on paper or even orally. It was a nightmare that compromised
both the Ukrainian clergy and the Austrian state.

The Rusyn clergy was in no better position, either. On a secret order from
the government, the bishops would not entertain a proposal to allow Rusyn

priests to come to their parishes. Even if someone did manage to get nominated by a bishop for an entry permit, the Austrian government would not approve it. Some bishops frankly advised "Don't be a Rusyn, and then you will get a parish." The value of a priest was determined by his political views.

The actions of Lemko peasants would sometimes approach heroism. Many of them deprived themselves of food to send their sons to school with the intent and conviction that the son would some day become a priest and the father would have a better lot in his old age. This was the dream of every father who sent his son to a gymnazium. But to the great disillusionment and sorrow of the parents, the dream would not come to pass. The son would not be accepted into a seminary. Ruined materially, the father would be unable to give his son even the most meager support to attend a university. For this reason, the talents of many Lemko youths, able and idealistic people, were wasted after their graduation from gymnazium. Many of them left the country. If this array of youth had had the opportunity to finish university training, they would undoubtedly have played a great role in the history of Lemkovyna. Yet despite their difficult material situation, many of them went on to serve their people and work faithfully for its good, leaving a good memory in the hearts of the people.

29. The Nationality Question and Ukrainian Separatism

Since the dawn of history, the population of Lemkovyna has considered itself part of the great Slavic family, and it has always called its nationality Rusyn [East Slavic]. The names Rus', Rusyn, Rusnak have to this day been closely associated with the Lemko people and have been defended as of the highest holiness. Lemkovyna is a tribal branch of the great Rus' people,[83] who occupy vast expanses of the Earth's globe.

Throughout history, Lemkovyna, like other parts of the Carpathian Mountains, has often gone under the name *Karpatska Rus'* (Carpathian Rus'), or *Prikarpatska Rus'*, designating both the nationality of the people and the

---

83   [That is, all East Slavs form a common nation.]

territory they occupied.[84] To protect the historic name Rus', Lemkos have often had to fight and even sacrifice their lives, because enemies have tried by
various means to tear this name away from them and saddle them with another, so as to tear them away from the rest of the Rus' peoples.

As for the origin of the name Rus', scholars have proposed various theories.
It is commonly said that the word "Rus'" was brought by the Varangians, while
the word "Ross" comes from the Greeks. But some scientists claim that the
word "Rus'" existed in Rus' as far back as the eighth century, that is, before the
arrival of the Varangians. Still others hold to the hypothesis that the origin of
Rus' lies in the Scandinavian word *dros*, which meant "fraternity." They claim
that the Normans [Norsemen], who appeared in Rus' in the ninth century,
played a significant role in organizing the East Slavic tribes into a nation. One
of those Normans, Rurik, played a guiding role in establishing a national center at Novgorod. Adherents of this theory maintain that at first Rus' referred to
the prince's family and retinue, later to the tribe, and finally to all East Slavic
tribes and the territories where they lived. They cite the fact that even today
the Finns refer to Swedes as *Ruotsi*, which means shore or coast. [Or "rowers."]

The name Rus', and with it the people called by that name, has been tried
in fire and blood and has endured to this very day. The Polish gentry bathed
it in blood and scorched it in fire; the Germans tried to wipe it off the face
of the earth. But its most fearsome enemy has been its natural brother– that
monster, the independence minded Ukrainian, who for Judas's penny sold
himself into the service of its enemies and used every means suggested in
hell to erase the name Rus' from the face of the earth, and with it its people.

In 1654, the great Cossack hetman and Rusyn patriot, Bohdan Zinovyi
Khmelnytskii, succeeded in uniting Little Rus' with Great Rus'.[85] In 1709, to destroy this unity and split the Rus' people into two camps, another hetman, the
Polish lord Ivan Mazepa, betrayed Peter the Great and in the battle of Poltava
went over to the Swedish enemy with his entire Cossack army. Mazepa's effort

84   [In this case *Prikarpatska Rus'* refers to Rus' below the peaks of the Carpathian Moun-
     tains on both the north and south sides.]
85   [The terms "Little Rus'" and "Great Rus'," referring very roughly to modern-day
     Ukraine and European Russia, respectively, come from an old Greek and Roman pat-
     tern of nomenclature in which "Little" refers to an original or non-colonial area, and
     "Great" refers to a newer or larger area. For example, in Latin *Parva Graecia* (Little
     Greece) referred to Greece proper, while *Magna Graecia* (Great Greece) referred to its
     colonies in Southern Italy. A similar, but not identical, pattern can be seen in English
     in which "Greater Boston" (for example) is contrasted with "Boston proper"; in the
     Greco-Roman pattern, "Boston proper" would instead be "Little Boston."]

was in vain and he perished, as does every traitor. Many from Little Rus' followed in Mazepa's footsteps. From this comes the [Russian] term *mazepist*, that is, traitor to the people of Rus'. From the time of Mazepa's betrayal, there began within Russia a certain type of antagonism between Great Rus' and Little Rus', which [towards the end of the nineteenth century] was rechristened Ukraine.

The name "Ukraine" originally meant "the border," "the border country," or *okraina*, that is, the Rus' territory lying at the edge of the state. The word "Ukraine" was applied to border lands as seen from the national center in Rus'. It was exclusively a territorial and geographic title. In time this name was extended to include the lands of Kyiv, Poltava, Kharkiv, and in part Chernihiv, but it was always in respect to territory, not nationality.

However, the word "Ukraine" has never been applied to Podolia, or Volhynia, or the Kholm region, much less to Galicia, Bukovyna, or Hungarian Rus'. Even in the first World War, if a Russian soldier from Kharkiv was asked what he was, he would reply, "I am a Little Russian from Ukraine." Everywhere people counted themselves as Russian nationals. Even the Kyiv region, the present-day heart of Ukraine, has always called itself Rus', a Rus' land. Kyiv was ruled by Rus' princes. From Kyiv came the nationhood of Rus' and the Rus' faith [*ruska vira*], which spread throughout all Rus'. From Kyiv came Rus' literacy and Rus' enlightenment. Kyiv was called the mother of the cities of Rus'. The name "Ukraine" was a later and merely local name, just like our Lemkovyna, Hutsulshchyna, or Kholmshchyna. [Present-day] Ukraine is only a part of the lands of Rus'. It is dear to us just as are other names of Rus' lands. It is from there that the famous Cossacks were recruited, those champions of an oppressed people and its faith. The word "Ukraine" cannot be used for all Little Russian lands, but only for that portion that lies at the border, the edge of the nation to which it belongs. This name does not apply to an entire nation nor an entire people. But to the enemies of the Rus' people, this is not important. What is important to them is their goal of breaking up the peoples of Rus', of creating strife and hatred among them so as to weaken and conquer them.

To our sorrow and misfortune, our enemies have been able to find among us some blinded, greedy, and ambitious people, who for Judas's penny, like Mazepa, began to deny the name Rus', Rusyn, Russian, took up a bitter struggle against their brothers by birth and, by the same token, against their own people. What was primary for our enemies was to change the names Ukraine and Ukrainian, from their previous territorial designation to a title of nationality, to call all Little Russian peoples Ukrainian, thereby dividing Rus' and creating a fight about nationality, in other words "turning loose Rusyn on Rusyn."

Our greatest enemies have proved to be the Polish gentry, the Austrian government, and Germany.

As far back as 1848, the Galician governor Stadion changed the name of the Rusyns living in Austria from Rus' to Ruthenian: "*nicht Russe, russisch sondern Ruthenen, ruthenisch.*" ("Not Russia, Russian, but Ruthenia, Ruthenian.") In 1863, the Polish general Mirosławski called on Poles with these words: "Throw fire and bombs on the Dnieper and the Don in the very heart of Rus'; let waste, ruin, and devastation fall on Rus'. Let us create argument and strife among the Rus' people themselves. Let them destroy each other with their own claws, while we increase in size and strength."

Those bombs and flames soon did fall on Rus' land. The Austrian government gave birth to the Ukrainian party in 1891. In 1892, it introduced phonetic spelling into Rusyn [Cyrillic] script and forcibly pushed it into schools and offices. It gradually changed the term Rusyn into Ukrainian. And to give the latter a scientific basis, it commissioned gymnasium teacher Mykhailo Hrushevskii to write a history of Ukraine, promising him promotion to a university chair. Hrushevskii drudged away on this history and, after some time, brought it out in print. The story of this history is a characteristic one. Hrushevskii originally issued it in the Russian language as "History of Rus'," in which there was not a single mention of any Ukrainian people, only Rusyn. That was the first edition of this history. After a while, a second edition was issued in the Little Russian language as "History of Rus'-Ukraine," in which the term Rus' was retained in respect to Little Russians, with Ukrainian in parenthesis. Finally, a third edition was published in 1898, now "History of Ukraine," in which the term Rus' was replaced by Ukraine throughout. This was the conversion that Hrushevskii's history went through.

Nevertheless, all historians criticized it sharply as being false. Alfred Rozenburg, a minister of the German parliament, called it the fairy tale of the twentieth century, and V. Shulgin, a member of the State Council, said: "This is the wildest falsification of the century." And indeed, Hrushevskii's history of Ukraine is a story of betrayal, deceit, discord, and malevolence, and a great misfortune for his own people. Furthermore, the author himself admitted in one of the footnotes to this history: "Since we cannot accept the tales in the Kyivan Chronicle, and we have no other source, the early history of Ukraine remains unknown." With this, Hrushevskii owned up to fabricating history. Hrushevskii did not live to get a university chair, and he atoned severely for his diabolical work. He died in prison after suffering brutal treatment.[86]

The governor of Galicia, Count Gołuchowski, wrote in one of his administrative reports to Vienna: "It is necessary and imperative to contrive a difference between the language and script of the Little Russians in Galicia and that of the Russians in Russia." It is clear from these words that there was no such difference, since it had to be created. And despite strong protest from the Rusyn population of Galicia, in 1892 the Austrian authorities ordered the introduction of phonetic spelling [of Cyrillic] in all schools and government offices. They tried to show by this that the Galician tongue, as taught in the schools, is not Russian because it uses a different spelling, and the words are written and spoken differently than they are in the Russian literary language. By this means, the Austrians wanted to erase from the consciousness of the Galician Rusyns their sense of kinship with the rest of the Rusyn peoples and to make it easier to steer them toward separatism. The introduction of phonetic spelling into Little Russian writing brought undesirable consequences, because it differed from that in Russian books and literature and made it difficult to read church materials.

The harm of this phonetic spelling was perceived by P. A. Kulish, who was the first in Ukraine to use it, so that it later came to be called *Kulishovska*. In the Ukrainian newspaper Pravda [№ 9, 1865], published in Lviv, he made this announcement:

I declare that when the Polacks begin to use my spelling to signify a break between us and Great Russia, when our phonetic spelling is displayed not as an aid to people's learning, but as a banner for our Russian differences, then I shall go back to writing in the etymological [Russian literary] spelling.

Use of phonetic spelling in the Little Russian lands in Russia was not harmful, because there the Russian literary language and etymological spelling were taught in the schools, and it was often even useful when practiced by ordinary people. In Galicia, however, it was harmful, because it served the enemy by subjugating the Rusyn people. It was one of those bombs that General Mirosławski told the Poles to throw at the body of Rus'.

In the early days of the Russian revolution, the then Minister of Education in the Russian government, Manuylov, an Armenian by birth, also partially introduced phonetic spelling into Russian literary writing and abolished the letter *yat*. The Soviet government went even further with these changes

---

86 [Hrushevskii died in prison during the Soviet persecutions of the 1930s, having previously lost his sight.]

by ordering them to be used in schools everywhere. In those circumstances and in those difficult times when a new era for mankind was developing, this was perhaps even necessary. Today, however, this matter requires correction, which must inevitably occur someday.

In his commentary on this topic, Professor Bernadskii wrote:

The old orthography (etymological spelling) is a symbol of unity in Russian literary culture. Therein lies its greatest importance and, if only for this reason, it must be protected. The old orthography was adapted to the linguistic practice of the various dialects and vernaculars within the Russian language. The new orthography severely disturbs this equilibrium. It is adapted only to the Great Russian tongues, and by no means all of those. Therefore, the new spelling cannot properly be called Russian, and Great Russian only in part. Little Russians will have a new and serious reason to claim that the Russian orthography does not suit them. Hidden behind such innocent changes in letters lie great dangers.

All this leads to the thought of "some secret scheme against the unity of Russian culture."[87] The reason why Professor Bernadskii was so set against the introduction of the new phonetic spelling for Little Russians, and the spelling reform in the Soviet Union, is that the formerly single etymological spelling common to all Russians has been broken up into many different spellings, leading to chaos and confusion.

On terms similar to those offered Hrushevskii, the then professor Emiliyan Ogonovskii was commissioned to compile a Ukrainian grammar, while Smal-Stotskii was directed to compose a reader and a textbook on Ukrainian literature. The words Ukraine and Ukrainian were introduced gradually into school textbooks. In the first edition, the term "Russo-Ukrainian" was used; in the second the order of this expression was changed to "Ukraino-Rusyn," while in the third only the term "Ukrainian" remained. As Hrushevskii had falsified history, so were all schoolbooks for learning falsified. Under the patronage of Austria and Germany, and under the leadership of the Polish gentry, the Ukrainian party grew using lies and distortions.

We know of cases where the Austrians and Germans gathered Little Russian prisoners of war into special camps where they were brainwashed and taught that they are not Russians, but belong to a distinct Ukrainian people who should have their own separate nation. Such prisoners were better fed and better clothed in

87   *Russkaia Mysl'* (Russian thought), 1923.

special uniforms, were trained as agitators, and were sent to Russia. The Austrians and Germans helped in every way to build an "independent" Ukraine, providing it with both a central council and Hetman Skoropadskii.

On this subject of Ukrainian separatism, I quote the words of the Galician Ukrainian A. Kaminskii, who soberly and frankly analyzed and illuminated the Russo-Ukrainian topic in a brochure:

> Those interested in Ukrainian separatism are primarily the Polish element in right-bank Ukraine and the leading pioneers of Ukrainian freedom. This seems a little odd, but that's the way it is. The right-bank Poles sense and understand that Poland cannot extend as far as the Dnieper and the Black Sea. If they should attempt to build a Poland in the right-bank region, even from afar, they would merely stir up anti-Polish sentiment. They therefore strive with all their might to build a Ukraine, working with Ukrainian patriots. They know that a Ukrainian state would strengthen Poland's position and ensure its existence. A Ukrainian state would have to enter into all kinds of intrigues and would subordinate itself to them so as to withstand Russia. He who, in this situation, yearns to build a Ukraine beyond the boundaries of Russia is building not Ukraine but Poland.[88]

Ukrainian separatism penetrated Lemkovyna by way of Ukrainian priests, who were sent there not to proclaim the word of God, but rather to propagandize Ukrainian independence. The people quickly recognized these wolves in sheep's clothing and, except for a few weak souls, have stood firmly on the ground of their *ruskost* (Rus'ianness), maintaining to this day their national honor and faithfulness to their heritage.

30. Enlightenment in Lemkovyna

Throughout its history, Lemkovyna has been a source of many stories, legends, proverbs, poems, and songs. Lemkos are very musical and love songs. Lemko songs are extraordinarily melodious. Many Lemko melodies have been

---

88   *Halychyna Piemontom* (Galicia as a Piedmont).

Elementary school classroom. Krynica, late 1930s.

appropriated by their Polish neighbors. The sensitivity and sentimental nature of the Lemko, the picturesque scenery of his mountains, and in addition
his passionate love for his own people and faith, as well as his hills, have given
rise in Lemkovyna to some profound poetry and lovely melodies. Reflected
in these songs are the Lemko joys and sorrows, his dreams, his yearnings, his
customs, and above all, his deep patriotism. It would be very desirable if some
young Lemko would gather up all these Lemko songs and publish them in
print. Such a national treasure must not disappear.[89]

The first books in Lemkovyna appeared with the adoption of Christianity.
They were written in the Cyrillic alphabet and the Old Slavonic language.
These were liturgical books, the two testaments of the Holy Scripture, which
were published and printed in Cracow and Kyiv.

Schools

The first schools in Lemkovyna were established near the end of the sixteenth century. Some large parishes organized parochial schools, where
reading was taught from the Holy Scripture and other liturgical books.
The teachers at these schools were initially priests, and later there were

---

89   [See Bogdan Horbal and Walter Maksimovich, *Lemko Folk Music on Wax Cylinders (1901-1913) and American Records (1928-1930)*, Lviv, 2008; http://lemko.org/
books/78.html.]

cantors. They were paid in produce, most often oats. As far back as 1638, such a school was established in Powroźnik. It was authorized by the bishop of Cracow, Jakub Zadzik, in a document dated February 13, 1638 in Radłów; he designated the local priest as teacher, who was to be paid a bushel of oats per year from each resident in the parish. For this, as it says in the document, the priest was to "accustom the children of the village chief [*sołtys*] and all his subjects to Polish and Rus' learning and teach them Polish writing, prayer, and church ritual."[90] Similar schools were set up on the Hungarian side of the mountains. Supervision over these schools was exercised by Przemyśl bishops on the Galician side and Prešov bishops on the Hungarian side of the mountains. The government of aristocratic Poland cared nothing at all about schooling in Lemkovyna and kept the people in darkness, but Austria did go a little further. When a "Regional School Council" was established in Lviv, with "County School Councils" in the counties, the parochial schools were gradually replaced by state schools, with [Lemko] Rusyn as the language of teaching. However, the number of such schools in Lemkovyna was very small at first and was increased very slowly. Such schools were also set up in Rusyn villages on the Hungarian side, but there the teaching was only in the Magyar language.

The first teachers in Lemko schools were Poles. When a teachers' college was opened in Krosno, in Lemkovyna, many Lemko students applied and on completion were posted to Lemko villages. The material situation of a village teacher was very poor. His initial stipend barely came to five hundred kronen. This was less than the pay of a gendarme, caretaker, or postman, and even less than the maintenance of a government horse. A teacher's working conditions were catastrophic. To support their often large families, some of them had to take up humiliating work, such as school janitor, village field worker, or even cowherd. In addition to their school duties, Lemko teachers usually worked in agriculture or as village scribes. Many teachers died prematurely from tuberculosis. More than a few of them had to leave the teaching profession. The hopelessness of their situation, persecution, and contempt led more than one to despair and suicide. To earn a meager pension it was necessary to work in teaching for thirty-five years.

Many Lemko teachers have rendered great service to our people and have left some good memories. To preserve their everlasting memory, here are some

---

90 Manual (Schematism) of the Apostolic Administration of Lemkovshchyna for 1936. [Available at http://lemko.org/pdf/shem1936.pdf.]

of their surnames: Savchak in Krynica, Chervynskii in Łabowa, Milianych in
Powroźnik, Hreniak in Brunary and Banica, Rusyniak in Hańczowa, Ustskii
in Żdynia, Krynytskii in Binczarowa, Stanchak in Polany and Olchowiec,
Nalisnyk in Krasna, Hurko in Małastów, Kuzmich in Izby, and in more recent years Iurkovskii in Skwirtne, Poloshynovych in Wysowa, Vyslotskii in
Hańczowa and his daughter in Kwiatoń, Trokhanovskii in Krynica, Barna and
Enkala in Wróblik, Gaida in Trzciana, Baiko in Barwinek, and many, many
more. They maintained their faith in their people, worked zealously for them,
and left a good memory in the hearts of the Lemko people.

　　In aristocratic Poland, if someone wanted to give his child a secondary
schooling he would have to send him to some monastery, where the teaching
was entirely in Latin. With the coming of the Hapsburgs to Austria, German
was added. Later, the Poles managed to get secondary and higher schools for
themselves, where Polish was taught in addition to Latin and German; or
Magyar in Hungary. Lemkos eagerly took advantage of these Polish or Magyar schools and sent their sons to gymnasiums and universities. On the Galician side, the secondary schools were located in some of the county seats,
such as Nowy Sącz, Sanok, Jasło, Krosno (a technical school), Gorlice, and
on the Hungarian side, Bardejov, Prešov, and Uzhhorod. Initially, students

*Students including (1) Stefan Zabawski from Skwirtne with Prof. Roman
Maksymovych, headmaster of this Ruska Bursa. Gorlice, 1935.*

went to university in Vienna, later in Cracow and Lviv. The Lemko people gave the world many illustrious, renowned, and highly educated people, including some with doctorates, who gained high standing in the world, but more about them later in this history.

Student Hostels

To make it possible for sons of poor parents to study at secondary schools, and get some reliable protection, *bursas* or student boarding hostels were set up in some towns, where the students would get all their sustenance for a small payment. These hostels were supported by donations from all over Lemkovyna, donations from America, membership dues, and student fees. The first such hostel was established in Nowy Sącz in 1898. The story of this hostel was told earlier in the section entitled "Nowy Sącz." Members of the societies "Rus' National Home" and "Beskid" established another in Sanok. Fifteen gymnazium students were housed in this hostel. It was supervised by Father Iosyf Moskalyk, gymnazium catechist, and Dr. Mykhailo Ladyzhinskii, gymnazium professor. This hostel housed a "Circle of Gymnazium Youth," which had a library containing Russian books. There were weekly meetings of all Sanok youth attending gymnazium, at which they studied the Russian literary language, Russian literature, and Russian history. The Russian language teacher was Evhenia Lastochkin from Russia. This circle had to be secretive; in Austrian times, teaching of the Russian language was prohibited. A student caught with a Russian book was immediately expelled. The Ruska Bursa in Sanok lasted until World War I. The Sanok gymnazium graduated many Rusyn intellectuals with high honors, among them Dr. Emilyian Fedorenko, who became a Russian general and chief commander on the western front during the Second World War.

The third Lemko student hostel was the "Ruska Bursa in Gorlice," which was established a few years before World War I on the basis of funds provided by the Lemko intelligentsia and peasantry. In the course of time, a second story and a large courtyard were added. This hostel accommodated forty Lemko secondary and public school students and was superbly operated. The students were taught Rusyn language and Rusyn history. Of great service to this hostel was its long-time director, gymnazium Professor Dr. Roman H. Maksymovych, a preeminent teacher and a benefactor of youth. Considerable service was also rendered by the Gorlice lawyer, Dr.

Iaroslav Siokało, chief organizer in the Gorlice area. This hostel graduated many Lemko patriots, including the widely known American activist, Dr. Symeon S. Pyzh, a man of great wisdom, a scholar, organizer, and patriot.[91] The Gorlice hostel suffered the same fate as the one in Nowy Sącz. During World War I, all of its property was appropriated by Dr. Przybylski. After the war, the matter was taken to court, and the property was returned to its rightful owners after lengthy litigation. Major repairs were made to the building, and in 1930 a new hostel was reopened. It lasted until 1939, that is, until World War II began.[92]

In 1908, a "Boarding School for Girls" was established in Sanok. This accommodated thirty girls from the public schools and the teachers' college. It recruited primarily from among the daughters of Lemko priests, who were taught literary Russian and Russian literature. Its mistress and teacher was the Russian lady Evhenia Lastochkin, who managed the school very well. The director was Dr. Aleksander Saviuk, a lawyer and principal organizer of Rusyns in the Sanok area. This school did not play much of a role in the life of Lemkovyna. It ceased to exist in 1914, at the start of World War I.

Journalism

Articles in the Lemko idiom began appearing in various Russian periodicals about sixty years ago. The first one was in the monthly *Slavianskii Viek* (Slavic era) published in Vienna. It was a humorous piece entitled *Yaki u Nas Liude Mudry* (How wise are our people). The Rusyn public that read this journal became aware of Lemkos for the first time. Several short stories about Lemkos appeared in subsequent issues.

A few years before World War I [in 1911-1914] came the first Lemko newspaper, "Lemko," published in Nowy Sącz and printed by Jakubowski's print shop. The publishers and editors were Dymytrii Vyslotskii, under the pseudonym "Hunianka," and Ivan Rusenko. This was a newspaper of national enlightenment, illustrated and with a humorous appendix embellished with caricatures drawn by Rusenko. It was delightful reading for Lemkos and it

---

91   [Pyzh was active in the North American Lemko Association. See his entry in the Encyclopedia of Rusyn Culture for more information.]

92   [The *Ruska Bursa* in Gorlice was reconstituted in the 1990s. In the first decade of the twenty-first century, Gorlice region Lemko-Rusyns gained full legal control of the building and land. A cultural and publication program is being carried on.]

Various newspapers vying for readership in Lemkovyna during the interwar period.

had a wide circulation. Dymytrii Vyslotskii also published "calendars" [annual almanacs] and Lemko songs. Hunianka enjoyed great rapport with the Lemkos. World War I interrupted the publication of this newspaper. Vyslotskii was arrested and sent to Vienna, where he was incarcerated in a military prison and, along with other Lemko activists, was put on trial in a political atmosphere; more on this in another section.

The Lemko people also benefited from Rusyn publications issued in Lviv. Almost every thinking Lemko was a member of the Mykhailo Kachkovskii Society, which published a *Listok* (Leaflet) along with monthly brochures on educational and economic subjects. Other periodicals read were *Halychyna*, *Prikarpatska Rus'* (Carpathian Rus'), *Russkii Holos* (Rusyn Voice), *Holos Naroda* (Voice of the People), *Vola Naroda* (Will of the People), *Zemledilec* (Agriculturalist), and *Selrob* (*Selski Robitnyk*, Village Worker.)

Libraries

Just about every Lemko village had a Mykhailo Kachkovskii reading room with a small library containing Kachkovskii brochures, Father Ivan Naumovych's publications, the journal *Nauka* (Learning), a history of Rus', Duda's publications, stories and scholarly articles on science, and books on religion and morals such as the *Poslannik i Knizhochki Misiiny* (Messenger and missionary booklet) published by Father Bilous.

In larger libraries one could find Russian classics by such authors as Pushkin, Gogol, Lermontov, Turgenev, Dostoevskii, Tolstoy, Saltykov, Shevchenko, and others. The Lemko libraries became victims of confiscation by Austrian gendarmes during World War I. When a brochure printed by Kachkovskii [in Austrian Lviv] was found in a Lemko cottage, that was enough for the gendarmes to declare the owner a "Moscophile" who should be arrested. Mykhailo Kachkovskii had been a councilor at the court in Stary Sambir. After long years of hard work and modest living, he retired and donated all his savings for the purpose of educating ordinary villagers. These funds were used to establish the Mykhailo Kachkovskii Society in Lviv and to publish booklets for the people. For the Austrian authorities, who wanted to keep the people in eternal darkness, this was salt in their eyes.

Educational Movement

Lemko youths swarmed to education and learning. They enlisted en masse as members of reading rooms and organized amateur groups, choirs, and various undertakings such as theatrical shows, concerts, lectures, and lessons. A new world opened up for the people, who had until then been kept in darkness. A new spirit flowed over our mountains. Everywhere was heard Rusyn song, everywhere was new life.

In some villages there arose "Fire Brigades," in which Lemko young men were organized for a special purpose. The motto of all these organizations was one proclaimed by that great lover of the Rusyns, the priest Ivan Naumovych: "Pray, study, sober up, work."

World War I brought an end to all the educational and cultural activities of the Lemko people. All their gains fell victim to the Austrian butchers. The people were enslaved, and their brightest stars were forced into prisons and the infamous Talerhof compound, where they stayed until the breakup of the "all powerful" Austrian Empire.

*Teodor Goch, the founder (in 1968) of the Lemko Museum in Zyndranowa.
Zyndranowa, 2002.*

Members of the German-commanded OUN(B) regiment "Nachtigall-Solovii" marching down the street near their training center in Krynica, 1941.

PART III:
FROM WWI THROUGH WWII

View on the grounds of Muzeum Budownictwa. Nowy Sącz, 2005.

Prologue to Part III

В Сараєвіморд зділано	There was a murder in Sarajevo
И цілый світ порушано,	That disturbed the whole world,
Якийсь жыван, може банда	Some kind of criminal or a gang
Застрілила Фердинанда.	Shot Ferdinand.
Загучало, зашуміло,	Buzzing and roaring followed,
В світі крику наробило,	Causing an outcry around the world
Вельку войну спричынило,	And starting a big war,
На людях ся всьо отбило.	It impacted everyone.
Австрия войну выдала	Austria declared war
Сербии, што была мала.	On Serbia, which was small
Не могла ся боронити,	And was unable to defend herself.
Мусіла о помоч просити	Therefore she had to ask for help
Россию, державу сильну,	From Russia, a powerful country,
До помочы завсе пильну.	Always eager to help
Німец з Турком на Россию,	Germans with Turks against Russia,
На Францию и Бельгию.	France and Belgium.
А Талиян на Австрию,	And Italy against Austria,
А незнати в корість чыю,	It is unknown to whose advantage,
А потом ся так звязали,	Later they made alliances,
Вельку войну розпочали.	They started a big war.
Отчули зме внет ворога.	Soon we heard from the enemy.
Война была дуже строга,	The war was very fierce,
Як лем довга Лемковина,	All across Lemkovyna,
Для никого не новина,	It was no surprise to anybody

Як Германцы з Мадярами
Знущалися над Лемками:
Єдных, як собак, стріляли,
Другым рукы звязували.

До арештов спроваджали,
На шыбеницях вішали,
Иншых били и копали,
Многых в обозах тримали.

Люде барз голодували,
Бо істи им не давали.
Знущалися, як злы духы,
Люде гынули, як мухы.

Шибениці, шыбениці,
На них вісят без ріжниці
Найліпшого Лемков роду,
Без причыны и доводу.

Нич невинны, а их вина,
Што их край то Лемковина,
Што то єст славянска земля
На ней жыє русске племя.

Зарыдала Лемковина
В морю крови вся краина.
Всядый боль, плач, всядый горе,
Слез и крови ціле море.

А далеко за горами
В швабском краю за лісами,
Находится лагер смерти,
Де было найлучше вмерти,

How the Germans and Hungarians
Tormented the Lemkos:
Some were executed like dogs
Others had their hands tied.

They escorted them to jail,
And sent them to the gallows,
Others they beat and kicked,
Many were kept in concentration
    camps.

People were starving
Because they did not feed them.
Mistreated them, like devils.
People were dying like flies.

Gallows, gallows,
They hang them there unconcerned
The best sons of Lemkovyna,
Without a cause or proof.

Though innocent, they are guilty
That their homeland is Lemkovyna
That it is a Slavic land and
On it reside Rusyn tribes.

Lemkovyna is wailing
The whole country is covered with
    blood.
There is pain everywhere, crying and
    sorrow,
Tears and blood to fill an ocean.

And far behind the mountains
And forests, in the land of Krauts
You find a death camp,
There it was best to die,

Штобы уйти швабскых рук,	In order to escape those Kraut hands,
Позбытися страшных мук.	And avoid dreadful torture.
Талергоф каждому званый,	Talerhof is known to everyone
Там Лемко в крови скупаный.	There the Lemko was bathed in blood.
Высміяный и скопаный,	Disgraced and kicked,
И там збитый, скатованый,	And there, beaten and tortured
Горш от пса трактованый,	Treated worse than a dog,
А слезами все заляный.	Always covered with tears.
В Талергофі под соснами	In Talerhof under the pine trees
Земля скута могилами,	The earth is etched with graves
Де заснули сном спокойным	Where they fell asleep in a tranquil dream
Мученикы, жертвы войны.	Martyrs, victims of the war.
Соткы Лемков загынуло,	Hundreds of Lemkos perished,
З Талергофу не вернуло.	They didn't return from Talerhof.
Соткы Лемков повішено,	Hundreds of Lemkos were hanged,
Русске знамя поганьблено.	The Rusyn banner put to shame.
А в Горлицях у вязниці,	And in a prison in Gorlice
На подвірю от улиці,	In the backyard away from the street
Розстріляти Сандовича,	They executed Sandovych
Без процесу, без облича.	Without a trial, without cause.
Впал до тюрмы з револьвером,	Entered the jail with a pistol
Якись ротмистр под ордером,	An unknown captain with an order,
Казал вязня выкликати,	Ordered the inmate be brought out,
Без процесу розстріляти.	And executed him without trial.
На подвіря поставили,	They stood him in the courtyard
Штырі кулі выстрілили,	Four bullets were fired
Отец Максим без памяти,	Father Maksym became unconscious
З лицьом ясным, як бы святый.	With a bright face, like on a saint.

На знак креста зложыл рукы,
Проголосил такы звукы:
Да жывет Русь, віра свята,
Ты Австрийо буд проклята!

По тых словах склонил главу,
Упал в крови на мураву,
За лемковску долю кроваву
Отдал Богу душу праву

За край, за народ, за віру,
Отдался Богу в офіру.
З Брунар декан Петр Сандович,
Сын його Антон Петрович

Были разом увязнены
В Новом Санчи уміщены.
Над ними был суд войсковый,
Выдал вырок барз суровый.

Вывезли их на стрільницю,
Святой Гелены околицю,
Там из вырок отчытано
И обидвох розстріляно.

Обох, хоц не виноватых,
Засудиди сендзі-каты,
Што над нами ся знущали
И жытя нас позбавляли.

Теофиля Мохнацкого
В ничом невинуватого

He placed his hands in the sign of
   the cross
And proclaimed these words:
Long live Rus', and the holy faith,
Austria, may you be cursed!

After these words he bowed his head
Fell on the wall covered in blood
For the Lemko bloody plight
Gave his just soul to God

For his country, for his people, for
   his faith
He offered himself to God.
From Brunary, Deacon Petro
   Sandovych
His son Anton Petrovych
   [Sandovych]

Were imprisoned together
Locked up in Nowy Sącz.
They had a military trial
And received severe punishment.

They were driven to an execution site
In the district of Saint Helen,
There they read them their sentence
And both were executed by firing squad

Both, though innocent
Were sentenced by
   judge-executioners
Those that tormented us
And deprived us of our lives

Teofil Mokhnatskii
Innocent of everything

В Грибові жбіры злапали И го збили, скатували.	Was caught by thugs in Grybów Beaten up and tortured.
А потом го розобрали, З чого втіху вельку мали. На рынку го повісили, Потом трупа согыдили.	Later he was undressed, From that they got great joy. They hanged him at the market square, Later they desecrated his corpse.
Много иншых трупом пало, Меже нами их не стало, А што правы были з роду, Одойшли по нагороду.	Many others also died, They are no longer with us, But since they were righteous from birth, They went to their reward.
Боже, им милостив буди Не памятай за их блуды, Чисты душы воз оттуды, Дай им небо за их труды.	Lord, have mercy on them Do not remember their sins, Take innocent souls from here Give them heaven for their troubles.

....

Царскы троны ся запали, Цары з тронов поспадали, Свой маєстат пострадали И карі ся дочекали.	Tsars' thrones collapsed, Tsars fell from their thrones, Their Majesties got it in the neck And their punishment came.
Такий был епилог войны, В котрой стогнал весь світ збройный: Николюшку розстріляно Вічну памят заспівано,	That was the epilogue of the war In which groaned the armed world: Nicholas was executed Eternal memory was sung.
Вилюсьови наказано, На то пят минут му дано З цисарства абдыкувати И до Бельгии утікати.	Wilhelm was punished In that he was given five minutes To abdicate his kingdom And to run to Belgium.

Там мусіл дырва рубати,
Штобы з голоду не сконати.
Франц Йосифу шнурок дано
И остро му наказано

В Бургу тихо сой сідити
И до Бога ся молити.
Одного дня вчасно вранці,
Повісился на фіранці.

Кєпско было и з Карольом
И з його остатньом рольом,
Пришло му ся бідувати,
Бо уж не мал свойой хаты.

Ани істи, ани пити,
Ани в што ся приодіти,
Ни пінязи, ани поля,
Ах, несчастна його доля.

Горка судьба, впрост неволя,
Прийшла біда на Кароля.
Благородна його жена,
Маєстату позбавлена,

Колись бідных ратувала,
А днесь сама в біду впала.
Велький нам жаль пані Зиты,
Але так мусіло быти.

Прийшол конец пануючым,
ВельBy'ым владзом и могучым.
Днеска дзядом жебруючым,
Пановати уж не суцым.

There he had to chop wood
In order not to die from hunger.
Franz Joseph was given the rope
And he was severely punished

To sit quietly in Schönbrunn Palace
And pray to God.
One day early in the morning,
He hanged himself from
   a curtain-rod.

Karl did not fare better either
In his final act,
The time came for him to suffer,
Since he lost his [royal] house.

Nothing to eat or to drink,
And nothing to wear,
No money and no land,
Oh, unlucky is his plight.

A bitter fate, just like servitude,
A bad time came for Karl.
His noble wife
Was deprived of her majesty,

She assisted the poor in the past,
And now she was poor herself.
We feel sorry for lady Zita
But that is how it had to be.

An end came to the masters,
Great authorities and those with
   power,
Are today's panhandling beggars,
No longer fit to rule.

Колись в світі панували,
Днесь дзядами позостали.
Sic Transit gloria mundi,
Hodie rex, cras sors vagabundi.

Before, they ruled the world,
Today they are beggars.
Thus goes the glory of the world,
Today a king, tomorrow a vagabond.

....

Народ почал розмышляти,
Яку бы власть с себе мати,
Кого до власти выбрати,
И як тот строй ма ся звати.

People began to think
What kind of government to have
Whom to elect to authority
And how this government should be
    called.

Строй Річпосполитом назвали,
Президента сой выбрали,
Высшы рангы фельдфеблями
Полковников министрами,

They named it the Polish Republic,
They elected a president,
To high ranks, sergeant-majors,
As ministers, colonels

Назначыли и выбрали
И уж полный ряд мали.
Всяка драмь голос мала,
А лівиця втяж мовчала.

Were designated and elected
And they had full power.
All sorts of bastards had a voice
And the left remained silent.

Як лівиця ся озвала.
Пилсудчина и Ендекы,
Береза ся отверала.
Ридзы, Славой, ріжны Бекы.

When the left spoke up,
Followers of Piłsudski and NDs
Opened Bereza Kartuzka.
Rydzes, Sławojs, various Becks

Польшом так овладіли,
Же никто другий не мал силы
Клику тоту розогнати
И порядок ту зділати.

Ruled over Poland in such a way,
Nobody else had any power
Let's disperse this clique
And bring order here.

Двадцет роков аж минуло,
Нове горе ся всунуло,

Twenty years already passed
New sorrow came upon us

Котре гитлеризмом зване | Which was called Hitlerism
И до тепер отчуваме. | Whose pain we feel even today.

....

Засмутилися Карпаты, | The Carpathians were saddened
Як прийшли до нас псубраты, | When those bastards arrived,
Гитлеровцы, дрань германска, | Hitlerites, German scum,
Каты, горшы от поганьства: | Executioners, worse than the pagans:

Людей били, катували, | People were beaten and tortured,
До роботы наганяли, | They forced them to work,
И над каждым ся здзівали | Everyone was abused
И невинных мордували. | And the innocent were murdered.

Близ Кракова в Освєнцімі, | Close to Cracow in Auschwitz
При так зв. «Смертной Стіні» | Near that "Death Wall"
Там знущалося гестапо, | There the Gestapo maltreated us
Ище горше было капо. | But the kapo was even worse.

Там то людей мордовано, | There they murdered people
И палено, и стріляно, | They burned and shot them
Много там жертв з Лемковины: | There are many victims from Lemkovyna
З Ясла, Санча, Горличины. | From Jasło, Nowy Sącz, and the Gorlice region.

Отец Шалаш из Мысцовы, | Father Shalash from Myscowa
И Попадюк, зять Корновы, | And Popadiuk, son-in-law of Kornova
Отец Борыс з Вороблика, | Father Borys from Wróblik.
Ціла украинска клика | The whole Ukrainian clique

Вірно Гитлеру служыли, | Faithfully served Hitler.
На нас Лемком доносили. | They denounced us Lemkos.

Сам Подсадник и Корнова,
Знає о том вся Лабова.

Even Podsadnyk and Kornova
   themselves;
All know about it in Łabowa.

Много людей полапали,
А Німці их выстріляли.
Людей гынуло цілы масы,
Бо настали тяжкы часы.

They caught many people
And the Germans executed them.
Whole masses of people died
A difficult time came upon us.

Священников цілы гурмы
Пхали людей там до тюрмы.
Заміст Богу ся молити,
Пошли Гитлеру служыти.

Groups of priests
Steered the people to prison.
Instead of praying to God
They went to serve Hitler.

Люде до лісов втікали,
Жытя своє ратували,
По певницях часто спали,
На ялицях ночували.

People ran off into the forest,
Trying to save their lives,
Quite often they slept in cellars
Some slept among fir trees.

А як то ся надоило,
Патриотизм в них впоіло,
Взяли вилы и лопаты,
И зачали швабов прати.

And once they were fed up,
They became patriotic,
They took pitchforks and shovels,
And started to attack the Krauts.

Пак ліпше ся узброили,
В партизанов замінили.
А в Горлицях у Донского,
Штодня партизанов много.

Later they armed themselves better
And became guerrillas.
And in Gorlice under Doński
Every day there were more
   insurgents.

Ту радятся, узброюют,
Свои силы умоцнюют.
Сам Гомулка там заходит
И нараду з ними водит.

Here they plan and arm themselves
Strengthening their forces.
Gomułka drops by in person
And consults with them

Як отчызну боронити,
Гитлеровцов в задок бити.

How to defend our land
Kick the Hitlerites in the butt.

Тож лемковска партизана
Вшиткым добрі была знана.

Бо Лемкы Гитлера прали,
До Берлина го загнали.
Много Лемков в бою впало,
Але Німцьом ся не вдало

В нашом краю позостати
И в неволі нас тримати.
Як Совіты ся зъявили,
Лемкы им то заявили:

Што в их войску хтят служыти,
Штобы Німців ліпше бити.
Лемковский полк ся народил,
Лемковину освободил.

С того барз мы рады были,
Штобы Гитлера ся позбыли,
Што го дябли з собом взяли,
Бы ним пекло замітали.

Бо гитлеризм то неволя,
Несчастлива людей доля.
А сам Гитлер родом з пекла,
Бо натура в него встекла.

Хотіл славян вынищити,
Пришло му як псу згынути,
На могылі в його псярни,
Зросли Німці Федеральны.

It was those Lemko guerrillas
They were well known to everybody.

Because Lemkos fought Hitler,
They drove him back to Berlin.
Many Lemkos lost their lives fighting
But the Germans did not succeed

At remaining in our homeland
And keeping us enslaved.
When the Red Army arrived
Lemkos declared to them:

That they want to serve in their army
So they could also fight the Germans
A Lemkos regiment was born
And Lemkovyna was liberated by
them.

From that we were very happy,
To get rid of Hitler,
So that the devils took him with them,
Let them sweep hell with him.

Because Hitlerism equals slavery
An unhappy fate for people.
Hitler's birth is straight from hell
Because his nature is rabid.

He wanted to exterminate the Slavs
So he had to die like a dog
On the grave of his kennel
Federal Germany grew.

(Из *Пісні о Лемковині*)　　(From *A Song About Lemkovyna*)

The Krasovskii family: parents Maria and Dmytro and children Anna, Mykhailo, Kateryna, and Ivan. Deszno, 1941.

Vasyl Maksymovych (1) with other villagers and the German soldiers taking these photos. Deszno, 1941.

Celebrations in Krynica, 1942.

German soldiers and Lemko women peeling potatoes. Besko, 1942.

1. The International Atmosphere Before The First World War

By the beginning of the twentieth century, the international situation had become very tense. The capitalist nations of England and France reigned over large areas in all parts of the world. The Germans, on the other hand, had started developing capitalism much later and found the world already divided up. However, they soon overtook the older capitalist nations of Europe with regard to industry and exports, and began intensive preparation for war and a new division of the world. German imperialism was directed primarily against the interests of England. The Germans began building a navy in order to challenge England's might and its supremacy on the seas. They gained a hold on Turkey, so that from the Near East they could threaten the British dominions in Asia and Africa. They also heightened their antagonism with France. They threatened France's control of its colonies in Africa, while France wanted to regain the province of Alsace- Lorraine and the Saar Basin grabbed by Germany in 1871.

Not only did the Germans strive to gain control of the colonial dependencies of England and France, but their aggressive policy was also aimed at conquering the lands of Poland, Ukraine, Belarus, and the Baltic states.

Tsarist Russia wanted to acquire the Dardanelles and Constantinople and to gain patronage over the Slavic peoples in the Balkan Peninsula. Russia's plans also included occupation of Galicia and Carpatho-Rus'. The principal incendiary elements in international relations were the Balkans and the Near East, where the interests of four imperialist powers collided: England, Russia, Germany, and Austria-Hungary.

All these conflicts led to the formation of two hostile camps. As far back as 1882, a bloc of countries– Germany, Austria, and Italy– formed the so- called Triple Alliance. Feeling threatened by Germany, France and Russia agreed on a pact in 1893, which England also joined in 1907. Thus was formed the so- called Triple Entente to counteract the Triple Alliance. When other countries joined in this alliance, it came to be known as the Coalition or Entente, while the Triple Alliance took the name of the Central Powers.

The governments of all these nations began preparing for war with increasing energy. The number of separate armies grew like yeast, and expenditures on armaments ate up enormous sums in national budgets. Ordinary people, oppressed and exploited both politically and economically, were not happy and waited impatiently for change in this feudal system.

The situation in Europe became one that needed only a spark to ignite the flames of war instantaneously. Such a spark was not long in coming. It was soon struck and it inflamed the whole world.

2. The Direct Cause of the War

On June 28, 1914, in Sarajevo, the capital of Bosnia, which had been seized by Austria, Archduke [Franz] Ferdinand, heir presumptive to the Austro-Hungarian throne, was assassinated by a Serbian student named Gavrilo Princip. Germany decided to take advantage of this murder. Under pressure from Germany, Austria gave Serbia a sharp and humiliating ultimatum. Although Serbia, on advice from Russia, made considerable concessions, Austria's pride was not satisfied and on July 27, 1914, it declared war on Serbia.

Russia, allied with Serbia, announced a mobilization, and Germany declared war on Russia. When German troops invaded neutral Belgium, England declared war on Germany. This was a painful blow to the German government, because it had not expected England to go to war. Japan soon joined the Coalition and declared war on Germany. Japan's aim was to take over the German possessions in the Far East. Turkey and Bulgaria joined the Central Powers. The war encompassed more and more countries and became a world war.

To bring their people into active support of the war, the various governments roused their publics to a sense of nationalism and hatred of other peoples.

The guilty parties in World War I were the imperialist powers of both blocs, above all the insatiable German imperialism.

Military drafts began immediately on the announcement of mobilization. A time of grief and despair began in Lemkovyna. With tears in their eyes and pain in their hearts, wives sent their husbands off to war, children their fathers, parents their sons, all going to fight for their most illustrious lord, the Austrian Kaiser [emperor]. A black cloud settled over the Carpathian Mountains.

Sorrow, pain, and despair filled the hearts of the Lemko people. Gendarmes soon began appearing in Lemko villages to make sure that all those drafted went off to the army. The start of world war became an incontrovertible fact. Austrian soldiers were assigned to two fronts, Russian and Italian. The majority of Lemkos were sent to the Russian front.

3. Victims of the War's Terror in Lemkovyna

World War I cost the Lemkos a large number of victims. In addition to those who fell at the front in the interests of the German and Austrian kaisers, thousands perished in prisons, in concentration camps, on the gallows, and in their homes from mercenary bullets. All of Lemkovyna was dotted with hangman's scaffolds, on which its best sons died. From the very beginning of the war, Austrian prisons were filled to overflowing with Lemkos. Austrian gendarmes, using lists with Rusyn names that were given to them by Ukrainian agents and provocateurs, ran around Lemko villages like hound dogs, dragging innocent people out of their homes and deporting masses of them to jails and then to concentration camps.

In addition to Ukrainian nationalists, a dastardly role was played in Lemkovyna by some Jews, who helped the gendarmes find "Moscophiles" among the villagers. Whoever happened to be such a Jew's personal enemy was arrested and charged as a Moscophile. The Austrian authorities paid the gendarmes five kronen apiece for every Moscophile they found. The gendarmes took advantage of this bounty and supplied the military authorities with hundreds and thousands of completely innocent people who were dubbed "Moscophiles." This is how all of the Rusyn intelligentsia and all well-informed peasants were arrested. There was not a single Rusyn priest or teacher left in Lemkovyna.

The right arm of the Austrian gendarmes in arresting Lemkos were Ukrainian priests and teachers. Just as in the Second World War they served Hitler, so in the first one they served Austria. Particularly notorious as scourges

Father Maksym Sandovych, summarily executed by the Austrian-Hungarian military at the outset of WW I (August 6, 1914).

of the Lemko people were the priests Vasyli Smolynskii of the Nowa Wieś parish and Mykhailo Dorotskii of the Złockie parish, as well as the teachers Hutsuliak of Izby, Shvedyk of Brunary, Havrilo Merena of Florynka, Vovk of Berest, Lopadiuk of Sołotwiny, and the ex-gendarme Kluchnyk of Florynka. The first victims of these Ukrainian criminals were that unforgettable priest, Petro Sandovych, dean and pastor in Brunary, father of eight children, and his son Antonii Sandovych, graduate student in philosophy. They were arrested and brought before a drumhead court in Nowy Sącz, accused of high treason. Testifying as witnesses were Father Smolynskii, Father Dorotskii, and the teacher Hutsuliak. All three of them testified falsely and at great length. They wanted to prove the guilt of the accused by their false witness. On the basis of their testimony, the military court, which was composed entirely of Magyars who did not understand our nationality problems, sentenced both of the accused to death by firing squad. After the prisoners received the Holy Mysteries, this sentence was carried out that same day in St. Helen Square outside the city.

A few days later, the Orthodox priest Maksym Sandovych[1] was executed in the prison yard in Gorlice by a Hungarian captain on a tip from a Ukrainian provocateur, without any trial whatsoever. Maksym Sandovych was widely known throughout Lemkovyna. He was the son of Timko Sandovych, cantor in Żdynia. He completed lower-level gymnazium at the Ruska Bursa in Nowy Sącz. Feeling a call to the priesthood, he entered the [Orthodox] Pochaevska Lavra Monastery, from which he was called by Bishop Antonii [Khrapovyt-

1   [See http://orthodoxwiki.org/Maxim_Sandovich .]

skii] of Volhynia to the religious seminary at Zhitomir. After completing the
theological course there, he married the daughter of a priest and was ordained
by the same Bishop Antonii.[2] He returned to Lemkovyna as a priest and chose
the Orthodox parish in Grab, Jasło County, happy that he could work for
his native Lemkovyna. His happiness did not last long. Reported by Ukrainians to the Austrian authorities, he was arrested in 1913 and sent to prison
in Lviv. In 1914 we find Father Maksym Sandovych, together with journalist
Semen Bendasiuk, student Vasyl Koldra, and another Orthodox priest, Father Godym, before the bench in a famous political trial in Lviv, which was
completed before the outbreak of war. This trial was inspired by Ukrainian
nationalists and it went on continuously for three months. Several hundred
witnesses, mostly Ukrainian politicians, passed through the courtroom. The
trial ended in acquittal of all the accused.

Father Maksym went back
to his former position. But
he did not enjoy his freedom
very long. Early in the war he
was arrested again and was imprisoned in Gorlice, together
with his wife, his child, his father, and his brothers. On September 4, 1914, some Hun-
garian captain entered the
Gorlice prison, steered there
by Ukrainians, and with revolver in hand tried to shoot
Father Maksym right then and
there. When the chief warden
of the prison protested, he was

"This is the resting place of executed Fr.
Maksym Sandovych, who gave his life for
Holy Orthodoxy." Zdynia, 2000.

threatened with the revolver. The frightened warden, with pain in his heart,
led Father Maksym out of his cell. The captain ordered him to stand in the
center of the courtyard, posted four privates with carbines a few steps away,
and yelled "one, two, three." The soldiers fired their carbines. Father Maksym
stood motionless, his eyes on the mountains and his hands on a cross. Not
a single bullet had hit him.

---

2   [According to some other sources, he was ordained by Metropolitan Antonii Vad-
kovskii of St. Petersburg.]

Prayer at the burial site of St. Maksym Sandovych. Zdynia, 2000.

The captain repeated his command, and the carbines fired again. Father Maksym staggered, exclaimed in a loud voice "Long live Rus' and Holy Orthodoxy," and fell to the ground. The corporal ran over to him, and with the words "die, like a dog," aimed his revolver and fired two shots. Father Maksym gave up his soul to God. His body was taken to the cemetery and buried there.[3]

4. Talerhof

Transports full of arrested Lemkos traveled to the Talerhof[4] concentration camp, located in Styria [province], near Graz in southern Austria. This was a large area [a military airfield] by pine forests and enclosed within barbed wire fences. There were no buildings there [except for a few hangars], so most prisoners spent three months under the open sky.

3   See *Karpatska Rus'* (Carpathian Rus' [newspaper]), Nos. 5 & 6 for 1959.
4   [The original German name was *Thalerhof.*]

Their situation was desperate because it was autumn, with frequent rains and strong winds. They were encircled by barbed wire, which they could not cross on pain of death. They had to stand on their feet all day long, and in the evening they would fall down from exhaustion, sometimes on top of each other, to get through the night. In the morning they would get up on command from the guards. Humanitarian consideration was at such a low level that there was no proper place for basic physiological needs. After a few months some dug-out barracks were built, rotting straw was brought in, and the prisoners were housed there.

Some examples make apparent the depth of the degradation suffered by the prisoners. People would sit in front of the barracks picking lice off their bodies and shaking them out of their clothing, and inside the barracks the straw was alive with the rustling of hordes of insects. It is not surprising that under these unsanitary conditions typhoid fever broke out in all the

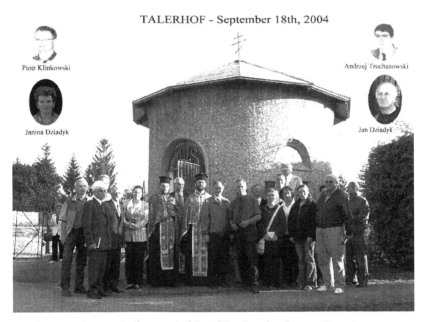

The Mausoleum in the front yard of the Feldkirchen church, near Graz, Austria, which contains the remains of almost two thousand Talerhof victims. 2004. From front/left: Alla Wozniak, Yaroslav Khomiak, Petro "Murianka" Trokhanovskii, Yaroslav Trokhanovskii, Monika Vorhach, Fr. Roman Dubets, Ivan Kosovskii, Fr. Lubomir Vorhach, Andrii Kopcha, Stefan Dychko, (behind him) Ianina Dziadyk, Stefan Dziamba, Yulia Trokhanovska, Ivan Fesh, Maria Broda, Anna Luchkovets, (hidden) Andrei Trokhanovskii, Teodor Goch and Yaroslav Horoshchak.

barracks. Every day scores of bodies were carted out to a grassy spot "under the pines." There were even cases of people dying from insect bites. While the prisoners suffered from hunger, deprivation, and filth, the camp officials would often indulge at night in feasts and drunken sprees. Saturated with alcohol, they would then order some young women to be brought out from the camp and, despite the quarantine, would rape those poor wretches. If one should dare to resist the rape, she would be shot on the spot by some drunken officer. For the prisoners' physiological needs, there was a long and deep ditch with a long pole over it. Latrine visits were made in groups, under guard, and at appointed times. The prisoners would sit down on that pole and get up from it on command. If someone should be either too slow or too quick, he would be shot immediately. Many of them met their deaths in that ditch full of human excrement.

When news of this Talerhof hell reached the world outside the borders of Austria, an international commission visited the place, and camp conditions improved rapidly. The barracks were enlarged, a latrine was built, a chapel was constructed, food improved, and people were better treated.

This concentration camp contained tens of thousands of prisoners from all over Galicia. There were about five thousand Lemkos alone. When the camp was closed down, only a handful returned home. The others all lie in blessed sleep "under the pines" of Talerhof.

Much has been written about Talerhof since the war. Those who lived through it and returned home safely have published an account of their sufferings as a group, thick volumes entitled Talerhof Almanacs[5]. Also a series of pictures of Talerhof martyrs was published. However, nobody can adequately describe orally, and no hand can effectively pen the full story of Talerhof with its Tantalian torture and the sufferings of the people that cry to heaven for vengeance. Talerhof will forever shame twentieth-century German culture. The worst torturer of the Talerhof martyrs was an Austrian officer named Chirovskii, a Ukrainian, who surpassed all the German monsters in

---

5   [*Talerhofskii Almanakh– Propamiatnaia Kniha avstriiskikh zhestokostei, izuvvertsv i na-silii nad karpato-russkym narodom vo vremia vsemirnoi voiny 1914-1917 hh.*, Lviv, Iz-danie "*Talerhofskaho Komiteta*," 1924 (and subsequent volumes.) These publications were combined into one volume by Peter Hardy, entitled *Galitskaia Golgotha: Voennie Prestupleniia Gabsburgskoi Monarkhii, 1914-1917* (Galician Golgotha: War Crimes of the Habsburg Monarchy, 1914-1917), Trumbull, Connecticut, 1964. It contains photo-offset copies of the four Talerhof Almanacs of 1924, 1925, 1930, and 1932. It is available at http://lemko.org/pdf/TalAlmanakh1-4.pdf .]

Talerhof Memorial at the Lychakiv Cemetery. Lviv, 1971.

cruelty toward defenseless people. He was a sadist of the first order, devising for his subordinates vicious ways of tormenting people. A memorial in the shape of a triple-bar cross has been placed over the burial ground of the Talerhof martyrs.[6]

5. Talerhof Congresses

"Talerhof congresses" were instituted after the war to preserve the memory of the victims of Talerhof. Such a congress would begin with a solemn liturgy for the souls of those who perished at Talerhof and other places of Austrian torture. During the liturgy, a priest who was a survivor of Talerhof would give a sermon in which he described the crucifixion of our people during the war, with appropriate responses. After the service there would be another meeting

---

6 [Eventually most remains were transferred to a mausoleum in the churchyard in nearby Feldkirchen. See *Thalerhof: The First Twentieth Century European Concentration Camp* (Lemko Association, forthcoming.)]

Fifteen thousand turn out to celebrate the dedication of the Talerhof monument at Lychakiv cemetery. Lviv, 1934.

in a reading room. One of the Talerhof survivors would present a report, which was followed by discussion and the resolutions of the congress. A third meeting would include academic studies and theatrical presentations, following which there was some friendly entertainment.

Masses of people took part in these congresses and returned home with patriotic uplift of their spirits. The largest such congress was held in Lviv in 1934. About two hundred priests and several thousand people from all parts of the former Galicia took part. After the liturgy, which was conducted in the Preobrazhenskii Cathedral, there was a grand march through the streets of Lviv to the Lychakivskii Cemetery, where a blessing was conferred on a memorial inscribed: "To The Victims of Talerhof 1914-1918. Galician Rus." This was a magnificent demonstration by the people of Galicia in the royal city of Lviv.

Many other Talerhof congresses were held in Lemkovyna, the largest of them in Sanok, Ustrzyki, Pielgrzymka, and other places.[7]

The Przemyśl bishop, Iosafat Kotsylovskii, prohibited priests from taking part in these congresses under threat of suspension. Father Panteleimon Skoromovych of Dyniska immediately sent a protest to Rome and had the interdiction rescinded. Many Ukrainian priests, filled with hatred towards Rusyns, would not allow Talerhof-survivor priests to hold services in their

7   [Reports of these meetings were printed in the Talerhof Almanacs.]

churches and locked people out. Because of this, Rusyn priests had to ask Roman Catholic priests for permission to hold services in Polish churches. Polish priests readily agreed to this. Such incidents occurred in Sanok, where Father Emilyian Konstantynovych was the Greek Catholic rector, and in Ustrzyki, where the rector was Father Mykhailo Zharskii. The people were frustrated and disturbed by such behavior on the part of Ukrainian priests.

6. The Garrison Prison in Vienna

Some of the leading scholars and villagers in Lemkovyna were arrested and transferred under heavy guard to Vienna, where they were confined in the garrison prison. This was the highest security prison in the entire Austrian nation. Among others jailed there were: Father Roman Pryslopskii, pastor in Żegiestów and chairman of the Ruska Bursa hostel in Nowy Sącz; Father Ioann Stanchak from Wysocko; Dymytrii Vyslotskii, student from the village of Łabowa; Ivan Andreika, student of philosophy from Tylicz; Teodor Mokhnatskii, farmer from Mochnaczka Niżna; Metodii Trokhanovskii, teacher in Krynica; Volodymyr Kachmarchyk, student from Binczarowa; Ivan Hassai, judge in Nowy Sącz; Father Mykhailo Iurchakevych, pastor in Czarne; Harasym Hromosiak, farmer from Krynica; Dr. Aleksander Saviuk, lawyer in Sanok; and others, about twenty all told. They were subjected to a long political trial at a military court in Vienna. Scores of witnesses were heard, mostly Ukrainians from Galicia. Foremost among these were the priests Vasyli Smolynskii and Mykhailo Dorotskii, already familiar to us. The trial ended with all the accused being sentenced *Zum Tode durch den Etrang veruvtiett* (to death by hanging) as traitors to the Austrian state.

The sentence was not carried out, thanks to the intervention of the British King and of Countess Zofia Potocka Zamoyska, who was in the service of Karl, Crown Prince of Austria at that time. Countess Zamoyska was the patron of Wysocko, where Father Ioann Stanchak was pastor. She gained an audience with Prince Karl through the Papal Nuncio in Vienna and managed to get the sentence rescinded, pledging her life and her property for the prisoners and testifying that they had not engaged in any spying but were involved only in cultural and educational work within the framework of registered institutions. The prisoners were granted amnesty and were freed. The proceedings of this trial and related documents are in the possession of the family of one of the accused, Sofia Stanchak Venhrynovych in Krynica-Zdrój. They make very interesting reading for historians and lawyers.

7. Slaughter of Common Folk

In their reports from the front, Austrian officers blamed all kinds of failures on the local populace. Whole groups of people were slain after every such failure. Before a coming battle, the Austrians would gather up a few or a dozen hostages, hold them at some special place, and then hang them on the nearest trees after the battle was lost. Hundreds of completely innocent people perished by the rope. Many Lemkos died at the hands of individual soldiers, mostly Hungarians. It often happened that a Hungarian private would encounter one of our villagers and ask him "who are you?" The villager would answer "I am a Rusnak." Then with a Satanic, diabolical cry of "Rus, Rus," the Hungarian soldier would draw his carbine and shoot the guiltless person

From "The Talerhof Almanacs."

dead. Nobody would come around to see whether the victim was guilty or innocent, because no army man was ever held responsible for killing a civilian. Many people died through the actions of Ukrainian provocateurs. The hanging of the members of the Wierchomla Wielka village council was well known. In the early days of the war, when Russian troops began to take over Galicia, some Ukrainian type appeared in Wierchomla out of the blue and declared himself a Rusyn patriot. He showed up at the village hall where the council members were in session, praised Russia, and sharply criticized Austria. He talked about the easy life in Russia, the nobility of the Russian tsar, the freedom there, and so forth. On the other hand, he spoke of oppression in Austria, of the Austrian kaiser's hatred of our people, Austrian bondage, and so on, and so on. Finally, he posed the question, "Who would you rather belong to, Austria or Russia?" The council members replied: "If it is as good in Russia as you say, then of course we would rather belong to Russia than to Austria." With that, the man left the hall. The same man appeared in the village late that night, but this time in the uniform of an Austrian gendarme and with a carbine in his hand; with him were several other gendarmes. All the members of the council were rounded up, chained, taken to Piwniczna, a neighboring village, and there they were all hanged on trees as traitors to their most illustrious lord. There were many similar scenes in Lemkovyna. Masses of people died at the hands of soldiers, gendarmes, provocateurs, and other such scum.

Lemkovyna was a principal arena of military activity. The front remained there from halfway through November 1914 until the end of May 1915, more than six months. Decisive battles were fought in Lemkovyna. It was the scene of the most military fatalities and the most civilian fatalities in the war. It suffered the most in both human and property losses. The war machine gutted Lemkovyna through its entire length and breadth. Many villages were burned, many demolished, and many denuded of grain, cattle, and every other means of livelihood. The war played havoc with the Lemko's material and moral resources, but it did not destroy his spirit. In a book entitled *Na szlakach Lemkowszczyzny* (On the trails of Lemkovyna)[8], the Polish publicist Dr. Krystyna Pieradzka describes this historic time thus:

> The commander of any army unit had the power of life and death over the people. Hundreds of Lemkos were put to death by the Austrian cowards to mask their defeats, and thousands were sent off to Talerhof,

---

8   [Available online at http://lemko.org/pdf/pieradzka.pdf.]

an Austrian concentration camp. Ukrainians played a sorry role as informers for the Austrian gendarmerie. So far, none of the perpetrators of these atrocities have been brought before any court. This tragedy of an innocent people must be understood and honored.

This is the testimony of a Polish historian and observer of the events in Lemkovyna.

8. Lemkovyna as an Arena of War

In the first two years of the war, Lemkovyna became the arena of some of the most notable events of the war, namely the Russian counteroffensive in the Carpathian Mountains after November 1914, and also a four-day battle at Gorlice on May 2-6, 1915.[9] These two events weakened the Russian army so badly that as a consequence Russia lost not only the part of Galicia it had occupied but also the [Polish] Congress Kingdom, Lithuania, and Volhynia. From the viewpoint of strategy, the geographical location of Lemkovyna was very favorable for the Austrian armies, but became a trap for the Russians. Lying on the north side of the middle Carpathians, which are not very high, Lemkovyna has several low mountain passes into the broad valleys of Subcarpathia. Roads lead from these passes along the lines of: (1) Dynów-Czeremcha, (2) Dukla-Barwinek, (3) Żmigród-Ożenna, (4) Gorlice- Konieczna, (5) Ropa-Wysowa, (6) Grybów-Tylicz, (7) Nowy Sącz- Krynica-Muszyna. Cutting across these roads was a main road along the line Nowy Sącz-Gorlice-Dukla-Sanok. Any army that entered these valleys would find itself trapped in a pocket. This is exactly what happened to the Russian army when it came into this region. The consequences were catastrophic for the Russians.

---

9   [See "Book Review Article: World War I in the Carpathian Mountains," *Karpatska Rus'*, Vol. 80, 2008-2010, No. 3/4, where nine books about the Carpathian Winter War are discussed.]

9. Military Operations in Lemkovyna

In September 1914, the Austrian armies, defeated at the battle of Lviv, began retreating toward the Dunajec River and out of the Carpathians. The Third Army retreated toward Gorlice. A part of the Second Army, hampered by a wave of refugees, went through the Carpathians by way of the Dukla and Rymanów passes. A week later, however, these armies returned to the offensive in the San valley. After another defeat in the San-Vistula sector, the Third Army retreated on November 10 into western Lemkovyna and took up positions in the wide valleys of the Gorlice area. This army was exhausted, demoralized, tattered and hungry, thinking only of how to get as far away from the enemy as possible.

An army headed by [the Russian] General Brusilov appeared with the first snowfall. In the vanguard came a cavalry patrol, moving carefully; behind them came rank upon rank of giants wearing sheepskin hats and with song on their lips, heading for Hungary. Everyone was overjoyed that with the march into Hungary there would be a victorious end to the war. This colossal army wound its way through all the passes of Rymanów, Dukla, Krempna, and Gładyszów.

On November 27, a battle broke out in the Dukla-Konieczna pass. Russian troops drove far to the south, thirty kilometers from the crest of the Carpathians. On December 1, they captured Bardejov, Muszyna, and Rytro, and on the following day Nowy Sącz. To the west, they reached the Cracow-Myślenice-Mszana Dolna-Krościenko line, and were threatening German Silesia.

On December 6, the Austrians put all their forces into a counter offensive. Battles fought at Chabówka and Limanowa ended favorably for the Austrians. Austrian troops, with the help of Polish legions led by Piłsudski, regained Nowy Sącz and pushed the Russians back. They managed to occupy the Jasło-Sanok plain to the Tuchów-Odrzykoń-Besko line, but could go no farther. In the course of 10 days, the Russians regained the main crest of the Carpathians but could not reach the roads to Wysowa and Krynica nor the Poprad and Dunajec rivers. Under these circumstances, in early January 1915 the front was strung along the road from Gorlice through Gładyszów and Konieczna to Zborov. There it remained for four months until May 2, 1915 without major changes, except for bloody thrusts to either side, mainly in the region of Konieczna-Regietów-Banica-Jasionka. The high ground to the east of this road was held by the Russians, that to the west by the Austrians. For four winter months the Gorlice and Krosno regions of Lemkovyna were in the hands of the Russians, who were preparing there to mount a decisive offensive that would open the way for them through Hungary to Vienna.

After four weeks of defending the passes, from January 26 to February 5, 1915, the Russians pushed the Austrians thirty kilometers to the south and threatened to break through into the Hungarian plain. The Austrian front was shaken. The Czech 28th Infantry Regiment [from Prague] went over to the Russian side on Good Friday near Zborov. Surrounded at Przemyśl, [Austrian] General Kusmanek surrendered on March 24 with his garrison of 150,000 men. The winter war in the Carpathians was fought under terrible conditions for the troops on both sides. Men froze to death in their trenches by the score. Deep snow made any kind of movement impossible. An unexpected thaw turned the roads into swamps. Men were soaked to the skin. A return to freezing weather changed clothing into icy armor. Hunger (at best there was frozen canned food) and lack of warm clothing killed more men than did bullets. Losses on both sides made it necessary to bring in more troops, new divisions. Two thirds of the Austrian army became casualties in the Carpathians in April. Austrian losses came to more than 600,000, of which 80,000 were fatalities. Russian losses were just as high. A total of 160,000 men went to their eternal rest in Western Lemkovyna. The offensives produced no results. They did not open the way to Vienna for the Russians, and they did not enable the Austrians to come to the aid of the garrison surrounded in Przemyśl.

The battle of Gorlice was an entirely different matter; it was of utmost importance for the outcome of World War I. The front extended from the mouth of the Dunajec through Tarnów, to south of Gorlice, where it made a right-angled turn to the east along the Carpathian Mountains. Gorlice was the terminus of the trans-Carpathian route which barred the way into the valleys the Russians were using to get to Hungary. A detailed plan of attack was drawn up by the Austrian General Conrad and the German General Hindenburg, while the breakthrough was in the hands of General Falkenhayn. Massive artillery fire was to be used for the first time on this front.

According to this plan, the Eleventh Army, composed of four German corps and one Austrian corps, was to hit the Russian front in the area of Gorlice over a line of thirty-two kilometers. At the same time, the Austrian Ninth Army, coming from the mouth of the Dunajec, and five divisions of the Austrian Third Army south of Gorlice, were to attack between Małastów and Konieczna. In the whole area, the entire Austrian army had half a million men and over a thousand artillery pieces. On the other side, the Russians were about a third weaker in men and much weaker in artillery, and, worst of all, were short of ammunition. In the region of Gorlice, they had only three divisions against the Austrians' ten. Between Małastów and Konieczna, they had one division facing five.

The Russians did not expect that they would have such a hard time repulsing the armies of the Central Powers. They were confident of their own strength, and over four months they made no further preparations. While the Russian governor, Count Bobrynskii, was reorganizing Galicia into the Russian system and while Tsar Nicholas II was making a triumphal visit to Lviv, the Austrians were secretly moving masses of German troops by fast train to the rear of the Ciężkowice-Gorlice sector.

10. The Battle of Gorlice

The battle of Gorlice commenced with great force on May 2, 1915, at six o'clock in the morning. For the first time on the eastern front[10], there was a hurricane of cannon fire, which destroyed all the Russian trenches and nearly the entire city of Gorlice. At ten o'clock that morning, one hundred thousand bayonets began attacking on a line over thirty kilometers long. The Russians put up a strong defense. Only after heavy losses were three tactical points captured by the Austrians, but with heavy losses: Pustki Hill, the cemetery and the castle. By the afternoon, the bombed ruins of Gorlice were also taken. Of all the Galician towns, Gorlice suffered the most in this war.

After the capture of Rypnik and positions around Małastów, the Russian front was broken for a distance of forty-five kilometers, that is, from Gromnik to Pętna, to a depth of four kilometers. The Russians underestimated the seriousness of the threat, as attested to by the fact that General Dimitriyev, headquartered in Jasło, committed only a small amount of reserves to Gorlice.

The Third Caucasian Corps advanced on May 3 to break through in the Żmigród-Jasło sector, but this help was too late. The Germans and Austrians

---

10   [A similar thing happened at the Battle of Tannenburg-Grunwald in 1914 with similar results.]

kept attacking continuously. On May 3, they occupied other positions and advanced an additional five kilometers to the east. The German Combined Corps drove a narrow wedge thirteen kilometers to Cieklin, on the third Russian line of defense. On May 4, it took the last Russian position in the Cieklin-Wał sector and drove a wedge sixteen kilometers farther, right up to Żmigród itself, cutting off the Russians fighting in the hills and preventing them from withdrawing to Krempna. The front was broken, and on May 4 it was pushed back six kilometers farther.

On May 5, the Combined Corps pushed up to Dukla and cut off the Dukla pass. The Russians doggedly defended the approaches to Jasło, but in the north they withdrew about ten kilometers. Jasło fell on May 6 and Krosno on May 7. In battles at Lubatówka and Iwonicz, the Combined Corps reached Rymanów. There the troops returning from Gorlice met cavalry coming from the mountains to Czeremcha. A third route for Russian withdrawal was cut off.

The Gorlice area of Lemkovyna now became a boiling cauldron in which half the Russian forces fighting on the north slope of the Carpathians were caught. These units, numbering nearly twenty thousand men, were being pursued from the east by five divisions through Krempna and Żydowskie, by two divisions and a brigade of cavalry from the Dukla pass, from the north by three divisions on the Żmigród-Iwla-Dukla line, and from the east by a cavalry division on the Jasło-Czeremcha road. In attempts to break through, the Russians became scattered and surrendered in small

Vladek Petryshak in Austrian military uniform, sent as a postcard to Marysia of Krynica selo. Vienna, 1913.

groups in the area between Dukla and Chyrowa. The well-known General Kornilov was captured. The last military action in Lemkovyna was the formation of an eighty-kilometer front on a line from Wisłok Górny to Frysztak on May 8 by twenty divisions, and counter attacks by the Russians on the following day. After that day, the Russians were no longer able to withstand the increasingly strong enemy forces.

It must be realized, however, that the Germans and the Austrians had expected an easier victory. Despite excellent preparation and superb strategy, they found it hard to bring down the Russians, who fought with uncommon bravery. The battle of Gorlice opened up great possibilities for further action by the Central Powers. Important events now followed each other closely. Lviv fell on June 22 and Warsaw on August 6, followed rapidly by Brest, Vilnius, and Lutsk. By the fall of 1915, the Russians had lost, in addition to Galicia, all those parts of Poland they had previously controlled, plus Lithuania; they halted at the border of the postwar Poland. The action between May 2 and May 12 that took place between the Dunajec and San rivers was the turning point in the war between Russia and the Central Powers.

The brutal plowshare of war had torn up Lemkovyna from end to end. The name of almost every village there is a synonym for at least one battle. The flames of war had scorched this formerly peaceful land and left memorials in the form of cemeteries all over Lemkovyna. In some Lemko villages, such as Gładyszów, Żydowskie, and others, church services were still being held in temporary chapels as late as 1938, because churches had not yet been rebuilt. Remnants of trenches dug during the Great War can still be seen in the hills, and in many places there still are roads paved with fir logs that were used for moving cannon into position. In all of Lemkovyna there are fifty-four cemeteries where soldiers were buried. One of the most striking of these is close by the road from Gorlice to Konieczna, while the largest is at Pustki near Gorlice. The Ropa River and its tributaries are thickly dotted with cemeteries on both sides, right up to the border. There are seven such cemeteries between Ropica Górna and Sękowa, indicating how fierce the fighting was there.

Austria kept fighting until 1918. Little by little the front lines of the Central Powers began breaking down, and in November 1918 World War I came to an end on both the eastern and southern fronts. Rebellious Austrian troops, seeing the futility of further war, threw down their arms and returned to their homes in chaotic disorder. New nations rose out of the ruins of the Austrian Empire.

Wartime Cemeteries in Lemkovyna

In World War I, Lemkovyna was the theater of a long-lasting Austro-Russian front. Fierce battles were fought there in the early days of May 1915, which resulted in defeat of the Russian forces and their withdrawal from Lemkovyna. The land of the Lemkos was left scarred with trenches and cemeteries as memorials to those battles. Although much time has gone by since they were fought, military trenches, huts and a variety of other shelters, and roadbeds laid with lumber that were used to move artillery into position can still be seen in the hills and forests. Most of the trenches were dug on a hill called Magura near Małastów.

Many men fell in those battles, on both sides of the confrontation. Their bodies were buried hurriedly in shallow temporary graves in fields and woods, near cottages, and even close to wells. Villagers often found uncovered and decomposing bodies in the forests. The most elementary principles of hygiene were violated in those burials.

To prevent a variety of epidemics, the Austrian government organized in Cracow a special unit called the *Kriegsgraberabteilung* (war graves commission), whose task it was to build the necessary number of military cemeteries, exhume the bodies, and rebury them in these new cemeteries. Austria hurried to build these cemeteries before peace was signed, so that it could use Russian prisoners of war for the work.

This special unit was divided into twelve crews, each of which was assigned a different job. One was supposed to clean up war debris, another to establish the identities of the bodies, a third to find evidence of burials, and the rest to do the technical work of building cemeteries. Among the officers in this unit there were

WW I military Cemetery No 60 atop Magura Hill, near Malastów. 2005.

WW I military Cemetery № 51 atop Rotunda Hill near Regietów. 2011.

architects, masons, painters, and all the other professions needed for this kind of work.

To speed up the work as much as possible, it was decided to start building simultaneously over all the territory where battles took place. To this end, ten *Kriegsgrabbezirk* (military cemetery districts) were established within the region from Żmigród to Tymbark and Szczucin. Lemkovyna was divided into three districts: Żmigród, Gorlice, and Limanowa.

On the territory of Lemkovyna there are fifty-four wartime cemeteries containing 1,260 individual graves and 617 mass graves, with each of the latter holding several dozen bodies of soldiers, mostly Russians.

Each military cemetery district was headed by a "district chief." These chiefs were officers trained as architects or painters who designed the cemeteries for their districts. For some of the cemeteries, contests were held in which artists, painters, and architects from other districts took part. Because of this, all these burial grounds in Lemkovyna look similar architecturally. The most interesting of all the cemetery districts is the one at Żmigród. The man in charge there was the well known architect Dušan Jurkovič. He built his cemeteries in the Old Slavonic style, and so they harmonize with the Lemko style and form. The most attractive of his cemeteries is the one on top of Magura near Małastów, near the road from Gorlice to Konieczna. It is built in the form of an ellipse and surrounded by a row of thick logs of fir topped with caps made of shingles, in the style of Lemko churches. Inside the cemetery are small wooden crosses, and on the back wall is a small chapel also made of logs. At the ends of the ellipse there are shingled canopies. On top of each canopy are is three crosses, joined together, with an image of the Mother of God between them. The whole impression is that of being framed by the fir trees of the nearby forest. This cemetery reminds one of a small, cozy Lemko village cemetery.

Not far from there is another cemetery on a hill that can be seen from far off on the road to Gładyszów. This one is also built of wood and is similar to the one on top of Magura, except that instead of a small chapel it has a steeple in the center of a round cemetery. The steeple is fifteen meters high and rests on a massive stone base. The upper part is made of wood covered with shingles. A cemetery on top of Rotunda Hill east of Regietów contains five such steeples, arranged so that the one in the center is the highest with the other four around it being a little lower.[11]

In Konieczna, right by the Slovak border, is a third cemetery with a steeple built by Dušan Jurkovič similar to those on Rotunda Hill but made entirely of stone except for a cap of wood shingles.

Among the cemeteries built by Jurkovič, mention should also be made of one at Grab. It departs in style from the others, but by a happy combination of stone and wood it makes a strong impression. A stone roof capped with wood shingles covers the cemetery in the form of a rosette, while the gateway is in the form of an small chapel, also of stone and with a steep roof of wood shingles. There also are two other small chapels in the side walls. At the back wall there is an altar-like structure above which rises a nineteen-meter steeple.

Jurkovič's work where he built entirely of stone is not so good, for example the cemetery in Krempna. In the center is a weighty memorial in the form of a round wreath of oak leaves, lying flat on four high pillars. If it were not for its overpowering mass, the whole thing would resemble a garden arbor. Around this memorial are circles of radially arranged graves, among which stand two large crosses.

In addition to those described above, there are a large number of cemeteries in various localities around Żmigród.

In the southeast corner of Gorlice County, there is scarcely a single village without a wartime cemetery. These are in the form of a square with low walls

---

11 [See http://www.beskid-niski.pl/index.php?pos=/obiekty/cmentarze/rotunda .]

and an iron gate. Within the walls are rows of graves marked by iron crosses. On the west wall is a stone structure shaped like a triangle or a throne from which rises a high wooden cross.

In the third or Gorlice military cemetery district, which lies north of the Żmigród district, the work was directed by Hans Mayer, who put primary emphasis on strength and impressive facades. Mayer built with stone. The cemeteries he designed can be recognized by their thick stone walls covered with stone slabs. The front walls and the driveways are decorated with high pylons that can be seen from a distance. There is one such cemetery on a hill east of Małastów. Others are located between Małastów and Ropica Górna, and in Sękowa.

It is easy to get a sense of the ferocity of the battles between the Austrians and the Russians from the number of cemeteries. There are seven of them on the hills between Ropica Górna and Sękowa. There are mass graves in the fields in many places, e.g., in Binczarowa at the foot of Jawor Hill, on the Chełm side of Wawrzka, in Florynka beside the main road, and in other places.

Johann Eger, the builder and director in the Jasło cemetery district, showed some originality in his approach to the task. On "Walachy Hill" near Cieklin, he found over twenty mass graves scattered through the woods. He did not move them, but just walled them in where they were and left behind a crooked little road about four kilometers long. From a distance, the place where these graves are located looks like a little chapel with a steeple at the edge of the forest.

Similar to the Lemkovyna wartime cemeteries are two large and prominent ones on Polish land, one in Gorlice and the other on Pustki Hill near Łużna. The Gorlice cemetery is situated on a high hill above the city and is visible from all directions. Leading up to it is a road lined with trees and some small benches. Its gateway is a large structure in the old style. This gigantic cemetery is traversed by little paths between which are stone crosses in straight rows. In all, there are 140 individual graves and 161 mass graves. In the center of the cemetery is a stone cross on top of a high steeple, designed by Gustav Ludwig; to which are affixed two tablets, one honoring the Poles who died for their native land and the other honoring the Germans.

Another cemetery notable for its tremendous size is located north of Łużna on Pustki Hill. This hill was the site of the most stubborn Russian defense. There was a furious battle here. This Pustki Hill cemetery is by far the largest of all. In separate clearings in the forest lie Russians, Austrians, Germans, and Hungarians. Each group has its own section with a stone memorial and a forest of wooden crosses. Throughout each clearing, there are paths, stair steps, handrails, and benches. On top of the hill is a wooden tower twenty-four meters high, decorated with shingled canopies. On the tower is an oratory with a carved figure of Christ carrying a cross. In this cemetery, there are 829 individual graves and 46 mass graves, each of the latter containing a few dozen or a few hundred bodies.

The wartime cemeteries in Lemkovyna are the fruits of fratricidal warfare among Slavic peoples fighting for the interests of dominating rulers— the old man and idiot Franz Joseph, the *hochstapler* (con-man) Wilhelm, and the mystic Nicholas [II of Russia]. The blood of the slaughtered soldiers cried to heaven for vengeance. And this revenge was not long in coming. Even before the final end of the war, the thrones of all three of these monarchies had crumbled to dust. The liberated peoples began a new life.

11. After World War I

Once the Austro-Hungarian monarchy and the Kaiser's Germany were shattered, all the Slavic peoples began building their own states. After being disappointed in an attempt to build a democratic state, some Lemkos turned their sights toward Russia, while others started looking to America, from which they expected aid and support. Russia was undergoing a revolution and civil war; there was little to hope for from there. The chances for help from America were better, especially after President Wilson promised self-determination for all peoples. Lemkos put their trust in this concept of self-determination and began forming committees that created "national councils" on both sides of the demolished Austro-Hungarian border. The representatives of the old regime had fled from Lemkovyna, and the people sensed freedom.

The focal point of Lemko organizing was Prešov. Convening there was the "Carpatho-Rusyn National Council," which was composed of representatives from the various local councils in all of Lemkovyna, that is, all of western Carpathian Rus'. The chairman of this Council was Dr. Antonii

Beskyd, former delegate to the Hungarian Parliament. He went to the Paris Peace Conference to present the wishes of the Carpathian people. The principal desire of these people was to unite all of Carpathian Rus' into a single entity and gain autonomy. However, nothing came of all these efforts. In the end, Carpathian Rus' was divided into three parts, with Lemkovyna divided in two, one part on the Polish side and the other on the Slovak side. The American Lemko delegates to the peace conference at Saint-Germain-en-Laye also achieved nothing.

In the meantime, in the part of Lemkovyna on the Polish side of the Carpathian Mountains, there began to arise Lemko republics, evidence of the strong desire of Lemko people for freedom and independence. Such republics sprang up in Florynka, Grybów County; in Gładyszów, Gorlice County, and in Wisłok Niżny, Sanok County. At first, the Poles were favorably inclined toward these republics (an example was Dr. Ramolt from Grybów). But when they strengthened their own organizational forces, these republics were put down and their organizers and administrators arrested and charged with treason to the Polish state. In his "Czerwona Kalyna" almanac, Fr. Kokovskii mentions other republics such as those in Przemyśl and Tarnobrzeg. Soon to be published in Lviv is a work by Petro M. Kohut with more details on this matter.[12]

12. Lemkos In "Sanation" Poland

After the war the Poles in all three partitions of the country were united into a single entity and a free and independent Polish state was declared. The Lemkos accepted this development with enthusiasm, because they had hopes that life would be easier in a Slavic state than it had been under the former Austro-German rule. However, they were soon disappointed. [After 1926] Poland became a fascist state, antagonistically inclined toward all other Slavic peoples. It tried in every way possible to denationalize the Lemkos. As in the old days of aristocratic Poland, so too now the Polish prefects and their gendarmes persecuted the Lemkos and denigrated their

12 [Unfortunately this book was never published.]

faith, their nationality, and their mother tongue. The fascist authorities acted to remove all Lemko-born teachers and other intellectuals from educational work among Lemkos, forcing them completely out of their profession or transferring them far away, to somewhere in Pomerania to work among Germans and Poles.

School officials set up purely Polish schools in purely Lemko villages, and chose the most chauvinistic teachers for these schools. There were incidents where a Polish teacher who knew no Lemko-Rusyn language did not want to go to a Lemko village, explaining to the school inspector that he could not communicate with the children since he did not know their language. They would not understand him and he could not understand them. The inspector replied: "In time, you will learn this language from the children, and that will suffice." And so an illiterate teacher went off to a Lemko village.

Well known at the time was the case of a teacher in Skwirtne, Nikolai Iurkovskii, an admired Lemko activist, whom the authorities transferred far away to Kielce Province to do his teaching. When Iurkovskii was leaving the village to go to his new position, a crowd gathered from neighboring villages and tearfully escorted their beloved teacher to the village limits, where police used carbines to disperse them. The Skwirtne villagers stopped sending their children to school, which resulted in more terror, arrests, and heavy fines.

Polish teachers tormented Lemko children. It often happened that a teacher would beat a child to unconsciousness merely for using a Lemko word. All

kinds of protests and complaints were ignored. And if such complaints became frequent, then police or even troops would be sent to pacify the village. The police or soldiers would beat the most prominent villagers unmercifully and even plunder their property. There were even some Polish pseudo-scholars who maintained that Lemkos are not Rusyns but just "some lost Polish tribe." Even birth and death certificates had to be made out in Polish. To make it impossible for Lemko students to get into Polish universities, a *numerus clausus* (literally, "closed number"; a quota) was

Nikolai Silvestrovych Iurkovskii (1895-1956), teacher from Skwirtne.

put into effect, limiting the number of university admissions. Only Poles could be admitted to universities. This explains why there are so few Lemkos who completed university studies in "Sanation"[13] Poland. Our people could get administrative jobs only by signing a declaration to convert to the Roman Catholic faith. This tactic was gradually also applied to physical laborers. Only Roman Catholics could eat bread in "Sanation" Poland. Lemkos were shut out from military promotion. Only a Pole, and a Roman Catholic at that, could become an officer. Rusyn

*Polish propaganda leaflet from 1939,
"Lemkos— Forgotten Poles."*

professors at universities were relieved of their posts, which meant that they were fired. One of these was a Lemko, Dr. Tyt Myshkovskii, born in Pielgrzymka, who was in the top tier of scholars at the University of Lviv.

"Sanation" Poland tried by every means to destroy Lemko Rus', which was salt in its eyes. Noteworthy is the procedure followed in voting for the Sejm [Parliament], as well as that for taking a census. All kinds of laws and rights were violated here. The local polling site was the school. The election was certified by the chairman of the elections commission or his deputy. The ballot urn lay on a table, guarded by two policemen. The chairman had the key to this urn. Voters made their selections on cards, which they then put into the urn. The voting took place before noon. At noon there was a lunch break, and the chairman went out to lunch, leaving his deputy and the policemen to watch the urn. While the chairman was gone, the policemen sent the deputy out for cigarettes, opened the urn with a duplicate key, and dumped out all the cards, replacing them with their own prepared

---

13   [After an attempt at democracy from 1918-1926, a *coup d'état* led by Józef Piłsudski established an authoritarian regime. Piłsudski's political movement was commonly referred to in Polish as *Sanacja*, or in English "Sanation," a word derived from the Latin *sanatio* (healing), in reference to the "healing" of public life that it preached. *Sanacja* has also been translated "Sanitation," in reference to the movement's calls to "clean up" society.]

cards and re-locking the urn. All of their replacement cards had the name or number of the government's candidate. At nine o'clock in the evening the votes were counted. The urn was unlocked, the cards were pulled out, and counting began. All the votes turned out to be for the government candidate, despite the fact that not a single person had actually voted for him. Also surprising was the fact that more cards were taken out of the urn than there were voters. Nobody protested or raised any objections. The prefect commended the chairman of the elections commission "for properly conducting the election." A similar honor was accorded the author of this farce, despite sharp protests against such illegality and demands to invalidate the election.

When a census was taken, the entry on the "religion" line of the form was always "Roman Catholic," regardless of whether the person was Greek Catholic or Orthodox. The "nationality" line said "Polish," even if the individual was Rusyn. By such means, solidly Lemko villages appeared in census reports as Polish and Roman Catholic. Data from these reports were used for various computations and statistics. It is thus no surprise that on the basis of such data the number of Lemkos did not increase but decreased. The officials and functionaries of "Sanation" Poland were good at lying and deception.

13. Lemkos Under Slovakia

The position of Lemkos [called Rusyns or, usually derogatorily, Rusnaks] in Slovakia was even worse. The Slovaks recognized absolutely no rights for Lemkos. They didn't even admit the existence of Lemkos. When they revised their statistics, they unceremoniously converted every Lemko into a Slovak, and there was no appeal. Teaching in schools was entirely in Slovak. Cyrillic was replaced by Latin script, even in church documents and private correspondence. The Slovaks recognized neither the faith, nor the speech, nor the written language of the Lemkos. "There are no Rusnaks in Slovakia, only Slovaks," proclaimed Slovak politicians. But the Slovaks learned the truth of a principle voiced by Lenin: "He who oppresses other people loses his own independence."

14. Socio-Political Relations in Transcarpathia

During World War I, when Hungarian gendarmes arrested hundreds of Rusyn villagers and shipped them to concentration camps, the Uzhhorod Bishop Chernokh called a conference of the clergy subordinate to him. At this conference it was decided to eliminate the Slavic alphabet in Transcarpathia and replace it with Latin script and Magyar phonetics [that is, using the Hungarian writing system]. Soon after that, the Mukachevo bishop, Antonii Papi, a rabid Magyarophile [also called "Magyarone"], followed Chernokh's example. The aim of this change of writing system was nothing less than to transform the Transcarpathian Rusyns into Magyars and open up a deep chasm between Uzhhorod and Mukachevo on one hand, and Kyiv and Moscow on the other.

On November 19, 1918, as the Austro-Hungarian empire was hurtling into the abyss, its loyal vassals, the Greek Catholic clergy headed by their bishop, announced the organization of a "Council of Rusyns in Hungary," which issued the following manifesto: "The Rusyns must support their old homeland (Hungary) and protect its territorial inviolability. By the same token, they reject all attempts to tear the Rusyns from their Magyar homeland," and so on.

As a consequence of the decision to eliminate Cyrillic script in Transcarpathia, the priest Avgustin Voloshyn, a teacher and educator, published a whole series of textbooks in a Magyar transliteration for Rusyn schools. Budapest paid him handsomely for this.

Soon, however, the Magyarophiles concluded that any hope of continued Hungarian dominance was an empty dream, and they began to flirt with Prague. These traitors tried by every means to have Czechoslovakia, the only power that could save them from popular wrath, take over Transcarpathia. The compromised renegades faded into the shadows, and their place was taken by new figures, previously unknown. These felt that it would have been more convenient to have Hungarians in charge rather than Czechoslovakia, about which they had their doubts and which they regarded as only a "seasonal state" [one springing up in the fall and gone by spring]. They soon linked up with Galician Ukrainians who believed strongly in a revival of the German empire. Under the influence of the latter, the Magyarophiles came to the conclusion that the best regime for them would be a German one, because only a German hand would keep a stranglehold on the throat of the people while treating the Magyars graciously. Transcarpathian politicians were divided on this point. The eyes of some were turned towards Budapest; others, towards Prague and even Berlin. The people, instead, dreamed of being together with the other peoples of Rus'.

Prague proved generous to Transcarpathian politicians. It established a Central Rusyn Council and appointed the American capitalist Zhatkovych[14] as governor of Transcarpathia. His assistants Beskyd and Voloshyn each received two thousand acres of fertile land from the Prague government. Nor did others of their henchmen, especially the Greek Catholic clergy, go unrewarded. But the Czechoslovak authorities took a different tack in respect to the Transcarpathian poor. Now that the Hungarian gendarmes had left the country, the villagers could follow their own inclinations. Now that the Czechoslovak constitution had proclaimed "freedom of conscience," they felt that they could get rid of their despised priests. But when they tried to drive them out of their parishes, they were bitterly disillusioned. The arguments of the Greek Catholic hierarchy were more convincing to the Czech authorities than were those of ordinary people. The Prague government sent police, troops, and punitive expeditions against the rebellious villagers, who were dealt with harshly while the deposed priests were restored to their former positions. Despite the terror of 1930, however, about a third of the villagers broke with the Greek Catholic church and went over to Orthodoxy.

Years went by. Rapacious Germany got up on its feet again under the leadership of the cannibal Hitler. The Holy See concluded a concordat with Hitler's German Reich [on July 20, 1933]. Under the black flag of fascism, Hitler went on the march to conquer the world. The reactionary forces of fascism began stirring in all corners of Europe, and they did not forget Transcarpathian Rus'. The principal organizers of "fifth columns" and principal agents of the fascist forces were the Greek Catholic priests. They ordered the political parties subordinated to them to work for Germany, Poland, and Hungary. Their main political support during the Czech domination was the so-called "Autonomous Agricultural Union." Operating under this benign banner was a cabal of Magyarophiles whose aim was to prepare the soil for a Hungarian takeover of Transcarpathia. The leaders in this effort were Kurtiak and Brodii. Brodii was a cantor and teacher, as well as a paid agent of Budapest. Until 1918, he

---

14   [Zhatkovych was actually a lawyer.]

published in Košice a Magyar revisionist newspaper, thus earning himself appointment as secretary of the Autonomous Agricultural Union. Brodii's party was subsidized by the Hungarian government, which every month sent him fifty thousand Czech koruns through Bishop Stoyk in the guise of a "fund to defend the faith."

Another "ace" renegade was the above-mentioned Father Avgustin Voloshyn. In 1903, he was editor of *Misiatseslov* (The monthly word), in which he castigated Ukraine as "a frightful plague that alienates Rusyns from the church." For thirty years, he published a series of school books using Latin letters in Magyar transliteration instead of Cyrillic letters, which Budapest had ordered for Rusyn schools on the initiative of Greek Catholic church leaders. Then in the winter of 1919-1920, we find him in the position of president of a Directorium led by Zhatkovych. Sensing how the political winds were blowing, Father Voloshyn became one of the directors of a Czechophile Central Rusyn National Council, and for his efforts received from the government a large allotment of land. When the western winds brought news of the re-emergence of the German army, he joined up with Galician Ukrainian nationalists similar to Evhen Konovalets. When Adolf Hitler became chancellor of Germany, Avgustin Voloshyn was appointed Gestapo resident in Transcarpathia.

A third example of this sort of politician was the most ambitious of Rusyn political leaders, Stefan Fentsyk. While Brodii was serving in the Hungarian espionage apparatus and Voloshyn in the German, Fentsyk performed the functions of a secret agent for both Hungary and Poland at the same time. He was an almost daily guest of the Polish consul in Uzhhorod, Chałupczyński. In the style of the Italian Mussolini, Fentsyk organized young men and dressed them in black shirts. When the Magyars took over Transcarpathia, he put his black shirts at the disposal of the Magyar counter-espionage apparatus, which made use of them in dealing with the villagers.

All three of these "aces" and their parties operated under a single command and for a single purpose designed by Berlin and carried out by its satellites– Miklós Horthy in Hungary and [Minister of Foreign Affairs] Józef Beck in Poland.

15. The Economic Situation of Lemkos After WWI

The economic situation of the Lemkos deteriorated significantly after the first World War. Life became much more difficult. The long war had materially ruined the people. There was no way to improve the material situation of the villagers. Mass immigration to America was closed off. The prewar emigrants, surrounded by family, had become American citizens and no longer thought of returning to the old country. They also gradually forgot about their kin in the old country and stopped sending monetary aid to their countrymen. Emigration was reduced to a minimum. Only those who had been born in America and brought up in the old country could go to America, because they were considered American citizens. An American citizen could also bring out his wife or children or parents. But this had no effect on the general welfare of the Lemkos in the old country.

In that time of exploitation and depression there could be no thought of any American aid. Nor was there any chance of earning some money in the old country. When some job did come up, for example, in the manorial forests or on the roads or in health resorts, our people could not get it. Preference for any such work was given to a Pole on the Polish side, or a Slovak on

Cows, roaming free, destroying memorial markers at a WWI cemetery. Czarna, 2005.

the Slovak side. A Lemko could get only the jobs that a Pole or Slovak would not take. Workers were required to have a birth certificate showing their nationality and religious affiliation. In order to hold on to their jobs, many poor people declared themselves to be Poles.

The political authorities took advantage of the situation and would notify church officials that so-and-so had left the Greek Catholic or Orthodox church and had become a Roman Catholic. Such a person was then officially a Pole and Roman Catholic. This policy created large numbers of pseudo-Poles and pseudo-Roman Catholics. This fabrication of Poles was carried out by all local governments. Only those Lemkos who signed statements that they were Polish could get jobs in the administration. Such a declaration also had to accompany every purchase and sale contract.

The Lemko was thus restricted in his religion, his nationality, and his material life. Forced by extreme necessity, Lemkos began to divide their land among family members, and this had a disastrous effect on their economic situation. Such an attitude toward a minority could not develop sympathy for the government of "Sanation" Poland.

16. The Lemko Delegation to Premier Składkowski

Lemkos could not achieve anything in government circles, and all their rights as citizens were restricted. To improve at least somewhat their dismal situation, they sent a delegation to Premier [Felicjan Sławoj] Składkowski to describe their situation and present their demands to him personally. They gained an audience with him through an influential person in the government.

The premier himself set the date for May 29, 1938. On the day of the appointment, the delegates were told that the premier would probably not see them himself. They were received instead by a department head named Sawicki, who told them at the very outset that the premier could not receive the Lemko delegation, even though he had promised to do so, because that would offend the Ukrainians and he had to take that into consideration. The audience with Mr. Sawicki lasted half an hour. All the wishes and requests that

the delegates presented to him were rejected and ignored. In his final statement to the delegates, Sawicki stated that the government did not need to
consider Lemkos, because they represented no force and, furthermore, "stank
of communism." The delegates left in very low spirits, and one of them sang
in a low voice, "To Thee, oh Lord, we raise our prayer; deign to punish this
'Sanation' Poland," and this prayer was soon answered.

Among the members of this delegation were: Dr. Orest Hnatyshak, lawyer in Krynica; Iosyf Iavorskii, notary in Bukowsko; Metodii Trokhanovskii,
teacher in Krynica; and Father Ioann Polianskii, priest in Wróblik Królewski.

17. Ukrainization of Lemkovyna

Ukrainian nationalists tried by every means to Ukrainize the Lemkos, who
put up a strong resistance. Przemyśl Bishop Iosafat Kotsylovskii came to
the aid of the nationalists. He ordered the clergy under his jurisdiction to
Ukrainize Lemkovyna; they carried out his orders fervently and brought an
unhappy religious war to Lemkovyna.

Bishop Iosafat Kotsylovskii was born in Pakoszówka, Sanok County. He
completed his theological studies in Rome at the "Gregorianum" [the Pon-
tifical Gregorian University]. As a young priest he taught dogmatics at the
seminary in Stanisławów [today Ivano-Frankivsk] and then in 1911 joined
the monastic Order of St. Basil. He spent World War I in Vienna, where he
organized the clergy of the Przemyśl and Lviv eparchies and for them created
a provisional seminary located in the Moravian town of Kromeriz. Here he
made the acquaintance of the parish priest, later a bishop, Dom Stojan, who
enjoyed great influence in the Emperor's household in Vienna. Thanks to this
acquaintance, Father Kotsylovskii was appointed bishop of Przemyśl in 1917
(during World War I). He displayed smoothness and sophistication, was ath-
letic, friendly, and good-hearted, yet very tactless, stubborn, rash, rigid, and
in politics an adamant Ukrainian nationalist.

The Ukrainian community in Przemyśl twice complained about Kotsylovskii to the Curia in Rome for what the Ukrainian intelligentsia considered his
inconsiderate behavior. In his reckless way, Bishop Kotsylovskii decided to

Portrait photo of Bishop Iosafat Kotsylovskii, Przemyśl, Poland.

Ukrainize Lemkovyna. First, he suspended two Rusyn priests, so that they could not interfere with his plans. Father Karol Voloshynskii and Father Ioann Voitovych were canons, members of the Przemyśl Cathedral Assembly, and highly meritorious priests; an appeal to the Roman Curia was resolved in their favor. The Curia revoked the suspensions and ordered Kotsylovskii to apologize to the priests.

Bishop Kotsylovskii transferred older Lemko priests from Lemkovyna to the eastern parts of his diocese and replaced them with young, inexperienced priests whom he ordered to Ukrainize the Lemkos, promising them rich parishes as a reward for success. The new priests went to work eagerly, not only in the churches but also in reading rooms and even in private homes. The pulpit became a political rostrum, a place to hurl thunderbolts and maledictions at damn Russkis, Moscophiles, Bolsheviks, schismatics, heretics, etc. Instead of the word of God, the faithful had to listen to lectures on Ukraine. The people hated these priests, who, incidentally, proved to be good at collecting fees for spiritual services, so they stopped attending Divine Liturgy.

So began an intense struggle between priest and parishioners. The parishioners expected to hear the Word of God from their priest, and when the subject became Ukraine they would walk out of church. They wrote requests

and complaints to the Consistory, sent delegations to the bishop, asked for
a change of priest, threatened to return to Orthodoxy, but all this was in vain;
they might as well have been throwing peas at a wall. The bishop was immov-
able. In his mind, these priests were faithfully following the dictates of their
bishop and should be rewarded rather than chastised. Getting no justice from
the bishop, and running out of patience entirely, the people decided to break
with the Catholic Church and go over to Orthodoxy.

18. Orthodoxy and the Religious Struggle

The first parish to convert to Orthodoxy, in 1926, was Tylawa, near Dukla,
Krosno County, where the [Greek Catholic] priest was Father [Ivan] Szkolnyk, despised by the Lemkos. Other parishes followed Tylawa's example. The
newly created Orthodox parishes began building churches, typically next to
the Greek Catholic church, and inviting Orthodox priests from the Metropolitanate in Warsaw. The Orthodox churches were overflowing with people, while the Catholic ones were empty. Donations for building Orthodox
churches were great, in some cases even heroic. Two Catholic priests remained
with the people and also returned to Orthodoxy. They were Father Dymytrii
Khyliak and Father Onufrii Orskii. Father Khyliak was a Lemko, born in
Binczarowa, and had the parish in Izby.

However, not all the parishes returned to Orthodoxy in entirety. In most
of them, only a portion of the parishioners returned while the rest remained
Greek Catholic. The latter were still under the influence of Ukrainian priests.

Under the influence of both Greek Catholic and Orthodox priests, a fierce
struggle erupted among the people. In time, this became a religious war.
Armed with clubs and axes, Orthodox believers attacked Greek Catholic
churches, breaking the locks and removing church furnishings, justifying their
actions by the argument that these things had been bought with their donations and were therefore their property. Armed even better than the others,
the Greek Catholics would attack the Orthodox churches on the next night
and regain the removed articles. It sometimes happened that the two parties
met and began bloody fighting. The mutual animosity became so great that

one would inflict various kinds of pain on the other. They would break each other's windows, throw manure into wells, destroy new plantings, etc.

The administrative authorities were deaf to these rumblings, and it seemed that they were even pleased with the situation, in line with the old Polish slogan "turn Rusyn on Rusyn." In some instances, the officials even incited one against the other. These attacks and damages would end up in long court trials with fines, prison terms, and other penalties. This was one of the most grievous scenes in the history of Lemkovyna. What a great harm resulted from the tactlessness and political chauvinism of the bishop! This fraternal strife laid the foundation for establishing Lemkovyna's own [Greek Catholic] diocese with the Administrator's residence in Rymanów-Zdrój.

19. The Polish Sejm Abolishes the Word "Rusyn" and Introduces "Ukrainian"

Based on a petition by delegates belonging to the "Ukrainian Club," whose members were Dr. Zahaikevych, Dr. Baran, Levitskii, Chrutskii, Paliev, Liangh, Maksymovych, Zubritskii, Strupinskii, Yuchnievych, Vyslotskii, Dr. Blazhkievych, Dr. Pelych, Dr. Biliak, Tertakowets, Kochan, Velykanovych, Lutskii, Kunka, and Rudnitskii, the Polish Sejm on June 15, 1928 passed a law introducing use of "Ukrainian" in place of the heretofore used "Rusyn" [spelled "Rusin" in Polish]. This law was comprised of four articles, translated here:

Article 1: For the designation of residents of Ukrainian nationality in the lands of the Republic of Poland, the name Ukrainian will be used instead of the former name Rusyn. Accordingly, the names *Rusin, Rusinka* will also be replaced with *Ukrainiec, Ukrainka*. The names *Ukrainiec, Ukrainka, ukraiński* instead of *Rusin, Rusinka, ruski* will be used in all laws and all decrees of the President of the Republic, the Council of Ministers, and individual Ministers.

All government and private authorities and officials will use these names in all orders, proclamations, circulars, signets, etc. In particular, these names will be used by school authorities in all acts, registers, certificates, etc. These names will also be incorporated in school work and school books. Also, all publications, whether government, private, or issued with the aid of or for the approval of officials, will use the above names.

Article 2: In conformity with Article 1, and with regard to regulations that are binding on laws and decrees, these changes of the names *ruski* to *ukraiński* and *Rusin* and *Rusinka* to *Ukrainiec* and *Ukrainka* will be entered into all relevant laws and decrees. (There follows a list of all the existing laws and decrees in which these changes are to be made.)

Article 3: The President of the Council of Ministers and individual Ministers are assigned the implementation of this law.

Article 4: This law shall take effect on the day of its announcement.

With one stroke of a pen, and without the least bit of discussion, the Sejm of "Sanation" Poland, composed of Polish and Ukrainian nationalists who were following the path of the German cannibals, liquidated the Rusyn people within the borders of Poland. In its place, they raised a Ukrainian idol, which did not last long, because eleven years later Hitler's blitzkrieg drove its bloody sword deep into the heart of the Pole.

20. Protest by Galician-Rusyn Institutions

Against that criminal pronouncement of the "Sanation" Sejm, ten Rusyn institutions located on the territory of Poland sent the following protest to the Polish government:

In the course of the last decade, that is, from the very beginning of the new Polish State to this very moment, the Government of the Republic of Poland, irrespective of changes in personnel and programs, has always and steadfastly used and is still officially using the names Rus', Rusyn, *ruskii*. This is the name by which the Government defines that portion of the Little Russian nationality that became, by virtue of the Great War, a part of the present Polish State.

The name "Rusyn," *ruskii* officially adopted by the Government is not only based on the traditions of historical Poland, which had from ancient times used it constantly, but more important, also corresponds completely to the historical traditions of the very people affected by it.

Although proving the authenticity of this thesis would be merely the equivalent of rediscovering America, there nevertheless are instances when even an obvious truth, besmirched by some people's evil wills, must be illuminated. This is the state of affairs with the name Rus', *ruskii*.

Thanks to a fortuitous conjunction of external affairs, namely, material and moral support from Austria and Germany and the revolution in Russia, within the last two decades in the life of the Little Russian peoples a strident Ukrainian party has appeared on the stage. Having met with total defeat in its activities, this party is trying by all possible means to hold on to the hegemony that is slipping out of its hands, and among its political aims is an attempt to move the Polish Government to change officially the names Rus' and *ruskii* to Ukraine and Ukrainian.

For these reasons, the undersigned cultural and economic societies consider it their duty to call the attention of the Polish Government to the following:

I.

From very ancient times, the terms Rus' and *ruskii* have been used not only in reference to the entire Kyivan State but also to its separate parts and to all its inhabitants. This is attested to by ancient trade treaties negotiated between [Kyivan] Rus' and the Byzantine state in 911 and 944, and also attested to by all of the literature of Rus' during its historical development. "Should a Rusyn hit a Greek or a Greek hit a Rusyn," we read in the great Prince Ihor's agreement with the Greeks in 944 (*Complete Collection of Chronicles*, Vol. I, p. 19), "with sword or spear, or any other weapon, for this sin he shall pay five liters of silver, to comply with the Rusyn law."

The terms Rus' and *ruskii* are found very frequently in the most renowned monument of Rusyn writing from the period of princes, namely, "The Tale of Ihor's Campaign." For example, "Grief shall spread over the land of Rus'," "Deep sorrow flows through Rus' lands," "Beyond Rus' land, beyond Ihor's limits."

These terms were used not only within the borders of the Kyivan State, but also during the existence of the Galician-Volhynian State that arose on the lands of the Cherven fortified cities. The principal architect of this

new state was Prince Roman "the Great" Mstislavych, who called himself "Autocrat of all Rus." After the fall of the Galician-Volhynian State
in 1340, its people continued using the terms Rus' and *russkii* and have
retained them to our times.

The leaders in the literary renaissance of Galician Rus' in the first half
of the nineteenth century, namely, Markian Shashkevych, Iakov Holovatskii, and Ivan Vahylevych, not only were not ashamed of their nationality
but even emphasized their Rusyn origin with extraordinary force in their
political tracts: "A Rusyn mother gave us birth, a Rusyn mother nurtured
us, a Rusyn mother gave us love." Throughout the former Galician-Volhynian State, wherever Rusyns live, even in the most remote and inaccessible parts of the Carpathian Mountains, they define their nationality by
the word Rusyn or Rusnak, from which, dropping the *yn* and *ak*, comes
the adjective *ruskii*.

Thus, it is not at all surprising that the leader of the Ukrainian movement, Prof. Mykhailo Hrushevskii, in his work *An Outline of the Ukrainian People's History*, had to admit that the tradition of the name Rusyn
has held out in Galicia and is still in effect to the present, and that here
both Poles and Rusyns consider the Ukrainian language and its tribes
to be Rusyn (p. 427).

In his brochure "Where Did the Names Rus' and Ukraine Come
From and What Do They Mean" (Lviv, 1907), L. Tsehelskii, the political
leader of the Ukrainian party, stated frankly: "We Galicians find it impossible to reject the names Rus' and Rusyn, because having used these
words in speech and in writing we know very well that these terms have
the same exact meaning as Ukraine and Ukrainian."[15]

II.

For centuries, the Popes have used in their bulls the term *rutheni*
(Ruthenian), which is identical to Rusyn, to designate the entire Rusyn
population.

III.

In Polish state decrees and in the writings of Polish chroniclers and
historians, the terms Rus' and Rusyn are found constantly. For example,

---

15   [This identification of plain "Rusyn" with "Ukrainian" is why the term "Carpatho-
Rusyn" is needed to identify inhabitants of Carpathian Rus'.]

in the agreements between Casimir the Great and the Lithuanian princes, we read, "If any Rusyn or *Ruska* [female Rusyn] runs away to Lviv, turn him or her over." After the fall of the Galician principality, Poland under Casimir the Great created from it a Rusyn Province, which was headed by a "General Prefect of Rusyn Lands."

Similarly to Poles, the Austrian government used the terms *Russen* and *Ruthenen* to designate the Little Russian peoples of Galicia, Bukovyna, and Transcarpathian Rus'. This usage lasted from the end of the eighteenth century until 1917, when Emperor Karl I used the term "Ukrainian" in an official document for the first time.

IV.

The name "Ukraine" was introduced into Poland for the first time after the Lublin Union in the second half of the sixteenth century, but only in a geographical sense, to designate the farthest eastern districts: Kyiv, Chernihiv and Bratslav, which were located on the edge (*na kraiu*) of the Polish state. This is similar to the present use of the term *kresy* (edges/borders), from which it would follow that the nationality of these people [from the Kresy region] ought to be "Kresovtsy."

The term "Ukraine" was used purely in respect to geography, not nationality. This is attested to the fact that even in such circumstances as the stormy period when a surrogate Ukrainian state was being created in the seventeenth century, Bohdan Khmelnytskii styled himself a "Rusyn Autocrat." "I am a small and slight person," he said to the Polish commissioners, "but by the will of God I have become a Rusyn despot and autocrat." (Mykhailo Hrushevskii, History of Ukraine, p. 303.) Similarly, Poland, on the basis of the Treaty of Haidach, was obliged to reject "Ukraine," that is, to form an autonomous "Grand Principality of Rus'" from the three provinces noted above.

The names "Ukraine" and "Ukrainian" came into wider use for the first time during the Great War, when a "Greater Ukraine" arose on the basis of the Russian Revolution and the Brest peace treaty that followed on the one hand, and on the other hand a portion of the Galician lands was proclaimed to be "Western Ukraine" after the fall of the Austro-Hungarian empire on November 11, 1918.

Thus, the old geographic term has in recent years become a political one, but not at all a national one.

On the basis of the arguments presented above, the undersigned

Societies request:

1. That the terms Rus' and *ruskii* be used officially to designate the Little Russian peoples living within the borders of the Polish State, which is in accord with historical truth as well as with the name used by the people themselves for centuries.

2. That, in conformity with the rules of grammar, the adjectival form of the noun *Rusyn*, after the suffix *-yn* is dropped, become the adjective *ruskii*, not *rusynskii*, as is done in similar cases where the adjectives *slovyanskii*, *tatarskii*, and *bolharskii* are formed from the nouns *slovianyn*, *tataryn*, and *bolharyn*.

3. That the term "Ukrainian" be used only in its political meaning to designate that political party which has set as its main purpose the creation of an "Independent United Ukraine" stretching from the Carpathians and the San to the Caucasus and the Don.

Signed:
Stauropegial Institute in Lviv
Society of Rusyn Ladies in Lviv

Tymotei Fuchyla (center), caretaker, with other villagers in front of the first Kachkovskii Society location in Zawadka Rymanowska. 1937.

Rusyn Refuge Society in Lviv
National Union of "Dnistro-San" Cooperatives in Lviv
Land Protection Credit Union in Lviv
Galician-Rusyn "Matitsa" Scholarly Society in Lviv
"Friend" Society of Rusyn Students in Lviv
Mykhailo Kachkovskii Society in Lviv
"Rusyn Club" Society in Lviv
Rusyn Examination Society in Lviv

This appeal was never answered. It became a voice crying in the wilderness. The Polish-Ukrainian mafia set a trident [the Ukrainian national symbol] over the grave of the Galician-Rusyn people. After the fall of the wretched "Sanation" Poland, People's Poland adopted the terms *Ukrainiec* and *ukrainski* for the Little Russian people living on the territory of the present Polish Republic.

21. The Apostolic Administration of Lemkovyna

When Orthodoxy began growing at a rapid rate in Lemkovyna and there was fear that all Lemkos would turn to Orthodoxy, the Curia in Rome was informed of the losses in Lemkovyna by the Polish primate August Józef Hłond [1926-1948] and became alarmed. To save what was left of the [Greek] Catholic Church in Lemkovyna, on February 10, 1934, the Apostolic See, in concert with the Polish Government, issued a decree *"Quo aptius consularet"* from the Sacred Congregation For the Eastern Church, cutting ten deaneries out of the Przemyśl diocese. For these ten, it created a separate administrative district headed by an Apostolic Administrator, *"ad nutum S. Sedis"* or directly dependent on the Holy See. This district was given the name *Apostolica Administratio pro Lemkis* (Apostolic Administration of Lemkovyna), and was placed under the direct control of the Roman Curia. The [Polish] Ministry of Religious Faith designated the villa of Count Jan Potocki in Rymanów-Zdrój as the residence of the Apostolic Administrator and his Curia. Appointed as the first Apostolic Administrator was a Lemko, Father Dr. Bazyli Mastsiukh, former professor of canon law at the religious seminary in Przemyśl and docent at Lviv University. The new Administrator began his official duties on

Jordan Festival. Blessing of the Waters by the first Apostolic Administrator Dr. Bazyli Mastsiukh. Sanok, January 19, 1935.

January 19, 1935 with a solemn blessing of the water (the "Jordan" service), in the San River at Sanok.

To assist in the administration of the new eparchy as Curia clerk and reviewer, Father Mastsiukh brought in Father Ioann Polianskii, former parish priest in Smolnik. The entire burden of administration fell on these two men. The work was hard and the problems many. Bishop Iosafat Kotsylovskii with the Ukrainian priests in the eparchy, the Ukrainian press, and even some of the Orthodox priests took an antagonistic attitude toward this new Administration.

The Orthodox priests did exercise tact and good sense, and there were no unpleasant incidents between them and the Apostolic Administration. The principal enemies of the new Administration were Ukrainian priests led by Bishop Kotsylovskii, and the editors of Ukrainian newspapers. The priests scrutinized every step of the Apostolic Administrator, spread all kinds of false rumors and calumnies about him, and reported everything to Bishop Kotsylovskii. The latter, in turn, sent numerous reports to the Roman Curia, painting Father Mastsiukh in the blackest colors. The Ukrainian press seconded all this slander. Everyone who had the opportunity tried to nip at his authority and his opinions. Even today, more than twenty-two years after his death, there are all kinds of [Ivan] Krasovskiis who dishonor his memory in vulgar ways in the Ukrainian press.[16]

When all the efforts of his enemies could not undermine Father Mastsiukh's position, some evil Ukrainian hand put poison in his food. Thus his work-filled life ended tragically on March 10, 1936, and he was buried in the cemetery of his native village, Nowa Wieś in Nowy Sącz County. His funeral was conducted by Bishop Kotsylovskii with the assistance of two Roman Catholic bishops. All the other Greek Catholic bishops boycotted the funeral and did not attend.

The news of Dr. Mastsiukh's death delighted all his enemies, who were convinced that with his death the Apostolic Administration would either be abolished or that eventually his successor would be a Ukrainian. The word went out everywhere that candidates were being sought for this office. But disappointment set in when news came from the Apostolic See by way of the Apostolic Nuncio office in Warsaw that Father Ioann Polianskii, the incumbent Curia clerk, had been named Acting Administrator of the Apostolic Administration with the rights of a vicar until such time as a new bishop or Apostolic Administrator would be appointed.

Father Polianskii took over the office on March 12, 1936, and held it until October 7, 1936. During this period Ukrainian nationalists twice passed a death sentence on him. Once they sent it to him in the form of a letter, the other in the shape of a skull with a Ukrainian trident painted on cardboard and nailed to the door of the curia office. Ukrainian nationalists flooded the Roman Curia with all kinds of denunciations and slanders of Father Polianskii.

One evening as Father Polianskii was returning from a trip, a gang of Ukrainian hooligans attacked him and beat him severely. It soon became apparent that these bandits were directed by a Ukrainian priest. In such an atmosphere the work of the Apostolic Administration was a burdensome task.

The next Apostolic Administrator, appointed by the Roman Curia [on July 13, 1936], was Father Dr. Iakov Medvetskii, former professor of religion at the seminary in Stanisławów and archpriest at the Stanisławów cathedral. Father Medvetskii was a good man but often displayed a weak will, due to his diabetic condition. Educated in the east, he knew nothing of Lemkovyna or the Lemko people, which made him less effective in the office of Apostolic Administrator than had been his predecessor, Father Mastsiukh, a man of great energy and iron will.

While Father Polianskii was in charge, the Curia of the Apostolic Administration published a "Manual (Schematism) of the Greek Catholic Clergy in

16 See for example *"Leninska Molod"* (Leninist Youth), newspaper of the Lviv district branch of the Communist Union of Youth, Lviv, 1959.

Nash Lemko (Our Lemko). 1936.

the Apostolic Administration of Lemkovyna For the Year 1936"[17] which was compiled by Father Stefan Iadlovskii, Counselor of the Apostolic Administration. This directory is very valuable to us because it contains a history of Lemko parishes and is illustrated with photographs of Lemko churches. Unfortunately, only two hundred copies were printed due to a lack of funds.

In evaluating the work of Father Polianskii as director of the Apostolic Administration, the Apostolic See sent him the following commendation:

[From] The Apostolic Nunciature in Poland, Warsaw, July 13, 1936. No. 13599.

To the Right Reverend Ioann Polianskii, Provisional Administrator of the Apostolic Administration of Lemkovyna.

Most Reverend Sir,

May we take this occasion, in the name of the Holy See, to congratulate you on your difficult labors in promoting the spiritual welfare of your curial commission. May God repay you for your continuous labor.

To you, most reverend sir, in the name of the Lord, A. Pacini.

While he was directing the Apostolic Administration, Father Polianskii published two theological works of his own: *On the Dignity of a Priest* and *On the Supreme Authority of Saint Peter the Apostle and His Successors in the Church of Christ.*

---

17 [See http://lemko.org/books/shem1936.pdf]

22. Education in Lemkovyna During the Interwar Years

After World War I, an organization called *Lemko Soyuz* (The Lemko Union)[18] was formed in Lemkovyna, aiming to unite all Lemkos into one entity. The president of this organization was Dr. Orest Hnatyshak, a lawyer in Krynica (murdered in Auschwitz), and the secretary was Metodii Trokhanovskii, a Krynica teacher.[19] For a while, the Lemko Union organized assemblies in various towns of Lemkovyna, in which numerous Lemkos participated. All kinds of topics pertaining to the cultural, educational, and economic life of Lemkos were discussed; high on the list was defense against "mazepinism" (Ukrainian nationalism).

The organ of the Lemko Union was the weekly *Lemko*, edited by Metodii Trokhanovskii. This paper was poorly edited, so it was not as popular as the prewar *Lemko* edited by Dymytrii Vyslotskii. This *Lemko* had a fascist slant, since it was subsidized by the Cracow provincial government and the County Council in Nowy Sącz. With its bias, and in an atmosphere hostile to Lemkos, this paper could not support itself with its own funds. The Lemko Union was able to exist and conduct its activities only because of the favor of the Cracow Deputy Administrator Malaszyński, who was a good friend of Lemkos and a protector of Lemko interests.

At the same time, Ukrainian nationalists, who were trying to Ukrainize the Lemkos, published a Ukrainian newspaper for Lemkos, called *Nash Lemko* (Our Lemko). This paper was printed in Lviv and was distributed in thousands of copies throughout Lemkovyna. The editor was M. Taranko, of very dubious identity. Lemkos did not care for reading this paper because they found in it nothing but falsehoods and slander.

With the concurrence of Polish school authorities, textbooks in the Lemko vernacular were introduced in Lemko schools a few years before World War II. The author of these school books was the teacher Metodii Trokhanovskii, who was later granted the right to teach the Lemko language at the teachers' college in Stary Sącz. These books were well written, and the children liked them.

The aim of the Polish authorities in putting Lemko books in the schools

18   [The European *Lemko Soyuz* was founded in Sanok in December 1933. A North American *Lemko Soyuz* (Lemko Association) was founded in Winnipeg, Manitoba, Canada in 1929.]
19   [See http://en.wikipedia.org/wiki/Metodyj_Trochanovskij .]

Local school children with teacher Metodii Trokhanovskii. Krynica, 1934.

was to alienate Lemkos from the Russian language, just as they had earlier introduced phonetic spelling for the same reason. However, when they noticed that these books were not having the desired effect, in the last year before World War II they removed the Lemko language books and replaced them with Ukrainian books. Trokhanovskii's right to teach the Lemko language was rescinded. This was one of many experiments towards the "destruction of Rus." At a conference in Krynica, in the presence of several of our scholars, school superintendent Gadomski expressed it thus: "Lemkos don't need schooling. It is enough for their children to learn to read and write just a little." That's how much "Sanation" Poland cared about our people.

The Lemko Union did not really play a major role in Lemkovyna, but it had some achievements to its credit. Its principal accomplishment was the establishment of the Apostolic Administration of Lemkovyna and termination of the religious war in Lemkovyna. It made the first moves toward reducing Bishop Kotsylovskii's Ukrainian influence and establishing a separate diocese. Both Greek Catholics and Orthodox participated in its gatherings, where both sides called for consensus and love of each other, notwithstanding their religious division. Although the work of the Lemko Union was not carried out on a large scale, it still attained some success. Among the active members of the Lemko Union were: Iaroslav Siokało, attorney in Gorlice; Dr. Iosyf Perelom, attorney in Sanok; Dr. Evhen Shatynskii, attorney in Sanok; Dr. Symeon Vozniak, attorney in Krosno; Dr. Teofil Kuryllo, attorney in

Cracow; Dr. Iosyf Hukevych, gymnazium professor in Sanok; Roman Maksymovych, gymnazium professor in Gorlice; Dymytrii Hensiorskii, notary in Sanok; Iosyf Iavorskii, notary in Bukowsko; Teodosy Iadlovskii, medical student; Teodor Voitovych, magistrate in Uście Ruskie; Stefan Barna and Iosyf Enkala, teachers in Wróblik; Aleksei Vyslotskii, teacher in Hańczowa; Aleksei Milanovych, teacher in Powroźnik; Pavlo Gaida, teacher in Trzciana; Ivan Baiko, teacher in Barwinek; Emanuil Mokrytskii, financial counselor in Sanok; Mykhailo Muzychka, government official in Sanok; Mykhailo Perelom, insurance agent in Sanok; Aleksander Hnatyshak, court official in Grybów; Aleksander Hukevych, merchant in Sanok; Nikolai Iurkovskii, teacher in Skwirtne; Iuri Poloshynovych, teacher in Wysowa; Aleksandra Vyslotskii, teacher in Kwiatoń; the Ianovitskiis in Krynica; and many others.

In 1936-1937, "Sanation" Poland put intense pressure on Lemko education by transferring Lemko teachers to Polish villages and by removing Rusyn signs from cooperatives and reading rooms. This led to a variety of complaints, protests, and strikes.

The most important event was a school strike in the village of Skwirtne in 1937. This was a protest against the transfer to Kielce Province of Nikolai S. Iurkovskii, an exemplary and beloved teacher well known as a Lemko patriot and activist. When he was leaving the village, a procession of people escorted him to the village limits. After that, no children went to school for several months. As if it sensed the coming end of its reign, "Sanation" Poland thrashed around in all directions, venting its frustrations on our poor people.

Of great importance in the development of cultural and educational work in Lemkovyna was the "Lemkovshchyna" museum in Sanok, founded by Professor Lev Getz of Cracow who devoted an entire decade of hard work to it. This museum was located in Sanok Castle, which was restored by the museum founders. It contained many valuable exhibits, the number of which grew day by day. A few years later, another museum was established, called "The Museum of Sanok Land." After the war, the two were merged, and now there is a single combined museum in Sanok. This Lemko museum has aroused great interest among the people in their cultural achievements, and has become an important institution of learning that even foreign scholars have made use of. Of great service to this museum were Professor Dr. Iaroslav Konstantynovych, Professor Irena Dobrianska, Professor Fr. Stefan Venhrynovych, and others. Dr. Konstantynovych made use of the museum in writing several valuable works.

When the Lemkos were exiled from the Carpathians, there were left in their churches many historical artifacts, which some unseen hand has removed. It is a shame that these Lemko valuables did not get into a museum. In the church in Izby, there was a marvelous painting of the Izby Mother of God, dating back to the early seventeenth century. This painting was taken from the Izby church by Franciszek Ignac, the Roman Catholic priest in Berest, who then replaced it with a copy. The original is still in the possession of Father Ignac.

23. The International Political Situation Before WWII

When the first World War (1914-1918) ended, the Versailles Treaty, signed in 1919, did not eliminate all the misunderstandings and antagonisms that had provided the basis of the conflict in 1914. Germany suffered great losses by virtue of losing the war. Italy and Japan, despite having participated in the war on the side of the victorious Allies, did not get enough of the spoils to satisfy their needs and aspirations. A struggle began for new markets and for disputed territories that remained sore spots. These three powers formed an alliance that came to be called the Rome-Berlin-Tokyo Axis. Agreeing on mutual assistance among themselves, they began a series of aggressive acts. After gaining possession of Manchuria in 1931, Japan began encroaching on Chinese territory. Italy seized Abyssinia in 1935-1936. Germany instituted compulsory military service, which had been prohibited by the Versailles Treaty, in 1934, annexed Austria in the *Anschluss* of March 1938, occupied the Sudetenland in September of the same year, took over the Klaipeda area of Lithuania in the following spring, and finally advanced territorial claims against Poland.

The Western Powers, England, France, and America, did nothing to counteract these aggressive moves by the Axis partners. Such indulgence merely encouraged the Axis powers to undertake increasingly more adventuristic steps that threatened the freedom and peace of the world. The high point of this policy of appeasement was the Munich Pact of 1938, by which the governments of England and France acquiesced in Hitler's plan to annex the Sudetenland. The main reason behind this attitude of the Western Powers was to maneuver Germany and its allies into a war with the Soviet Union, which they regarded as a dangerous competitor on world markets. Furthermore, they feared the Soviets' cooperation with revolutionary workers' movements, which became a very great danger for capitalism during the great economic crisis of 1929-1933.

The ruling circles in Italy and Germany, as well as in some other countries, learned that the best way to quiet their restive masses was to establish fascist regimes that exercised power by means of terror and military-police dictatorships. In Japan, the existing autocratic and militaristic power structure had for ages suppressed all signs of any revolutionary action. Fascism considered its principal enemy to be communism, which it strove with all its might to eradicate.

In 1936, the fascist nations concluded an "Anticomintern Pact" aimed at the Soviet Union. Under the pretext of fighting communism, they often dealt harshly with all progressive organizations, even cultural ones that had nothing to do with communism. In time, however, the governments of England and France became aware of the results of the Munich accord and of the danger from the fascist powers, which threatened the world. In March of 1939 the English and French governments promised to guarantee Poland's borders and to begin negotiations with the Soviet Union on military cooperation. They did not, however, take a single step to deter German aggression. It was not until Hitlerism had inflamed all of Europe that western politicians decided who was the greatest enemy of mankind and who threatened destruction of the culture and freedom of all peoples.

World War II began with Germany's imperialist attack on Poland. In early 1939, the Germans made territorial claims against Poland, demanding that the free city of Danzig be handed over to Germany and that a "corridor" be created in Polish Pomerania. These demands could not be accepted, as the Germans knew very well. These demands were only a pretext, while in the background was the age-old German desire to destroy Poland entirely, as a nation and as a people. Hitler often mentioned this when talking with his accomplices. For example, on May 23, 1939, Hitler said, "Danzig is not the matter in dispute. This is a matter of enlarging our living space (*Lebensraum*), of providing resources for living, of solving the Baltic problem." And again on August 22, just days before the attack on Poland, Hitler divulged his intentions with respect to Poland. "Extermination of the Poles," he said, "is our first and most vital duty. Even if war should break out in the west, destruction of Poland must be our primary objective. This decision must be carried out

within the year. For propaganda purposes, I will give some excuse for the outbreak of war. It does not matter if this is believed or not. In starting and conducting a war, it is not truth that counts, but victory. Be merciless! Be brutal!"

Most of the Polish people were aware of the feelings and intentions of the
German imperialists toward them. The tragedy of Poland lay in the fact that
its government did not understand, and didn't even want to know about, the
danger to Poland from Hitler's insatiable fascism, which had absolutely no
regard for international rights.

The shortsightedness of Poland's politicians and their total disregard of
their responsibility for the fate of the nation are attested to by their actions,
such as sending Polish troops to occupy the Zaolzie area of Czechoslovakia
while Hitler was starting to divide that country and giving Poland ultimatums
that threatened its sovereignty. The downplaying of Germany's annexation of
the Czechoslovak territories [by Western governments] enabled the Germans
to conduct blitzkrieg operations in the early stages of the war and made it
possible for them to take over the entire continent of Europe in short order. It
was Hitler's attack on the Soviet Union in June of 1941 that awakened public
opinion to the danger of the situation and united all the anti-fascist forces to
fight this most dangerous enemy of humanity, the like of which history had
not known heretofore.

24. Hitler's Occupation of Poland

Early on the morning of September 1, 1939, military warplanes with those
ominous swastikas painted on their wings roared over Poland and bombs began sowing death and destruction. This was the beginning of World War II.
The people could not yet believe that this was really war, because the newspapers, radio, and all of Polish propaganda had kept proclaiming right up to
the last moment that, on the one hand, Hitler's threats were just extortionary,
and on the other, that "we are strong, united, and ready" and that England and
France will immediately come to our aid. Meanwhile, a deluge of bombs fell
on cities and villages, on mansions and cottages, on roads crowded with refugees, on communication lines, killing civilians and spreading conflagration.

Anastazia Khomko of Wisłoczek and Aleksander Maksymowicz (1911-1942), a woodcarver from Wołtuszowa, killed in Auschwitz during the German occupation of Poland.

This was a new kind of war, one fought against an entire people.

On September 7, Warsaw was evacuated, and on the following day it was encircled by German armies. Thousands of men volunteered for military service; none were accepted, because there was a shortage of weapons, ammunition, uniforms, and transport. There was total chaos and disorganization from the very first day of the war. Soldiers wanted to fight the enemy, but at the border they were ordered to retreat without firing a shot. Government notables fled in fright, packing up their trunks and carrying off money and valuables, both personal and state. Instead of fighting alongside the soldiers at the front, generals, colonels, and majors fled in limousines packed with all kinds of valuables, trying to get to Zalishchyki in two weeks and then across the border [to Romania] to avoid the wrath of the people.

The traitorious government fled the country and left the people to the mercies of Hitler's invaders. Fighting continued, however, with both soldiers and civilians carrying on. They fought bravely, but the enemy forces were immeasurably stronger. Warsaw surrendered on September 27, and a few days later all of Poland was in the hands of the occupier.[20]

---

20 [The Soviet Union attacked Poland on September 17, 1939 and seized the eastern half of the country.]

In keeping with long established plans, Hitler now set out to completely exterminate the Polish people, both culturally and biologically. He said that Germany had to take the path of age-old aggression, had to go up against Russia and its neighboring nations, must Germanize all those lands. In May 1941, Graizer, who was sentenced to death by a Polish court after the war, said it thus: "Poles can work for us, but only as laborers," and to the Germans he said, "I emphatically require that you be savage, be cruel and more cruel." Governor General Hans Frank, who after the war would be sentenced to death by the International Tribunal in Nuremberg, put it in these words: "The difference between the German master race and the Poles must be expressed with great clarity. Poles will be given just enough education to make them realize the utter hopelessness of their national existence."

The occupied area of Poland was divided into two parts. One part (Silesia, Greater Poland, Pomerania, and parts of the Warsaw and Łódz provinces) was annexed directly to Germany. The rest went into a *Generalgouvernement* (General Government), which was divided into four districts: Warsaw, Radom, Lublin, and Cracow, with its capital in Cracow. The governor was the same Hans Frank who had defended Hitler during his legal trials. Frank lived like a king in the former royal castle on Wawel Hill.

In the first part of this divided country, the people lost their right to have an opinion. Property rights, land, and industry were taken over by German magnates. A system of confiscation and destruction was applied extensively. Some village families were resettled to the General Government, and many young people were forcibly sent to work in Germany. The rest of the populace were left on their own lands as laborers, while their land was taken by the German colonizers.

To keep everybody in submission, the occupiers resorted to a policy of unprecedented terror, oppression, and persecution. All schools were closed. Young people were forced to work in factories and on farmsteads. Priests were led off to concentration camps. University professors were arrested. A crematorium was built on the grounds of one university, for burning the bodies of those who died in the camps and prisons. Multitudes of people were brutally resettled. During the severe winter of 1939-1940, many were forced out of their homes and cast to the whims of fate, together with their children and their sick, taking nothing with them but hand baggage. Those who were not evacuated were forced into a labor regimen handled by the *Arbeitsamt* (Work Administration), in which working conditions were extremely harsh. They had to work for twelve hours every day, with no compensation. Food rations were miserly, below the level of nourishment needed for survival. Many concentration camps were constructed, some of them in the Radogoszcz district of Łódz, in Żabików, and in Chełm. Over three hundred thousand people were slaughtered there.

In the General Government, large quotas of meat, milk, fats, grain, and potatoes were levied on the villagers. Large estates were put under German management. Public property and Jewish possessions were confiscated. The plunderers took great wealth out of the country and sentenced the people to starvation.

To intimidate the population, the German authorities applied the principle of mass responsibility. In exchange for the death of one German, several dozen Poles would be executed. These would be picked up on the street, at home, or taken from among those previously arrested and held on the basis of lists prepared by confidential agents, mostly Ukrainians. In this way, every day many hundreds of innocent people were slaughtered.

The largest extermination camp in Europe was built on marshes near Oświęcim (Auschwitz). Polish labor was used in its construction. This camp held about two hundred thousand prisoners of all nationalities, not to mention the millions of victims who were taken from the railroad station directly to the gas chambers. From the spring of 1940, there was a steady stream of political prisoners of all nationalities from all over Europe, sent directly to their death. There were transports full of Jews and Gypsies, and even of Soviet prisoners of war. None of them ever walked out through the Auschwitz gate. The Auschwitz complex comprised a group of three concentration camps–Auschwitz, Auschwitz II-Birkenau, and Auschwitz III-Monowitz. The inmates worked in thirty *Kommando* or work details: coal mines, factories, camp agriculture, etc. The entire complex covered 465 hectares. Living conditions were dreadful. People died of hunger, of epidemic diseases, and of exhaustion brought on by overwhelming labor, as well as from beastly torture and downright murder.

In 1941, this forced labor camp became an extermination camp. The first ever structure for killing people with poison gas was built in Auschwitz II-Birkenau. Four gigantic crematory furnaces were set up for burning human bodies. Even today, it is still not known just how many people perished in Auschwitz. Estimates range up to five million. Hitler's minions worked hard to extract every bit of value from their victims, even after death. The inmates' belongings were meticulously sorted and sent off to Germany. About 240 railroad carloads of clothing alone were shipped out, even two carloads of nothing but eyeglasses.

Using the most modern methods of technology, there were committed repeated acts of murder, mass extermination of millions of people, and attempts to annihilate entire races. Hitler's vile plans included the biological annihilation of all Slavic peoples. But the primary target of these extermination plans were the Jews. As far back as January of 1939, Hitler had said that the new world war would result in eradication of all the Jews in Europe. And in September of 1939, he issued a secret order in preparation for carrying out this plan. Jews from the provinces were gathered together in major cities and interned in specially prepared living areas called ghettos. Imprisoned behind walls, crowded into small areas, sentenced to starvation, decimated by epidemics, denied elementary human rights, masses of Jews perished. The rate of extermination, however, did not satisfy Hitler's genocidal murderers. In mid-1942, they began eliminating the ghettos by killing hundreds of thousands of people. The ashes of the bodies incinerated in the crematoriums were shipped to Germany by the boxcar load and used to enrich German gardens. Today, Auschwitz/Oświęcim is visited by tourists from all over the world to view the site of Hitler's hell on earth.

25. The Hitler-Mazepa Terror in Lemkovyna During WWII

As soon as the Germans occupied Western Galicia, a large number of escapees from the [Soviet-occupied] east began flowing into Lemkovyna, mostly Ukrainian nationalists. Most of them were priests, teachers, journalists and bureaucrats. They were fleeing from Soviet rule and seeking sanctuary with the Germans. They settled mostly in towns, but there was no lack of them in Lemko villages. The Germans welcomed them with open arms as allies and collaborators, and handed over to them the properties of local teachers, school supervisors, translators, village officials, trustees, etc. They were especially pleased with Governor General Frank, who helped them set up their own organization in

Cracow called the Ukrainian Assistance Committee. The purpose of this committee, as its title suggests, was to help the Germans in ravaging the Slavic people. It became the right arm of Hitler's cannibals.

The efforts of the Ukrainian Assistance Committee soon brought results. All kinds of incriminations, denunciations, and slander against the Lemko intelligentsia and village elders poured into the files of the German authorities. The mazepists characterized Lemkos as Polonophiles, Moscophiles, Bolsheviks, and communists. A wave of individual and mass arrests followed. Where defamation did not suffice, provocations were incited. Here are a few examples.

In an effort to get village priest Polianskii arrested, the rumor-monger and provocateur Zakharivskii, who had been given the property of a teacher in Wróblik, removed from a wall in the school an icon of the Mother of God and hung in place of it a Ukrainian trident. When Father Polianskii came to the school for a class in religion, he had the children remove the trident

and put back the Mother of God image. Zakharivskii then reported to the Gestapo that Father Polianskii had taken down a German swastika, trampled it, and told the children that only the Devil can wear such a symbol. However, investigation revealed the falsity of these charges. Father Polianskii was exonerated, but Zakharivskii was not done. He hired a hooligan to go to the village well and pour some kerosene into it, for which he paid the man thirty zlotys. The latter did as he was told and poured in several buckets full of kerosene. The next day, Zakharivskii reported to the German military authorities that Father

Hryhory Petsukh from Florynka posing for the German Arbeitskart work card in 1940.

Polianskii had polluted the water in the well to poison the German troops stationed in Wróblik. Polianskii was arrested and was sentenced to death by firing squad. Just before the execution was about to be carried out, however, the truth of the matter was revealed, thanks to some German. Father Polianskii was released, and Zakharivskii lost his credibility with the Germans.

In another example, the teacher Baiko in Zyndranowa was framed by mazepists who hid a rifle in his barn. Next day they reported to the German authorities that Baiko was concealing weapons and ammunition. A search was immediately begun, and the hidden rifle was found. The teacher Baiko was arrested, along with his entire family.

Many such examples could be presented. The most active informer and provocateur in Wróblik was a priest named Horchko, a refugee from the east whom Father Polianskii had befriended, providing him with free room and board. He joined up with Zakharivskii and denigrated Father Polianskii at every opportunity, trying to get rid of him and take his place as parish priest in Wróblik. In such ways, the very best sons of Lemkovyna fell victim to Ukrainian denunciation.

On June 21, 1941, the day that Hitler treacherously attacked the Soviet Union, mass arrests began in Lemkovyna, based on blacklists compiled by the Ukrainian Assistance Committee. Brought to the prison at Nowy Sącz that very same day were Father Volodymyr Mokhnatskii of Tylicz, Father Evhen Khyliak of Krynica, Father Volodymyr Venhrynovych of Wierchomla, Father Emilyian Venhrynovych of Mochnaczka, Father Iuliian Sembratovych of Złockie, Father Vasyli Bartko of Złockie, Father Andrei Orshak of Krynica, Metodii Trokhanovskii of Krynica, Antonii Stanchak of Muszyna, Emilyian Milianych of Powroźnik, and many others whose names no longer come to mind. Imprisoned in Jasło were Father Ioann Detko, Father Ioann Polianskii, and Father Iaroslav Mirovych. A short time later it was the turn of Nikolai and Pavlo Iurkovskii, Petro Sobyn, N. Rusenko, Vasyl Koldra, Petro Saifert, Pavlo Gaida, Rusyniak, Sobolevska, Fedorek, and many others.

During the time that Lemkos were active in the guerrilla movement, imprisoned in Jasło were: Volodymyr and Ivan Tkach, Ivan and Mykhailo Romec, Iuri Rogots, Stefan Peiko, Myroslaw Vyslotskii, Aleksandra Vyslotskii, Danylo Porutsydlo, Vasyli Polivka, Ivan and Tymofei Doński, and Teodor Serniak.

The situation of the inmates in the Jasło prison was full of suffering and mortification. Hitler's minions set dogs on them, beat them with metal whips, knocked out their teeth, nailed through their hands, poured salt into their wounds, submerged them in boiling water, poured cold water on those who were badly beaten as they recovered consciousness, and then beat them some more until they lost consciousness again. Every night they led several or a score out into the woods and shot them. Weeping and bitter lamentations resounded throughout Lemkovyna, because there was not a single family that did not have at least one member who had fallen victim to the Hitler-Mazepa torture. The prison in Jasło echoed with continuous suppressed groaning, as did all of Lemkovyna. One of the most fearsome executioners in Jasło was the Polish renegade Dżazga, while at Nowy Sącz it was Johann.

Gestapo agents among the Ukrainian committees raced around the Lemko villages like hound dogs, sniffing out "Moscophiles" and communists. These lackeys of the Germans robbed the people, taking not only foods but also church items such as bells and chalices. The Ukrainian Assistance Committee gathered up copper bells and gold monstrances from all over Lemkovyna and presented all this to the Jasło *Kreishauptmann* (district administrator) as a birthday present. The latter, however, was not pleased with this gift, considering the bells to be a symbol of unexpected death. The ceremony of presenting the gift was conducted by one Nychka, a lawyer from Krosno, and the school supervisor Zwiryk, who has scores of Lemko victims on his conscience.

Many Lemkos perished at the hands of the Hitlerite and Ukrainian butchers. Murdered at Auschwitz were Aleksander Hnatyshak, magistrate in Grybów, and a little later his brother Dr. Orest Hnatyshak, attorney in Krynica and president of the Lemko Soyuz. Executed in Jasło were Ivan and Mykhailo Romtsio, Volodymyr and Ivan Tkach, Iuri Rogots, Teodor Serniak, Stefan Andreychyn, Miroslav Vyslotskii, Aleksandra Vyslotskii, Danylo Porutsydlo, Matsiiovskii, Vasyli Polivka, Ivan and Tymofei Doński.

Written in bloody letters on the hearts of the Lemko people are the surnames of Ukrainian hangmen such as: Zwiryk, school supervisor; Petruk, lawyer in Zmigród and agent of the German high command; Batiuk, deputy school supervisor in Wysowa and Gestapo agent; Petrushko, chief of the Ukrainian police in Uście Ruskie; Rusynko, chief of the Ukrainian police in Ropica Ruska; Boiko, deputy land commissar in Gorlice; Volodymyr Lishchynskii, assistant to the land commissar in Gorlice; Ivan Lishchynskii, storekeeper; Zhemelko, storekeeper in Gorlice and Gestapo agent; Mykhailo Hamula, teacher in Pielgrzymka; Nychka, lawyer in Krosno; Father Stefan Shalash, parish priest in Myscowa; Zakharivskii, teacher in Wróblik; Dr.

Lutsiv, village bailiff in Wróblik; Pasichynskii, prosecutor in Nowy Sącz; Stefan Varkholak in Wróblik; Father Pakhomii Borys, Basilian abbot in Wróblik; Father Stefan Kornova, parish priest in Łabowa; Father Pidsadniuk in Czyrna; Father Teofil Kmitsikevych, parish priest in Surowica; Father Mykhailo Zhemplinskii, parish priest in Zawadka Rymanowska; and so many others that they cannot all be listed. Father Stefan Shalash has thousands of innocent victims on his conscience, while Father Kornova and his son-in-law Fr. Pidsadniuk have hundreds.

When the German armies on the eastern front began falling back, the Ukrainian nationalists organized an "SS Galizien" division and sent it off to help Hitler. They forced Lemko youths to join this division, using unprecedented terror for this purpose. The young men battled against this as best they could, fleeing to the forests to join up with Lemko guerrilla fighters.

The Ukrainian nationalists in Lemkovyna played the same role in the second world war in Lemkovyna as they had in the first: that of Cain.

The war ended. The Ukrainian division could not save Hitler. The Soviet Union, together with the armies of its allies, brought victory over the cannibal Hitler. His loyal servants, the Ukrainian nationalists, afraid that the hand of justice would reach them, saw no other way out but to shamefully flee their native land with the remnants of the German armies into exile in Germany. One who kills his brother is not worthy of living in his native land but must wander forever all over foreign countries.

26. The Apostolic Administration of Lemkovyna During the German Occupation

In February of 1940, the Apostolic Administrator, Father Dr. Iakov Medvetskii, was visited by a Greek Catholic priest of German nationality, Father Peters of the Order of Studite Fathers. This priest presented documents showing that he was a trusted emissary of Governor General Frank, and he demanded that Father Medvetskii appoint Father Aleksander Malynovskii as his deputy with the title of Vicar General. Father Medvetskii refused to comply with Father Peters' strange request, saying that he did not know Father

Malynovskii at all and he could not give such an important post to the first priest that happened by. Father Peters persisted and threatened Father Medvetskii with arrest. Frightened, Father Medvetskii agreed to do as Father Peters demanded, but he did not hurry to comply. Finally in August, in despair and with his back to the wall, Father Medvetskii gave in to the pressure and appointed Father Malynovskii to the position of Vicar General of the Apostolic Administration of Lemkovyna.

Who was this Aleksander Malynovskii? Simply put, he was a Ukrainian provocateur and Gestapo agent. In World War I, he was a captain in the Ukrainian Sich Riflemen.[21] After unsuccessful battles against the Poles, Captain Malynovskii went to Prague with the surviving remnants of the Sich Riflemen and stayed there for ten years. In about 1930, he returned to Lviv and was accepted into a religious seminary. A few years before World War II, Malynovskii was ordained a priest by Metropolitan Sheptytskii, and was appointed the seminary's household manager.

When World War II began, Father Malynovskii fled before the Soviet advance and went from Lviv to Cracow. In Cracow he met a German officer with whom he had served in World War I. By virtue of this acquaintance, he got a well paid job in the General Government and began energetic Ukrainian activity. He founded the Ukrainian Assistance Committee and imported a whole Ukrainian colony into Cracow. Governor General Hans Frank saw in Father Malynovskii an organizational ability and a dedication to the Fuehrer, and decided to put the fate of the Lemko people in his hands. Frank sent Father Peters to Father Medvetskii to get a hierarchical position for Father Malynovskii. The latter contrived to repay his patron's generosity a hundredfold.

On becoming Vicar General, Malynovskii reorganized the entire Apostolic Administration. He shunted his superior, Dr. Medvetskii, off to the hospital of the Boniface Fathers in Cracow. He fired all of the Curia personnel and replaced them with rabid Ukrainians. He asked the Rusyn parish priests to sign a formal declaration, pledging to serve Ukraine and to work exclusively for Ukraine. The Rusyn priests replied that they had made a solemn vow to serve God, the Church, and the immortal souls of their faithful, not some kind of Ukraine. Father Malynovskii ordered all these priests to be arrested and imprisoned. He had a Gestapo[22] identification card, which meant that he

---

21 [This group fought for the Austrians. See *Ukrainski Sichovi Striltsi, 1914-1920* (Ukrainian Sich Riflemen, 1914-1920), Lviv: Nakladom Iuvileinoho Komitetu, 1935.]

22 [Actually, a *Sicherheitsdienst* (Security Service) ID.]

had the power of life and death in his hands. Having disposed of the Rusyn priests, he was now free to build Ukraine in Lemkovyna. The Germans themselves soon saw that there was something wrong with this Ukraine, because after being held in prison for a month the arrested priests were moved to the city of Kielce, where they were confined/interned and compelled to report to the Gestapo office every day.

Father Dr. Medvetskii died in the hospital in Cracow. Through the influence of Governor General Hans Frank in the Apostolic Nunciate in Berlin, Monsignor Orsenigo nominated Father Malynovskii to the post of Apostolic Administrator of Lemkovyna to succeed the deceased Father Dr. Medvetskii. The nomination was approved furtively and illegally. And so, hierarchical authority over the Lemko people was exercised by a Gestapo figure in priestly robes.

How zealously Father Malynovskii served Hitler and his butchers is demonstrated by the following fact. When Hitler invaded the Soviet Union, Father Malynovskii immediately sent him, in his own name and in the name of the Lemko people, a congratulatory message through Governor General Frank, expressing best wishes for a victory over the Russians. In translation, this shameful document reads as follows:

> To the Honorable Governor General Dr. Frank in Cracow. With the indescribable joy of all Ukrainian people, I and the clergy and the faithful of my eparchy hasten to tell the Great Leader of the German people, through you, of our deep feelings of thankfulness for his courageous declaration of war against the Bolshevik enslavers of peoples. We will accompany the glorious German Army on the field of battle with sincere wishes for success and with fervent prayers. May the Lord God keep you under His protection and blessing and lead to an illustrious victory, so that you will be crowned and immortalized with even greater glory as the great savior of humanity from Bolshevik bondage.
>
> Sanok, June 29, 1941
> Aleksander Malynovskii
> Apostolic Administrator of Ukrainian Greek Catholic Lemkovyna

Father Malynovskii published the German language text of this message in the official monthly "Annals of the Apostolic Administration of Lemkovyna in the General Government," vol. XVII, section 45, July 1941.

In addition to this telegram to Hitler, Father Malynovskii issued the following edict to the priests of Lemkovyna:

Invocation to the Most Honorable Clergy Concerning the Anti-Bolshevik Drive, No. 2295/41.

The glorious German Army, on order of the Great Leader of the German people, has entered on a crusade against Bolshevism, which during the twenty years of its domination over the lands of Eastern Europe has engaged in brutal enslavement of the peoples subject to it, including our Ukrainian people, and has proved to be an unparalleled enemy of the Christian faith and church. At this extraordinarily historic moment, when the fate of the Christian Church and our people is being decided, we cannot dare to remain passive in this conflict. We must show, by our sentiments and our actions, that we stand in the ranks of those who are fighting for Christian, universal human, and our own rights. In view of this call to our Christian and national conscience, we command the Most Honorable Clergy to do the following, throughout the entire anti-Bolshevik military campaign:

1. Introduce into all Divine Services during the "litany of fervent supplication" prayers to lift the faint-hearted and to orient the Church toward the success of the German Army and its allies.

2. Instruct the faithful in the Godless and inhuman doctrines and practices of Bolshevism.

3. Take immediate steps– within a week of announcement– to collect donations in the churches for the Red Cross, which collections are to be sent directly to the Apostolic Administration.

4. Train the faithful so that they willingly fulfill their wartime obligations, keeping always in mind that in the contribution of labor and belongings, no procrastination can be tolerated when so many brave souls are offering their lives in defense of justice.[23]

To cap his faithful service to Hitler, Father Malynovskii issued an order to his priests to organize the Lemko youth in their parishes into a military unit called "SS Galizien." The eager and energetic efforts of the Ukrainian clergy in this regard were not crowned with success. Instead of going into the German army, young Lemkos fled into the forests and joined the guerrilla units fighting against the German forces.

---

23 Annals of the Apostolic Administration of Lemkovyna in the General Government, vol. XVII, sec. 46, July 1941.

Father Malynovskii did not get to see a German victory over the Russian armies. At war's end, disappointed in his hopes and dreams, like the fratricidal Cain, he wandered from place to place, trying to hide from justice and to soothe his own conscience. He first went to Slovakia, then to Krynica and Wróblik, and returned again to Sanok. From there he dashed off to Germany, selecting Munich for his permanent residence.

With Hitler's suicide, all of Father Malynovskii's services and exploits for the glory of Hitler's butchers came to an end. He turned over his ordination authority to Father Andrei Zlupko, parish priest in Gładyszów. However, Father Zlupko could make no use of this authority, because the Apostolic Administration of Lemkovyna soon [in 1946] ceased to exist. The Lemkos were deported from their ancestral hills, some [in 1945-1946] to the Soviet Union [Soviet Ukraine], others [in 1947] to the western parts of Poland. There will be more on this in Part iv of this work.

27. Statistics on Losses During the Occupation

World War II, the most extensive and terrible of all wars, was most destructive of Poland and its people. Poland was the first country to resist Hitler's Germany. The entire impact of the enemy's war machine was concentrated on Poland. From the very first day of the war, the Germans used the most barbaric methods of waging war, violating all the principles of international rights.

Poland was attacked in a most piratical way, with no declaration of war. German aircraft conducted mass bombing of the defenseless population, killing civilians and destroying homes and historic memorials. The German airmen did not even honor the flags of the Red Cross, bombing even hospitals filled with wounded. For example, in Warsaw they hit the Christ Child Hospital, killing two hundred patients, six physicians, and twenty-six nurses. At the Holy Spirit Hospital, over a hundred patients were burned alive and two hundred died under falling debris. Incidents of prisoner torture were the order of the day.

During the occupation, "extermination camps" were constructed in

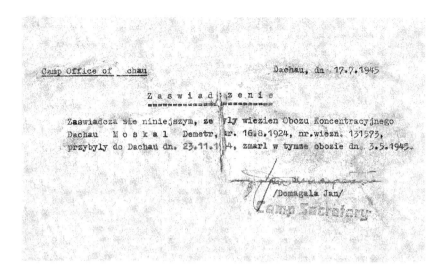

Notice of death of Demitr Moskal from Wysowa on May 3, 1945 at the Dachau concentration camp in Germany.

Poland, where innocent people were put to death by use of poison gas. The salvos of firing squads crackled through the streets of the cities. In the prisons and Gestapo death chambers, the most refined methods of torture were used. As a result of these repressions, 5,384,000 people perished, that is, over 19% of the population of Poland, not counting military casualties. When the latter are added, the death toll comes to 6,028,000, or 22.2 % of the population. No other country in the world suffered losses as high as did Poland.

Along with annihilating its people, the Germans also denuded Poland of its material resources. There was expropriation of property, forced contributions, pillage of assets in mines and forests, demolition of machinery and equipment, entire villages and cities laid in ruins, devastation of livestock, transport, communications, cultural institutions, and so on. All this resulted in impoverishment of the nation and its inhabitants. According to estimates by the Polish Bureau of Wartime Costs, the total material losses in Poland came to about 49 billion dollars. This amounted to 628 dollars for each person living in Poland. Thus, the cost of the war for Poland was the highest in the world.[24]

---

24 [Polianskii's figures here do not add up. If 22.2% of the population was 6,028,000, that suggests a population of about 27.1 million, which is roughly equal to the 1921 Polish census figure of 27.177 million. But the 1938 census had a 34.489 million population. The 1946 census counted 23.930 million. Whichever figure is used, 628 dollars per person comes to much less than 49 billion dollars.]

There are costs, however, that cannot be expressed in numbers. Primary among these is the loss of representatives of science and culture. Hitlerism murdered 700 (30%) of the professors, docents, and assistants at Poland's institutions of higher learning, 104 actors and directors, 235 artists, 156 writers, 122 journalists, and thousands of teachers, ministers, physicians, and lawyers. Furthermore, no one can count the number of old manuscripts, books, documents, compositions, museum articles, historic artifacts, etc. that were destroyed or plundered.

This is a brief and sad picture of the losses suffered by Poland during Hitler's occupation. Lemkos also suffered great losses in all aspects of governmental, religious, and cultural life. Poles were ruined by the Germans, Lemkos by the Germans and the Ukrainians.

28. Lemko Participation in the Struggle Against Hitler's Occupation

When the first wave of Hitler's terror and destruction passed through Central Europe, all the Slavic peoples, including the Lemkos, took up arms against the invaders. Only Ukrainian nationalists sided with Hitler.

The struggle against Hitlerism was hard, and Lemkos played a significant part in it. Considering the proportion of Lemkos in the total population, the number of Lemkos engaged in fighting the enemy, and the number of Lemko casualties, we can say without exaggeration that Lemkos took first place among the peoples fighting Hitlerism. Lemko participation in this struggle took three forms: guerrilla activity, voluntary service in the army, and material assistance. Because of its mountainous terrain, covered with forests and grooved by ravines, Lemkovyna provided favorable natural conditions for guerrilla action.

The first Lemko organizer of underground resistance was the fearless and unforgettable Hryhory Vodzik, born in Mszanna and a resident of Myscowa. Arrested by Ukrainian police, he escaped and soon made contact with Polish patriots. An anti-fascist organization called "Subcarpathian Patriots" was formed on his initiative. Its purpose was to unite all anti-Hitler and anti-fascist elements and prepare them to fight the invader. Among the first members of this organization in Subcarpathian Rus' were Hryhory Vodzik, Ivan Doński, Mychał Doński, Tymofei Doński, Stefan Peiko, Ivan Serniak, Fedor Serniak, Vasyl Olenych, Pavlo Shved, Tymik, Beskydniak, Iaviliak, Maltsev, and several others. Party committees and combat units were organized in the villages of Pielgrzymka, Kłopotnica, Wola Cieklińska, Myscowa, Uście Ruskie, Rozdziele, Brzozowa, Macyna Wielka, Hańczowa, Skwirtne, Bartne, Sołotwiny, Leszczyny, and Banica, and in the towns of Gorlice, Jasło, Żmigród, Krynica, Krosno, and Sanok. The Lemko committees became part of Subcarpathian District No. 1, with Stefan Peiko as district secretary and Hryhory Vodzik as chief of staff.

A conference of the party activists in Subcarpathian District No. 1 was held in Gorlice in March of 1942. Also participating in this conference were the party chiefs of the Cracow district, as well as members of the Central Committee of the Polish Workers Party, particularly Władysław Gomułka.

Lemkos from Zawadka Rymanowska in Red Army uniforms. 1945.

The conference adopted a resolution to start direct action against the invaders. In conformity with this, a military group of twelve men, headed by Hryhory Vodzik, was formed for Lemkovyna. This group was assigned to first, acquire weapons and go through Lemkovyna at night to search out fascists and their lackeys and to proclaim the inevitable downfall of Hitlerism and fascism in all Slavic lands; second, conduct hearings with those who consciously or unconsciously cooperated with the fascists and warn them of retaliation by the underground; third, put all Gestapo agents to death on the spot, destroy

Lemko villager Ivan Maksymovych (left) from Wołtuszowa, part of a slave labor force in Austria, carrying a bale of hay down from an Alpine meadow. Iselsberg, Ost Tirol, 1940.

telephone lines and all forms of communication between such agents and their superiors, confiscate and destroy official village documents concerning supplies for the German forces; fourth, wreck all facilities for processing agricultural products, such as wineries and milk plants, destroying stocks of grain, potatoes, and other food products destined for supplying enemy troops; and fifth, remove typewriters, printing equipment, and radio and telegraph apparatus.

And so the work of the underground began. The Gestapo agents soon learned that they were in enemy country and that, besides them, there was another force operating in the Carpathian Mountains that could deal them a fatal blow at any moment. Even more deadly were guerrilla actions against Ukrainian nationalists, those traitors to Slavic interests. The activities of the Lemko partisan guerrilla units were conducted with great difficulty. They were short on weapons and ammunition. In many cases they had to make do with old and decrepit Polish and Austrian carbines.

In April 1943, the Lemko partisans launched an operation to free two thousand Soviet military prisoners held in a death camp near Rymanów and guide them into the mountains. This operation did not succeed, however. In the camp there was a Gestapo agent dressed as a Soviet army major who sabotaged the plan. Many Lemkos died in this operation, among them Hryhory Vodzik, the commander of Subcarpathian District No. 1. Ivan Doński was selected to replace him as chief of staff. A short time later, he too had to leave the area, and Mychał Doński took his place.

Ukrainian nationalists tried all kinds of intrigue to sow discord between Lemkos and Poles, but the ties between the Subcarpathian District and the Central Committee stayed close. The Central Committee regarded the District as being important, cooperated with it, helped with instructions, and kept the two sides in harmony. This was due in large part to Władysław Gomułka, the present secretary of the Polish United Workers Party. He often came here with others to acquaint our organization with the situation on other fronts and to show the way to our objective. The help given the Subcarpathian District by the Central Committee was useful in maintaining friendly relations throughout the entire Second World War.

In Lviv, underground activity was carried out by Lemkos Iuliian Dziamba, Vasyli Dziamba, and Panchak, under the direction of D. N. Medvediev. In Ternopol Oblast, a group of Lemko emigrants organized an underground committee headed by Tkachenko. In this group were Ivan Romtsio, Volodymyr Tkach, Seman Peiko, Maksym Karpiak, and other Lemko emigres. After Tkachenko was killed by the fascists, this group returned to Lemkovyna where they continued fighting the invaders. Volodymyr Tkach was elected secretary of the Subcarpathian District.

Ivan Fudzhak, Jasło, 2002.

In early June 1943, a conference of representatives from the organizations in the Subcarpathian District was held in Mychał Doński's apartment in Gorlice; there was a discussion in detail on the situation in Lemkovyna. Setbacks on the eastern front had enraged the Germans and the Ukrainian police, and they stormed through the villages. Sensing their own ruin, they vented their rage by savage treatment of captured partisans and Soviet prisoners of war who had escaped from death camps. Especially rabid were the Ukrainian police in Uście Ruskie and Ropica Ruska, who killed partisans and soldiers unsparingly.

Not wanting to become slaves to the Germans, many young Lemko men fled to the mountains and hid out in the forests. Caught in the nets of various informers and provocateurs, they often became innocent victims. That is what happened to Petrushko in Uście Ruskie and the Nosal brothers in Krynica. The Ukrainian police broke the arms and legs of their captives, beat them unconscious, and threw them into the water, keeping them there until they revived, and then finally shot them. There was no end to the brutality of the Gestapo and the Ukrainian police.

Near the end of June 1943, a group organized by the Subcarpathian District was ready to fight the invaders. In the group were Lemkos Iaviliak, Shkymba, Maltsev, and Labyk, with some Soviet escapees, including Vasyli V. Nazarenko, Ivan Tetenov, and Sergei Tetenov. Seven partisans headed by one "Stakh" came to the mountains from Dembica. These two groups formed a single partisan unit of twenty-five men commanded by Stakh. This unit began operating in the Gorlice and Jasło areas and fought a number of battles. In the woods on Mt. Magura, near Gładyszów, they attacked a German transport, capturing large amounts of guns and ammunition. The Germans wanted to eliminate the Stakh unit, but they were afraid to go into the woods themselves so they sent in a number of spies. One of these was a Ukrainian activist, a bailiff in the village of Świerzowa Ruska, who entered the woods with a basket, as though looking for mushrooms. He discovered the location of the Stakh unit and signaled the Germans following him, who hurled hand grenades into the partisan camp. Stakh and his men were surrounded on all sides. They fought hard but were forced to retreat and left two men dead on the battlefield, Shkymba and Ivan Tetenov. Realizing that the partisans were poorly armed, the Germans pursued vigorously, so Stakh with his remaining men returned to the Dembica area. Stakh sent two of his men to report to the District headquarters, but they turned out to be traitors. Using information provided by them, the Germans made arrests in all the villages of Lemkovyna on June 28, 1943. Imprisoned at Jasło were some of the best people of Lemkovyna, among them Volodymyr Tkach, Ivan Romtsio, Mykhailo Romtsio, Iuri Rogots, Stefan Peiko, Iaroslav Vyslotskii, Aleksandra Vyslotskii, Danylo Porutsydlo, Vasyli Polivka, Ivan Doński, Tymofei Doński, Teodor Serniak, and dozens of other Lemkos and Poles. The prisoners suffered indescribable cruelties and humiliation. Often at night, some of them would be led out and executed. Bitter tears and loud wailing broke out all over Lemkovyna. The entire region wept, because there was not a single village without some victim of this fascist terror.

On the warm and quiet night of August 8, 1943, Polish partisans dashed into the Jasło prison to rescue the desperate inmates. They cut the telephone lines, disarmed the guards, burst into the jail, distributed weapons, and led the men out to liberty, 120 of them. This daring guerrilla attack enraged the Gestapo and the Ukrainian police even more. They arrested relatives of the freed partisans and confined them in a concentration camp at Szebnie near Jasło, where the prisoners were subjected to vengeful retaliation. Only four Lemkos escaped from Jasło prison; all the others had already been executed.

A partisan detachment, called *Bortsi za Svobodu* (Fighters for Freedom)[25] and composed of Lemkos and Soviet prisoners of war, was organized in the vicinity of the village of Myscowa. In this unit were such former prisoners as Lt. Boris Dranishnikov, who became the detachment commander, Ivan Mikhoev, Ivan Silchenko, Aleksander Burdov, and other escapees from the death camp. This unit took part in a number of actions. In the fall of 1943, it fought

---

25 [The published 1969 edition of *Lemkovyna: A History* incorrectly calls this detachment *Bortsi za Sovity* (Fighters for Soviets). Ivan Fudzhak, one of only two teenagers in the unit to survive the German occupation (six teenagers did not), describes their activities in more detail in Jarosław Zwoliński, *Lemkowie w obronie własnej* (Lemkos in their own self-defense), Koszalin, 1996, p. 26, available at http://lemko.org/pdf/obrona.pdf.]

a battle against German and Ukrainian police on Mt. Dziurdz, between Tylicz and Trzciana, in which many fascists were killed and much weaponry and ammunition was captured. In revenge for this defeat, the Germans took twenty men out of Jasło prison and executed them, including Lemkos Ivan Doński, Tymofei Doński, and Vasyli Polivka. At the Krynica prison, they executed Matsiiovskii. Danylo Porutsydlo from Czyrna also died there under frightful conditions. To avoid informing on his comrades, he slashed his wrists and his throat. His brother Volodymyr Porutsydlo managed to escape and exacted revenge for the death of his brother. Together with Antonii Kryl and others, he organized a unit that made the fascists and their lackeys pay a high price. They succeeded in freeing twenty Soviet prisoners from a factory in Nowy Sącz.

In the spring of 1944, a meeting of the partisans in the Subcarpathian District, together with delegates from the Cracow District of the Polish underground, was held in the forest between Pielgrzymka and Folusz. This meeting elected Petro Pavliak of Pielgrzymka as secretary and Mychał Doński as commander of the Subcarpathian District. Doński thus became the commander of all the partisan units in Lemkovyna. Now the pot really began to boil. Increasing numbers of escaped prisoners were brought into the forest. Partisans Dymytrii Labyk and Vasyl Chulyk managed to bring in some Slovak soldiers and officers: Jan Dubkalo, Jan Durilo, and others. The gunner Puterka joined the Lemko group, bringing his machine gun, and soon recruited fifteen well armed Slovaks. In Zyndranowa, a Slovak officer brought in twenty men

Dedication of the monument "To those from Lemkovyna who fell fighting the invader, 1939-1945." From left: Teodor Madzik, Maryna Shkurat and Mykhailo Madzik, all from Bartne. Uście Gorlickie, July 22, 1962.

"Returned from the war" in Red Army uniforms are Ivan Koval and Ivan Koropchak from Wysowa. 1945.

plus four machine gunners with their guns. Volodymyr Porutsydlo's detachment made contact with Slovak partisans led by Demko of Bardejov.

The partisan movement in Lemkovyna grew day by day. By the spring of 1944, there were hundreds of armed men fighting in the forests. They destroyed several police stations belonging to the Organization of Ukrainian Nationalists,

Orhanizatsiia Ukrainskikh Natsionalistiv (OUN). They attacked German transports carrying weapons and provisions. A vehicle with three staff officers was demolished on the Gorlice-Ropica road, killing the officers and recovering a number of important documents and a military map. On the Gorlice-Żmigród road, a motorcycle and its driver were captured; the driver was taken into the woods and the motorcycle was destroyed. A daytime battle was fought near Bodnarka, with many fascist casualties and no partisan losses. By the time German panzer units arrived, the partisans had disappeared into heavy woods. The Germans burned some cottages in Kłopotnica and shot the wife of partisan Stefan Olenych. Many homes were burned and many people arrested.

Right about that time, the [pro-]Soviet "Gottwald" partisan detachment came into the Carpathians. Its commander was Captain Kvitynskii. He captured Myscowa and several other Lemko villages. All the residents greeted him joyfully. The Lemko partisans joined this detachment and went with it to Czechoslovakia. They were of great help, especially Maltsev, Iaviliak, Ivan and Stefan Doktyr, Dymytrii Labyk, Vasyl Chulyk, Mykhailo Kotyrha, and others. Maltsev and Iaviliak fell in battle at Moravska Ostrava.

Captain Kvitynskii was a renowned partisan organizer. His detachment grew to brigade strength, because entire companies and battalions of Slovaks joined him. For his successful operations and battlefield exploits he was promoted to major, and the Soviet government awarded him a Hero of the Soviet Union medal.

When the Gottwald detachment left Lemkovyna, it was replaced by one commanded by Leontov. He also stopped in Myscowa, where he was greeted warmly. He spoke briefly to the villagers: "I have crossed through Ukraine and Poland, but nowhere have I felt as relaxed and secure as here in Lemkovyna, where every man tries to help his Soviet brethren in any way he can and empathizes with them through sorrow and through joy. Here there is only a true Russian spirit that has suffered the oppression of strangers and has not welcomed a liberator until today." The Leontov unit crossed the Slovak border and fought the fascists there until Czechoslovakia was liberated. General Baranov's guards regiment, hurrying to help the insurgent Slovak army [as an anti-fascist uprising was going on in Slovakia], drove a wedge into the Carpathians through Tylawa near Dukla. There it met up with the Lemko guerrilla fighters. The Germans were strongly entrenched in Dukla Pass, and General Baranov's troops had a hard time forcing through. The Germans knew that Baranov's regiment would be a great help to the Slovak army and did everything they could to prevent the two forces from combining. Despite all the difficulties, General Baranov broke through into Czechoslovakia, but with heavy losses. A portion of his men became separated and could not break through. However, they did not surrender to the Germans but joined the Lemko guerrilla fighters and continued fighting in the rear until both Poland and Czechoslovakia were liberated.

A Soviet partisan unit headed by Grigori Gladilin appeared in the area of Krynica. It was joined by Volodymyr Porutsydlo's unit. A detachment commanded by Lt. Col. Zolotar, who directed all partisan units in Poland, stayed for a month in Lemkovyna. His chief of staff was Lt. Col. Perminov. Zolotar's detachment conducted reconnaissance and fighting operations in the region of Nowy Sącz and Krynica. Petro Rusyniak rendered valuable service to the underground in Krynica. At the risk of his life, he systematically followed the movements of German troops and reported wherever appropriate. In the fall of 1944, the Zolotar detachment crossed the Slovak border. With it went the unit of Volodymyr Porutsydlo, who knew the territory and spoke both Russian and Slovak, rendering valuable service to the Soviet partisans.

A partisan unit headed by Pavlo Iurkovskii and composed of Lemkos and escaped Soviet soldiers and officers operated in the vicinity of Gorlice. Inestimable service in underground activity and the fighting around Krosno was rendered by Petro M. Kohut, Lena Kohut, and Havryil Levytskii.[26]

At nine o'clock on the morning of January 15, 1945, the artillery and rockets of the Red Army roared out. A cloud of black smoke hung over the German fortifications, with tongues of flame flashing through it. The whole earth seemed to be in flames. Deafening bursts of thunder merged into one long continuous roll that shook the air and the hills. It seemed that the mountains would all disappear. Suddenly, everything went quiet, but only for a minute. Then, a tremendous "hurrah" from the Soviet armies rolled over the Beskid Mountains, and the war on Lemko land was over. The people rejoiced with tears in their eyes, thanking God for their liberation from Hitler's oppression.

One of the most praiseworthy Lemko fighters in the war against the invaders

---

26 [See Petro Kohut, *Wojenne Ścieżki* (War Footpaths), Krosno, 2003. Available at http://lemko.org/pdf/kohut.pdf.]

was Mychał Doński, the very best son of Lemkovyna.[27] Together with his two brothers Ivan and Tymofei, Mychał fought valiantly and fearlessly for the betterment of his downtrodden people, from the very beginning of the guerrilla movement to its final end, as a partisan, commander, organizer, and instructor. Under harsh battle conditions, suffering shortages and hunger, wounded in battle several times, imprisoned for months, beaten and humiliated, but released through an unbelievable confluence of circumstances, and despite severe illness while in prison, he never relaxed for a moment, until the matter came to an end. His brothers died in battle as national heroes. Their names and their feats will remain forever inscribed in gold on the hearts of their people.

In addition to the glorious activity of the partisans, the contribution of Lemkos to the liberation of their homeland also includes the fact that many of the young men of Lemkovyna volunteered[28] for service in the Soviet regular army, and under the command of Soviet officers dealt the enemy a crushing blow. The number of Lemko volunteers in the Soviet army exceeded twenty-five thousand. About a third of them never returned to Lemkovyna. They fell as heroes on the field of battle, giving their lives for their people.

Mention should be made here of that great officer of the Soviet army, General Dr. Emilyian Iosafat Fedorenko, a Lemko born in Kostarowce[29] in Sanok County. As the supreme commander on the Ukrainian front he fought the enemy with superhuman strength, hoping that he could bring freedom and glory to his beloved Lemkovyna and that he would see his native village and greet his relatives in joy and happiness. However, fate did not permit him to see Lemkovyna. Severely wounded in battle, he was taken to a hospital and, suffering greatly from his wounds, ended his honorable life in 1945.

American Rus' also made a great contribution in the struggle against the

---

27 [Mychał Doński, pseudonym "Stańko", was born March 15, 1919 in Wola Cieklińska as Mykhailo Tsap. "Mychał Doński" was his nom de guerre during WW II and became his legal name after 1944, when he began working for the Polish security services. He immigrated to Soviet Ukraine in 1954 but returned to Poland in 1956 and immigrated to Yonkers, New York in 1975. He died March 2, 2001 in Gorlice.] See *Karpatska Rus*, Nos. 21, 23, 24, 25 for 1959.

28 [Most, possibly all Lemkos in the Red Army were in fact drafted by force, vacuumed up and sent to the front lines after two week training; many died in Slovakia. The editors have not encountered a single surviving veteran who has claimed that he volunteered. See e.g. Adam Barna and Teodor Goch, *Lemky v borbi za svoiu i ne svoiu svobodu* (Lemkos in the struggle for their own freedom and for the freedom of others), Legnica - Zyndranowa, 2005 (in Lemko), http://lemko.org/pdf/dobrovoltsy.pdf.]

29 [Part IV and Part V have him born in nearby Czerteż.]

German invaders. In addition to the fact that many young Lemkos served in the American army, mostly in the air war, and that many of them gave their lives, American Lemkos also contributed their savings to the Soviet army, thus expressing their solidarity with the people who were fighting fascism. With the Lemko Soyuz [of North America, the Lemko Association] as an intermediary, the Lemkos of the United States and Canada collected and sent to the Soviet Union about half a million dollars in cash, clothing, food, and medicine. The principal organizer of this effort was the late Dr. Symeon Pyzh.

29. The Tragic Balance of World War II

The second World War was the largest, most brutal, and most destructive of all wars up to the present time. From the very first days of the war, the Germans used the most barbaric methods, in contradiction of the principles of international rights. They invaded other countries without any declaration of war. Their air forces conducted mass bombardments of defenseless cities and villages, killing masses of civilians. German airmen did not even honor the flag of the Red Cross. They bombed infirmaries and hospitals. Crashes of firing squad salvos resounded through city streets. In prisons and death chambers, the German police and Gestapo tortured people using the most highly re-fined modern methods. Innocent people were burned alive in concentration camps. Priority in selection of murder victims was assigned to leading figures in science and culture, such people as university professors, artists, literary persons, teachers, physicians, spiritual people, lawyers. Historic art was either destroyed or carted off to Germany. Material resources were wiped out, and so on. However, a look at Hitler's ways of waging war shows clearly that the balance in this war was tragic for both sides.

Sixty-one nations took part in World War II, while only six remained neutral. The total population of the warring countries came to 1,700 million, of which 110 million were mobilized for war. Armies of 110 million men faced each other on the various fronts of the war. The extent of the fighting covered twenty-two million square kilometers. Battlefield casualties came to thirty-two million killed and thirty-five million wounded. Poland estimates its human losses at 6.028 million. Material losses in the war amounted to 260 billion dollars, of which 120 billion fell to Russia, 48 billion to Germany, 21 billion to France, 20 billion to Poland, and not quite 7 billion to England. During the war years, America produced 296,000 aircraft, Germany 104,000, England 102,000, and Russia 40,000.

Unmaintained Eastern Rite church on the verge of collapsing. Chyrowa, 1979.

The cemetery of the now no longer existing Lemko village Nieznajowa, whose inhabitants were forcibly resettled after the Second World War. Nieznajowa, 2003.

Iconostasis of the church in Królik Wołoski (above) as it looked in the mid-1950s after the 1945 deportation of that village's inhabitants, and its condition in 2002 (below).

PART IV:
AFTER WWII

Roadside religious monument near Krampna, 2001.

Prologue to Part IV

Хоц як война остра была,	No matter how fierce the war was
Але в конци ся скончыла,	It did come to an end
Войско домів повертало	Soldiers returned home
Гитлеровцов добивало.	The remnants of Hitlerites were being finished off
Тюрмы стали отворены,	The prison gates were opened
Вязні от смерти звольнены,	The imprisoned were saved from death
Повертают до свых родин,	They're returning to their families
Рахуют лем кілько годин	But wonder for how long
Знайдутся уж в своим домі,	They'll find themselves in their homes
По так тяжком сердця громі.	After such a heavy-hearted time.
Всядый радост, всядый втіха,	Everywhere is happiness, joy everywhere
Же по войні уж до лиха.	That the evil war is over
Же позбылися Гитлера,	That they got rid of Hitler
Же уж взяла го холєра.	That hell has taken him
Здавалося идут часы,	It appeared that a time is coming
Уж без страху, світлой красы.	A time without fear, of radiant beauty.
Но инакше ся судило,	A different judgment came,
Векше горе наступило,	Greater sorrow came upon us,
Аж нам в очах потемніло,	We were hardly able to see,
На Лацкові зашуміло.	Wind roared all over Lackowa.

Новий смуток, чорна хмара,
Пришла на вас нова кара
Зато, же мы вірны были,
Вірно Польші все служыли.

Пред ворогом боронили,
Николи єй не здрадили.
Горка наша русска доля,
Лучша єст смерт, як неволя.

Хцете знати, як то было,
Як выселение ся отбыло?
Тож уважно послухайте
И добрі сой спамятайте:

Може и вас то споткало,
З выселеньом так ся стало:
Село войско обступило,
Нове горе спричынило.

Пан капитан войска того
Наробил нам смутку много,
Казал нам ся позберати
И в дорогу рыхтувати.

З гор будеме выселены
И далеко вывезены.
Пару годин лем дал на то
И карами загрозил за то,

Кто был выжылся спознити
Або з села выдалити.
За то был бы барз караный,
Навет войском розстріляный.

New sadness, a dark cloud,
A new curse came upon us
Because we were faithful,
Faithfully we always served Poland.

Defended her against enemies,
Never betrayed her.
Bitter is our Rus' plight,
Death is better than being without
    freedom.

Do you want to know how it was,
How deportation took place?
So listen closely
And make sure you remember:

Maybe you were also touched by it,
This is how deportation was done:
The soldiers surrounded the village,
New sorrow took place.

The captain of this [Polish] army
Created a lot of grief for us,
He told us to get dressed
And be ready to travel.

We will be removed from our
    mountains
And be deported far off
He only gave us a few hours to pack
And threatened us if we don't hurry,

Anyone who entertained being late
Or running away from the village
Would be severely punished for that
Possibly even executed by the
    soldiers.

З собом вшытко можна взяти,
Што лем дастся спакувати.
Такий розказ был выданый,
Людми в страху выслуханый.

Кождий Лемко о том знає,
Што як войско не слухає,
Буде за то штрофованый,
Навет смертьом укараный.

Тож никто ся не противил,
Лем заплакал и ся скривил.
Ой, повічте, добры люде,
Што то з нами тераз буде.

Нас вывезут, арештуют,
Або нами проганддюют.
Річ окрутна, доля страшна,
Судьба наша барз несчастна.

Боже Благий и Могучий,
И Ты колись был страдучий,
Дай нам горе пережыти,
Будем вірно Ти служыти.

Пред нами крестна дорога,
Але уповайме в Бога.
Бог нам поможе, Бог наша сила!
Правда на кривдом все побідила.

Сміло з Исусом аж на Голготу,
Майме надію, віру и охоту.
В морю терпіний, в плачу и болю
Благайме Бога о лучшу долю.

You can take everything with you,
If you can pack it,
That is the order they gave us,
Heard by the people with fear.

Every Lemko knows that whoever
Doesn't listen to the soldiers,
Would be punished for that,
For sure, threatened with death.

Therefore nobody antagonized them
Only cried and winced.
Oh, tell us, good people
What will become of us?

They'll deport us, arrest us,
Or barter for us.
This is frightening, a terrible fate,
Our judgment is very bleak.

Benevolent and Almighty God,
You too at one time suffered,
Help us live through this calamity,
We will faithfully serve You.

The Way of the Cross is ahead of us
But look to God.
God will help us, God is our strength!
Truth always wins over wrongdoing.

Boldly with Christ all the way to
      Golgotha,
Let's have hope, faith, and will.
In a sea of suffering, full of crying
      and pain
God grant us a better plight.

О справедливост, правду и волю
Отче Небесний о то Тя молю,
Дай нам то горе передержати
И лучшой долі ся дочекати.

Пречыста Діво, Найлучша Мати,
Дай нам то горе перетимати,
Божы Ангелы и вшыткы Святы
Звольте нам а горю помоч дати.

Што ся в селі пак діяло
Коли вшыткым ясным стало,
Што зме з села вышмарены,
На погыбель презначены.

То не дастся описати,
Ни устами розказати.
Люде выли и кричали,
Слезами ся обливали.

Небіщыков споминали
И земличку цілували.
Слабшы мліли, их чутили,
Ишы з розуму сходили.

И вішати ся хотіли,
Люде анормальны были.
Ціле пекло ся озвало,
Людям розум помішало.

Єдны летят, як шалены,
Як бы Богом потуплены,
Гевсот кричыт, тамтот плаче,
А ворона все лем краче.

For justice, truth and liberty,
Heavenly God, I pray to you,
Give us strength to survive our sorrow
And to hope for a better plight.

Pure Virgin, Best Mother
Let us survive our grief,
God's Angels and all the Saints
Give us help in our grief.

What followed in the village
When it became clear to all
That we are being thrown out of the
    village,
Destined for destruction,

This can't be described,
Nor verbally expressed.
People wailed and shouted
Awash in tears.

They recalled their ancestors
And they kissed the ground.
Weaker ones fainted and were being
    revived,
Others were losing their minds.

Some wanted to hang themselves,
People did not act normally.
All of hell was speaking out,
And it mixed up people's minds.

Some were running like crazy,
As if condemned by God,
This one is shouting, that one crying,
And the crow crows as usual.

Баба копат свою грядку,
Нигде не видно порядку.
Хлопец з поду до сін скаче,
А ворона все лем краче.

Всядый гамор, всядый крикы.
Всядый розпач, всядый рыкы.
И звірята ся озвали,
Нибы концерт людям дали.

Концерт дикий и понурий,
Розпочал го Тарка бурий,
Бо як зачал он брехати,
Не мож было вытримати.

Хоц он все был на узвязи,
Урвал ся сам из ретязи.
Потом зачал страшно выти
И землю ногами рыти.

А корова ту тымчасом,
Зарычала контрабасом.
За ньом когуты запіли
И з банту сой выскочылы.

Куры зачали гдакати,
А гуси им вторучати.
Як телята забечали,
А паскудный голос мали.

Дітиска ся розплакали,
Потом козы забечали.
Такий концерт люде мали,
А вороны втяж кракали.

Granny is digging in the garden,
You can't see order anywhere.
A boy is jumping from the attic onto
		the corridor,
And the crow just crows.

Everywhere horror, everywhere
		shouting
Everywhere despair and howling,
Even the animals were heard
As if performing a concert for the
		people.

A wild and gloomy concert
Started by Tarka, the dog
Because when he started to bark
It was not possible to endure it.

Though he was always on a leash,
He broke loose
Then he began to howl dreadfully
And burrow into the ground.

And the cow, in the meantime
Roared in low bass.
After her the roosters crowed
And jumped from their perches.

Chickens began to cluck
And the geese answered them
When the calves lowed
And they made a nasty sound.

Children began to cry,
Later the goats began to bleat.
That is the kind of concert people had,
And the crows continuously crowed.

Внет молоты ся озвали,
Бо ними скрині збивали,
Штобы до них лахы дати
И зеренцьом присыпати.

Молоты бют, нервы грают,
А псы выют, сердце крают.
Была то ноч дуже грозна,
Без морозу а морозна.

Ничым то ноч Бартомлея,
Ничым конец был Гитлера.
Таке ото было пекло,
Што з памяти нам не втекло.

Довго будем памятати,
Покля буде жыти Мати,
Наша люба Лемковина,
Богом дана нам краина.

Весь добыток оставили,
Бо го взяти не успіли.
Ци можливе в том гаморі,
А до того в ночной порі

Каждой річы памятати,
Жебы єй зо собом взяти.
А ци дастся весь маєток,
Одіж, лахы, хліб и статок

До торбы на плечы взяти
И в світ помашерувати...

Soon hammers were heard,
Because chests were being made
To place clothing
And grain in them.

The beat of hammers, nervous tension,
And dogs' howling, slicing through
    the heart,
The night was terrible,
Without frost but freezing

As if it were St. Bartholomew's night,
Hitler's end pales in comparison
That's the kind of hell this was
Something that won't leave our
    memory.

We will remember for a long time,
As long as our Motherland lives
Our loving Lemkovyna
The land given us by God.

All property was left behind
Which they did not succeed at tak-
    ing with them.
It was not possible in this hell,
In addition this was at night.

Remember every thing,
So you can take it with you.
But will that be possible for all
    possessions
Attire, clothes, bread and animals?

To put them into a sack on your
    shoulder
And march into the world...

Як солнце сходило о 6-ой годині,
Памятам добрі, як бы было нині:
Вшыткы ся сходили на пляц
  презначеный
Через польскє войско вколо
  окруженый.

Як з хыж выходили жалостно
  плакали,
Порогы и стіны в слезах
  ціловали.
Ціловали землю, по котрой
  ходили,
Котру оробляли и єй барз
  любили.

«Горы нашы, горы, пращамеся
  з вами,
Бо уж отходиме, жаль нам єст за
  вами.»
Отходили смутны в далеке
  незнане.
Сердце у них было з жалю
  покраяне.

Остали грунты, хаты,
Господарскы всякы граты,
И зеренце, и жывину,
Озимину и ярину.

Поле красні пооране,
И зеренцьом засіяне,
Уж дакадый зеленіло,
Бо уж дост высоке было.

Аж ся сердце радувало,
Же не буде браковало

When the sun was rising at six
  o'clock
I remember as if it were today
All gathered at the designated place
Completely surrounded by Polish
  soldiers

They cried coming out of their
  houses
Threshold and walls were kissed in
  tears
They kissed the ground which they
  walked upon
Which they tilled and loved very
  much.

"Mountains, our mountains, we bid
  you farewell,
Because we are leaving, leaving you
  in sorrow."
We were leaving in sadness, to a distant unknown,
Each heart sliced to pieces by sorrow.

The land and houses were left behind
All farming tools,
And grain and animals
To plant for winter and for spring.

Fields already nicely plowed
And seeded with grain,
In some places it was getting green
Because it was already pretty high.

Our hearts were full of joy
That we wouldn't lack anything

Хліба, грульок и омасты,
Буде што до стодол класти.

Bread, potatoes, and grease,
And plenty to put in the barn.

Земля Лемкам все родила,
Одівала и кормила,
Аж ту вшытко нам пропало,
Бо мало ся взяти дало.

This land always produced for the
    Lemkos
It clothed us and fed us,
And now we have lost everything
Since we carried so little away with us.

Полемковскє добро взяли,
Тоты, што нич не вартали,
Неробы драбы и злодіи,
Працувати не хотіли.

They took Lemkos' goods,
Those who were worthless.
Loafers, hoodlums, and thieves,
They did not want to work

Ціле майно внет пропили,
Лемковину вынищыли
И цілком ей спустошыли,
И в джунглю ей замінили.

Soon they drank away everything,
They destroyed Lemkovyna,
Laid her to waste
And turned her into jungle.

Бы ей загосподаровано
Ріжны пляны укладано,
Пегееры закладано,
Миллиярды ту вкладано.

In order to farm her again,
Various plans were conceived,
Collective farms were set up,
Billions were spent.

Миллиярды дябли взяли,
Нич ту не вымудрували.

The devils took those billions,
But nobody got any wiser.

(Из *Пісні о Лемковині*)

(From *A Song About Lemkovyna*)

Villagers in front of local "Kachkovskii" Society, headed by Tymotei Fuczyla, Zawadka Rymanowska, 1937.

Holy Family along the road in the no longer existing village of Petna, 2004.

1. Hopes and Dreams for a Better Future

The Second World War was finally brought to a long-awaited end. The oppressor of nations and war criminal Adolf Hitler committed suicide on April 30, 1945. His defeated army ultimately surrendered to the Allied Powers on May 8, 1945. Those enslaved by Hitler breathed a sigh of relief and started to live a new life. It seemed that nothing could disturb the peaceful existence of men. Everybody hoped that the war, cruel and horrible in its consequences, would bring together united nations; that the Slavs would become honest brothers to each other; and that between the nations there would be Christian love. One might have thought that the time of all atrocities and injustices was finally over. Unfortunately, all these hopes turned out to be the wishful thinking of those who had lost most in the war. The demon of war did not rest, but continued to rage on, making various efforts in order to further its cravings for human blood; floods of tears covered the earth. On the Lemko horizon, black clouds gathered over the Carpathian Mountains, predicting that the people would experience new pain and suffering. Hardly had the Russian *katiusha* rockets fallen silent, hardly had fire been extinguished in Berlin and Wrocław, hardly had mothers' tears dried after the loss of their sons (either [drafted] volunteers or guerillas), when rumors, like thunder from the skies, were heard in the villages, claiming that the Lemkos were to be deported to the Soviet Union. To their horror, the news turned out to be true. Resettlement started in March, 1945, in stages. Those in the first stage were resettled voluntarily; those following were deported forcibly. In general, the people did not want to leave. They felt a strong emotional connection both to their native land and the mountains, and so they resisted deportation with all their might.

2. Use of Terror To Encourage Resettlement

Low-ranking government officials, the great majority of whom had not even the least bit of morality, were determined to have the Lemkos exiled to the Soviet Union by hook or by crook; they used a variety of methods to achieve their aim. First of all, they imposed heavy duties on peasants, requisitioning agricultural products which the villagers were obliged to carry to town free of charge. As a result, villagers were weak with hunger, and no one was there to lend them a helping hand. Furthermore, they were forced to do backbreaking physical labor, despite hunger and without any compensation. Because of hunger, various illnesses arose. To keep from starving to death, the Lemkos ate stinging nettle and other types of herbs, just as did people facing famine in the time of cholera.

Arrests were also used to intimidate the Lemkos into resettlement. The police spent entire days combing Lemko villages for men to arrest, taking from a dozen to several dozen prisoner until their families paid ransoms for them. In case an arrestee had nobody to pay a ransom, he would be taken to police custody in a district town and handed over to a specially appointed prosecutor. Arrested this way were the author of these words and Osyp Porutsydlo, a cantor from the village of Czyrna and the father of Danylo and Volodymyr Porutsydlo, both guerillas who fought fearlessly for democratic Poland and died as heroes in combat with the enemy.

The warehouses at police stations were bursting with food products (such as meat, flour, poultry, dairy products, eggs, honey, etc.) collected from Lemkos as ransoms for their freedom. Consequently, they threw lavish parties, with drunken feasting all night, at the expense of Lemko people who were left without even a crumb of bread and suffered excruciating hunger. This is how the police and all sorts of scum contributed to building a democratic Polish state in Lemkovyna: it grew out of human suffering and tears. One of the most severe persecutors of Lemkos was Mr. Gogol, the head of the local office of the *Urząd Bezpieczeństwa* ([State] Security Service) in Krynica, who arrested hundreds of people falsely.

These events took place in Nowy Sącz and Gorlice Counties. Further east, the situation was more terrifying, as witnessed to by the dozens, or perhaps hundreds, of burned-down villages, and the people swept off the face of the earth. Dozens, perhaps hundreds of Lemko villages, which until recently were full of life, are today a barren desert covered with weeds, inhabited only by stray feral cats.

3. Armed Bands Using Terrorist Tactics

When news of the Lemkos' deportation and their negative reaction to it reached Polish villages, some Poles decided to organize armed bands in order to force the Lemkos to leave for the Soviet Union; they wanted to plunder the Lemkos' possessions and then divide the spoils. Such armed bands were successfully formed in the following Polish villages: Mrzygłód, Bircza, Kuźmina, Borownica, Bukowsko, Nowotaniec, Głęboka, Jędruszkowce, Markowce, Niebieszczany, Zarszyn, Prusiek, Wróblik, and others, those formed in Niebieszczany, Prusiek and Wróblik were exceptionally ruthless. The villages of Prusiek and Niebieszczany were surrounded by barbed wire and trenches, with bunkers built in the middle. The band from Niebieszczany consisted of five hundred strong men armed with the newest weapons, having thirty modern cannons at their disposal. The band from Prusiek was composed of three hundred selected men armed from head to toe.

As wild as beasts, these bands raided Lemko villages and drove their inhabitants to emigrate to the Soviet Union. They struck terror in people's hearts just as Tatars and Huns did. When opposed by villagers, they would set a whole village on fire, beat its people, then expel them and steal their property. As for those who agreed to go to live in the Soviet Union voluntarily, while they were on the road to their destination these bands would rob them at gunpoint of whatever property they were bringing along. Not even Hitler, during the German occupation, caused as much harm to the enslaved nations as these bands of criminals did to the Lemko people. To convince the reader that the author of these words is an impartial storyteller who does not exaggerate facts, I am going to quote what an eyewitness of these events, Mr. Oleksa Konopadskii, born in Hłudno near Dynów, Lemkovyna, wrote down in his memoirs entitled *Spomny Ostroverkha* (Ostroverkh's Memoirs).[1]

---

1   Oleksa Konopadskii, *Spomyny Chotovoho* "Ostroverkha", Munich, 1953. [Reissued in *Litopys UPA*, Series 1, Vol. 30, Toronto, 2000; http://infoukes.com/upa/series01/sum30.html.]

4. An Eyewitness Written Record of the Events

This is what Oleksa Konopadskii wrote in his memoirs:

- Every day I encountered refugees from the left bank of the San River, the majority of them women and children, since their men had been murdered by Poles.
- The Polish bands have reached the right bank of the river; they've been sacking our villages with impunity, murdering people, looting and burning down houses.
- Poles raided the village of Leszczyna Górna, burned several houses, plundered the area, brutally beat the priest Fedorkevych, the cantor Naidukh and the head teacher Stepan Krenta. They took the latter to the village of Leszczyna Dolna; after breaking his arms and legs, they burned him alive. While he was burning to death, he cried out: "People, I'm dying for Lemkovyna!"
- The Poles from the village of Bircza set Mykhailo Tovarnytskii's house on fire; inside were the corpses of his mother and wife, both stabbed to death, and his brother, gravely wounded by a shot.
- Twenty Polish thugs from the areas of Leszczawa and Kuźmina raided the lower part of the village of Lachawa, beat and battered its people, then rushed off to the hamlet known as Podlesie.
- A group of roughly four hundred Polish thugs raided the village of Grąziowa, set about a dozen houses on fire and killed all the male inhabitants.
- In the village of Grąziowa, over two hundred thugs coming from the villages Wojtkowa, Leszczawka, Kuźmina and Bircza fatally shot a few men. Nine villagers were tied to stakes while another nine were ordered to beat them. Then the situation turned around and those who had been beaten were made to take revenge on their fellows. Several of them died at the stakes from their beatings.
- In the town of Jamna, thugs set fire to several villages and murdered some peasants.
- Thugs arrived at Leszczawa Górna with carts and plundered the village, taking whatever they could pile onto the vehicles while killing about fifty villagers.
- In the forest west of Bircza lay a village of Polish thugs known as Borownica. There were about three hundred thugs there, so there was no peace nearby.

Every day gangs of thugs launched assaults on our areas in which about ten villages (including Brzeżawa, Ulucz, Jaworów) were burnt nearly to the ground and thoroughly plundered of cattle, horses and grain; nearly two hundred young boys and girls were murdered.

- All through May and June, Lemkos were being chased out and forcibly resettled. While the pacification and resettlement were taking place, villages were set on fire.

- People who managed to survive could not return to their houses. Their villages lay in ruins, plundered by thugs coming from the villages of Głęboka, Nowotaniec, Pobiedno, Jędruszkowce, Bukowsko, Markowce, Niebieszczany, and others. In the towns of Zagórze and Zarszyn, bands of thugs attacked the expelled Lemkos, robbing them of whatever they had rescued from their villages. These bands took people's of money and possessions, including underwear, clothes, shoes, cattle and horses; they also arrested peasants, mostly young people, many of whom where taken to an unknown spot and killed.

- In the woods, one would come across many huts made of pine branches as well as peasant carts loaded with possessions, cattle, and horses. Every village had its own encampment or bunch of wagons around which constant guard was kept; but when thugs would attack, people would flee deep into the forest, leaving their belongings to their fate. Many peasants hid in Slovak forests.

- The village of Rubatowo was burnt three times by Poles. The Lemkos lived either in dugouts or in shelters made of planks and pine boughs.

- When forced resettlement intensified, Lemkos fled their houses and hid in the woods along with their belongings. Some of those who escaped reached Slovak forests; there, in the shade of fir trees, they erected shrines made of bark and decorated them with the image of the Mother of God, placing icons and crosses beneath it. At these shrines, they would kneel down and fervently pray to the Suffering Mother of God, placing their fate in her hands. This testifies to the high moral stands and the piety of the suffering Lemko.

- Czechoslovak State Security Service spread the rumor that the Czechoslovak government would admit all Lemko exiles into the state, providing them the farmland from which Hungarians had been expelled. Many Lemkos believed the rumors, but once they crossed the border, State Security caught them and handed them over to the Poles. So did Slovak partisans and Czechs.

- Many Lemkos were held in Polish prisons and suffered grievous conditions. A peasant who was released from prison in Sanok gave a firsthand account of Lemko prisoners' life. The food was simply terrible, and during interrogations prisoners were severely tortured; they were beaten and had their finger bones broken.

Here, I will stop relating the words of Konopadskii as an eyewitness to the terror and suffering of the Lemko people. They give a fairly clear picture of the moral decline of the rural Polish population.

This extermination of the Rusyn people had the peculiar characteristic that the organizers and leaders of the Polish bands who carried it out were for the most part Roman Catholic priests. To put some flesh on this statement, we introduce two of these priests, Franciszek Żurawski and Jan Szul.

5. The Priest Franciszek Żurawski – Organizer and Leader of a Polish Gang

The priest Franciszek Żurawski, a former Armia Krajowa (Polish Home Army) chaplain, organized a terrorist gang. It was composed of a thousand men marching from village to village, murdering Rusyn priests and peasants, burning down houses, stealing possessions, and perpetrating the most dreadful crimes. Dozens of clergymen were killed, among them the pastor of the village of Babice, Anatol Sembratovych; the pastor of Tarnawka, Mazur; the pastor of Skopów, Demianchyk; the pastor of Brzuska, Bilyk; etc. Apart from clergymen, approximately a thousand innocent people of both Rusyn and Polish origin were murdered. Here is the copy of the accusation against Żurawski of committing crimes, made by one Kosińska, a Polish woman living in the village of Babice. The accusation was to be read by the bishop of Przemyśl. Translated, it reads as follows:

Your Excellency Bishop of the Diocese of Przemyśl:
In front of Your Excellency, I accuse the priest Żurawski from the village of Drohobyczka (Dubiecko) of the following crimes, committed during and after the German occupation between 1942-1946. As captain of

a Home Army unit, he is responsible for murdering Father Mazur, the pastor of the village of Tarnawka, near Dubiecko. Everybody knows that it was Żurawski who had ordered two thugs, fellow inhabitants of the Drohobyczka village, to kill Father Mazur. Having killed the priest, they plundered his house of all possessions and abducted his young house-keeper, Maria Król. The girl was kept as Żurawski's lover with whom he had a five-year sexual relationship. At the same time, he had another lover, Janina Duduś from the village of Babice; he is currently living with her in the west. The priest Żurawski arrested the husband of Janina Duduś with her assistance after he had been released from a five-year captivity; though a Polish Catholic, he died in prison in December, 1951.

Apart from the crimes mentioned above, the priest Żurawski is guilty of slaughtering thousands of people with the help of his thugs that were sent out to neighboring villages. By the order of Żurawski, some thugs were directed to the village of Babice and told to murder Father Sembra-tovych, a friend of the Polish population. Owing to the villagers of Babice who interfered with the thugs, Father Sembratovych's family escaped alive.

In Skopów, the priest Żurawski along with his gang participated in murdering the Greek Catholic priest, Father Demianchyk, as well as other clergymen and their families. The band led by Żurawski also killed several peasants while robbing them of their carts and horses; a peasant who was threshing grain nearby was slaughtered too.

The thugs smashed Father Demianchyk's head in so violently that his brain matter splattered across the wall. After the brutal murder of the priest, Żurawski and his gang had a drinking binge, paid for with their victims' money. After they had been drinking heavily for a couple of days, the party gradually turned into an orgy and adultery since Żurawski had many guerrilla girls within his group. The party's becoming an orgy was encouraged by Żurawski who with his lover set an example in front of his people's eyes. His fellow thugs followed his example and soon the orgy was in full swing. Having no partner, a village official, Tomasz Golenio-wski, left the party and hurried to tell people what had happened, so the whole parish knew the details. With his lover, Maria Król, Żurawski stole all of the priest Demianchyk's possessions; he also installed her father at Demianchyk's parish house where he is still living now.

When the Skopów parishioners put the murdered villagers on a raised bier, the thugs commanded by Żurawski emerged and desecrated the bodies; their clothes were torn off, bones broken, and they were thrown to the ground. And yet, even these dozen or more corpses did not satisfy Żurawski, who was still thirsty for blood. In the beginning of April, 1945, he summoned all his people, an estimated thousand villains, and launched a savage assault on the villages of Bachów, Brzuska, and Sufczyna. Before they marched out, he prayed for a long time, then blessed the thugs and sprinkled them with holy water. He spurred them into carnage, urging them to kill in the name of Christ and burn down whatever they would encounter in their way. Armed to the teeth, the thugs slaughtered eighty Poles in the village of Bachów as well as the rest of the inhabitants, who were of Rusyn nationality. In the village of Brzuska, 180 people were butchered, among them Father Bilyk; over seventy unarmed civilians, both women and men, were massacred in the village of Sufczyna. Hundreds of homesteads were burnt to the ground. The thugs plundered thousands of cattle, cows, horses, sheep, pigs, hundreds of sacks filled with grain, furniture, clothes, vessels, farming tools, etc. Both Poles and Rusyns were murdered regardless of their age or sex; drunken thugs cut them dead with pitchforks, axes, metal sticks, or chains. And as the butchery raged on, the thugs robbed whatever they could. The whole family of Father Bilyk in Brzuska was murdered. The thugs returning from their mass killing expedition were solemnly welcomed by the priest Żurawski awaiting them in the market square of the village of Babice. Dressed in a cassock, he thanked God for the victory, praised his people's courage and addressed the children who were nearby, reminding them to "follow in these heroes' footsteps," that is, to follow murderers and butchers from his guerrilla unit. Four thugs were brought back dead to the village; being drunk, they had fatally shot themselves. They were to be buried in a cemetery in their parish of Dubiecko, but its pastor did not want the cemetery to become the final resting place of criminals. In the end, the bodies were taken back to Babice and buried by Żurawski who conducted a formal funeral service. After the funeral, he divided the wealth plundered from the villages of Sufczyna, Brzuska, and Bachów among the members of his bands, with the lion's share (including dollars, horses, clothes, and other valuables) left for himself. The priest Żurawski was in need of money for his lovers, for women of loose habits, and for presents for them.

Today, the priest Żurawski is living on the "Recovered Territories," in the village of Srokowo, Kętrzyn County, Olsztyn Province, where he is under another name, hiding from the hand of justice.

I have described here the misdeeds of the priest Żurawski that I am familiar with. However, my account does not exhaust the subject of his heinous crimes. He is a villain who ought to be deprived of his priestly dignity as he does not deserve to be regarded as a priest. For years, he has been committing adultery and other sins. His hands are stained with the blood of hundreds of victims, among them over a dozen clergymen, as well as being marked with the tears of a few thousand people grieving over their relatives killed either by him or by his order.

I would appreciate it if Your Excellency could look into the crimes of the priest Franciszek Żurawski committed during the German occupation and until 1946, and the sins that he commits to this day. I expect Żurawski to be severely punished for his atrocities. This felon cannot be a priest since he has the blood of innocent people on his hands; he has hundreds of clergymen on his conscience. He violated the law of God and the laws of the Church.

Babice, April 24, 1952. Kosińska.

This is the accusation Mrs. Kosińska leveled against Żurawski to the Roman Catholic bishop of Przemyśl. The banditry described in the letter is the best characterization of the morality of the priest Żurawski and other Roman Catholic priests like him. There arises the question of how the bishop responded to Mrs. Kosińska's letter. According to canon law, after committing these murders, robberies, and profanities, the priest Żurawski should have been deprived of priestly rank, or in the most lenient case suspended from his duties until the end of his life. As it turns out, there was no reaction from the bishop. Conversely, the villain was given a false identity paper issued by the Episcopal Curia and went to live in the Olsztyn Province where he continued to carry out the duties of a priest. How could that be? A segment of the Roman Catholic clergy, of extremely nationalistic sentiment, coined a new, chauvinist golden rule: "Kill and rob people of different nationality and you will do your homeland a favor and be worthy of respect. Who serves their homeland serves God." It's as simple as that. Obedient to this rule, Żurawski killed and robbed our people and our priests, firmly convinced that he did what God and his homeland expected of him.

Here we will provide an illustration of how the Roman Catholic [Latin Rite] bishops approach the Greek Catholic church. A Greek Catholic priest, Father D., came to live in a female convent where he served as a priest in exchange for board and lodging. One day, the convent was visited by a diocesan bishop. Seizing a rare opportunity, D. asked the bishop to be granted an audience. The

bishop agreed. At the meeting, when D. raised the subject of the Greek Catholic
Church and rite, the bishop flushed with anger. Convinced that D. was a Latin
Rite priest, he addressed him frankly: "You probably know that the Eastern Rite
is to be liquidated as soon as possible. I am surprised that you care about that.
You'd better not concern yourself with it." Once the bishop finished his speech,
a nun came in and invited him for dinner. Before dinner was served, the bishop asked the nuns why their priest was concerned about the Eastern Rite. The
nuns explained to him that D. was a Greek Catholic priest. When the bishop
learned this, he grew anxious and yelled out with regret: "I shouldn't have spilled
the beans! What is the priest going to think about us?!" And he was so worried
about what he had said that he did not even touch the food.

   Although unintentionally, the bishop clearly expressed the intention to liquidate us; that is, to destroy us. And Żurawski found a way to destroy us, and
destroyed us in his way. He acted in agreement with the bishop's intention.

6. The Priest Jan Szul –
Organizer of Terrorist Gangs

Another Latin Rite priest who has been praised to the skies in public forums
strictly followed the golden rule mentioned above. He is Jan Szul, the former
pastor of the Radziechów village, the present parish priest and dean of the village of Stare Bogaczowice, Wrocław Province. In 1945, the priest Jan Szul and
his parishioners settled in villages neighboring the parish of Wróblik Królewski,
within Krosno County. He planned to use terror to capture Wróblik with the
assistance of the gang that he had organized, force all its inhabitants of Rusyn
nationality to emigrate to the Soviet Union, and then settle there with his parishioners. The band led by Jan Szul consisted of three hundred thugs, including
his relatives and parishioners, and was well equipped with all kinds of weapons,
including cannons. During the whole month of June, 1945, the village of Wróblik was the scene of fierce fighting between the priest's thugs and the inhabitants of the village. Each evening the thugs attacked the place, surrounding it;
the village came under fire from all sides. Houses were ignited by shots and the
explosions of hand grenades. The local residents took defensive positions; some

guarded the homesteads while others fought the fires. Those who had a gun returned fire in order to keep the thugs out of the village's central area. The noise of the shots was accompanied by the cries of children and the wailing of dogs, of which there were many in Wróblik. Fighting lasted all night until the break of dawn. The fighters were sleepy, exhausted, depressed, and anxious about what would happen the following night. Nobody was able to do any work. The situation lasted a month. Eventually, the villagers were forced to capitulate and register for emigration to Russia [Soviet Ukraine].

The bandits took over Wróblik. Of its long-time residents only one villager remained. On their first night in Wróblik, Szul's bandits attacked him and beat him so severely that he died before morning; his property was robbed. The Wróblik priest, Fr. Polianskii, was left alone in the parish house, to which he had recently returned after four years in confinement. The priest Jan Szul appeared at Polianskii's door and declared that he was the new pastor of Wróblik and that the church, parish house, and all the crops gathered from the parish field belonged to him; therefore, Polianskii had to move out immediately. In response to this declaration Polianskii demanded the paper stating that the parish had been assigned to Szul by the bishop. Szul replied that it was now not the bishop who ruled, but physical force. He threatened Fr. Polianskii that his parishioners (the bandits) would force Polianskii to emigrate. The priest Szul followed through on his threat and the following night he set his thugs on Polianskii. The band surrounded Polianskii's house and fired several shots into the windows of the bedroom where he slept. The assault resulted in windows smashed to pieces and Polianskii's last cow stolen. The following day, Szul repeated his demand. After protracted negotiations, he allowed Polianskii to stay in the parish house for a couple of days; meanwhile, Szul moved in with his family and occupied the rest of the house.

A few days later, Polianskii was attacked once again. The attack was led by two bandits dressed up in military uniforms. At about eleven p.m., they broke into Polianskii's bedroom and told him to produce an identity paper. Then, they made him turn his face to the wall and on pain of death they forbade him from turning around. This time, the priest was robbed of all the valuables he kept in his bedroom. After locking Polianskii in, the bandits plundered the house methodically, room by room. Finally, the priest was told to leave the place within twelve hours; otherwise he would be killed. He was given twelve hours to leave the Wróblik village forever.

As soon as the village had been wiped out of its inhabitants, the band led by Szul broadened the scope of their crimes. Night and day, they attacked

Lemkos leaving for the Soviet Union, robbing them of their last possessions. When rumors of these assaults reached military authorities, they sent army and police units to Wróblik to examine the case. The army surrounded the parish house, searched the building and seized hundreds of rifles and other weapons that had been hidden inside; in the stable, they discovered the cows and horses robbed from the Lemkos. As a result, the priest Szul's family was immediately arrested; the weapons and cattle were confiscated. The chief bandit, Jan Szul, managed to escape and left for the Recovered Territories; in spite of his heinous crimes, clerical authorities assigned him to a thriving parish and gave him the rank of dean. Similar activities by Latin Rite clergymen took place in other villages of our unfortunate Lemkovyna.

7. The Ukrainian Insurgent Army (UPA)[2]

As mentioned above, Polish bands marched through Lemko villages, killing, burning, and plundering. The members of these bands, recruited from fascist scum, forced people to leave for the Soviet Union. If the inhabitants of a village refused to obey, they were driven out by violence; their houses were

2   [There are grave doubts that Sections 7-12 of Part IV are the product of Fr. Polianskii's hand. It seems that the printing and binding of *Lemkovyna: A History*... could not be completed at the Yonkers, New York Lemko Association print shop and that final production was moved to the Ukrainian Svoboda printing press in New Jersey. An informant, who was in a position to know, states that a UPA delegation appeared from Canada and insisted on the inclusion of these sections on threat of stopping production, or worse. A fall 2011 enquiry into this matter to the executive of the *Ukrainskii Narodnii Soyuz* (Ukrainian National Union), the owner of the Svoboda press, elicited no response. Whatever the case, it seems that Fr. Polianskii, a well known anti-Ukrainian, was not and could not have been in a position to know the operational details of UPA activities in the Lemko Region. Such details have been published for all UPA operational areas in the fifty-plus volumes of *Litopys UPA* (Chronicle of the UPA), which began appearing in Toronto, Canada in the 1980s. Toronto was the final destination for many UPA refugees after WWII and it was there that an archive and publication office was established; see www.litopysupa.com. Given the anti-Soviet stance of the UPA, the political perturbations in the Lemko Association leadership (see "The Lemko Association and *Lemkovyna: A History*..." in Appendix I of this volume), and the Lemko Association's return to a pro-Russian, pro-Soviet, and pro-Communist line for the next twenty years, it would seem that the two thousand or so copies of Polianskii's *Lemkovyna: A History*... became a liability. They were relegated to the basement of Lemko Hall in Yonkers for some thirty years.]

burned, property stolen. The people found themselves in a grave situation. In this tragic moment, the Ukrainian Insurgent Army operating in the Hutsul region came to the Lemkos' rescue. It made an effort to fight against the bandits, and a fierce, bitter guerilla war broke out. After long struggles, the UPA started to liquidate the Polish bands. As this liquidation neared completion, the regular Polish Army entered Lemkovyna, and a new war between the army and the UPA developed. It is worth mentioning that the UPA came to aid the Lemkos of its own volition, without intervention from the Lemkos.

8. The Organization of the UPA

Formed in 1943, the Ukrainian Insurgent Army, *Ukrainska Povstanska Armiia* (UPA) grew out of the pre-war OUN). During the German occupation, they were engaged in fighting against Polish and Soviet guerrillas. The leader of the national movement was Stepan Bandera, the son of the priest in the village of Nowica situated near the city of Kalush; Bandera headed the Ukrainian Supreme Liberation Council (UHVR). Roman Shukhevych, under the pseudonym "Taras Chuprynka," was the UPA's Supreme Commander. Subordinated to Stepan Bandera, he was in charge of the Supreme Military Headquarters (HVS) as well as Regional Military Headquarters (KVS).

Following the four compass points, the UPA was divided into four operational regions:

1. UPA "East" encompassing the region of Podole;
2. UPA "West" covering the area of the Lwów and Stanisławów Provinces;
3. UPA "North" based in the regions of Polesie and Wołyń;
4. UPA "South" encompassing the area of Transcarpathia.

Each operational group was subdivided into military districts, which in turn split into tactical sectors. In 1945, the Operational Group UPA "West" operated in Poland. Its units were included into the Sixth Military District (*okruha*) which comprised the following tactical sectors: "Lemko," covering Przemyśl County except for its northern part, Sanok County, Lesko County, and Nowy Sącz County; "Bastion," covering territory west of the San River and the northern part of Przemyśl County; and "Danyliv," encompassing the western part of Tomaszów

Lubelski County as well as Włodawa County, Hrubieszów County, and Biała
Podlaska County. The UPA's basic combat unit was the company. The "Lemko"
sector was comprised of *sotni* (companies) known as "Bir," "Brodych," "Burlaka,"
"Hromenko," "Khryn," "Krylach," "Lastivka," and "Stakh." Similarly, the "Bastion" sector consisted of companies named "Bryl," "Kalynovych," "Kruk," "Shum,"
and "Tucha." The companies within the "Danyliv" sector were named "Chansa,"
"Davyd," "Duda," and "Yar." Each company (*sotnia*) comprised between 80 and
180 riflemen (soldiers) and contained three or four platoons (*chotas*); each platoon consisted of three squads (*roii*). Three or four companies (*sotni*) made up
a battalion-size unit (*kuren*). Each military district and tactical sector had its own
headquarters with a commander, a chief of staff, a political instructor, a secretary,
and an armed militia. The headquarters of a battalion and a company included
the commander, political advisers, quartermasters distributing supplies to troops,
and army men. Battalions and companies had military police at their disposal.

The OUN was led by the *Kraiovii Provid* or directorate which consisted
of the leader (*kraiovii providnik*), the UPA's military commander, the heads
of the administrative units (the organizational, economic, and propaganda
units), and the secret police (*Sluzhba Bezpeky*, abbreviated SB). Regional and
local leaders (*providniks*) of the OUN were subordinated to the *Kraiovii Provid*. All in all, the OUN was the underground organization in charge of administrative duties, whereas the UPA constituted its military wing. The UPA's
members numbered roughly 2,500 soldiers and 3,500-4,000 civil servants.

In 1945, the UPA's units operating in Poland constituted the group code-
named "Sian" commanded by Iaroslav Onyshkevych, a co-founder of the
Ukrainian Insurgent Army. He adopted various pseudonyms of which "Orest" was the most famous. Iaroslav Starukh, the son of the mayor of the village of Baligród, was the main OUN *providnyk*; he adopted the name "Stiah." *Sluzhba Bezpeky* was headed by Petro Fedorov, code name "Dalnych."

9. The UPA's Military Strategy

The UPA's units were well-equipped and led by well-trained officers. They hid in
bunkers and raided neighboring villages and towns. They often attacked Lesko,

Baligród, and Sanok. They gained control of the frontier region and inspired terror in the population. Mothers mentioned them to threaten their naughty children. Even today, deep in the mountains, their bunkers and dugouts can be seen; they were designed and constructed with artistry. For example, one huge hideout was built under an enemy headquarters swarming with soldiers and closely guarded. The entrance to the bunker entrance was concealed in the well from which the enemy drew water every day. Nevertheless, the insurgents passed unnoticed for months. With the use of covert listening devices, they eavesdropped on all the conversations being held at the headquarters.

The UPA's soldiers would endure hunger, cold, and other hardship without complaining. Since they fought stubbornly and fiercely, the struggle against them was bitter and inflicted heavy casualties. The UPA's units were composed of people of different nationalities. There were Germans, Czechs, Italians, General Vlasov's soldiers, Poles from the Blue Police, and many other foreigners among them, although some of these foreigners turned out to be provocateurs or traitors. In battles against the UPA, many of our villages were burnt to the ground and many people perished.

10. The Death of General Świerczewski

On March 28, 1947, Karol "Walter" Świerczewski, commander of the Polish Second Army and a hero of the Spanish Civil War, was assassinated while on his way to inspect the troops. On his way from Jabłonki to Baligród, he was caught in an ambush that had been set up by the UPA's "Khryn" and "Stakh" companies.

Since the death of General Świerczewski's assassination is linked to the deportation of the Lemko population, it is worth taking a closer look at the circumstances of his death.

On March 27, 1947, at ten o'clock p.m., the colonel Szerpyński, a division commander, called the major Grodzicki, the chief of staff of the Polish military forces in Lesko, to inform him that the following day at six o'clock a.m. an important figure was arriving in town with the purpose of inspecting the troops in Lesko and Baligród. Yet nobody knew who the figure was. The major

Pawlikiewicz and the lieutenant Osiewski were issued the orders to make preparations for the visit. A guard was posted at the top of the castle in Lesko and was told to wave a red flag to indicate that the guest was approaching the site. The guest, General Świerczewski, turned up exactly at six a.m., emerging from the green Opel that belonged to the commander of a division. Świerczewski's armed escort occupied a Dodge. Once the troops had given him a respectful salute and all reports had been received, the general entered the headquarters and was offered breakfast which he refused. After a short conversation with the captain Ciszewski, the general said that he wished to be taken to Baligród; he was in a hurry as he should have been in the town of Sanok by noon. Two Dodge cars had been prepared for a drive; these were to be followed by the Opel and a ZIS, the latter with the lieutenant Osiecki at the wheel. Having been saluted by the troops, the general got into one of the Dodges; he was accompanied by the colonel Sierpiński, the major Grodzicki, the captain Cichowski, and two soldiers armed with machine guns. The car was driven by Hipolit Kaleń. Other officers piled into the remaining cars. All the passengers numbered about thirty people.

It did not take them long to get to Baligród. After a company within the battalion commended by the general Muszyński tipped their caps to render honor to Świerczewski, the officers mentioned another garrison stationed further to the south, in the town of Cisna, namely the operational maneuver group of the Border Protection Corps. The general decided to review it immediately. The officers tried to dissuade him from his idea, pointing to the difficult access to the village, the lack of time, and danger, but to no avail. He insisted on going to Cisna. So they did as he wished.

They set off for Cisna in the following order: the lead Dodge was occupied by the armed escort composed of the soldiers who had arrived from Sanok; right behind the escort, the second Dodge with Kaleń at the wheel carried the general (taking the passenger seat), the colonel Sierpiński, the major Grodzicki, the captain Ciszewski as well as a sapper platoon lieutenant and the two soldiers equipped with machine guns; the last ZIS, driven by the lieutenant Osiecki, contained Lieutenant Rafałowski and the soldiers of a non-commissioned officer school.

At first, the road was smooth. The general was in a good mood. The town of Cisna was a twenty-kilometer distance from Baligród. During the course of conversation, Świerczewski promised to supply more troops for the officers so that they could utterly destroy the UPA by autumn. The lieutenant Sierpiński explained to the general that it would be difficult to get rid of the

UPA since some mountain villages had been providing them with help and protection; whether voluntarily or under threat, the local population served as the UPA's base of support.

"They will have to be resettled then," said the general, "I know it's hard, but it can't be helped. For their lost property, they will receive compensation and be given modern farms in the 'Recovered Territories.' It is a common policy to resettle people; peasants around the world are relocated by industrial development (whenever railroads, dams, etc. are to be built). In the Bieszczady mountains, the resettlement will be linked to the struggle against bandits. In this regard, it seems justifiable."

The first Dodge suddenly came to a halt and made the following two vehicles stop. The drivers leapt out of the cars and leaned over the dead engine. The general, who was getting impatient, decided to continue the drive without his escort, saying that they would catch up when the car had been repaired. The Dodge that carried the general passed around the damaged vehicle and drove off; the ZIS driven by Osiecki followed it. As both cars reached the village of Bystre, the landscape turned into a barren desert. Bystre and Jabłonki do not exist anymore as villages. They have been burned to the ground by Polish bandits.

They were driving along the narrow mountain road. The peak of a lofty mountain towered over the area on the right; on the left, the river Jabłonka wound its way through the clearing; behind the clearing another mountain summit covered with dense coniferous forests rose from the ground. What they could see in front of them was the river bend, a bridge and undulating land. Complete silence hung over the place.

As the cars approached the bridge, everyone heard bullets whistle in the air. The cars screeched to a halt. The general, the officers, and the drivers burst onto the road. It suddenly dawned on them that they were caught in an ambush prepared by the UPA. The guerrillas couldn't have chosen a better place to fight. A fierce battle began. Using automatic weapons, the UPA units continued spraying the Poles on the road with bullets. While the officers were trying to shield themselves from shots, the general was standing upright with his hands clasped behind his back and his head lifted up to look at the mountain occupied by the UPA gunmen. Anxious for him, the officers bellowed: "Sir, lay down on the ground! on the ground!" To their despair, he did not react, but stood in place. He behaved as if he were bullet-proof. Several shots hit the cars. The lieutenant Osiecki was shot dead. The captain Ciszewski, the lieutenant Rafałowski, the driver Hipolit Kaleń, and many others were severely wounded.

Yet, the general kept standing on the bridge. Indifferent to the battle raging on, he undid his coat, lowered his head and started to examine a point below his breast. When the captain Ciszewski asked him if he had been hurt, he replied that a bullet had only grazed him. Then, he fastened his coat and uniform, and told his people to descend to the river. The guerrillas, however, did not let them gain an advantage; they ran down the mountain, crossed the road, and clashed with the Poles at the riverbank. Afterwards, they climbed up the hills and continued shooting. The river crossing became extremely dangerous since the officers were constantly under enemy fire. All of the sudden, the general shivered with cold and slumped onto the ground. The captain Ciszewski darted towards him, crying desperately, "General, General!", but in vain. Świerczewski breathed with difficulty. His face was pale, eyes closed.

The major Grodzicki ordered that the general be taken to Baligród, but none of the vehicles was accessible. The driver Niebylski volunteered to go and fetch a car, but once he approached it, he was hit by a shot. The struggle was bitter. There was no chance to get out of this hell. The UPA companies "Khryn" and "Stakh" numbered about two hundred, whereas the Polish group was made up of hardly thirty soldiers, among them several already wounded. At that very moment, the Dodge that had gone dead on the road turned up, carrying Świerczewski's armed escort. The soldiers jumped out of the car and plunged into fighting. Thinking that the Polish army had come in relief, the UPA insurgents retreated to the mountains. The battle was over. The general was dead. His corpse was placed in the car that Kaleń had driven him in earlier. That was the general's last battle as well as his final journey. Next to him, the corpses of Kaleń and Osiecki were laid. The second car was occupied by the wounded officers, captain Ciszecki and lieutenant Rafałowski, and the two riflemen, Rudak and Niebylski, injured as well. The other soldiers went on foot behind the cars.

In the place where General Świerczewski breathed his last, a lasting memorial was built.

The general's death resulted in the forced relocation of the Lemkos. On April 24, 1947, the Council of Ministers decided to resettle the Lemkos to the western provinces of People's Poland. A sum of sixty-five million zlotys was allocated for the implementation of resettlement. The goal of the deportations was the liquidation of the UPA military organization and the punishment of the local people for supporting this organization, which in reality had no basis in fact.

11. The Stages of the UPA's War

The guerilla war that the Ukrainian Insurgent Army made on Poles in the Carpathian Mountains can be divided into three stages. Its initial phase covered the period from summer 1944 until spring 1946; the second stage of the war lasted from spring 1946 to spring 1947, overlapping it was the final stage which continued until the end of 1947, or even to March, 1948. During the first stage, the UPA soldiers fought against Polish bandits who were forcing the Lemkos to resettle in Soviet Ukraine.

The UPA operated in Lemkovyna, winning battles and gradually taking control over the area. They didn't hide, but lived in cabins built in the woods, from which they emerged to raid the neighboring villages.

The second phase of the fighting began when the Polish military forces engaged in combat. Violent tactics and unexpected attacks were employed, with both sides determined to crush each other. The situation for the UPA units got worse each day. Due to significant combat losses, they were forced to retreat to the woods. It was impossible for them to even think about gaining control of the region. During this stage, forests and various inaccessible places were converted into a network of UPA bunkers, dugouts, and hideouts.

During the last stage of the war, the UPA was completely liquidated. Surviving units fled across the border to Soviet Ukraine.[3]

12. The Organization of Polish Military Forces and the Final Liquidation of the UPA

From April, 1946, the theatre of operations encompassing Lemkovyna was divided into operational sectors under the authority of Regional Security Committees, which in turn were subordinated to the Polish State Committee on Public Security. The committees included officers of the Polish Army (*Wojsko Polskie*, abbrev. WP), Internal Security Corps (*Korpus Bezpieczeństwa*

---

3   [Other units fled through Czechoslovakia as best they could to the American occupation zone of Germany.]

Wewnętrznego, KBW) as well as members of the Office of [State] Security (*Urząd Bezpieczeństwa*, UB) and the police (*Milicja Obywatelska*, MO).

The operational sectors split into smaller sections within which the military units of KBW, WP, MO, *Wojsko Ochrony Pogranicza*, WOP (military section securing borderlands), etc. operated. From April to October, 1946, the Operational Group "Rzeszów" (derived from the Eighth and Ninth Divisions of the Polish Army) was charged with fighting against UPA units, but it did not succeed in destroying them. On April 17, 1947, therefore, after Świerczewski's assassination, the Operational Group "Vistula"[4] was called to action, headed by Gen. Stefan Mossor. Eventually, a few divisions of the Polish troops and the Internal Security Corps defeated and destroyed the UPA *sotni* led by the officers known as "Ren" (Sanok County, Przemyśl County, Krosno County, Jasło County), "Baida" (Sanok County, Lesko County), "Zhelizniak" (Przemyśl County, Lubaczów County), and "Berkut" (Hrubieszów County, Tomaszów Lubelski County). By the end of 1947, the UPA and the OUN ceased to exist. Until March, 1948, KBW, MO, and ORMO (Voluntary Reserve of MO) units continued to apprehend UPA remnants. The UPA's leaders, Iaroslav "Stiah" Starukh and Petro "Dalnych" Fedorov, were arrested and sentenced to death. Ivan Mizernii, the commander of the "Ren" company, Minister Piernacki's assassin, stepped on a mine planted near the Chryszczata forest and was blown to bits.

13. The Battalion of Death

In Lemkovyna there also operated a Polish band known as the "Battalion of Death." It was commended by a Major Michalski and included about three hundred Belarusians, and even Russians. Like all other such bands, it was armed. Along with Poles, there were Jews and Gypsies within its ranks, and it was purely predatory. Since the UPA commander known as "Khryn" [Stepan Stebelskii] attended the same school as Michalski, these units were neutral towards each other. Michalski said, "I don't want to fight with 'Khryn'; let him not look for me, and I won't look for him. I don't desire his death, just as I want to live, too." But what Michalski said did not prevent his people from robbing poor Lemkos.

4   The "Vistula" group forcibly deported the Lemkos to the 'Recovered Territories.'

14. The "Burning Hearts"

In alliance with the UPA, another Polish military organization known as "Burning Hearts" operated in the Lemko region. Their motto was "Freedom and Independence." Since the band was commanded by Major Żubryd, its members were called "Żubrydowcy." Captain Piskorz served as the second-in-command of the group. Their main goal was to fight against democratic Poland. Therefore, they raided police stations, blew up bridges, set fire to factories, and killed peasants who bought a piece of land that had been parceled off, attacked trucks carrying food supplies, murdered Jews, and tortured innocent people. Not only did the Polish Army quickly liquidate the "Battalion of Death," but it also got rid of the "Burning Hearts."

After General Świerczewski's assassination, but before the UPA was thoroughly destroyed, the saddest chapter of the Lemko history began, a chapter of the national tragedy with a whole sea of tears, suffering, and despair. Even Jews mourning the fate of their nation over the ruined walls of the Holy Temple in Jerusalem were not as devastated as we are when describing our nation's recent suffering. Our people's misery cannot properly be expressed using perishable letters from a pen, or properly told by human lips, but can only be felt by an open and honest heart.

* * *

During his university years, the author personally knew such figures as Stepan Bandera, Roman Shukhevych, Iaroslav Onyshkevych, Iaroslav Starukh, Stefan Mossor, and Michał Żubryd.

15. The Expulsion of the Lemkos From Their Beloved Mountains

The spring of 1947 came. Spring is the most enchanting time of year. Every day, the sun rises higher and shines brighter. In spring, peasants start their work at dawn and finish it late in the evening. They plough the field, preparing it for sowing seeds; then, they plant grain, potatoes and cabbage, which were the most essential crops in mountain villages. A peasant's heart grows happier when he goes into the field in the springtime to see that his work has paid off and the seeds he sowed and planted have begun to sprout. That gives him hope for a bumper harvest. The sun is shining brighter and warming the soil; birds are singing cheerfully above, accompanied by frogs croaking in the pond. "How beautiful is God's world!," thinks the grower glowing with happiness. He bows before God and whispers a prayer to thank Him for His gifts. May in Lemkovyna is marvelous.

Yet May 1947 in Lemkovyna differed from the usual May. In the spring of that year all the duties of a grower were done; fields were sowed with seeds and crops were planted. Yet, for some unexplained reason, the Lemko grew sick at heart and was tortured by some great pain. He could not rejoice at the beautiful world, at the bright sun, at the cornfields. Instead there were only premonitions of terrible tragedy, which was not long in coming.

Late one night in May 1947, unexpected guests arrived at Lemko villages. They were the penal detachment of the Polish troops. Coldly, their commander announced that the military authorities had issued a decree expelling all the Lemko villagers from their land as punishment for the assassination of General Świerczewski; by six o'clock a.m., they were to be ready for their departure from the area. The villagers, however, were not told where they were to be taken. There were various speculations. Some Lemkos thought that they would be resettled in the Soviet Union, some feared that they would be sent to prison, and others were convinced that they would be taken to a detention camp or subjected to slave labor. A ghastly night descended on Lemkovyna. This night cannot be compared to any other night recorded in human history, neither to the night of St. Bartholomew's Day [when thousands of Huguenot Protestants were killed in France], nor the massacre at Uman [when thousands of Jews and Poles were slaughtered by the rebellious haidamaks]. The people sunk into despair. Cries and screams broke the silence of the night, mingling with the barking of dogs. All these sounds were accompanied by the hard blows of the axes and hammers with which the villagers were nailing together boxes to pack their things in. Even the cattle kept in the stables were bawling hysterically, trying to bolt from their tethers as if they felt some imminent danger. Horrified by their unhappy fate, some Lemkos went insane and some were hitting their heads against the wall, while others fainted, or ran around chaotically as mad people do. These terrible scenes, which continued until morning, can by no means be adequately described by the pen. Those who stayed calm and conscious asked themselves, "Are we capable of packing all the belongings that we've gathered through centuries, with only a few hours to pack? How are we to carry these things with neither a horse nor a cart?" Why are we being punished so severely by Poles? Haven't we remained faithful to Poland? This is how they repay us for our sons fighting and dying for a democratic Poland..."

At six a.m., all were ready to depart. Those who possessed a horse-drawn cart could take with them as many belongings as a small mountain vehicle could contain and a horse could deal with. Those without a cart were even more limited as they had to carry things on their backs. Consequently, the Lemko property was left to fate. The deportees abandoned what generations had worked whole centuries to collect. They left the fields that they had sowed and planted with crops as well as their houses, farm buildings, agricultural machinery, farming tools, kitchenware, and household appliances. They took with them only a small part of what they once possessed.

Precisely at six o'clock a.m., they set forth on a journey into nowhere with tears of grief and hearts filled with sorrow. Each of them gave a farewell kiss to the threshold of their cottage and the soil that used to feed them. What they felt within their hearts when leaving their villages and beloved mountains is impossible to describe. Pain and torment of soul pushed some people to the edge of despair; others entrusted themselves to God's will. They prayed to God, whispering a Psalm of David, "My help comes from the Lord Who made heaven and earth." Never before had any of the deported Lemkos been struck with such a tragedy, such struggle, such sorrow and suffering, even while standing over the grave and bidding farewell to their dearest ones who were setting out on the road to eternity.

Only after the deportees were brought to the railway station were they finally told where they would be taken. That reduced their anxiety a bit, and they sighed with relief.

Days and nights passed and they still were on the way to their destination. The train transporting Lemkos stopped at every station; sometimes it remained at a station a couple of days. After weeks on board, the Lemkos were running out of food and money; as a result, they were threatened by death from hunger. Struggling to survive, they helped each other as much as they could. Yet they developed dry stomachs, emaciated faces, and hollow eyes. After the hardships of the rail travel and many sleepless nights, the train finally drew into the station. The Lemkos had the terrible appearance of people from another world. Getting off the train, they scared everybody away with

The Petronchak family with Atanas Petronchak on the lap. After 1945 the family lived in Lviv. Królik Wołoski, 1933.

their appearance. A rumor spread that a train transporting wild Africans had arrived in the "Recovered Territories." Other gossip began circulating that Russia had sent cannibals to slaughter all the Poles.

Two reasons for the deportation of the Lemkos have been given: the assassination of General Świerczewski, and easier liquidation of the UPA. The first idea is implausible because everyone knows who killed the general. The other solution accuses the Polish troops of incompetence: was it really necessary to resettle a half million inhabitants to get rid of a handful of bandits? The Polish army had many other ways of dealing with the UPA. And if that had really been the reason, then after the liquidation of the UPA the Lemkos would have returned to their ancestral lands. There was another reason. The surviving fascists contrived the deportation.

16. The Lemkos Settle In The "Recovered Territories"

The deported Lemkos were transported to the "Recovered Territories" and dispersed across nearly all its provinces. Most Lemkos were moved to the provinces of Wrocław, Zielona Góra, Szczecin, and the Pomerania region. However, they were scattered throughout various villages so that they did not form a large group in any of them. They were given the poorest land to cultivate and the most decayed buildings to live in, those which no Polish settler wanted. The farms set aside for the Lemkos were either without buildings, or dotted with buildings that crumbled away, lacking doors, windows, or roofs. There was no furniture in the homesteads and no farming implements, not to mention the lack of agricultural machinery. Without food or the bare necessities of life, they were in an exceedingly difficult situation. At the same time, they were not allotted any benefits from the government; neither provisions, clothing, nor money. A priest attempted to persuade the head of the charity organization "Caritas" to support the starving Lemkos, but to no avail. Although stores run by "Caritas" were full of food and clothes sent from America and meant for people in dire straits, the Lemkos' needs were ignored. At least some of these goods must have been intended for the Lemkos as they were donated by their countrymen in America. Unfortunately, the Lemkos got nothing. It was the leaders of "Caritas" who most benefited from the donations; they stole things and engaged in fraud. That is why the government began to supervise and finance the organization.

In order to not starve to death, the Lemkos took on the hardest jobs, enduring humiliations and insults hurled by their Polish brothers. For nearly half
a year they suffered hunger and poverty until they finally gathered the first
harvest. This slightly ameliorated their situation; at least they weren't hungry. Over time, their living conditions improved. They built new buildings
and repaired the old ones; they bought indispensable farming tools; later on,
they acquired farm machines, too; more livestock was raised, and intensive
agriculture eventually started.

Today's Lemkos have more success farming their hilly land than their Polish neighbors have on better land. Similarly, Lemkos are better citizens of Poland than the Poles themselves. The Lemkos fulfill all their duties as citizens;
they pay all taxes on time and provide the country with part of their harvest;
the authorities want everybody to follow their example. The Lemkos live soberly and morally. They stopped drinking ether, known as *kropka* (droplet),
which had been their favorite beverage. Living in the difficult mountain conditions influenced the Lemko character; they became hardworking, honest,
and noble people. It would not be an exaggeration to call them the worthiest group of people in Poland. In the "Recovered Territories," their material
conditions are far easier than they had been in the mountains.

*Lubin continues to serve as a magnet to descendants of those deported to the
"Recovered Territories" in 1947. Aleksandra and Oleh Hereichak's wedding ceremony
at the Orthodox church in Lubin, 1989.*

Fiftieth anniversary celebrations at the Orthodox church in Legnica, Lower Silesia, in the former German "Recovered Territories," 1998.

With church choir in the background, Fr. Eugeniush Boiko bids farewell to his successor Fr. Lubomyr Vorhach. Lubin, the largest agglomeration for deportees of 1947, located 20 km from Legnica, September 28, 1997.

Remains of a house as of 1959. Wołowiec. (Photo © J. Madzik)

Nevertheless, they miss living in their mountains and dream of returning to their native places. The Lemkos no longer lack wheat loaves, but they would find more savor in their former oat bread or *adzymka*.

17. Why Do The Lemkos Dream Of Returning To Their Mountains?

There are many reasons for posing this question. Most importantly, Lemkos are indigenous to the Carpathian region. Polish scholars unsuccessfully tried to prove that Lemkos are vagabonds. Such an effort, for example, was made by a professor at Warsaw University, W. Maciejowski. In his work *Pierwotne dzieje Polski i literatury* (The early history of Poland and its literature) he claimed that King Casimir the Great had allowed Lemkos to settle in the Carpathian Mountains. His view was contradicted by Mykhailo Krynytskii, the parish priest of the town of Tylicz, who dug through various archives, court judgments, and offices, and collected many documents, on the basis of which he wrote his famous work entitled "The Historical Status of the Muszynka Vice-Regency: A Physical, Political and Religious View on the Basis of Fifty-One

Existing Purely Rusyn Villages and the towns of Muszynka and Tylicz." With this work, the priest refuted all the claims made by Maciejowski and, on the basis of documents, was able to show that Lemkos are the indigenous inhabitants of their homeland.[5] As a result, even Maciejowski did not have the courage to continue to voice support for his theory.

Contemporary Polish and Soviet scholars and historians who did the same research concluded that the Carpathian region (today's Lemkovyna) was the cradle of Rus', not Kyiv as was alleged until now. From the Subcarpathian area, Rus' spread towards the east, reaching the Dnieper River and Kyiv. Since the dawn of Slavic history, Rusyn people, the ancestors of Lemkos, have inhabited the area of today's Lemkovyna.

Putting aside historical proofs that the Lemkos are the autochthons of the Carpathian land, Lemkos feel instinctively, in their blood, that they have originated from the Carpathian Mountains. They may wander around the world, but eventually they always end up returning to their mountains, as though drawn there by some inner force. They miss their mountains, forests, and pastures; in them they see peaceful life, happiness, and joy. The Lemkos feel this yearning all the more today, when they are dispersed over the whole world. In Poland, they are scattered across a wide area, not forming clusters anywhere, and living long distances from each other, they cannot satisfy their cultural, educational, and religious needs. To them, it is torture and slavery living in the midst of a foreign people with different customs, culture, character, and even a different religion. Such conditions evoke even greater yearning for their native place.

Freedom of religion is a constitutionally guaranteed right in Poland. Members of each rite have their own recognized places of worship where they can fulfill their spiritual needs. Only the Lemkos are excluded from this privilege. The deportees left behind hundreds of beautiful Eastern churches in the mountains, which were changed into Roman Catholic ones, but they were given none in the "Recovered Territories." As a result, they were deprived of Divine Service and their rite's religious practices. Their yearning for their native land includes a thirst for their Church, their fine rite, their language, as well as their material and spiritual culture. While living in the mountains, the Lemkos had been involved in educational and cultural work; they had their own press, publishing houses, reading rooms, and literary circles as well as economic and commercial organizations. Now they have none of these. Yet, what humiliated them most is that the historic name applied to their nation, "Rusyn" or "Rusnak," was officially banned, and

5   See Zborowski, ed., *Otechestvennii Sbornik* (A collection of native works), Vienna, 1853.

Consecration of the first Eastern Rite church in Poland since the interwar period. Zyndranowa, 1985.

they started to be identified as "Ukrainian." Every people has its own nationality and name; this is a law of nature. Yet with Lemkos, even the laws of nature were flagrantly violated. This cries out to heaven for vengeance.

Poland is inhabited by citizens of different nationalities, among them Germans, Czechs, Belarusians, Jews, Gypsies, and others. They all have their own organizations, newspapers and committees. Only the Lemkos have none of them; they were denied these rights. A policy of rapid "Ukrainization" was adopted. To trigger off the process, the Lemkos were given a page in the Ukrainian newspaper *Nashe Slovo* ("Our Word"). To deceive Lemko eyes, the page was entitled *Lemkivske Slovo* ("The Lemko Word"), but over time the title was changed into *Lemkivska Storinka* ("The Lemko Page").[6] Not many Lemkos took the bait. Some Lemkos published their articles on the page out of pure necessity, since they were not allowed to issue their own press.

The Lemkos have many reasons for their dissatisfaction with living in the "Recovered Territories" and desire to return to their mountains, but among them are the hostile, even belligerent attitude of Polish peasants and Roman Catholic clergymen towards them. For the most part, Polish society is uninformed about and poorly disposed towards Lemkos, identifying them with the Ukrainian nationalists who had committed many dreadful crimes

---

6   [There were periods when even that one page was suspended for months.]

From left: Maxim Sandovych Jr. with wife, head of the Polish Orthodox Autocephalous Church Metropolitan Basil (Doroszkiewicz) of Warsaw and all Poland, and Bishop Adam (Dubec), of the Przemyśl-Nowy Sącz Eparchy. Zyndranowa, 1985.

against Poles during the German occupation and after the war. Thirty thousand Poles were murdered by Ukrainian hands in the eastern borderlands of pre-war Poland. Still, Poles have a distorted picture of the Lemkos; they are wrong to blame them for these heinous crimes. Ukrainian fascists inflicted as much suffering upon Lemkos as they did on Poles. As early as World War I, Ukrainian nationalists along with Austro-Hungarian military authorities created the Talerhof concentration camp where thousands of Lemkos were imprisoned, tortured, and killed. During the Second World War, Ukrainian nationalists acting as agents, military policemen, and trusties for Hitler persecuted Lemkos even more severely than they did Poles.

The hatred of Poles, especially young ones, for Lemkos, is so deep that under the influence of alcohol, the youth launched assaults on Lemkos and perpetrated awful crimes against them. Lemkos have been beaten by the Polish youth and cases of murder have even taken place. God forbid a Pole hear Lemkos speaking their language; an assault would be unavoidable. In 1960, for example, several Lemkos were beaten unconscious by young Poles at the railway station in the village of Gwizdanów; the police sided with the hooligans while the poor Lemkos, residents of a village near Gwizdanów, faced charges of assault and were taken to court. Such beatings and murders happened quite often in the "Recovered Territories." Other cases are also worth mentioning: Petro Zoryla was killed in the village of Gawronki; a Pole from this village seriously wounded Ivan Perun; Pavlo Mytsovskii from the village of Niszczyce was brutally murdered; members of the Demai family were attacked and beaten black and blue near the village of Modła, in Bolesławiec County; with the chauvinist shout "Ivans!" Poles savagely beat our boys in the village of Krzydłowice, Głogów County; in the vicinity of the villages of Rychlik and Siedliska, located in Trzcianka Lubuska County, vicious attacks and fights occurred continuously for many years. There are hundreds of other examples of crimes against Lemkos which would take entire volumes to describe. Although the Constitution of Poland protects freedom of speech in all languages, woe to the Lemko who tries to speak to another Lemko in his own language. Young Poles would not hesitate to threaten to kill and hang them as soon as given an opportunity, even though Lemkos have never given Poles the slightest reason to hate them and have always tried to live in harmony with Poles. The life of a Lemko in the "Recovered Territories," therefore, is an uneasy and bitter one, as they live in constant uncertainty about their future.

For the reasons mentioned above, the Lemkos wish to return to their mountains. Since their arrival in the "Recovered Territories," they have been trying to fulfill their dream, but various civil and county officials put obstacles in their way. Appeals and complaints lodged with central authorities also, for the most part, turned out to be to no effect. Last year, a small group of Lemkos finally succeeded in coming back to Lemkovyna in the following manner: they bought back from Polish settlers the lands that used to be theirs before they were forced to abandon everything and leave. But the fate of these returning Lemkos is nothing to envy. The demon of national chauvinism triumphed here, too. In Izby, on Christmas Eve, Poles set fire to the house where two Lemko families were sitting at the table and singing Christmas carols. Shocked at such violent hatred from his Polish neighbors, the owner of the burned-down house returned to the "Recovered Territories."

18. To Whose Advantage Was the Resettlement of the Lemkos?

The deportation of the Lemkos did not bring any good to anybody, but rather did harm to the deportees as well as to the Polish government. It was precipitous, reckless, and not well thought out. The Lemkos suffered extensive material and moral damage. They left the labor of generations behind on their estates in the mountains, for they could take only which a small cart could contain or, for those having no cart, what they could carry on their backs. The rest of their property had to be abandoned. Their farms were mostly taken over either by idle settlers who didn't want to work, or who were incapable of cultivating mountain fields. Their deserted cottages and buildings were pulled down and used as fuel for heating houses. Valuable furnishings and farming tools were either lost or squandered on drink. The harvest towards which Lemkos had labored was reaped and eaten up; when the next spring came, the new settlers had nothing to sow and plant their fields with. Consequently, they left the lands uncultivated; eventually the barren fields were overgrown with weeds and went to waste. The new settlers faced severe famine. In order to not starve to death, a whole procession of hungry people lined up at the county administrative office to beg for bread, claiming that their mountain fields did not want to grow anything. The chief executives of the county replied, "Until recently, before your arrival, these fields were farmed by Lemkos who never came here for bread. Each year, they gathered in a bumper crop since they cared about their fields. Work as the Lemkos did, and you will not be short of bread." It was a wise and fair response, but the lazy settlers did not follow this advice, letting their fields go even further wild.

The government, which was striving to improve rural agriculture, did its best to recover the Lemko farms. In some villages, "State Agricultural Farms" (*PGR* in Polish) were created; in some, collective farms or *kolkhozy* emerged; in others, cattle were raised and vegetables were grown. But all this effort proved in vain as there was a shortage of people willing to work. The government paid out millions for agriculture, but it all came to nothing.

At the Polish Academy of Sciences, a committee on mountain land management was established. After examining the matter, the committee held a conference which was attended by a wide variety of specialists and scientists, among them the director Bodnar, the professor Krzysik, Dr. Kubica, Dr. Nowak, the engineer Dąbek, Dr. Szmagała, and many others who were knowledgeable about the matter. At the conference, its participants were virtually unanimous that only the Lemkos were capable of farming these areas, as they were hardworking people who from their grandfathers' and great-grandfathers' time had been skilled at cultivating mountain fields. The committee launched a project that was aimed at setting up four thousand new settlements (along with the five hundred already existing) by 1960; each year, the number of new villages was to be increased. This plan still has not been implemented.

If the Lemkos had not been expelled from their beloved mountains, the mountain areas would look different today, managed with advanced agricultural techniques. With the strong support of the Polish government, the hardworking, resourceful, and hardened Lemko nation would have expanded the mountain economy to such a degree that it would have become a lucrative source of income both to the local people and to the state. The deportation of the Lemkos, therefore, turned out to be a bad move by the government of that time.

Today, thanks to the renewal of its policies, the People's Republic of Poland has been making up for old mistakes and repairing the damage it caused. It should also let the Lemkos return to their native lands so that they could contribute their great knowledge and industry to the recovery of the mountain economy. Such an action would be beneficial for both sides: by erasing the harm done to faithful citizens of the People's Republic of Poland, its authority would be strengthened not only abroad, but also in the eyes of the Lemkos.

19. The Situation of the Greek Catholic Church in People's Poland

The expulsion of the Lemkos from their beloved mountains is linked to the fate of the Lemko nation and its religious confessions, both Greek Catholic and Orthodox, a fate that never before took place in any Christian country. By the time deportation started, Divine Liturgy and all other church services in the Eastern rite had been strictly forbidden in Lemkovyna. The ban was announced orally by district leaders and subsequently enforced by the police

(Milicja Obywatelska). Enforcement was strict. As a result, by the second half of 1945, all the Lemko Eastern Rite churches had been closed. At first priests continued to conduct Divine Liturgy silently, behind closed doors, but this was at great risk, since such priests were in constant danger of being persecuted and arrested.

At the end of 1945, all our clergymen were deported from Lemkovyna either to the Soviet Union, or to western Polish territories. The people were deprived of their priests and liturgy. In May 1947, there followed the deportation of the entire remaining population of Lemkovyna, which resulted in empty churches without priests, faithful, or care. The Lemko people had sacrificed in order to build their churches, which became their pride and their soul. These churches had their own special Lemko style and architecture. Their interior was abundant with the treasure of centuries of folk culture. There were wonderful historic icons depicting the Mother of God, Christ the

In 1945-1946, 60,000 Lemkos were deported to what is now Ukraine. Consecration of the first Lemko church in Ukraine. Lviv, 1992.

Saviour, and those pleasing to God, painted on canvas, wood, or glass, mostly by Lemko painters. Almost each parish could boast beautiful folk carvings and an iconostasis made by famous carvers and painters, as well as a library containing valuable and rare charters, manuscripts, chronicles, parish histories, and artistically adorned service books, Gospels, Books of Hours, and menaions. The churches were furnished with precious ritual objects such as gold chalices, crosses, candle-stands, and many more. These were priceless national treasures. When the Lemko people were deported from Lemkovyna, all these liturgical objects were carried away by some invisible, but evil hand. Today, the Lemko churches stand empty (or have completely disappeared) and are falling apart due to their age. Adherents of modern culture converted the church of the village of Ropki into a sheep barn.

In the church in the village of Izby was a wonder-working icon of the "Mother of God of Izby," dating from the seventeenth century. Today the church no longer has that icon. It fell victim to theft. (It is probably held in the [Eastern] church of the city of Brest and looked after by a Polish priest, Ignac...) Other historic icons dating back to the times of outlaws and confederates were robbed as well. That very church of Izby, which was once the pride of the Lemko Beskids, nowadays has been sagging to the ground because of its age, as if saying to the Lemko souls, "If you are gone, then I, too, do not want to live." In the village of Łabowa, a beautiful brick [Eastern] church toppled entirely to one side. Some blasphemous hand dug a hole under one side of its foundations, while under the other side a huge stone was inserted in order to trigger its collapse. This was the unlucky fate of Lemko churches. Those Eastern churches which were converted into Latin Rite ones underwent extensive changes: iconostases and Byzantine icons were thrown away and murals were whitewashed in order to cover up any trace that might reveal that these temples had once been of the Eastern Rite. Rusyn *phelonion* vestments were turned into Roman chasubles, liturgical books were destroyed, and so on.

Not one Eastern church was set aside for the Lemkos resettled in western lands. The Greek rite was liquidated, while the Lemko people were assigned to Latin-rite churches with Latin services.

One of our priests made a request to the [Polish] Council of Ministers, asking them to allow the celebration of Divine Service in the Eastern Rite on Christmas Day and Epiphany Day (1953) for the Greek Catholic faithful. A negative answer was received; the government said that they could not

Before remnants of Lemkos were deported to the former German territories in the west in 1947, twice as many were deported east in 1945-1946. Luminaries in the Lemko community in Lviv are (back/left) Volodymyr Shurkalo, Andrii Sukhorskii, Ihor Rusyniak, Anatol Petryshak, Andrii Barna, Yaroslav Shvahla, and Andrii Tovpash, (front/left) Dmytro Solinko, Ivan Chelak, Hryhory Sydoryk, and Ivan Krasovskii. Lviv, 2006.

agree on introducing another calendar. It was also noted that the Ukrainian question in Poland had been liquidated in 1947, while the Lemko question had never existed and did not exist. The above-mentioned priest, despite the explicit denial issued by government bureaucrats, on the Christmas and Epiphany Days of 1953 conducted solemn services in the Eastern rite, which were attended by many people, mostly Lemkos. It is impossible to describe the enthusiasm and happiness as the assembled thousands, with tears in their eyes, joyfully sang their favorite carol, *"Boh Predvichnii"* (Eternal God), to newborn Christ. The priest, however, paid dearly for his courage. Government officials had no reaction. Instead, the reaction came from a clergyman, Father Łagosz, who was then acting as diocesan bishop. He sent for the disobedient priest and announced his verdict, which reads as follows:

"Due to the fact that you dared to celebrate holy Mass in the Greek-Catholic rite, I dismiss you from your parish and the local diocese. *Roma locuta, causa finita.* (Rome has spoken, the case is closed.)"

The priest was denied the possibility of appeal and ended up on the streets. He applied for different parishes within various dioceses for months, but to no avail. Celebrating liturgy in the Eastern rite was considered a serious crime.

From the very beginning, the lack of Roman Catholic clergymen was noticeable in the Polish western territories; the German priests who used to administer local parishes were deported to Germany, whereas there were not enough Polish ones to fill all the posts available. Therefore, Roman Catholic bishops gladly assigned Greek Catholic priests to Latin Rite posts. The Greek Catholic clergymen who had been resettled to the Polish territories were in dire financial straits and could not afford the basic necessities of life. They gladly took the posts offered to them, but they adhered to their own rite. At the beginning, there was nothing to envy about these Rusyn priests living among Polish parishioners, many of whom were secretly nationalists and chauvinists. These priests were treated as adherents of Bandera and the UPA. They had to continually overcome many obstacles. To get rid of them, Poles would organize attacks, make complaints to the Curia, hurl abuses and cast aspersions on them, send various delegations to powerful people, and simply persecute the priests until church authorities finally somehow got rid of them. Latin-rite bishops generally sided with the nationalists against Rusyn priests. In September 1952, an Ordinary [the administrator in charge of a diocese] accompanied by a canon unexpectedly arrived at the village of Gniechowice. During the church service, they openly incited parishioners against their parish priest, a Greek Catholic clergyman. Although he hadn't done anything wrong, he was moved to another parish. On other occasion, a Greek Catholic priest was transferred to another parish because he dared to sing a *panakhida* [an Eastern Rite prayer for the dead] for his deceased family members on All Souls' Day. During one bishops' conference held at Jasna Góra, one of its participants was literally jumping with joy and clapping his hands while repeating the words, "Praise God, we've done away with the Union!" Then, Cardinal Sapieha replied, "You should rather be sad... Just as the Union is gone, we will disappear as well."

So chauvinist were some Latin-rite bishops that they considered any Greek Catholic priest as deserving punishment simply for being Greek Catholic. As proof, we quote here a letter sent from a bishop's Curia to one of our clergymen, in response to a parishioner's complaint to the bishop that his parish priest is of Rusyn origin, and he wants a Polish one. Instead of reminding this parishioner, who lacked a conscience, of the Gospel's command to love a neighbor as oneself, the bishop proved himself a Pharisee by issuing a decree transferring the priest to a lower post. The text of the decree is as follows:

No. 334/46
7th April, 1946
To the Very Reverend Prelate,

Despite your goodwill and the great effort that you have been making for the glory of God and the salvation of immortal souls, I have been informed that your parishioners are dissatisfied with your work. I am sure you know what this discontent may stem from. As a spiritual man of deep faith you must realize that a shepherd who is incapable of developing a bond with his sheep cannot perform his duties properly. I feel obliged to tell you that, however unpleasant it is. Yet, I hope you will understand my decision as a true disciple of Christ as you are a man of rich inner experience and strong faith. I suggest you take up a post as chaplain at the convent of the Sisters of St. Joseph in the village of Bliżanowice. You will be assigned limited responsibilities at the independent Bliżanowice-Trestno congregation. As for the parish of Prochowice, it will be given to a priest who I am going to designate soon.

I pray to the Lord so as you endure the ordeal like Paul the Apostle who not so long ago bore similar things as befits a soldier of Christ Jesus.

Sincerely yours in Christ,
the signature of the Ordinary

How much falsehood, cynicism, and hypocrisy is in this letter! Rusyn priests working in Latin Rite parishes were constantly exposed to persecutions launched by parishioners, bishops, or the Latin Rite clergy. Some Roman Catholic priests were filled with chauvinism to such an extent that they prevented the Greek Rite faithful from coming to church for services. With the permission of the Primate, Father Iatskov began holding liturgy in the village of Rudna for Greek Catholics, who made up forty percent of the village's population. The people were happy to take part in services celebrated in their rite. The local Latin Rite parish priest felt otherwise and began making various excuses to keep Rusyn services out of the church. First, he forbade the Lemkos to come to church, using the pretext that their offerings were far too small to cover the costs of repairing the building. In response, the Lemkos donated a considerable amount of money to the church. For a short time there was peace. After a while the parish priest came up with another excuse for not admitting the Lemkos into the church: he accused them of making the church dirty. In order not to miss any services, the Lemkos decided to sweep the building after every service. But that also proved insufficient for the parish priest. He didn't give up, but hit below the belt, saying that the Lemkos stunk and polluted the air in the church. There is no resolution to such an accusation. Father Iatskov had to cease holding services in the church of Rudna; the miserable people were deprived of Divine Liturgy and pastoral care. Many similar cases could be found. Due to such hostility of Latin Rite clergymen towards our faithful, our faith fell into decline and our religious practices were neglected. It is worth emphasizing that out of all Latin Rite clergymen only the Salesian fathers were well-disposed to our rite and people. Only the Salesians tried to meet our Lemkos halfway.

From the beginning of the People's Republic of Poland, the Orthodox Church and the Greek Catholic Church were in the same position, i.e. they were both inactive. Later on, Orthodox bishops obtained permission from the Polish government to revive the Orthodox Church. Now, it has its own structure, hierarchs, parishes, priests, and seminary. The government seems to have a positive and friendly attitude towards it. The administration of the Orthodox Church has been growing quickly. The Church has three deaneries and two bishops, besides the Metropolitan in Warsaw. The main sees of the Orthodox hierarchy in Warsaw, Wrocław, Szczecin, and Sanok.

Relations between Orthodox and Greek Catholics are friendly; they live in harmony. Both one and the other consider themselves brothers of the same nation and rite, the sons of one mother Rus'. Their shared fate has planted brotherly love in their hearts.

After the October 1956 revolution [the "Polish Thaw"] by the First Secretary of the Polish United Workers' Party, Władysław Gomułka, the situation of the Greek Catholic Church in Poland improved slightly. The government granted Greek Catholics permission to form "Greek Catholic outposts" as assistants to Latin Rite parish priests. A Greek Catholic priest in one of these "outposts" is allowed to hold a service in his rite, and the faithful are permitted to freely participate in it. Latin Rite clergymen, however, do not observe this decree and prevent priests from celebrating liturgy in the Eastern Rite even in those churches which had been converted from Eastern Rite ones. This spirit of implacable hatred towards the Eastern Rite pervaded the whole Polish country, especially Lemkovyna and—to an even greater extent— the Recovered Territories. In the summer of 1962, one of our pastors arrived at his native village to hold a service for his deceased relatives buried in the local cemetery. The service, which was also aimed at re-consecrating the freshly cleaned graveyard, was to be celebrated in the church where he had once managed by this pastor. So he asked the Latin Rite pastor, Father Franciszek Ignac,[7] for permission to hold Divine Services in the Eastern Rite, but he was cruelly denied. In spite of Ignac's refusal, the pastor held the service in his own rite. Immediately after the service was celebrated, police (MO) officers turned up. The local people had informed them that Lemkos had arrived from across the whole country to kill Poles, and that the pastor, in the church, had consecrated the knives that were to be used to kill with. As the police officers were civilized people with common sense, they checked the Lemkos' identity cards, recognized the situation, and closed the case.

The Primate Stefan Wyszyński, to whom the Greek Catholic Church is subordinated, has an unfavorable attitude towards it and seems reluctant to allow its "outpost" pastorates to be created. It is often necessary to wait a long time for his permission. On the other hand, the government of People's Poland reacts indifferently to the matter; we do not know of any case where the government took action to prevent a priest from holding a liturgy in the Eastern Rite or to bring him to account for celebrating one. Yet we know of many cases where Latin Rite clergymen have done so.

It is extremely difficult for a Greek Catholic priest to be granted an audience with the Primate. Whenever one of our priests arrives at his Curia and wishes to be received, he is told that the Primate has gone somewhere, that he is not receiving anyone, or that he has fallen ill. If a priests is lucky enough to be received by the Primate, it means absolutely nothing. He will leave with no more than he came in with. The Primate is always blaming the government for any obstacle that the Greek Catholic Church encounters. Meetings with government officials are completely different. The government has concluded an agreement with the episcopate, according to which it is not allowed to interfere in the internal affairs of the church; they are the responsibility of the Primate. Senior government staff have often been heard to make the statement that the government does not care at all in which rite Divine Services are held. It is as plain as day who considers it to their advantage to completely liquidate the Greek Catholic Church in Poland.

---

7   [The 1969 editorial board added the note:] We believe that this is the same Father Ignac that A. Tsislyak wrote about in one of last year's issues of the *Karpatska Rus'* newspaper.

LEMKOVYNA

We are quite familiar with the means, lawful and unlawful, which the Latin Rite clergy and the Polish nobility used in the past to enforce the Union in the Rus' lands. Nowadays, the descendents of these clergymen are destroying the idea spread by their forefathers. We do understand the cause of this phenomenon. The Union was promulgated in order to bridge the gap between the two confessions, following which our nation was to be Latinized and Polonized. Since this aim hasn't been achieved, the Union is useless and must be destroyed.

How will you respond, destroyers of the Union, to the words of the leader of the Roman Catholic Church, Pope Urban VIII: *"Per vos, Rutheni, orientem convertendum spero* (Through you, Ruthenians, I hope to convert the East)"? Or to the words of Pope Benedict XIV: *"Volumus, ut omnes catholici sint, non, ut omnes latini fiant* (We wish that all be Catholics, not that all become Latin)"?

Latinizers, read the decrees issued by the Congregation for the Propagation of the Faith, and you will find the following words: *"Transitus de ritu graeco unito ad ritum latinum prohibitus per decretum Sanctissimi Domini Nostri faelicis recordationis Urbani octavi."* ("For a Greek Catholic to convert to the Latin rite is forbidden by a decree of His Holiness, the late Pope Urban VIII.")

What kind of Catholics you are, gentlemen, if you ignore the words of your spiritual leader and violate his decrees! By destroying the Greek Catholic Church you are preventing the unification of all Christians. Can the Orthodox Church place its trust in you if you destroy its rite? A word to the wise (*sapienti sat*)!

20. The Polish Government in the Early Years of the People's Republic of Poland

Having considered the tragedy of Lemkovyna, the question arises automatically as to why the People's Republic of Poland— basing its national relations programme on the doctrine of Marx and Lenin, proclaiming itself [Communist] International, pronouncing equal treatment of all its citizens, peace and friendship between nations, justice and respect for the human dignity of each person, and fighting against abuses and injustice as well as striving for its citizens' happiness— turned out to be cruel, merciless, even savage to the Lemkos, its most loyal citizens.

To address this question, it is necessary to consider the circumstances in which the first government of the People's Republic of Poland was formed. In its ranks were not only many irresponsible and immoral people, but even secrets opponents of socialism and communist government. Into the government there also crept full-blooded fascists, disguised as communists. The burdensome struggle with all these intruders had to be carried out by a handful of highly respected people in the government, idealists with a pure Communist orientation. It should be kept in mind that Hitlerism exterminated the worthiest people in Poland, professors, doctors, lawyers, officers, economists, politicians, etc. In short, a multitude of educated people and idealists were slaughtered. Various troublemakers and careerists strove to find their way into the government. Cold-blooded fascists wearing Communist overcoats found themselves in the government ranks. It was necessary to stabilize the government, but getting rid of these intruders was difficult. While the central authorities were preoccupied with their own problems and not paying attention to what was happening around the country, low-ranking government officials indulged in abuses and crimes against Lemko villagers. Every official and policeman considered himself the lord of life and death. Had anyone dared to complain to a higher authority, he would never again have been seen on God's earth.

The main culprit behind the deportation of the Lemkos from their ancestral lands was the Marshal of Poland, Michał Rola-Żymierski. Incited by the fascists, he issued an order to deport all the Lemkos. But he didn't enjoy his high rank for long. His scheming was unraveled by the government. He was removed from his position [in 1949] and replaced by a Soviet general, Konstantin Rokossovsky, a person of impeccable character and a kind-hearted fellow.[8]

The Polish government understands the damage inflicted on the Lemkos, but for some reason it is unwilling to allow them to return to their old lands. Its current attitude towards the Lemkos seems positive. The future fate of the Lemko people remains to be written.

---

8   [Not all would agree with this statement. Konstantin Rokossovsky was assigned duty in post-WW II Poland by Stalin.]

21. The Lemko Contribution to the Building of the People's Republic of Poland

Lemkos made colossal contributions, out of proportion to their numbers, to the building of the People's Republic of Poland. Among others:

1) They organized and led the first guerilla units that fought against fascist Germany. Their operations were described in Section 28 of the third part of this book, following an account given by their commander Mychał Doński.

2) To fight against fascist Germany, an estimated twenty-five thousand young Lemkos joined the Soviet army as volunteers.[9] Only half of them returned home. The other half died in combat; they gave their young lives for the People's Republic of Poland [and Czechoslovakia].

3) During the German occupation, the Lemko Association (Lemko Soiuz) of Yonkers, New York, which was composed of Lemko immigrants, sent the troops fighting against fascist Germany about one million U.S. dollars' worth of food, clothing, medicine, and cash; all these goods were delivered via the Polish Red Cross and were a great help to those fighting Hitler's army.

4) A general in the Soviet Army, Iosafat Emilyian Fedorenko, was of Lemko origin and was born in the village of Czerteż, near the town of Sanok. As the commander of the Ukrainian Front, he urged his soldiers on, striving to enter his beloved Lemkovyna as soon as possible in order to unfurl the flag of freedom in his native village. Unfortunately, he did not live to see this happy moment. Before they entered the village of Czerteż, an enemy bullet wounded him gravely, following which he died in a hospital in agony. Many Lemkos who remained in Russia after the First World War served in the Soviet Army [during WWII]. Many of them were sent to the Ukrainian Front. They all fought bravely against fascist Germany.

5) During the German occupation, almost all the members of the Lemko intelligentsia were arrested and taken to concentration camps spread over various towns. Many of them were killed in Auschwitz or in other places of torture. Nearly all of them were denounced by Ukrainian nationalists, including Ukrainian clergymen. But the leading part was played by the priest Aleksander Malynovskii, who was known as Berlin's Apostolic Administrator of

---

9 [While the official communist government position was that they volunteered, in reality they were drafted. See the fourth note to Part III, Section 28, above.]

Lemkovyna. He was a Ukrainian ataman with a bishop's miter and a Gestapo membership. He gave Hitler's authorities a list of unreliable priests who were then taken to prisons in the towns of Jasło and Nowy Sącz.

Whatever Lemkos had that was valuable, they dedicated to the building of the People's Republic of Poland. In return, three shots were fired right at their hearts: deportation, liquidation of the Greek Catholic Church, and the changing of the name of their nationality from "Rusyn" to "Ukrainian."

Those shots were fired off by opponents of socialism who held high positions at the time when the People's Republic of Poland was coming into existence; they tried by various means to do it harm. They quickly lost their jobs, which were then filled by people strongly influenced by the principles of socialism.[10]

In accordance with the Constitution of the People's Republic of Poland, all its citizens have the same rights and have equal treatment, and internationalism places all nationalities on the same footing.

22. The Difficulties that the People's Republic of Poland Had to Overcome at the Beginning of its Existence

One of the most important and at the same time most difficult tasks for a new government to undertake is to fill positions in its administrative apparatus with people who are qualified and moral. To complete this task properly, there must

---

10 [It is possible that this and similar communist propaganda found in Part IV was not part of Polianskii's original manuscript and may have been added by certain "progressive minds" within the Lemko Association as the manuscript was readied for printing in 1969. On the other hand, in the late 1960s it would have been very impolitic for someone living in Poland to do other than praise the Polish People's Republic if he wanted to stay out of jail, have a job and a place to live, etc. And after all, there were many, even in the USA and Canada, who believed in the promise of socialism. Of course, if things were really so good, then why was the communist government overthrown so quickly in May-December 1989?]

be a sufficient number of such people. If there are few of them, then not all positions can be filled; or if positions are filled with unsuitable people, then the state apparatus will function improperly. A similar story took place in People's Poland at the beginning of its existence. Hitler's terror had destroyed the most valuable elite of the Polish intelligentsia. The fascist Germans treacherously murdered the leading intellectuals, including professors and university docents, lawyers and politicians, statesmen and men of letters. Doctors, local officials, engineers, and technicians also fell victim to Hitler's terror; in brief, a whole generation of valuable people was destroyed. So, when it came time to establish a state administrative apparatus in Poland, there turned out to be a lack of qualified candidates for some positions. Out of pure necessity, these posts were filled by the unqualified, or even by immoral people with a hostile attitude towards the building of socialism. The consequences of this were suffered almost immediately. The highly-positioned leaders of the state, however, quickly noticed the offenses committed by these people and removed them from their posts as harmful to the country; their positions were filled by people trained by the state to have the necessary qualifications. All the damage, offenses, and injustices were done by precisely these people, who misused their power for immoral purposes. Among them were some Jews who made contacts with the international Zionist movement, intending to do harm to the state.[11]

Each year new cadres of qualified people graduate and take up posts in the state apparatus. Under the close supervision and wise leadership of the Government, the state administration has been functioning well and bringing better and better order and justice to the country, and contentment to its citizens. Despite difficult beginnings, Poland continues to develop and become an important authority among other countries and nations. This provides the best evidence that it stands on a firm socialist foundation.

In the beginning, the People's Republic of Poland faced the difficult problem of feeding its population, but that problem has been successfully dealt with. Millions of citizens returned to their beloved homeland, but

---

11 [This book originally appeared in 1969, a year after the Polish government conducted an anti-Semitic campaign after student riots in Warsaw in March 1968. This campaign drove as many as twenty thousand Jews from the country. It is generally assumed that party conservatives opposed to changes and hoping to oust Władysław Gomułka, who was then party chief, seized on anti-Semitism and anti-intellectualism as a means of attacking him indirectly. See Walter Maksimovich, "The Lemko Association and *Lemkovyna: A History*," appearing in this volume, for further discussion of communist influences on the text.]

found it ragged, oppressed, devastated, stripped of its old charm, and starving, with the life squeezed out of it. The government stood empty-handed in the face of this great need, but energetically called on society for help. The sacrifices that people made proved to be powerful: they closed wounds, dried tears, fed the hungry, dressed the naked, and were a tremendous help to people in need. This period is written in golden letters in the history of postwar Poland. From widespread poverty, new life grew. The rebuilding of the country progressed. Faith in a better future became stronger. In those hard times, the Polish diaspora in America and the Lemko Association (*Lemko Soyuz*) of Yonkers hurried to offer the country a helping hand. Every day, ships carrying food, clothing, and medicine anchored at the ports of Gdańsk and Gdynia, which was an enormous help. For these gifts, the émigrés have our heartfelt thanks. Food supplies were so wisely distributed among the people that after the war no place in the country suffered hunger, except for some villages in Lemkovyna.

Industry started to thrive on a large scale, and everyone who wanted to work could be employed. As a result, unemployment declined considerably.

Over a quarter century, Poland was transformed into an industrial and highly developed country.

Nearly all European countries, and many from other continents on our globe, maintain commercial relationships with People's Poland. Much of what is produced in the country is exported.

23. Living in People's Poland

People's Poland is a socialist country with a new system for governing its citizens. The distinguishing characteristic of this system is that all citizens enjoy the same rights and are treated the same, and that all income derived from citizens' work shall be spent on citizens' needs. In other words, the citizens are the owners of the state's money. In a socialist country, each citizens can be reassured about his future, as the state guarantees that all of his and his family's needs will be satisfied not only while working, but also during sickness and in old age.

We remember the old times when one encountered whole masses of beggars, the disabled, tramps, and the unemployed on the street, at the market, or in front of churches. Today this sight is no longer seen. People's Poland has solved this problem remarkably well. Special institutions were opened to accommodate all these disadvantaged people, where they are provided with essential support and loving care under the guidance of clergymen and nuns. Each year, the government allocates half a billion zlotys for this purpose. For the sick, it founded many hospitals, equipped with the latest technologies, where every patient can receive treatment under a doctor's care without any payment. Whenever a person gets sick, whether at home or away from home, after calling a Health Center an ambulance is sent to provide first aid, then take him to a hospital where he can stay under a doctor's care until recovered.

In large towns, there are "first-aid stations" where doctors of all specialties are on duty every day, waiting for patients and providing emergency treatment. Treatment is free; all costs are covered by the government. Disabled and sick children are placed in special institutions and given special treatment. The chronically ill are sent to health spas situated in the country or abroad.

People's Poland also cares a great deal about the education and cultural enlightenment of its citizens. In every village, even the tiniest one, there is a school for first through fourth grade, and through eighth grade in larger villages. After completing primary education, children may attend trade school or a four-year vocational secondary school or lyceum. After graduating, students can apply for university or other institutes of higher education. Everyone is allowed to study; every person has free access to education. The government grants scholarships and various benefits to talented students. Lyceums, vocational secondary schools, and boarding schools are located in almost every district town. Many students go to school by bus. Vocational schools offer a variety of job skills. As youths enjoy learning, schools are grossly overcrowded.

"Houses of Culture" are located in many villages, and in some "coffee bars" have been started to enable teenagers to congregate and entertain each other in their free time. People's Poland pays special attention to young people.

Each diocese is presided over by at least three bishops and has a seminary from which hundreds of young priests graduate every year. Besides seminaries, there are also the Theological Academy in Warsaw and the Catholic University in Lublin, where priests can earn academic degrees.

In People's Poland, the freedom of religion is safeguarded. Everyone can profess their faith without obstruction by the authorities. The government has the same attitude towards all religions. In 1949, the Council of State of the Republic of Poland issued a decree guaranteeing the liberty to practice any religion. Under threat of severe sanctions, it strictly forbids religious discrimination. Religious classes are held in special classrooms outside the school or in churches. The government pays priests a salary for teaching religion, and a pension after retirement. All religious ceremonies with processions are performed without any obstacles. Priests are treated with respect by officials. According to the principles of internationalism, people of all nationalities enjoy equal treatment.

Two houses were designated as clergymen's rest resorts by the government. They are well equipped and staffed, allowing priests the health benefits of relaxation during holiday breaks. These facilities are situated in the towns of Zakopane (in the mountains) and Sopot (by the sea.) They offered free stay for priests. All costs are covered by the government.

In People's Poland, all citizens can feel financially secure. Those who are incapable of working due to disease or age are paid a state benefit so that they can live comfortably for the rest of their lives. A farmer who is not able to work anymore, either because of disease or age, gives his fields over to the government in exchange for a state benefit paid regularly; however, he is allowed to keep his house and a piece of his land.

The ill are entitled to free medical treatment at a sanatorium or health spa. Those who draw the state benefit or are insured are privileged to fill prescriptions at a pharmacy without payment. Sick workers and farm laborers are under special state medical care.

The public transportation system works effectively. One could get to any spot by bus or on the motorcycle that all citizens possess. Bus fares are fairly low.

The state pays special attention to children and teenagers. During a holiday break, those living in towns and some living in villages are sent to holiday camps where they can relax in the fresh air and spend an enjoyable time under the care of tutors. These holiday camps positively influence their health; they are free of cost and widely accessible.[12]

---

12 [What's presented is, of course, the standard justification for a communist regime. Needless to say, all of the above depended on one's political reliability. If you were considered unreliable, you got nothing.]

24. How Many Lemkos Live On Earth?

It is difficult to answer this question without proper statistics at hand. To a large extent, we use consistorial censuses (Schematisms [of the Greek Catholic Church]) and occasionally statistics. However, we do not have recent data. So we decided to use sources from 1924 and update them using the percentage of population growth for the nearly fifty-year period since then.

In 1924, the number of Lemkos on Earth was as follows:

1.	Galicia (according to [Greek Catholic] Schematisms)	314,755
2.	Romania	69,191
3.	Bosnia and Herzegovina	8,579
4.	Yugoslavia	20,860
5.	Croatia	9,150
6.	Dalmatia	300
7.	Czechoslovakia and Hungary	404,659
8.	The United States of America	870,000
9.	Canada	300,000
10.	Brazil	31,000
11.	Russia	50,000
	Total	**2,078,484**

Only Greek Catholic Lemkos were taken into consideration in these statistics; Orthodox ones were not counted. Neither were Lemkos inhabiting other countries than those enumerated above, and many people of Lemko origin have been living in France, Germany, England, and other countries. Keeping this in view, we can arrive at the conclusion that in 1924 there were over three million Lemkos in the world.

Now, add the percentage of population growth for forty-four years to the figure given above, and we can see that the number of Lemkos has dramatically increased since 1924. Let's say that over the past fifty years the population has grown by ten per cent; that would mean that the number of Lemkos amounts to many millions. That's quite a lot. If all the Lemkos who had been hiding during both wars as well as the interwar and post-war years came out, a huge army of worthy people would appear.[13]

---

13   [Unfortunately Fr. Polianskii seems to be including many Ukrainians and other Rusyns in his statistics.]

A roadside chapel in the now no longer existing Lemko village Czarne, whose inhabitants were forcibly resettled after the Second World War. Czarne, 2003.

Primitive painter Epifan "Nykifor" Drovniak. Krynica.

PART V:
LEMKO CONTRIBUTIONS TO CULTURE

Paining by Teodor Kuziak. Barne, 2000.

Prologue to Part V

Лемковина много мала	Lemkovyna had plenty
Велькых геній свого духа,	Great talents of her spirit,
Ними то удуховняла	By them she inspired
И вченого, и пастуха.	Both the educated and the shepherd.
Много людей мала вченых,	She had many educated people,
Науковцев, просвіщеных,	Scholars, enlightened people,
З кількома докторами,	Many holders of doctorates,
Одзначеных медалями.	Decorated with medals.
Меже ними епископы,	Among them were bishops,
Священников цілы копы,	Priests by the dozens,
Пралатов и кардиналов,	Prelates and cardinals,
И войсковых генералов.	And military generals.
Велькой славы историков,	Historians of great importance,
Фильософов и медыков,	Philosophers and physicians,
Велькых знавцев свого рода,	Great experts of our kind
Бо така их была врода.	For that is what they were by birth.
Нихто з них не ділал чуда,	None of them performed miracles,
И не знали, што облуда.	But they did not know what is failure.
Хотяй дуже вчены были,	Although they were well educated
Украины не открыли.	They did not discover a Ukraine.
За Русинов всі нас мали,	They knew us as Rusyns,
Русскыми нас называли,	They called us Rusyns,
Бо Русь свята наша Мати,	Because Rus' is our holy Mother
Казали Ей шанувати.	They taught us to revere her.

Pavlo Maliv (1) with wife (2) on a pilgrimage to the Pochaiv Monastery by residents of Tylawa and Zawadka Rymanowska, Pochaiv, 1938.

Lemkovyna has produced a number of renowned people– eminent writers and poets, profoundly learned university professors, scientists in every field, authors of scholarly works of worldwide significance, brilliant men on bishops' thrones, eminent physicians, and renowned military commanders. Following are the names of some of them along with their works.

1. Scholars

Fr. Dr. Iosyf Iaryna

Fr. Dr. Iosyf Iaryna was born in Radocyna, Gorlice County, where his father was a priest. He completed gymnazium in Hungary and studied theology and philosophy in Vienna, where he earned two doctorates, in theology and philosophy, and became professor of theology at the university. He was a man of great learning and great authority who enjoyed a high reputation among students and professors. He died on September 15, 1817. A memorial dinner

Interior of a Lemko house. Nowy Sącz, 2005.

Interior of a Lemko house. Nowy Sącz, 2005.

was held in his honor on November 11, 1817. At this affair, Prof. Dr. Iosyf Maus read a special paper on Iaryna. One of the archpriests of the Latin Cathedral Assembly expressed it thus:[1] "Oh, Rusynki, Rusynki, you will never again have such Iarynki."[2] Iaryna wrote scientific essays on various matters in Latin and German.

Fr. Mykhailo Krynytskii

Fr. Mykhailo Krynytskii was born in 1797. After completing theological studies, he became a priest in Hańczowa and then in Tylicz. His grave and headstone can still be seen today near the church there. He collected historical documents and other materials about the Sącz area of Lemkovyna. He copied decrees and proceedings of the court in Krynica, as well as three volumes of deeds to Muszynka estates. On the basis of these documents he wrote "The Historical Status of the Muszynka Vice-Regency: A Physical, Political and Religious View on the Basis of Fifty-One Existing Purely Rusyn Villages and

1 "Recollections of Iosyf Iaryna", in Zborowskii, ed., *Otechestvennii Sbornik* (National collection), Vienna, 1855.
2 [This is a play on words; here *iaryna* = vegetable.]

the towns of Muszynka and Tylicz."[3] With this historical study he refuted a theory advanced by W. Maciejowski, a professor at Warsaw University, in his essay "Primary Annals of Polish Literature" (Warsaw, 1846), alleging that Lemko Rusyns were colonists that King Casimir the Great had permitted to settle here. On the basis of those historical documents, Krynytskii proved to the Polish scholar that he was mistaken, that Lemkos are really the autochthons of their homeland.[4] After Krynytskii's death, these materials disappeared without a trace.

Fr. Dr. Onufrii Krynytskii

Fr. Dr. Onufrii Krynytskii was born in 1793 in Krzywa, Gorlice County, where his father was a priest. He completed public school in Jasło, gymnazium in Hungary, and theological studies in Lviv. After earning a doctorate in theology, he became professor of church history at Lviv University. At the time of his death he was a *Hofrath* or State Councillor to the Emperor's household in Zoltancy. He wrote several works in the field of church history. He was a member of a delegation to the Austrian Emperor that petitioned for approval of the teaching of Rusyn in public schools.[5]

Dr. Vasyl Chyrnianskii

Dr. Vasyl Chyrnianskii was born in Złockie, Nowy Sącz County. He completed two courses, philosophy and medicine. For a short time he was a physician in Krosno. From 1852 on, he taught the natural sciences at the Academic Gymnazium in Lviv and later lectured on zoology and mineralogy at Lviv University. He wrote scientific treatises in his field of expertise.[6]

---

3   Zborowskii, ed., *Otechestvenniy Sbornik*, Vienna, 1855.
4   D. Zubritskii, *Granice między polskim a ruskim narodem w Galicji* (The boundary between the Polish and Rusyn peoples in Galicia), Lviv, 1849.
5   *Listy Rusyna* (Letters of a Rusyn), Poznań, 1850.
6   *Drittes Programm des K. u. K. Akad. Staats gymnasium im Lemberg amSchlusse des Schuljahres 1852* (Third program of the Royal Academy State Gimnazium in Lviv at the end of the 1852 school year).

Dr. Valery Sas Iavorskii

Dr. Valery Sas Iavorskii was born in Florynka, Nowy Sącz County, in 1848. He completed gymnazium in Przemyśl and university in Lviv. He was a teacher at a higher vocational school in Cracow and later professor at Cracow University. For 14 years before his death, he was director of the university's clinic. He was also a member of the Cracow Academy of Sciences. He died in 1924.

Iavorskii wrote many treatises that introduced new theories in medical practice. He wrote in Polish and German. His works include *Ueber Wirkung therapeutischen Werts und Gebrauch des neuen Karlsbader Quellsaltzes* (On the effects of therapeutic uses and customs of the new salt springs at Karlsbad), Vienna, 1886; *Ectasia ventriculi paradoxa* (Equatorial constriction of the stomach); *Zarys patologii terapii chorób żoąadkowych* (Outline of the pathology of therapy in stomach diseases); *Zestawienie krytyczne szczegółowej profilaktyki w terapii cholery* (A critical summary of particular prophylactics in cholera therapy); and *Przewodnik chorob zoladkowych* (A guide to stomach diseases).

Dr. Emilyian Chyrnianskii

Dr. Emilyian Chyrnianskii was born on January 20, 1824, in Florynka, Nowy Sącz County, in the home of his father Hryhory. After completing university

Interior of a Lemko house. Nowy Sącz, 2005.

courses and earning a doctorate, he was appointed docent in the chemistry faculty at Cracow University. He died in 1888 in Cracow, where his grave lies. He wrote in both Polish and German. His most important works are: *Słownictwo polskie chemiczne* (Polish chemical vocabulary), Cracow, 1853; *Wykład chemii neorganicznej w zastosowaniu do rolnictwa* (A lecture on inorganic chemistry in application to agriculture), Cracow, 1857; *Rozbiór chemiczny wód mineralnych lubilińskiej i warszawskiej* (Chemical analysis of the Lublin and Warsaw mineral waters), Cracow, 1860; *Odpowiedź na ocenę chemiczną teoryi* (Response to an appraisal of chemical theory) Cracow, 1871; *Chemische Theorie* (Chemical theory), Cracow, 1872; and *Niektóre uwagi nad teorią chemiczną* (Some remarks on chemical theory), Cracow, 1871.

Chyrnianskii's works and services were highly rated in *"Przegląd Polski"* (Polish Review), Cracow, May 1888.

Dr. Mykhailo Baludianskii

Dr. Mykhailo Baludianskii was born in 1769. He became a professor at Warsaw University and later rector of the Scientific Academy in St. Petersburg. He wrote scholarly articles in the field of law.

Dr. Andrian Kopystianskii

Dr. Andrian Kopystianskii was born in Śnietnica, in the home of his grandfather, Fr. Hryhory. He was director of the Lviv gymnazium during the interwar years. He wrote historical works, including a three-volume *History of Rus'.*

Iosyf Shchavynskii

Iosyf Shchavynskii was born in 1819. He completed gymnazium and theological studies in Hungary and was ordained in 1845. He served as a priest in Sołotwiny, Klimkówka, and [from 1874 until his death in 1890] in Korostno near Dobromil.

After the death of his wife, he took up the growing of mulberries and the history of Galician Rus'. He produced a volume entitled "The Beginning of the Story, or an Investigation Into Early Slavic and Rusyn History, With Particular Attention to Red Galician Rus." This work was printed by the "Kliros" Russian Council Press in Przemyśl.

Valuable manuscripts concerning the history of Tylicz and the oppression of its residents by the bishop of Cracow were taken to Vienna by his son Volodymyr, and their present whereabouts are unknown.

Fr. Dr. Toma Polianskii

Fr. Dr. Toma Polianskii was born in 1796 in Bartne, Gorlice County. In 1859, he took over the Przemyśl bishopric after Bishop Hryhory Iakhimovych died. He often conducted canonical visits to his eparchy. In 1863, he presented a report to the Apostolic See on the parishes of the Przemyśl eparchy and was instrumental in the issuance of the 1863 Papal decree "Concordia" [of 1863], which normalized relations between the Roman and Greek Catholic churches. He wrote works in German, Polish, and Rusyn, including *Słowo jedno w celu wzajemnego porozumienia* (One word for the purpose of mutual

Interior of a Lemko house. Nowy Sącz, 2005.

understanding), published in Przemyśl in 1848. A Rusyn translation of this appeared in the *"Literaturny Sbornik Galitsko-Russkoi Matitsy"* (Literary review of the Galician-Russian *Matitsa*) for 1886.

Bishop Polianskii's epistles were distinguished for their profound theological meaning and strong patriotism. The Little Russian journalist and poet Bohdan Diditskii dedicated several poems to him, and the church historian Dr. Iuliian Pelesh evaluated his services in the study *Geshichte der Union der ruthenischen Kirche mit Rom* (History of the Union of the Ruthenian Church with Rome), p. 969.

Fr. Dr. Iosyf Sembratovych

He was born on November 8, 1821, in Krynica, Nowy Sącz County, where his father Teodosy was treasurer. He went to gymnazium in Nowy Sącz and Przemyśl. Bishop Ioann Snihurskii sent him to Vienna, where he completed the theology course with honors. On October 7, 1845, he was ordained. The following year he obtained his doctorate in Rome and was appointed prefect at the religious seminary in Lviv and docent in biblical studies at the university there. In 1853, he became vice-rector of the religious seminary in Vienna but was soon called to Rome to serve in the Congregation for the Propagation of the Faith. In 1867, he returned to his homeland and was appointed suffragan to Bishop Toma Polianskii of Przemyśl. On May 18, 1870, he was named Metropolitan of Galician Rus', Archbishop of Lviv, and member of the Galician Sejm and the Austrian House of Lords.

After the famous 1882 trial of Fr. Ivan Naumovych, Emperor Franz Joseph ordered him to resign from the office of Metropolitan. His place was taken by his nephew Sylvester Sembratovych. Iosyf Sembratovych then went to Rome and lived there for fourteen years, far from his family, grieving for his homeland and his people. On the thirtieth anniversary of his appointment to the archbishopric, Galician Rus' sent a congratulatory delegation to him.

He died in 1896 and left the memory of a great patriot and beloved archpriest who defended the Eastern Rite. During his service as professor, he wrote many essays on religious themes, including his doctoral thesis, published in Vienna in 1850.

Fr. Dr. Sylvester Sembratovych

Fr. Dr. Sylvester Sembratovych was born on September 3, 1836, in the village of Desznica, Jasło County, where his father Antonii was priest. His mother, Anna Vyslotskii, came from Florynka. His parents died early, and he was brought up by his uncle Iosyf Sembratovych. He went to public school in Jasło, Gorlice, and Tarnów, and to gymnazium in Przemyśl, Lviv, and Vienna. He completed the theology and philosophy courses at Pope Urban VIII's college "for the Propagation of the Faith" in Rome, where he obtained his doctorate in 1861. He returned to his homeland and for a short time served with his grandfather Sylvester Vyslotskii in Florynka, and then as chaplain at the monastery in Slowity. In 1863, he was appointed prefect at the religious seminary in Lviv and professor of dogmatics at the university. In 1879, Pope Leo XIII appointed him suffragan to his uncle Iosyf Sembratovych. On the latter's resignation, he was appointed Metropolitan of Galician Rus' in 1885. In 1895, he was elected cardinal. Besides that, he was a Privy Councillor to the Emperor's household, a life member of the House of Lords, and knight of the Order of the Iron Crown. He had the deciding vote in the Galician Sejm and was deputy to the regional president.

In 1891, he convoked a provincial synod in Lviv to make some changes in the Greek Catholic Rite. Due to the efforts of Bishop Pelesh and strong opposition among the assembled clergymen, our Rite was not Latinized, as was ardently desired by Cardinal Sembratovych and the papal delegate Tsiaska, who was chairman of the synod.

Cardinal Sembratovych died of stomach cancer on August 4, 1898, leaving a sorry memory of building a career at the expense of our Rite. To his credit is his founding of the "Rusyn Zion," a journal for priests, as are many pastoral epistles, the most meritorious of which are "In Regard to Temperance" (1885); "Epistle on the 900th Anniversary of the Baptism of Rus'" (1888); and "Epistle on the Anniversary of Pope Leo VIII" (1888). He also wrote some essays: "Similarities and Differences in the Teachings of the Orthodox and Catholic Churches" (Lviv, 1869), and "A Speech at the Blessing of a Religious Seminary" (*Dushpastyr*, No. 19, 1889).[7]

---

7   Sources: *Novii Prolom* for 1885; Fr. Władysław Sarna, *"Opis powiatu jasielskiego"* (Description of Jasło County), *Przegląd Katolicki*, No. 34, 1898.

Fr. Dr. Iuliian Pelesh

Fr. Dr. Iuliian Pelesh was born on January 3, 1843 in the village of Smere-kowiec, Gorlice County. His father Hryhory was a cantor-teacher, and his mother Ioanna was the daughter of the priest Teodosy Shchavynskii. He went through elementary school in Jasło and gymnazium in Prešov and Przemyśl. He completed theological studies with honors in Vienna in 1867, and was ordained that same year by Bishop Toma Polianskii. He was immediately appointed prefect of the religious seminary in Vienna, where in 1870 he was awarded the diploma of doctor of theology. From Vienna he went to Lviv, where he became prefect of the religious seminary and adjunct professor in the theological faculty at Lviv University. In 1872, he was appointed professor of pastoral liturgy at Przemyśl. There he expanded his activities to include positions as judge at the Przemyśl Consistory and member of a commission for compiling schoolbooks in Rusyn. In 1874, he went back to Vienna, where he became rector at the religious seminary and also rector of the St. Barbara Church.

Pelesh's unusual talents, his erudition, his eloquence, and his pedagogical training brought him wide renown in Viennese society. Emperor Franz Joseph appointed him tutor to Crown Prince Rudolph, heir to the Austrian throne. Pelesh instilled democratic principles in the mind of his young pupil. He showed him the poverty and hunger of the common people, on the one hand, and the luxurious and dissolute life of the royal household, on the other. The young Prince listened attentively to his teacher, for whom he had great respect and sympathy.

In 1880, the Russian Tsar Nicholas II visited the Austrian Emperor in Vienna. This visit came at the time of the Easter holidays. The Tsar expressed a desire to take part in the Divine Service according to Russian tradition. There was no Orthodox church in Vienna, so both monarchs went to the Church of St. Barbara, and the Divine Service was conducted by Fr. Pelesh. After the service, the Tsar went up to Pelesh, gave him the customary Easter greeting, and kissed him on the cheek. Knowing nothing about this Russian custom, the Viennese talked extensively about the episode. Pelesh's prestige grew daily, and he became very popular in Viennese society.

Although the Austrian monarch valued Pelesh highly, he was not satisfied with him and even decided that his stay in Vienna was not in the best interests of the state. To get rid of him for good, the Emperor, with the collaboration

At the gate of the Museum of Lemko Culture. Zyndranowa, 2002.

of the Roman Curia, created a new eparchy in Stanisławów and in December 1885 named Iuliian Pelesh to be its first bishop. There was much work to be done in this newly created eparchy, and with no help whatsoever, Bishop Pelesh had a heavy work load. So this hardworking Lemko labored day and night without rest. The stress of this mental exertion undermined his health and sent him to his grave prematurely.

In 1891, Pelesh was appointed Bishop of Przemyśl. That same year, a provincial synod was held in Lviv, at which he played a major role as defender of the Eastern Rite. The synod was convened by Metropolitan Sylvester Sembratovych. More than three hundred priests from all three eparchies attended. The chairman was the papal delegate Tsiaska. The purpose of this synod was Latinization of our Rite.

As a member of the Synodal Board, Pelesh had advance knowledge of the program for each day. Every evening, he would visit the quarters of the participating priests, would encourage them and explain to them how to cope with the given subject, would even designate the most knowledgeable priests to enter into the discussion, and did everything in his power to defend the rights and privileges of our church at this synod. This activity organized by Bishop Pelesh resulted in rejection of all the unfavorable proposals, and the Latinizers were unable to carry out even a single one of their many projects.

At the conclusion of the synod, all of its proceedings were sent for approval to the Apostolic See, which kept them for six years. Then in the sixth year, all the churches and priests received a copy of each of the resolutions approved at the synod, in the form of a thick booklet with a cover inscribed "Resolutions of the Provincial Synod Held in Lviv, 1891." and strict orders that they be carried out. The eyes of the priests bugged out when they looked at the content of the resolutions that came back from Rome. There were resolutions there that had not even been mentioned at the synod, as well as others that had been proposed but had been rejected– not approved-- by a majority of votes. In the course of six years, all the resolutions of the synod had been falsified. But no one had the courage to speak out about this: *Roma locuta, causa finita.* ("Rome has spoken, the matter is finished.") It was not until after World War I that a dozen or so priests who had been at the synod and were still living, though standing on the edge of the grave, dared to expose this sham publicly in a brochure entitled "Clarification of the Lviv Conference." Metropolitan Andrei Sheptytskii pronounced the Lviv conference invalid.

Bishop Iuliian Pelesh died on April 10, 1896, leaving all of Galician Rus' in mourning. He was buried in the Przemyśl cemetery by Cardinal Sylvester Sembratovych, with priests from all three eparchies and a great crowd of people attending.

The literary work of Bishop Pelesh began at the time he became editor of the church journal *Ruthenian Zion*. He published many articles on theology in that journal. In addition to that, he wrote a textbook on the worship of God for the fifth and sixth grades in gymnazium; the book Pastoral Theology (Vienna, 1877); a textbook in three parts on the Catholic religion (Lviv, 1876); a treatise, dedicated to the priest Ioann Shchavynskii, on the spiritual style of

Rotating grinding stones for the making of flour. Zyndranowa, 2002.

administration (Vienna, 1878); and *Geschichte der Union der ruthenischen Kirche mit Rom* (A history of the Union of the Ruthenian Church with Rome)[8], published in two volumes in Vienna in 1880.

Pelesh's name became well known. His works brought him to the attention of the scholarly world. He was elected an honorary member of the Galician-Rusyn *Matica* and was invited to Freiburg to take part in compiling a German theological dictionary, *Kirchenlexikon oder Encyklopedie der katholischen Theologie und ihrer Hilfswissenschaften* (A church dictionary, or encyclopedia of Catholic theology and its auxiliary studies).

Bishop Pelesh was one of the greatest of scholarly administrators, a man of crystalline character and noble spirit. He was extremely hard working, modest, asking little for himself, ardently loving the people he came from, and detesting the nobility who oppressed simple people. He was a pure-blooded democrat in the true Christian sense

When Count Badeni, Viceroy at the time, once sent Pelesh a pair of beautiful horses, with sparkling harnesses and a luxurious coach, Bishop Pelesh declined to accept this lordly present and sent it back to the Viceroy with a note, "Thank you for the gift, but I cannot accept it because ordinary horses and a simple peasant cart are enough for me." Another time, the same Viceroy Badeni came to visit, and the Bishop refused to receive him, claiming lack of time.

Badeni swore to get even, and his revenge was not long in coming. Badeni vilified Pelesh to Pope Leo XIII, declaring the Bishop to be a habitual drunk. Pelesh had never consumed any alcohol during his entire working life. Overtaxed by his labors, he began having stomach pains, which none of the medications prescribed by his doctors could alleviate. Finally, some specialist advised him to take a small glass of French cognac when the pains came. This proved to be helpful; the pain went away after he took the cognac. Count Badeni explained this condition differently to the Pope. The Pope ordered Pelesh to come before him for censure. The Bishop explained the nature of his illness to the Pope and promised that cognac would never touch his lips again. And despite the urgings of physicians and friends, Bishop Pelesh never again touched any cognac, even though the attacks of stomach pain became stronger and stronger. He explained his attitude with the words "I promised the Pope, and I must keep my word." He kept his word, but this hastened his death.

---

8   This is a major opus, on par with that of the Jesuit Stanisław Załęnski, and it ranks among the most objective and meaningful of studies.

Fr. Dr. Nikolai Malyniak

Fr. Dr. Nikolai Malyniak was born on September 1, 1851, in the village of Kamianna, Nowy Sącz County. He received his elementary education from a cantor-teacher. With the support of Metropolitan Sembratovych, he completed gymnazium in Nowy Sącz and theological school at the Greek Catholic College in Rome, where in 1875 he earned a doctorate in theology and philosophy. He was an associate pastor in Wróblik for a short time, and worked for four years as adjunct professor in the theological faculty at Lviv University and prefect at the religious seminary. He was also village pastor at Nowica, Krystynopol, Złockie, Krynica, Szlachtowa, and finally at Śliwnica near Przemyśl. He was arrested during World War I and sent to Talerhof, where he died in 1915.

Malyniak wrote under the pseudonyms "Rymlianin," "NDM," and "Kamianyn." The largest of his works is *Mustard Seeds*, which was written in several parts, some of which were published while others were still in manuscript. In this collection of articles he wrote about his native village, his life in Rome, his journey to Jerusalem, and so on. The most interesting article is one entitled "Mustard Seeds From the Tree of Life," an autobiography from the beginning of his life to the time he came to the parish in Śliwnica in September 1890. It is interwoven with interesting observations describing various periods in the author's

View of the main living quarters. Zyndranowa, 2002.

life, as evidenced by the chapter titles: "Kamianna"; "Łabowa"; "Nowy Sącz"; "Intermezzo"; "Rome"; "Mentoreka"; "The Last Days of School"; "On the Way Back"; "Wróblik"; "Seminary"; "Nowica"; "The Matter of the Basilians' Reform"; "Krystynopol"; "Days of My Roaming"; "Złockie"; "Muszyna"; "Serving in Krynica"; "Szlachtowa." Malyniak's "Notes of a Roman" appeared in the journal *Rusyn Zion* and his "Church and State" in the *Church Herald*. In 1885, he published a number of articles on matters of our church in the French journal *Revue del' Eglise grecque unie*. These articles caught the attention of a wide audience. He was also a frequent contributor to the journal *Calendarium utrinsque Ecclesiae*, edited by Prof. Dr. Nicholas Nilles at Innsbruck. Malyniak also left an unfinished "Talerhof Diary," which is now in the hands of Dr. Roman Myrovych.

Fr. Dr. Tyt Myshkovskii

Fr. Dr. Tyt Myshkovskii was born in 1861 in Pielgrzymka, Jasło County, where his father Ioann was parish priest. His mother Ioanna's maiden name was Durkot. He completed public school and gymnazium in Przemyśl and theological studies in Vienna, at the "Barbareum." There he earned a doctorate in theology. In 1889, he became prefect at the religious seminary in Lviv and adjunct professor in the theological faculty. In 1891, he also performed the duty of teacher of religion at the technical school in Lviv. In 1894, he was nominated for professor at the religious seminary in Przemyśl, but Count Kazimierz Badeni, then Viceroy of Galicia, vetoed the nomination. In addition, Myshkovskii was even removed from his post as prefect of the Lviv religious seminary, and accepted a position as registrar at the Lviv Consistory. He also served as chaplain for a women's prison. In 1903, through the efforts of the Roman Catholic Archbishop [Józef] Bilczewski, he was appointed professor of Old Testament biblical studies and Oriental languages at Lviv University.

During the First World War, Myshkovskii was interned at Eger in Hungary and later was transferred to Faustenau near Salzburg. He was released and returned to Lviv at the petition of the university. In "Sanation" Poland he was dismissed from his professorship, and from that time on he taught theology at the religious seminary in Lviv. He died in 1936 and was buried at the Lychakivskii cemetery.

Professor Myshkovskii produced, among others, the following works:

- *Chronologice historica introductio in Novum Testamentum* (his dissertation for university docent);
- *De ratione litterarum A. T. in cantico Mariae conspiena, dissertatio exegetica*, Lviv, 1901;
- *Dvi nauky– istina edina* (Two sciences– one truth), Lviv, 1914;
- *Isaiac liber in versionibus Graeca LXX et latina Vulgata et Palaeoslavica exhibitus et explicatus, pars prior*, Lviv, 1906;
- *Vzgliad sv. Ioanna Zlatoustogo na verkhovnuyu vlast' sv. Apostola Petra* (St. John Chrysostom's view of St. Peter the Apostle's supreme authority), Lviv, 1908;
- Several scholarly reviews and essays that appeared in the *Bogoslovsky Vistnik* (Theological Herald) and the *Tserkovnii Vostok* (Ecclesiastical East);
- *Nash obriad i oblatinenie ioho* (Our rite and its Latinization), Lviv, 1912;
- *Izlozhenie Tsaregradskoy Liturgii sv. Vasyliya Vel. i sv. Ioanna Zlatousta* (The Constantinople Liturgy as explained by St. Basil the Great and St. John Chrysostom), Lviv, 1926;
- *Jugozapadnaya etnograficheskaya granitsa Galitskoy Rusi* (The southwestern ethnographic boundary of Galician Rus'), Lviv, 1934;
- A revised fifth edition of the book *Izbomik blagopotrebnykh tserkovnykh chynov i sluzhb* (Compendium of canonically required church orders and services), Lviv, 1914;
- *Evkhologion ili Trebnik, soderzhashchii v sebi chiny sv. Tain* (A Euchologion or Book of Needs containing the orders of the Sacred Mysteries), Lviv, 1926;
- An annual catalog of church laws;
- *Protiv vvedeniia v galitsky vydavnitstva fonetichnoi pravopisi* (Against the introduction of phonetic spelling into Galician publications), Lviv, 1930.

Fr. Dr. Bazyli Mastsiukh

Fr. Dr. Bazyli Mastsiukh was born in Nowa Wieś, Nowy Sącz County. He completed public school and gymnazium in Nowy Sącz and theological studies in Lviv and Przemyśl. He earned his doctorate in Vienna. Before the First World War, he was prefect and professor of canon law at the religious seminary in Przemyśl. At the same time, he was a docent at Lviv University. During the war, he was arrested and sent to Talerhof. Released at the request of the seminary, he returned to his former positions at Przemyśl.

In 1916, he joined the Austrian army as a field chaplain and was captured at the Italian front in 1918. Upon his return from Italy, he found his position as professor of canon law taken by someone else. Unable to get any employment, he wandered for nearly half a year among his clerical acquaintances, offering his services at various parishes. Finally, he obtained the administration of the parish at Horożanna Wielka in Komarno County, where he stayed until he was named Apostolic Administrator of Lemkovyna in 1935. He died on March 10, 1935 at the Administrator's residence in Rymanów-Zdrój, poisoned by Ukrainian nationalists.

Dr. Mastsiukh wrote a scholarly treatise entitled *Pravo Supruzhe* (Matrimonial law) in Rusyn, as a reference for ecclesiastics. Another of his works, "Church Law," was left in manuscript. His articles on church law and dogmatics were published in various periodicals. His name is listed in encyclopedias as an ecclesiastic.

Fr. Dr. Petro Lodii

Fr. Dr. Petro Lodii was born in 1764 in Transcarpathian Lemkovyna. He was a professor at the Studium Ruthenorum in Rome, later at Cracow University, and finally at St. Petersburg University. He produced several works in the fields of law and philosophy.

Final resting place of Fr. Dr. Bazyli Mastsiukh. Nowa Wieś, 2011.

Fr. Dr. Mykhailo Baludianskii

Fr. Dr. Mykhailo Baludianskii was born in Verkhnia Olshava in Western Transcarpathia in 1769. He earned a law degree in Budapest and was a professor at Warsaw University. He was invited to Russia in 1804 and in 1819 became the first rector of the Academy of Science in St. Petersburg. He wrote scholarly treatises in the fields of law, economics, and education. He died in 1847.

Fr. Teodor Kuryllo

Fr. Teodor Kuryllo was born on February 2, 1818, in Wysowa, Sanok County. His mother Anna came from the Smerek family. When a manorial estate in Wysowa was purchased by peasants in 1868, his father was assigned a large section of land and was able to send his son to school.

Teodor completed gymnazium in Hungary and theological studies in Przemyśl. He was parish priest at Lipie and Chaszczów in Turka County. He died on July 25, 1881. His grave with a marker is found in Chaszczów. He left several manuscripts in Latin: *Theologia pastoralis* (Uzhhorod. 1846); *Onomasticon Excellentissimo, lllustrissimo ac Reverendissimo Domino Ioanni Th. Snigursky, episkopo gr. cath. Premyslensis*; *Carmen, lllustrissimo ac Reverendissimo Domino Gregorio Jachimowicz, nominato episcopo diaecesis gr. cath. Premyslensis*; *Synopsis sacrae Scripturae utriusque Foederis*; and *Actus Apostolorum*.

Fr. Oleksii Toronskii

Fr. Oleksii Toronskii was born in 1838 in Zawadka, Sanok County, the son of priest Ioann. He was ordained in 1862. He was a professor of religion at the gymnazium in Drohobych and later at the Academic Gymnazium in Lviv. He died in 1901.

His publications include, among others, the following:

- *Rusyny-Lemky* (Rusyn-Lemkos), Lviv, 1860;
- *"Hantsia,"* a story about the lives of the people of the Beskid Mountains;
- *Ruskaya chitanka dlia vysshoy gimnazii* [A Rusyn reader for upper-class gymnazium], Lviv, 1868;

- *Rukovodstvo do nauky malogo katekhizmu* (A guide to teaching the Small Catechism), Lviv, 1885;
- *Luzhytsko-Serbskii narod* (The Lusatian Sorb people), 1888;
- *Spory o pravopis u Rusynov i Rumunov* (Spelling disputes among the Rusyns and Romanians), 1888;
- *Proskurka po koliadi (Dilo)* (Blessed *prosfora* bread after Christmas caroling, a work);
- *Prichinok do zhit'episi O. Tomy Polianskoho* (A supplement to Fr. Toma Polianskii's biography), 1889;
- *Obiasnenie chtenii apostol'skykh v prazdniki nepodvizhni* (Explanation of the Epistle readings for fixed holidays), 1889;
- *Khrist-kat. dogmatyka fundamental'na dlia uchenikov gimnazii* (Fundamental Christian and Catholic dogmatics for gymnazium students), Lviv, 1893;
- *Dogmatika fundamental'na i apol'ohetyka* (Fundamental dogmatics and apologetics), Lviv, 1893;
- *Katekhism* (A catechism), Lviv, 1896;
- *Istoria bibliina Novoho Zavita* (A Biblical history of the New Testament), Lviv, 1901.

Fr. Ioann Pryslopskii

Fr. Ioann Pryslopskii was born in the early eighteenth century in Kamianna, Nowy Sącz County, and died there as priest in the middle of that century. Some time about 1736, he wrote the "Liturgicon of St. John Chrysostom" and the "Irmologion," and gave both of these books to his church in Kamianna. Also among his works is "Church Songs For All Holidays," in the compilation of which he used Pamva Berynda's dictionary of 1627. He translated the Psalter of David from Church Slavonic to the Lemko vernacular, adding his own explanatory comments. He also translated an entire Gospel into Lemko. He translated from Polish into Lemko two parts of the *"Zertsalo,"* that is, 289 examples of great and small sins and good deeds, as well as "St. Patrick's Description of Torment in Purgatory." In his translations from Church Slavonic to Lemko, he incorporated many Polish words. Dr. Nikolai Malyniak asserts that Ioann Pryslopskii was one of the first to write in Little Russian and merits the attention of those doing research into our popular folklore. Ivan Franko

View of the main living quarters. Zyndranowa, 2002.

also mentions Pryslopskii in his *Carpatho-Rusyn Writings of the Seventeenth and Eighteenth Centuries*, Lviv, 1900. Some of Pryslopskii's manuscripts were borrowed by Prof. Ivan Orienko and incorporated into his *Samples of Cyrillic Writing of the Tenth to Eighteenth Centuries.*

Fr. Ioann Pryslopskii

Fr. Ioann Pryslopskii was born in 1831 in Kamianna, Nowy Sącz County, the great-grandson of the Fr. Ioann Pryslopskii above. After completing gymnazium and theological studies, he married Anna Pryslopskii from Regietów. He was parish priest in Wysowa, Binczarowa, Żegiestów, Brunary, and Florynka, where he died in 1909. He was a journalist for all the Galician-Rusyn newspapers. He wrote *Sandetska Rus'*, published by Iosyf Marko. It contains his observations on some of the villages, churches, and priests of Nowy Sącz County. He signed his works with the pseudonym "Ioann Petrovych."

Fr. Roman Pryslopskii

Fr. Roman Pryslopskii, son of Fr. Ioann Pryslopskii, was born in 1866 in Florynka, Nowy Sącz County. He was parish priest in Dubiecko and Żegiestów. He wrote many articles, mainly in the fields of politics and economics, which were published in all the Rusyn newspapers in Galicia. Particularly noteworthy is his brochure *"Primir latinizatorskoy gakaty na rubezhakh Galitskoy Rusi"* ("An example of Latinizer stuttering on the borders of Galician Rus'"), Przemyśl, 1902. There he describes an abominable example of the Latinization of our people by the Polish clergy. He also wrote an extensive manual for managing an exemplary farmstead under the title *Hospodarskii ukazatel'* (A management guide). As the longtime chairman of the Ruska Bursa in Nowy Sącz before World War I, he argued before the City Council for the overturning of an illegal increase in the assessment of the Bursa's property. Before the hearing, he wrote *"List otwarty do Panów Radnych Gminy Miasta Nowego Sączu w sprawie realności T-wa Ruska Bursa w Nowym Sączu"* (An open letter to the honorable members of the Nowy Sącz City Council in the case of the property of the Ruska Bursa Society in Nowy Sącz), Tarnów, 1922. Fr. Pryslopskii lost the case at the first hearing, then won on appeal; the case is still pending a second appeal. Meanwhile, the Bursa is under the control of the City Council.

The memorial wall: wrought-iron crosses from destroyed Lemko churches. Zyndranowa, 2002.

Fr. Mykhailo Konstantynovych

Fr. Mykhailo Konstantynovych was born on July 21, 1790, in Żydowskie, Jasło County, where his father was the priest. His mother, Maria Wapińska, came from Desznica. He went to the German gymnazium in Lviv and the theological school there. In 1849, he married Iulianna Hoinatskii from the village of Hodynie near Mościsko, where he was first assistant. For a time, he was parish priest at Krempna near Jasło and later at Rostajne. Together with Adolf Dobrianskii, he received a gold cross from the Austrian Emperor for services rendered to Austria in 1849, when Russian troops were going through Lemkovyna to crush the rebellion in Hungary. He died on September 19, 1875, in the eighty-fifth year of his life. He left a manuscript entitled "Genealogy of the Ostrozheskii-Konstantynovych Family." He traced his ancestry to the Ostrog and Konstantynovych princes, and to this end he searched for source material in the library of the Przemyśl bishop and in the ecclesiastical offices in Wysowa and Polany. This manuscript is in the hands of the Konstantynovych family. It was the first attempt at genealogical research in Lemkovyna.

Ivan Konstantynovych

Ivan Konstantynovych was born on December 26, 1821, in Krepna, Jasło County, where his father Mykhailo was priest. His mother was from the Hoinatskii family. After completing law studies in Lviv, he served for forty years in the Ministry of Internal Affairs in Vienna. He married a German lady named Maria Weber. He died suddenly on September 26, 1889, while still with the Ministry. He wrote *Opisanie ikon po tserkvakh Russkykh v stolichnom gradi Lvivi* (A description of icons in Rusyn churches in the capital city Lviv), Lviv, 1858. A review of this study was published in the Vienna *Vistnyk* (Herald), No. 9, 1859.

Fr. Iosyf Hoinatskii

Fr. Iosyf Hoinatskii was born on January 7, 1806, in Czyrna, Nowy Sącz County, where his father Ioann was priest. His mother Maria was from the Chyrnianskii family. He was parish priest in Czyrna, Roztoka Wielka,

Roztoka Mała, and Berest. Before the war, there were in the Berest parish library the following manuscripts that he had written: "On Composing and Delivering Sermons"; "A Chronicle of Churches in Berest and Polany"; "On the Celebration of Saints' Days in Berest and Polany"; "The Rusyn People of Berest," with statistical data; and "A Census of the Rusyn Population in Polany," 1851. None of these manuscripts have been published, but they are of great importance for the history of Berest and Polany.

Dr. Benedykt Mokhnatskii

Dr. Benedykt Mokhnatskii was born in Banica, Nowy Sącz County, near the end of the eighteenth century. After completing gymnazium, he studied at Vienna University, where he earned a doctorate in medicine in 1814. His dissertation was entitled *"Dissertatio inauguralis medicopolitica de Pharmacoplis,"* Viennae, Typis. Antonii Schmid, 1814, and was divided into an introduction, chapters, and theses. He dedicated it to his grandfather Ioann and to the knight Radwan Jarzębiński, director of a school in Żembocina near Kielce. He also wrote other studies in the field of medicine.

Damian Savchak

Damian Savchak was born in Nowa Wieś, Nowy Sącz County. He was a member of the judiciary and a delegate to the Vienna parliament. He wrote several essays in his specialty, among which are: *Sbornik zakonov administratsiynykh* (A compendium of administrative laws), Lviv, 1893; *Novy zakon dorogovy* (The new highway law), Lviv, 1898; " A Speech On the Confirmation of Ambassador Polianskii's Election"; and "A Speech On Motives For Adjudication in Cases of Cattle Disease." Both of these speeches were published in *Dilo* (Business), Nos. 224 and 241, 1889.

Frants Levynskii

Frants Levynskii came from Olchowiec in Krosno County. He was a judge in Dukla. He wrote an interesting treatise entitled "Aeronautics," 1895, and illustrated it with seven sketches.

Samples of the woodcarving skill of Andrii Sukhorskii of Wólka (Lviv after 1948.) Zyndranowa, 2002.

Dr. Teofil Kuryllo

Dr. Teofil Kuryllo was born in 1891, in Rozdziele, Gorlice County, where his father Vasyli was priest. His mother was of the Konstantynovych family. He completed gymnazium in Jasło and the study of law at Cracow University, where he earned a doctorate in law. He became a lawyer in Cracow. He was killed by Polish thugs in 1945 after the war had ended. He wrote "A Brief Review of Writers and Journalists in Lemkovyna" (Part I, Lviv, 1937); "Lemkos on the Bishops' Thrones of Galician Rus'"; and "On Lemko Highwaymen." Besides these, he published several articles in various journals and newspapers, mostly on Lemko life. In the last few years of his life, he compiled over a thousand biographies of the most famous Lemkos and was planning to publish this valuable work after the war. However, his unexpected death frustrated these wishes. This was extremely valuable material that cost the author much labor and would have been of great utility for the history of Lemkovyna. Some of these manuscripts are still kept by his son in Cracow. Dr. Teofil Kuryllo was a grandson of the Fr. Teodor Kuryllo noted above.

Among the very oldest scholars, of whom we know very little, are the following:

Mykhailo of Sanok

Mykhailo of Sanok was the son of an archpriest in Sanok. In the mid-sixteenth century, he translated, on order of a Holshanskii princess, the Gospel from Bulgarian into Rusyn. This translation is known as the "Peresopnytska Gospel," [written 1556-1561] because it was found in the Peresopnytsia Monastery [near Rivne] in Volhynia. He also translated four other Gospels from Church Slavonic into the Galician dialect. He is mentioned by Pavel Jozef Šafarik in his *Sloviansky Drevnosti* (Slavic Antiquities).

Tymofei of Wysoczany

Tymofei of Wysoczany lived in the mid-seventeenth century and left *Evangelie uchitelnoe* (A teaching Gospel), 1635. It is now in the Library of the National Home in Lviv. It is mentioned by Antonii Petrushevych in his *Svodnoy halitsko-russkoi litopysy* (A summary of Galician-Rusyn manuscripts), 1874.

Stefan of Rychwałd

Stefan of Rychwałd lived during the middle of the seventeenth century and also wrote "A Teaching Gospel." This is now kept in the library of the Przemyśl bishop. It is also mentioned by Antonii Petrushevych in his *Summary*.

Miniature of St. Matthew from the
Peresopnytska Gospel, circa 1556-1561.

2. Writers and Poets

Pavlo of Krosno

Pavlo of Krosno was born in the latter half of the fifteenth century and died in November of 1517. In Polish and Latin literature he is known as "Paulus Crosnensis Ruthenus," "Paul de Crosno," and "Paul de Russia." In 1500, he obtained a baccalaureate degree at Cracow University and a master's degree six years later. Toward the end of 1508 he made a trip to Baradyn in Hungary and returned to Cracow. He continued his professorial work there until 1517 when he went to Sanok for treatment of pestilential plague. He died there of apoplexy.

Pavlo of Krosno was a poet steeped in Latin literature. He started writing poems in about the year 1500. There are many of them, and they were published in an individual anthology, dedicated to his compatriot Havryil Peremii, in Vienna in 1509. His poetry is religious and secular in content and shows the marked influence of Horace and Ovid. His poems include about 2,500 elegies and about 1,500 panegyrics, epigrams, and other short stanzas in Phalaecian hendecasyllables and asclepedeans in alcaic and Sapphic strophes. There are also some odes and various topical verses, but all of them bear the mark of humanism.[9]

Damian Levytskii

Damian Levytskii lived in the middle of the eighteenth century. He was born in Nowa Wieś, Nowy Sącz County, where his father was priest. He compiled a *Sbornik dukhovnykh stikhov i pisnei* (Anthology of spiritual poems and songs). This volume takes up 326 sheets of paper. Among them is an ode (chant) to the battle of Poltava. He wrote secular songs about love. These poems and songs

---

9   Details on the life and work of Pavlo of Krosno can be found in H. Galle, *Zarys dziejów literatury polskiej* (Historical sketch of Polish literature), Warsaw, 1913; Dr. Bronisław Kruciekiewicz, *Rozprawy wydziału filologicznego Akademii Umiejętności* (Proceedings of the Philological Division of the Academy of Sciences), R. XII, scey. 111; Władysław Sama, *Opis powiatu Krośnieńskiego* (Description of Krosno County), pp. 331-335.

Return in time to the bygone days. Museum of Lemko Culture, Zyndranowa, 2002.

were reviewed by Dr. Iuliian Iavorskii, a professor at Kyiv University, in his *Novyie danniia dlia istorii Starinnoy malorusskoy pisni i virshi* (New data on the history of ancient Little Russian song and verse), Lviv, 1921.

Volodymyr Khyliak

Volodymyr Khyliak was born on July 15, 1843, in Wierchomla Wielka, Nowy Sącz County, where his father Ihnaty was priest. His mother Efrozinia, of the Parylow family, died when he was barely two years old. He completed public school and six grades of gymnazium in Nowy Sącz and then transferred to Prešov, where he finished his gymnazium studies. He completed theological studies in Przemyśl. He served as priest in several parishes: Doliny, Izby, Bartne, and Litynia, where he died on June 13, 1893.

Khyliak was a prolific writer. He signed his works either with his proper name or with a variety of pseudonyms: "Neliach," "Ya sam" (I am), "Lemko-Semko," "Nikyi," "Ieronim Anonim," "Quidam," "W." His writings soon made him famous in our mountains. Among his best works are "A Polish Patriot" (1872); "An Attraction to Hearts" (1874); "Matrimony and Four Faculties" (1870); "The Rusyn Fate" (1880); "A Great Renegade on a Small

The wall of memory to Volodymyr Khylak and poet Ivan Rusenko. Zyndranowa, 2005.

Scale" (1881); "The Hangman's Peak" (1883); "Do Not Take the Name of Your Lord God in Vain" (1888); "The Last Cup" (1888); "Seven Slips at One Sitting" (1888); "Happiness Lies Not in Money" (1889); "Of Sin and Punishment" (1889); "First Love" (1891); "Do Not Judge and You Shall Not Be Judged" (1893); and "Marriage From Carelessness" (1893).

Also of interest are his novellas: "Andrey's Day," "Death and Wife Are From God," "To Cry or to Laugh," "Stubborn Oldsters," "Mail Call," "The Deceased Wife Was Better," "My Cantor of Blessed Memory," "On the Advice of the Doctor, "Choose Not Only a Wife But Also a Mother-in-Law," "Cause and Consequence," "An Engagement in a Swamp," "Not All Things Are Equal," "Both Funny and Sad."

Khyliak's humorous tales are full of life and compassion: "Also a Jubilee," "Clara Milych Turgenev," "Fish," and "He Recognized His Wife." So are his satires: "What Rusyn Eyes Wonder At," "On the Growth of Men," "New Year's Greetings," "She and I," "Prophecies For 1876," "Grandfathers and Grandmothers," "Comedies and Wonders," "The Wise Letter of a Rusyn Fool," "The Duel," "The Lviv Provincial Synod," and "The Waters of Wysowa." Volodymyr Khyliak's works were published in such Ruthenian journals as *Slaviansky Viek* (Slavic Age), *Russky Vistnik* (Rusyn Herald), *Iliustrovany Svit* (Illustrated World), and others. A scholarly analysis of his writings was written by the Rusyn scholar and critic, Academician A. Pypin. Khyliak's complete works were published in Lviv, edited by the Academic Circle.

Klavdia Aleksovych

Klavdia Aleksovych was born on November 20, 1830, in Krasna, Krosno County, where her father Ioann was priest. Her mother was the daughter of Trokhanovskii, parish priest in Grab. Her parents died when she was a child, and she was brought up by her grandfather Bishop Toma Polianskii in Przemyśl. There she completed a theological program with the Benedictine Sisters. Later she was an active member of a "sisterhood" founded by Bishop Polianskii in Przemyśl. She herself organized *Obshchestvo Russkykh Dam* (the Society of Rusyn Ladies) and a Shelter for Rusyn girls in Lviv. She was also an active member of the Mykhailo Kachkovskii Society and the Muza Society. She died in 1916. Her body is buried in a cemetery for Galician-Rusyn authors and journalists.

Klavdia Aleksovych wrote "The Song of Oldina" (1860); "A Befuddled Girl," a play that has been successfully performed by Lemko groups; "Popular Support for Great Rus'"(for school children); "The Bewitched Bear" (a folk tale); "Two Little Sisters" and "Arendar" (both folk dramas); and "With Andrei, I Am Sowing Flax; Let Me Know, God, With Whom Shall I Reap It," a farce, published in *Istoriia Obshchestva Russkykh Dam vo Lvivi* (A History of the Society of Rusyn Ladies in Lviv), Kolomyia, 1905.

Fr. Vasyli Chernetskii

Fr. Vasyli Chernetskii was born in 1837 in Wola Cieklińska, Jasło County. He was a parish priest. He wrote "Recollections of 1846," wherein he described, as an eyewitness, the slaughter of Polish gentry by Polish peasants in the Mazury region, with Sholom as leader of the mob.

Fr. Aleksander Dukhnovych

Fr. Aleksander Dukhnovych was born in 1803. He was canon of the Prešov cathedral. He is one of the greatest Carpatho-Rusyn writers and poets. In addition to compiling an entire series of school textbooks on religion and teaching, he wrote many tales and poems on the life of the Carpatho-Rusyn people.

Fr. Iuliian Stavrovskii

Fr. Iuliian Stavrovskii was parish priest in Czertyżne. He wrote under the pseudonym "Popradov." He wrote marvelous poetry, in which he describes the beauty of the Carpathian lands and the area of the Poprad River. Among the best of his poems are: "On the Beskids," "A Winter Evening," "Native Land," "Spiš," "Recollections of the Poprad," "The Sufferings of Slavs," "To Uhro-Rusyns," "To My People," and "The Genius of Rusyns."

Adolf Dobrianskii

Adolf Dobrianskii was born in 1817. He was widely known as a social worker, statesman, politician, poet, and writer. He was a delegate to the Vienna Parliament and Councillor to the Emperor. He wrote much, but it was mainly stories and poems that were more suitable for the intelligentsia than for ordinary people.

Volodymyr Shchavynskii

Volodymyr Shchavynskii was born in 1853 in Klimkówka, Gorlice County. His father Iosyf was a priest. After completing gymnazium, he studied medicine at Vienna University, but did not finish. He devoted all his talents to journalism. In Vienna he was the life of the Rusyn community. He never lost contact with his native land and would return to our mountains every summer, most often to visit Fr. Rusyniak in Królowa Ruska. The last time he left Lemkovyna, he took with him a clump of dirt, requesting that it be placed on his grave. He died in Vienna on February 4, 1913. He never ceased writing up to the very moment of his death.

Volodymyr Shchavynskii was a correspondent for all the major Galician-Rusyn newspapers: *Galichanyn* (The Galician), *Chervona Rus'* (Red Rus'), *Prikarpatskaia Rus'*, and others. He signed his articles with the pseudonym "vo". He loved to travel. In addition to articles and feuilletons, he compiled a *"Samouchitel' nimeckoho iazyka"* (Teach yourself German), and wrote "The Christening of Rus'," "Through Northern Italy," "From Nice" [referring to the city in France], and "From the Paris Exposition." All of these articles were published in the pages of *Chervona Rus'*.

Dr. Modest Humetskii

Dr. Modest Humetskii was born on April 3, 1842 in Tokarnia, Sanok County, where his father was priest. His mother Melania, a descendant of Russo-Galician boyars, came from Śnietnica. She was a very conscientious woman, and she superbly reared fourteen children. Modest went to school in Krosno and Rzeszów. After completing gymnazium, he matriculated in theology but soon transferred to medicine, first at Cracow and later in Vienna. In 1871, he obtained a doctorate in medicine. He practiced medicine in Lesko, Dobromil, and for twenty-five years in Krosno, where for a time he was mayor. He purchased Ripnik and was buried there in the family mausoleum. He died on December 9, 1899. He wrote in both verse and prose in Russian, Polish, and German. His works were published in Galician periodicals under the pseudonym "Maria of Zion," and also in Polish and German journals. Among his better writings are "Poetry Through the Unknown" (Jasło, 1876; Lviv, 1879); "Aphorisms With Nature in the Background" (Lviv, 1877); "Darwinism" (Lviv, 1878); and "Ideas and Opinions" (Lviv, 1881). There are twenty poems in this collection, some of which have the author's comments added. His patriotic poem "Zion, Or Rusyn Song" was left in manuscript.[10]

The village of Klimkówka, prior to start of work on an artificial lake in the 1970s. Klimkówka, 1962.

---

10   *Kalendar To-va Mikh. Kaczkowskoho za 1901 hod* (Calendar of the Mykhailo Kachkovskii Society for the year 1901), pp. 266-268.

Fr. Aleksander Pavlovych

Fr. Aleksander Pavlovych was born in 1819 in the village of Czarna, Bardejov District. He went to public school in Lviv where, as the orphan of a priest, he lived with the Hladyshovskii family. He went to gymnazium in Bardejov, Miskolc, and Eger, and completed theological studies in Trnava. He worked as librarian for the bishop in Prešov for two years, and then became parish priest in Biała Wieża and Svidnik. He lived in the latter village for thirty-six years, i.e., until 1900. He wrote mostly poetry. His first poems were published by Dukhnovych in his almanac *Pozdravlenie Rusynov* (Greetings to Rusyns). After that his poems appeared in Carpatho-Rusyn publications. Some were also published by his compatriot, the teacher Ivan Polivka, in Uzhhorod in 1929, under the title *"Vinets stikhotvorenii o. Aleksandra Pavlovycha"* (Fr. Aleksander Pavlovych's garland of poetry). Pavlovych was the only Carpatho-Rusyn poet who tried to write in the Lemko native vernacular. He wrote about village life as seen by a priest.

Dr. Symeon Pyzh

Dr. Symeon Pyzh was born on February 14, 1894 in Wapienne, Gorlice County. He went to public school in Wapienne and gymnazium in Gorlice and Nowy Sącz, where he passed the final exam with honors. When he began preparing for university studies, World War I broke out in 1914. Because he was of Rusyn nationality, he was arrested and sent to Talerhof. [To extract himself] from Talerhof he enlisted in the Austrian army and was sent to the Italian front. There he escaped from the Austrian army and voluntarily joined a Czechoslovak legion that was organized to fight for the independence of Czechoslovakia, which had arisen on the ruins of the Austro-Hungarian monarchy. Then he entered the university at Prague, graduating in March 1922 with a doctorate in law.

The next year, a group of Lemko students in Prague sent Dr. Pyzh to America as one of the few Lemko emigrants allowed to go there. He was to organize a national effort and collect the funds needed to battle the opposition to independence for Lemkovyna. In Philadelphia in 1923, he became editor of the newspaper *Pravda*, organ of the Society of Rus' Brotherhoods (RBO). He continued this editorial and organizational work for ten years. Meanwhile, a new organization, the Lemko Soyuz, came into being, with its newspaper

Lemko published first in Cleveland, then in New York and Yonkers and re-named *Karpatska Rus.* In 1934, Dr. Pyzh joined the Lemko Soyuz and be-came editor of its organ. He continued in this position to the end of his hard-working life. He died unexpectedly on June 10, 1957, in Yonkers.

Dr. Symeon Pyzh was gifted with a great mind, was highly educated, and ardently loved the people he stemmed from, and lived and worked only for those people. He did not restrict himself to just his editorial duties, but also took an active part in every aspect of the growing organizational work. He was secretary of the Lemko Soyuz and secretary of the Carpatho-Russian American Center [in Yonkers, NY]. He was director of the Carpatho-Russian American Center during the Second World War and the principal rep-resentative of the Lemko Soyuz and other Carpatho-Rusyn organizations to the Slavic Congress and to the American Committee for Russian War Relief. The American Lemko Park Corporation was organized with his assistance. He prepared a memorandum to the Polish Government on the harm done to the Lemkos in banishing them from their beloved mountains. He lived for his native Lemkovyna with all his spirit and dreamed of improving its fate.

In addition to writing newspaper articles, Pyzh published essays on vari-ous political, historical, and juridical themes that evidenced great knowledge of the subject matter and a practical mind. Most notable are his essays enti-tled "Two Fronts (Russia and Germany)," and "The Struggle for Nationality Rights and the Fight for Social Justice."[11]

Dymytrii Vyslotskii

Dymytrii Vyslotskii was born on November 4, 1888 in Łabowa, Nowy Sącz County. He came from a poor peasant family. He completed gymnazium in Nowy Sącz and then matriculated in the law school at Lviv University. Lack of financial resources kept him from completing the course, and he devoted himself to socio-political work. He took a job as director of the Ruska Bursa in Buczacz. After two years, he took up political and public work. In 1912, he began publishing the newspaper *Lemko*, first in Nowy Sącz and a year later in Gorlice. In 1914, he moved to Przemyśl and began the newspaper *Ruska Ze-mlia* (Rusyn Land), but the First World War interrupted this. Vyslotskii was arrested and sent to the military prison in Vienna. There he and other Lemko

11 *Karpatorussky Kalendar* (Carpatho-Russian Calendar), 1958, pp. 21-26.

An outdoor classroom. Krynica, 1943.

activists were tried, and all were sentenced to death. Through the intervention
of the British king, they were granted amnesty. When the war ended, Vyslotskii returned to his native village and began cultural and educational work.
The Polish authorities started to harass him for his political views. Due to
difficult circumstances, he immigrated to Canada in 1922. After living there
for five years, he moved to the United States. There he engaged in extensive
organizational work. Among other things, he edited the Carpatho-Rusyn
newspaper "Lemko," which soon became the leading organizational agent
among the working people in the US and Canada.

During World War II, Vyslotskii organized considerable aid for the Soviet Union in the form of money, clothing, and food products. During his
stay in the US, he published an entire series of calendars, collections of his
own articles, feuilletons, humorous stories, and scenic illustrations. In 1937,
he translated into Lemko N. Ostrovskii's *"Yak Hartuvalasia Stal'" (How Ste-
el Was Forged)* and in 1938 the *"Istoriia Sovietskoho Soyuza"* (History of the
Soviet Union). His translation of Nikolai Gogol's *Taras Bulba* enjoyed considerable popularity. He expressed his great love for all Slavic peoples in his
own *Slavianske Bratstvo* (The Slavic fraternity).

In 1934, Vyslotskii made a trip to the Soviet Union, where he became better acquainted with the life of the Soviet people and their achievements and

took part in celebrating the seventeenth anniversary of the October Revolution in Moscow. After returning from this trip, he traveled all over America and gave speeches on today's Russia. Among the products of his pen are hundreds of sketches, poems, publicistic articles, dramatic works, and letters of correspondence. Among the best of his works are *"Pravda o Rossii"* (The truth about Russia), *"Za narodniu pravdu"* (For the people's truth), and *"O Lemkakh"* (About Lemkos).

After World War II, Vyslotskii returned to his Lemkovyna in 1946. He spent a very short time in his native village and a little longer in Uzhhorod, where he was welcomed warmly. He then went to live permanently in Lviv, where, after fifty years of intellectual work, he lived [quietly] with his wife until 1968, near the end of which he left us forever. Dymytrii Vyslotskii wrote under the pseudonym "Vanio Hunianka."

In addition to those listed above, other Lemko writers of poems, stories, and articles include: Antonii Doshna, Konstantyn Kuryllo, Teofil Kachmarchyk, Mykhailo Nesterak, Ivan Rusenko, Stefania Verbytska, Vasyl Didovych, M. Voloshynovych, Stefan Pilkh, Hryhory Hanuliak, Mykhailo Vatslavskii and Kyryll Chaikovskii. Among the journalists were: Mykhailo Hnatyshak, Roman Pryslopskii, Iosyf Fedorenko, Hryhory Hanuliak, Vasyl Koldra, Iuliian Iurchakevych, and many others.

3. University Professors

1. Fr. Dr. Mykhailo Baludianskii, at the universities of Warsaw and St. Petersburg.
2. Fr. Dr. Onufrii Krynytskii, at Lviv University.
3. Fr. Dr. Petro Lodii, at Cracow University.
4. Fr. Dr. Nikolai Malyniak, at Lviv University.
5. Fr. Dr. Bazyli Mastsiukh, at Lviv University.
6. Fr. Dr. Tyt Myshkovskii, at Lviv University.
7. Fr. Dr. Iuliian Pelesh, at the universities of Lviv and Vienna.
8. Fr. Dr. Sylvester Sembratovych, at Lviv University.
9. Fr. Dr. Iosyf Sembratovych, at Lviv University.
10. Dr. Vasyl Chyrnianskii, at Lviv University.
11. Dr. Emilyian Chyrnianskii, at Cracow University.
12. Fr. Dr. Iosyf Iaryna, at Lviv University.
13. Dr. Valery Sas Iavorskii, at Cracow University.

4. Bishops

1. Fr. Dr. Toma Polianskii, Bishop of Przemyśl.
2. Fr. Dr. Iosyf Sembratovych, Archbishop of Lviv and Metropolitan of Galicia
3. Fr. Dr. Iuliian Pelesh, Bishop of Stanisławów and Przemyśl.
4. Fr. Dr. Sylvester Sembratovych, Archbishop of Lviv, Metropolitan of Galicia, and Cardinal.
5. Fr. Dr. Bazyli Mastsiukh, Apostolic Administrator of Lemkovyna.
6. Iosafat Kotsylovskii, Bishop of Przemyśl.

5. Military Leaders

1. Dr. Emilyian Fedorenko, born in Czerteż, Sanok County, General and Marshal of Soviet armies, Commander-in Chief at the western front, died in a hospital of wounds suffered at the front in 1945.
2. Danylo Talpash, born in Nowa Wieś, Sanok County, Major in the Austrian army.
3. Ivan Pukhyr, born in Świątkowa, Jasło County, Colonel in the Austrian army.

* * *

From all of the above, it is clear that Lemkovyna, the most forlorn and forgotten corner of the Carpathian Mountains, produced a whole series of highly learned scholars, renowned writers and poets, illustrious bishops and military men, who performed great service not only for the Lemko people themselves but also for all of humanity. Regardless of the positions they held or the places they worked, they stayed true to their origins and the traditions of their people, and they gravitated heart and soul toward those always oppressed people. We look in vain through their scholarly works for any evidence that Lemkos are Ukrainian, as is proclaimed by Ukrainian separatists. They were in agreement with scholars of all other nationalities that Lemkos are a part of the great Slavic-Rusyn family.

Bride and groom in regional costumes. Wola Michowa, early 1940s.

BIBLIOGRAPHY

Works cited by Fr. Polianskii

On pp. 267-279 of the 1969 text, Father Polianskii cites works as of the 1960s, in Russian, Ukrainian, Polish, Slovak, Czech, German, Latin, English, French, and Italian. The reader is urged to start further research into the Lemko question there.

Polianskii's writings

Besides the present *Lemkovyna: A History...* and his autobiography, also included in this volume in translation, Polianskii alludes in his History to his *Piesn o Lemkovyni* (Song of Lemkovyna, or A Song About Lemkovyna) and two theological works: *"O dostoinstvi sviashchennyka"* (On the merit of a priest) and *"O verkhovnoi vlasti vs. Apostola Petra i ioho naslidnikov Khristovoi Tserkvi"* (On the supreme authority of St. Peter the Apostle and his successors in the Church of Christ). In his letter to Teodor Dokla, Polianskii mentions another poem, "Yearning after Lemkovyna." Unfortunately these items were not available to us and may be lost.

Biographies of Polianskii

Besides those included in this volume there are only two very, very short thumbnail sketches of Ioann Polianskii: in Polish, Jerzy Starzyński, *"Proboszcz z Rudnej"* (Rector from Rudna), in *Wersja: miesięcznik Legnicki* (Version: a Legnica monthly), vol. 9, No. 19, *Wrzesien* (September) 1999, p. 10-12; and in Rusyn, Petro Trokhanovskii, *"Sviashchennyk inchii od inchykh"* (A priest of a different sort), *Lemkivskii Kalendar* (Lemko Calendar) 1998, pp. 84-87, available at http://lemko.org/books/LKK/LKK1998.pdf .

Евакуаційний лист
Karta ewakuacyjna

_____ 194 5 р.

Дано громадянинові
Wydano obywatelowi

жителю села (міста)
mieszkańcowi wsi (miasta)

області (воєводства) в тому, що він за дозволом Головного Уповноваженого Уряду Української
obwodu (wojewódstwa), iż za zezwoleniem Głównego Pełnomocnika Rządu Ukraińskiej SSR

РСР (Польського Комітету Національного Визволення) по евакуації на території Польщі (Укра-
(Polskiego Komitetu Wyzwolenia Narodowego) dla ewakuacji na terytorium Polski (Ukraińskiej SSR)

їнської РСР) евакуюється в _____ району (волость) _____
ewakuuje się do   rejonu (gminy)

області УРСР (воєводства Польщі).
obwodu USSR (wojewódstwa Polski).

З ним разом евакуюються такі члени його сім'ї:
Wraz z nim ewakuują się następujących członków jego rodziny:

ПРІЗВИЩЕ, ІМ'Я, ПО БАТЬКОВІ NAZWISKO, IMIĘ, IMIĘ OJCA	Відношення до голови сім'ї Stosunek do głowy rodziny	Місце і рік народження Miejsce i rok urodzenia	Примітка Uwaga
Михневич Юлія Лук.	дружина	1910	
— Семан Степ.	син	1936	

Громадянин _____
Obywatel

з собою перевозить коней ____, великої рогатої худоби 2, свиней ____, овець 1
przewozi z sobą koni, rogacizny, świń, owiec

кіз ____, інвентарю плугів ____, возів ____, збиральних машин ____
kóz, inwentarz: pługów, wozów, żniwiarek

продовольчих продуктів 7, дитяч. з них зерна і зернопродуктів 2, штук, речей домаш-
produktów żywnościowych, ctn.: w tym ziarna i produktów zbożowych, ctn., przedmiotów użytku

 нього вжитку 15, штук
domowego ctn.

М. п.   Районний Уповноважений по евакуації
М. р.   Rejonowy Pełnomocnik dla ewakuacji

по _____ району
rejonu (підпис) — (podpis)

Представник сторони по _____ району
Przedstawiciel strony   rejonu (підпис) — (podpis)

History of the Lemko Region

The only other history than that of Polianskii known to the editors is that of Iuliian Tarnovych, *Iliustrovana Istoriia Lemkovshchyny* (An illustrated history of the Lemko Region) (Lviv, 1939, reprinted in New York in 1964 by the *Kultura* publishing house), available at http://lemko.org/pdf/tarnovich1. pdf. This book contains one hundred black and white illustrations and 286 pages of text in a small pocket-sized paperbound format on inexpensive paper. Tarnovych (pseudonym Iuliian Beskyd), 1904-1977, was a very strong Ukrainophile. He was active in inter-war Poland, mostly in Lviv. During the German occupation he worked in Cracow on the Ukrainian language newspaper *Krakivski visti*, which was supported by the Germans. After fleeing to the west at the end of WW II he migrated to Canada. He died in Toronto after reactivating his interest in the Lemko Region.

ПЕТРО ТРОХАНОВСКІЙ

СВЯЩЕННИК ІНЧИЙ ОД ІНЧЫХ

Кажде жытя трудне єст до зрозумліня, бо — як повідали дідове — „єден чловек в другым не сідит", але жытя того чловека, о котрым тепер замірюю дакус написати, представлят ся особливі таємничо.

Вродил ся в Баници, давного ґрибівского повіту, 1888 рока, дня 20 січня. Понеже было то дораз по сьвяті Йордану, родиче - Поляньскы, Тевдор і Мария дали му імено Йоан, в чест св.Йоана Крестителя. Ріс малий Ванцьо з братом Митром і трьома сестрами — як сам споминат — „весело при родичах". Та недолго было того веселого дітиньства. Уж в осмым році взял го няньо за ручку і зо словами: „*Ід сыну до школы і вчий ся, жебыс в жытю не бідувал так тяко як я*" — попрова-

Petro Trokhanovskii, "Sviashchennyk inchii od inchykh" (A priest of a different sort).

Deportation

MILITARY OPERATION code named "VISTULA"

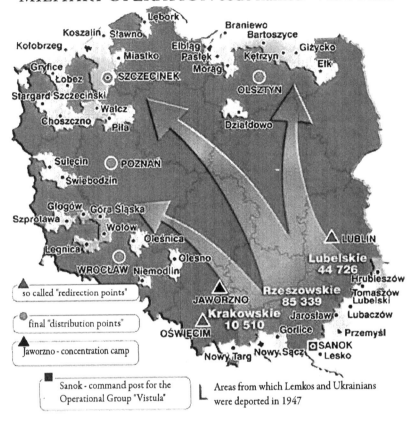

Logistical map of the military Operation "Vistula" showing the number of those deported from three districts of Poland. For additional reading, see http://en.wikipedia.org/wiki/Operation_Vistula and http://lemko.org/lih/olszansk.html .

Encyclopedia

While there is mention of the Carpathian region in Russian and Ukrainian encyclopedias, there is only one compendium of knowledge devoted solely to that part of central Europe: Paul Robert Magocsi and Ivan Pop (eds.), *Encyclopedia of Rusyn History and Culture (second edition, revised and expanded)* (Toronto, Buffalo, London: University of Toronto Press, 2005). There is now a Ukrainian language version with a bit more information (Padyak Publishers, Uzhhorod, Ukraine, 2011). This encyclopedia contains many entries related to the Lemko Region.

Books

Horbal, Bogdan, *Lemko Studies: A Handbook* (New York: East European Monographs, distributed by Columbia University Press, 2010). This book is placed first in this listing since it is the most necessary book to have for someone interested in things Lemko. It covers not only the Lemkos and the Lemko homeland but also the whole of the Lemko Diaspora. References include not only English language sources but also those found in Polish, Ukrainian, German, Czech, Slovak and Russian. This is the very best book available about the Lemkos and we will not reproduce its very extensive bibliography here.

Best, Paul and Stanisław Stępień, *Does a Fourth Rus' Exist? Concerning Cultural Identity in the Carpathian Region* (Przemyśl and Higganum: Carpathian Institute, Southeast Research Institute, 2009).

Best, Paul and Jarosław Moklak (eds.), *The Lemkos...Articles and Essays* (Cracow and New Haven: C-SSG [Carpathian Institute], 2000). [Second edition, revised and expanded, Carpathian Institute, Higganum, Connecticut, 2012.]

Best, Paul and Jarosław Moklak (eds.), *The Lemko Region, 1939-1947: War, Occupation and Deportation* (Cracow and New Haven, C-SSG [Carpathian Institute], 2002).

In Magocsi, Paul Robert, *Of the Making of Nationalities there is no End* (New York: East European Monographs, distributed by Columbia University Press, 1999):

"The Lemko Rusyn Republic, 1918-1920 and Political Thought in Western Rus' Ukraine" (Volume 1);

"Nation-Building or Nation Destroying: Lemkos, Poles and Ukrainians in Contemporary Poland" (Volume 1);

"On Lemko Identity" (Volume 2).

In Magocsi, Paul Robert (ed), *The Persistence of Regional Cultures: Rusyns and Ukrainians in their Homeland and Abroad* (New York: East European Monographs, distributed by Columbia University Press, 1993):

Olena Duc'-Fajfer, "The Lemkos of Poland."

In Rusinko, Elaine (ed), *Committing Community: Carpatho-Rusyn Studies as an Emerging Scholarly Discipline* (New York: East European Monographs, distributed by Columbia University Press, 2009):

Michalasky, Susyn, "Rebuilding a Shattered Community: the Lemkos after the 'Akcja Wisła'";

Horbal, Bogdan, "The Rusyn Movement among the Galician Lemkos";

Hann, Christopher, "From Ethnic Group to Sub-Sub Ethnicity: the Lemko-Rusyn-Ukrainians in Post-Socialist Poland."

Magocsi, Paul Robert, *Our People: Carpatho-Rusyns and their descendants in North America* (fourth revised edition) (Wauconda, Illinois: Bolchazy-Carducci Publishers, 2005). See especially the best Carpatho-Rusyn gazetteer (place finder) in any language in the "Root Seeker's Guide to the Homeland," pp. 110-206.

Periodicals

Carpatho-Rusyn American (newsletter/forum), published 1978-1997 by the Carpatho-Rusyn Research Center. See especially "The Lemko Rusyns: Their Past and Present," Vol.10 (1987), No.1, p.5-12.

Karpatska Rus', begun as *Lemko* in 1928, the oldest more or less continuously published Carpatho-Rusyn periodical. Since Vol. 80, No.2, a quarterly published by the Lemko Association, Inc. of Higganum, Connecticut, USA.

Lemkivshchyna, a quarterly devoted to the Lemko Region as "Western Ukraine," has been in print for twenty-two years and is written in standard Ukrainian. Lately a few pages in English have been appearing in the central section of the magazine. Published by the Organization for the Defense of Lemkivshchyna Western Ukraine, Clifton, New Jersey, USA.

The New Rusyn Times is published by the Carpatho-Rusyn Society of Munhall, Pennsylvania, USA. The Society is the largest Carpatho-Rusyn oriented organization in North America.

APPENDIX I:
HISTORICAL AND LINGUISTIC
CONTEXT

The Language of *Lemkovyna: A History*

We opened I. F. Lemkyn's *Istoriya Lemkovyny* (History of Lemkovyna, published by the Lemko Association, Yonkers, New York, 1969) with great interest, and we are unable to put it away.

Our modest goal is to provide a brief linguistic analysis of this text. The emotional charge with which Lemkyn approached work on his book, an above all heartfelt reinterpretation of the lives of his people, laid out two styles of description of their long history: an artistic style of poetry in the prologues to its five parts, and a scholarly, journalistic style of presenting the principal events of Lemko history.

Our challenge will remain unfulfilled and our conclusions will not be understood if we do not answer the main question: what language is being used in *Istoriia Lemkovyny*?

Even having no biographical information about the author and his scholarly and social activities, in the course of analyzing his book we can say a lot of positive things about his personality. He is of an emotional nature, possessing a wide store of knowledge. He is an ardent patriot of the Lemko-Rusyn people and their unique culture. His use and analysis of sources (383 items comprising Russian, Ukrainian, Polish, Czech, Slovak, German, Latin, English, French, and Italian publications) testifies to his meticulousness and responsibility towards historical truth. The author belongs to the category of fair, good and just people. With undisguised pride, Lemkyn refers to the land of the Lemkos:

Because this is our Rusyn land
It is our fatherland
It is our inheritance
It is the cradle of Holy Rus'.

All that is best in the world can be found only in Lemkovyna, says Lemkyn: "Although simple, the Lemko cuisine is very tasty. Nowhere in the world can you find bread as flavorful as Lemko paskha, or sausage as savory as Lemko *kolbasa*, or pasta as tasty as Lemko *pirohi*. Similarly, you won't find any tastier drinking water than that in the Lemko highlands." (p. 22)[1] "...The marvelous natural setting of the Carpathian Mountains has left its mark of beauty on the Lemko soul. No other peoples are characterized by such great spiritual gifts, such virtue, and such high integrity as the Lemko people." (p. 27)

To clearly understand the entire linguistic position of the author, one should also address this matter: what is the Lemkos' nationality? To this question the author answers:

In terms of nationality, Lemkos belong to the large Slavic Rus' family. The name Rus' has always been sacred to them, and Slavic ideals have always been close to their hearts... They call themselves Rusyns, Ruthenians, Rusnaks, or Lemkos. (p. 24)

If Boikos and Hutsuls, the author notes, were influenced by Galicia, then Lemko-Rusyns felt Polish and Slovak influence. Locally, they are Lemkos, but in the world space, in the author's opinion, they are a part of the Rusyn family of people, which numbers in the millions. According to the author, the population of Lemkovyna has always considered itself to be a part of the great Slavic family, whose concept of "nationality" is linked to the concept whose root word is Rus':

The names Rus', Rusyn, Rusnak have to this day been closely associated with the Lemko people and have been defended as of the highest holiness. Lemkovyna is a tribal branch of the great Rus' people, who occupy vast expanses of the Earth's globe. Throughout history, Lemkovyna, like other parts of the Carpathian Mountains, has often gone under the name *Karpatska Rus'* (Carpathian Rus'), or *Prikarpatska Rus'*, designating both the nationality of the people and the territory they occupied.

---

1   Page numbers refer to the 1969 edition.

Lemkos had to fight and often sacrifice themselves for their historically-given name, in order not to be torn away from the rest of the "Rus'" (Rusyn) world. "The Polish gentry bathed it in blood and scorched it in fire; the Germans tried to wipe it off the face of the earth." (p. 121)

Among his Little Russian [Ukrainian] brothers, Lemkyn finds so-called Mazepists, i.e., those similar to Mazepa, turncoats, the worst hangmen, black sheep, Ukrainian independence seekers who for one penny went into the service of our enemies. Lemkyn perceives the renaming of everything "Little Russian" (the people and the area) to "Ukrainian" as creating conditions for inter-ethnic hostility, "to sic one Rusyn on another". A similar position was taken by other enemies of Rusyns– the Polish gentry and the Austrian and German governments. Thanks to the Austrians, the Ukrainian party was created in 1891, and in 1892 phonetic spelling was forcefully introduced into schools and institutions. Then the term "Ukrainian" was gradually introduced. To this end, Mykhailo Hrushevskii was invited to write a history of Ukraine. At first he wrote a *History of Rus'* in which he does not even mention the Ukrainian people. The second edition followed, this time in the Little Russian language and entitled *History of Rus'-Ukraine*, and the third edition, *History of Ukraine* (1898), was in Ukrainian. (p. 123) Such was the evolution of Hrushevskii to the Ukrainianist side. Lemkyn makes the following categorical charge: "Hrushevskii's history of Ukraine is a story of betrayal, deceit, discord, and malevolence, and a great misfortune for his own people." (p. 123)

But that's not all. In the book we find more compelling cases of *mazepivshchina* when Ukrainian nationalists openly went into the service of outsiders and promoted the Ukrainization of Lemkovyna. Lemkos desperately resisted. But the power was in the hands of landowners and the ruling class. Bishop Iosafat Kotsylovskii used the clergy to implant Ukrainization into ecclesiastical matters: he removed honest Rusyn priests from their positions, and in their places put his devoted followers. The church, where Christian morality and truth had been preached, turned into an anti-Rusyn political rostrum. Not finding any other way to fight, people decided to break with the Catholic Church and turn to Orthodoxy. On June 15, 1926, the Polish Sejm abolished the term "Rusyn" and replaced it with "Ukrainian."

The persecution of Lemko-Rusyns was intensified during the Second World War. When the Germans occupied Galicia, many Ukrainian nationalist refugees appeared in Lemkovyna, predominantly priests, teachers, and civil servants. The Germans greeted them with open arms. A "Ukrainian Assistance

Committee" was created in Cracow to assist Germans in the destruction of the Slavic nation. Frequent arrests of Lemko-Rusyns began. A lot of agents provocateurs appeared, among whom the most zealous was Zakharivskii, a teacher in the village of Wróblik. He set himself the goal of provoking the arrest of Fr. Polianskii. To this end, he hung a Ukrainian trident in the classroom in place of the icon of the Mother of God. During religion class, the priest noticed the replacement of the icon, so he took off the trident and again hung up the icon of the Mother of God. Zakharivskii denounced him to the Gestapo, reporting that the priest took a German swastika off of the wall and trampled it underfoot. Unmasked as a liar, Zakharivskii did not stop, but came up with a new provocation: he persuaded a swindler to pour diesel fuel into a drinking well, and then told the Germans that the priest poisoned the well, which was drunk from by German soldiers. Polianskii was arrested and sentenced to death by firing squad. Lemkyn cites many similar examples (pp. 178-181).

At the beginning of World War II, Hitler's Gestapo man, a Ukrainian provocateur and former captain of the Sich Riflemen [in the Austro-Hungarian army], Fr. Malynovskii founded the "Ukrainian Assistance Committee". Governor-General Hans Frank noticed Malynovskii's organizational skill and succeeded in assigning him to the highest position in the hierarchy of the Apostolic Administration of Lemkovyna. The faithfulness of Malynovskii's service to Hitler can be seen in the congratulatory message he sent to Hans Frank on the occasion of the German attack on the Soviet Union, with wishes for victory over the Russian people:

With the indescribable joy of all Ukrainian people, I and the clergy and the faithful of my eparchy hasten to tell the Great Leader of the German people, through you, of our deep feelings of thankfulness for his courageous declaration of war against the Bolshevik enslavers of peoples. We will accompany the glorious German Army on the field of battle with sincere wishes for success and with fervent prayers. May the Lord God keep you under His protection and blessing and lead to an illustrious victory, so that you will be crowned and immortalized with even greater glory as the great savior of humanity from Bolshevik bondage.

Sanok, June 29, 1941

Aleksander Malynovskii

Apostolic Administrator of

Ukrainian Greek Catholic Lemkovyna

In addition, there were a number of practical undertakings to demonstrate allegiance: at all church services, Fr. Malynovskii inserted into the "Litany of Fervent Supplication" petitions for the success of the German army, organized fund raising for the German Red Cross; sent donations for "the brave German soldiers who sacrifice their lives fighting for justice," and offered to organize military formations in all parishes for the SS "Galizien" Division. (p. 184).

All these circumstances could not help but influence the formation of the author's anti-Ukrainian worldview and his negative attitude towards renegade priests and intellectuals. He poured out all his thoughts and feelings as beautiful poetry:

Отец Шалаш из Мысцовы,
И Попадюк, зять Корновы,
Отец Борыс з Вороблика,
Ціла украинска клика
Вірно Гітлеру служыли,
На нас Лемков доносили.
Сам Подсадник и Корнова,
Знає о том вся Лобова.
Много людей полапали,
А Німці их вистріляли. (р. 135)

Father Shalash from Myscowa,
And Popadiuk, son-in-law of Kornova,
Father Borys from Wróblik,
The whole Ukrainian clique
Faithfully served Hitler.
They denounced us Lemkos.
Even Podsadnyk and Kornova themselves,
All know about it in Łabowa.
They caught many people
And the Germans executed them.

Lemkyn's ideological position has clearly affected the style of this book. The scholarly-publicist style has intertwined itself, as mentioned above, with the artistic and poetic one, as is seen in the prologues to each of the five parts. Lemkyn's verses are distinguished by their high level of emotion, their sincere feelings about the fate of his people. The verses are written in the form of folk songs. But these are not folk songs, but original poems, filled with profound political content, intertwining pictures of peaceful working life with Lemkos' worries about their destiny during the war and even more so during the period of forced eviction from their native places. Lemkyn's verses, as prologues to each chapter, are the author's poetic memoirs on behalf of the long-suffering Lemko-Rusyn people.

In Lemkyn's versification, trochaic meter, predominately tetrameter, prevails (trochee is a two-syllable foot with a stress on the first syllable). The trochaic meter endows the verse with extraordinary dynamism: one event is replaced by another in a flash. People, nature, wildlife change like images in a newsreel, and create an exciting psychological atmosphere:

Што ся в селі пак діяло,
Коли вшыткым ясно стало,
Што зме з села вышмарены,
На погыбель презначены.
То не дастся описати
И устами розказати.
Люде выли и кричали,
Слезами ся обливали (p. 200)

What followed in the village
When it became clear to all
That we are being thrown out of the village
Destined for destruction
This can't be described
Nor verbally expressed.
People wailed and shouted
Awash in tears.

The autology (in poetry, autology is the usage of words and expressions in their direct, immediate meaning) of Lemkyn's verses ensures that what is occurring is exceptionally realistic and transparent. Let us look at and feel the disturbing picture of the eviction of unfortunate Lemkos into the unknown, and see how the household animals, livestock and poultry react to it. The author ironically calls this picture a concert:

Концерт дикий и понурий,
Розпочал го Тарка бурий,
Бо як зачал он брехати,
Не мож было вытримати.

А корова му тым часом
Зарычала контрабасом,
За ньом когуты запіли
И з банту сой выскочили.
Куры зачали гдакати,
А гуси им вторувати.
А телята забечали,
А паскудный голос мали.
Дітиска ся розплакали,
Потом козы забечали.
Такий концерт люде мали,
А вороны втяж кракали. (p. 200)

A wild and gloomy concert
Started by Tarka, the dog
Because when he started to bark
It was not possible to endure it.

And the cow, in the meantime
Roared in low bass.
After her the roosters crowed
And jumped from their perches.
Chickens began to cluck
And the geese answered them
When the calves lowed
And they made a nasty sound.
Children began to cry,
Later the goats began to bleat.
That is the kind of concert people had,
And the crows continuously crowed.

There are no metaphorical words and turns of speech here. By its tragic, lyrical tension the anthological style of the prologues, as an expression of realistic accuracy, brings it close to folk poetry (it is no accident that at the end of each prologue we read: "From *A Song about Lemkovyna*.")

In the poetic parts of the book, heroic verse is predominant. But at the moment of greatest tension, when people reflect on their plight, think about the possibility of salvation, and hope in God and his omnipotence, the author switches to dactylic stanza (dactylic refers to ternary feet with stress on the first syllable):

Бог нам поможе, Бог наша сила!
Правда над кривдом все побідила
Сміло з Ісусом аж на Голготу,
Майме надію, віру и охоту,
В морю терпіний, в плачу и болю
Благайме Бога о лучшу долю. (pp. 199-200)

God will help us, God is our strength!
Truth always wins over wrongdoing.
Boldly with Christ all the way to Golgotha,
Let's have hope, faith, and will.
In a sea of suffering, full of crying and pain
God grant us a better plight.

The picture of peasants bidding farewell to their homeland takes on an even more tragic character, and the author enters a new form of versification— six iambic trochee, thanks to which he reaches the apogee of the psychological state of those condemned to suffering:

Як з хыж выходили жалостно плакали,
Порогы и стіны в слезах ціловали.
Цілували землю, по котрой ходили,
Котру оробляли и ей барз любили.

They cried coming out of their houses,
Threshold and walls were kissed in tears.
They kissed the ground which they walked upon,
Which they tilled and loved very much.

The last lines remind us of the famous song by sub-Carpatho-Rusyn poet Aleksander Mytrak:

Горы наши, горы,
Наши бідны горы,
На вас я печально
Устреляю взоры...

While from Lemkyn we read:

Горы нашы, горы,
пращамеся з вами,
Бо уж отходиме,
жаль нам ест за вами.

The ideological positions and worldview in the book, as well as lexical analysis and the form of versification give us the opportunity to outline the position of the author, a Lemko, relative to his mother tongue. The language of Lemkos, affirms Lemkyn, is "the most singular of all Rusyn local dialects," and we can add that it has Rusyn pronunciation and etymological spelling. The basis of this dialect (language) is old Church Slavonic, but in a process taking place through historical time it "has become so well developed and independent that it is used not only by the common people but also by Lemko intellectuals." (p. 25). Over the centuries, books, magazines, and newspapers have been printed in this language; it possesses its own grammar, and dictionaries have been collected. That is, it has taken on the form of a literary language and has the right to exist alongside the Russian and Ukrainian languages. An important feature of the Lemko-Rusyn language is that it is understood by every Slav. During modern times dictionaries for other Slavic languages are being published (Ukrainian-Polish, Czech-Polish, Russian-Polish, etc.). For the Lemko language, maintains Lemkyn, there is no need for such dictionaries. It is understood by Great Russians and Little Russians (Ukrainians), Czechs, Slovaks, Poles and all other Slavs. And all this is thanks to its Old Church Slavonic foundation: "None of the other Slavic languages has been able to preserve so well the character of the Old Slavonic language, the forefather of all Slavic languages, as the Lemko language has." (p. 25)

Lemkyn dreams about a time when, based on the Lemko language, it will be possible to create a new literary Slavic language (by which we are to understand a single common Rusyn language – M.A.) He motivates his thought by stating that the Lemko language already has a beautiful heritage behind it. "Although it finds itself in very unfavorable circumstances, Lemko literature is growing daily." (p. 25) The diversity of dialects ("There are many localisms, many names for the same object...") is, in Lemkyn's opinion, proof of the ongoing development and enrichment of the Lemko language.

Lexical analysis of the book *Lemkovyna: A History* indicates that due to historical conditions, proximity to and contact with different peoples (Poles, Slovaks, Hungarians, Russians, Germans) the Lemko language is filled with many non-native elements. But despite this, in his book the Rusyn language dominates and it can be divided into the following thematic groups:

Abstract concepts - благодарность (p. 27), отчизна (135), широкость (69), пространь (13), даровизна (49, 51), достоинство (27), посылость (61), жерело (источник познания) (61), зомста (190), воспитание (27), новина (133), высокость (14), стараня (52), сколькость (15), ясности (205).

Designation of locality: звалище (202), посылость (50), ключ (объежинение сел) (53), площа (63), ущелье, скалиця (11), пасовиско (106), стерниска (106), ровы (106), панскый ліс (107), площа (63), прабочный (правобережный((13), довкола (10), границя (11), стрільниця (134), околиця (134); лемковина (163), Моравия (25), ламана лінія (13), рольничый край (17), кошара (18), посылость (61).

Features of the Lemko character: гоноры (214), проповідальниця (162), дарование души (27), благодарность (27), достоинство характера (27), честноты (27), трудолюбивый (27), заботливый (27), совістнъй (27), честный (27), мирный (27), терпеливый (27), ощадный (27), солидный (27), даровитый (27), твердый темперамент (27), привязанье до своей истории (27), чувство чести (27), моральный (27), спрыт (21).

Words in religious use: катехет (63), катехетура (63), побожность (26), привязаность до св.церкви (26), богослужение (26), священник (26), парохия (26), дорадник-священник (26), целибат (26), прихожан (26), иконостас (46), священникы-целибаты (26), православие (163), свічкы-трийці (21), римскый папа (88), іезуит (88), уния (88), Божа помоч (89), патер (89), кардинал (89), схезматик (89), костелы (89), вселенский архиерей (88), священство (26).

Moral categories: почести (63), фалыповати (37), зрадник (121), мазепинець (в см. изменник) (12), ненависть (163).

Public administrative terminology: строй (135), структура, повітова рада (33), воєводство (33), Річ Посполита, магистр (33), волоскый (49), повітовый (99), делегація (161), администратор (48), староство (107), громада (107), урядованя (99).

Consumer vocabulary relating to food and beverage: адзимка (22), киселиця (12), варянка (12), стеранка (12), яшниця (12), солонина (12), картофля (22), брынзя (18, 20) пирогы (30) різанок (30) крупы (30), масло (22), овсяный пляцок (22), подпалок (22),чыр (22), мастило (22), ярчаный хліб (22), лемковска паска (22), пенцакы (29), палюнка (22), кропля (22) оронжада (22), питя (22).

Consumer vocabulary relating to clothing: калап (12), керпці (23), наволоки (23), настрочанкы (23), криса (12), онучы (23), скірні(23), ціжмы (23), кошеля (23), гуня, гунька (23), шапка баранкова (23), баранячі кожухы (23), басамункы (23), кожушаны рукавиці (23), куртак (23). вовняна хустка (23), баранковый кожух (23), кабат (23), сердак (23), сукняна шапка (23), кожушаны сардакы (23), чепец (23), чуга (23), фацелик (23)

Consumer vocabulary relating to housewares: мотовило (12), скірні (12), кериці(12), фрашкы (12), воз (29), лопаты (135), вилы (135), ложкы (19). варихы (19), веретена (19), масничкы (19), коробкы (19), пищалкы (19), касеткы (19), тацкы (19), тарелкы (19), паличкы (19), полотно (21), бито сукно (21), різак (17), віяк (17), ціп (17), палиця (15).

Occupation, type of activity: обшарник (109), партизант (135), рыболовство (104), лісоводство (104), рольництво (104), жандарм (68), пастух (29), різьбярство (18), каменярство (18), вандрованый промисел (20), торговля (21), мазярство (21), ткацтво (21, пасічництво (21), спортовец (22).

Legal relations: свідок (86), карность (110), замкненя (98), совітник (83), грошева кара (15), ліцитация (106), справоздание (42,106), звычайове право (18), зажаление (162), жадати (162), просьба (162), виноватый (134), засудити (134), назначити (135), одшкодованя (107). Tools: орчик, костур, маглярка (110)

Domestic animals: куры (107), гуси (107), волы (18) яловик (18)

Wild animals (fauna): волкы (15), медведі (107), дикы (107), елені

(107), лисы (197), звірина (197).

Plants (flora): ялиці (15), смерекы (15), сосна (15), бук (15).

Fruits: ягоды (15), малины (15), яфиры (15) черниці (15), грибы (15).

Hydronyms (rivers): Попрад (14), Камениця (14), Біла (14), Ропа (14), Вислок (14), Ясьонка (14), Ослава (14), Сян (14).

Toponyms (mountains): Яворина (14), Ланцова (14), Магура (14), Холм (14), Церкова (14), Букавиця (14), Каминь (14), Пасічна (14), Хрещата (14).

The numerous place names are interesting. They are important material which provides evidence of Lemkos being the indigenous peoples of their homeland since distant times.

Settlements: Шляхтова, Яворкы, Біла Вода, Чорна Вода, Чорнорікы, Ріпник, Петруша Воля, Братовка, Лончкы, Опаровка, Гольцовка, Бережанка, Высока, Красна, Лютча, Ванівка, Бонарівка, Близянка, Гвоздянка, Барычка, Жарнова, Небылец (13), Ропа (50), Ропиця (14, 50), Ропка (50), Ропянка (50).

Names of settlements have different origins: from the name of the founder: Гладышов (Гладиш), Андреивка (Андрей), Яшкова (Ясько), Богуна (Богуна), Юрковцы (князь Юрий II), etc.; from forest flora: Дубне (дуб), Смерековец, Смеречне (смерека) Яворкы, Яворье (явор), Грабы, Грабовка (граб), Липова, Липна (липа), Ольховец, Ольховцы (ольха), Черемха (черемха), Ожина (ожина), Ліщины, Лыско (лыска), Берест (берест, береза); from hydronyms (rivers): Сянок (Сян), Ропкы (Ропка), Вислок, Вислочок (Вислок), Ясьонка (Ясьонка); from the type of soil: Вапенне (вапнистая земля – soil full of lime), Камяна (камянистая почва – soil full of stones), Скальник (скалистая поверхность - rocky surface), Заболотцы (болотистая земля – marshy land), Суровиця (сырая земля – raw land); based on folk art: Поворозник (производство мотузов - manufacture of ropes), Боднаркы (производство бочок – barrel making), Фолюш (битье сукна - beating of cloth), Шкляры (производство стекла – glass production); based on landform features: Криве, Довге, Глубоке, Крыжовка, Розстайне; villages of royal origins: Королева, Королик, Вороблик Королевский; villages of noble origins: Шляхтова, Добра шляхотска, Вороблик шляхотский; based on a historical event: Більцарева (having sheltered a queen), Баниця (place for banishment of criminals), Избы (based on first human settlements) (pp. 87-88).

Onomastics (origin of surnames): Etymology of surnames is mostly based on the names of settlements: Баницкий (Баниця), Баранский (Баране), Бортнянський (Бортне), Веселовский (Весола), Волянский (Воля), Грабский (Граб), Грушевский (Грушевка), Долинский (Долины), Дубинський (Дубне), Завадский (Завадка), Каминский (Камяна), Крыницкий (Крыница), Липницкий (Липна), Малиновский (Малиновка), Новицкий (Новиця), Полянский (Поляна), Ростоцкий (Ростока), Синявский (Синява), Тарнавський (Тарнава), Флоринский (Флорика), Чертежинский (Чертеж), Щавницкий (Щавник), Яблонский (Яблоница), Яворский (Яворье) (87).

Ethnonyms: русины, руснакы, русаки, лемки, карпатороссы (24), поляки, словаки, чехи, украинец (34).

Folk rituals: крестины, кстины (29), кум, кума (29), положниця (29), роженица (29), дарункы (29), булка (29), гостина (29), кума-положниця (29), весіля (30), молодый, молода (30), молодиця (30), молодята (30), новоженці (30), топорець (30), сват, свашка (30), міртовый вінець (30), барвінковий вінець (30); похорон (30), ліхтары з свічками (30), деревяный крест, павіса (30), труна (30), просатор (30), цвинтарь-теметів (30) небіщик (30), помершый (30), парастас (30), панихида (30), свята вода (30), повісмо (30).

Military terminology: офицер королевскых войск (82), войско (18, 82), напады (82), спустошеня (82), региментарь (83), вымарш撃ровати (83), генерал (83), розбити (83), позиции (83), шпионы (92) диверсанты (93) героична оборона (92).

Words indicating action: мельдуватися (183), убиратися (23), розобрати (134), злапати (134), полапати (135), пхати (135), прати (in the context of fighting) 135), умоцнюют (135), згынути (136), перелапувати (43), пересуватися (48), отновил (43), завозвали (43).

Great Russian (Russian) Language Lexicon

Б: Богатырь (34), больше (37), борьба (47, 163), богослужение (60), большинство (17), брак (45), братья (41),

В: Введение (13), взгляды (33, 50), властитель (63), власть (47, 135), всегда (25), вселенский (88), влияние (40, 115), вольность (89), вопрос (233), восток (13, 24), восточный (46), враждебно (42), выборы (21), выводы (43), выселение (34),

Г: Географический, граница (13), город (городами) (40), государство (289), группа (81).

Д: Дарование (19, 21), движение (174), делегация (161), доброволец (257), доказательство (25, 46), должность (258), донос (42), достаточно (14), духовенство (42).

Ж: Желательный (126), жизненный (41), жизнь (42), житье, жертва (135), житель (22), женщины (23).

З: Заострение (137), запад (13), западный (34, 39), запрещение (43), защитник (46), знание (21), знаток (13).

И: Индивидуальность (47), иностранный (48), интересный (13), историк (13), изъятие (17), исключительно (21, 63), интеллигенция (21), июнь (180).

К: Каждый (15), колбаса (22), континентальный (14), крещение (46),

Л: Людность (167).

М: Мечта (47), миссионер (45), миссия (46), монета (49), мучения (190).

Н: Наконец (99), народ (99), народность (53) народный (21), направление (13, 14), начальство (41, 81), невольник (15), несчастье (28), ноябрь (182).

О: Обвинение (42), обособленность (40, 47), обстоятельство (16), образование (42), объявлено (99), ограды (16), одновременно (24), оккупация (62), оттуда (13), окрестность (13), организация (61), основатель (63), острый (14), от (47), отличие (241), оттуда (43).

П: Прелесть (9), патриотизм (135), пространный (43), письмо (43), письменность (44), подданство (99), политик (99), полный (135), поселение (49), потом (30), прекрасный (46), принадлежность (47,257), принятие (47), природа (13), пространство (25, 40, 47), профессор (13).

Р: Размышлять (135), русский народ (13), русская культура (40),

С: Свой (21), сегодня (69, 34), сейчас (46), селение (13), сентябрь (242), скоростный (291), слеза (133), славянский (44), смотрят (37), собрание (63), содержание (244), союзник (47, 97), способ (21), справедливый (183), страна (13), судьба (34), существовать (50,51).

Т: Территория (13), террор (139), теперь (14), торжественно (29, 43), труд (21), трудности (44), трудный (14), трудолюбивый (258),

У: Ученик (44), ударение (25), условие (14), украинизация (161), узкий (13), управитель (41), ученость (13), ужасна (202).

Ф: Фронт (257), фонд (258).

Ц: Церковь (46).
Ч: Чешский (45), чувство (183).
Ш: Школьный (63).
Я: Язык (25, 99).

Phonetic features

Lemkyn's book to some extent reflects the particular phonetic features of the Lemko language. The system of vowels differs from the Ukrainian and Russian languages. The Lemko language contains seven vowel phonemes: А, О, У, І, И, Ы, Е, and also three of the "yot" type: Я, Ю, Є (єдник (120), єй (121), єст (25), єден (25), уживає (25), єсли (103), остаєся (123), язык (43).

The "yotated" Ukrainian Ї is conveyed as the grapheme І: істи (133), выіхал (211), ізда (215), поіздка (259). In place of Ukrainian Ї in the genitive personal pronoun ЇХ (вони), the Lemko language uses ИХ (ОНИ) (135).

The "yotated" О is written using two graphemes (йо): Йосиф (256), його (257), or by using "мягкій знак" Ь (всьо (133), Ясьовка (87).

The "yotated" А is conveyed as the grapheme Я: Яра (212), Сян (212).
The "yotated" У is written using grapheme Ю (перевюл (59), Юлиян Юрчакевич (259).

Spelling (orthography)

Letter И is written in its natural form in these cases:
- the roots of words: зима (11), робити, обнимає (13), гостина.
- the end of infinitives: встидати (37). глядати (40), наклонити (89), спочати (38), поправляти (37), упадати (11), утікати (11).
- the end of prefix при: прикарпатскых (13), приходство (15).
- the endings of third-declension feminine nouns' dative and prepositional cases (?): груди, долони, мысли, пути, церкви (88).
- the end of plural nouns in instrumental case: Врагами (93), Габсбургами (92), единомышленниками (90), епископами (88), представителями (88), провиницями (91), словами (93).
- the endings of adjectives, ordinal numbers, participles, and pronouns:

веселий, мудрий, молодий, шестий, сидячй, битий,

- the beginning of a word: историк (237), история (86), Исус (200), Иван (190), и (союз).

Letter Ы is written:
- In the stem of a word according to pronunciation: быти (12), высший (17), гыну (9), жытя (11, 184), гынути, гыкати, кыртиця, Кычера, хыжа (5), отчына (135), погыбель (90), шыроко (299).
- At the end of prefix ВЫ- : вывезены (199), выкупити (15, вынищили (17), выселены (199), выслухана, выстріляли (135), вытягнены.
- In nominative adjectives, ordinal numbers, singular participles: выслуханый (191), вышмареный (34), добрый (34), зложеный (190), знаный (133), караный (199), лояльный (34), народный (21), окруженый (200), покорный (34), скатованый (133), скопаный (133), скупаный (133), спокойный (34), сухый (14), трактованый (133). Note that according to Myroslava Khomiak and Henryk Fontański, *Hrammatika lemkovskoho iazyka* (Grammar of the Lemko language), Warsaw, 2004. p. 49, in this type of ending one should use -ИЙ.
- in the short form of plural adjectives, ordinal numerals, participles and pronouns in the nominative case: вредны (37), царскы (134), выведены (199), выселены (199), выданы (199), окрещены (38), нашы (43) такы, котры.

Among the consonants, we note the traditional spelling of Л verbs in the masculine past tense: вернул (43), вступил (43), выслал (43), достал (50), начал (47), передал (43), побил (50), повстало (51), подносили (57), позостала (55), перешло (51), ходили (57).

Spelling consonants in prefixes:

З- is written before voiced consonants or before a vowel: збирати, здерати, зорвати;

С- is written before voiceless consonants: стогнал (134), стріляно (135), строй (135), стяти, сходити.

prefixes РОЗ-, БЕЗ- are written in all cases with letter З: роздерти, розбити, розбити, розобрати, розпалити, розколоти, розмышляти (135), розпорол (190), розстріляно (134), розстріляли (190) безпощадно (182), безпосередный (82), безсмертным (183), безстрашно (190).

Consonants С and Ц are always written as hard: днес (11), жебыс (11), горнец (11), конец (200), окраєц (10), отец (135, 203), хоц (200), ялиц (10, 21), ярец (10).

Capital (upper case) letters are written just as in the Russian and Ukrainian languages, but in Lemko it is also used when writing names of nationalities: Русин, Поляк, Лемко, Словак, Мадяр, Чех, Лех, Рус, etc., and also for academic titles: professor - Проф., doctor - Др.: Д-р Симеон (258), Д-р А.Бескид (41) Д-р. Михаил Ладыжинский (75), публіцист Д-р К. Тверадска (145). However, as exceptions, Lemkyn also writes профессор (238), доцент (239) starting in lower case.

Sufixes -СК-, -ЦК, unlike in Ukrainian, are written without the soft sign: германска своłоч (10), дворскы (83), земский (5), збойницкой (290), королевскых (82), (82), німецке (43), польскыми (82), праславянска земля (10), славянска (133), словацкой (290), Украинска (135), французкого (245), царскы (134), Швабском (133).

The sound of Т in the Lemko language is always hard: радост (199), смерт (199), находится (133), грают (200), крают (200), пят (134), десят (134), двадцет (135).

In the poetry part of the book (the prologues) there is clearly visible a fixed stress in words– on the second syllable from the end of a word (under the influence of the Polish language.) Stress is a determining factor in the author's choice of verse in rhyme with trochaic foot (this was mentioned above): не зрадили, послухайте. (Ukrainian would have "не зрадили" with stress on А and "послухайте" with stress on У.) Here the Lemko language is differs not only from the Russian and Ukrainian languages, but also from the language of the Rusyns living in Subcarpathia (Ukraine), Romania, Hungary and Serbia.

We come across various ways of writing the prefixes ОВА- УВА-. For example, мордовано (135) and мордували (135), катували (135), ратували (135), шанувати (237).

We also find inconsistency in Lemkyn's use of names of months of the year. In some cases, he utilizes Russian names: от 2 мая до 6 мая 1915 р., дня 2 мая 1915 р.(148), дня 7 мая (148), меже 2 а 12 майом (149), дня

19 ноября 1918 р. (157), день 29 мая 1938 року (161), дня 23 мая 1939 р. (175), в марті 1945 р. (202), дня 27 марта 1947 р. (214), дня 27 марца 1947 р. (214), от апріля 1946 р. (217), дня 17 апріля 1947 р. (218), дня 18 мая 1870 р.(241)

In many other cases, Ukrainian names of the months are being used: 20 січня 1939 р. (71), дня 24 червня 1914 р. (138), в листопаді 1918 р. (149), дня 7 вересня, 2 лютого 1818 р. (248), 15 липня 1843 р. (254), 14 лютого 1894 р. (257). Double names of the months also occur– Ukrainian with Russian in parenthesis: 21 червня (июня) 1941 р. (175), в грудни (декабрю) 1885 (243), 10 квітня (апріля) 1896 р.(244), 1 вересня (сентября) 1851 р. (245), 21 липня (июля) 1790 р. (250), листопада (ноября) 1830) р. (255), 3 квітня (апріля) 1842 р. (256). Finally, the reverse also occurs– the Russian name with Ukrainian in parenthesis: 21 июня (червня) 1941 р. (180), 8 ноября (листопада) 1821 р. (241), сентября (вересня) 1836 р.(242).

As far as spelling goes, in Lemkyn's book there dominates an etymological principle that steers the Lemko language toward the Russian literary language. Compare Lemko "сердце" (5) with Ukrainian "серце", "счастливо" (5) with Ukr. "щасливо", "солнце" (10) Ukr. "сонце, "несчастный" (164) - "нещасний", "жалостно" - "жалісно" and so on.

In proper and common nouns of feminine gender ending in IЯ we come across various spellings of the endings: Марія (257) but Моравия (25), and надія (86) but гімназия, мемориял (183).

We also encounter in the book some peculiar morphological features, particularly in the endings of nouns, adjectives, ordinal numbers, and feminine participles in the dative case: they end with -ОМ: Балтика - Балтиком (39), Божья помоч, Божом помочом (89), Велтава - Велтавом (39), гола рука - голом руком (30), горяча молитва - горячом молитвом (184), грамота - грамотом (61), Лаба - Лабом (39), наша доля - нашом дольом (9), нога - ногом (11), ріка - ріком (62), оселя - осельом (61),

From Galicia Lemkos borrowed a form of complex future tense - a combination of auxiliary words in the future tense and the main verb in the past tense: буде мусів (29), буде хотіла (29).

This analysis of the language of Lemkyn's Istoriia Lemkovyny is far from complete. The length of this article does not permit the listing and investigation of all the grammatical phenomena reflected in the book. The book is so interesting with respect to the language used that one could write a major scholarly work about it, but this would require time and a clear definition of the research topic. Based on this book, one could develop separate topics such as "Vocabulary and phraseology," "Phonetics," "Spelling of the Lemko language," "Word and structure formation in the Lemko language," "Syntax of the Lemko language," "Comparative analysis of the language of Rusyns in Lemkovyna and Transcarpathia," etc.

Nevertheless, having read Lemkyn's book, it is definitely possible to conclude that the language of the book is Lemko-Rusyn, similar only in general characteristics to Ukrainian and Russian. This is the Lemko-Rusyn people's original language, rich in vocabulary that is different from other Slavic languages (see the thematic groups above.) The author himself talks about this on page 25, and his words are confirmed by all linguistic elements of the book (phonetics, morphology, syntax, vocabulary, phraseology, imagery system.) Numerous place names, hydronyms and ethnonyms testify to the richness and authenticity of the language.

In the poetic parts of the book, which are close to folk songs, the living spoken language of the Lemko Rusyn people predominates. In the scholarly-publicistic part of the book we find a significant number of Russian and common foreign words of Greek and Roman origin. The explanation for this phenomenon is very simple: a living colloquial language generally lacks many scientific terms related to philosophy, history, law, and forms of government. The author's use of this scholarly and philosophical terminology could lead to incorrect conclusions about his possible sympathies to the Great Russian language, though we cannot fail to notice such symptoms as: "Lemkos by nationality belong to the large Slavic Rus' [slavianorusskoi] family" (p. 24). As far as the Ukrainian language's relation to the Lemko language goes, he says almost nothing, but the nationalistic sentiments of many renegades, the so called mazepintsy, along with Polish and German national-fascists are clearly unacceptable since they brought a lot of grief upon his people (see Part II, Section 29; Part III, Sections 17, 19, and 25-28; and all of Part IV.) Lemkyn's attitude toward Ukrainians should not be considered a hostile one. This book is an assertion of national identity not only of the author himself, but of all Lemko-Rusyn people. This is evidenced by the fact that Lemkyn repeatedly addresses the issue of Transcarpathia, talks about the processes occurring in the territory of fellow Rusyns on the other side of the Carpathian Mountains from the position of an expert (see pages 90 - 99), and names the best representatives of the Rusyn people in Transcarpathia: Iuliian "Popradov" Stavrovskii (255-256), Dulyshynovich (95), Fr. Mykhailo Andrella (93), Sylvai-Meteor (95),

Petro Lodii (248), Mykhailo Baludianskii (248) , Aleksander Dukhnovych
(255), Adolf Dobrianskii (256), Fr. Aleksandr Pavlovych (257).

Lemkyn also does not forget the luminaries of the literary revival of Galician Rus' in the first half of the nineteenth century: Markian Shashkevych, Iakov Holovatskii, and Ivan Vahylevych, who were not ashamed of their national name, actively underscored "their Rusyn ancestry" and openly declared (p.
166): "Русска матка нас родила, русска матка нас повила, русска матка нас
любила– A Rusyn mother delivered us, Rusyn mother swaddled us, Rusyn
mother loved us." [Markian Shashkevych, 1811-1843]

Mykhailo Almashii
Honored Teacher of Ukraine
Chairman of Transcarpathian Regional Scholarly-
    Cultural Society of Aleksander Dukhnovych
Senior Lecturer, Kyiv Slavonic University
    Transcarpathian Branch, Uzhhorod, Ukraine

Bishop Adam (Dubec), head of the Przemyśl-Nowy Sącz Eparchy (for the Lemko Region) of the Polish Autocephalous Orthodox Church. Wysowa, 2005.

Świerżowa Ruska, 1928. The first anniversary of Return to Orthodoxy celebrations.

The Lemko Association
and *Lemkovyna: A History*

The Lemko Association of the USA and Canada (informally, *Lemko-Soyuz*) moved its headquarters to Yonkers, New York after being founded in 1929 in Winnipeg, Canada and holding its first congress in 1931 in Cleveland, Ohio. The founders were Rusyn immigrants from an area of the Carpathian Mountains that had been annexed by the Austrian Empire during the first partition of Poland in 1772.

It was the largest social and cultural organization among Lemko-Rusyn immigrants and their descendants in North America.

Dymytrii "Vanio Hunianka" Vislotskii. Yonkers, NY. 1938.   *Symeon Pyzh. Yonkers, NY. 1938.*

After 1934, under the influence of Symeon S. Pyzh[1] and Dymytrii "Vanio Hunianka" Vyslotskii[2], the Lemko Association became pro-Communist in orientation. Already before the start of World War II, and then again after the war's end, it promoted a plan to resettle Lemko-Rusyns from Lemkovyna (along with returning immigrants from North America) to the Soviet Union, in order to ease this group's national and socio-economic difficulties. It adopted an anti-fascist political platform in the late 1930's, and during World War II the Lemko Association was the leading leftist organization among all Slavic immigrants in the United States.

Dymytrii Vyslotskii left the United States in 1946, as if to set an example, and eventually settled in Lviv during the time of unrest in his native Lemkovyna. Symeon Pyzh, then the editor of *Karpatska Rus'* newspaper, died suddenly in 1957. A later publication of the Lemko Association admitted that:

> After the departure of D. Vyslotskii and the death of S. Pyzh the Association's activity declined, which was evidence of the great role the two personalities played in the organization. The fact remains that no one can replace them completely. Those that succeeded them possessed neither their education nor their practical experience. In addition, those substituting for Vyslotskii and Pyzh had families to take care for and therefore they could not possibly dedicate their entire lives to the Association as their bachelor predecessors had.[3]

Until the late 1950's the organization's membership consisted mostly of American born, Depression era Lemko-Americans or of those who were born during the interwar period, either during the semi-democratic 1918-1926 period in Poland or in militarily ruled *Sanacja* Poland (1926-1939). Some Lemko-Rusyns who were American citizens by birth returned to the United States before September, 1939. Starting in the late 1950's, when immigration under a quota was resumed from "People's" Poland, this older membership body became exposed to post World War II Lemko-Rusyn immigrants.

---

1   See "Pysh, Simeon / Pyzh, Symeon" in Magocsi, Paul Robert and Ivan Pop (eds.), *Encyclopedia of Rusyn History and Culture*, 2nd ed. (Toronto: University of Toronto Press, 2005), pp. 406-407.

2   See "Vyslotskii, Dymytrii / Vislocky, Dmitri (pseudonym Van'o Hunianka" in *Encyclopedia...*, p. 538.

3   *Iubileinii Almanakh 50-lityia Lemko Soyuza v SShaA i Kanadi / Fiftieth Anniversary Almanac of the Lemko Association of USA and Canada* (Yonkers, 1979), p. 38. Available at http://lemko.org/pdf/LS50.pdf

Lemko Park, Monroe, NY. 1979.

Unlike the earlier immigrants, the latter had already experienced living in post-World War II communist Poland, years of civil war in 1944-47, "voluntary resettlement" to Soviet Ukraine from Lemkovyna in 1944-47, and the forceful deportation in 1947 to western and northern Poland of those fifty thousand remnants who were not sold on being Ukrainian and on promises of better life in Soviet Ukraine. Despite this differing life experience, political wisdom and financial standing appeared on the surface to lead at first to a friendly coexistence between these two factions for the most part.

On July 21, 1958, Lemkos established a separate for-profit stock corporation/legal entity to purchase for $175,000 a 126 acre piece of already-developed property fifty miles from New York City in the vicinity of Monroe, New York. The purchase of what later became known as Lemko Park/Lemko Resort, which appeared to most immigrants from the Carpathians as a small piece of Lemkovyna that magically appeared in the Catskills, was a major achievement for those members who bought stock in the venture.

During the following decade, as a later publication of the Association recounted:

[In 1965] Nikolai Tsisliak, editor-in-chief of *Karpatska Rus'*, became seriously ill. Stephen Kychura[4] became editor and sought collaboration

---

4   See "Kitchura, Stephen / Kychura, Shtefan" in *Encyclopedia...*, p.237.

with the reactionary Ukrainian nationalists. At the Twenty-Third Congress of the Lemko Association at Lemko Resort, Monroe (September 4-6, 1965), and at the following two Congresses [in 1967 and 1969], the attention of the delegates was distracted from acute organizational and cultural problems. They were lured into discussing a World Lemko Congress and protests concerning the evicted Lemkos in Poland, many of whom made it clear they did not want to move from their new place of residence.[5]

The Twenty-Fourth Lemko Association Convention was held in Lemko Park on September 23-24, 1967. Unlike at past conventions, this time two "reactionaries" were elected to major positions in the Central Committee. Teo-

dor Dokla[6] became the General Secretary, while Stephen Kychura, who two years earlier succeeded Nikolai Tsisliak as editor of *Karpatska Rus'*, became co-editor of the newspaper with Michael Savchak.

In 1968, Kychura led a delegation to Poland and Soviet Ukraine, believing that Lemko-Rusyns in the United States should play a greater role among the Lemko-Rusyns scattered all over behind the Iron Curtain. Together with the Lemko Association's newly elected General Secretary, Teodor Dokla, Kychura broke with the Association's long standing sympathies toward communist rule over Lem-

Stephen Kychura (1912-1997), Yonkers, NY. 1938.

ko-Rusyn communities in Europe. Under his leadership, the Lemko Association for the first time openly condemned the post-World War II deportations of Lemko-Rusyns from Lemkovyna, along with the infamous military operation Operation "Vistula" of 1947. They began to criticize Communist Poland's policy of national assimilation toward Lemko-Rusyns, the forced ukrainization policy against Rusyns in the Prešov region of eastern Slovakia

5   *Almanac*, p. 43.
6   See "Doklia/Dokla, Teodor" in *Encyclopedia...*, p.94.

(then Czechoslovakia), and the So-
viet-led invasion of Czechoslovakia
by the Warsaw Pact countries (with
the exception of Romania). There
is no doubt that these "revisionist"
or "reactionary" moves did not escape the watchful eyes of "progressive" activists, along with Dymytrii
Vyslotskii, who passed away in Lviv
on December 1, 1968.

The policy of Dokla and Kychura was short-lived. Two years after
being elected, both were removed
from their positions during the
Twenty-Fifth Congress, which was
held in Yonkers, New York, August
30 through September 1, 1969. The

*Theodore Dokla (1931-1982), 1979.
(Photo © J. Madzik)*

Lemko Association returned to its pro-Soviet orientation, to "time-tested principles dating back to the early days of the organization's activity," a position that
was ratified again by the subsequent Twenty-Sixth Congress held in Lemko
Park on September 4-6, 1971. It was during this later Congress that both Kychura and Dokla were actually thrown out as members, with 35 out of 49 delegates
voting in favor of the proposal as recommended by a young delegate named Alexander Vostok, whose previous surname was Wan. *Vostok* means "The East"
in Russian. This odd character, a member of the Central Committee, was even
later sent to Moscow and Kyiv for training to become the future editor of *Karpatska Rus'*, but returned quickly and was seen in Lemko Park for about ten
years, though he was apparently dismissed from a seminary for school-related
reasons. The Twenty-Sixth Congress, under the leadership of the elected Central Committee, declared that "the newspaper *Karpatska Rus'* again becomes
the true medium of the Lemko Association, that it will follow a predetermined
policy and guidelines of the organization." Instead of reflecting views of its editors, as in the past, the newspaper once again became the "truthful" mouth-
piece of the Association, adhering to instructions and requirements from above.

This outdated stand was maintained by the organization at least until the
end of the Soviet Union in 1989 and its forty-five year hold over Central and
Eastern Europe.

*Central Committee of the Lemko Association, 1983-85. (1) M. Lohoida, (2) I.
Porada, (3) Janet Fuchyla, (4) I. Chupashko, (5) M. Meri, (6) John Adamiak,
(7) Aleksander "Vostok" Wan, (8) O. Vostok, (9) A. Porada, (10) M. Lohoida, (1)
Theodore Rudawsky, (12) A. Berezhna, (13) I. Frytskii, (14) A. Chelak, (15) V.
Zaviiskii, (16) Dymytrii Vislotskii and (17) Symeon Pyzh. Monroe, NY. 1983.*

The internal strife was viewed cautiously by the newer, post-1960 immigrants.
With different life priorities in front of them, they were not eager to become
members of the Association. They might visit Lemko Park only once a year for
a major festival. The income for Lemko Park from the once a year purchase of
a general admission ticket was not what stockholders were counting on. These
were the early warning signs that the future for this undertaking did not look
bright. With property taxes mounting, the natural attrition of older dues-paying
members and a drought in attracting younger members led to Lemko Park's de-
mise. Lemko Park was auctioned off on the steps of the Orange County court-
house in 1997 for $400,000. A similar fate awaited the Carpatho-Russian Ameri-
can Center's Lemko Hall building in Yonkers, NY: it was sold in 1999. Perhaps
because people incorrectly thought of it in connection with these separate, failed
ventures, the Lemko Association shrank to a few branches with only a handful of
members. There were no more Lemko Association congresses held. Alex Herenchak, who had been President of Lemko Park, the Carpatho-Russian American
Center, and the Lemko Association, died of cancer in April 2010.

It is against this background that one has to look at the publication of Io-ann "Lemkyn" Polianskii's book in 1969 in the then-prevailing atmosphere of intrigue within the Lemko Association. Polianskii mentions in his letter dated January 2, 1971 to Dokla that he had visited the United States; the specific date of his visit is not known. He writes that he has been paralyzed since September 1970 and is confined to bed. In this letter he acknowledges receipt of one copy of the book, which was sent to him by Dokla by regular mail. This probably happened in 1968, after the election of Dokla to the General Secretary's position in the fall of 1967. Most of his manuscript appears to have been written long before 1968, maybe even during the interwar period. Ioann Polianskii was assigned by the Vatican to head temporarily the Apostolic Administration of Łemkoszczyzna in 1936, following the suspicious death of Reverend Vasyl Mastsiukh, who was the first Administrator, assigned to that position in 1934. At this time Polianskii probably had access to private sources and the staff to assist him in this kind of work. After having had a chance to read the first copy of the book, Polianskii complains that portions of his text have not been published and that the texts of other authors have been added.

John Madzik of Ansonia, Connecticut was able to recover Polianskii's letter to Teodor Dokla and his observations on the printed book from Dokla's records after Dokla's death. The editors thank him for bringing them to our attention. They are included below.

Lemko Park, Monroe, NY. 1972

Peter S. Hardy. Trumbull, CT. 1985.

It was a long standing belief of the Lemko Association that "People's" Poland would eventually realize that it erred in deporting all Lemko-Rusyns out of the Lemko region. The Lemko Association bent over backwards not to take any steps which that regime might interpret as offensive, hoping that it wouldn't be hindered in rendering help to the deportees at their new places of residence.

A fourth Lemko entity, The Lemko Relief Committee of the USA and Canada (LRC), was established for this purpose in 1946. In 1957, four delegates of the LRC, headed by Peter S. Hardy, were finally received in Warsaw and an agreement was reached with the Polish government to permit the American Lemko aid program to assist their brethren in Poland. A collection campaign was started to benefit Lemkos in Poland. It was planned to collect $1,000,000 to purchase farm machinery, cattle and materials. Reality frustrated all these plans. Only $12,000 was raised. Later Peter S. Hardy stated that they failed to attract to the campaign the prosperous fraternities of the Russian Brotherhood Organization and churches. The Uniate/Greek Catholic and Orthodox clergy refused to set a good example. The contributions of Lemko businessmen to the LRC proved minimal.[7] This program faltered shortly thereafter.

It is therefore hard to say whether Part IV, Sections 19 ("To Whose Advantage Was the Resettlement of the Lemkos") through 22 ("Life in People's Poland"), dealing with the wonderful living conditions that citizens of People's Poland began to enjoy after 1945, were written by Lemkyn himself or were inserted in the book by the crew at the print shop in Yonkers. I am very apprehensive because they read as if they were copied straight from a brochure provided for that purpose by the propaganda section of the Polish, or more likely, the Soviet Embassy in Washington, DC.

7　　*Almanac*, p. 43.

In addition, the book is full of "Great" Russian words, real and contrived. Polansky's letter to Dokla is written in decent Ukrainian, even though most of the book is written in Lemko-Rusyn, but how can we explain that it does not contain a single *"vshytko"*, everything? It uses "всьо/ *vsio*", which is a Russian word. Instead of *"vetse"*, more, it uses "больше/ *bolshe*", again a Russian word. From *"bolshe"* (more) it even invents a word "поболшевать/*pobolshevat*", when the Russian word for "to enlarge" is "увелічывать/*uvyelichyvat*".

Stephen Kychura, on the doorstep of his childhood house. Wierchomla Mała, 1968. (©J. Madzik)

To show to what extent somebody within the Association went to make the language of the book closer to Russian than to Lemko-Rusyn, I list Russian, or distorted Russian, words found just within page 226 of the original book:

- Выселение/*vysielenie* (eviction) – instead of Lemko выселіня/*vyselinia*
- Правительство/*pravitielstvo* (government) – instead of уряд/*uriad*
- Нерозважный/*nyerozvazhniy* (hasty) – instead of непередумани/*neperedumany*
- Труд/*trud* (labor) – instead of робота/*robota*
- Потерять/*potyerat'* (to lose) – instead of стратити/*stratyty*
- Следующего от слідуючого/*sleduyushchevo* (following) – instead of наступного/*nastupnoho*
- Объединены/*obyedinieny* (united) – instead of обєднані/*obyednany*
- Скотоводство/*skotovodstvo* (cattle breeding) – instead of скотарство/*skotarstvo*
- Всьо/*vsio* (everything) – instead of вшытко/*vshytko*
- по точном/*po tochnom* (after detailed) – instead of по докладним/*po doklanym*
- дела/*dyela* (cases) – instead of справы/*spravy*
- больше/*bolshe* (more) – instead of веце/*vetseh*
- народ трудолюбивый/*narod trudolubiviy* (work loving people) – instead of робітны люде/*robitny liudeh*
- согласно/*soglasno* (in accordance with) – instead of згідно/*zhidno*
- существуючых (существующих)/*sushchestvuyushchykh* (existing) – instead of існіючых/*isniyuchykh*
- побольшувати число/*pobolshuvaty chyslo* (increase the number, Russian увеличивать) - instead of повекшати кількіст/*povekshaty kilkist*
- Оречение/*orechenyeh* (attainment) – no such word. достижение/*dostizhenye* is a better candidate.
- з (из от с) их любимых гор, сегодня/*s ikh liubimykh gor, sievodnia* (from their beloved mountains, today) – instead of з іх улюблених гір, гнеска/*z ikh ulublenykh hir, hneska*
- до такого уровня/*do takovo urovnia* (to such level) – instead of до такого рівня/*do takoho rivnia*
- оказалось фатальным передвижением тогдашних правительственных сфер/*okazalos fatalnym peredvizheniem togdashnikh*

pravitelstvyennykh sfer (was a fatal move of the then-governing circles) – instead of был смертельным посуніном урядовых сфер на тот час/*byl smertelnym posuniniom uryadovykh sfer na tot chas*

• благодаря возрожденной политики Народной Польши/*blagodarya vozrozhdennoy politiki Narodnoi Polshy* (thanks to the renewed policy of People's Poland) – instead of вдяки відродженой політикы Народной Польщы/*vdyaky vidrodzhenoy polityky Narodnoi Polshchy*

• горожанам/*horozhanam* (townspeople) – instead of міщанинам/*mishchanynam*

• Правления/*pravlenya* (management) – instead of уряд/*uriad*

It was on the second day of the Twenty-Sixth Congress held in Lemko Park on September 4-6, 1971 that a young female delegate rose and asked the Presidium, "Where is this young man who make so much trouble here the previous day [by asking that Kychura and Dokla be thrown out from the Association]? That this is the third time that he has done this; he asks to speak,

Elected officers of the Lemko Association's 2010-2012 Executive Committee. From left: Walter Maksimovich (VP), Ivan Madzik (Treasurer), Paul Best (President). Secretary Mary Barker not pictured.

shouts a lot and then disappears." Iaroslav Kaban got up and replied, "That young man [Aleksander Wan, later "Vostok"] is our future editor. We will send him to Moscow to study and he'll return as a real falcon-editor."[8] Having had a chance shortly before this book went to the printer to review additional correspondence of Ioann Polianskii from the late 1950s, that correspondence shows that Polianskii was a very skilled communicator in Russian.[9] It is very hard to decide whether the large percentage of Russian words that appeared in the 1969 printed edition of Polianskii's book were there due to the author's background as a priest, or whether they were inserted by certain individuals such as Alexander Vostok from Lemko-Soyuz.

Although Lemko Park has ceased to exist and the Carpatho-Russian American Center is now a small for-profit social club, the Lemko Association (www.lemkoassociation.org) continues, now as a tax-exempt, non-profit, non-political, non-partisan organization for promoting Lemko and Carpatho-Rusyn history and culture.

Walter Maksimovich
Lemko Association Executive Committee
Webmaster, lemko.org

8   *Lemkovyna*/Lemkovina, No. 2(18), Yonkers, New York, May 1975, p. 3. Stephen Kychura, editor.
9   Zwoliński, Jarosław, *Rapsodia dla Łemków* (Koszalin, 1994). http://lemko.org/pdf/rapsodia.pdf.

Letter from Ioann Polianskii to Teodor Dokla

Rogi [Poland]
January 30, 1971

Highly respected Mr. [Teodor] Dokla,

I have received your letter and am replying to it. I also wish to acknowledge that I have received [one copy of] *History of Lemkovyna*, which you sent me via regular mail. Thank you sincerely for both. As an attachment I am enclosing my observations about the published book, i.e. its content and cover. Even though it contains many shortcomings, I must however point out your enormous input to have it published. You have provided a great service. Without your presence in the States, this book would not have been published. Several years have elapsed with the manuscript resting in a drawer and nobody eager to have it published. You alone succeeded in this mission. It is unfortunate that you did not stop by during your last visit to Poland. We could have gone over this matter, and many of these errors could have been avoided. Now a second edition needs to be considered, but without those bad pages that have crept in into the first edition. I can perform the proof reading and provide supplemental material, but it is necessary to send me another copy of the book without blank pages. What I have received contains eight blank pages. If it is your wish to print my "A Song About Lemkovyna" or the other poem "Yearning after Lemkovyna" I can send them to you since what you have are just excerpts. "A Song About Lemkovyna" or happy and tragic moments from the life of Lemkos is a poem which portrays the entire history of the Lemko people. They could be published since people do enjoy reading poetry. I also have ready to publish manuscripts which deal with various Lemko subjects. If Lemko-Soyuz is interested in publishing them then I can provide this material. My advice is to print as much as possible because our ideas are best propagated by being published. Only worthwhile themes should be published, not just any junk, but mostly scholarly works.

If possible, be kind enough to send one additional copy of the *History* to Haitko in Żdynia and one to Olesnevych in Brodowice. Also Fr. Volodymyr

Borovets from Szczecin is asking for one copy. He is the only Russian priest in Poland and he will write to you separately.

Since September 15th, 1970 I am paralyzed and confined to bed, but I am still able to write.

I am happy that my effort was well received by the American Rus'. That this version of history will be attacked by our enemies I already knew, since truth is very prickly. I have exposed that their work of Cain as is pertains to the Rusyn society and they like wasps, when their nest is disturbed, fly out and do not act timidly but start stinging as painfully as possible. They are doing it now and will continue screaming into the future, but to me that is the best proof that I have exposed the truth.

Let me warn you. [Lemko-Soyuz] should be wary, since they are endearing themselves to you, with an intention to ally themselves with you, then they will in mass join you as members and eventually, after the passage of time, they will take over Lemko-Soyuz, just as they have done with all other Rusyn organizations in America. When I spoke with them during my last visit to America, they did not conceal anything from me. They thought that I am also a follower of Mazepa, that they will eventually take over Lemko-Soyuz, since "the billy goats [Russians] are just like the dying skeletons. There are not many of them left". They have many mischievous methods to destroy those "billy goats" and their organizations.

Because of this you must be very cautious and astute, but best of all is not to enter into any compromises with them, since nobody can be successful in any kind of dealings with them. Individuals such as Żeleńskyj are very dangerous.

The Ukrainians in America have reprinted the Schematism of the Apostolic Administration of Lemkovyna for 1936, which I originally published. It contains history of many Lemko villages. This is very important to us. Maybe we can exchange one copy of History of Lemkovyna for a copy of their Shematism [1970]. They are selling it for $5. It was published by some Ukrainian museum. Address: Dr. Vasyl Łencyk, Ukrainian Museum and Library, 161 Glenbrook Road, Stamford, CT, USA. I recommend that this copy of the Schematism be acquired for Lemko-Soyuz. It contains a listing of all Lemko parishes, churches, clergy and villages, as well as their history.

At the same time I am writing to Mr. [Stephen] Kychura and Mr. [Peter S.] Hardy. I convey to you all my sincere greetings and wish you further success in your public work for the good and benefit of the Lemko population.

/signed by Ioann Polianskii/

Rohy dnia 30 sicznia 1971.
MNOHOUWAŻAJEMYJ HOSPODIN DOKLA !
Wasze piśmo oderżał ja i otsym otwiczaju na nioho.soobszczaju riwnoż,szto
połuczył ja ot Was Istoriju Łemkowiny,kotru wysłałyste pocztom.Za list i za н
kniżku serdeczno błahodarju.
Wpryłozi peresyłaju Wam moi zamiczania na wydanie reczenoj Istoriji to
znaczyt na wypeczatanie i oprawu kniżky.Chotiaj tam mnoho newłastiwostej,odnak
muszu zaznaczyti Wasz wełyczeznyj wkład Waszoj praci pry wydaniu toj kniżky.Wasza
zasłuha w tim weżyka.Nebyłoby was w Ameryci,ne byłoby Istoriji.Minułoż kilkanajciat
lit,jak materjał do toj Istoriji łeżał w biurku,a ne było komu wziati sia do pecza-
tania.Wy toje diło perewełу.Żałko,szto w czasi Waszoho pobytu w kraju ne zajszły
Wy do mene dla obhoworenia diła,a byłoby ne wyjszło stilko newłastywostej w kniżci.
Teper treba podumati o druhom wydani toj Istoriji uże bez tych złych storon,kotry
wkrały sia w perszim wydaniu.Korrektu mohu perewesti i Istoriju dopożnyti.Treba
odnak prysłati meni odin prymirnyk Istoriji bez opuszczenoho druku,bo w tim,jakyj
maju jest 8 storin opuszczenych druku.
    Jesły chotiły byste peczatati moho autorstwa " Piśń O Łemkowini 0 I druhyj
stich "Tuha za Łemkowinoją "nto ja możu Wam wysłati,bo tam majete łem urywki,a
ciłosti ne majete,." Piśń o Łemkowini"abo radosni i tragiczni momenta łemkowskoho
naroda jest stichom predstawłena ciła istorija łemkowskoho naroda.Możny byłob to nap
peczatati,bo narod lubyt czytati poezyi. Maju toże hotowi opracowania na riżni
łemkowsky tematy.Jesły Łemko-Sojuz chotiłby peczatati,mohu toj materyał dostarczyti.
Moja rada jest,sztoby jak najbilsze peczatati,bo peczatju najlipsze propaguje sia
ideju.Peczatati łem wartisni riczy,a ne szmelc,pobilszoj czasti naukowy wydania.
    Jesły nema pereszkody,to budte łaskawi peresłati po odnomu prymirnyku Istori
Hajtkowi do Ždyni i Olesniewiczowi do Brodowic.Prosyt takoż o tuju Istoriju o.Wła-
dimir Borowec z Szczecina. To odynokij russkij swiaszczennyk w Polszczi.Win do Was
napisze.Ot 15 weresnia 1970 ja żeżu w łiżku sparaliżowanyj,no jeszcze piszu.

    Duże tiszusia,że mij trud zistał życzływo pryniatyj czerez
Amerykansku Ruś.Szto worohy budut atakuwaty totu Istorju - ja znał napered,bꝙ
prawda w oczy kołe..Ja im wykazał ich kainowu robotu wzhladom russkoho narodu
to oni,jak toty osy,koły im hnizdo poruszaty,wylitajut i ne pereberajut w sr
sredstwach,aby tylko zażałyti i to jak najbolesnijsze.Kryczat i budut kry-
czati,a dla mene to najlipszym dokazom,żem prawdu w ocz wykazał.
    Odna dla W as perestoroha ot mene. Majte sia na bacznosty /Łemko-
Sojuz /,bo oni teper umizgajut sia do Was w toj ciły,żeby sobi Was zjednati,
a potim ingremo zapisuwati sia do Łemko-Sojuza i po jakims czasi zaharbyti
Łemko-Sojuz,jak zaharbyli w Ameryci wsi russki organizacyi.Koły ja z nimi
rozmawłał,buduczi w Ameryci,to ne ukrywali pered mnom,dumajuczi,szto ja maze-
pinec,że oni z czasom pereberut Łemko-Sojuz bo "kacapy to wże trupy na wymer
tiu,i ich mnoho nema.Oni majut riżni djawolsky sposoby na nyszczenie kacapiw
i ich organizacyj. Treba buty w wydu toho ostorożnyi i chytrym,a najłuczsze
z nymi ne wchodyti w żaden kompromis,bo z nymi nikto ne dohoworytsia.Taky typy
Żełankyj-to duże nebezpeczni.
    xxx   Ukrainci w Ameryci peredrukowali Szematyzm Apostolskoj ADMINISTRAC
cyi Łemkowszczyzny na rik 1966,kotryj ja wydał w roci 1936.Atam jest historia
dekotrych łemkowskich seł.Dla nas ważne.Można bude zrobyty łaminu.Daty im
odin prymirnyk Istorii Łemkowiny,a w zamin distaty ot nich Szematyzm.Ony prod
dajut Szematyzm po 5 am.dol. Ne maju adresy pod rukom.Waśl Wydało jakieś
ukrainskie muzeum . Wże maju adres: Dr Wasyl Łencyk,ß Ukrainian Museum and
Library / 161 Glenbrook Road, STAMFORDß,Connecticut,USAaßyßißmexyßmdyßixxx
Radyłbym toj Szematyzm nabyti dla Łemko-Sojuza.Tam mistyt sia spis wsich
łemkowskich parochij,cerkwej,swiaszczennikiw i seł,jak takoż ich istoria.
    Riwnoczasno piszu   do Hospodina Kiczury i Hospodina Hardoho
Serdeczno pozdorowlaju Was i żełaju dalszych uspichiw w narodnoj roboti
na cześć I polzu łemkowskoho naroda.

Letter from Ioann Polianskii to Teodor Dokla, dated January 30, 1971

Observations on History of Lemkovyna

THE EXTERNAL APPEARANCE OF THE BOOK IS GENIAL
AND ATTRACTIVE. Clearly printed on a good quality paper, the binding is good, decorated with an embossed in gold title of the book. The IN-
TERNAL APPEARANCE OF THE HISTORY, however, presents itself
much worse. The chaotic placement of material, lack of following the basic
rules used in book printing, some material is missing, many errors, eight blank
pages, erroneous placement of footnotes within the text, typos, etc., etc.

1. Each part of the *History* should have included a short summary, in other words, what will be discussed in each part. Specifically: Part I should
   have been entitled *Geography of Lemkovyna*; Part II, *History from early
   times until WWI*; Part III, *From WWI until the end of WWII*; Part IV,
   Lemkovyna under the rule of People's Poland; Part V, *Literature of Lemkovyna*, all of which has been omitted.

2. The footnotes should have been placed at the bottom of the page instead
   of being in the middle with an asterisk or a number. The text contains
   an asterisk or a number but an explanation to this is scattered if not in
   the middle of the page, then frequently on another page. This is encountered on pages: 45, 67, 71, 104, 111, 112, 113, 116, 117, 118, 119, 124,
   204, 210, 238, 242, 247, 253 and 257. This creates a bad impression.

3. Pages 81, 84, 85, 88, 89, 91, 92 and 96 are blank, the text is missing. Such
   book cannot be marketed since it is not complete. The missing text has
   to be added.

4. The bibliography, i.e. works dealing with Lemkovyna should have been
   placed as a supplement at the end of the book. After bibliography there
   should have been no other work placed, just an index of all the works
   that the book contains. Here however, after the bibliography, text dealing with Prešov Rus' has been inserted. That is not allowed. Work of
   others cannot be inserted into a book without permission of the author.
   [This added text has been omitted from the English translation.]

5. The article of religious nature should be placed in Part IV and not at the
   end of Part V. [This text now appears as Part IV, Section 19. Sections
   following it in Part IV have been renumbered.]

6. Bibliography should have been started on a new page and not on the
   same page which contains material from Part IV. In the book it appears
   as if the bibliography is a continuation of History.

ZAMICZANIA DO HISTORII
ŁEMKOWINY

WNISZNYJ WYD ISTORII SIMPATYCZNYJ I PRITIAHAJUCZYJ Papir choro-
szyj,druk czetkij,perepłetnia chorosza ukraszena zołotym wytyskom.No o mnoho hirsze
predstawlajetsia WNUTRISZNYJ WYD ISTORII.Chaotycznyj rozkład na.eryał
brak znania podstawowych zasad peczatania knih,brak dejakich referatiw,mnoho oszybok
wisim storinok ciłkowyto nezapisanych,czystych,oszyboczne umiszczenie żereł do textu
oszybky ortograficzny itd,itd.
1/ W kożdoj czasty istorii dołżno byti korotke soderżanie ioj czasti,inszymi słowa-
mi o czim bude besida w kożdoj czasti.Imenno:Persza czast,dołżno byti:Geografjałemk.
Druha czast: Istoria ot perszych jej poczatkow do perszoj wojny switowoj.Treta czast
Ot perszoj wojny switowoj do konca druhoj wojny switowoj. Czetwerta czast:Łemkowina
pod władinijem Narodnoj Polszczi. Piata czast:Literatura Łemkowiny.To wsio zostało
opuszczene. Ne zachodyka potreba połyszyti ciłu storonu na "czast"
2 / Żereła dołżny byti wypisany ne w seredyni tekstu a na dołżyni toj storinky,
w kotrij zwizdkom abo czysłom byli naznaczeny.W teksti jest zwizdka abo czysło,a
pojasnenie do toj zwizdky wzhladno żereło dołżno umistyti sia na dołżyni pid tekstom
Tymczasom żereła sut porozkidany w seredyni tekstu,a czasto na inszoj storinci.T aki
newłastywosty nachodiatsia na storonach:45,67,71,,104,111,119,112,113,116,117,118,
124,204,210,238,242,247,253,257.To robyt nemiłe wpeczatlinije.
3/ Storony:81,84,85,88,89,91,92,96 sut nezapisany,brak tekstu.Taka knyżka ne może
ity w prodaż bo jest nepowna.Należyt druk dopołnyti.
4/ Bibliografia/to jest trudy traktujuczy o Łemkowini/ POWINNA BUTI UMISZCZENA
jako dodatok na samim koncy knyżki.Po bibliografii ne powinno sia umiszczati żad-
nych referatiw,a tylko maje buty umiszczenyj indeks to jest spis wsich referatiw
)nachodiaczych sia w knyżci.Tymczasom w Istorii po bibliografi zostali umiszczeny
statyji z Priaszewskoj Rusy.To ne wolno.Statyj inszych autoriw ne wolno pomiszczu-
wati bez dozwołu autora
5/ Statiaiz cerkownoj obłasti powinna buti umiszczena w czasti IV A NE na kincy
czasti V
=6/Bibliografia dołżna była maty poczatok na nowoj storinci,a ne na toj samoj,na
kotroj predstawlało sia materyał czasti IV. W Istorii wyhladaje tak,naczeb biblio-
grafia była peredowżeniem historyi
7/ Czomu ne buli umiszczeny w Istorii moi znymki,kotri ja pisław Redakcyi około
100 sztuk.Byli to znymki specyalno robżeni do Istorii i ony predstawlały folkor
łemkowski.Knyżka czerez toje duże utratyła na jej wartosty
8/ Mnoho materyału,jaki ja wysław do Redakcyi ne zostało umiszczeno w Istorii,a
materyał toj był duże ważnyj
Moja propozycya byłaby taka: ISTORJU w takim wydi,w jakim wyszła z peczati
starati sia jak najskorsze rozprodaty znyżajuczi jej cinu,bo ona za doroha,a prystu-
pyty do pryhotowania druhoho wydania toj Istorii,ałe wże poprawłenoho,pobilszenoho,
usoweszennoho,sztoby tak wnisznyj wyd jak i wnutrisznyj był prytiahajuczyj,sztoby
workohy ne mohły takomu wydaniu wyrok. Ja podijmu sia perewesti korrektu toj
Istorii,poprawlajuczi wydanyj tekst.Muszu połuczyti ot Was odin prymirnyk Istorii
bez biłych plam /nezapisanych 8 storin/,bo mij prymirnyk jest z biłymi plamami.
                                        JOHAN TEODOROWICZ ŁEMKIN

7. I sent to the editorial board about one hundred photographs. Why were
they not placed in the book? These photographs were made specifically
for this book and dealt with Lemko folklore. The book has lost a lot of
its quality because of this omission. [The fate of these photographs is
unknown.]

8. A lot of material which I sent to the editorial board, was not included
in the book, and this material was very important.

I recommend the following: the History as it currently appears, having already been printed, to sell it as fast as possible. Let's lower its price because

it is too expensive and prepare another edition of the History, but this time corrected, enlarged and improved in such way that makes it attractive in both its external appearance and internal content. This way our enemies will have nothing to criticize. I will take it upon myself to proofread this version and correct the already printed text. For that I must receive from you those eight missing pages of text that are not in my copy of the book.

Ioann Teodorovich Lemkyn
/signed/

Final resting place of Fr. Ioann Polianskii. Rogi, Opole County, 2011.

Regional Ternopil District Museum of Lemko Culture and Art. Monastyryska, Ukraine, 2007. Monastyrska has become the center for the largest Lemko community in Ukraine.

Who Are the Lemkos? Where is Lemkovyna?

Who are the Lemkos?

The general question of national identity needs to be dealt with especially in relation to Carpatho-Rusyns and Lemkos. No matter what the political/national orientation of the author, historical literature is in agreement that the Lemkos are a part of the Carpatho-Rusyn group of East Slavs. The main subgroups are generally considered, in the 21st century, to be the Lemkos, whose origins could be found in the Polish controlled Carpathians, the Boikos (some of whom formerly existed in the Polish-controlled Carpathians in the very southeast of today's Poland but today live in Ukraine) and the Sub-Carpathian Rusyns who live to the south of the Carpathian ridges in Transcarpathian Ukraine. There are compact Rusyn communities in Serbia and Croatia as well as a large diaspora in northern and western Poland and the Czech Lands and a widely dispersed diaspora in North America, Argentina, Brazil and other areas of the world. Lemko leaders in North America recognized by 1940 that the term Lemko did not and could not encompass all Carpatho-Rusyns so they joined with the newly formed (1939) Carpatho-Russian National Committee in Manhattan to form a single unit. While retaining the name Lemko Association the Lemko newspaper was combined with the new *Karpatska Rus'* one and was produced under the *Karpatska Rus'* name but retained the *Lemko* papers numbering. Thus in January 1940 the No .2 issue of Lemko was renamed as Volume XIII, No .2 of *Karpatska Rus'*; apparently that was sufficient for both sides to recognize both a Lemko and a Carpatho-Rus' identity and that Lemkos and Rusnaks were the same people. As anyone who has dealt with Lemkos in emigration will know, in the very same family, members will claim they are, in origin, Slovak, Russian, Ukrainian, Austrian (from a civil point of view) or even Hungarian (if assimilated to Magyar culture) and finally Lemko/Rusyn. Since the collapse of the Soviet Union's large scale but failed attempt to foster an overarching "Soviet" nationality from a multi-ethnic— though, assuredly, Slavic dominated— society (Russians at about 50%, Ukrainians 20%, Belarus 10%), Yugoslavia (South Slavia) also failed. Why did these experiments fail when "American" as well as "Canadian" nationality projects, so far, have proved successful? Obviously some force or feeling drove people to establish fifteen separate states out of the Soviet ruins and five states plus Kosovo out of Yugoslavia. That force is nationalism— a topic of enormous outpourings of research, writing and discussion, a field too deep and vast to go into here. We need only look at some elements of nationalism.

As far as we are concerned we may point to severally agreed points of departure. First there are objective factors in determining national affiliation and, second, there are subjective ones. Just as someone of Chinese ethnic origin cannot pass as a Russian because he/she will not be accepted by Russians nor any non-Asian American be accepted as Japanese, certain features are minimally necessary to be a Lemko. Membership in the Caucasian Indo-European population would be one feature. Further being Slavic, or East Slavic, would be necessary. A family origin in the Carpathian mountains is also basic along with a family history of attending an Eastern Rite Christian Church, whether or not one attends any church today. After these, subjective factors enter in. The most important one would be does an individual identity, minimally, with the Carpatho-Rusyn, Lemko people. Does that person use the ethnonym (self identity label) Lemko? The inhabitants of the Lemko homeland in Central Europe, whether of Russian, Ukrainian or Rusyn political /grand national orientation knew that they were different enough to have a special self identifier to differentiate themselves from other Slavs and they rather universally, in the Lemko Region, accepted the ethnonym Lemko before WW I. Almost every researcher who has dealt with the origins of the Lemkos accepts that the term originated in the local inhabitants frequently and noticeably using the Slavic word *lem* (if/only/but) in conversation and that Lemkos spoke with word accents landing on the second to last syllable. There are other complicated explanations for "Lemko" which we choose not to go into here, using William of Ockham's concept of going toward simplicity rather than contrived explanations. There were/are other East Slavic language speakers who also use the Cyrillic alphabet, if literate, and/or who attended an Eastern Rite Christian Church, if religious, in the Carpathian region but the key is: did they identify themselves as Lemkos or Rusyns (or Rusyn-Lemkos)?

Another problem about the term "Lemko" is its attribution by some to other people who were very similar to the Lemkos but who did not use the term. The population on both sides of the Polish-Slovak border were the same

people (up through the deportation of the last Lemkos in 1947 and 1951 on
the Polish side). On the Polish side (that is, in the Galician-Austrian portion
of the Austro-Hungarian Empire) and in emigration, the population seized
on Lemko to identify itself and even applied that name to all East Slavs west
of the Uzh and San rivers (that is, to the Slovak side too) while, in general
the south of the Polish-Slovak (that part in the Hungarian Kingdom of the
Austro-Hungarian Empire) the population did not, preferring to continue to
use the older terms "Rusnak," "Rusyn" which had been used on both sides of
the border (to the confusion of many). It will be noticed in this book that Fr.
Polianskii occasionally mentions the south. The editors of the 1969 edition
included illustrations from the Slovak side, and they even added an appendix dealing with the Slovak side's Prešov region which had really nothing to
do with Fr. Polianskii's text. Fr. Polianskii protested against its addition and,
according to his written wishes (see his letter to Teodor Dokla, included in
"The Lemko Association and *Lemkovyna: A History*" by Walter Maksimovich), we do not include it in this edition.

Additionally, it appears that the name "Lemko" may be in use by a few
East Slavs who, living in Poland in the post-WW II period of bitter Polish-
Ukrainian mutual dislike (hatred), preferred to call themselves "Lemkos"
since the term "Ukrainian" had become pejorative. With "Ukrainians" often
called backstabbers, the word "Lemko" may have become fashionable, and
may still be.

Where is Lemkovyna?

[also known as: *Lemkowszczyzna* (Polish), *Lemkivshchyna* (Ukrainian),
Lemkovshchina (Russian), *Lemkin Land* (German), The Lemko Region
(English)]

A packet of maps is available from the Lemko Association to help in the
following discussion. In examining these aids the reader will note that there
is no great issue as to where is Lemkovyna.

It is in the Carpathian Mountains in the very center of Europe. On the
northern side of Lemkovyna, as all writers agree, there was a rather sharp
distinction between the Polish foothill dwellers (the *"pogorzancy"*) and the
Lemko highlanders with relatively little intermingling. The western part of
the Lemko Region came to a narrow end in the Szlachtowa area where four
Lemko villages existed as an island, at least on the Polish side of the border,

these villages were connected to Rusnak villages on the Slovak side, however. The southern border of Lemkovyna was/is defined as the Polish-Slovak (formerly Hungarian) political border, from one point of view, or where the Rusnak and Slovak inhabitants met and intermingled, from another point of view. In general most "Lemko" organizations claimed Lemkovyna started at the Uzh and San rivers and ran west to Szlachtowa. (Interestingly enough, local proponents of the *"Russka Idea"* [the notion that there was a single East Slavic Rus' unit] conceived of the borders of Rus' as running from the "Poprad [river] to Vladivostok" or from "the Carpathians to Kamchatka.") There also was a Lemko island north of Krosno, referred to as the *Mieszancy* (Mixed) area where the majority appeared to have been Lemkos. The real matter of contention is where the Eastern border lies: where does the Boiko Region begin? The differences between the Boiko and Lemko regions are based on linguistic analysis— vocabulary and fixed accent versus movable accent; dress— clothing patterns; cultural norms and especially sacred (church) architecture and secular buildings. (Admittedly both groups are made up of Carpatho-Rusyns.) The majority of researchers place the Lemko-Boiko shift or transition zone in the Osława and Solinka river valleys while a few place the border further east in the San and Uzh (sometimes Laborec) river valleys. See the following:

Entsiklopedicheskii Slovar (Encyclopedic Dictionary), vol. XVIIa (St. Petersburg: Brochhaus and Efron', 1896): "Lemki- a part of the Little Russian population of the Carpathian mountains, between the Ropa and San rivers, of about 109,000, members of the Greek-Catholic (Uniate) Church. The call themselves Rusyns or Rusnaks..."

Encyclopedia of Ukraine, vol. II (Toronto: University of Toronto Press, 1984): "Lemkos: A Ukrainian ethnic group which... lived ... on both sides of the Carpathian mountains and along the Polish –Slovak border".

Encyclopedia of Rusyn History and Culture, Second Edition (Toronto: University of Toronto Press, 2005): "Lemkos: the farthest western ethnographic group of Carpatho-Rusyns... lands they inhabited in present day Poland are referred to as the Lemko Region and in Slovakia as the Prešov Region. There is no consensus regarding its eastern boundary: according to linguistic and ethnographic criteria that boundary lies somewhere between the Osława and Solinka rivers, according to political activists, the boundary is the upper San, i.e. the present day Polish-Ukrainian border."

In *Lemko Studies: A Handbook* (New York: East European Monographs, distributed by Columbia University Press, 2010), the author, Bogdan Horbal, devotes the whole of Chapter 6 to the Lemko territory. While he mentions the San river as a possible eastern departure point for Lemko territory and that it goes on to the west to the Poprad and Szlachtowa, citing the work of Ivan Krasovsky of Lviv which supports the idea found "in some Lemko circles... that the region actually extends as far as the San river... and is reflected in Lemko consciousness of many second and third generation [displaced] persons," he mainly uses the works of the late, famous Polish ethnographer Roman Reinfuss (see picture on page 361, top, of the 1969 *History*), Adam Fastnacht, Jan Falkowski, and Zdzislaw Stieber as to linguistic and cultural indicators and calling on the aforementioned scholars he concludes, "considering the latter it would be appropriate to regard the basins of the Osława and Solinka as the transitional Lemko-Boiko territory."

We may also state that there are several other factors that militate towards Dr. Horbal's conclusion:

Prof. Volodymyr Kubijovich, on his map (V. Kubijovich and M. Kulintskii, *Lemkivshchyna I Nadsyannya* (Lemkovshchyna and On-the-San) (Cracow: Ukrainian Publishing House, 1940(?)) clearly differentiates Lemkovyna from the On-the-San area— again, see the 2012 Lemko Association map.

Ukrainian nationalists make much of the existence of the *Zakerzonnya* (Beyond, i.e., to the west of, the Curzon Line) area. The Curzon Line was proposed by Lord George Curzon, Foreign Secretary of Great Britain, by telegram, to the Soviet Union in 1919 and 1920 as a cease-fire line during the Polish-Soviet War, hence the "Curzon Line" (see: "Curzon Line," Wikipedia. com, accessed January 13, 2012.) In fact the Line, which was based on a supposition that the majority of the Poles lived to the west of it and the majority of Ukrainians east of the Line, was the brain child of Sir Lewis Bernstein Namier (1888-1960) who had emigrated to Great Britain in 1906 and had become a professor of history (see: "Lewis Bernstein Namier," Wikipedia. com, accessed January 13, 2012.) While the Curzon Line was not used in the inter-war period it became more or less the eastern frontier of the Nazi General Government from 1939-1941 and the 1945-present Polish-Ukrainian border. This line divided the 1772-1918 Austrian province of Galicia in half. Lemkovyna was/is in Western Galicia while Eastern Galicia was overtly or covertly in contention between the Ukrainians and Poles for almost 145 years and then for the twenty years of the inter-war period. That the Lemkos took no part in this struggle certainly helped to establish a mind-set about who a Lemko was.

Along the Curzon Line and to the east of it, from late 1942 to 1946, a horrific ethnic slaughter/ethnic cleansing took place as the Ukrainian nationalists endeavored to get rid of non-Ukrainians in any way possible in order to establish a *"Samoistiena Ukraina"* (Independent Ukraine) free of foreign taint. See Timothy Snyder, *Bloodlands: Europe between Hitler and Stalin* (New York: Basic Books, 2010). On the northern end of the Curzon Line there was a massacre in 1941 in the town of Jedwabne of perhaps five hundred Jews who were, in the main, burnt to death in a synagogue by local Poles seeking revenge and loot, to be sure egged on by the Germans; see Jan Gross, *Neighbors: the Destruction of the Jewish Community in Jedwabne, Poland* (Princeton, NJ: Princeton University Press, 2001). Near the southern end of the Line there was the case of the revenge liquidation of the On-the-San Ukrainian village of Pawłokoma by Poles, based on claims that local Ukrainians had "disappeared" a number of local Poles and even refused to state where their bodies could be found so that they could receive a proper burial. (see Peter Potichnyj, *Pawłokoma: A History*, in Ukrainian, for the Ukrainian side of the story and Zdzislaw Konieczny, *Those were the Times: the origin of the Revenge Action in Pawłokoma*, in Polish, for the Polish side.) Regardless of how one judges those two incidents, we may state that Lemkos did not commit any

Recruitment Poster in German and Ukrainian for "14. Waffen-Grenadier-Division der SS." Sanok, 1943.

acts of aggression against their neighbors. Certainly Lemkos were not angels but the propensity toward ethnic violence was not there. To be sure there was anti-German resistance but only after the Germans were driven out did lawless bandit groups (*bandy*) appear, guns in hand, to pillage throughout the Lemko territory; see Polianskii's comments on this phenomenon. Also in the 1944-1947 period the *Ukrains'ka Povstancha Armia* (the Ukrainian Insurgent Army), known in historical literature in Polish, Ukrainian and English as the "UPA," started to send raiding parties into Zakerzonnia to recruit local East Slavs to the Ukrainian cause. They were successful in the On-the-San area and deep in the central and eastern Bieszczady mountains.

However, much to the UPA's surprise, they were unable to root their cause west of the Osława and Solinka valleys. Unfortunately in the immediate post-WW II period the new Polish communist authorities were unable to or did not want to differentiate Lemkos from UPA supporters and Lemkos were forced east to Soviet Ukraine or, in 1947 and 1951, to the Recovered Territories of western and northern Poland.

Also in the 1947 to 1949 period, after the forced deportation of those Lemkos who had not been pushed to Soviet Ukraine, this inability or lack of will to differentiate Lemkos from others caused a number of Lemkos of all ages and sexes to end up in the COP-Jaworzno labor camp (*Centralny Obóz Pracy w Jaworznie*).

To those who perished in Jaworzno and Talerhof. Zyndranowa, 2002.

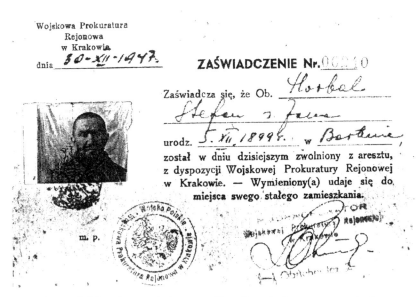

Stefan Horbal from Bartne, discharge certificate from the Jaworzno concentration camp. Jaworzno, 1947.

Volodymyr Fedak from Polany near Krynica, discharge certificate from the Jaworzno concentration camp. Jaworzno, 1948.

To the memory of those who perished at the concentration camp in Jaworzno (1947-1949). Jaworzno, 2005.

This camp, a reused sub-camp or branch camp of the German Auschwitz concentration camp which had not been damaged during WW II, was in general a place to put "inconvenient people": Silesians who had signed onto the Volksliste (declared themselves to be Germans), Austrians, Dutch, Yugoslavs, etc. A special sub-sub-camp *(Podobóz Ukrainsko-Lemkowski)* was maintained for Lemkos and Ukrainians, where Eastern Rite clerics (both Orthodox and Greek Catholic) and people suspected of cooperating with or being sympathetic to the UPA or OUN were placed in forced labor conditions. If they survived the ordeal and were released, they were *de facto* kept under surveillance until the end of the communist regime in 1989. Actual, provable members of the UPA or the OUN were tried by the military and usually executed, or else were imprisoned for long periods of time elsewhere, thus never in fact getting to COP-Jaworzno. The camp for Lemkos and Ukrainians was run by the *Urząd Bezpieczeństwa Publicznego* (Office of Public Safety), the security/political police, and physical and psychological terror were in use. The Lemko/Ukrainian camp was officially closed on January 8, 1949, but clerics were held until February 15, 1949, when they were shipped off to the town of Grudziądz. At its peak in 1947, COP-Jaworzno held over fourteen thousand prisoners in all categories.

Today Lemkovyna is a historical artifact with few (ten thousand?) ethnic Lemkos actually living there. We may conclude that historical Lemkovyna ran from Szlachtowa on the west to the Osława and Solinka river valleys in the east; the northern border can be determined by historical/ethnic village maps (see *Mapping a Stateless People* and the map published by the Lemko Association. The southern border of Lemkovyna is the ancient Polish/Austrian-Slovak/Hungarian political (not ethnic) border which runs along the crests of the Carpathians. People to the south do not use the ethnonym Lemko but rather the older term Rusyn/Rusnak, formerly used on both sides of the border. Reasons for this frontier determination include linguistic, sociological, anthropological, architectural, religious, historical and certain mental formative factors as outlined above.

The Lemko Association in North America had and the Lviv, Ukraine association has, a rather grandiose notion of the eastern extension of Lemko ethnic territory, which is also reflected in the Lemko Association map. This is probably reflective of the lack of a clear distinction between the Lemkos and Boikos, who are, after all, parts of the same people. Fr. Polianskii does often mention Sanok on the river San, but nothing beyond it, so one may conclude that he tacitly supports the San-Uzh/Laborec boundary. The lemko.org Web site mentions the Beskid Niski (Lower Beskid [hills]) as the Lemko homeland. Names used for the various parts of the Lemko territory include: on the west side, the eastern parts of the Beskid Sadecki; all of the Beskid Niski in the center; and portions of the western end of the Beszczady range as the eastern end of Lemko territory. All of these are part of the great arc of the Carpathian mountains of central Europe which run from Vienna in the west to the Iron Gate district in Serbia in the south. The approximate length of Lemkovyna is one hundred miles with a narrow western end of ten to fifteen miles to the wide eastern end of some fifty miles. Again, see the maps available from the Lemko Association.

Paul Best
Professor Emeritus of Eurasian Studies,
Political Science Department,
Southern Connecticut State University,
New Haven, Connecticut
President, Lemko Association

View looking outward through the front entrance of the Greek Catholic Church in Bartne, 2003.

Portrait photo of Fr. Ioann Polianskii as Acting Apostolic Administrator of the Lemko Region.

APPENDIX II: IOANN POLIANSKII, HIS LIFE AND TIMES

The Thorny Path of an Eastern Rite Catholic Priest
(Autobiography of Ioann Polianskii)

Photo © Kyczera

I was born on the feast day of St. John Chrysostom [the "Golden Mouth"] on January 20, 1888 [January 7, old style] in Banica, a small mountain-village in Grybów County, Cracow District, in the Lemko Region [at that time in the Galicia province of Austria].

My parents, Teodor and Maria (of the family Prycik), had a farm of about ten morgs [about six hectares or fourteen acres] of the old type [a farm made up of separated strips of land]. I had four sisters, Anna, Joanna, Juliana, Maria and one brother Dymytr– I was the third child. I had a happy childhood. Because there was no room in the local school and my father was illiterate, he had a deep desire for me to study. So he sent me, as an eight-year-old child, to school in the county seat, some twenty-one kilometers from home, with the words "Go to school and study so you won't be so deeply impoverished like me." He rented me a space with a poor widow who became my guardian, for which my father paid with farm products and one Austrian crown a month. It was very hard to become acclimated to an unknown house far from my parents. Nevertheless, I became accustomed to the situation and I felt comfortable in the school. The teachers showered me with praise and in the second term I was advanced to the second class; that's how I completed two classes of primary school in one year. Because a Bursa [boarding house] was opened in Nowy Sącz for students from poor families, my father placed me in it, and I completed third and fourth classes there.

After that, I took the entrance exam to the gymnazium [a type of secondary school] and I completed the first and second year without trouble. However, in the third year, I ran afoul of a sadistic teacher of history, Błażej Gawor Sławomirski , who hated non-Polish students. He would not allow even the best pupil of another nationality to pass onto the next level.

Having thus fallen victim to this, I moved to the gymnazium in Sanok, which was run by an extraordinarily sympathetic director, Volodymyr Bankovskii, who took under his wing every pupil who had been treated badly. In 1911, I finished studies at the gymnazium and took the graduation examination with a "Good" result.

In October 1911, I registered in the Theological Department of the Jan Kazimierz University in Lviv [Polish Lwów; German Lemberg; Latin Leopolis; Russian Lvov, Galicia, then in the Austrian part of Austria-Hungary]. I lived in the Greek Catholic Seminary at 36 Kopernik Street and attended University lectures. The stay in that seminary was the most tragic period of my youth.

The collegial atmosphere in the Greek Catholic seminary before World War One was simply terrible because of the tensions between two Rus' orientations in Galicia. The first view was that of a radical Ukrainian orientation whose aim was to artificially convert the Galician Rus' population into Ukrainians in order to found an "Independent Ukraine" [Samostijna Ukraina] without peasants, priests or landlords. The means to that end was falsification of history, changing our ethnic name, changing the writing system, changing the language, changing vocabulary, etc. That party was negative toward other Slavic peoples and favorable to the Germans. Of a completely different nature was the Rus' party, which was friendly to all the Slavic peoples (Panslavism) [especially all East Slavs] and loyal to its history, its national name and the national culture.

Both parties were poles apart and battled each other. The Habsburgs and the Hohernzollerns supported the Ukrainian side and, along with the [Greek Catholic] church hierarchy, they tried to stamp out the Rus' orientation. During the Austrian period, the bishops didn't like to accept Rus' candidates into the seminary, only Ukrainian ones, and all administrative positions were held by Ukrainian oriented priests. Because of this, in the 1911-1912 school year, out of three hundred candidates for the priesthood in Lviv, only eleven were Rus' oriented and they were terrorized by their Ukrainian colleagues.

In December 1911, the Ukrainians sent a delegation to the Rector [head of the seminary] with the demand that the Rus' be expelled or there would be a boycott [of classes]. Fr. Dr. Bocian, despite being a Ukrainophile, refused the demand, stating that he didn't see the reason to put them out because they were fulfilling all their seminary and university obligations. The delegates called an immediate strike and didn't eat [in the seminary cafeteria] or attend classes. On the third day, in the evening, they gathered in the chapel under the leadership of Fr. Kunicki and they decided to throw the Rus' out the second floor window[1] that very night onto Sykstynski Street. By chance, a seminary guard overheard and warned those under threat. They approached the rector for help but he said "get away from the seminary because I can't protect you." Thus, in the freezing night, eleven seminarians found themselves out on the street and the seminary was shut down for a month. The guilty were not punished, however, and after the month the boycott was repeated, and in the next academic year there were only three Rus' left.

As has been stated, things were terrible; one couldn't write down all the hooliganism that took place and there was even fear for life. One can imagine how hard it was to study.

Hooliganism was carried out not only by seminarians, but also by a few of the professors. One teacher, Drov Tarnovskii, even rapped one on the legs and back if one used the word *ruski* in place of *ukrainski*. The whole period of

---

1   [This is the third floor window by American count, which could have killed or crippled the Rus' students.]

my life in the seminary is written on my heart in bloody letters. Of the eleven, only myself and one other priest [now] in Szczecin, Volodymyr Borovets, still live...the boycotters have all died.

After the end of my third year of theological studies in Lviv, there was a heavy atmosphere. In ... [June] 1914 in Sarajevo, Archduke [Franz] Ferdinand was assassinated and World War One began [in August] with Austria attacking Serbia. Russia stepped forward in defense of Serbia and Germany supported Austria. Others attached themselves to these principals, and a great struggle took place and the map of Europe was changed.

From the very beginning, Austria suffered one defeat after another. In order to justify the lack of success of the Austrian leadership and to conceal the lack of preparedness of the Austrian armed forces before the world, the [Austrian] German generals came up with a story that the guiltless population was committing treason and thus, the defeats. Therefore, before every important battle, the Austrian leadership had locals arrested and in case of failure on the battlefield, gallows were built, these hostages were hanged, and it was reported that the loss was caused by treason and the local leaders had to pay the price, according to martial law. Thus, in the first year of the war, Galicia was covered with thousands of gallows from which hung guiltless people.

It was publicly announced that for every discovered traitor to His Majesty or every Moscophile uncovered, the person who turned them in would receive ten crowns... [Many] took advantage of this. Tens of thousands of denunciations poured in. Whoever had an enemy had a chance for revenge. All it took was an accusation of Moscophilism and your life could be finished. Whole groups of people were also arrested. People who had no idea about politics ended up in jails, concentration camps and prisons.

During [prisoners'] transportation, Dantesque scenes took place caused by the worst classes. [The prisoners], in chains or tied together, were stoned, beaten with clubs or even murdered. In Przemyśl on Siemieracki Street, a group [of over fifty people] was massacred so that all that was left was a mass of flesh, with brains splattered on the walls of nearby houses. This bestiality was carried out with cries of "Traitors!", "Moscophiles!", "Spies!", "To the hook with them!", and "To the gallows!" Thus it was not strange that the Carpathian region was filled with gallows and the cries of guiltless people.

We should add that the Austrian gendarmes [police] were particularly good at torturing and beating with clubs, kicking and depriving people of food and water. On the whole, morality disappeared.

In terrible physical conditions, those arrested were dragged from prison to prison starving, beaten and without any way to resist. Thus the First World War showed how far people can fall.

In the village where I spent my summer vacation of 1914 with my parents, on the night of August 7-8, there was a meeting in the local inn of four people, two gendarmes and two Jewish owners of inns or pubs... they decided who among the locals were Moscophiles and which ones to arrest... I was added to this list. The next day, three other gendarmes with a list of names went around to arrest people.

All the arrestees except me were taken away by foot some fifteen kilometers; I was taken by cart. About three hundred prisoners were assembled in a school hall under control of fifty police led by a certain Commandant Bac', of Ukrainian orientation. The gendarmes were armed with carbines with mounted bayonets. In order to scare everyone they'd let off a shot every now and then.

New transports of arrestees came in the same evening. About eleven o'clock p.m., horse carts from neighboring villages showed up, and the prisoners were loaded up, with shouts, shots, and cries from the families of arrestees. The gendarmes prevented family members from getting too close, and accompanied by barking dogs, cries, shots and heavy rain, the carts departed with the arrestees, who were given to know what a dangerous situation they found themselves in. I was in the second load and we were taken to the train station, loaded up, and sent off into the unknown.

We met the same fate as others, as previously mentioned: clubs to the back and stones to the head from all sides. We traveled for three days and three nights to where we were going. Many never made it. Victims fell in Galicia, Hungary and a few [Austrian] German provinces. On the other hand Czechs, who still felt their Slavic blood, treated us as well as they could. Women brought us food and fed the starving prisoners, a truly Christian act. Our arrival point was a field surrounded by barbed wire called Talerhof[2] in Steiermark (Styria) [Province] south of [the city of] Graz [in Southern Austria]. This was a camp for people Austria did not trust. [Nearly] all people arrested were sent to Talerhof. It is a place hard to speak of. Was it a place of extreme suffering, or was it a Satanic work of people, or the worst construction of a depraved clique of rulers in the twentieth century? Was it a place deprived

---

2   [The original German spelling was Thalerhof.]

of all ethics, humanity or moral values, or a place where every evil was practiced in one accursed location?[3]

Conditions of existence for the prisoners in Talerhof were beyond compre-
hension, horrible, simply sadistic. From August to the beginning of December 1914 the victims were held under the open skies,[4] squeezed in by barbed
wire to such an extent that nobody could change his standing position for
another. Every evening a sign was given, usually a carbine shot or the command *neider* (down), and every prisoner had to fall to the ground, one on top
of another, and stay there until morning when an *auf* (up) signal was given.
Anybody who couldn't get up was forced up by a carbine [with a bayonet] of
a patrolling soldier. Every day, those who died were hauled out and buried in
a common grave "under the pine trees."

In summer clothes without a change, without washing, in wind, rain, snow,
frost and starvation, in pain and lamentation and loss of strength by standing
all day while waiting three months for barracks was obviously beyond human
strength. Thus it wasn't odd that people fell like flies. A cart came through
daily to take out the dead bodies…the single daily meal was made up of some
uncertain smelly liquid with something floating in it along with a small slice
of bread, baked from poor flour.

In order to satisfy one's bodily functions there were ditches of ten meters
length, two meters deep and one meter wide with a rail on one side. Prisoners were brought to a ditch in groups of twenty and on the order *sitzen* (sit)
everyone sat on the rail. After a few minutes the order *auf* (up) was given
whether one was finished or not. If you didn't get up immediately then a soldier would push you into the ditch with a carbine; you couldn't get out and
you'd die right there in the sewage. In that way hundreds died. After the first
group the next group was brought and then a third and a fourth, etc. One got
a chance to use the latrine only once a day.

During my stay in the camp there were thirty thousand people of different
nationalities, of different ages, both sexes, of different professions and jobs.
There were more then eight hundred priests incarcerated, mostly of the Greek
Catholic variety, victims of the Ukrainian party. If by mistake a Ukrainian
found him/herself in Talerhof he or she [made a declaration to the resident

---

3   [See *Thalerhof: The First Twentieth Century European Concentration Camp* (Lemko As-
     sociation, forthcoming.)]
4   [The camp in Talerhof was within the bounds of a military airport. A few lucky prison-
     ers got into the hangars present, the rest were outside.]

Ukrainian *Vertrauensmann* (confidant) and] was immediately freed. The camp was open three and a half years and most internees never returned home but rather lay permanently "under the pines."[5]

In December 1914 barracks made of boards were constructed, but they were only a small step toward bettering the condition of the camp inhabitants. There was now a roof over their heads to keep off the rain and snow, but the barracks, far from hygienic, were a sort of joke because rotten straw served as the floor, brought in after being used in horse barns and thrown about on top of the damp soil.[6]

Because of a lack of space in the barracks the internees were so tightly packed that one could only sleep on one's side and the body couldn't be straightened out. The straw wasn't covered; neither were the people [there were no blankets] and everybody slept together, men, women and children. As may be supposed, after a few days insects started to infest the straw which became a plague for the prisoners. In fact the straw could be seen to be moving and one spoke of "living straw". The result of this was typhus. There was no medical assistance available, much less medicine. People started to die like flies. Hundreds were hauled out "under the pines" on a daily basis. Often one could see people taking their shirts off and picking insects off them. Several prisoners died from bites alone, so the "living straw" was taken out and burned.

The situation got a bit better after a visit from a foreign delegation sent by the English King. There was an investigation by General Baczynski who condemned the camp directorate, and many officers who committed criminal acts against female prisoners were sent out of the camp under escort. During this period the Austrian army suffered defeat after defeat. The army got smaller and smaller as whole units gave themselves up to the enemy. This had an effect in Talerhof as traitors to his Royal Highness were converted into his defenders, and that's how I got out of the camp— I was drafted. Along with others, we were transported to Graz, where we received uniforms including a hat... with the initials "F.J.I" on it which some vicious people read as "for Jewish interests". In the beginning I was happy to get out but that soon left me because I couldn't forget that camp.

After some weeks of training in Graz we were sent off to the front. Traveling through Lviv I jumped off the train to buy a few cigarettes nearby but the

---

5   [Austrian authorities only admit to the deaths of about two thousand.]
6   [The Austrians initially built *erd hutte* (earth huts), dugouts with some sort of roof. In summer 1916 actual above-ground barracks with floors were built.]

train left right away and there I was absent without leave and no other unit
wanted me, so I stayed in Lviv.

The next day while crossing through Jesuit Park I met Fr. Dr. Tarnawski, a lecturer on church history at the University. He recognized me right away... and in
a half hour discussion I learned what a difficult situation I was in. He brought
me to Archbishop Bilczewski and we talked about what to do. The Archbishop
had me enrolled in the *Clericalverband* (clerical union) which gave me an exemption from military service as a candidate for the priesthood. I was then able
to visit my family and after one year's break I returned to the seminary. After
completing the 1915-1916 academic year in theological studies I was ordained
in December 1916 by Bishop Grzegorz Chomyszyn in Stary Sambir. My first
liturgy was in the village of Piorunka with the assistance of five... other clerics.

My first parish was Tuligłowa in the deanery of Sądowa Wisznia, diocese of Przemyśl, county of
Mościska. I was there one
and a half years and I was
able to repair the church
building and the rectory.
I then was sent to Smol-
nik on October 15, 1918
as a temporary adminis-
trator. On May 8, 1922
I became permanent and
I was there for the next
sixteen years which were
the best of my life because
I was in the mountainous
territory I knew from my
youth, with all its beauty...
A person could see out his
window the works of the
all powerful and merci-
ful God. The world of the
mountains is the chapel of
God and people can there
appreciate his strength
and power.

*Ioann Polianskii with sister Maria after being
ordained to the priesthood by Bishop Grzegorz
Chomyszyn. Stary Sambor, 1916. © Kyczera.*

Eastern Rite church in Roman Catholic use. Brunary, 1968.

The local population was similarly beautiful and honest with the best character despite their being materially poor. This simple people, often not being able to read and write, had great understanding, intuition, native intelligence, and good will. They were able to truly praise God. Pastoral work was a blessing. The authority of the parish priest was very high because the pastor was everything: a spiritual father, a leader, and an advisor; a judge, a physician, and a defender. Nothing happened in the parish without his knowledge and agreement and no bad influences could penetrate the parish.

As a result of our mutual work our parish developed with a beautiful church, a three-room school, and a cooperative building which had a food store, a dairy house and a reading room. Also different sorts of educational, economic and cultural societies were organized such as an amateur circle, a brick kiln, a forestry cooperative, etc. The funds for building were drawn from gifts and free labor. The parish also owned 450 morgs of high quality forest [about 256 hectares or 640 acres.]

It's so nice to remember those days among the fine parishioners of Smolnik...but today [ca. 1972] I can only remember those poor people and that tragic parish for it does not exist today; so it is also with the other two nearby villages... The whole area where such happiness existed has been turned into an African jungle... because of the post-World War Two fighting. Armed groups stole everything, burned the buildings and drove the people to Soviet Ukraine or other places. This was an evil occurrence which cries out to heaven. We must look at how this happened objectively. In the post-World War One years an abnormal religious situation developed, driven by the actions of the Przemyśl bishop Iosafat Kotsylovskii. That bishop, who took his post in 1917, came from the Lemko Region and turned his attention to it when he took over the diocese. He didn't like the antagonism of the Lemkos toward the Ukrainians and their politics. In order to break this antagonism he sent young [unmarried] priests of strong nationalistic Ukrainian views to Lemko parishes with an order to Ukrainize them.

According to this order, the church pulpit became a political platform. The word of God was replaced by Ukrainian issues. A people who survived the hell of Talerhof and other concentration camps in World War One, a people who, thanks to Ukrainian support [of the Habsburgs], left "under the pines" hundreds of their relatives and dozens of their beloved pastors, who were given over to death by Ukrainians, with great bitterness heard words about Ukraine spoken from the pulpit by these disliked preachers. These people were asked to stop preaching politics and to return to the word of God based on the Bible. Unfortunately no requests or threats in this direction yielded any result.

People, moved to the quick, sent a delegation to the bishop but he not only rejected them but also complained that they were wasting his precious time with an unnecessary complaint. When all these means to get rid of an evil proved unsuccessful and there was no other path, the only way out was to convert to another faith.

Taking advantage of this situation, Orthodox monks who had moved from Pecherska Lavra [the Kyivan Caves monastery] to Čertižné in Slovakia, began a strong agitation in favor of the Orthodox rite.

The first parish which returned to Orthodoxy was in Tylawa, in Krosno County, where the pastor was Fr. Szkolnyk. After Tylawa other parishes followed.

The conversion of Lemkos to Orthodoxy had fatal consequences. In fact no parish returned completely but only in part. A battle began between the Orthodox and [Eastern Rite] Catholics which was deprived of all sense and limits. People began to break each other's windows, poison each other's wells, destroying each other's property. Orthodox worshippers, armed with clubs and scythes, broke into [Eastern Rite] Catholic churches and stole the liturgical books, chalices and church paraphernalia and carried off these items to Orthodox churches, stating that these items had been bought with their money. The next night the Catholics armed with better weapons, took back the church furnishings from the Orthodox church. Of course sometimes they clashed directly and life and limb were at risk. Crippled participants with broken skulls

Jordan Festival. Blessing of the Waters by the first Apostolic Administrator Dr. Bazyli Mastsiukh. Sanok, January 19, 1935.

Jordan Festival. Blessing of the Waters by Bishop Adam (Dubec). Sanok, January 19, 1979.

returned from the field of battle and, of course, court cases followed, with fines and imprisonments. Every day brought news of fresh outbreaks.

A mission to the parishes damped down the situation a bit but not completely. The situation was very painful to me but I was without strength or capacity to do anything. I came up with different plans. One time, taking advantage of the presence of the Primate Fr. Hłond [the head of the Latin Rite Catholic Church of Poland], in Krynica on vacation, I organized a delegation, made up not only of me but also two influential Lemko people. The Primate received us very graciously, and with attention listened to our explanation of the situation and was very interested. After a short discussion, we went into details. The Primate promised to look into the situation. The Roman Curia and the government of Poland would have to agree to separate the Lemko region from the diocese of Przemyśl and to establish a separate church unit, dependent directly on the Apostolic See [Rome].

The Primate asked me to send a weekly report about what was going on. From that time I did send weekly reports on the Orthodox movement and about fresh conversions to Orthodoxy. After a few months the results came in. Primate Hłond arranged that the Apostolic See, in agreement with the government of Poland, would separate the nine deaneries of the Lemko region from the Przemyśl diocese and would create a church entity under the name *Administratio Apostolica pro Lemkis* [The Apostolic Administration of the Lemko Region, hereinafter AAL.] This occurred by a decree of the Congregation for the Eastern Church, entitled Quo Aptius Consularet, dated February 10, 1934. The Polish state Ministry for Religion... in Warsaw designated the town of Rymanów-Zdrój as the seat of the Apostolic Administration and his Curia, and count Jan Potocki offered his large villa as a residence: The first Administrator [not a bishop but a priest with near-bishop powers] directly dependent on the Holy See was Dr. Bazyli Mastsiukh, former professor of canon law in Przemyśl and docent of Jan Kazimierz University in Lviv. He began his activities with the blessing of the waters of the San [River] in Sanok, January 19, 1935. By a decree of February 27, 1935 I was confirmed as the Chancellor and Advisor to the Curia of the Administration and thus I cooperated with the Administrator.

In the beginning work in the Curia was not easy because it fell on the shoulders of only two people, one of whom was a theoretician and the other not familiar with the work of a chancellor of a Curia. It was necessary to sit at a desk, without a break, in order to settle questions which had sat at the Przemyśl Curia for half a year without action.

In June 1935 the Administrator went to Rome, called by Pope Pius X. After his return, based on a decree of June 25, 1935, he gave me the right to wear a cassock with a cape and gloves, a violet waist sash and a violet hood. [Thus Polianskii became a "Monsignor" or archpriest.] A diocesan consistory was established, with six consultors. By a decree of July 17, 1935 I became

Апостольский Адміністратор
Лемківщини в Риманові - Здрою.
Ч. *176.*

Д о
Всечесного Отця
Йоанна Полянского
в Риманові - Здрою.

Сею граmotою поставляємо Вашу Всечесність канцлером Курії тутешної Апостольскої Адміністрації Лемківщини.

В тій ціли явиться Ваша Всечесність перед місцевим Ординаріем дня I. марта с.р. для : I/ зложеня віроісповідання , 2/ зложеня проти модерністичної присяги ,3/ зложеня присяги ,що обовязки свого Уряду совістно сповняти будете .

Для улекшення сповнювання обовязків уряду з огляду на сторони ,сим уділяємо Вашій Всечесности право уживати реверенди з крилошаньскими ознаками т.е. з пелериною і рукавцями і чорного пояса зі золотими френзлями .

Мир з Вами ./

Дано в Риманові -Здрою , дня 27. лютого 1935 р.

Ioann Polianskii becomes a monsignor/archpriest. Rymanów Zdrój, February 25, 1935.

Clergy of the Apostolic Administration of Lemkivshchyna. (1) Fr. Volodymyr Vakhnianyn of Deszno and Administrator Dr. Bazyli Mastsiukh (holding hat). Deszno, 1935.

a synodal judge and by a decree of July 27, 1935 a member of the Council for the Purity of the Faith and Morals (*consilium a vigilanta*).

For protection of [my] material existence (by decree of January 17, 1936.) I got additional work as pastor of Wróblik Królewski and Wróblik Szlachecki [two neighboring villages], to which I went on Sundays and holy days. This nomination certainly increased my workload considerably.

The Apostolic Administration had many dangerous enemies, among whom, as one may suppose, was Bishop Kotsylovskii, all the Ukrainian clerics and the Ukrainian press. Orthodox priests, obviously, were also opposed but the general population was rather indifferent. The greatest enemies were Ukrainian politicians and the Ukrainian press. Ukrainian priests followed every step of the Administrator and spread around false stories and lies. Bishop Kotsylovskii reported all of them to the Roman Curia... attempting to portray the activities of the Administrator in the darkest colors.

The Ukrainian press repeated all the rumors and lies. He was presented as a religious and social criminal. Everyone who could, tried to put the screw to his person. When his enemies were not successful in putting down his authority, a criminal Ukrainian hand placed poison in his food and he tragically died on March 10, 1936. He was buried in the cemetery of Nowa Wieś, Nowy Sącz County, with the assistance of [Catholic] bishops and priests of both rites [Roman and Byzantine]. Nationalistic Ukrainians from the very beginning blamed the existence of the Administration on the person of Fr. Administrator Mastsiukh. Unfortunately civil authorities, even though they should have, did not assign personal guards to the Administrator. The reason for his death was never made public in order to prevent an autopsy [and scandal].

The news of the death of the first Administrator of the Lemko Region was met with great joy by his enemies, because they thought at his death the Administration would be liquidated or the second Administrator would be Ukrainian. They sought out candidates and sent proposals to the Apostolic Nuncio [in Warsaw], without result. During the burial of Fr. Dr. Mastsiukh I received a telegram, from the Nunciature, of condolences, dated March 14, 1936..., signed by Cardinal Marmagio, in which I was also nominated as the Acting Administrator by the Holy See, which gave me the rights of a *Kapitular Wikariusz* (vicar) during the time of *sede vacante* (vacancy of the seat of Administrator).

With great fear I reviewed the news but, trusting in help from God, I took on my shoulders the weight of running the diocese in very difficult circumstances, in the midst of a battle between two political parties and the two religious points of view— that is, Orthodox and Catholic. The main reason for the creation of the Apostolic Administration was the liquidation of [the presence of] Orthodoxy in the Lemko Region which was caused by the unfortunate policy of Bishop Kotsylovskii and the Ukrainian clergy. Enemies of the Administration now doubled their attacks and now on my person. The devil had a wide field for action: plots, conspiracies, slanders and denunciations, right and left. The most active now were Ukrainian organizations and their press. Ukrainian politicians burned with hatred for the Administration because the creation of the Administration forced them out of the Lemko region, which they wanted to possess according to the intentions of Bishop Kotsylovskii. Like rabid dogs they searched every corner to find ways to attack me in every way, spreading around fantastic news about the Administration and its representatives. In time "revelations" appeared in the Ukrainian press which had no relation to reality... there even, from time to time, appeared at the Curia representatives of Ukrainian newspapers promising better press coverage if money changed hands; in short, bribery. When they were asked to leave (I didn't want to talk to them) attacks continued with greater intensity. Only after I brought a case to the local court in Sanok for libel and after a hearing and a verdict the editor Taranko got a few months in jail and a requirement to repay court costs was there an effect on some of the editors of Ukrainian newspapers and Ukrainophile priests.

The accused editor, Taranko, as part of the court process, called as witnesses three Ukrainian priests, who in writing claimed I had committed certain acts. They were called to the court for an open hearing. All three repeated their libels. The court required them to take an oath as to the veracity of what they said. All three made a false oath. The court, in giving its verdict, did not accept the false oath and gave a verdict against the editor Taranko. After an appeal to the provincial court in Cracow the punishment was increased.[7] All three priests, in the space of a single month, in different ways, suddenly died. One was shot accidentally while coming out of a church by a... soldier... a few days later another was called to the bedside of a sick man... an unknown person hit him over the head... and he died immediately. The third traveled to town in a horse carriage which was hit by an auto... and he was killed. The sad facts had an additional effect, calming down the excited clergy.

Into the arena of struggle now stepped the Ukrainian underground, from whom I received a written death sentence with two signatures and the *tryzub* Trident seal [the Ukrainian national symbol]. Another time a skull and cross-bones was nailed to the chancery doors with the same seal but two different signatures. Besides these, different provocative curses were stuck on the doors. I had to endure a thousand different insults. Every day was filled with dangers from evil people. One day, returning by train in the evening I was badly beaten up by a group of attackers and I had to spend two weeks in bed. I tried very hard to discover who had attacked me. It turned out that a Ukrainian pastor had inspired the attack. A life under such pressures wasn't a very happy one and work under such circumstances was difficult, but due to God's help, I survived. During the whole time when I was the Acting Administrator I worked without assistance. In one person I was the Administrator and the Curia. A housekeeper took care of the house and cooked and typed [for me] in her free time. Every letter issued by the Curia was edited by me personally. In my heart and soul I was convinced that I served the good of God and the people from whom I came.

---

7   [This is possible in some European law.]

Portrait photo of Apostolic Administrator Dr. Iakov Medvetskii. Rymanów Zdrój, 1936.

All my difficulties were known to the Holy See because I had to respond to all the written claims against me lodged by Ukrainian politicians; also Cardinal Hłond personally told the Holy Father about the situation in which the Apostolic Administration of the Lemko Region found itself and the difficulties connected with its work.

I was [then] informed by the Nunciature in Warsaw that, as of July 13, 1936 Fr. Dr. Iakov Medvetskii of Stanisławów [today Ivano-Frankivsk in Ukraine] had been nominated as the Administrator. I also received thanks for carrying out my duties in a time of great difficulties. On October 28, 1936 I handed over the post of Administrator to Fr. Dr. Medvetskii and moved to my parish in Wróblik Królewski and Wróblik Szlachecki, thanking God I ended my work happily. In Wróblik I was able to build a two story house without special help from the parish. I now lived in Wróblik and carried out my pastoral duties, traveling to the Curia occasionally to settle a few unresolved issues.

The new Administrator, with the agreement of the government, switched the seat of the administration to Sanok, which was more historic, easier to get to and better presented itself.

The German occupation brought with it a whole ocean of new sufferings, troubles, bitter tears and much suffering and many victims. There wasn't a corner of the country where the people didn't cry out from under the German boot, with beatings and murders carried out by these "bearers of culture". At the very beginning, October 5, 1939, I was arrested by the Germans and threatened with a death sentence for supposedly poisoning the parish well in order to poison the Germans stationed in Wróblik. The accusers were Ukrainian nationalists who had fled from the Soviet occupation zone [of Poland] and who had volunteered for German service. Among them was a Greek Catholic pastor whom I had received with an open heart as a brother and whom I helped with whatever he needed. In a short while, under the influence of his comrades, forgetting I was a fellow priest, he performed such a service: with the help of one peasant he poured a few buckets of kerosene into the parish well, then went to the German headquarters and accused me of putting chemical agents into the well in order to poison the army. This accusation had the aim of getting rid of me and his taking over the parish as pastor. The witnesses were the comrades of the accuser and I had no defense. Five other people added their voices against me and I was likely to be shot in [the city of] Jasło where I was taken by train. In the court processes a German by the name of Max was the translator for those who didn't know the German language. This German wanted to get into the German police service by showing his ability, and he quickly figured out what was going on. He researched the issue from the beginning and went to the judge. Thus before the arrival of the train the Commandant showed up at the station and when I arrived stated that I was free since the actual perpetrators had been uncovered. I didn't take revenge, but the opposite, and I asked the Administrator to issue an order placing that priest in a neighboring vacant parish. That pastor and his conspirators couldn't believe my act. Thus for a short time I was left in peace.

After awhile another accusation against me showed up at the Gestapo office in Krosno, signed by the Ukrainian nationalist Zakharivskii, a teacher at a local school, also a recent arrival from the east. He accused me of taking a picture of Hitler down from the wall of the school and, in the presence of pupils, throwing it into the furnace. Further, I supposedly walked on a swastika saying it was a satanic symbol. The chief of the Krosno Gestapo himself showed up at my house and gave me the accusation to read. My heart skipped a beat as the Gestapo man demanded an explanation. My explanation was that I once came to school for religious education and I noticed that in place of the icon of the Mother of God, which had been thrown into the furnace, there hung the Ukrainian trident. Disturbed, I asked the children who had done it and they said Mr. Zakharivskii. I ordered the trident to be taken down and the icon to be replaced, which the children gladly did. The trident I threw in the furnace, where, I suppose, it burnt up. The state secret policeman said, *"Haben sie gut getan! Alles ist in besten ordnung."* ("You have done well! Everything is in the best of order.") He put the accusation back into his briefcase and left. That policeman, a Lutheran, had given a sign of respect to that Mother of God whom Zakharivskii had thrown out, recognizing the correctness of hanging the picture on the wall.

During the occupation a lot of changes took place in the Lemko region. Ukrainians moved against the Rus', especially the Lemkos, exactly as they had done in World War One. History repeats itself.

The Ukrainians were now in the saddle and a field of activities was open to them. They spread falsehoods right and left and used the Germans against a guiltless people.

In the first phase the Administrator fell a victim because he was like salt in the eyes of the bestial Ukrainian politicians. The Ukrainian nationalists who from the first days of the war controlled Cracow established organizations there. Governor Hans Frank [administrator of the "General Government," the Nazi German regional government] sent to Dr. Medvetskii a German, Johann Peters, who, calling himself a Greek Catholic confidant of Frank, was to be the intermediary between the governor and the Greek Catholic church. That Peters gave the Apostolic Administrator a copy of an order nominating Fr. Aleksander Malynovskii as the Associate Administrator, to sign under the threat of arrest. Fr. Dr. Medvetskii delayed issuing the document, though he did stick it on a wall, because he did not know Malynovskii.

Fr. Aleksander Malynovskii had been a captain of the Sich Riflemen [in WW I] and had had some sort of a position in Lviv. At the beginning of the war [World War Two] he fled to Cracow and there, thanks to the help of a German officer with whom he had served in the army, got the job of an assistant. He became an important person. He was a confidant of Governor Frank,[8] ran the Ukrainian Aid Committee and held the identity card of a captain in the *Sicherheitspolizei* (security police).

When finally Fr. Dr. Medvetskii accepted Fr. Malynovskii as Associate Administrator, he [Malynovskii] began immediately to run the Apostolic Administration and also immediately made many changes in favor of Ukrainization. Dr. Medvetskii was taken to Cracow and put into a hospital of the Order of Friars. The whole staff of the Administration was changed; Malynovskii selected people in favor of his policies. Having seized control of the top position and with a police ID card in his pocket, he became the lord of life and death over his clerical subordinates. For the Rusyn priests he couldn't stand he instituted rigorous control. He ordered the arrest, by individual name, of:

---

8   [Frank was hanged after the war for war crimes.]

1. Fr. Volodymyr Mokhnatskii, advisor to the AAL and dean and pastor in Tylicz;
2. Fr. Evhen Khyliak, advisor to the AAL and pastor in Krynica;
3. Fr. Emilyian Venhrynovych, advisor to the AAL and pastor in Mochnaczka;
4. Fr. Ioann Polianskii, advisor to the AAL, Chancellor of the Curia, and pastor in Wróblik Królewski;
5. Fr. Stefan Bartko, Curial Notary and chaplain to the Administrator;
6. Fr. Iuliian Sembratovych, pastor in Złockie;
7. Fr. Andryi Orshak [b. 1915 in Węglówka (Waniwka), Krosno County];
8. Fr. Volodymyr Venhrynovych, advisor to the AAL and pastor in Wierchomla Wielka; and
9. Fr. Zenon Kalimiuk, a Studite monk.

The arrestees were put into the infamous German prison in Nowy Sącz where special torture was applied by the well known torturer Johann.

Interned by German authorities until 1945 for lack of pro-Ukrainian sympathies are: (front row, from left) Fr. Evhen Khylak from Krynica; Fr. Emilyian Venhrynovych, priest from Mochnaczka and head of the Muszyna deanery (d. June 4, 1961 and buried in Krynica); Fr. Dymytrii Khyliak, Orthodox priest from Izby; Fr. Ioann Polianskii; and (back row, fourth from right) Metodii Trokhanovskii, teacher from Krynica. Kielce, 1941.

Somehow other Germans discovered we were in prison as victims of the hated Ukrainian nationalists. After a hearing, all of us were freed. When Fr. Malynovskii heard of this he immediately went to Cracow and, after a week, got all of us arrested again. This time we were sent to Kielce and quartered in an old school building. We were required to register once a day at the Gestapo

Sanok. Proclamation of the establishment of the Ukrainian SS Division "Galizien", May 9, 1943 in front of an Apostolic Administration church. Apostolic Administrator Aleksander Malynovskii blessing the process. (Photos © Sanok Museum.)

headquarters plus we were forbidden to leave the city. After six months we were allowed to live separately. Through the intervention of Dr. Teofil Kuryllo we sent a request for our freedom to the General Government. We got a positive answer but Fr. Malynovskii wouldn't allow it and we sat in Kielce to the end of the war. We returned to our places only after the German capitulation.

The four year stay in Kielce, while the worst of the fascist terror was raging, was not a happy time for us. Every day we had to go to the Gestapo, wait at an electrified fence for a *hereinkommen* (come in) command, go inside and register and make an exit, which was not always a certainty. It was certainly not fun. Inside the Gestapo building many fell victim. Those were frightening moments but God protected us and we are grateful to him for life. During our stay in Kielce we were protected by Bishop Czesław Kaczmarek, a man with a golden heart. We have to thank him since we had no money and he supported us so we weren't orphaned. We could daily serve mass and take advantage of recollections and all services of God's mercy. Following the example of brotherly love, Bishop Czesław Kaczmarek, Bishop Franciszek Sonik and other Kielce priests were for us true friends. The Kielce believers showed us sympathy and understanding. Such support made our bitter life more bearable and we have fond memories of it.

Fr. Malynovskii faithfully served Hitler and his clique, as the following telegram sent [in German], to Dr. Hans Frank in Cracow, shows:

To the Governor General Dr. Frank in Cracow,
     The undersigned wishes to express joy on behalf of all the Ukrainian people that the great *fuehrer* (leader) of the German people has attacked the Bolshevik torturers of people. We hope for the success of the German army on the field of battle. May God protect it and grant it victory... against the Bolsheviks.

Sanok, June 29, 1941
Aleksander Malynovskii
Apostolic Administrator of the Ukrainian Greek Catholic Church
of the Lemko Region.

This telegram and letter can be found in the Acts of the Apostolic Administration, No. 45, July 1941.

This sort of character with a miter on his head, a staff in his hand, and a revolver in his pocket became the head of the [Greek] Catholic Church in the unhappy Lemko Region on June 6, 1940.

Ioann Polianskii receives permission from Administrator Malynovskii to request facilities to carry out ceremonies in the Roman Rite. Sanok, July 14, 1945.

When I returned to my home in Wróblik Królewski, imagine how surprised I was when I came to my house and I found Fr. Malynovskii in my bedroom. That poor fellow, not imagining my return, since I had been sent off by him to the Gestapo, had taken over the house as a refugee from justice. Greeting him I said, "Well, Excellency, I see the wheel of fortune has turned, as the saying goes. You were the lord of life and death. You sent me to die but I still live and as you can see I feel fine. I am happy to see you. You tarnished my reputation but since you are comfortable, as if in your own home, you may stay as long as you like." Malynovskii, shocked by my sudden appearance, could only say "Excuse me" and he felt rather disconcerted. I spoke with him openly. On the second day he left my house and went to Sanok by horse accompanied by Borys Pakhomii, a Basilian monk, who during my absence was the pastor in Wróblik Królewski. He, the close friend of Malynovskii, was of the shady type often found among the Ukrainian clerics. Afraid of local justice, he registered for departure to Soviet Ukraine, and when he left he took as many expensive church objects as he could.

Malynovskii, after he returned to Sanok, lived in the local church rectory and acted as a pastor. Two months later Polish and Russian officers came to arrest him but he was clever enough to escape from the house and never returned. The next day [Polianskii does not mean this literally] he was already in Munich.[9]

The war ended and the Germans lost it badly as a just verdict of history. In a free fatherland began a free life. All of Poland lay in ruins. There developed a desire to rebuild but there was yet to be another strong earthquake. When the capital was liberated, a People's government was formed but chaos reigned throughout the country. The worst elements, with arms in hand, began stealing, plunder and murder. One could bitterly observe that situation of anarchy in the Carpathian Mountains. People used to armed conflict did not willingly give it up and some decided to fight further. Gathering weapons abandoned on the fields of battle, they would attack defenseless villages. They plundered and burned, driving the villagers over the border into the Soviet Union. Thus we see on today's maps blank spaces where conflict took place.

A few villages such as Niebieszczany and Prusiek dug trenches, surrounded the village with barbed wire, and made bunkers where weapons were stored. In such villages three hundred to five hundred people of different ages could be assembled for defense. Habitations with armed people, ready for battle, included villages such as Bukowsko, Mrzygłód, Nowotaniec, Andruszkowice and Zarszyn. From such places emerged armed bands which went into the Carpathian Mountains, into the Lemko Region, to force people, under threat of burning the place down, to abandon their homeland. Fires burned, whole villages disappeared in flames, smoke could be seen from afar, in which went up what wealth people had spent their whole lives acquiring. By necessity and with bitter tears, frightened people said goodbye to their beloved mountains and left into the unknown. What wasn't burned was looted.

To battle with these bands came other units from the East under the name of the Ukrainian Insurgent Army (UPA). Fights between the two were bloody; villages burned and the people died or fled. After a heavy struggle the UPA controlled the territory until the Polish Army arrived and after heavy battle, liquidated the Ukrainian groups. During this last struggle the Polish general Karol Świerczewski was killed by the UPA near Baligród. Then the worst time for the Lemkos arrived— deportation.

---

9   [Malynovskii (1888-1957) went to England via Germany, assisted by UPA units heading in 1945 via Czechoslovakia to the Western Allies' sectors of Germany. He was Papal Prelate and Vicar General for Ukrainian Catholics in Great Britain. He is buried in Acton, near London. See http://www.findagrave.com/cgi-bin/fg.cgi?page=gr&GRid=5903672 (accessed January 31, 2012).]

The deportation of the Lemkos happened in the following way:

At the end of May 1947, after the end of spring sowing in the fields, in every Lemko village there appeared in the evening a unit of the Polish army. The unit's officer called all the population together and declared that everyone had to be ready to depart by six o'clock a.m. the next day. Everyone could take what they wanted but the rest of their goods had to be left behind. No one would be able to return and everyone would be sent far away. But the officer didn't say to where. As you can imagine everyone thought the worst and people went crazy.

In the dark deaf night one could hear crying and shouts, the howling of dogs and the sound of hammers building boxes to pack things in. Even the cattle in the barns added their sounds, seeming to understand their fate. People fell into madness, beat their heads against the wall, ran around like crazy, kissed the earth, raised their hands to the heavens and prayed. A few even wanted to hang themselves. I was an eyewitness to these terrible scenes and personally lived through that painful moment. I can't really describe these night scenes, how they looked in reality, I don't have the words for it. The pain of losing one's own ground, one's mountains, one's life's work, and the unknown future sent the hearts of these people into pieces.

Nobody could bring their whole life's work. Some brought the least useful items. One woman left everything except an old down blanket, others pulled the holy pictures from the walls and tied them up to carry on their backs. One carried a big wall clock, and so forth. People lost their heads and stood dumb. At six a.m. the march started towards the county seat, to the railroad station, with bitter tears and prayers. Suddenly thousands started to sing a song to the Mother of God, *Prechystaya diva maty* (Immaculate virgin mother), and the marching column quickly disappeared from the village.

At the railroad station one had to wait three days [or more] for the train to arrive. There was no extra food and nobody had any cash. On the third day the train arrived, deportees were loaded onto the wagons and off they went to Wrocław [formerly Breslau, in German], the ride lasting a whole month. At a few stations wagons were decoupled and sat for a few days without food. Then they sat in Wrocław for a few days. The starved and tired people looked like they were not from this planet, in a word, terrible, and it's better not to write further.

In the city rumors began to circulate that some wild people had arrived, and teachers would not let pupils out into the street so they wouldn't meet with cannibals. Knowing that [the Catholic charity] Caritas had received a lot of American gifts for poor people, I went to the director, Fr. Samulski, and presented him with the deportees' situation and asked for food from [Caritas'] reserves. He promised to give them something as long as the local [Apostolic Administrator of the Wrocław Archdiocese], Fr. Karol Milik,[10] agreed. I returned for an answer and got the statement "I can't help the Lemkos since his Excellency has forbidden it"— so they got no help. At that very time, dozens of petty merchants were selling American Caritas gifts on the market. So that's how Caritas handled American food packages and material assistance.

The deportees arrived at their designated places without any strength. They received no help, neither food nor money. They got the worst places, those which Polish settlers refused.[11] They got farmsteads without buildings or inventory, or with buildings laying in ruins, and land that was marginal for agriculture at best. They arrived in late June, a time too late to plant. In any case the deportees came without food to eat, much less seed grain or straw.

Now began really hard times. There was nothing to put in one's mouth and famine began. Whoever was healthy enough went off to work at richer neighboring farms for a crust of bread to feed the family. Lemkos could eat their own bread only after a year, after spring planting. Today they are exemplary; because of their hard work and careful planning they eventually were able to make a go of it. They were the first to take care of their obligations to the state and [today] hold important offices. By their orderliness you can recognize Lemkos. By means of work and thrift the people enriched themselves.

However, the people who got the former Lemko homesteads made a mess of them. They took bank loans, drank up the proceeds and didn't pay back the funds, and converted the Lemko region into African jungle.

After my return to Wróblik from German internment I saw the results of the various groups prowling around. The worst groups were these organized by [Roman] Catholic priests, one of which was led by a Franciszek Żurawski who was chaplain to a [Polish] AK [*Armia Krajowa*, Home Army] band of some one thousand members. That group moved about through villages and

---

10   [More on Milik is available (in Polish) at http://pl.wikipedia.org/wiki/Karol_Milik .]
11   [The Soviet Union had seized the eastern half of inter-war Poland in 1939 and, in 1945, required those who wished to retain Polish nationality to leave for Poland; those remaining became Soviet citizens. Poland, in turn, expelled the German population living east of the Oder and western Niesse rivers— territory received in exchange for the eastern land lost to the Soviet Union— and repopulated the area with Poles. The last to arrive in these "Recovered Territories" were the deported Lemkos. They got the worst land, with the type of soil that was left over after the Poles were settled.]

towns murdering people and stealing property. That servant of God did not even hold back from murdering [Greek Catholic] priests. Fr. Anatol Sembratovych, pastor in Babice, Fr. Mazur in Tarnawka, Fr. Demianchyk, pastor in Skopów, Fr. Bilyk, pastor in Brzuska, and others fell at his hand. More than one thousand members of the civilian population were murdered during robberies. The property of the dead was carried off as loot. For such crimes no one was ever brought to justice including Fr. Żurawski; he sits quietly in a parish under an assumed name.

I personally was not touched by that band [of criminals] but I did obtain a document describing the activities of that chaplain. I, however, was bothered by another group also organized by a [Roman] Catholic priest, a certain Jan Szul, pastor of Radziechów, of Lviv diocese. That character, consecrated by God, came along with his parishioners after the war's end to the Rymanów area, a place from which his family originated. He organized a group of bandits and set up near my parish. During a three month period he organized attacks on the peaceful inhabitants of Wróblik Królewski. Since my people had no weapons, after three weeks they gave up and registered for departure to the Soviet Union.[12]

After the parishioners left for Soviet Ukraine, Szul's followers took over the abandoned farmsteads and Fr. Szul began attacks on my rectory. At first they stole my cow, then my food. Next he demanded that I move to the second floor while he took over the first. He wasn't satisfied with that for long and at eleven o'clock p.m. he sent his brother and brother-in-law, dressed in officers' uniforms, to search my things. They demanded I leave by midnight under threat of death, so I went to relatives in Nowy Sącz.

Szul's bandits also stole from Lemkos leaving for Russia [Soviet Ukraine]. They stole from them the things that people took with them on departure. The militia [police] and army were called; they did a search and found arms in the rectory basement and stolen cattle. Those in the rectory at that time were arrested while Fr. Szul, who meanwhile was teaching religion in school, fled to Silesia where he got a parish near Jelenia Góra where he is to this day

---

12   [According to an agreement between People's Poland and the USSR, or more specifically the Ukrainian Soviet Socialist Republic, populations were to be exchanged— Ukrainians to Soviet Ukraine, Poles to Poland, in the 1944-1946 period. In 1947 the remnants of Lemkos and Ukrainians in Poland were deported to the Western and Northern territories of post-WWII Poland. See http://en.wikipedia.org/wiki/Repatriation_of_Ukrainians_from_Poland_to_the_Soviet_Union .]

[1972]. He was appointed dean [the administrator of a group of parishes] by... [Administrator] Milik, as a reward for his services. After a peace conference in Warsaw in 1950 I was sent to give a lecture in Jelenia Góra. Priests from the whole of Jelenia Góra province came, along with Fr. Szul, and I extended my hand in friendship and we had a friendly conversation.

Having gone to relatives I thought I would have peace in this mountain town [Nowy Sącz], which had no easy access. Unfortunately my hopes came to nothing. Misfortunes pursued me like a dog. I had to pay for the sins of my predecessors [Ukrainian priests] who fled abroad to escape justice.

The People's Militia [People's Police], made up of the worst elements, patrolled around Lemko villages and on a daily basis they would arrest a few or a dozen men and lock them up until someone would pay a ransom for them. One had to bring eggs, butter, cheese, salt pork, honey, chicken, sausage and vodka— cash was accepted too. The ransom was paid to a Mrs. Gogol, wife of the head of the local security service, and the victim was immediately released. Those not ransomed were sent to the county prison and they had to wait months for release. At one point I, too, got arrested and since nobody could buy me out I stayed in prison for several days. Thanks to Fr. Duchnowycz, pastor of Krynica-Zdrój, I was finally released, and as I left prison I asked Mr. Gogol why I was arrested. He said, "You'll never know, and if you find out you'll be back in here, and then you won't get away so quickly." It seems, though, that Gogol didn't remain in his post so long, since I later saw him selling newspapers on the street.

The People's Police didn't always act correctly and they demanded a large amount of agricultural goods from a Lemko population already squeezed dry by the Germans. The population carried out orders without resistance and brought, without payment, wheat, potatoes, cabbage, chickens and butter. The militia sold these articles for cash, buying alcohol. There were daily orgies accompanied by shouts and yelling.

I lost weight while in Krynica because of Gogol. Beside the roof over my head I had no means of support, nor even any money. I couldn't leave Krynica and I suffered from hunger. At night I had to steal potatoes from the fields which saved my life. I told no one of my catastrophic situation, and I put my fate in God's hands.

I cannot forget the evening vigil of Christmas I spent in Krynica Zdrój in 1945. The city was illuminated by vigil lights, as was the park. In windows you could see Christmas trees and hear the singing of carols. The atmosphere was happy. Even the drunks rushed home to their families, shouting incomprehensible words. The whole holiday was filled with happiness but for a few days all I had in my mouth was mineral water and a few potatoes baked on ashes. However, holiday cheer was so deep and I felt such joy in my heart that I strangely felt happy and prayerful, forgetting my hunger.

On the first day after Christmas an unknown priest visited me. While wishing me the best holiday greetings, he pulled out of his briefcase a whole bunch of food supplies, gifts from the local pastor, Fr. Wojewoda. I have no idea how they found me, who told them of my need, or who directed them to me. Fr. Wojewoda helped the poor and forgotten...

Unfortunately I had to live with the news that Gogol had forbidden me from serving holy mass. When he heard that I was starving, he categorically ordered me to leave town, either east or west. Naturally I chose the latter. While in Krynica I made contact by mail with Primate Hłond. In his last letter he [authorized me to perform Roman Rite services and] sent me an order to take over a clerical position in the [Roman Rite] Apostolic Administration in Gorzów and recommended me to the Apostolic Administrator[13] Fr. Drow Edmund Nowicki. Nowicki gave me a place in the Curia and asked me to come quickly to Gorzów to begin work. In the first days of January 1946 I went off to Gorzów but I had to stop in Wrocław since I didn't have money for a ticket. I went to the Curia of the Administration of Wrocław for information and by chance I met an acquaintance, Fr. Alphonse Przybyła, the newly appointed chancellor of that [church] administration. So it happened that I was appointed pastor in Prochów (formerly called Browchow), a town in the suburbs of Wrocław. Fr. Dr. Nowicki did inform [Wrocław Administrator] Fr. Milik.

At the time, Prochów was in complete ruin, as was all Wrocław.[14] From the very first, I began intensive work to remodel the church and the rectory and a new roof was put on the church. The interior was also renewed...the parish was made up mostly of railroad employees that were also attached to the Church. They trusted me and gave assistance whenever I asked for it.

At this time, Fr. Wacław Jabłoński, former Chaplain in the Polish army, and his colleague from the army and friend paid a visit to Fr. Administrator Dr.

---

13 [Regular bishops were not yet established in western Poland.]

14 [Wrocław, German Breslau, had been a German *festung* (fortress city) at the end of World War Two and fell only after the fall of Berlin. It was one of the most ruined cities of Europe since *"Festung Breslau"*, besieged for three months by the Soviet army, fought to the bitter end.]

Milik with a request that I be given a good position but not near Wrocław, or Prochów. The one problem for both of them was that I had already been installed in Prochów. After a discussion, they put together a letter with the following contents:

The Apostolic Administration of Lower Silesia, Wrocław
No. 3034/46
Dear Monsignor,
Despite your good will and great effort in the service of God...certain rumors have come to my ears about dissatisfaction of parishioners with their pastor.
You, yourself, can best understand the source of this dissatisfaction, and understand deeply in your heart that a pastor who cannot move the heart of his parishioners cannot work positively in his position.
I have the sad duty to inform you of this and have the hope that as a disciple of Christ, you'll accept this in deep faith.
Therefore, I propose that you take a position as the Chaplain of the Sisters of St. Joseph in Bliżanowice, and as part of this, become the pastor of Bliżanowice and leave Prochów to another priest who will soon be appointed. I pray to God that He will help you to bear all the blows you have received in the recent past, like St. Paul.
Given in Christ, Fr. Milik

From my side I must draw attention that the words "certain rumors have come to my ears" are a fantasy of Fr. Milik, who was simply lying. No complaints came from the parishioners about this, as the Chancellor of the diocese later informed me in detail. The real reason for Fr. Milik's dissatisfaction was my nationality and rite.

Anyway, I immediately went to the position offered me, but it turned out that there was no clerical post there, but rather a large farm which the authorities had given to Caritas for use, and which was run by Fr. Samulski, a friend of Fr. Milik. Samulski kept his cows and horses there.[15] The Sisters of St. Joseph were supposed to run the place, however, buildings lay in ruins and there was no place for the Sisters to live or anything to eat. There were, however several cottages used by railroad workers who returned in the eve-

15   [Regular clergy do not have a vow of poverty, only clergy belonging to specific orders take such a vow.]

nings to sleep there. There was no church or chapel and it turned out Milik really wanted me to pasture the cattle of Samulski.

As soon as I figured out what was going on, I sent a letter of refusal to Milik. In two weeks, Fr. Colonel Jabłoński showed up with an order, signed by Milik, sending me as a vicar [temporary administrator] to Prochów. I couldn't understand what was going on. At that time, the diocese of Wrocław had such a lack of priests that each priest had to administer several churches in the deanery, but I was to have only one church and one school and furthermore, I was to be a vicar only.

I went to the Curia to request an explanation. It was perhaps his mistake but Milik had left on a one week journey, leaving full powers to his Chancellor. Thus, I called on the Chancellor from whom I found out secretly that Fr. Jabłoński gave me a vicar's position in order to push me to the brink; then Milik could punish me by sending me off to yet another parish and Jabłoński could be the pastor of Prochów. The Chancellor advised me, and issued me an order, to go to the parish in Żurawin. A year and a half later, Milik put another priest in Żurawin leaving me without a position. After a month, I simply moved to a parish in Gniechowice and there Milik left me...During my stay there, Fr. Milik paid me an official visit. I sent one hundred bicycle riders and two hundred on horses to meet him and he was satisfied...Although it was forbidden [during Communist times] to set up a permanent triumphal arch to greet his visit [as the de facto Bishop] I prepared three movable gates and the visitation went off well... From that time, his relations with me were correct. Honors and flattery of certain hierarchs are effective and his weak character didn't suit a proper hierarch. Generally, he was not liked by his clerics. He was even called a bad actor. In 1950, he was forcefully taken to Poznań along with other Administrators. Later, in an audience with Premier Józef Cyrankiewicz, I heard these words:

> My dear Apostolic Administrators. My point of view is that you are attempting to sit on two chairs and you're playing a double game, which the state cannot agree to. The chairs will be pulled out and you'll fall down and your places will be taken by others.[16]

Returning from Warsaw, I repeated these words to Fr. Milik. That is, I warned him of an impending catastrophe, which a short time later occurred. Fr. Milik left and his place was taken by another, of whom it was said he

16 [The year 1950 was the height of Communist oppression and the Communists wanted the church to serve them only and not try to serve both God and man.]

was the embodiment of the Devil. *De mortius nihil sine bene* (about the dead
say nothing but good). His deeds showed who he was.

The Apostolic Administration of Wrocław didn't have new members of
its Curia (central administration), only older ones. Fr. Canon Niedzbała remained and the others, of German nationality, had been deported. When
Fr. Milik left [he was forced out], Fr. Niedzbała tried to put Fr. Bilczewski
in as a temporary replacement but Bilczewski refused, feeling he couldn't
do it in the situation that then existed. The next candidate, Fr. Jaroszek...for
the same reasons, refused. Then...Fr. Józef Kazimierz Lagosz[17] appeared and
volunteered...and Niedzbała appointed him, to the astonishment of all the
priests who knew him.

Who was this Lagosz? He was a Catholic priest of the Lviv Diocese, a religious teacher in schools, who was twice suspended for leading an immoral life.
He fled in the face of the Russians [Soviets] to Złoczów [now Zolochiv]. Later,
he went to Wrocław fearing the consequences of misleading the Russians. In
the city of Złoczów, he had built a large building of the Association for People's
Schools (*Towarzystwo Szkoły Ludowej – TSL*) and on the top part of the school
were the letters "TSL." One time, a Russian officer passed the school and asked
what those letters meant. Supposedly, Fr. Lagosz said, "*Towarzyszowi Stalinowi,
Lagosz* (To Comrade Stalin, Lagosz)." When the Russians found out the truth,
he fled to Wrocław while the city still was in German hands. He was the first
[Polish] priest in Wrocław. After the German capitulation, Lagosz took over
the church of St. Boniface, the only church in good shape after the war. After
a few days, he gathered a few assistants and he held continuous services from
six o'clock a.m. until two o'clock p.m. All believers came to his church because
all the rest were in ruins. Four church workers collected offerings for rebuilding churches and they got a great sum but Lagosz complained. According to
one of his assistants, when a Sunday collection got less than a million zlotys,[18]
Fr. Lagosz, not content with the offerings, bought himself a horse and wagon
in which he could carry items dug out of the ruins. The entire two-story rectory of St. Boniface became a great repository of all sorts of recovered things.
That went on for too long, however, and the state seized the goods and locked
up Lagosz. Completely resigned to his fate, he sat in prison without hope of re-

---

17 [Kazimierz Lagosz was Vicar Capitular (administrator of a vacant diocese) in Wrocław
     from 1951 to 1956. Dismissed from this function in 1956, he died in 1961 while in
     retirement.]
18 [It would be hard to calculate what that was in U.S. dollars in 1946 or today.]

lease. He was visited occasionally by assistant priests. At about that time the first priestly societies were established, attached to ZBoWiD (*Związek Bojowników o Wolność i Demokrację*, Association of Fighters for Freedom and Democracy)[19] The head of the organization was Fr. Colonel Mróz and the secretary Fr. Zaleski. These two went to the prison warden and in agreement with state authorities got Lagosz out. From that time, those three priests were best friends...Lagosz, as the pastor of the largest parish is Wrocław, visited Administrator Milik frequently and every so often handed over some thousands of zlotys.[20] Since Administrator Milik loved money, he rewarded Fr. Lagosz with all sorts of medals, titles and offices. And since Milik was the Ordinary [the man in charge], he designated him the dean [head of a group of parishes in a district or "deanery"] of Wrocław, so it wasn't really extraordinary that Fr. Niedzbała appointed him the Acting Administrator of the Apostolic Administration of the Wrocław diocese.

In a short time, Niedzbała discovered his mistake when he received a letter from his German priests saying: *"Quod fecisti Domine? Ad regentium Ecclesiae Sanctae pessimus ommium sacerdotum sacerdos, a te nominatus est...!"* (What have you done, Master? The worst of all priests was named by you to govern the Holy Church!) These were painful words for that saintly soul, Niedzbała, and he soon passed away. Fr. Józef Kazimierz Lagosz, a fellow with great ambitions and aspirations, clever, nervous and liable to lose control, without culture or ethics, couldn't unite his clergy and left a sad memory behind him. His only service was the rebuilding of the cathedral destroyed in the war and the designation of funds to restore all the churches of the diocese.

Thanks to the work of the whole of the clergy and many appeals to church authorities... the temporary nature of the church administration in the "Recovered Territories" was stabilized.[21] The church was now on firm ground.

---

19 [ZBoWiD was a Communist front organization which until 1956 excluded members of the AK (Armia Krajowa or Home Army) underground. The AK was the largest anti-Nazi, anti-Communist force in Poland during WW II. The priestly societies mentioned were formed of "patriotic" priests who were willing to assist the Communist regime.]
20 [Remember, no vow of poverty for ordinary priests.]
21 [During German times the Catholic Church, was, obviously, run by a German Catholic hierarchy with the blessing of the Vatican. In the immediate post-WW II years, the "Recovered Territories" were technically part of the German church and only temporary Apostolic Administrators could administer the church there. Eventually, West Germany (the Federal Republic of Germany) saw the light and recognized Germany's eastern border as the Oder-Niesse Rivers. The German Democratic Republic, the Communist state, had always recognized the post-World War II status. Once the political ground had been set, the Vatican moved the church in the "recovered territories" officially from German to Polish control.]

Once everything was straightened out, priests could ask for permanent assignments.

Fr. Lagosz set up two different kinds of parishes to which priests could present themselves as candidates. The first type was parishes with a better material foundation; the second type had worse conditions. The first type was not openly advertised; they were handed over to Lagosz's friends. The second type was announced. One of Lagosz' truest friends was Fr. Colonel Władysław Mróz, Chaplain and pastor of the Garrison Church of St. Elizabeth in Wrocław. He was a fellow with a great heart, with a good soul, friendly with everybody, and he gave his all for God and the Fatherland. To me, he was very nice. He secretly told me about the lists and advised me to apply for one on the first list, with the recommendation of Fr. Mróz [himself]. After hearing that advice, I applied for the parish of St. Dorothy...on Swidnicki Street in Wrocław, not anticipating the storm that would arise. When Lagosz received my petition, he fell into a fit, jumped about, shouted and threatened revenge and blamed Fr. Mróz with the worst words. Fr. Mróz told me about the character of Fr. Lagosz and I didn't wait long for revenge to strike. On the next Sunday, I came to the church in Grzechowice with Fr. Szukalski. When I returned after Mass in the neighboring parish, where I was substituting for the absent pastor, a church assistant run up to me shouting, "The Bishop has arrived, the Bishop has arrived." I pointed out to the church assistant that we didn't have a bishop and the diocese was administered by an ordinary priest who didn't have the title of bishop. I went into the church and I left Fr. Szukalski walking outside and on the bench in the presbytery sat Fr. Lagosz with a file of papers in hand. Going into the sacristy, I nodded to him, reading danger in his face. He did not return the gesture. I waited half an hour, then dressed for a service and went to the main altar. It was the Sunday of the Pharisee and the Tax Collector. After the New Testament reading, I preached a sermon about the Pharisee and the necessity of good prayers, not holding back about high officials imbued with arrogance.

After serving Mass, when I was already in the sacristy taking off my garments, I heard Fr. Szukalski saying "Dear parishioners, perhaps you have some complaints about your pastor. If you do, then go to the Bishop in the sacristy and he'll hear you out." I couldn't believe what I heard, because this would diminish the authority of the pastor in relation to church authorities. After giving thanks in church I went to the rectory. There I found two people in the office. When I stood at the desk, the first question I got was from Fr.

Lagosz: why had I not greeted the Ordinary from the pulpit, why? I said "because I didn't know why you had come, as the parishioners should have been informed. I waited for the Ordinary in the sacristy and since I thought he had come incognito, it was not right to publicly greet somebody incognito."

"Why didn't you, going to the ambon, ask for a blessing before delivering your sermon?" asked Lagosz. "Because," I responded, "my Ordinary is not a bishop and a bishop's blessing is only delivered by a bishop." At such a response, Lagosz' eyes screwed up and his face turned white as he went on: "Today's sermon was on a different theme than was ordered by the Ordinary." I said that for a sermon, I answer only to God, not the Ordinary. I choose those topics which I consider the best for the parish. And you yourself had ordered that the priest's sermon ought to be in accordance with the Gospel, thus the best sermon for today was what I spoke; is there anything better?

Fr. Szukalski, in his Judas voice, broke in, saying, "We came because we heard that you had done a *panakhyda* [an Eastern Rite prayer for the dead] here." My reply was, "That's strange. Since you were a priest in Sokal where the majority were Greek Catholic and where, often, priests of both rites carried out burials and other services together, you don't know what a *panakhyda* is? If you don't know, I'll happily explain it. A *panakhyda* is a beautiful, moving one to tears, Catholic service of the Byzantine Rite, done for the souls of the dead. Maybe I committed a crime carrying out that service for my dead parents who were Greek Catholics. A *panakhyda* I sang, and in the future I will sing one again. Nobody has the right to forbid me. Now I have to go to Zachowice for my third Mass today; a cart is waiting for me."

"Go, then," said Lagosz "I will send you a letter in this matter."

"I don't expect any response," I said," since I didn't send any problem for the Curia for resolution," and saying "*Laudetur Jesus Christus*" (Glory to Jesus Christ), I left and went to Zachowice. In the meantime, Szukalski ran out to see if anyone came to complain but nobody did.

After I left, the two searched through the rectory, probably for a weapon, in order to denounce me to the state authorities. My housekeeper told them to stop the search. "Don't seek anything here, because you won't find anything, but if you steal something then our priest will have something to complain about. Different priests have visited us, but none were like you. Maybe you aren't priests?" In a while, Szukalski went to the kitchen and asked the housekeeper for something to eat because they were hungry. She gave them coffee, bread and butter, but rather unwillingly. They sat for a moment and then left.

The highest council of priests in Wrocław decided to expel me from the diocese using various methods. Thus, I received a letter dated August 12, 1952 signed by Fr. Lagosz stating, "In an attachment I am sending you a letter allowing you to seek work in another diocese since further stay here would cause you to meet with more and more difficulties. By the first of September please send me your promise to seek admission to another diocese. If I don't get such a letter of the fifteenth of September, I will send you to another parish for your good. Wrocław Ordinary, Fr. Kazimierz Lagosz".

I did not respond to that letter and on the first of September, 1952, I got the following order: "I transfer you to be administrator of the parish in Krzepielów in the deanery of Głogów effective September 15, 1952. The parish memorandum book you should get personally from the dean in Bytom, Fr. Odrzanski. The Ordinary of Wrocław, Fr. Kazimierz Lagosz." To that letter, I replied that I couldn't fulfill the order in the indicated term because I wasn't a winged bird and I couldn't get from one end of the diocese to the other so quickly. The response, dated September 8, 1952...said, "The transfer stated in my letter of September 1...is not literally binding. I agree to your stay in your present place...but only to the end of September. I clearly state that at that time your jurisdiction in Gniechowice becomes invalid. I wish you the blessings of God and personal happiness."

Because my jurisdiction expired on September 30, my pastorate was left empty for two months, but I continued to live in the rectory. The priest from the nearby parish of Tyniec Mały, Fr. Józef Lisiewicz, did what he could during that time. In the meantime, I got a letter from the Curia dated November 5, 1952 granting me the administration of the parishes of Rudna and Gwizdanów with the obligation to take them over by November 28. The reason for giving me these two parishes was the fear of the expansion of Orthodoxy in those parishes. On the territory of the parishes, there were two churches served by two Orthodox clerics.[22] The population of this territory belonged to three faiths, Roman Catholic (fifty percent), Greek Catholic (forty percent), and Orthodox, about ten percent more or less. However, Greek Catholics attended Orthodox services due to their similarity with Greek Catholic

---

22 [There is some reason to believe that the Communist authorities, in spite of being officially atheist, supported Orthodoxy in the struggle with the Roman Catholic Church. The Greek Catholic church officially did not exist after 1946 when the pseudo-synod of Lviv claimed to have transferred the Greek Catholic church to the jurisdiction of the Russian Orthodox Patriarch in Moscow.]

services which they could understand, rather than Latin Rite services which they could not understand.[23] At that time there were neither a Greek Catholic church nor clergy, and Greek Catholic parishioners were served by Roman Catholic and Orthodox clergy.

My predecessor was Fr. Jan Schmied, of German extraction, who was suddenly called away by Fr. Lagosz. Changing parishes caused a very unpleasant atmosphere. Since I was not yet known, rumors appeared about me: "You have traded away a German and brought us one of the Ukrainians who was murdering us in the East." About these events taking place in Eastern Galicia, we don't need to elaborate.[24]

On my arrival in the parish on Sunday, I went immediately to the church and the parishioners stood outside the building. Taking off my hat, I greeted them with *"Niech będzie pochwalony Jezus Chrystus* (Glory be to Jesus Christ)." The response should have been *"Na wieki wieków* (Forever and ever)." I noticed the threatening posture of the parishioners and I couldn't get to the church doors, since no one made way for me. I was in a silly situation. Then suddenly I heard a loud male voice, "Step back— make way to the church." Later I found out it was a militiaman [policeman] who spoke. He had been sent especially so as not to allow an attack on me planned by Fr. Schmied. I got into the church, carried out a Mass, and greeted the parishioners at the end of the service. From that day, I had no trouble with the parishioners. I did start parish work with some fear but every day relations became better. Relations not only got better with the parishioners but also with others, who belonged to two nationalities and three faiths. I extended my hand to everybody I met, but the enemy didn't sleep.

At the urgent request of parishioners, I conducted a service in the Greek Catholic (Byzantine) rite on Christmas according to the Julian calendar (January 7) and the blessing of waters (Jordan) (January 17). The aim was to draw back to the Catholic Church Greek Catholics who had been going to Orthodox services or none at all, like lost sheep. On January 7, a few thousand

---

23   [At that time, Orthodox services used the same Church Slavonic language as did Greek Catholic ones, though with a slightly different pronunciation, while Roman Catholic services were in Latin. The Second Vatican Council (1962-1965) promoted more active communal participation in the Mass and by 1971 this included the replacement of Latin by vernacular languages.]

24   [Polianskii is referring to the slaughter of Poles by Ukrainians, and vice versa, in the Wołyń (Volhynia) region during the later stages of WW II. See http://www.thefullwiki.org/ Massacres_of_Poles_in_Volhynia (accessed January 31, 2012).]

showed up and they couldn't all fit into the church, therefore some had to stand outside. People came from all corners of Lower Silesia to hear a service not heard for five years, since their deportation in 1947; even Orthodox worshippers came.

I began the service with *"Boh predvichnyi"* (God Eternal), and a thousand breasts burst out with song, and people wept... and their faith was renewed in joy and hope for a better future. That carol led to another world, being a reminder of their former homeland, dear Lemkovyna, and their thatch-covered houses... and the small churches, and the wonderful flora among the sky-touching mountains, and the sound of trees, and the green fields and streams. That carol has enough strength to treat wounded hearts. I also delivered a sermon appropriate for the occasion. After the liturgy, everyone said they would attend church regularly as long as I would hold an Eastern Rite service on major holidays according to the Julian calendar, which I said I would do. I felt a great satisfaction. I could draw people to church and I thanked God. I also carried out the Jordan service in a similar fashion.

Normally, I should have been recognized positively by church officials but the Devil didn't sleep and the issue took a fatal turn. I got a letter, dated February 13, 1953, calling me to appear before Fr. Kazimierz Lagosz. I showed up on February 26, 1953 and Lagosz met me in the corridor without a greeting, saying "I've gotten news you carried out a Greek Catholic liturgy in Rudna. By what right did you do that?" I responded that I am a Greek Catholic priest in good standing, not suspended, and have the right to do that and no one except the Holy Father can forbid me. In any case, it wasn't my idea but that of my Greek Catholic parishioners, and it was my duty to do a service for them, certainly on at least two of the greatest holidays. After my explanation, Fr. Lagosz put the blame on Minister [of Religious Affairs Antoni] Bida saying: "But you did it. Minister Bida has ordered me to put you out of the parish and the diocese; that's why I called you here to communicate this decision from above. When do you want to leave, before or after the [Easter] holidays?" I responded, "After meeting with Minister Bida," and that was the end of the conversation. Already on the next day, I got an official Curial letter dated February 27, 1953, saying, "You are released from the parish of Rudna and Gwizdanów as of March 1 with the recommendation that you go to Bishop Franciszek Sonik[25] in Kielce who has promised you a post. We wish

---

25   [See http://pl.wikipedia.org/wiki/Franciszek_Sonik .]

to thank you for your many years of service to the Archdiocese. Kazimierz Lagosz." Effective the same day, Fr. Stanisław Walachowski from Sobieszów was appointed the administrator, but he didn't accept. Then Fr. Dr. Jerzy Rumak was appointed and he did accept.

The very next day, I went to the provincial administrators and asked to see the highest authority in the province [of Lower Silesia], where I found out that Bida did not issue, and had no authority to issue, an order to Lagosz putting me out of the parish. Fr. Lagosz had done it himself, but covering the deed by calling upon the name of Bida. In the provincial administration, I learned that the state was indifferent to the rite a priest, used in service— that was an internal church matter. They advised me to go to Lagosz with an expression of sorrow, since he appeared to have been insulted, and that he would withdraw the order. They said Lagosz was very sensitive on this point. I stated that I would never do that even if it meant I died from starvation. Because I had been thrown out on the curb by Fr. Lagosz, I had no means of existence, so I took a position as Fr. Dr. Rumak's servant. I cleaned and cooked and he gave me enough to live on. However, Lagosz got wind of this arrangement and sent me an order to vacate the premises by April 18 or be suspended from priestly functions. In the meantime, I had fallen ill and I used that to justify remaining in the rectory at Rudna. A response came, dated April 27, 1953, that I could stay until I got better but I could carry out no duties; I could say a private Mass but one of the Salesian priests would take the parish book away from me. I handed over the book and that was the end of my dealings with Lagosz. The wheel of fate turned and Lagosz was relieved of his post [in 1956] and retired to Warsaw to work as a cab driver. He bought a car and carried passengers for a living. *Sic transit gloria mundi.* (Thus passes worldly glory).

I finally left Rudna and went to Gliwice to live with a friend, to await what came my way next. I did apply to the Katowice (at that time called Stalinogród) Curia for a post, but was turned down due to a lack of openings (a letter of September 27, 1953, signed Fr. Filip Bednorz, Vicar.[26] I presumed that all my problems had to do with Lagosz, so I wrote to Cardinal Stefan Wyszyński, Primate of Poland, outlining my difficulties. The Cardinal wrote directly to Vicar Bednorz; what exactly was said I don't know, but when Bednorz received it, he was clearly unnerved. Finally I got a letter assigning me to the Stalinogród [Katowice] diocese for a three year probationary period. I informed Bednorz

---

26 [See http://www.encyklo.pl/index.php5?title=Bednorz_Filip .]

that [based on my experience on the job] he should not treat me as some sort of trainee, like a minder of cattle or an apprentice to a master craftsman.

Anyway, I got substitute positions while priests were on vacation...in one place, as long as four weeks...in one place, where the priest usually got one hundred zlotys for a Mass, I got only twenty-seven zlotys, in cash (they deducted the cost of wine and hosts)... Finally I went to Bednorz for another assignment but heard there were none to be had, and that I'd have to wait from half a year to a full year for something else. He suddenly said there's a chaplaincy in a hospital. I went right away but found out there was no such position, though if I wanted to stay, I could get one hundred zlotys a month, but from which I'd have to pay for my own living expenses (room, food, travel, etc.) I returned to Bednorz and told him flat out, "May God pay you back for the way you've treated me in my tragic situation," and I left, never to return. I had a few scruples about those words later when I heard that he was involved in a fatal automobile accident on January 13, 1954.

I then went around to various bishoprics to find work, starting with Cracow, Tarnów, Kielce. I was always turned down due to lack of openings, though I knew a bishop could make a place if he wished.

I chalked it all up to being a Greek Catholic priest. Hatred for the Greek Catholic rite started under the influence of Franco-German clergy, and in Poland in 1018 after the return of Bolesław Chrobry from his expedition to Kyiv to subjugate it, and this pursuit has lasted to this day. A witness to this is the pile of complaints which were sent to the bishops' Curias. I heard of one bishop no longer living, who, at a bishops' conference, on hearing of the liquidation of the Union of Brest [by the Soviet Union in 1946], jumped up and shouted, "Praise God, we got rid of the Unia!" What kind of logic is that? It's all supposed to be the same church. He was happy about the fall of a part of the Catholic Church. The Devil has his supporters. What a sad witness that bishop gave.

After four dioceses had refused me, I went to Opole and it turned out that the Curial Vicar Fr. Emil Kobierzycki[27] was an old colleague from our university days. He offered me an unfilled spot in the deanery of Niemodlin, the parish of Rogi, for which I was grateful. During the time he was in charge of the diocese, I didn't have the slightest problem. He was a true friend and a great person.

The parish of Rogi was made up of Poles from every part of Poland, but mostly from the Eastern borderlands and the Kielce region. There were only

---

27   [See http://www.encyklo.pl/index.php5?title=Kobierzycki_Emil .]

ten German families. Most immigrated to West Germany rather soon. Only one German family remained and it soon moved to another place. The material and moral situation of the parish wasn't very good. In all the villages, there were cooperatives [collective farms] and there was no real development. People working in the cooperatives were dissatisfied because they didn't like that sort of survival. Work was forced and nobody cared about anything. Everyone tried to get as much as he could for himself. Fights among collective farm members were a daily occurrence. Members got lazy and they didn't try to put together any property investment for themselves. Most people didn't go to work, claiming illness; they were completely demoralized. On the other hand, every Sunday evening there were dance parties with a full buffet and plenty of alcohol. There were fights among the youth ending in court sentences.

The first priest in this place was Władysław Przygodziński and even though he tried, he didn't get much respect. He did try to raise moral standards but without much result. When a canonical visitation occurred in 1949... the parishioners used the occasion to accuse the priest of all sorts of errors and omissions having nothing to do with reality. In answer, the visitor, Fr. Bolesław Kominek,[28] promised a better priest and sent Stefan Juszczyk of the [Greek Catholic] Basilian Order, the former Vicar of Niemodlin. He came to the Rectory in Rogi from which everything had been carried off by the parishioners. The last German pastor had left everything, luxurious furniture, pictures, rugs, dishes, clothing, tablecloths, and crystal. The parishioners even took out the doors and windows. He lived in an empty building and he begged the people, from the pulpit, to return at least, the doors and windows, so he could live there. Only the worst junk was returned. Thus the rectory stood empty and devastated from 1949, and the local government seized the building as abandoned property. From that point, every pastor in Rogi had to pay rent to use the building. That situation lasted until 1971 when all such properties were returned to the church.

Fr. Juszczyk lived like a monk, very simply, very ascetically, but when parishioners found out he was a Greek Catholic, they started a boycott and complained about him...not only to church authorities but also to the militia and the security service. Finally he was transferred to another parish. Today, he is in Canada as a missionary.

That's the parish I got, with the bad luck that I was the second Greek Catholic priest in a row. For a long time, the parishioners thought of me as

---

28   [See http://www.encyklo.pl/index.php5?title=Kominek_Bolesław .]

a Latin Catholic and were open and trusting towards me. But as soon as they heard from a neighboring priest that I was a Greek Catholic, things changed. I felt rejection and a negative attitude at every step. I suffered from this but attempted to be good and open to everyone and didn't react to any provocation. As I determinedly carried out my church and school obligations, things slowly got better. For my pastoral work, I got a small sum but I acted with everybody in such a way as to give no one a chance to be dissatisfied.

The stupidity connected with hatred showed itself in connection with a celebration of the pilgrimage of the Czestochowa Mother of God Icon [which was exhibited at various churches]. As part of this activity, we conducted a Greek Catholic liturgy. I did the service on the last day of the celebration at eight o'clock a.m. The church was full, and as soon as I started, on a sign given by one of the missionary fathers (Wojtaszek) the parishioners, disregarding the Holy place, began a revolt against the Eastern Rite service. The lights were turned on and with a great amount of noise, the people left the church shouting "We don't want any Ukrainian Mass." Inside, only a few were left and I continued to the end with the assistance of some Sisters who escaped in fear as soon as they could. The groups taking part in the protest poured hatred on me and the Eastern Rite. They sent a delegation to the militia and the secret service charging me with being a traitor to the Republic because I carried out a Liturgy of St. John Chrysostom. A delegation also went to the dean of the region.

On Sunday, I explained the liturgy issue and pointed out their disbelief and stupidity. Finally things settled down. This feeling among the common people was caused by a few priests, who over the ages built a hatred for the Eastern Rite. One of the French bishops, lecturing about indestructibility, said, "For close to two thousand years, priests have tried different methods to overthrow the Catholic Church but it stands to this day, and it will stand to the end of the world, because it was instituted by God, indestructible, and that is the best proof that it is indestructible." How much truth is in those words?

A few priests are the greatest destroyer of the Catholic Church. Doesn't a priest spreading hatred for one of the Catholic Rites[29] become one of its destroyers? Sad but true.

In the meantime, there was a sudden change in the leadership of Opole diocese. Bishop Franciszek Jop[30] from Cracow became the diocesan Ordinary and Fr. Emil Kobierzycki took over a parish in Bytom. Finally we got

29   [The Catholic church recognizes seventeen rites, only one of which is the Latin Rite.]
30   [See http://www.encyklo.pl/index.php5?title=Jop_Franciszek .]

a bishop. In the first year of his administration, before the academic year began, I brought one of my parishioners to meet him with the request that he be accepted into the seminary...but he was turned down. Next, I took him to the Archbishop in Wrocław and he was accepted without a problem. This young man carried himself well in all things, better than his colleagues. I later asked the seminary director how he was doing and was told "Cleric Rudawski is the pride of the seminary". Antonii Rudawski finished the Higher Seminary in Wrocław, passed his examinations with high marks and was ordained. His first Mass was in Rogi and his first position in Oława, a place where his predecessors didn't last more than a couple of months— he spent five years there. Today, he heads one of Wrocław's churches and is recognized as an exemplary chaplain. Thus, the question comes up, why didn't Bishop Jop accept him into the diocesan seminary? That was my first and last audience with that Bishop.

Anyway, I have carried out pastoral duties in Rogi for fifteen years and fulfilled all priestly duties laid upon me. Obligation has first place with me, whether services or catechism. Our dean, Fr. Joniec, visiting during religious classes was pleased with the children's answers and after the visit said that such a level of understanding he had yet to meet elsewhere. It wasn't worse when Bishop Henry Grządziel came. My pupil Bahrii even won a first award in a religious contest. Canonical visits always turned out well.

As a pastor, I took part in charitable activities, in the spirit of encyclicals of Pope John XXIII and Paul VI. Based on an understanding arrived at on April 14, 1950, signed by the Polish episcopate and the Polish People's Republic...the Central Administration of the "Caritas" Organization asked me to join...since that organization's aim is to help those in difficulties due to fate. In order to be correct, I wrote church authorities in Opole for permission but for a whole month got no answer. Based on the notion *"Qui tacit, consentire videtur"* (silence means assent), I joined. In that institution, I carried out the obligations of a vice president and president of the Priests' Circle. For me and for others, Bishop Jop's attitude towards Caritas cannot be understood. He looked crossly at participation in Caritas, refusing advancement to members, not even attending their funerals and even removing member priests if anything bad came up... [yet] working with Caritas is of the highest value in the Christian ideal...Work in Caritas houses for old people without homes, work with the sick, orphans and partial orphans, with special-needs people and even imbeciles shows the great hearts of clerics...and show their love of God and His people. I would be happy if someone would explain why it is wrong that priests take care of Caritas units and that orders of sisters actually run

Russian Orthodox church of St. Michael the Archangel (1898 - 1923) central Warsaw, Poland, prior to demolition in 1923. (Photo courtesy of the Library of Congress, LC-F82-996.)

them, especially since the sisters do get a small pay but send the money to their Mother Houses because they live in the Caritas units. Is it better for lay people to run these operations rather than Catholic Sisters?

These problems should be openly discussed. If work in Caritas is seen as a great sin by some bishops, then these bishops ought to publicly state the nature of the sin. Such a step by bishops would discharge the tension felt among priests. The bishops need not divide priests into first and second categories, good ones and bad ones...

I once read [the Russian language book] *Pouchenie* (Sermons), of the famous Orthodox archpriest John of Kronstadt, who the Orthodox faithful feel is a great saint, due to the miracles which took place after his death. In one sermon, he says: "the greatest human offense is that offense committed by a bishop who was consecrated by God."

I remember that archpriest because he foresaw the destruction of Warsaw. During Tsarist times, the Russians built the Russian Orthodox Church of St. Michael the Archangel [at 12 Ujazdowskie Ave.], in Warsaw.[31] It was one of the most beautiful holy places that the Tsarist regime built in the Russian Empire. The church was consecrated by John of Kronstadt in 1894 and in his sermon he said: "Whoever puts his hand on this church will bring destruction on this city and the people will die." Years passed by and Poland regained its independence. There was a new government and a new set of rules. The leader, Józef Piłsudski, ordered that the church be torn down and in its place a military parade square be built...unfortunately, the church's construction was so solid that it couldn't be knocked over, so a foreign apparatus called a "Devil's Machine" was brought in and with the help of dynamite, the cathedral was blown up in 1923... In the process, three hundred people were killed.[32] The flat area made on the spot was called Piłsudski Square and Piłsudski himself ended tragically. World War Two came which led to the outbreak of the Warsaw uprising and during that uprising, the words of John of Kronstadt came true. Piłsudski offended the temple and the city of Warsaw was destroyed and its people died. A temple built to serve God should remain to the end of its existence and serve God, not human passions.

The celebration of my eightieth year of life fell in 1968, to which I added a celebration of my consecration as a priest [1916]. The main celebration was to be the following year. I only celebrated the fiftieth anniversary of my consecration, which I celebrated in the presence of a large number of parishioners. I received greetings from school children and parishioners. I received blessings from Pope Paul VI and Cardinal Primate Wyszyński, Cardinal Josyf Slipyi, Archbishop Jan Buczko, Bishop Wacław Wycisk [and many others] but my own bishop sent me nothing...there also was a celebration for me put together by...Caritas.

In July 1967, I asked the Curia in Opole for a vacation from the parish; I didn't get it, but rather they sent me an assistant priest, Stanisław Pelesz. He arrived on September 1, 1967 and told me that he had special orders from

31   [See http://pl.wikipedia.org/wiki/Cerkiew_św._Michała_Archanioła_w_Warszawie .]
32   [This story appears to be apocryphal.]

the Ordinary to, in fact, take over and not allow me to carry out any pastoral functions...so I wrote to the Curia asking just what the assistant was supposed to do. The reply was that I was still the pastor and the assistant was to work under my direction until such time as I could no longer carry out my duties— then he was to take over and I was to retire. Seeing that the Curia's reply was not in accordance with what Pelesz had told me, I went to Opole to see the Bishop personally. I waited for half an hour in a dark corridor outside his apartment. He finally appeared and advanced toward me to enter his apartment but then he recognized me. He turned around and ran down the stairs in such a way as to break a leg. My God, the bishop is running away from his own priest, I thought. I returned home. The double meaning of information coming from the Curia was explained to me later by the brother of Stanisław Pelesz, Wiktor Pelesz. In the Curia there was a double game going on. On the one side, the personnel of the Curia scrupulously followed canon law and every document coming out of the Curia was one hundred percent in order. A second set of orders was given by the bishop himself orally, often not in accordance with correctness. That's when I understood the conundrum.

Anyway, I received Fr. Pelesz in a brotherly fashion and assigned him half the rectory, though I didn't have to because as it was a government building, I paid the rent. For the first month, I fed him for free but he treated me as his worst enemy. During the year he was in Rogi, he caused me a lot of trouble. In the worst way, he put me down in front of my parishioners and organized people against me...he presented himself as the right-hand man of the bishop, a person who was to put priests in order. He, however, showed himself to be a common *Hochstapler* (swindler, con artist). He could fool good people and bishops and bring praise on himself and make himself a hero. As a priest, he was dishonest and didn't carry out his obligations. Religious services were theatrical in nature and sermons were banal and not well prepared. He had no time to teach religion in school, because he was gone from the parish from Tuesday morning to Saturday evening or Sunday morning, telling people he was with the bishop. Sometimes he disappeared for a whole week or all summer. Vespers on Sundays were rare and Holy Days were served without preparation.

Finally I appealed to the Curia, and the dean of our area...after an investigation, removed Fr. Pelesz. Fr. Josef Onyszków became the pastor but the ill done by Fr. Pelesz took a long time to heal. Everything got better and I began to be treated nicely; nothing was happening. I owe a lot to two auxiliary bishops, Adamiuk and Wyciskōw, who treated me well. However, even

Grave of Archpriest Ioann Polianskii, Jan. 20 1888-Nov. 6 1978, Eternal Memory. Rogi, 2011.

though they visited me with blessings during my illness, I was still feeling low from the way Fr. Pelesz treated me and I became very sick. I had high blood pressure and half my body became paralyzed...and glaucoma threatened my sight. I lay for days on end in bed and had to be moved to a chair by others. But my mental abilities were still intact and I could at least do mental work.

I have no desire in this writing to insult anybody but rather to present the facts as they were...now I am eighty-six years old and I stand before my grave. At any moment I can leave this world, and I didn't want to leave any debts. I extend my hand to everyone everywhere whom I might have hurt or insulted, and to all those who hurt and insulted me. The first I beg to forgive me for all my sins and the second I forgive, with my whole heart, for their sins against me.

I hope that God will forgive me when I stand before him. In my life, I was arrested seven times by different political orders and once even condemned to death. Thanks to God, I survived it all.

In regard to my earthly fatherland, I carried out my duties and was decorated twice with the "Cross of Service," based on both interwar legislation of February 18, 1939 and postwar legislation of February 21, 1964.

[Father Ioann Polianskii died in Rogi on September 6, 1978 and he is buried there.]

Parishioners of the now nonexistent village of Kamianka on a festive occasion, 1930s.

Pastor to the Lemkos: Fr. Ioann Polianskii

What the archives tell us

Ioann Polianskii was born January 20, 1888 in the [now non-existent] village of Banica, Gorlice County, in the province of Galicia of the Austro-Hungarian Empire, into a family of middle class peasants. His father was Teodor and his mother Maria (née Prytsyk) Polianskii.[1] He had four sisters, Anna, Joanna, Juliana and Maria as well as a brother, Dymitr. His early childhood was spent in his native village. When he turned seven years old he went off to elementary school in Gorlice where he completed two years of elementary school and then two more in Nowy Sącz. In 1903 he began studies in the Imperial and Monarchial Middle School (*gymnazium*) in Sanok where he graduated on June 22, 1911, and in October of the same year he began studies at the Greek Catholic Seminary in Lviv and also enrolled in the Theological Department of that city's university. After the outbreak of WW I, though still a student, he was arrested (September 8, 1914) by the Austro-Hungarian authorities on suspicion of spreading pro-Russian propaganda and was sent to the Talerhof internment camp near Graz. What happened in that camp as well as the slights and threats he had to endure strengthened his separatist tendencies in relation to Ukrainians.[2] He saw himself as a Lemko. After release from internment he continued his education in the Greek Catholic Seminary in Przemyśl. After completing his studies in June 1916 he married Stefania Papp, the daughter of Fr. Orest Papp, Greek Catholic pastor in Wierchomla Wielka, and Sofia Lipska.[3] On December 19, 1916 he was ordained in Stary Sambor by the Stanisławów bishop Hryhorii Khomyshyn.[4]

On the first of January, 1917, Fr. Polianskii was appointed the Administrator [a temporary post] of the Tuligłowy parish in Mościska county. He

---

1 Archiwum Państwowe w Przemyślu (further APP), Archive of the Greek Catholic Eparchy, sign. 9329, p. 123.
2 See Fr. Polianskii's autobiography in this volume.
3 APP, Archive of the Greek Catholic Eparchy of Przemyśl.
4 See: *Manual (Schematism) of the Apostolic Administration of Lemkovshchyna for 1936*, Lviv, 1936, p. xvi. Available at http://lemko.org/pdf/shem1936.pdf .

stayed there until October 15, 1918, when the bishop of Przemyśl, Iosafat Kotsylovskii, appointed him Administrator of the parish of Smolnik, in Lesko County. He remained Administrator until May 18, 1922 when he became the pastor/rector [priest-in-charge] after passing the pastor's exam.[5] In 1926 his wife died.

In his parish he was heavily engaged both in pastoral and civic work. He was, among other things, on the local school board and before the parliamentary elections of September 13, 1930 he served as head of the local electoral commission.

Fr. Polianskii played a very active role in the 1930s in the Apostolic Administration of the Lemko Region [hereinafter "AAL"] which was established to halt the expanding "return to Orthodoxy" movement in the Lemko Region.[6] This process became public on November 16, 1926 when practically the whole of the Tylawa parish converted to Orthodoxy [to the Polish Autocephalous Orthodox Church derived from Russian Orthodoxy]. Between 1926 and 1934, according to Catholic count seventeen thousand people converted,[7] or by Orthodox count, twenty-five thousand.[8]

Actually plans to set up a separate Lemko diocese first appeared in the second half of the nineteenth century,[9] but only after whole parishes went over to Orthodoxy, based on dissatisfaction with the policies of modernization and Ukrainianization followed by Bishop Kotsylovskii of Przemyśl, did the Apostolic See [Rome] decide to act. Lemkos had reacted against the sending of celibate priests of decidedly Ukrainian orientation to Lemko parishes, which attacked the heretofore strong Lemko priestly clans, and the bishop's order to cease using in the liturgy the phrase *i vas pravoslavnikh khristiian* (and

5   See: Dmytro Blazejowskyj, *Historical Šematism of the Eparchy of Peremyśl including the Apostolic Administration of Lemkivśćyna (1828-1939)*, Lviv, 1995, p. 808.

6   Archiwum Akt Nowych w Warszawie (further AAN), Ministerstwo Wyznań Religijnych i Oświecenia Publicznego (further MWRiOP), sign. 1158, p. 229.

7   See: Anna Krochmal, "Stosunki między grekokatolikami a prawosławnymi na Łemkowszczyźnie w latach 1926-1939," in *Łemkowie w historii i kulturze Karpat*, ed. Jerzy Czajkowski, cz. 1, Rzeszów 1992, p. 289, http://lemko.org/pdf/LHKK1. pdf; Krzysztof Z. Nowakowski, "Sytuacja polityczne na Łemkowszczyźnie w latach 1918-1939," ibidem, p. 324; Jarosław Moklak, "Kształtowanie się struktur Kościoła prawosławnego na Łemkowszczyźnie w II Rzeczypospolitej," [in:] *Przez dwa stulecia: XIX i XX wiek. Studia historyczne ofiarowane prof. Wacławowi Felczakowi*, ed. W. Frazik, B. Nykiel, E. Orman et al., Kraków 1993, p. 56-57.

8   Anna Krochmal, "Stosunki między grekokatolikami a prawosławnymi...," p. 290.

9   See Part II, Section 4 of this volume.

you rightly-worshipping [orthodox] Christians). [Parishioners knew the liturgy by heart and any change was immediately noticed]. The mass character of the conversions is seen in a letter of the mayor of Gorlice to the governor of Cracow Province in 1928. He wrote, "I ask that you order that birth certificates not be issued because whole communities are massively seeking such documents" [which were needed to register a change of church adherence in government offices].[10] Beyond this, a change in church affiliation brought on violent strife: seizing control of churches, battles between villagers and theft of church accoutrements. In many cases the police had to intervene in strength to separate battling sides.[11]

In this situation, Lemko activists met with Apostolic Nuncio Francesco Marmaggi [in Warsaw] (October 22, 1932) and gave him a petition , signed by representatives of all Lemko villages in Nowy Sacz county, requesting the establishment of a separate Lemko church unit.[12] The same petition was sent in the next year to the Polish Primate [chief bishop] August Cardinal Hłond asking him to support a separating out of a Lemko church unit from the Przemysl diocese and making it directly dependant on the Holy See.[13] One of the delegates was Ioann Polianskii.[14] On February 10, 1934 a decree of the Holy See *Quo aptius consularet* was issued, creating the AAL;[15] 111 parishes with 136 clerics and 127,305 parishioners were separated from the Przemyśl Greek Catholic diocese.[16]

The first Apostolic Administrator appointed by the Holy See was Fr. Dr. Bazyli Mastsiukh, Professor of Canon Law at the Greek Catholic Seminary in Przemyśl.[17] A residence for him was set up in Rymanow-Zdrój in Krosno County. Because the parish in Smolnik in Lesko County was not part of the

---

10 AAN, MWRiOP, sign. 354, p. 169.
11 APP, Administracja Apostolska Łemkowszczyzny (further AAŁ), sign. 41, p. 275; Archiwum Państwowe w Krakowie, sign. 32, p. 7; ibidem, sign. 279, p. 162.
12 P. Przybylski, *Rola duchowieństwa greckokatolickiego*, p. 77.
13 Again see Fr. Polianskii's autobiography. See also: Bohdan Prach, Administracja Apostolska Łemkowszczyzny, p. 301; Mariusz Ryńca, *Administracja Apostolska Łemkowszczyzny w latach 1945-1947*, Kraków 2001, pp. 13-14; Eugeniusz Senko, *Administracja Apostolska Łemkowszczyzny (1934-1947)*, Nieznane losy Łemków w Polsce, Nowy Sącz 2007, p. 58-60.
14 Eugeniusz Senko, *Administracja Apostolska Łemkowszczyzny...*, p. 60.
15 *I Decretum. Erectionis Administrationis Apostolicae*, "Acta Apostolicae Sedis" [1934], No. 27, p. 80.
16 *Manual (Schematism) of the Apostolic Administration of Lemkovshchyna for 1936*, p. 167.
17 Stanisław Stępień, *Masciuch Wasylij*, "Studia Polsko-Ukraińskie", Przemyśl 2006, Vol. 1, pp. 246-248. An extensive bibliography about his life is included there.

LEMKOVYNA

new Church unit, Fr. Polianskii, on January 23, 1935, asked the Administrator to admit him to the clerical staff of the new AAL. After consultation with bishop Kotsylovskii, the Administrator took him on and on February 27, 1935 appointed him Chancellor [chief administrator after the Apostolic Administrator himself] and reporter for the Curia [the AAL central administrative body].[18] At the same time he became the rector of the nearby parish in Wróblik Królewski.[19] Later Fr. Polianskii received additional appointments: Advisor to the Curia (June 25, 1935), judge of ecclesiastical matters (July 17, 1935), examiner in church affairs (July 27, 1935), and on July 27, 1935 member of the AAL Council for the Purity of the Faith and Morality.[20] Thus Polianskii became the closest collaborator of the Administrator. The very first pastoral letter of Administrator Mastsiukh, *"Do Lemków"*(To the Lemkos), informed believers about the reason for the establishment of a separate church organization for the Lemkos, explained the principles of the Catholic faith, and appealed to all to remain within the Greek Catholic fold.[21] Fr. Polianskii not only performed his pastoral duties but also assiduously carried out his advisory and Curial functions for the AAL. In 1935 he set up in Wróblik a school for "diaks" (cantors) who were especially necessary for the Eastern Rite [since services were sung, not spoken].[22] Unfortunately, despite his best efforts, not enough enrollees showed up so the school closed.[23]

After the unforeseen death of Apostolic Administrator Mastsiukh on March 12, 1936, Ukrainian newspapers immediately carried stories claiming that the AAL would be closed. The Apostolic Nuncio's office, however, as early as March 14, 1936 informed the public of Fr. Polianskii's appointment as Acting Administrator with the rights of Vicar *sede vacante* (during the vacancy of the position of Administrator).[24] Polianskii wrote a pastoral

---

18   *Schematism*, pp. xvii-xviii, 118,163.
19   *"Wisti Apostolskoji Administraciji Łemkiwszczyny"* (News of the Apostolic Administration of Lemkovyna, further as "News of the AAL"), 1935, no. I, p. 8. The official inauguration of Fr. Polianskii as pastor in Wróblik Królewski took place on January 17, 1936.
20   *Schematism*, pp. xvi-xviii.
21   See: *Pershe pastyrske poslanie Dra Vasylia Mastsiukha Apostolskoho Administratora dla Lemkivshchyny "Do Lemkiv"* ("To the Lemkos," First pastoral letter of Dr. Vasyli Mastsiukh, Apostolic Administrator of Lemkovshchyna), Lviv 1935.
22   APP, AAŁ, sign. 99, pp. 56-57.
23   Ibidem, pp. 65-71.
24   APP, AAŁ, sign. 1, p. 1-6; AAN, Ministerstwo Spraw Wewnętrznych, sign. 964, pp. 131-132.

letter in which he requested support in his new office and confirmed that the AAL would not be eliminated.[25] He also initiated the collection of data in order to publish a "Schematism" (manual or handbook) of the AAL. This handbook was printed in 1936 under the editorship of Fr. Stefan Jodłowski. It is a compendium of knowledge about Lemkovyna and all the parishes of the AAL. In the introductory part there is information about the territory of and the origins of the Lemkos which was stated to be based on the tribe of the *Bilo-Horvaty* (White Croats). Further, it was stated that Lemko Christianity was founded on the mission of Cyril and Methodius to Moravia, and, thus, started a hundred years before the Christianization of Kyivan Rus'. The larger part of the book listed each parish and, besides the usual data found in such publications, supplied information about the inhabitants of each village including how many Roman Catholics, Jews and sectarians lived there, plus a short history of the village and a picture of the village church. Also included was information about schools and about both secular and religious organizations.

During the comparatively short time of his being in charge, Fr. Polianskii was unusually active in publishing article in the church publication *"Visti Apostolskoi Administratsii"* (News of the Apostolic Administration) which started in 1935. In 1936 he published a thirty-two page brochure entitled *"O verkhovnoi vlasti sv. Apostola Petra i ioho naslidnikov v Khristovoi Tserkvi i priznavaniiu vlasti na Lemkovshchyni"* (Concerning the leadership of St. Peter and his successors in Christ's Church and its recognition in the Lemko Region), in which he explained the source of St. Peter's and his successors' primacy. He further laid out the history of the church in the Lemko Region, condemned national and religious splits, and called on Lemkos to be loyal to their church and the land in which they were born.

As advisor to the AAL he battled with every sort of Ukrainian nationalism. Priests active in the Ukrainian movement were deprived of any function in the AAL, which caused protests to be lodged with the Nuncio [in Warsaw] and even with the Vatican,[26] and he was publicly accused of Moscophilism.[27] His severe attitude toward Ukrainians probably torpedoed his chances of succeeding to the Administratorship. The Nuncio did not want to further

---

25 Ibidem, sign. 52, p. 107.
26 Eugeniusz Senko, *Administracja Apostolska...*, p. 83.
27 AAŁ, sign. 11, pp. 78-80. Fr. Polianskii did not represent Moscophile views, but those of Old Rus'.

inflame the religious situation in Lemkovyna and did not support Polianskii's candidacy even though it was pushed by the *Staro-Rus'* (Old Rus') movement among the Lemkos.[28]

On July 23, 1936 the Congregation for the Eastern Church issued the decree *Cum per obitum* appointing the Archdeacon of the Greek Catholic diocese of Stanisławów and professor in the seminary there, Iakov Medvetskii, as the new Administrator.[29] Fr. Medvetskii took over the AAL on October 3, 1936,[30] while concurrently the whole Curia received a letter of thanks from the Nuncio, A. Pacini.[31]

Fr. Polianskii remained at his pre-Acting Administrator posts and worked well with Medvetskii who, not being a Lemko, needed help in handling questions of local language, customs and mentality.

Fr. Polianskii always cooperated with Polish authorities and was active in civil and patriotic activities to the extent that he received a state medal in the form of the "Gold Service Cross."[32]

The outbreak of WW II began a very difficult time for Lemkos and the AAL.[33] After the designation of the border between the German "General Government" and the Soviet occupation zone, almost all the AAL lay in German hands, except for four parishes (Olchow, Załuż-Wujskie, Tyrawa Solna, and Międzybrodzie) which ended up in the Soviet zone. The war caused a substantial churning of populations. Onto Lemko land came a few thousand refugees from the Soviet side, a goodly number being intelligentsia and clergy.[34] Movement to the east also occurred. The Nazis and the Soviets signed a population exchange agreement on November 16, 1939, on the basis of which some five

---

28   Ibidem, pp. 165-168.
29   Stanisław Stępień, "Medwecki Jakiw," [in:] *Encyklopedia Katolicka*, Vol. XII, ed. Stanisław Wilk et al., Lublin 2008, p. 397.
30   Eugeniusz Senko, *Administracja Apostolska...*, pp. 85-86.
31   APP, AAŁ, sign. 11, p. 169.
32   APP, AAŁ, sign. 52, k. 106.
33   For more on this subject see: K.Z. Nowakowski, "Administracja Apostolska Łemkowszczyzny w latach 1939-1947," in *Polska-Ukraina. 1000 lat sąsiedztwa*, ed. S. Stępień, Przemyśl 1996, Vol. 3, pp. 231-232; S. Stępień, "The Greek Catholic Church in the Lemko Region in WWII and its Liquidation (1939-1947)," in *The Lemko Region, 1939-1947. War, Occupation and Deportation*, ed. P. Best and J. Moklak, Cracow – New Haven 2002, pp. 183-189.
34   See: V. Kubiiovych, *Ukrajintsi w Heneralnij Hubernii. 1939-1941. Istoriia Ukrainskoho Tsentralnoho Komitetu*, Chicago 1975, p. 289.

thousand Lemkos emigrated to Soviet Ukraine.[35] This population mixture had an immediate effect on the Lemko Region. Many of those of Moscophile or Sovietophile persuasion left for the USSR, while convinced Ukrainians flowed in.[36] These latter immediately tried to take over schools, cooperatives and social institutions and to eliminate those of Lemko orientation. The very first activity was to "Ukrainianize" the AAL.[37] Leadership in this activity came from the Ukrainian Central Committee headed by Prof. Volodymyr Kubiiovych in Cracow, which had been established at the end of October 1939 in cooperation with the German occupation authorities.[38] When it appeared that the Holy See would not agree to the liquidation of the AAL, the Cracow Ukrainians decided to take it over instead. A certain Greek Catholic archpriest, the former vice Rector of the Greek Catholic Seminary in Lviv and a refugee [from the Soviet occupation], Alexander Malynovskii, who was already busy in Ukrainian social activities in the German General Government [there was an unspoken alliance between the Nazi German authorities and Ukrainian activists] was recruited to take control of the AAL. Since Administrator Medvetskii was already gravely ill, Malynovskii was pushed forward to be his deputy. This was accomplished by Governor Hans Frank [who was executed after WW II for war crimes] who pressured the Apostolic Nuncio in Berlin, Archbishop Cesare Orsenigo, to send a letter to Fr. Medvetskii requesting the appointment of Malynovskii as his Vicar General [deputy administrator]. Medvetskii, wishing to avoid conflict, acceded on June 10, 1940.[39]

Malynovskii's situation was strengthened when the ailing Medvetskii was sent off to a hospital in Cracow and Malynovskii was left in charge. As may be supposed, relations with Polianskii were tense. Then on October 23, 1940 Malynovskii completely reorganized the AAL Curia, discharging Polianskii and replacing him with a fellow refugee from Lviv, Fr. Bohdan Lysk.[40] The

35   I. Hnat, *Doba Heneralnoii Huberni (1939-1944),* [in:] *Lemkivshchyna - zemla - ludy istorija - kultura,* ed. B. Struminskyj, New York, 1988, Vol. I, pp. 201-202. http://lemko.org/pdf/lemkivshchyna1.pdf
36   P. Potichnyj, "The Lemkos in the Ukrainian National Movement During and After WWII," in *The Lemko Region, 1939-1947...,* p. 149-169.
37   Archiwum Państwowe w Przemyślu (further as APP), Archiwum Biskupstwa Greckokatolickiego w Przemyślu (further as ABGK), sygn. 9485, k. 46.
38   V. Kubiiovych, op. cit., pp. 17-95; see also: R. Torzecki, *Polacy i Ukraińcy. Sprawa ukraińska w czasie II wojny światowej na terenie II Rzeczypospolitej,* Warsaw 1993, p. 56.
39   V. Kubiiovych, op. cit., p. 290.
40   E. Senko, op. cit., 138.

rest of the Curia was replaced with Ukrainophile clergy.[41] In January Deputy Administrator Malynovskii retitled the AAL newsletter as *"Visti Apostolskoi Administratsii Lemkivshchiny v General-Gubernatorstvi"* (News of the Apostolic Administration of the Lemko Region in the General Government) and announce that hereafter the language of church affairs would be Ukrainian while that of secular affairs, German.

Fr. Iakov Medvetskii died on January 27, 1941, and he was buried in Sanok on February 1.[42] Alexander Malynovskii, based on the support of the Berlin Nuncio, became the new fully empowered Administrator as of February 3, 1941.[43]

Father Polianskii was arrested on June 23, 1941, the day after the German-Soviet war broke out, along with seven other priests and one monk, all suspected of "Moscophilism" and imprisoned in Nowy Sącz. After interrogation, they were all freed on July 10 but with an order to send them to Radom Province. Polianskii was kept under police surveillance and on August 6, along with the others, taken off to Kielce [a city in Radom Province].[44] They were at first interned in an old schoolhouse with the necessity of reporting to the Gestapo on a daily basis. After six months they were allowed to seek separate accommodations but were forbidden to leave the city. The local Latin Rite bishop, Czesław Kaczmarek, received a special memorandum from the internees on September 16, 1941.[45] Several internees, including Fr. Orszak and Polianskii requested permission to celebrate service in the Latin Rite and to assist in pastoral duties in Latin Rite parishes [for which they could get some compensation] and Bishop Kaczmarek sent a positive reply.

The internees also sought to be freed from Gestapo control but this didn't happen until a few months before the end of the war. The situation of the internees was very comfortable for Administrator Malynovskii so he didn't ask for them to be released nor did he support their own requests for freedom. The internees were received very well in Kielce as can be seen from Polianskii's autobiography:

41   APP, AAŁ, sygn. 54, p. 46, 53; "News of the AAL," 1941, no. XVI.
42   See obituary of Fr. Medvetskii – "News of the AAL" 1941, no. XVI, p. 25-28.
43   V. Kubiiovych, op.cit., pp. 290-291.
44   Stanisław Nabywaniec, "The Greek Catholic Clergy and Lemko National Orientation," in *Does a Fourth Rus' Exist? Concerning Cultural Identity in the Carpathian Region,* ed. Paul Best and Stanisław Stepien, Przemyśl – Higganum 2009, p. 144.
45   This memorandum is kept at the Archiwum Diecezjalne in Kielce (*Akta kapłanów obcych 1940-1942,* sygn. OP-17/4), published in Fr. S. Nabywaniec, "The Greek Catholic Clergy...," op. cit., pp. 142-145.

During our stay in Kielce we were protected by Bishop Czesław Kacz-marek, a man with a golden heart. We have to thank him since we had no money and he supported us so we weren't orphaned. We could daily serve mass and take advantage of recollections and all services of God's mercy. Following the example of brotherly love, Bishop Czesław Kacz-marek, Bishop Franciszek Sonik and other Kielce priests were for us true friends. The Kielce believers showed us sympathy and understand-ing. Such support made our bitter life more bearable and we have fond memories of it.

The military changes in the second half of 1944, with the Soviets getting closer and closer, changed the behavior of Fr. Malynovskii towards the intern-ees. He asked the General Government authorities to release them. The first priests to return to the Lemko Region, on October 23, 1944, were Fathers Khyliak, Sembratovych, E. Venhrynovych, V. Venhrynovych and Vasyli Bar-tko. The longest detained was Polianskii who only returned to his parish after the Soviet army had passed though.[46] The land was not, however, peaceful, because there were attacks on Lemko villages from all sides: from Poles, the UPA, and all sorts of bandit groups. In fear of his life Fr. Polianskii had to flee from Wróblik Królewski to Krynica. He was appointed administrator of the parish in Czyrna in Nowy Sącz County.[47] However because [much] of the Lemko population had been deported to Soviet Ukraine he again requested to be bi-ritual [to be able to serve in both the Latin and Eastern Rites] and ob-tained them directly from the Polish Primate, Cardinal Hłond, on November 5, 1945. At that same time, wishing to escape deportation to Soviet Ukraine, he left for the "Recovered Territories" in Western Poland, going to the city of Wrocław [in German, Breslau] and applying to the Wrocław church Ad-ministrator [regular bishops were not yet assigned to the "Recovered Territo-ries"] for an assignment. On January 7, 1946 he was sent to a suburban parish in Prochów where he stayed until September 1946 when the local Admin-istrator sent him to Żórawina in Wrocław County. A bit later, on October 18, 1946, he also obtained a position as a religion teacher in that village and the neighboring Węgry. He also took upon himself the obligation of helping Lemkos who had been forcibly settled there as part of the *Akcja "Wisła"* (Op-eration "Vistula"), which angered local [Polish] parishioners who requested assignment of a different priest. While it is true Polianskii rarely performed

---

46   APP, AAŁ, sygn. 50, p. 129; Ks. J. Polański, op. cit., pp. 39-40.
47   Archiwum Wrocławskie.

Greek Catholic services he did not refuse to carry out Greek Catholic burials. Despite the fact that some parishioners defended him, on March 1, 1948
he was sent to a new parish in Gniechowice, also in Wrocław County. At this
time he tried to immigrate to the USA where a sister lived and where he supposed he could work in the Greek Catholic Church. Unfortunately for him
he didn't receive permission to leave, neither from state authorities nor from
ecclesiastical ones. The latter refused because of a great lack of priests in the
Recovered Territories.

Fr Polianskii was personally very sensitive to any perceived slight and at the
same time he was loyal to the state authorities. He naively believed that the
new Polish [communist] authorities really intended to establish a just society
and to struggle against poverty. He especially valued the literacy campaign
[a commonplace of all communist regimes] and thus he decided that together with his parishioners he ought to go along with positive social activities.
His difficulties began with his taking part in an open meeting of the People's
Council in Gniechowice. Encouraged to act publicly, he reminded himself
that the church and the pastor should be with the people, which he understood as meaning support for the current authorities. [Unfortunately for him]
the local newspaper, *Gazeta Robotnicza* (Workers' Newspaper), reported that
while recognizing papal authority in religious matters, he seemed to deny any
such authority in the secular sphere.[48] Polianskii was called in front of the
Wrocław church Curia to explain himself. He claimed his words were manip-
ulated and called upon witnesses, but he never recovered the trust he formerly
had. It isn't known whether it was from his own desire or from state pressure,
but he took part in other communist-initiated activities. On May 16, 1950
he again attended a public meeting and got himself elected to the community Committee of Defenders of Peace, an organization widely propagated by
the Communist authorities. For this he was punished by church authorities.
He wrote an explanation stating that the church had never issued orders for-
bidding membership in that organization and that he knew of other priestly
participants. The problem didn't quiet down because he wanted to take part
in charitable activities. He joined the *"Caritas"*(Charity) organization which
had formerly been a Catholic one but had been taken over by the state, and
"ZBoWiD," *Związek Bojowników o Wolność i Demokrację* (Union of Fighters
for Freedom and Democracy), an organization of ex-combatants, where he

---

48   The article was entitled *"My księżą na Ziemiach Zachodnich będziemy szli razem z lu-
dem"* (We priests in the Western Territories will walk together with the people).

became chairman of the county priests' commission. Nevertheless, despite all this, just as other former Greek Catholic priests, he was under constant observation by the political police. In 1951 the provincial Department of Public Safety began a permanent oversight operation called *"Wichrzyciele"* ("Troublemakers").[49] Being in a situation of conflict with the Wrocław church administration, Polianskii began to think of transferring to another diocese. On March 15, 1952 he applied to the Katowice diocese as well as the Kielce diocese, where he had many friends. At the same time he was transferred from the Gniechowice parish to the parishes of Rudna and Gwizdanów (November 27, 1952). That didn't settle the situation down, however, because Polianskii not only didn't cut his ties to regime organizations, but also attempted to minister to Greek Catholic deportees in the area by handling burials and hearing confession in Ukrainian and Lemko, an activity officially forbidden at that time. In order not to come into conflict with the state, the Wrocław Administrator removed him from both parishes on February 27, 1953 using as a pretext the fact that he had celebrated a Christmas liturgy on January 7, according to the Julian calendar.[50] He did remain in his parish for a while but finally left on April 7, 1953, to relatives in Gliwice where he lived for a few months while seeking a position in the Katowice diocese. He gave up on Kielce since there were no Greek Catholics there and he wanted to act as a bi-ritual priest and serve in both rites. Finally he was received into the Opole diocese and assigned first as the Administrator and later rector of the Rogi parish in Niemodlin county. His pastoral activities were highly appreciated by both his parishioners and the clerics he worked with. He was known for living very modestly with a great concern for others whom he eagerly helped. In 1967, because of progressive paralysis, he retired.

Fr. Polianskii tried very hard not to come into conflict with the communist authorities and even took part in pro-regime organizations in Opole, such as Caritas, Defenders of Peace and ZBoWiD. He even again received a Gold Service Cross (February 21, 1964). Nonetheless the secret police didn't trust

---

49   Igor Hałagida, *"A-O, Zakon, Wichrzyciele– działania aparatu bezpieczeństwa Polski Ludowej wobec duchowieństwa greckokatolickiego w latach 1944/1945-1956/1957"* (A-O, Zakon, Wichrzyciele: activities of the security apparatus of People's Poland towards Greek Catholic clergy in 1944/1945-1956/1957) in *Internacjonalizm czy...? Działania organów bezpieczeństwa państw komunistycznych wobec mniejszości narodowych (1944-1989)*, ed. Joanna Hytrek-Hryciuk, Grzegorz Strauchold, Jarosław Syrnyk, Warsaw – Wrocław 2011, p. 398.

50   Wrocław. Arch.

him and kept him under surveillance all the time. The church authorities weren't trusting of him, either, because they viewed negatively any Catholic cleric who had contacts with the Communists.

From the end of the 1960s, Fr. Polianskii was continuously ill. He died on November 6, 1978 in Rudna, Niemodlin County in his ninetieth year and he is buried in his last parish's cemetery in Rogi. He left a few unpublished works including his memoirs and a few works of a religious character.

Stanisław Stępień
Przemyśl, Poland
Professor of History at the State Higher
    School of Eastern Europe
Director, South-East Research Institute

Eastern Rite church in Leszczyny, 1968.

Symbol of Rusyn revival – the Carpathian bear in tricolor.

INDEX

Zharskii, Mykhailo 245
Zhatkovych, Gregory 264, 265
Zhehestovskii, Viktor 110, 111, 129
Zhemplinskii, Mykhailo 294
Zhitomir 239
Zielińska, Amela 183
Zielona Góra Province 351
Zita (Austrian empress) 228
Złockie 116, 238, 292, 385, 395, 396, 500
Złoczów 512
Zlupko, Andrei 298
Zmigród 293

Żmigród Estate 114
Zoikin (Orthodox bishop) 173
Zolotar (Red Army colonel) 309
Zoryla, Petro 358
Zubritskii, Denis 139
Zubrzyk 116
Żurawski, Franciszek 332, 335, 506
Zvenyhorodka 143, 144
Zwoliński, Jarosław 14, 305
Zyndram of Maszkowice (Polish knight) 114, 139, 168
Zyndranowa 114, 168, 292, 306, 310

The editors wish to thank the following individuals and publishers for supplying photographs and/or granting permission to reproduce them from existing publications. Their courtesy is gratefully acknowledged.

Paul Best, Higganum, Connecticut, USA, p. 430; Bogdan Gambal, Cracow, Poland, pp. 396, 467, 527; Bogumiła Gruszczyńska Kozan, Ostrów Wielkopolski, Poland, pp. 50, 79, 219, 222, 255; John Madzik, Ansonia, Connecticut, USA, pp. 83, 84, 105, 117, 118, 157, 290, 352, 354, 355, 451, 455, 456, 457, 476, 491(2); Maksymilian Maslej, Toronto, Canada, pp. 19, 51, 57, 58, 69, 81, 82, 154; Narodowe Archiwum Cyfrowe, Warsaw, Poland, pp. 52, 56, 66, 278, 418, 474, 480, 491(1), 497, 501; Sanok Historical Museum, Sanok, Poland, p. 150; Jerzy Starzyński, Legnica, Poland, pp. 13, 149, 423, 481, 488, 493, 503; *Voienniie Priestuplenniia Habsburskoi Monarkhii 1914-17* (The Talerhof Almanacs), Trumbull, Connecticut, USA, 1964, pp. 244, 246; *"Watra"*, Gorlice, Poland, p. 161; Wikimedia Commons, p. 407.

Unless otherwise noted, photographs came from the archive of www. lemko.org .

Yaroslav Trokhanovskii, founder of the Bielanka ensemble "Lemkovyna". 1967.

ABOUT THE EDITORS

Paul J. Best, Ph. D., is Professor Emeritus of Eurasian Studies in the Political Science Department, Southern Connecticut State University, New Haven, Connecticut, USA, and President of the Lemko Association.

Michael Decerbo has family roots in the Carpatho-Rusyn colony of Bridgeport, Connecticut. He is a graduate of the Massachusetts Institute of Technology, where his studies included Russian language, literature, and history. He is Vice President of the Lemko Association.

Walter Maksimovich was born to Lemko parents in Lubin, Poland (1949) and immigrated to the United States in 1964. The father of two, he is a retired electrical engineer from NASA/Goddard Space Center in Greenbelt, MD. Ever since his retirement in 2006 he spends time between homes in Miami Beach and Lviv, Ukraine. He regularly travels to Lemko  cultural events in Ukraine, Poland and Slovakia where he became a household name among Lemko-Rusyns. In 1996 he set up and still maintains a comprehensive and nonpartisan webpage, lemko.org. Through this web page and his personal connections he fosters contacts among Lemkos living in various countries. He has also published two books on Lemko wedding music and customs (*Lemkivske Vesilia*, 2002, with Ivan Madzik) and on commercial recordings of Lemko folk music in America during the Roaring Twenties (*Lemko Folk Music on Wax Cylinders (1901-1913) and American Records (1928-1930)*, 2008, with Bogdan Horbal).

Я Лемко і тым ся гоную!

А Ты ...?!

Narodowy Spis Powszechny 2011

I am a Lemko, and proud of it! And you...?! Advertisement posted in advance of Poland's National Census, 2011. Poster boy– Slavko Starzyński.